CONTENTS

8   **Gender, Crime, and Justice**   **234**

PREFACE

This edition of *Women, Men, and Society* is a year overdue. We have received many phone calls and e-mail messages from colleagues and even some students and former students, asking when the fourth edition would be ready. We'd like to take this opportunity to offer an apology for the delay, along with an explanation.

Early in 1996, Joe Renzetti, our father/father-in-law became sick and spent most of that year in the hospital. At the start of 1997, although he appeared to be getting stronger, he experienced heart failure and went into the hospital for the last time. He lived for three and a half months, usually conscious but unable to speak, communicating only by squeezing our hands, blinking his eyes, and sometimes nodding his head. Dad was a man who never let work interfere with family life, and he taught us to cherish that value as well. During his long illness, many projects were delayed—including this one—so we could be with him, Mom, and our extended family.

To those of you who have sent messages of support and sympathy, please know that we were touched by and are grateful for your kindness, understanding, and patience. We are grateful, too, to our "family" at Allyn and Bacon, who generously extended deadlines and did all they could to ensure that we had time to spend with Dad during his illness and time to grieve after his death.

When we finally got back to the business of revising this book, we looked to reviewers' suggestions for guidance. In response to these reviews, readers of this edition will find some significant changes. First, the text has been shortened somewhat, but this has been accomplished without sacrificing the thorough coverage of essential topics that reviewers praised. Chapters 3 and 13 have been eliminated; much of the material in Chapter 3 has been integrated into other chapters throughout the text, while the discussion of feminism, social movements, and social change has been moved to Chapter 1. All the statistics and citations, of course, have been updated, but more data on the intersection of gender with race and ethnicity, social class, sexual orientation, age, and ability/disability have been added whenever possible. We have also expanded our discussions of men and masculinities. Readers will also find some new, timely topics covered in this edition, such as pornography on the Internet, sex tourism and the sexual exploitation of children, welfare reform, women and economic development, and heterosexism in health care.

Despite these changes, we didn't make change simply for change's sake. We listened to reviewers, who basically said, "If it's not broke, don't fix it." We remain true to the goals we set for ourselves when we wrote the first edition of *Women, Men, and Society*. Our first goal continues to be to assist students in connecting a central element of their personal lives—their gendered experiences—with the social and political world in which they live. To do so, we present a broad, but thorough sampling of the wealth of recent scholarship on gender and gender-related issues. Most of this research is sociological, but we have also drawn on the work of biologists, psychologists, anthropologists, economists, historians, and others. This material often affirms students' observations that women and men *are* different in many ways, although perhaps less so than students might suppose. Clearly, women and men are treated differently in most societies, and much of the research we examine addresses this differential treatment and its significance in the everyday lives of women and men within the context of particular structural or institutional arrangements.

Our second goal is closely intertwined with the first. Specifically, we seek to persuade students to look beyond the boundaries of their own lives so as to understand the complexity and diversity of gendered experiences in terms of race and ethnicity, cultural context, social class, sexual orientation, age, and physical ability/disability. Although our primary focus is a critical assessment of gender inequality, we emphasize in every chapter the interdependence of multiple inequalities. We want students to understand how the constraints imposed on women and men by specific social constructions of gender may be tightened when combined with a devalued racial/ethnic status, sexual orientation, age, economic status, or physical challenge. Moreover, while the book is written from a feminist perspective, we expose students to the diversity that makes up contemporary feminism, turning the analytic lens so that they see an issue from various feminist *perspectives*.

Finally, we hope to accomplish these first two goals by presenting the material in a way that students find stimulating, clear, and highly readable. Together, we have brought to this project fifteen years of textbook writing experience and more than thirty-five years of experience teaching the sociology of gender, women's studies, feminist theory, marriage and family, and similar courses. During our years in the classroom, we have observed that students who take such courses often come from diverse academic backgrounds. Although most are juniors and seniors, many have had only one or two introductory-level social science courses. With this in mind, we have incorporated into the text a number of useful pedagogical tools. For instance, key terms or concepts are emphasized in boldface within each chapter, allowing students to study them in the context in which they are introduced. These key terms are also grouped at the end of each chapter, where they appear with a brief definition. At the end of the book, all of the concepts are alphabetized and defined in a glossary. Each chapter also concludes with a brief list of suggested readings. An instructor's manual for the text is also available. The manual contains a test bank, film and video suggestions, classroom exercises, and resources available in print form and through the Internet, including a list of helpful Web sites and listservs. In response to reviewers' suggestions, the instructor's manual, and in particular the test bank, have been expanded considerably.

As with previous editions of this book, we have been fortunate to have colleagues who are generous with both their time and their resources. We wish to thank those who reviewed all or part of the third edition and this manuscript, offered insightful comments and criticisms, suggested additional references, shared journals and other publications, and passed along other relevant information that crossed their desks. In particular, we wish to thank Betty A. Dobratz, Iowa State University; Clinton J. Jesser, Northern Illinois University; Rebecca F. Guy, The University of Memphis; Sheila Macrine, St. Joseph's University; Mark McMinn, Wheaton College; Ken Pope, private practice, Connecticut; and Richard Warren, St. Joseph's University. Thanks also to the librarians at St. Joseph's University, especially Chris Dixon; our graduate assistants, Karen McDonough and Carlyn Prisk; and our secretaries, Denise Shaw and Jane Downey.

During the course of our long association with Allyn and Bacon, we have had the good fortune of working with Karen Hanson, Editor-in-Chief, Social Sciences. Karen guided this book through three editions before turning that responsibility over to Series Editor Sarah Kelbaugh. Sarah has met the challenge with the kind of expert editorial skills and good humor that most authors only wish for. We have also been blessed with Kathy Smith, whose editorial production service is surpassed only by her warmth and camaraderie.

While we were working on this preface, our son, Sean, inquired about what we were doing. We explained that we were revising one of our books. *"Again?"* he asked. But instead of walking away in exasperation, he sat down with us and actually offered some advice about what we were writing. He was soon joined by his brother, Aidan, and before long, we were reduced to laughter by their outrageous suggestions. There are not enough words to thank our children for the sustenance they provide us, not only in our work, but in every aspect of our daily lives. They are our anchors, and we are forever grateful.

CHAPTER

1

Studying Gender:
An Overview

We describe ourselves in many different ways. One of the most fundamental ways is to say, "I am a man" or "I am a woman"—that is, to describe ourselves in terms of our sex. However, the information conveyed by these simple phrases goes beyond mere anatomical description. It also conjures up a configuration of personality traits and behavior patterns. Without ever having seen you, others are likely to draw conclusions about you—about the clothes you wear, the way you express yourself, and the various activities you pursue.

If you are a woman, for example, people would not be surprised to see you wearing slacks, but they might expect, and even be pleased, to see you in a dress. Most also expect you to be rather passive and dependent, emotional and given to crying easily. They will think of you as nurturing, preoccupied with romance and your appearance, and inept with things mechanical.

If you are a man, though, people will expect to see you wearing slacks, and they would be shocked, maybe even frightened, to see you in a dress. Most also expect you to be assertive and independent, always in control of your emotions. They will think of you as ambitious and competitive; preoccupied with your studies, work, or sports; and mechanically inclined.

In other words, a biological given, **sex** (i.e., maleness or femaleness) is used as the basis for constructing a social category that we call **gender** (i.e., masculinity or femininity). It may be that few of the socially defined characteristics of your gender describe you accurately, but this is perhaps less important than the fact that people believe these assumptions to be true or appropriate and that they act on their beliefs, treating women and men differently, even as opposites. Many people use gender stereotypes to guide their interactions with others. A *stereotype* is an oversimplified summary description of a group of people. There are positive and negative stereotypes, and virtually every group in our society has been stereotyped at one time or another; women and men are not exceptions. **Gender stereotypes,** then, are simplistic descriptions of the supposedly "masculine male" or "feminine female." Most people conceive of these stereotypes in bipolar terms; that is, a normal male supposedly lacks any feminine traits, and a normal female lacks masculine traits (Deaux & Kite, 1987). Thus, gender stereotypes are all-inclusive; every member of each sex is thought to share the characteristics that constitute their respective gender stereotypes. The reality, as we will learn throughout this book, is that many members of each sex do not conform to their stereotyped images. Sometimes this may be looked upon favorably by others, but often the nonconformist is labeled deviant, abnormal, or bad and is treated as such.

Significantly, this kind of differentiation occurs not only on an interpersonal level between individuals, but also on a structural level within a given society. Every society prescribes traits, behaviors, and patterns of social interaction for its members on the basis of sex. These prescriptions are embedded in the institutions of the society—in its economy, political system, educational system, religions, family forms, and so on. This institutionalized pattern of gender differentiation is referred to as a society's **sex/gender system.** An examination of sex/gender systems, as well as their consequences for women and men, forms the major focus of this book.

We will learn that sex/gender systems vary historically and cross-culturally. However, each system includes at least three interrelated components:

1. the social construction of gender categories on the basis of biological sex;
2. a sexual division of labor in which specific tasks are allocated on the basis of sex; and
3. the social regulation of sexuality, in which particular forms of sexual expression are positively or negatively sanctioned (Rubin, 1975; Thorne, 1982).

Of special concern to us will be the ways in which a sex/gender system functions as a system of *social stratification*; that is, the extent to which women and men, and the traits and behaviors respectively associated with them, are valued unequally in a society.

Given that social institutions are imbued with the power to reward and punish—to bestow privileges as well as to impose obligations and restrictions—a sex/gender system has a profound impact on the lives and life chances of women and men. Consider, for example, that in most countries throughout the world, during the last two decades, women have entered the paid labor force in dramatic numbers, yet across countries, economic sectors, occupations, and educational levels, women's wages are significantly lower than men's wages, and women continue to shoulder primary responsibility for traditional household chores (United Nations, 1997). These startling observations reflect the fact that most women and men worldwide live in societies with patriarchal sex/gender systems. A **patriarchy** is a sex/gender system in which men dominate women, and what is considered masculine is more highly valued than what is considered feminine. However, as we will learn in this text, patriarchy is by no means universal. Thus, one of our tasks here will be to examine alternative, more egalitarian sex/gender systems. We will also find that patriarchy does not benefit all groups of men equally, just as it disadvantages some groups of women more than others.

Before we undertake our analysis of gender and sex/gender systems, though, we should realize that not all sociologists agree on how to study gender or on what aspects of sex/gender systems are most important to study. Why the disagreement? To understand it better, let's look at some of the research on gender and the various theoretical perspectives that have informed it.

Sociological Perspectives on Gender

Broadly defined, **sociology** is the scientific study of human societies and cultures, and of social behavior. Not all sociologists undertake this work in the same way, however. Rather, a single social phenomenon—gender, for instance—may be researched and explained differently by different sociologists. This may be a bit puzzling, since it is commonly assumed that all sociologists by virtue of being sociologists share the same perspective. Certainly, the traditional image of science itself is one of a cumulative enterprise. That is, each scientist, whatever his or her specific field, supposedly works to solve the problems that the members of the discipline have agreed are most important. Each scientist's work progressively builds on that of others until the answer or truth is attained. The fact of the matter is, though, that scientists, including sociologists, conduct their research within the framework of a particular *paradigm*.

What is a paradigm? A **paradigm** is a school of thought that guides the scientist in choosing the problems to be studied, in selecting the methods for studying them, and in explaining what is found. This implies that research carried out within a specific framework is, to some degree, predetermined. The paradigm, in focusing researchers' attention on certain issues, simultaneously blinds them to the significance of other issues and also colors their view of the social world. This is not to say that there is no objective social reality or that sociology is simply what our favorite paradigm tells us it is. Instead, we can see that it indicates that sociological research, like all scientific research, is subjective as well as objective. This is an important point, and we will return to it shortly.

Sociology is a multiple-paradigm science; that is, it is made up of a number of different—and some would say, competing—paradigms (Ritzer, 1980). This observation solves our earlier puzzle of how a single social phenomenon can be researched and explained differently by different sociologists. At any given time, however, one paradigm tends to dominate the discipline. This does not mean that other paradigms are ignored, but rather that one paradigm seems to better explain current social conditions. Consequently, the majority of sociologists at that time will carry out their work within the framework of the dominant paradigm.

For much of sociology's recent past—especially from the 1940s to the 1960s—the dominant paradigm was structural functionalism. The structural functionalist perspective has been particularly influential in the study of gender, so it is important for us to examine it carefully.

Structural Functionalism

The **structural functionalist paradigm** depicts society as a stable, orderly system in which the majority of members share a common set of values, beliefs, and behavioral expectations that may be referred to collectively as *societal consensus*. The social system itself is composed of interrelated parts that operate together to keep the society balanced or, as a functionalist would say, in equilibrium. Each element of the society functions in some way to maintain social order. Change, then, must come about slowly, in an evolutionary way; rapid social change in any element would likely be disruptive and, therefore, dysfunctional for the system as a whole.

In their analysis of gender, structural functionalists begin with the observation that women and men are physically different. Of special significance are the facts that men tend to be bigger and stronger than women and that women bear and nurse children. According to functionalists, these biological differences have led to the emergence of different *gender roles*. More specifically, a social role, not unlike a theatrical role, includes a set of behavioral requirements expected of the person occupying the role. The concept of **gender roles** refers to the behaviors that are prescribed for a society's members, depending on their sex.

Functionalists maintain that for much of human history, women's reproductive role has dictated that their gender role be a domestic one. Given that women bear and nurse children, it makes sense for them to remain at home to rear them. It then follows that if women are at home caring for children, they will assume other domestic duties as well. In contrast, men's biology better suits them for the roles of economic provider and protector of the family. As one prominent functionalist theorist put it:

> In our opinion the fundamental explanation for the allocation of the roles between the biological sexes lies in the fact that the bearing and early nursing of children establishes a strong and presumptive primacy of the relation of mother to the small child and this in turn establishes a presumption that the man who is exempted from these biological functions should specialize in the alternative [occupational] direction. (Parsons, 1955, p. 23)

Structural functionalists point out that the work women do in the home is functional. In many ways, women reproduce society: by giving birth to new members, by teaching or socializing them to accept the culture's agreed-upon values and norms, and by providing men and children with affection and physical sustenance. However, some functionalists simultaneously devalue traditional women's work, referring to it as a "duty" and designating men as the instrumental leaders of their families.

Evaluating Structural Functionalism   Let's evaluate the central themes of the structural functionalist perspective of gender. First, functionalists see gender differences as *natural* phenomena deriving from human biology. Portraying masculinity and femininity as natural, however, confuses gender with sex and suggests immutability. The implicit message is that efforts to change our definitions of masculinity and femininity will have little, if any, effect on human behavior. Women and men cannot help that they think and act the way they do; it's in their nature. Moreover, men and women are opposites, and efforts to alter this natural dichotomy will likely do more harm than good. Yet, the fact is that gender is quite amenable to change; what constitutes masculinity and femininity varies tremendously throughout history and across cultures. That is because gender as we defined it at the outset is a social creation, not a biological given. Even if biological factors play some part in producing gender differences, available evidence shows that biologically determined traits can be modified or completely overridden by environmental influences.

We will discuss this point further throughout the text, especially in Chapter 2. For now, though, it is important to add that the functionalist rendition of the evolution of gender may also be inaccurate. Part of the problem stems from the fact that scientists confront several difficulties when trying to reconstruct evolutionary history. For one thing, archeological finds are relatively sparse and fragmentary and, as Ruth Hubbard (1990, p. 67) points out, "behavior leaves no fossils." Scientists must rely on a few, very general clues—a jaw or skull (but often just pieces of them), some teeth, or chipped stones—as they try to solve the puzzle of how our early ancestors lived hundreds of thousands of years ago. The further back in time we go, the less evidence we have and the more geographically spread out the puzzle is. Consequently, "[e]ven armed with the maximum amount of information currently available for study . . . the amount of knowledge we do *not* possess is so vast that no one can claim a definitive theory of the human origin and evolution, either morphological or cultural" (Bleier, 1984, pp. 122–123).

The theory of the origin and evolution of contemporary gender roles that structural functionalists have adopted is a familiar one known as *Man the Hunter theory*. According to this reconstruction of our evolutionary past, some time between 12 and 28 million years ago, our ape ancestors were forced down out of the trees as the climate became dryer, causing their subtropical habitat to recede. One of their most important adaptations to life on the ground was *bipedalism*, or the ability to walk upright on two feet. Their hands were thus freed for reaching, grasping, and tearing objects; for carrying; and eventually for using tools. There were other physiological consequences as well, including a narrower pelvis. As language developed, though, their brains and, therefore, their heads, grew larger. To compensate, offspring were born at an earlier stage of development, making them more dependent on their mothers' care for survival. Females burdened with helpless infants couldn't roam very far in search of food, so men became the sole breadwinners. They banded together for hunting expeditions, which led to the further development of language and to the invention of the first tools (weapons for hunting and defense). This sexual division of labor was adaptive; those who conformed to it enjoyed a distinct advantage in the struggle for survival. Moreover, these mutually exclusive gender roles gave rise to particular personality traits; women grew to be empathic, nurturing, and dependent, whereas men were daring, unemotional, and aggressive. Over time, these adaptive characteristics were also naturally selected for in the evolutionary process, which is why we continue to see them today (Lovejoy, 1981; Tiger & Fox, 1971).

There is an alternative interpretation of the archeological record, however. For example, some anthropologists maintain that our ape ancestors were not forced into the open savannah, but rather moved there as their numbers grew to avoid competition with other species. On the forest fringe, they found a plentiful variety of foods, including nuts and seeds, fruits and berries, roots and tubers, eggs and insects, and several species of small animals, some of which burrowed underground. Successful exploitation of these resources, as well as the need for protection and defense, required new survival strategies and adaptations. Bipedalism was one such adaptation, since it freed the hands for other tasks. Although bipedalism contributed to the need for offspring to be born at an earlier stage of development, this change did not force mothers and children to become dependent on males. Rather, it spurred females to be more innovative in their quest for food and in defense of their young against predators. The mothers' food-gathering task was made more difficult by other physiological changes, such as the loss of body fur, because this meant that infants could no longer cling to their mothers' fur the way ape offspring do; they had to be carried. Consequently, women had to invent something to carry their babies in, so they could keep their hands free for collecting food, and they may have extended the use of these carriers so they could collect more food than could be eaten on the spot. This suggests that perhaps the first material technology was not weapons for hunting, but rather slings or carriers for babies and food. Females, then, far from being passive, dependent childbearers, may have been active technological innovators who provided food for themselves and their young and defended against predators. Instead of living in male-headed families with a clear-cut gendered division of labor, our prehistoric ancestors may have lived in mother-centered kin groups with flexible structures (Bleier, 1984; Slocum, 1975; Tanner & Zihlman, 1976).

Which rendition of the evolution of contemporary gender roles is correct? We may never know. The point is, however, that there are multiple visions of prehistory based on the available evidence. By considering the alternatives, we raise important questions that the structural functionalist paradigm overlooks: "Has there always been a sexual division of labor? has there always been gender? what alternative forms of labor division might exist? how might such division of tasks, in fact, 'create' gender?" (Conkey & Gero, 1991).

Another serious consequence of depicting gender differences as natural the way functionalists do is that such a position traditionally has been used to justify inequality and discrimination on the basis of sex. History offers abundant examples. In the fifth century B.C.E., for instance, the Chinese philosopher Confucius declared that while women are human beings, they are of a lower state than men (Peck, 1985). In 1873, Myra Bradwell was denied admission to the Illinois bar and the right to practice law on the ground that "the natural and proper timidity and delicacy which belong to the female sex evidently unfits it for many of the occupations of civil life" (quoted in Goldstein, 1979, p. 50). More recently, some scientists have argued that men inevitably outscore women on IQ tests because men's brains are slightly larger than women's brains (see Blum, 1997, and Chapter 2).

It may well be the case that biological factors are responsible for many of the personality and behavior differences that we may observe between women and men. However, that does not mean that one sex or gender is better than the other or that members of one sex deserve a disproportionate share of society's resources and rewards because of their sex. In Chapter 2, we will more thoroughly evaluate claims regarding biologically based differences between the sexes; however, the problems of gender inequality and discrimination will occupy us throughout the text.

This brings us to another major theme in the structural functionalist perspective: the conception of gender in terms of roles. Although this position recognizes the importance of social learning in the development of gender, it also presents several problems. Stacey and Thorne (1985, p. 307) succinctly summarize them:

> The notion of "role" focuses attention more on individuals than on social structure, and implies that "the female role" and "the male role" are complementary (i.e., separate or different, but equal). The terms are depoliticizing; they strip experience from its historical and political context and neglect questions of power and conflict. It is significant that sociologists do not speak of "class roles" or "race roles."

A key concept in this critique is power. **Power** is the ability to impose one's will on others. The most powerful members of a society are usually those who control the largest share of societal resources, such as money, property, and the means of physical force. In hierarchically structured societies such as our own, these resources may be distributed unequally on the basis of characteristics over which individuals have no control, such as race and ethnicity, age, and *sex*. In overlooking the issue of power relations, then, the structural functionalist perspective neglects significant dimensions of gender: the structural causes of gender-based inequality and the consequences this inequality has for women and men in society.

This point of view also has serious implications with regard to social change. If we put too much emphasis on the process of individual learning, we may be tempted to assume that the solution to gender inequality lies simply in teaching people new social roles. Although much has been accomplished by individuals learning to reject the social constructions of gender that they find oppressive, we will see in the chapters that follow that far-reaching and effective social change requires a fundamental restructuring of society's basic institutions. A major weakness in the structural functionalist analysis of gender is its defense of the status quo.

A Paradigm Revolution

We noted earlier that structural functionalism was the dominant paradigm in sociology from the 1940s to the 1960s. Like most dominant paradigms, however, structural functionalism began to wear out; that is, it could no longer adequately explain social conditions or problems without being revised in some fundamental way (Harding, 1979). When this occurs, a *paradigm revolution* is likely. This means that members of a scientific discipline reject the dominant paradigm in favor of a competing paradigm that is better able to explain prevailing conditions (Kuhn 1970). What prompted a paradigm revolution in sociology during the 1960s?

The popularity of structural functionalism during the years following World War II is understandable, given the conservative political climate of the time. During the 1960s, however, structural functionalism began to lose its status as the dominant sociological paradigm. The decade of the 1960s was a period of widespread social protest and activism. Although opposition to the Vietnam War is usually viewed as the focal point of this unrest, other social problems mobilized various groups of people for collective action. At the heart of their concern was the widespread inequality that characterized American society. Some sociologists, for instance, documented the existence of pockets of poverty and malnutrition in the United States, a finding that showed that American affluence was not as widely shared as many people believed (Harrington, 1962). The African American Civil Rights movement vividly brought to the public's attention the fact that an entire segment of the U.S. population was systematically denied both full participation in society and equal access to society's resources and rewards simply on the basis of their race. And, as we will see shortly, the women's liberation movement, which also emerged at this time, raised public awareness of discrimination on the basis of sex.

Sociologists began to question the accuracy of depicting society as an orderly, harmonious social system. Many also rejected the notion of societal consensus and focused instead on how dominant ideologies developed out of the struggles between the haves and have-nots in a society. At the center of their analysis was the issue of power relations.

A number of different paradigms have emerged out of the turmoil. Particularly important to the sociological study of gender was the development of the feminist paradigm. Although it has been argued that feminism has had less revolutionary effects on sociology than on other disciplines, its impact nonetheless has been far-reaching (Abbott, 1991; Baca Zinn, 1992; Chafetz, 1988; Kramarae & Spender, 1992; Stacey & Thorne, 1985; Stanley, 1992). Table 1.1 summarizes the basic differences between the feminist paradigm and the structural functionalist paradigm.

TABLE 1.1   Sociological Perspectives on Gender

Perspective	Basic Assumptions and Central Principles	Key Concepts
Structural Functionalism	Society is a stable, orderly system in which the majority of members share a common set of values, beliefs, and behavioral expectations (societal consensus).	gender roles
	The social system is composed of interrelated parts that operate together to keep the society in equilibrium. Each element of the society functions in some way to maintain social order, so change must come about through a slow, evolutionary process.	
	Women and men are biologically different, and these biological differences, especially reproductive differences, have led to the emergence of different gender roles. These gender roles emerged early in human history and were institutionalized because they were adaptive and assisted in the survival of the species.	
	Women's and men's roles are opposite, but complementary. Because they are products of nature, social efforts to change them will be futile at best, but could also be harmful for society as a whole.	
Feminist Sociology	Gender is socially created, rather than innately determined. It is generated within the context of a particular social and economic structure and is reproduced and transmitted through a process of social learning.	sexism, sex/gender system, patriarchy, sexual politics
	Gender is a central organizing factor in the social world and so must be included as a fundamental category of analysis in sociological research. Researchers should take an empathic stance toward their research and acknowledge their personal biases, but maintain scientific standards in their research.	
	The consequences of gender inequality are not identical for all groups of women and men. Therefore, research must analyze the interrelationships among multiple oppressions, including sexism, racism, classism, ageism, heterosexism, and ableism.	
	A major goal of sociological work should be the development of effective means to eradicate gender inequality and to change those aspects of our social constructions of gender that are harmful or destructive.	

A Feminist Sociology of Gender

We must begin this discussion with a caveat: Feminism is not a single, unified perspective. Rather, as Delmar (1986, p. 9) points out, it is more accurate to think in terms of a "plurality of feminisms." The diversity within feminism is a benchmark of the extent to which it has developed and matured. But before we discuss some of the diverse perspectives that make up feminist sociology, let's consider some principles that virtually all feminist-identified perspectives share.

The **feminist paradigm** acknowledges the importance of both nature and learning in the acquisition of gender. However, feminist sociologists stress that it is virtually impossible to separate out the precise influences of biology because, as we will see in Chapter 3, the learning process begins immediately after birth. The complex interrelation between biological and cultural factors is also emphasized. Our genes, they tell us, "do not make specific bits and pieces of a body; they code for a range of forms under an array of environmental conditions. Moreover, even when a trait has been built and set, environmental intervention may still modify [it]" (Gould, 1981, p. 156).

The feminist perspective, therefore, begins with the assumption that gender is essentially socially created, rather than innately determined. Feminists view gender, in part, as a set of social expectations that is reproduced and transmitted through a process of social learning. In this way, the expectations become fundamental components of our personalities. But feminists also recognize that a complete understanding of gender requires more than an analysis of this learning process. They point out, in fact, that what we learn is itself a social product that is generated within the context of a particular political and economic structure. Consequently, feminist sociologists seek to answer research questions that set them apart from structural functionalists and other nonfeminist sociologists.

Feminists take issue with the inherent sex bias or sexism in traditional sociological research that we noted earlier. **Sexism** is the differential valuing of one sex, in this case, men, over the other. Historically, sexism in sociology has been in large part the result of the relatively low numbers of women faculty and students at academic and research institutions. However, it also reflects a broader societal prejudice against women, which is embodied in the assumption that what women do, think, or say is unimportant or uninteresting (Lorber, 1993).

The influence of these factors on sociological research has been threefold:

1. Most sociological studies were conducted by men, using male subjects, although findings were generalized to all people.
2. Gender was considered an important category of analysis only in a limited number of sociological subfields, such as marriage and family, whereas in all others (e.g., sociology of work, complex organizations, or sociology of law), it was ignored.
3. When women were studied, their behavior and attitudes were analyzed in terms of a male standard of normalcy or rightness.

A few examples should make these points clearer.

Consider, for instance, the classic research in the subfield of urban sociology. In her review of this literature, Lyn Lofland (1975, p. 145) found that "[women] are part of the locale or neighborhood or area—described like other important aspects of the setting such as income, ecology, or demography—but are largely irrelevant to the analytic action." Thus, although urban sociologists claimed to be studying community, their focus was limited to empirical settings in which men were likely to be present (e.g., urban street corners or neighborhood taverns). They completely overlooked the areas of urban life where women were likely to be found (e.g., in playgrounds with their children or at grocery stores), although few of us would deny that these locales are also central components of human communities.[1]

Sociologist Dale Spender (1981) provided another example. Studies on sex and language have shown differences in women's and men's speech. Spender found in her review of this research that many studies were designed to discover deficiencies in women's speech. The underlying assumption of the research was that there must be something wrong with women's speech if it is different from men's speech. In other words, men's speech has been considered normative, so speech that is different has been assumed to be deficient.

In short, feminist sociologists have shown that "most of what we have formerly known as the study of society is only the male study of male society" (Millman & Kanter, 1975, p. viii). Feminists, in contrast, include gender as a fundamental category of analysis in their research because they view the understanding of gender relations as central to understanding other social relations. This, in turn, has important implications for the research process and its outcomes. For one thing, it means that although feminist researchers strive to uncover similarities and differences in women's and men's behaviors, attitudes, and experiences, they do not do this so they can estimate the value of one relative to the other. Rather, their goal is to develop a *holistic* view of how women and men, because of their different locations in the social structure, encounter differential opportunities and constraints, and how they resist or respond to their relative circumstances (Hess & Ferree, 1987; Offen, 1988).

We are speaking here of the differential consequences of particular social arrangements on the lives of women and men, and of women and men as agents of social change. We will return to each of these issues momentarily. Notice first, however, that feminists do not exclude male experiences and perspectives from their research, but they do insist on the inclusion of female experiences and perspectives. Feminists deliberately seek to make women's voices heard in sociological research, where previously they have been silenced or ignored. To do this, feminists reject the traditional model of science "as establishing mastery over subjects, as demanding the absence of feeling, and as enforcing separateness of the knower from the known, all under the guise of 'objectivity' " (Hess & Ferree 1987, p. 13; see also Reinharz 1992). Feminist researchers instead take an *empathic stance* toward their research subjects. They frequently utilize more inclusive research methods that allow subjects to express their feelings and to speak for themselves, rather than imposing the researchers' own ideas or categories of response on their respondents.

The experiential emphasis in feminist research has frequently drawn charges of bias from traditional sociologists. However, feminists do not deny the partiality of their work; on the contrary, they acknowledge that it is intentional. Feminists recognize that sociological research is *dualistic:* It has both subjective and objective dimensions. On the one hand, no research, including that conducted within the structural functionalist paradigm as we have seen, is completely unbiased or value-free. No matter how objective sociologists may like to think they are, they cannot help but be influenced by values, personal preferences, life experiences, and aspects of the cultural setting in which they live. On the other hand, this does not mean that research is completely subjective either. While a researcher may be influenced by *values* (i.e., judgments or appraisals), her or his goal is the collection of *facts* (i.e., phenomena that can be observed or empirically verified). Feminists call for open acknowledgment by researchers of their assumptions, beliefs, sympathies, and biases. They question not only the possibility, but also the desirability, of a value-free sociology. While they reject the notion of value-free science, however, feminists do not reject "scientific standards" in their research (Reinharz, 1992).

The dualistic nature of sociological research makes it especially challenging, particularly for those of us interested in the study of gender. This is because of our intimate tie to what we are studying—after all, each of us has gender. But this duality also makes gender research very promising. Just as our values affect what we choose to study and how we choose to study it, they can also guide us in deciding how the facts we gather can be put to practical use. As we will show shortly, the scientific knowledge that feminist sociologists acquire through the research process empowers many of us to act to change behaviors and conditions that are harmful or oppressive.

Let's return for a moment to the issue of consequences. Feminist sociologists are fundamentally concerned with the question of how specific social constructions of gender impinge on the lives of women and men. The feminist research we will review in this text documents the serious and far-reaching effects of sexism in our society and in others. Chapter 7, for example, discusses how sexist beliefs that devalue women's labor have served as justifications for paying women less than men, and often as excuses for not paying them at all. This, in turn, is one of the major reasons women outnumber men among the ranks of the world's poor. Similarly, Chapter 11 shows that the notion that men should be stoic and unemotional has had profound consequences for their physical and mental health.

This latter example highlights an important point that was raised earlier, but is worth repeating here. Specifically, although many people tend to think of feminism as applicable only to so-called "women's issues," feminists themselves see their paradigm as relevant to the experiences of both sexes. Certainly, feminists' primary concern has been to study the position of women in society, largely because, as we have already noted, women and women's experiences have long been devalued or ignored in scientific research. Nevertheless, feminists have not left the social construction of masculinity unanalyzed. In studying men's lives, in fact, feminist researchers have found that, although virtually all men benefit from institutionalized patriarchal privilege, not all men actually have power in our society. As Bem (1993, p. 3) points out, "the term *male power* should thus be construed narrowly as the power historically held by rich, white, heterosexual men, for it is they who originally set up and now primarily sustain the cultural discourses and social institutions of this nation. It is thus not women alone who are disadvantaged by the organization of U.S. society but poor people, people of color, and sexual minorities as well."

Feminists, therefore, also recognize that the consequences of sexism are not identical for all groups of women and men. Instead, the effects of gender inequality are made worse by other types of discrimination. Consider, for example, the likely dissimilarities in the lives of a White, middle-class, middle-aged, gay man and a poor, Latina teenager who is pregnant and unmarried. Both may think of themselves as oppressed, but their objective circumstances are very different. Feminist research, therefore, attempts to account for the gender-based experiences of many diverse groups of women and men in our society. It analyzes the inextricable links among *multiple* oppressions: sexism, racism, classism, ageism, heterosexism, and ableism (Crenshaw, 1994; King 1988). An examination of these complex *intersecting inequalities* is a central theme of this text.

Finally, just as other sociological models, such as structural functionalism, have implications for social change, so does the feminist paradigm. Feminist sociologists, in fact, are advocates of social change. They seek to develop effective means to eradicate gender inequality and to change those aspects of our social constructions of gender that are harmful or destructive.

An important first step in this process is for people to develop a *group consciousness;* that is, they must begin to see that their problems are not personal ones, but rather are shared by others like them. Until a group consciousness develops, change is likely to be limited to the individual level. As one observer explained, "People tend to think that personal problems can be solved simply by working harder. Personal problems become political demands only when the inability to survive, or to attain a decent life, is seen as a consequence of social institutions and social inequality rather than personal failure, and the system is blamed" (Klein, 1984, p. 3). Once a group consciousness emerges and institutional arrangements are identified as the source of the problem, collective action can be taken to bring about structural change. A **social movement**— a group that has organized to promote a particular cause through collective action— may develop. Movement members take a stand for or against something and work together to get their position integrated into official public policy.

Feminist research serves to raise our consciousness about gender inequality, and it has spurred many people to work together for social change. This collective effort is usually referred to as the **feminist movement** or the **women's movement.** Throughout this text, we will examine the extent to which feminists have been successful in their efforts to reconstruct gender. Now, though, let's return to the issue of diversity in feminism. Although feminists share similar views with regard to the themes we have discussed so far, they also comprise heterogeneous factions with different interests and perspectives. This diversity has given rise to different tactics or strategies within feminism to achieve various objectives. However, before we discuss contemporary feminist theories and movement strategies, we will first put feminism in historical perspective.

Feminism in Historical Perspective

The First Wave of Feminism

Most of us have grown up uneducated about women's history. If, in fact, we rely only on the information in standard history texts, we are left with the impression that the sole preoccupation and accomplishment of nineteenth- and early twentieth-century women was winning the right to vote. Not surprisingly, then, to some people, the word *feminist* is synonymous with *suffragist* when discussed in the context of the nineteenth century. However, feminist historians who have studied the *woman movement*, as it was called back then, emphasize that the singular focus on suffrage emerged only after a decades-long campaign that addressed numerous dimensions of gender inequality. Even then, many feminists objected to making suffrage the primary goal of the movement and continued to draw attention to other aspects of women's oppression (Cott, 1987; Delmar, 1986; Goldsmith, 1998). Early feminism, like contemporary feminism, was far more diverse than has been depicted in traditional historical accounts (see Box 1.1 on page 16).

Feminist historian Gerda Lerner (1993) has also discovered that feminist ideas predate the period that is typically identified as the "first wave" of feminism, from 1830 to 1920 (see also Norton, 1997). In her analysis of historical documents dating back to the Middle Ages, Lerner uncovered a tradition of women's protest against patriarchal oppression, although it is fragmentary largely because, as she points out, women's actions and writings were not systematically included in the historical record. Indeed, women were systematically *excluded* from history-making because men have had the power to define what is history and what is important. Consequently, most women who resisted gender inequality were unaware of similar efforts by other women who came before them. This, in turn, inhibited the development of a *feminist consciousness:* a recognition by women that they are treated unequally as a group and that their subordination is socially created and maintained by a system that can be replaced, through collective action, with a more equitable social structure. Thus, although examples of feminist resistance can be found throughout history, a feminist social movement did not emerge until near the turn of the nineteenth century.

During the late 1700s, a number of women began publicly calling for equal rights with men, especially equal educational opportunities. These women, such as Judith Sargent Murray and Mary Wollstonecraft, were from the middle and upper classes. The men of their social station were espousing a political philosophy of individualism and democracy, asserting that "all human beings had equal rights by nature . . . and that everyone should have an equal chance of free development as an individual" (Klein, 1984, p. 530). But none of this seemed to apply to women, nor, for that matter, to anyone other than White men. Even as middle-class women acquired more education during the 1800s, they found most professions legally closed to them. Their alternative to filling hours at home with knitting and needlework was philanthropy and, as historian Lois Banner (1986) has observed, there were plenty of charitable voluntary organizations for them to join, particularly in the northern states.

Of course, to the targets of these social reform groups—that is, African Americans and European immigrants, the poor and the working class—the goal of equal rights for women must have seemed irrelevant at best. Black women were enslaved with Black men, both equal in a sense in their oppression, exploitation, and lack of any rights of citizenship. While upper- and middle-class women were demanding access to jobs and equality with men, working-class and poor women wanted protection and differential treatment from men (Klein, 1984). Poor women had no choice but to work outside the home for wages to help support their families. They typically earned $1 to $3 a week and labored in unsafe, unsanitary, and overcrowded factories (Banner, 1986).

Certainly, it is not difficult to understand, then, why the early feminists failed to attract broad-based support for their demands. (As we shall soon see, racism and elitism still plague some segments of the women's movement and are at least in part responsible for fragmentation within contemporary feminism.)

Ironically, it was their experiences in antislavery organizations that converted many White, middle- and upper-class women to feminism. Work in other social reform groups equipped these women with valuable organizational and administrative skills, but their focus tended to be local and their interests diverse. Abolitionism brought geographically dispersed women together and united them for a common cause. In addition, it has been argued that the ideology of abolitionism provided these women with a framework for understanding their own inequality relative to men. However, it is also likely that the way they were treated by supposedly liberal male abolitionists helped greatly to politicize them. In 1840, for example, at the first international antislavery conference in London, women delegates were prohibited from speaking publicly and were segregated from the men in a curtained-off section of the convention hall. Understandably, the women were outraged, and many, including Lucretia Mott and Elizabeth Cady Stanton, resolved to hold their own conferences in the United States—on women's rights as well as abolitionism (Banner, 1986; O'Neill, 1969; Simon & Danzinger, 1991).

Over the next twenty years, many such conferences were held, the most famous one being at Seneca Falls, New York, on July 19 and 20, 1848. There, led by Mott and Stanton, about 300 women and some sympathetic men—men originally were not to be admitted, but ended up chairing the meeting—adopted a Declaration of Sentiments, deliberately modeled on the Declaration of Independence, along with twelve resolutions. The latter were mostly general statements in support of the principle of equality between the sexes and in opposition to laws and customs that preserved women's inferior status. All except one—specifically, "*Resolved,* That it is the duty of the women of this country to secure to themselves the sacred right to the elective franchise"—were adopted unanimously. Those who opposed the call for women's enfranchisement expressed concern that such a radical demand would weaken public support for the more reasonable proposals and would possibly discredit the entire movement. Nevertheless, the resolution was finally accepted by the majority, and the Seneca Falls Convention became known as the official launch of the campaign for women's suffrage (Hole & Levine, 1984; O'Neill, 1969).

Still, it was not until after the Civil War that the drive for women's enfranchisement became paramount. In the prewar period, at women's rights conferences, before state legislatures, and in their own newspapers, feminists addressed a variety of issues such as dress reform, changes in divorce and custody laws, property rights, and the right to control their earnings. However, once the Civil War broke out in 1861, many feminists began to neglect the women's movement to devote their time and energy to the war effort. Although some, such as Susan B. Anthony, were openly pessimistic about this strategy, most assumed that the Republican administration would reward them for their wartime support by granting women the right to vote. They were wrong. In the aftermath of the war, Congress not only failed to grant women equal rights, but it also added a sex distinction to the Constitution by using the word "male"

BOX 1.1
Early Feminists

Although the first wave of feminism in the United States is often depicted as a single-minded social movement aimed at securing suffrage for women, the activities of nineteenth- and early twentieth-century feminists in this country demonstrate otherwise. They were involved in a wide range of political and social reforms, including public health and hygiene, "moral uplift," abolition, and public education. We offer a small sampling of brief biographies of some of these women to illustrate the diversity in their backgrounds, ideas, and goals.

■ **Elizabeth Blackwell** (1821–1910) The first female physician in the United States, Blackwell rejected marriage in favor of a career in medicine. She was a practicing physician, though, for only a short time before she moved into hospital administration and from there into public health. She was instrumental in the enactment and implementation of a number of public sanitation reforms that substantially improved the health and living conditions of the poor, the working class, racial and ethnic minorities, and immigrants.

■ **Charlotte Perkins Gilman** (1860–1935) As a professional writer, social critic, journalist, and public speaker, Gilman was one of the intellectual leaders of the first wave of feminism in the United States. She wrote and lectured on such topics as sex differences, social evolution, women and work, and child development. Although she preferred to be called a "sociologist" and not a "feminist," the influence of her work is evident in contemporary socialist feminist theory. At the turn of the century she advocated changes in traditional practices of child care and housework to relieve the double burden of women who worked outside the home. She was less concerned with securing formal legal rights for women than she was with bringing about practical institutional changes to improve the everyday lives of poor and working-class women.

■ **Margaret Sanger** (1879–1969) It is perhaps inappropriate to include Sanger here, since her work for women's right to control their bodies spans more than five decades of the twentieth century. Nevertheless, her pioneering efforts during the early 1900s are especially significant because she carried them out at a time when contraceptive devices and even the dissemination of information about birth control had been outlawed and deemed immoral; Sanger was arrested and prosecuted several times for her activities. Nevertheless, she remained committed to this cause throughout her life because she recognized that gender equality was impossible if women could not prevent and control the timing of pregnancy and childbirth. While she is best known for her advocacy of reproductive freedom, Sanger also labored to improve employment and living conditions for the working class, and was politically active for many socialist causes.

■ **Maria W. Stewart** (1803–1879) Orphaned at the age of five, this Black woman was bound out as a servant to the home of a White clergyman and his family, where she stayed until she was fifteen. In 1832, she became the first woman born in the United States to deliver a public lecture. In a series of four lectures that she gave that year in Boston, she encouraged women domestics and laborers to educate themselves and to strengthen their talents, which she saw as being dulled by women's servitude and subordination. She also defended women's right to speak in public. Later, she became a teacher and in 1863 she opened her own school in Washington, DC.

■ **Sojourner Truth** (1797–1883) Born a slave in New York, Sojourner Truth was sold several times during her childhood and suffered many indignities at the hands of her masters, including rape. When slavery was outlawed in New York, she began traveling as an itinerant preacher, and in her homilies she advocated abolition, protection and assistance for the poor, and equal rights for women. During the Civil War, she visited Union troops, and following the war, she worked for freedmen's resettlement and relief.

Frances Willard (1839–1898) Founder and early president of the Women's Christian Temperance Society (WCTU), Willard was active in a number of civic and moral reform movements, but is perhaps best known for her campaigning for strict laws regulating the sale and consumption of alcohol. One source of Willard's motivation in working tirelessly for temperance was her desire to protect women and children who were often abused by intoxicated husbands and fathers.

Victoria Claflin Woodhull (1838–1927) One of the most flamboyant and controversial first wave feminists, Woodhull is perhaps best known for her advocacy of free love and her illicit relationships with wealthy men, including Cornelius Vanderbilt. However, Woodhull is also notable as the first woman to operate a Wall Street brokerage firm, the first American woman to address Congress, and the first American woman to run for President (even though women could not vote and Woodhull herself was below the constitutional age requirement).

Sources: Compiled from Gabriel, 1998; Gray, 1979; Hill, 1980; Hine & Thompson, 1997; Lerner, 1972; and Rossi, 1973.

---

in the second section of the Fourteenth Amendment. The Fifteenth Amendment was passed with the specification that suffrage could not be denied on the basis of race, color, or previous condition of servitude; the word "sex" was excluded (Banner, 1986; Hole & Levine, 1984).

Disappointed and angry, feminists took up the fight for women's rights on a state-by-state basis, starting in Kansas. In 1867, Kansas voters were called on to decide two referendums, one to enfranchise Blacks and one to enfranchise women. State Republicans supported the former, but openly opposed the latter. The Democrats, hardly friends of feminism, allowed their racism to get the better of them and campaigned for women's suffrage with the hope of defeating the referendum for Blacks. Both measures lost at the polls, but the Kansas campaign caused serious divisions in the women's movement. Feminists such as Stanton and Anthony, who had sided with the Democrats, alienated other feminists, who were appalled by their blatant hypocrisy and racism. Because of this as well as other disagreements over strategies and goals, some of these women formed their own organization, the American Woman Suffrage Association (AWSA), with the sole objective of enfranchising women and Blacks. Stanton and her supporters organized the rival National Woman Suffrage Association (NWSA) which, despite its name, lobbied for a variety of causes in addition to suffrage. Neither group enjoyed much popularity with the general public, but the NWSA had the greatest difficulty because some of its members advocated "free love" and Marxism, which gave the organization an anti-American, antifamily image (Cott, 1987; Goldsmith, 1998). By 1890, though, both groups merged into the National American Woman Suffrage Association (NAWSA) to pool all their resources to win women the right to vote. (Black men were enfranchised in 1870.)

Expediency characterized the movement by the turn of the century, and some feminists appeared willing to exploit virtually every prejudice and stereotype, no matter how harmful, if it helped garner support for their cause. While some argued that women deserved the vote because in a democracy all people should rule themselves, others maintained that women should vote because they would purify politics. Women, the latter claimed, would bring to the political process natural talents, such as nurturance, which made them not men's equals, but their moral superiors (Cott, 1987). In a similar vein, the suffragists capitalized on the growing anti-immigrant sentiment of middle-class, native-born Whites, as well as their longstanding racism against Blacks (Caraway, 1991; Simon & Danzinger, 1991; "Suffragette's Racial Remark," 1996).

At the same time, however, there were some feminists, such as Charlotte Perkins Gilman, who successfully mobilized working-class women and men and new immigrants into suffrage organizations. According to historian Nancy Cott (1986, p. 53), "As never before, men and women in discreet ethnic or racial or ideological groups saw the advantage of doubling their voting numbers if women obtained suffrage" (see also Cott, 1987). Black women's organizations, such as the National Association of Colored Women's Clubs, the National Federation of Afro-American Women, and the Northeastern Federation of Colored Women's Clubs, established suffrage departments or committees and conducted classes on civics and the Constitution to prepare women for enfranchisement (Hine & Thompson, 1997). For Black women, suffrage was more than a women's rights issue; it was a means to address the often violent subversion of Black men's voting rights in the South (Cott, 1987; Yee, 1992). "[T]hey mobilized not only as a matter of gender justice but of race progress, despite [or perhaps because of] their awareness that White racist arguments were simultaneously being raised on behalf of woman's suffrage" (Cott, 1986, p. 53). Black women were systematically excluded from most White suffrage organizations (Caraway, 1991; Simon & Danzinger, 1991). Certainly, by the early 1900s, it was clear that "mainstream feminism" was not every woman's movement, but rather an explicitly White, middle-class women's movement.

During the 1890s, several Western states enfranchised women—for example, Wyoming in 1890, Colorado in 1893, and Utah and Idaho in 1896—but no other states were won until 1910. NAWSA and other groups, such as Alice Paul's National Women's Party (NWP), continued to stage petition drives, demonstrations, and other media events, but ironically, it took another war, World War I, to turn the political tide for women's enfranchisement. Most feminists supported President Wilson's position on the war and contributed to the war effort in many ways, but unlike during the Civil War, suffrage organizations remained active during World War I and targeted for election defeat senators who opposed suffrage. Finally, in a special legislative session held in the spring of 1919, both the House and the Senate approved the Nineteenth Amendment, sending it to the states for the two-thirds ratification. Ratification took little more than a year; on August 26, 1920, 26 million American women won the right to vote.

What followed can best be described as anticlimactic. For one thing, suffrage did not have the impact that feminists had promised, which is not surprising given that it was sold as a panacea for virtually all of society's ills. Once the vote was won, women did not go to the polls as often as men, and when they did go, they voted similarly to men (see Chapter 9). More importantly, the suffrage campaign cost feminism much of its active support since many women withdrew from the movement in the belief that equality had been won along with the right to vote. Young women in particular ignored the women's movement or rejected it outright, depicting feminists as lonely, unmarried women who needlessly antagonized men. In the politically conservative postwar era, social activism fell into disfavor and the "cult of Domesticity" was resurrected with a slightly new twist: The modern "emancipated" middle-class housewife was a "house-hold manager" who mixed science and "aesthetic inspiration" to produce an efficient and tranquil home for her family. As O'Neill (1969, p. 313) concludes, "femininity, not feminism, was increasingly the watchword."

This does not mean that feminism disappeared completely. For example, Alice Paul, who has been described as "a dedicated, iron-willed 'superfeminist,'" led a small following in the National Women's Party, which continued to lobby for women's rights in a number of arenas, but focused primarily on the Equal Rights Amendment (Taylor, 1990, p. 287). Other organizations, such as the National Federation of Business and Professional Women's Clubs, the National Association of Women Lawyers, and the American Medical Woman's Association, worked to get women elected to political office and appointed to policy-making positions in government. Thus, as Taylor (1990, p. 284) explains, the period following ratification of the Nineteenth Amendment into the early 1960s was not a time of mass mobilization for the women's movement, but the movement was also by no means completely dormant (see also Cott, 1987). The early 1960s, however, became a period of mass mobilization for the movement, both in the United States and abroad (see Box 1.2 on page 20); feminism was revitalized.

The Second Wave of Feminism

Several factors contributed to the resurgence of feminism in the early 1960s. One important impetus was the publication in 1963 of Betty Friedan's book, *The Feminine Mystique*. Friedan voiced the unhappiness and boredom of White, educated, middle-class housewives. Isolated in suburban homes, which Friedan referred to as "comfort-able concentration camps," these women found their personal growth stunted. After subordinating their own needs to those of their husbands and children, they were left with a profound sense of emptiness rather than fulfillment. This Friedan dubbed "the problem that has no name," but the real significance of *The Feminine Mystique* was Friedan's labeling this not an individual problem, but a *social* problem. The book quickly became a bestseller, but more importantly, it served as a springboard for developing analyses of **sexual politics,** that is, the examination of gender inequality as rooted not only in the public sphere, but also "in the 'privacy' of our kitchens and bedrooms," in the intimate relationships between women and men (Stacey, 1986, p. 210). From such analyses has come the much-quoted feminist slogan, "The personal is political."

However, even before the publication of *The Feminine Mystique*, the federal government took action that drew attention to the problem of sex discrimination. In 1961, President John F. Kennedy appointed a Presidential Commission on the Status of Women at the urging of Esther Peterson, whom he later named as an assistant secretary of labor. Interestingly, Kramer (1986) reports that Peterson advocated the

BOX 1.2
Feminism in Great Britain and Western Europe[2]

British and Western European feminists, like their counterparts in the United States, emerged out of particular social, political, and economic circumstances. The Enlightenment—with its emphasis on reason, progress, education, the fulfillment of the individual, and freedom from restrictions—has been identified as an important antecedent, although the major Enlightenment philosophers, such as Rousseau, were openly opposed to equal rights for women. Nevertheless, we can see the influence of Enlightenment ideals in the writings of early British and Western European feminists, such as Mary Wollstonecraft. In her 1792 treatise, *A Vindication of the Rights of Woman*, Wollstonecraft denounced traditional male authority and female subservience and called for equal educational opportunities for women as the means for their liberation and full development as individuals.

The French Revolution and the rise of liberalism also contributed to the emergence of nineteenth century British and Western European feminism. Women were actively involved in the French Revolution, leading protests and forming political clubs, and writers like Olympe de Georges argued vehemently for full economic political rights for women under the new government. (Unfortunately, de Georges was beheaded by Robespierre, and the Revolutionary Assembly outlawed all women's organizations.) The writing of John Stewart Mill in *The Subjugation of Women* illustrates liberalism's emphasis on removing legal barriers to equal rights, although Mill was one of the few liberal male philosophers who took up the cause of women's rights. At the same time, socialists such as August Bebel and Frederich Engels developed their critiques of the subordination of women in the family under capitalism and exhorted women to join the socialist movement to secure their emancipation.

With these diverse origins, it is not surprising that early British and Western European feminists tackled a range of issues, including the protection of women and children from battery and sexual abuse, prevention of the exploitation of women through prostitution, divorce reform, revisions in property laws, increased employment opportunities, equal access to education, and, of course, the right to vote, but their concerns were broader than formal legal rights. "Europeans focused much or more on elaborations of womanliness; they celebrated sexual difference rather than similarity within a framework of male/female complementarity; and instead of seeking unqualified admission to male-dominated society, they mounted a widespread critique of the society and its institutions" (Offen, 1988, p. 124). Still, British and Western European feminists exchanged ideas and experiences with their American sisters through participation in international feminist organizations, such as the International Council of Women, the International Women's Suffrage Alliance, and the Socialist Women's International (Cott, 1987; Lovenduski, 1986).

The success of British and European feminists' struggles depended to a large extent on specific conditions in the country in which they were waged (Chafetz et al., 1990). In most European countries, for instance, divorce laws were gradually liberalized during the nineteenth and early twentieth centuries, but in strongly Catholic-identified countries, divorce was prohibited until very recently. For example, it was prohibited until 1985 in Ireland, and many restrictions still remain. Most European nations enfranchised women during or shortly after World War I, although some had granted women full suffrage rights much earlier (e.g., Finland in 1906) and others much later (e.g., France in 1944) (Lovenduski, 1986; Rowbotham, 1997).

The upheaval of war in Europe and increasing political conservatism in its aftermath helped to suppress feminism in many countries and to drive it underground in others. During the 1960s and 1970s, however, Britain and Western Europe, like the United States, experienced a resurgence of feminism. Although a variety of factors undoubtedly contributed to this resurgence, it was due at least in part to widespread dissatisfaction among women regarding how little genuine equality they enjoyed despite several decades of formal legal rights that had been secured largely through the efforts of nineteenth-century femi-

nists (Lovenduski, 1986; Rowbotham, 1997). This dissatisfaction has given rise to a multiplicity of feminist groups and organizations, which, like those in the United States, have diverse philosophies, strategies, and goals (Bashevkin, 1996; Margolis, 1993).

establishment of the commission to placate members of the NWP and the Federation of Business and Professional Women's Clubs, who were intensifying their lobbying efforts for the Equal Rights Amendment. In its final report, the Commission focused primarily on the persistent and severe discrimination experienced by women in the labor force. The report subsequently provided the basis for the Equal Pay Act of 1963 (see Chapter 7), led to the appointment of two permanent federal committees on women's issues, and served as a model for the numerous state-level commissions that were established in its wake. The state commissions, in turn, became vehicles for gathering and distributing information on women's issues (Freeman, 1973; Kramer, 1986). The state commissions also helped give rise to the National Organization for Women (NOW), which was founded in 1966 by Betty Friedan and twenty-seven others who were representing state women's commissions at a national assembly in Washington. NOW became a model for a variety of other feminist groups, such as the National Women's Political Caucus, the Women's Equity Action League, the Congressional Caucus for Women's Issues, and the National Abortion and Reproductive Rights Action League.

At about the same time that NOW was being formed, a second, more militant branch of feminism was emerging from different sources. More specifically, this feminism had its origins in the political left, centered largely on college campuses, and developed among women who were active in other social movements during the 1960s, such as the Civil Rights movements and the anti-Vietnam War movement. The leadership of these latter social movements was male-dominated, but large numbers of women participated, running the same risks and fighting for the same goals as the men (O'Neill, 1969). Nevertheless, these women often found themselves relegated to traditional female roles, as cooks, typists, and sexual partners. They were struck by the glaring contradiction between the ideology of equality and freedom espoused by radical men and the men's sexist treatment of women (Evans, 1979; Freeman, 1973; Shulman, 1980). By the late 1960s, these women had formed their own feminist organizations, less formally structured and more radical than NOW and similar groups. The focus was on developing a theoretical analysis of women's subordinate status as well as engaging in political activism to end gender oppression.

Feminist groups at this time attracted many women who personally felt the sting of gender discrimination, including many lesbians. According to Pearlman (1987, p. 317), the feminist movement was central to lesbians' politicization as a group. "Feminism gave lesbianism a female-oriented political movement and a political understanding of the basis of their persecution. . . . Feminist political activity gave lesbians places to meet outside of the bars through consciousness raising groups, women's centers, and services such as rape crisis and women's health centers." A more open and supportive environment meant that lesbians could be visible and active. However, as lesbian feminists increased their participation in the women's movement and began to contribute their own critical analyses of heterosexual relations, straight feminists grew more defensive and argued that a visible and vocal lesbian presence would hurt the movement by delegitimating it. This eventually led to a lesbian/straight split in the women's movement, with lesbian feminists forming their own organizations, such as Radicalesbians (Cruikshank, 1992; Faderman, 1991; Pearlman, 1987). Although in recent years this split has mended somewhat, there remains an uneasy alliance between lesbian and straight feminists within some segments of the women's movement.

Like the first wave of feminism, then, the second wave was hardly homogeneous. These differences and divisions have given rise to the many perspectives that make up feminism today, including, as Box 1.3 on page 24 shows, a pro-feminist men's movement. Let's consider some of these perspectives now.

Contemporary Feminisms

Sociologist Judith Lorber (1998) has developed a useful way of categorizing the diverse perspectives that make up contemporary feminism. She identifies three major categories of feminist theory: gender-reform feminisms, gender-resistance feminisms, and gender-rebellion feminisms.

According to Lorber, *gender-reform feminisms* emphasize the similarities rather than the differences between women and men. Their goal is for women to have the same opportunities as men to fully participate in all aspects of social life, reflecting personal choices, not society's sexist dictates. Lorber identifies four feminisms—liberal, Marxist, socialist, and development—as gender-reform feminisms. Liberal feminism focuses on securing the same legal rights for women that men enjoy, whereas Marxist and socialist feminisms see women's oppression as caused by economic dependence and thus emphasize increasing women's employment opportunities and bettering their wages and working conditions. Development feminism reflects the concerns of women in economically developing countries and strives to improve work and educational opportunities for women there, while often operating within the constraints of their traditional cultures.

Gender-resistance feminisms argue that formal legal rights alone cannot end gender inequality because male dominance is too ingrained into everyday social relations, including heterosexual sexual relations. These perspectives not only focus on how women's ideas and experiences are different from those of men, but also urge women to break away from male dominance by forming separate, women-only organizations and communities. Lorber calls these perspectives "gender resistant" because while this separatist strategy resists the gendered social order, it does nothing to change it. Lorber includes radical feminism, lesbian feminism, psychoanalytic feminism, and standpoint feminism in the gender-resistant category. Radical and lesbian feminisms focus on the sexual exploitation of women by men and especially on men's violence against women. Psychoanalytic feminism uses the ideas of Sigmund Freud to explain gender inequality in terms of sex differences in personality development, while standpoint feminism attempts to examine all aspects of life from a woman's unique standpoint.

Finally, *gender-rebellion feminisms*, Lorber notes, are sometimes called *third wave feminisms* because they represent a major break in the way sex and gender have been conceptualized by the perspectives that grew out of the first and second wave feminist movements. Gender-rebellion feminisms focus on the interrelationships among inequalities of gender, race and ethnicity, social class, and sexual orientation, and analyze gender inequality as one piece of a complex system of social stratification. Gender-rebellion feminisms include multiracial feminism, men's feminism, social construction feminism, postmodern feminism, and queer theory. Multiracial feminism and men's feminism highlight how one's various social locations within the stratification hierarchy privilege or disadvantage groups of women and men in different ways. Social construction feminism examines the ways that people construct varying identities and social labels through their everyday interactions with one another. Postmodern feminism and queer theory conceptualize sex and gender as social scripts and then rewrite the parts and alter the props as they see fit for specific situations. Gender, from these perspectives, is fluid.

Lorber's classification scheme is not exhaustive, however. Within each of these branches or categories of feminism, there are still other divisions. And, of course, many of these perspectives are not mutually exclusive. Our brief discussion of divisions within feminism is, by necessity, overly simplistic—a presentation of *ideal types* or characterizations of the essential elements of each category, which does not do justice to the multifaceted nature of a movement in which differences often are not so clear cut and factions frequently unite. Our intent here was merely to give readers a sense of the rich diversity of contemporary feminism, a diversity that we pointed out earlier has given the movement strength and resiliency.

However, diversity also has generated problems for feminism. One of the most serious problems is what one observer calls a "sclerosis of the movement" in which segments "have become separated from and hardened against each other. Instead of internal dialogue there is a naming of the parts: there are radical feminists, socialist feminists, Marxist feminists, lesbian separatists, women of color, and so on, each group with its own carefully preserved sense of identity. Each for itself is the only worthwhile feminism; others are ignored except to be criticized" (Delmar, 1986, p. 9). The "discourse of difference," in other words, has not been accompanied by an "ethic of conflict or criticism" (Hirsch & Keller, 1990). The criticism and conflict that erupt around differences of perspectives and strategy have sometimes disintegrated into censorship or trashing of competing feminist viewpoints. There exists, then, a tension within feminism between the felt urgency to present concerns and grievances as a single, unified group of women, and the need to give voice to the variations in concerns and grievances that exist among feminists on the basis of race and ethnicity, social class, sexual orientation, age, physical ability/disability, and a host of other factors. Consequently, what feminists must recognize, as Childers (1990, p. 70) points out, is that "practicing conflict is also practicing feminism." Or, to paraphrase Hirsch and Keller (1990, p. 380), although feminists may be invested in the possibility of speaking with a

BOX 1.3
Men and Liberation

To many women, the term *men's liberation* sounds a bit ironic. After all, men certainly do not seem to need liberating, given that they benefit most from our patriarchal social arrangements. Still, as we will learn throughout this text, there are many ways that traditional masculinity harms men. For example, men's higher rates of heart disease and their lower life expectancy are linked to traditional masculinity (see Chapter 11). Moreover, as we have already pointed out, the social category "man" is as diverse as the category "woman." Although all men benefit to some extent from male privilege, the distribution of societal resources—most importantly, wealth, prestige, and power—varies among men according to their race and ethnicity, social class, age, physical ability, and sexual orientation.

In the early 1970s, some men, mostly White, educated professionals in colleges and universities, began to meet in small informal groups to discuss their experiences as men, their interpersonal relationships, and their notions of masculinity and how these impinge, for better or for worse, on their lives. These men formed consciousness-raising groups that focused initially on how gender norms and stereotypes were limiting them (Messner, 1998; Segal, 1990). By the end of the 1970s, though, "men's liberation" had divided into two branches, each with very different emphases and goals. Harry Brod (1987), a leader in the field of men's studies, labels these two branches *male-identified* and *female-identified*, respectively.

The male-identified branch of the men's movement has continued to focus on the harms and constraints of the traditional masculine role. This branch of the men's movement is composed largely of men's rights groups. According to supporters of this perspective, male privilege is an illusion; it is women who are advantaged in our society. They argue, in fact, that men are victimized by women: that is, men are seduced by women and then falsely accused of rape; men are routinely denied custody of their children following a divorce; and men are expected to be protec-

tors and economic providers, while women are exempted from the military draft and do not have to pay for drinks or meals when on dates (see, for example, Farrell, 1993; Thomas, 1993). "Thus, to men's rights advocates, while the women's movement now allows a woman to 'have her cake and eat it too,' the continued imposition of a rigidly narrow male sex role results primarily in costs to men (and ultimately to the family, schools, and other institutions). For these men, what is now needed is a movement that will free men, who will then counter these destructive effects of feminism" (Messner, 1998, p. 270).

In short, the men's rights branch of the men's movement is clearly anti-feminist. Michael Kimmel (1995) includes in this branch of the men's movement the Christian men's group, the Promise Keepers (see Chapter 10), Louis Farrakhan's Nation of Islam, and the mythopoetic men's groups. Each of these groups takes a different approach, but they share a common objective. At Promise Keepers rallies in large sports arenas, at Farrakhan's Million Man March, and at mythopoetic retreats in the woods where men beat drums to get in touch with their "masculine essence," leaders exhort men to return to their homes to assume their "rightful" place as head of the household. Although they are encouraged to be respectful of women, women are nevertheless seen as potential victimizers of men (in the eyes of the mythopoetic men's groups) or are expected to be subordinate to men (according to the Promise Keepers and the Nation of Islam).

In contrast to the male-identified branch of the men's movement, the female-identified branch is explicitly pro-feminist. Pro-feminist men agree that traditional masculinity is harmful, especially for men of color and working-class men (Connell, 1995; Seidler, 1991). But sexism is a *system* of male domination, so in order to bring about change, it's not enough to just give women some of what men have. Instead, it's necessary to *reconstruct* gender and gender relations in our society, and to do this, men must promote and engage in *antisexist* behavior (Christian, 1994). A central focus of the pro-feminist men's movement, for example, is addressing men's violence, especially men's violence against women. In both the United States and abroad, pro-feminist men's groups have formed cooperative alliances with feminist rape crisis centers and battered women's agencies, providing counseling and other programs to change the behavior of violent men (Messner, 1998; Segal, 1990).

Of course, it is not surprising that some observers, particularly women in the feminist movement, regard the men's movement in general with suspicion and skepticism. There is the very real concern, fueled by the rhetoric and actions of men's groups, that "men's liberation" is simply a strategy "for repairing men's authority in the face of the damage done by feminism" (Carrigan et al., 1987, p.100). And some question men's commitment to genuine social change in gender relations (Hagan, 1992). Indeed, the challenge to pro-feminist men's groups is to mobilize men for social change when such change will result in gains for women—but at the cost of some loss of privilege for themselves. It remains to be seen whether they will be successful in meeting this challenge, and in overcoming the anti-feminism of the men's rights branch of their movement.

---

common voice, they must also give equal value to the integrity of diverse voices. This attention to the plurality of voices within feminism is becoming increasingly important for young women and women of color, who bring their own concerns and strategies to the feminist movement.

The Future of Feminism: Young Women and Women of Color

During the 1980s and 1990s, media reports have pronounced feminism dead. In light of our discussion thus far, they obviously were wrong. In fact, as we see in Box 1.4 on pages 26 and 27, feminism has grown into a global social movement. But what prompted the media to make such a claim?

One reason the media sounded the death knell for feminism was survey results that showed a dramatic decline in support for feminism among young women. According to the press reports and other journalistic accounts, "feminism" and "feminist" had become "dirty" words among young women aged eighteen to twenty-nine. Feminists had come to be seen as whining, humorless manhaters who practice the "politics of victimization" and who are out of touch with the concerns of the younger generation. According to these reports, most young women considered the women's movement an anachronism, no longer necessary because women now had the greater freedom they had been seeking (Bellafante, 1998; Denfeld, 1996; Faludi, 1991; Roiphe, 1993; Wallis, 1989).

Empirical research has substantially qualified this negativism. In studies of college students and other groups of young women, researchers have found that most young women do not hold negative views of the women's movement and, although they believe that the status of women has improved over the last twenty-five years, most also feel that gender discrimination is still a serious social problem. But while these young women hold positive views of feminism, they are nonetheless reluctant to identify themselves as feminists (Miller-Bernal, 1992; Renzetti, 1987). In one survey, for example, the

BOX 1.4
Feminism in Developing and Undeveloped Countries

Feminism in the economically undeveloped and developing countries of Africa, Asia, and Latin America is sometimes referred to as *Third World feminism*, reflecting the traditional designation assigned by sociologists and economists to impoverished countries of these regions.[3] Histories of feminist activism in these countries are relatively scarce, however. Although there is now a sizable body of scholarship on women's involvement in liberation movements in these countries, this work usually does not focus on feminist activism per se (Mohanty, 1991). For many people in low-income countries, the struggle for women's liberation has been inseparable from the one for national liberation from Western imperialism or for liberation from political dictatorships. And while writers have recently begun to document the history of women's activism on behalf of women *as women* in the developing and undeveloped world (see, for example, Jayawardena, 1986; Lobao, 1990), there is still much more known about contemporary feminism in these countries than about feminism historically.

In the impoverished countries of Africa, Asia, and Latin America, daily economic survival usually takes precedence over any attempts to win formal legal rights for women. Men in these countries are also oppressed by imperialism, racism, and social class inequality, so many women in these countries view the goals of Western feminism as separatist and ethnocentric. As Johnson-Odim (1991, p. 320) writes, "In 'underdeveloped' societies it is not just a question of internal redistribution of resources, but of their generation and control; not just equal opportunity between men and women, but the creation of opportunity itself; not only the position of women in society, the position of the societies in which Third World women find themselves" (see also Margolis, 1993; Moyo, 1996). Nevertheless, women in these societies experience oppression not only because they are citizens of countries oppressed by economic exploitation and racism, but also because they are women oppressed by patriarchy. In other words, women in these countries experience a *double deprivation:* the deprivation of living in a poor country and the deprivation imposed because they are women.

Consider, for example, economic development policies. Training and support programs, technology transfers, and agricultural extension programs typically benefit men in developing countries rather than women, even though women are responsible for much of the economic production (Curran & Renzetti, 1993; Rowbotham, 1989). Women comprise the majority of the work force in low-income countries where foreign corporations have moved their production processes to keep costs down and profits up. The Nike Corporation, for instance, has numerous factories in Indonesia, where indigenous workers, most of whom are women from rural areas, earn slightly more than $2 a day. Such wages are not enough to allow the women to return to their villages more than once a year to visit their children. Meanwhile, Nike's holdings in Indonesia are estimated at more than $5 million, and Philip Knight, Nike's president, is one of the 400 wealthiest Americans with a personal net worth of $5.3 billion ("The *Forbes* Four Hundred," 1996, p. 111; Herbert, 1996). Meanwhile, Nike advertisements in the U.S. are praised for promoting gender equality. And it is women and girls in low-income countries, especially in Asia, who are the victims of sex tourism, the mail-order bride business, and the international prostitution trade (Goering, 1996; Kristof, 1996; Sherry et al., 1995; U.S. Department of State, 1994; see also Chapter 8).

In the Western world, as we have noted, one of the central feminist goals has been reproductive freedom. This has largely taken the form of freedom from childbearing. However, for women in low-income countries, reproductive freedom sometimes has a different meaning. In some countries, where women are exhorted to bear many children to populate a small labor force or to staff revolutionary armies, reproductive freedom often means access to contraception and abortion. But in other countries where women gain status and material security through childbearing, they also often encounter pressures from Western agencies such as the World Bank and the International Monetary Fund, as well as from their own governments, to use contraceptives (some forms of which have not been approved for use in the West) or to undergo sterilization (Chesler, 1994). In these countries, reproductive freedom is the right to *have* children. In addition, in countries where women are weakened by pregnancies and births spaced too close together and where malnutrition and disease make it unlikely that most of their children will live into adolescence, reproductive freedom may simply mean the right to give birth to healthy babies whose lives may be sustained through adulthood (Bulbeck, 1988).

These, then, are some of the central concerns raised by feminists in developing and underdeveloped countries (Johnson-Odim, 1991).

However, Mohanty (1991, p. 6) cautions that to locate these women solely in the contexts of underdevelopment, oppressive traditions, poverty, overpopulation, and similar problems is to mask the diversity among them and to collapse the fluid and dynamic character of their everyday lives into "a few frozen 'indicators' of their well-being" (see also Moyo, 1996). Brah (1991) gives us some sense of this problem when she writes about her experiences of racism as an Asian woman living in Great Britain. She notes, though, that her membership in a dominant caste also affords her a position of power relative to lower-caste Asian women living in Britain. Consequently, she argues that feminist politics necessarily requires women in industrialized, developing, and undeveloped countries to "examine the ways in which their 'womanhoods' are both similarly and differently constructed within patriarchal, racial and class relations of power" (Brah, 1991, p. 73).

number of women who identified themselves as feminists hovered around 20 percent, while those who did not consider themselves feminists rose over 60 percent. Although most respondents said they considered "feminist" a neutral term, 21 percent think it is an insult (up from 16 percent in 1992) and just 10 percent think it is a compliment (down from 18 percent in 1982) (Boxer, 1997). Goldner (1994) found that women who hold feminist beliefs nonetheless anticipate a negative reaction from others to the label "feminist," so they avoid this stigmatized identity. The media, Goldner (1994) and others (e.g., Faludi, 1991) maintain, are a primary source of negative images of feminism. However, Rhode (1997, p. 227) points out that other sources of resistance to the feminist label are a deep-seated reluctance on the part of most Americans to view themselves "as victims or perpetrators of injustice; our desire for roles that provide power, status, security, and a comfortable way of life; and our anxiety about alternatives. For many of us, feminism seems to put too many issues up for renegotiation."

There is evidence that during the 1990s the involvement of young women in the feminist movement has increased substantially. Analysts tie this renewed feminist groundswell to a number of events: assaults on abortion clinics and providers by anti-abortion groups, which are dramatically curtailing women's reproductive freedom; widely publicized sexual harassment cases, including those involving Supreme Court Justice Clarence Thomas and President Clinton; the sexual assault trials of William Kennedy Smith, Mike Tyson, and Marv Albert, as well as the murder trial of O. J. Simpson; the AIDS epidemic; and the repeal of affirmative action programs and policies in a number of states (De Witt, 1996; Manegold, 1993; Powers, 1993; Schrof, 1993). Significantly, the result has been not only an increased individual commitment to feminism among many young women, but also a growing willingness to take collective action to bring about change, leading some observers to argue that these young women constitute a distinct "new wave" of feminist activism (for a different view, however, see Sigel, 1996).

An important concern of many young feminists is inclusion. Although most feminist groups still attract a majority of members who are White and middle class regardless of their age, many groups of younger feminists have a multicultural emphasis and attempt to address problems resulting from racism, social class inequality, and homophobia as well as sexism. The inclusiveness of these groups may prove to be the key to their continued viability—and the continued viability of the feminist movement in general. If the movement is to remain strong and make up ground lost as a result of the conservative backlash of the 1980s and 1990s, then the needs and experiences of diverse groups of women must not just be taken into account by the powers that be within feminism, they must reshape the focus and course of the movement itself (Hurtado, 1996; King, 1988).

Research indicates that women of color are more likely than White women to identify as feminists, and the strength of their feminist identification appears stronger than that of White women as well (Goldner, 1994; see also Hunter & Sellers, 1998). Historically, as we have seen, mainstream feminism has largely ignored the concerns of non-White women unless its own ends were also served by addressing them, and White feminists have not infrequently been racist. Women of color confront a double oppression in the forms of sexism *and* racism, an oppression that frequently generates a third burden: poverty. Their objective life experiences as people of color frequently lead them to conclude that they have more in common with non-White men, who also have been victimized by racism, than White women who, despite sexism, enjoy numerous privileges because of their race (King, 1988). Women of color have confronted such problems as forced sterilization, inadequate and unaffordable housing, and the degradation of welfare. It is no wonder that they often (rightly) perceive White feminists as pursuing liberation defined as "access to those thrones traditionally occupied by White men—positions in kingdoms which support racism" (Hood, 1984, p. 192; see also hooks, 1990; Hurtado, 1996; King, 1988).

Women of color are infusing contemporary feminism with alternative ways of understanding gender oppression, understandings that are generated from their lived experiences as marginalized members of society. Sociologist Patricia Hill Collins (1986), one of the leading theorists of multiracial feminism, has pointed out that members of marginalized groups—those who live in the dominant society, but are shunned as outgroups—can provide unique insights from their vantage point as "outsiders within." "Most basically, research by and about marginalized women has destabilized what used to be considered universal categories of gender. Marginalized locations are well suited for grasping social relations that remained obscure from more privileged vantage points" (Baca Zinn & Dill, 1996, p. 328). Women of color are themselves a diverse group, composed of African Americans, Latinas, Asian Americans, and Native Americans, categories that also mask numerous differences in history, culture, and contemporary opportunities and barriers. This research is generating new data on women—and men—who occupy diverse social locations, not only in terms of their race and ethnicity, but also their social class, sexual orientation, age, and other factors. With these heretofore silenced voices raising new issues and injecting fresh perspectives, the future of feminism promises to be richly diverse indeed.

The Perspective of This Text

We have discussed feminism at length because it is the paradigm that informs this book. We do not propose to resolve the debates that divide feminists of different perspectives. For the most part, we see these differences as beneficial to the development of the paradigm and the feminist movement. Instead, our goal in this text is to highlight and analyze these differences and debates in the context of available empirical research. In the chapters that follow, you will hear diverse feminist views as we examine gender relations within specific areas of social life.

Despite the diversity of perspectives that are labeled feminist, there are themes or principles shared by all feminists. We think that these themes, coupled with the diverse interests and emphases within feminism, broaden the utility of the paradigm. The fact that feminism is interdisciplinary—that feminist sociologists share their research with, and learn from the work of, feminist psychologists, biologists, historians, and others—further adds to the paradigm's ability to account for the many observed variations and similarities of gender. We second Kramarae and Spender's (1992, p. 6) point that

> Whatever the approaches used most frequently these days—postmodernism, French feminisms, deconstructionism, ecofeminism . . . —we should not overlook the role that feminist scholarship has played in shifting the criteria of knowledge making. Feminist scholarship has helped formulate a model which values plurality and commonality, which presupposes diversity as well as interconnectedness.

In short, the feminist paradigm, taken as a whole, offers a comprehensive and insightful framework for the analysis of gender and gender inequality.

KEY TERMS

feminist movement (women's movement) a social movement that spans more than a century of U.S. and European history and that is represented today in most countries of the developing world as well; it is composed of many diverse segments, each committed to eliminating gender oppression as well as other inequalities

feminist paradigm a school of thought that explains gender in terms of the political and socioeconomic structure in which it is constructed and emphasizes the importance of taking collective action to eradicate sexism in sociology as well as in society, and to reconstruct gender so that it is neither a harmful nor an oppressive social category

gender socially generated attitudes and behaviors, usually organized dichotomously as masculinity and femininity

gender roles social roles that are prescribed for a society's members, depending on their sex

gender stereotypes summary descriptions of masculinity and femininity that are oversimplified and generalized

paradigm a school of thought that guides a scientist in choosing the problems to be studied, in selecting the methods for studying them, and in explaining what is found

patriarchy a sex/gender system in which men dominate women, and what is considered masculine is more highly valued than what is considered feminine

power the ability to impose one's will on others

sex the biologically determined physical distinctions between males and females

sex/gender system   the institutionalized traits, behaviors, and patterns of social interaction that are prescribed for a society's members based on sex; the system incorporates three interrelated components: (1) the social construction of two dichotomous genders on the basis of biological sex; (2) a sexual division of labor; and (3) the social regulation of sexuality

sexism   the differential valuing of one sex over the other

sexual politics   analysis of gender inequality as rooted not only in the public sphere, but also in the supposedly private sphere of the family and intimate male/female relationships

social movement   a group that has organized to promote a particular cause through social action

sociology   the scientific study of human societies and cultures, and of social behavior

structural functionalist paradigm   a school of thought that explains gender as being derived from the biological differences between the sexes, especially differences in reproductive functions

SUGGESTED READINGS

Each chapter of this text will conclude with a list of books that we feel will enhance your understanding of the issues just discussed. We begin with several that provide a good introduction to the study of gender and to the theoretical perspectives that inform it, both in the United States and abroad.

Buckley, S. (1997). *Broken silence: Voices of Japanese feminism.* Berkeley, CA: University of California Press.

Ferree, M. M., & Martin, P. Y. (Eds.) (1995). *Feminist organizations: Harvest of the new women's movement.* Philadelphia: Temple University Press.

Findlen, B. (Ed.) (1995). *Listen up: Voices from the next feminist generation.* Seattle: Seal Press.

Lorber, J. (1998). *Gender inequality: Feminist theories and politics.* Los Angeles: Roxbury.

Rhode, D. L. (1997). *Speaking of sex: The denial of gender inequality.* Cambridge: Harvard University Press.

Shah, S. (Ed.) (1997). *Dragon ladies: Asian American feminists breathe fire.* Boston: South End Press.

Stein, A. (1997). *Sex and sensibility: Stories of a lesbian generation.* Berkeley, CA: University of California Press.

Young, G., & Dickerson, B. J. (Eds.) (1994). *Color, class, and country: Experiences of gender.* London: Zed Books.

NOTES

1. Sociologist Liz Stanley (1992) points out that urban sociology remains one of the subfields of the discipline that is most resistant to feminist critiques and suggestions for more inclusive sociological work. Abbott (1991) argues that the areas of greatest resistance are sociological theory, the study of social class, and political sociology. These three disciplinary subfields, she maintains, are high status and male-dominated.

2. Our focus on British and Western European feminism is not meant to diminish the struggles and achievements of feminists in other industrialized countries in other parts of the world, such as Eastern Europe, Japan, Australia, and New Zealand. For a comparison of feminist movements in some of these countries, see Buckley, 1997; Drakulic, 1991; Eisenstein, 1991; Funk & Mueller, 1993. Our goal here is simply to emphasize the international character of feminism; a complete cross-cultural examination of feminist movements is beyond the scope of this book.

3. The term "Third World" is often used in everyday speech and academic writing to refer to the poor, nonindustrialized countries of Africa, Asia, and Latin America. However, many sociologists object to this term for a number of reasons, one of the most important being that this term groups over one hundred highly diverse countries into a single category, masking not only significant variation in their relative wealth, but also important differences in culture and traditions that affect life conditions, including gender relations.

2 Biology, Sex, and Gender

The Interaction of Nature and Environment

We all probably have childhood memories of meeting some of our parents' friends for the first time and of having to stand by with a tolerant smile while they chattered on about how much we resembled Mom or Dad or Aunt Tilly or Uncle Ned. Thinking about it for a moment, you can probably recall innumerable instances of being told you have your mother's eyes or your father's chin.

In recollecting these experiences, we are doing more than just reminiscing about the little indignities of childhood. Rather, we are beginning to get an inkling of the extent to which most people incorporate the idea of inheritance into their understanding of the world around them. Not only do we hear from others how much we physically resemble our kin, but also we often hear about the behavioral traits we have inherited as well. You may have been told, for instance, that you are stubborn like your father, or outgoing like your mother. Of course, this kind of explanation for our actions and appearance can come in handy at times. It allows us to rationalize, for example, that the inability to find a pair of jeans that fits properly is because of the large bone structure passed on from our mother's side, rather than recent overindulgence in pepperoni pizza. Undoubtedly, the notion that genetics or, more generally, biology, is responsible for who we are socially, as well as physically, holds considerable appeal. Not surprisingly, it has been very popular as a way of explaining many of the differences we observe between men and women.

Documenting differences between women and men has long been a preoccupation of many scientists (see, for example, Caplan & Caplan, 1994; Turner & Sterk, 1994). Drawing these comparisons, however, often goes beyond simply cataloging difference; particular attitudes, aptitudes, and behaviors are imbued with differential value. One trait or behavior is typically, even if only implicitly, considered superior to the other—the "other" almost always being associated with the female. Moreover, like the general public, scientists have not infrequently explained sex differences solely in terms of "natural" or biological differences between women and men, without recognition of the interaction between the biological and social dimensions of life. Psychologist Carol Tavris (1992, p. 24) offers an explanation for this state of affairs:

> Views of women's "natural" differences from man justify a status quo that divides work, psychological qualities, and family responsibilities into "his" and "hers." Those who are dominant have an interest in maintaining their difference from others, attributing those differences to "the harsh dictates of nature," and obscuring the unequal arrangements that benefit them.

Tavris maintains that "there is nothing *essential*—that is, universal and unvarying—in the natures of women and men" (1992, p. 21; see also Lorber, 1993). And, as we will see shortly, the social may influence the biological as much as the biological influences the social.

In this chapter, we will examine some of the available scientific evidence on the impact of biology on gender. We will discuss the significance of studies of genetic abnormalities for our understanding of sex differences, and we will examine the possible effects of other biological factors on gender, particularly the role of hormones and the influence of the size, structure, and organization of our brains. In short, we will be discussing in greater detail the relationship between (biological) sex and (social) gender that we introduced in Chapter 1. To make sense of all this, however, we need some background of how we become male or female in the first place. Let's begin, therefore, by discussing the process of sexual differentiation—a process that begins not long after conception.

The Sex Chromosomes and Sexual Differentiation

Human development is extraordinarily complex. Consider the process of sexual differentiation, for example. Typically—although not always, as we'll see shortly—a person is born with forty-six chromosomes arranged in twenty-three pairs, one of each pair contributed by the individual's mother and one by his or her father. One pair of chromosomes is referred to as the **sex chromosomes** because it plays the primary role in determining whether a fertilized egg will develop into a male or a female fetus. The sex chromosomes of a genetically normal male consist of one X and one Y chromosome, while genetically normal females have two X's. Thus, since the mother of a child always contributes an X to the sex chromosome pair, it is the father's genetic contribution that determines the child's sex.

It is not until the sixth week of embryonic development that the process of sexual differentiation begins. This means that from the moment of conception until the sixth week of their development, all embryos, be they XX or XY, are *sexually bipotential;* they are anatomically identical, each possessing the necessary parts to eventually develop as a male or a female. During the first six weeks, the embryo develops a gonad (called the "indifferent gonad" by scientists because it looks the same in XX and XY embryos) and two sets of ducts, one female (the Müllerian ducts) and one male (the Wolffian ducts). What happens during week six? Scientists are not entirely certain, but they have isolated a gene on the Y chromosome that appears to trigger a sequence of events, beginning in week six, that leads to the development of a fully recognizable male fetus. The gene, which scientists have labeled *SRY* (sex-determining region of the Y), seems to stimulate the transformation of the indifferent gonad into fetal testes. It is still unclear how SRY operates; it may, in fact, work in conjunction with other genes located on the Y chromosome that have not yet been isolated. Nevertheless, SRY seems to be a key component in the sexual differentiation of an embryo into a male (McLaren, 1990; Page et al., 1990; Sinclair et al., 1990).

Once developed, the fetal testes begin to synthesize a whole group of hormones called *androgens.* (Hormones are chemical substances secreted by organs to stimulate a variety of biological activities within the body.) Two of the most important androgens are *Müllerian inhibiting substance* (*MIS*) and *testosterone.* MIS causes the degeneration of the female duct system, while testosterone promotes the further growth of the male (Wolffian) duct system. The secretion of another hormone, *dihydrotestosterone* (*DHT*), during week eight prompts the formation of the external genitals. The genital tubercle (another bipotential structure like the indifferent gonad) develops into a penis and the surrounding tissue becomes a scrotum. DHT also contributes to the "masculinization" of the male brain—a topic to which we will return later in the chapter (Hoyenga & Hoyenga, 1993).

What about the development of a female fetus? Unfortunately, scientists are even less clear about this process. Traditionally, it was argued that the absence of a *Y* chromosome and the subsequent lack of testosterone production prompt the indifferent gonad of an *XX* embryo to transform into ovaries at about the twelfth week of gestation. In other words, female development was conceptualized in terms of a *lack* of the male or *Y* chromosome. More recent research, however, suggests a more balanced alternative hypothesis: that a genetic parallel to male gonadal development exists for females and spurs the formation of ovaries (Eicher & Washburn, 1986). Some scientists have theorized that estrogen (often referred to as one of the "female sex hormones") synthesized by the fetal ovaries may be responsible for the development of the female genitalia in much the same way that androgens are involved in male genital development (Fausto-Sterling, 1985). This hypothesis, though, is refuted by evidence that shows that the ovaries actually develop after the female external genitalia have begun to develop (Hoyenga & Hoyenga, 1993). Obviously, much more research is needed before the entire puzzle of sexual differentiation is solved.

Figure 2.1 summarizes the process of sexual differentiation in the human embryo. We know that males and females are identical in their development until the sixth week of gestation, when genetics, along with various hormones, come into play to help produce those physical differences between the sexes of which we are all very aware. However, several questions remain: Do chromosomes or hormones contribute in any way to the behavioral and personality differences we often observe between males and females? If so, to what extent? And given that these are biologically based differences, are they immutable? There are a variety of ways scientists have tried to answer these questions, and a discussion of their work will occupy us for the remainder of this chapter. Let's begin by taking a brief look at studies of individuals with genetic and hormonal abnormalities.

Chromosomal Abnormalities and Gender

Before an egg is even fertilized, chromosomal errors can occur during sperm production that later result in the birth of individuals with an abnormal complement of sex chromosomes. During sperm production the chromosomes divide and duplicate themselves in a two-stage process called *meiosis*. This usually produces two kinds of sperm— those that carry a *Y* chromosome and those that carry an *X* chromosome. (Remember: A woman always contributes an *X* chromosome to her offspring.) Sometimes, however, the sperm fail to divide properly, a problem called *nondisjunction*. If nondisjunction occurs during the first meiotic division (stage one), two kinds of sperm are produced: those with both an *X* and a *Y*, and those with neither an *X* nor a *Y*. If one of these sperm fertilizes a normal egg, the offspring will be either *XXY* or *XO*. If nondisjunction occurs during the second meiotic division (stage two), three kinds of sperm are produced: *XX*, *YY*, and those with no sex chromosomes. Eggs fertilized by these sperm

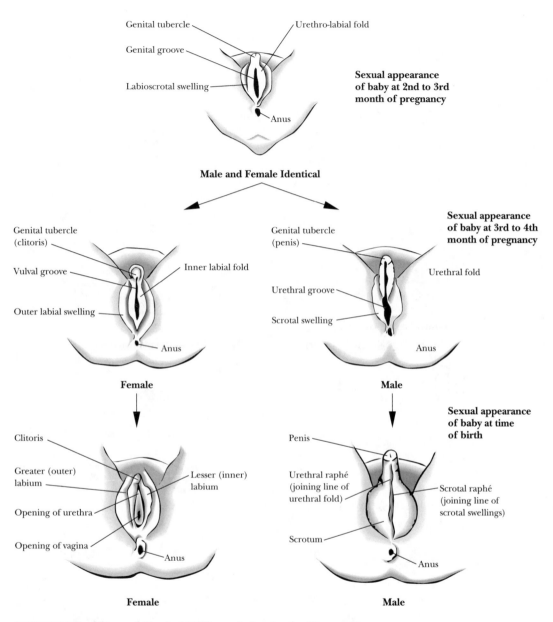

FIGURE 2.1   External Genital Differentiation in the Human Fetus.

Source: Money, John and Anke A. Ehrhardt. *Man and Woman, Boy and Girl.* The Johns Hopkins University Press, Baltimore/London, 1973, Fig. 3.2, p. 44. Reprinted by permission of John Money.

would produce offspring that are *XXX, XYY,* and *XO* respectively. Figure 2.2 on page 36 depicts both normal and faulty meiotic divisions. Do these chromosomal abnormalities have any effect on gendered behavior or personality traits?

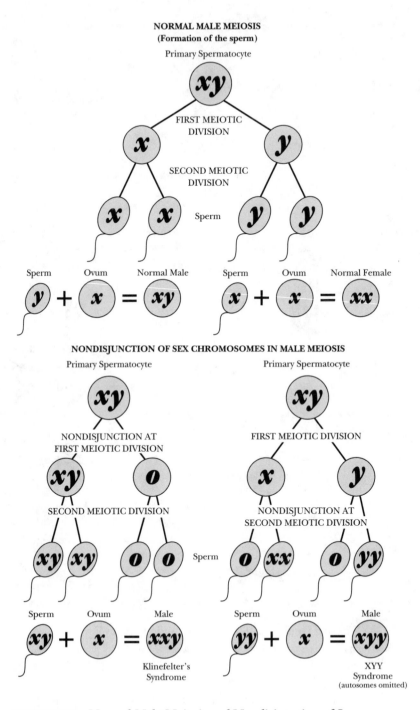

FIGURE 2.2 Normal Male Meiosis and Nondisjunction of Sex Chromosomes in Male Meiosis.

Source: M. F. A. Montagu. "Chromosomes and Crime." *Psychology Today* October, 1968, p. 47.

Individuals who are *XO* have **Turner syndrome.** Because they do not have a *Y* chromosome, they do not develop as males. However, without a second *X* chromosome, they have no gonadal tissue and produce no sex hormones. They are reared as females because their external genitals appear to be female. Despite the absence of sex hormones, however, research with Turner syndrome females reveals an exaggerated femininity in their behavior and personalities. In one study, for example, Turner syndrome females were very unlikely to be described as "tomboys," either by themselves or others. Compared with chromosomally normal girls, they liked to wear "frilly dresses" more, strongly preferred girls over boys as playmates, played only with girls' toys (e.g., dolls) rather than boys' toys (e.g., trucks and building blocks), and expressed an intense interest in caring for babies (Baker, 1980; see also Money & Ehrhardt, 1972). There is no biological explanation for these behavioral and personality differences. Instead, it may be that parents of Turner syndrome girls, determined to compensate for the missing *X* chromosome, intensified the feminine socialization of their daughters.

Women and men with an extra *X* chromosome (that is, those who are *XXX* and *XXY,* respectively) differ considerably. *XXX* women show few visible signs of abnormality, although they tend to be taller than *XX* women and have a higher incidence of learning disorders (Hoyenga & Hoyenga, 1993). In contrast, the *XXY* chromosome combination, a condition known as **Klinefelter syndrome,** produces a number of physical anomalies. Individuals with Klinefelter syndrome physically look more male than female, although they usually have small penises and testes. At puberty, although they tend to grow taller than average, their hips usually feminize, they may have some breast development, their testes do not enlarge, they do not produce sperm, their voices do not deepen, and they develop little or no pubic and facial hair. It has been reported that these men tend to be timid and socially isolated; at an increased risk for developing emotional and interpersonal problems; and uninterested in women, dating, or sex. Of course, such difficulties could very well be related to their condition in an indirect rather than a direct way. Instead of Klinefelter syndrome causing these problems, the problems may result from individuals' trying to cope with their abnormality in a society that is not especially kind to deviants, especially sexual deviants. Nevertheless, most researchers report that many *XXY* men are no different from *XY* men in terms of social and emotional characteristics (Hoyenga & Hoyenga, 1993).

During the 1960s, scientists became interested in another chromosomal abnormality known as *XYY syndrome.* Their interest was aroused by research reports of an unusually high incidence of the abnormality among institutionalized and incarcerated men: Some studies showed a frequency ten to twenty times greater than in the general population. Add to this the fact that offenders in at least two well-publicized murder cases—Daniel Hugon in France and Richard Speck in the United States—reportedly had *XYY* syndrome, and it is not difficult to understand how this chromosomal abnormality attracted the attention of both the scientific community and the general public.[1] By 1970, more than two hundred scientific articles and books had been written on *XYY* syndrome (Ellis, 1982).

Why would having an extra *Y* chromosome predispose men to behave violently? As we stated earlier, the presence of a *Y* chromosome is associated with the secretion of the hormone testosterone and, as we will discuss in greater detail shortly, testosterone has been linked with aggression. Consequently, it was hypothesized that an extra *Y* chromosome would lead to elevated testosterone levels which, in turn, would increase the likelihood of aggressive, even violent behavior. However, subsequent research showed that *XYY* offenders committed primarily petty property crimes and that rather than being especially aggressive, they were somewhat less aggressive than chromosomally normal men (Sarbin & Miller, 1970). Although animal experiments, in particular, have found a link between high testosterone levels and impatience, even a readiness to fight, the extra *Y* chromosome in *XYY* men does not appear to elevate testosterone levels. The overrepresentation of *XYY* men among the institutionalized and incarcerated can be explained instead by social and psychological factors. For example, because *XYY* men tend to be unusually tall, they may look "dangerous," thus biasing criminal justice officials toward arresting, convicting, and institutionalizing them (Sarbin & Miller, 1970). The high institutionalization rate of *XYY* men has also been associated with their low level of intellectual functioning (Witkin et al., 1976). What we see in both of these explanations, however, is an emphasis on the interaction between biology and environment: The extra *Y* chromosome (a biological factor) produces unusual height and low intellectual functioning in the men who have it, which may lead to negative social reactions to their appearance and behavior (an environmental factor), thus resulting in a high probability that *XYY* men, if identified, will be institutionalized or incarcerated. The interaction between biological and social factors is an important point to which we will return throughout the chapter, but first let's discuss several other prenatal mishaps that have been examined for their possible effects on gender.

Prenatal Hormones and Gender

Earlier in the chapter we said that during the sixth week of pregnancy, the presence of a *Y* chromosome in a fetus causes the indifferent gonad to develop into testes, which produce a group of hormones called androgens that, in turn, promote the formation of male sexual organs and genitalia. What if somehow a female fetus gets exposed to androgens? Will such a child grow up to be masculine or feminine? Or, suppose the cells of a male fetus are insensitive to the androgens it secretes. Will that child behave like a "typical" boy or like a girl? Mishaps such as these actually do occur, although fortunately they are rare. When they occur, however, they provide researchers with a unique opportunity to gauge the effects of hormones on the development of gender.[2]

The first situation we described is referred to as **adrenogenital syndrome** (**AGS**); it is also called *congenital adrenal hyperplasia* (*CAH*). It occurs in 1 in 5,000 to 1 in 15,000 births and is caused by a malfunction in the mother's or the fetus's adrenal glands or from exposure of the mother to a substance that acts on the fetus like an androgen (Hines & Kaufman, 1994). Individuals with AGS are exposed to abnormally high levels of androgens prenatally, but if the condition is detected at birth, their androgen levels can be regulated throughout their lives with regular doses of cortisol, another hormone (Hoyenga & Hoyenga, 1993). Both males and females may have AGS, but genetic females are more severely affected.[3] These are individuals whose genetic sex is female and who were exposed to androgens in the womb *after* their internal reproductive organs (ovaries, fallopian tubes, and uterus) had developed. Consequently, the androgens have a masculinizing effect on their external genitals (i.e., the clitoris is enlarged and may resemble a small penis, the labia may be fused, and the vagina may be closed). Because their internal reproductive organs are normal and they are often fertile, surgery is typically used to redesign their external genitals so they are consistent with their genetic sex. AGS females also usually undergo hormonal replacement therapy, so they experience normal female pubertal development (Ehrhardt & Meyer-Bahlburg, 1981; Hoyenga & Hoyenga, 1993).

Researchers have studied AGS females to determine whether their excessive exposure to male hormones in utero affects their gender identities or behavior. Most of these studies involve interviews with fetally androgenized girls who are receiving medical treatment for AGS or related health problems. The girls are questioned about such things as clothing, toy, and playmate preferences as well as their future goals. In comparing the AGS girls' responses with those of other girls similar in age and other social characteristics but without AGS, many researchers have found some striking differences between the two groups. For one thing, AGS girls describe themselves (and are described by their parents) as tomboys more often than normal girls, and they prefer slacks and shorts over dresses and skirts. They are also more likely to prefer toys considered more appropriate for boys (e.g., trucks, building blocks), prefer boys as playmates, and enjoy rough-and-tumble play. Older AGS girls also express a greater interest in pursuing a career than non-AGS girls do (Baker, 1980; Berenbaum & Hines, 1992; Dittman et al., 1990a, 1990b). Nevertheless, most researchers report that AGS girls are not more physically aggressive than normal girls, and that older AGS girls do express a desire for romance, marriage, and motherhood in their futures (Baker, 1980; Money & Ehrhardt, 1972). At least one study found no differences in desire for rough-and-tumble play between AGS and non-AGS girls (Hines & Kaufman, 1994).[4]

In a follow-up study with twelve AGS women who had been studied as adolescents, Money and Matthews (1982) reported that four had married and that none showed any difficulty in establishing relationships with men. Other researchers, however, have noted that AGS women begin dating and engaging in sexual relations later than non-AGS women (Hurtig & Rosenthal, 1987), and some report dreams or fantasies involving bisexual sexual relations (Ehrhardt & Meyer-Bahlburg, 1981). It may be that a delay in dating and sexual behavior is related to the extensive hormonal replacement therapy these women undergo, and there is no evidence that their experiences of bisexual dreams or fantasies occur with greater frequency than those of non-AGS heterosexual women. Indeed, research indicates that women as a group are more flexible with regard to sexuality than men are (see Chapter 6). Before we discuss interpretations and difficulties of the AGS research, let's consider two other prenatal hormonal mishaps.

Sometimes an *XY* fetus has a genetic defect that causes it to be unresponsive to the androgens its testes secrete, a condition known as **androgen-insensitive syndrome.**[5]

Individuals who are androgen-insensitive are sometimes referred to as "*XY* females" because even though they possess the sex chromosomes of normal males (*XY*), they are born with the external genitalia of females. They look like girls at birth, so they are typically raised as girls by their parents. In fact, their condition is sometimes not discovered until puberty when, because they have no uterus, they do not menstruate. But do their *XY* chromosomes predispose them to behave in a masculine manner? According to researchers, androgen-insensitive individuals are as feminine (and sometimes more feminine) than normal *XX* females. In one study, for example, androgen-insensitive subjects expressed as pronounced an interest in dolls, dresses, housewifery, and motherhood as normal girls who were identical to them in terms of age, race, social class, and IQ test scores (Baker, 1980; Brooks-Gunn & Matthews, 1979; Frieze et al., 1978; Money & Ehrhardt, 1972).

Another condition, which involves partial rather than total androgen insensitivity, is **DHT deficiency syndrome,** also called *5-alpha-reductase deficiency,* In individuals with this condition, an enzyme (5-alpha-reductase) responsible for converting testosterone into dihydrotestosterone (DHT), is abnormally low or absent. Recall that DHT is the hormone that prompts the formation of the external genitalia—the scrotum and the penis. Individuals low in DHT or who lack it completely are born with normal undescended testes and internal male accessory organs. Externally, they have female genitals that are partially masculinized (an enlarged clitoris that resembles a small penis and sometimes an incomplete scrotum that looks similar to the female labia). Because of the presence of normal testes, however, at puberty, when the testes begin to produce large amounts of testosterone, the external genitalia change: The penis grows, the scrotum descends, and the body becomes more muscular (Blum, 1997; Hoyenga & Hoyenga, 1993).

Imagine the havoc this condition must wreak on an individual's gender identity. However, some researchers who have studied these cases report that DHT-deficient individuals experience little difficulty in changing their sex and gender identities at puberty when their external genitalia become masculinized. Not surprisingly, other scientists have questioned this finding. For instance, in a small rural village in the Dominican Republic, the deficiency seems to occur with unusually high frequency, perhaps due to inbreeding. Imperato-McGinley and her colleagues (1982) studied eighteen males from this village who had the syndrome and reported that although they had been reared as girls, they easily switched their identities when their genitalia masculinized: At puberty, they became men. Imperato-McGinley's controversial explanation for this ease of transition is that their brains, having been exposed to prenatal testosterone, had been masculinized in utero, thus allowing them to quickly ignore or reject seven to twelve years of socialization as a female (see also Moir & Jessel, 1989).

A number of scientists have challenged this conclusion, as well as the research itself. For one thing, they have questioned the extent to which affected individuals were reared as normal females prior to puberty. There is considerable evidence that they were recognized as "different" or "special" at birth and treated accordingly (Herdt & Davidson, 1988; Rubin et al., 1981). In fact, in the Dominican Republic, boys who have the condition are called *guevedoces* ("eggs" or testes at twelve) or *machihembra* (man-woman). Research with DHT-deficient individuals in other societies indicates that not only are they treated differently than normal boys during childhood, but their attempts to change their sex and gender identities at puberty or in adulthood are sometimes not as smooth as Imperato-McGinley and others maintain (Herdt & Davidson, 1988; Hoyenga & Hoyenga, 1993).

Prenatal Mishaps: What Can They Teach Us about Gender?

We must be cautious in applying findings from research with very small, atypical groups of individuals to women and men generally (Rogers & Walsh, 1982). These studies are often plagued by serious methodological difficulties inherent in this type of research. For example, although researchers usually match subjects with a control group similar in various social characteristics, other important factors are sometimes ignored or are simply not controllable. Consider, for instance, that AGS females who have participated in studies were familiar with the researchers and were already comfortable with the clinical setting in which the research took place. It's possible that the results reflect a greater willingness on the part of AGS girls to talk about sex-atypical behavior and attitudes, rather than reflecting a genuine difference between AGS and non-AGS girls (Frieze et al., 1978). In addition, the researchers themselves are aware of which subjects have chromosomal or hormonal abnormalities and which do not. This knowledge might unconsciously bias their assessments of the attitudes and behavior of the patient-subjects (Fausto-Sterling, 1985; Longino & Doell, 1983).

Despite these problems, though, the research does offer us important lessons with regard to the relationship of chromosomes and hormones to gender. It suggests that the development of a masculine or feminine gender identity is quite independent of either the presence of a pair of *XY* or *XX* sex chromosomes, or the production of particular hormones. More importantly, this research indicates that neither sex nor gender is dichotomous. When we speak of sex, we may be referring to chromosomal sex, hormonal sex, gonadal sex, or genital sex. Although for most individuals these are consistent with the category male or the category female, the research we have discussed so far shows vividly how they may sometimes be inconsistent, so that, difficult as it may be for us to do, we should stop thinking of sex as a unidimensional characteristic with dichotomous attributes. Similarly, gender—what we generally call masculinity and femininity —far from being an either/or phenomenon, includes a broad spectrum of attitudes, behaviors, and social expectations that we acquire during our lifetimes, through interactions with one another and experiences in various environments.

Suzanne Kessler (1996) has criticized physicians who rush to surgically "correct" genital ambiguity, pointing out that their decisions are influenced as much by cultural factors as by medical ones: They use medical technology to convert the non-normative (intersexuality) into the normative (one of two sexes/genders). "[G]enital ambiguity is 'corrected' not because it is threatening to the infant's life, but because it is threatening to the infant's culture" (Kessler, 1996, p. 362; see also Angier, 1997). In other societies, the fluidity of sex and gender is accepted as natural, and multiple genders are the norm: In some societies, there are three genders, in others, four. In some Asian, South Pacific, and North American Indian societies, for example, individuals may choose to adopt the gender behavior ascribed to members of the opposite sex without fear of being stigmatized as abnormal or deviant. Such individuals are often collectively referred to as *berdaches*.

Berdaches live, work, and dress as members of the opposite sex, although they may specialize in tasks associated with both sexes (Gailey, 1987; Martin & Voorhies, 1975; Roscoe, 1991; Whitehead, 1981; Williams, 1986). Anthropologist Will Roscoe (1991) has conducted extensive research on Zuni *berdaches*, called *lhamana* by this American Indian nation. Roscoe points out that although *berdaches* cross-dressed, it is inaccurate to label them transvestites or transsexuals as some researchers have done. This is because their cross-dressing was routine, public, and without erotic motives. Nor were *berdaches* necessarily homosexual as we think of this sexual orientation today. There were Zunis who were sexually attracted to the opposite sex, some who were sexually attracted to the same sex, and still others who were sexually attracted to *berdaches*. Roscoe attributes this openness to the traditional Zuni conception of gender acquisition, which maintains that gender is not something one is born with, but rather something that develops over the course of a person's life. In fact, until about age six, gender was not seen as an important attribute of a child, and children of both sexes were referred to simply as "child," rather than "boy" or "girl." All Zunis could combine or temporarily adopt roles and experiences of more than one gender, but *berdaches* did enjoy a special status because in Zuni culture they represented "an affirmation of humanity's original, pre-gendered unity—representatives of a form of solidarity and wholeness that transcended the division of humans into men and women" (Roscoe, 1991, p. 146).[6]

Other examples of such gender crossing can be found in Tahitian culture (Gilmore, 1990); among the Omani Muslims (Wikan, 1984); and with the Hijras of India (Nanda, 1990). Among the Hua of Papua New Guinea, gender is perceived as changing throughout an individual's life, with both men and women possessing varying degrees of masculinity and femininity at different life stages (Gailey, 1987; Meigs, 1990). The Hua bestow high status on masculine people, but view them as physically weak and vulnerable. Feminine people are regarded as invulnerable, but polluted. When children are born, they are all at least partially feminine because the Hua believe that women transfer some of their own femininity to their offspring. Thus, the more children a woman has, the more femininity she loses. After three births, she is no longer considered polluted. She may participate in the discussions and rituals of men and share their higher status and authority, but she must also observe their diet and sanitation customs since she is now vulnerable like them. Meanwhile, Hua men gradually lose their masculinity by imparting it to young boys during growth rituals. As this happens, they are thought to become physically invulnerable, but polluted. Consequently, older men work in the fields with young women and have little social authority. "Among the Hua, then, gender is only tangentially related to sex differences; it is mutable and flows from person to person" (Gailey, 1987, p. 36).

The cross-cultural data illustrate not only the fluidity of gender, but also the creativity that humans bring to the process of social organization. This is not to say, however, that biology plays no role in shaping gender identity and behavior. To paraphrase science writer Deborah Blum (1997), it's not a question of "if" biology influences human behavior, but rather of "how" and "how much." Let's continue to explore these questions by examining recent research on the structure and function of women's and men's brains.

The Case for His and Hers Brains

The notion that men and women have different brains is an old one. Nineteenth-century scientists maintained, for instance, that women were less intelligent than men because their brains are smaller. When it was pointed out that elephants, then, should be more intelligent than men given the relative size of their brains, the argument was quickly modified. It was subsequently argued that the best estimate of intelligence could be obtained by dividing brain size by body weight. However, this hypothesis, too, was abandoned when it was discovered that according to this measure, women were more intelligent than men (Fausto-Sterling, 1985; Gould, 1980; Harrington, 1987). Today, there are few scientists who argue that size differences in men's and women's brains make one sex intellectually superior to the other (but for examples, see Lynn, 1994; and Rushton & Ankney, 1996). Still, an interest in how sex differences in the brain might contribute to differences in men's and women's behavior remains strong. The focus of research nowadays, though, is primarily on how our brains are organized. Indeed, it has been hypothesized that the differential organization of the brain is not only the source of behavioral differences between women and men, but also it may be responsible for the development of sexual orientation (see Box 2.1 on page 44).

One of the difficulties in looking for sex differences in the brain is that much of the research uses the brains of animals, usually rats, not humans. Are rat brains comparable to human brains? No one can say for sure, but researchers looking for sex differences in human brains that have been identified in rat brains are often unsuccessful (Blum, 1997). A second problem is that the human brain changes as people age and in response to experience and environmental conditions. For example, although men's brains are, on average, larger than women's brains, men lose brain tissue three times faster than women as they age, but it is unclear at this point why (Cowell et al., 1994). Nevertheless, new nerve growth can be stimulated in the brains of both elderly women and men by introducing new challenges into their environment (Blum, 1997). A third, related problem is that scientists do not yet fully understand how the way specific parts of the brain are structured affects how they function. Interestingly, some scientists speculate that the relationship may actually be the opposite of what we might think: Instead of structure determining function, the way the brain works causes it to build or alter its structure (Blum, 1997). Keeping these issues in mind, then, let's consider the findings on sex differences in the brain.

As Figure 2.3 on page 45 shows, the brain is divided into two halves or *hemispheres*, one on the right and one on the left. In the late 1960s, Dr. Roger Sperry and his colleagues, working with a group of patients suffering from severe epileptic seizures, discovered that each hemisphere appears to "specialize" in certain functions or tasks

BOX **2.1**

Sexual Orientation and the Brain

In the August 30, 1991, issue of the prestigious journal *Science*, neuroscientist Simon LeVay reported the results of a study he conducted in which he examined the post-mortem tissue of the brains of six women and sixteen men that he presumed had been heterosexual, and those of nineteen men who had been homosexual. LeVay found that one node of the anterior hypothalamus (an area of the brain that scientists speculate may play a part in sexual behavior) was three times larger in the heterosexual men than in the homosexual men, whose nodes were closer in size to the ones found in the heterosexual women's brains. Soon after LeVay's findings appeared in *Science*, major national newspapers and news magazines ran prominently placed articles with titles such as "Brain May Determine Sexuality; Node Seen as Key to Gay Orientation" (*Washington Post*, August 30, 1991); "Zone of the Brain Linked to Men's Sexual Orientation" (*New York Times*, August 30, 1991); and "Born or Bred?" (*Newsweek*, February 24, 1992). One year later, another study reported that the anterior fissure (a cord of nerves that is thought to facilitate communication between the two hemispheres of the brain) is larger in homosexual men than in either heterosexual men or women (Allen & Gorski, 1992). These findings, like LeVay's, not only triggered a storm of media attention, but also added fuel to a heated debate over whether sexual orientation is innate or learned.

On the one hand, there are those—including members of the gay community—who welcome such findings, arguing that they will reduce prejudice and discrimination against gays. If homosexuals cannot help what they do—if their sexual behavior is biologically programmed and not freely chosen—then they are not responsible for their orientation and should therefore be granted the same basic rights as other minority groups (e.g., racial minorities) whose minority status is based on a biological trait (Herek, 1991). On the other hand, there are those—also including members of the gay community—who maintain that

negative attitudes toward homosexuals are not likely to be changed by research findings indicating that homosexuality is biologically based. Rather, they maintain that such findings have the potential for doing more harm than good to gay people. They warn, for instance, that the research could be used to support a eugenics movement to eliminate homosexuality through genetic engineering, surgery, or some other interventionist strategy (Zicklin, 1992).

Members of the scientific community are also divided in their assessment of these studies. Some claim that the studies provide support for the hypothesis that sexual orientation is biologically determined, while others are more skeptical. Nearly everyone cautions that researchers simply do not yet fully understand how humans (or even other animals) develop sexual orientation. There are too many unanswered questions and the behavior involved is too complex to reduce to a cause-and-effect relationship with one minute area of the brain (Blum, 1997).

One hypothesis linking brain structures with sexual orientation suggests that a genetic mechanism (i.e., a gene or genes) triggers hormonal secretions prenatally that organize the brain in such a way that a person is later attracted to the opposite sex or the same sex (Blum, 1997). There is research showing a genetic link to sexual orientation (Bailey & Pillard, 1991; Bailey et al., 1993; Hamer et al., 1993; Hu et al., 1995). However, other researchers have been unable to replicate the findings of these studies as well as those of LeVay (Blum, 1997; Marshall, 1992; Risch et al., 1993; Spanier, 1995). The research has also been criticized on methodological grounds. For example, lesbians have been largely left out of the research. When they are included, the findings are nonconfirming, although some scientists argue that this is because sexuality in females is governed by a different "genetic scenerio" than sexuality in males (Blum, 1997). A second methodological problem is that most of the studies are based on very small samples: LeVay, for instance, examined a total of 41 brains; Allen and Gorski studied 193 brains, but only 34 came from known homosexual men. Furthermore, the relationship between brain and behavior is unclear; it is possible that the differences observed by LeVay and Allen and Gorski are caused by homosexuality rather than the reverse.

Despite these cautions and the tentative nature of the research that has generated them, many people have come to accept the findings as scientific "facts." Science—even rather shaky science—carries considerable weight in our society because it is considered "objective" and this ascribed objectivity often makes it a powerful political tool (see, for example, Gould, 1981; Hubbard & Wald, 1993). As the public debates show, the findings of the studies discussed here became politicized almost instantly. What remains to be seen are their political consequences for homosexual people (see Chapter 6). As one scientist observed, however, "in an ideal world . . . it shouldn't matter whether there's a biology to sexual preference or not; we should merely respect each other" (quoted in Blum, 1997, p. 135).

(Sperry 1982). This specialization is referred to as hemispheric asymmetry or **brain lateralization.** The left hemisphere (which controls the right side of the body) is responsible for language, among other things, whereas the right hemisphere (which controls the left side of the body) is thought to handle such functions as emotions. In working with patients recovering from strokes, other researchers found that women tend to recover more quickly than men and to show less profound impairment from brain damage. It was hypothesized that the reason for this difference may be that men are more lateralized than women—that is, they are more dependent on one hemisphere of their brains to complete certain tasks, whereas women draw on both hemispheres (Gazzaniga, 1992).

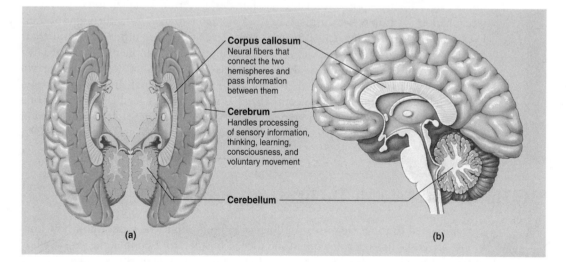

Corpus callosum
Neural fibers that connect the two hemispheres and pass information between them

Cerebrum
Handles processing of sensory information, thinking, learning, consciousness, and voluntary movement

Cerebellum

(a)

(b)

FIGURE 2.3   The Human Brain

Subsequent research using sophisticated technology, such as Magnetic Resonance Imaging (MRI), provides support for this hypothesis.[7] For example, in one study that asked subjects to complete a rhyming task, MRI images showed men's brains glowing in a small frontal center on the left side of their brains as they worked, whereas women's brains glowed on both sides in this area (Shaywitz et al., 1995). In another study comparing the electrical activity in men's and women's brains while they performed a series of word selection tests, most women had equal activity in both hemispheres, while most men had activity in just the left hemisphere (Blum, 1997). Related to this is the finding that the *corpus callosum*—the mass of tissue and nerve fibers that connect the two hemispheres of the brain (refer back to Figure 2.3)—is as much as 23 percent larger in women than in men (Allen & Gorski, 1992). It may be that the greater size of women's corpus callosum allows more communication between the brain's two hemispheres.

In practical terms—that is, in terms of men's and women's everyday lives and interactions—what do these findings mean? One writer suggests that the sex difference in brain lateralization may account for why women have an easier time expressing emotions; there is connection and cross-talk between the two halves of their brains, one of which controls speech and the other emotion (Blum, 1997). This theory, though, remains untested and is complicated by the fact that other structures of the brain also play a role in emotional expression. Others speculate that the brain differences we've discussed explain why women outperform men on tests of verbal ability, while men outperform women on tests of spatial ability (see Chapter 4). Greater communication between the two hemispheres may facilitate verbal skills, but research also shows that such cross-talk may impede spatial skills (Gorman, 1992).

However, regardless of what behaviors these differences may account for, the larger question looming in the minds of many concerns the source of the differences. Are sex differences in the brain present at birth, the products of innate biology? Or, do they develop in response to males' and females' differing socialization experiences (see Chapter 3)? It may be, for instance, that women and men *learn* throughout their lives to process language and interpret spatial relationships differently, and their brains have adapted to these socialization experiences. Indeed, the discovery of a difference probably reveals as much about culture as it does about biology, since the two spheres, as we have already noted, are not separate and distinct. Instead, it appears that their relationship is best conceptualized as an *interactive* feedback loop. As one scientist put it, "Everything is biologically determined at one level, but its expression is always an interaction with an environment" (Wallen, quoted in Blum, 1997, p. 279).

"My Hormones Made Me Do It"

Not unrelated to the issue of sex differences in the brain is the question of how hormones affect the behavior of women and men. Consider, for example, the case of a boy initially studied by John Money at the Johns Hopkins University Gender Identity Clinic in Baltimore, Maryland. The boy, who, along with an identical twin brother, was born a chromosomally and physically normal male, had his penis almost completely destroyed when he was eight months old as a doctor tried to repair the foreskin. Following the accident and in consultation with physicians, his parents decided in favor of sex reassignment; at seventeen months of age, the boy was surgically reconstructed as a girl and lifelong hormone replacement therapy was planned. Money and his colleagues reported in 1973 that the reassigned twin had been "successfully" socialized as a girl: She preferred to wear dresses rather than slacks, had feminine toy and play preferences, and, in contrast to her brother, was neat, clean, and enjoyed helping with housework.

In 1997, two other researchers, Milton Diamond and H. Keith Sigmundson, reported the findings of their follow-up study with the child. They found that at about the age of twelve, the child began to experience serious emotional problems because, even though she was receiving estrogen treatments that promoted breast development and other female secondary sex characteristics, she had a decidedly masculine appearance and was the brunt of much cruel teasing by her peers. Her parents had not told her about the accident, nor about the fact that chromosomally she was male. Her early feminine behavior was simply an attempt to win social approval, but at fourteen, the child decided to stop living as a female and refused further hormonal treatments and genital surgery. When her father finally told her about her medical history, the teenager said she felt relieved. Eventually, she decided to undergo male hormone therapy and a mastectomy, and had a penis surgically constructed. At the age of twenty-five, this person married a woman who already had children and, most recently, he was reported to be happy and well-adjusted as a man (Diamond & Sigmundson, 1997).

Certainly, caution is in order in interpreting the significance of this case, given that it is only a single incident—and one embedded in highly unusual circumstances at that. However, Diamond and Sigmundson's controversial explanation as to why this child could not be "successfully" socialized as a girl was that her brain had been exposed to the male hormone testosterone, making her ineradicably male. No matter how hard people worked at making her female, her brain knew otherwise (Diamond & Sigmundson, 1997). Testosterone, we know, does contribute to differences in the physical appearance of males and females. Earlier in this chapter, we discussed that testosterone is largely responsible for building a male body out of a sexually bipotential embryo. But does the secretion of testosterone also produce a male brain which, in turn, generates those distinctive personality traits and behaviors that we, in our culture, associate with masculinity? Let's consider some of the research on the effects of testosterone on behavior, and then turn our attention to a discussion of the effects of the "female" sex hormones.

Testosterone and Gender

If you were to ask others what they consider to be the most fundamental behavioral difference between males and females, most would likely say aggression—specifically, that males are more aggressive than females. Research on aggression, in fact, has yielded some of the most consistent findings of sex differences in behavior, from preschoolers to adults. One explanation for sex differences in aggression centers around the fact that males secrete higher levels of the hormone testosterone. (It is important to note here that both males and females produce the same sex hormones, but in different amounts. Males secrete more testosterone and other androgens, while females produce more estrogen and progesterone. All the steroid hormones are derivatives of cholesterol.)

The evidence linking testosterone to aggression has come primarily from animal studies. Typically, in these experiments, laboratory animals (rats, mice, or monkeys) are injected with testosterone. The usual outcomes are that, regardless of their sex, the animals show a significant increase in impatience, rough-and-tumble play, and fighting behavior. A variation on this theme is to castrate newborn animals, with the result that as they mature, they display little aggressive behavior.

Some people accept such findings as strong indicators that males are biologically programmed to be aggressive. However, there is reason to be cautious in interpreting these results. For one thing, there is tremendous variation in behavior across animal species. Female gerbils and hamsters, for instance, are just as aggressive as the males of their species, without being injected with hormones (Fausto-Sterling, 1985). Clearly, this variation points to the difficulty in generalizing about behavior from one species of rodents to another, let alone from rodents to human beings (Angier, 1992).

In research with humans, findings do indicate that high levels of circulating testosterone are correlated with edginess, competitiveness, and anger. This result holds for both men and women. For example, in a study of female athletes who had taken synthetic testosterone during training, researchers found that the women were more easily irritated and more quickly angered than women who had not used testosterone (Van Goozen et al., 1994). However, scientists have not been able to pinpoint the relationship between testosterone and specific behaviors in humans for a number of reasons. One is that the hormone fluctuates dramatically over the course of a day and in response to environmental stimuli (Blum, 1997). For instance, we noted that testosterone is correlated with competitiveness, with the traditional hypothesis being that high testosterone makes a person more competitive. But recent research shows that testosterone levels rise and fall *in response to* competitive challenges. In one study, researchers found that testosterone rises in male tennis players before a match, goes down as the match is being played, and then rises dramatically in players who win, but drops just as dramatically in those who lose (Booth et al., 1989; Mazur & Lamb, 1980). A similar pattern was found in chess players (Mazur et al., 1992).

Such findings have led some scientists to hypothesize that it is not the relationship between testosterone and aggression that is significant, but rather the relationship between dominance/eminence and testosterone. *Dominance* "refers to an elevated social rank that is achieved by overcoming others in a competitive confrontation, and *eminence* is where the elevated social rank is earned through socially valued and approved accomplishment" (Kemper, 1990, pp. 27–28). Thus, Booth and his colleagues (1989) discovered a rise in testosterone in male medical school graduates the day before graduation—that is, the day before they achieved an eminent status. This research not only reframes our understanding of the relationship between testosterone and aggression, but it also illustrates how biology itself is affected by social factors (Kemper, 1990).

Finally, scientists have had difficulty specifying more precisely the relationship between testosterone and human aggression because testosterone is only one of several chemicals interacting in the body that affect human behavioral response. Two other important chemicals are the neurotransmitters serotonin, which appears to have a calming effect, and noradrenaline, which helps us react almost instantaneously in a crisis. Like testosterone, both neurotransmitters fluctuate in response to environmental stimuli. For instance, serotonin levels can be raised and noradrenalin levels lowered by placing an individual in a relaxed, secure environment or through interaction with others behaving calmly and kindly (Blum, 1997).

Such research indicates that human social behavior is highly governed by the situation or context in which it occurs, and that this, in turn, may override or alter the potential effects of various hormones. Studies with women, for example, show that they can be just as aggressive as men in certain situations, such as when they are rewarded for behaving aggressively or when they think no one is watching them (Frieze et al., 1978; Hyde, 1984). This research suggests that females may simply inhibit aggression because of social pressures to conform to a feminine or ladylike ideal; in the absence of such pressures, they may be as likely as males to express aggression. Cross-cultural research, in fact, indicates that women may behave as aggressively as men, but how they express aggression (for example, verbal versus physical aggression) may be structured by their culture's gender norms (Bjokqvist, 1994; Lepowsky, 1994; see also Crick & Grotpeter, 1995). A related finding is that females are more likely than males to perceive aggressive behavior on their parts as posing a danger to themselves and, therefore, they may inhibit aggression when the likelihood of retaliation is high (Bettencourt & Miller, 1996; Eagly, 1987; Eagly & Steffan, 1986). Moreover, for both males and females, aggressiveness decreases as age and education increase (Harris & Knight-Bohnhoff, 1996).

While testosterone and its impact on aggression has probably been the most widely studied hormonal gender difference, the "female" sex hormones have not escaped scientific—and popular—scrutiny. Let's consider, then, the effect of the "female" sex hormones on behavior.

Women, Hormones, and Behavior

We've all heard stories and jokes about changes in women's personality and behavior that result from the fluctuation of hormones in their bodies every month. The stereotype is of a woman out of control; she is depressed, enraged by the slightest perceived transgression, and overcome by the need to satisfy her cravings for sweets or salty foods—all signs that her menstrual period will start in a few days. The official name given to this malady is *premenstrual syndrome*, or PMS for short.

The notion that women's personality and behavior are dictated by their hormones is an old one. After all, as science writer Deborah Blum (1997, p. 189) reminds us, the word *androgen* comes from the Greek word for "man," while *estrogen* comes from the Greek word for "frenzy." Premenstrual syndrome, however, was not discussed in the medical literature until about sixty-five years ago. It captured the attention of the general public during the 1980s, largely as a result of media coverage of two

British homicide trials. The first case in 1980 involved a thirty-seven-year-old woman who drove her car at full speed directly at her boyfriend, pinning him to a telephone pole and killing him. She was subsequently convicted of manslaughter instead of murder and was released on probation because of a mitigating factor in her case: At the time of the crime, her defense attorney argued, this woman was suffering from premenstrual syndrome, a condition that may cause those afflicted to behave violently. Also in 1980, a twenty-nine-year-old woman was convicted of killing a coworker at the London pub where she tended bar, but she too was sentenced to probation on the basis of the premenstrual syndrome defense. As a condition of probation, both women were required to receive monthly hormone injections to control their PMS symptoms (Glass, 1982; Parlee, 1982).

These cases undoubtedly reinforced the image of the premenstrual woman as under the influence of "raging hormones." Certainly, the treatment of PMS has become a thriving business, with more than seventy-five PMS clinics operating in the United States and numerous over-the-counter medications and self-help books available (Chisler & Levy, 1990; Markens, 1996). Moreover, the American Psychiatric Association has added PMS to its *Diagnostic and Statistical Manual* (the *DSM*) under the name *late luteal phase dysphoric disorder* and classifies it not as a gynecological problem, but as an "unspecified mental disorder" that is insurable (i.e., treatment may be covered by medical insurance). But while PMS and other hormonally caused syndromes (see Box 2.2) have been receiving a great deal of attention in recent years, the crucial question that remains unanswered is whether women really are transformed each month by fluctuations in their hormones. Let's consider the *scientific* evidence.

As we noted earlier, both men and women secrete the sex hormones, which, besides testosterone and other androgens, include the "female" estrogens (estrone, estradiol, and estiol) as well as progestins. Of the estrogens, men secrete only estradiol, whereas women produce all three estrogens. Of the three, estradiol has been the most extensively studied and, unlike testosterone, levels of this hormone in a woman's body do not fluctuate as much over the course of a day nor in response to environmental stimuli, such as competitive challenges. Instead, female hormone production is influenced by the monthly reproductive cycle as well as the cessation of reproductive capacity (menopause) during the life course.

A woman's monthly cycle is twenty-eight days, although for some women it is slightly longer and for others, slightly shorter. During the first two weeks of the cycle, estradiol production increases as an egg matures in the ovaries. When ovulation occurs at the end of this period, progesterone production increases, which prompts another surge in estradiol. But if the egg is not fertilized, both progesterone and estradiol production drop and within a few days menstrual bleeding occurs. Many women report a number of physical changes about a week before their menstrual period begins. These include acne flair-ups, an increase or decrease in appetite, fluid retention, headaches, forgetfulness, and irritability. But do these changes constitute a *syndrome*, that is, a medically diagnosable physical abnormality?

One of the difficulties in answering this question is that much of the research on PMS is plagued by serious methodological difficulties. Indeed, Blume (1983, p. 2866) has argued that available data on PMS are "seriously flawed." For instance, the major-

BOX **2.2**

Postpartum Depression Syndrome

Depression after the birth of a baby, also called the "maternity blues" or the "baby blues," is not uncommon. Studies indicate that in the United States 50 to 80 percent of women report feelings of sadness, tension, and irritability during the first two weeks after the birth of their babies. However, for these women, the symptoms also disappear quickly, often within just a few days. About 10 to 20 percent of women who give birth report more severe symptoms, including feelings of inadequacy, guilt, fatigue, and an inability to care for the baby. These symptoms—usually referred to as *postpartum depression*—may appear from two weeks to three months postpartum and may last from several weeks to several months. For a very small number of women—1 to 2 percent who give birth—the symptoms may be so severe as to constitute *postpartum psychosis*, involving hallucinations, mental confusion, panic attacks, suicide attempts, and attempts to kill their babies. Although it appears that the incidence of baby blues and postpartum depression has increased in the United States and Great Britain over the last several decades, the rate of postpartum psychosis has remained fairly stable (Giovannini, 1992; Taylor, 1996).

The most widely cited theory of the causes of postpartum disorders focuses on hormonal changes following childbirth, especially the sudden drop in progesterone (Gitlin & Passnau, 1990). However, the scientific data directly supporting this position are limited. Moreover, as Giovannini (1992) points out, the exceptionally low incidence of postpartum depression and psychosis reported in cross-cultural studies indicates that sociocultural or environmental factors may also be important contributors to these disorders.

Giovannini's (1992) research shows that the incidence and severity of postpartum emotional disorders are directly related to the amount of social support available to new mothers, as well as the amount and type of socioenvironmental stressors (e.g., financial or housing difficulties, marital problems, the number and ages of other children in the household) to which they are exposed. Women who are isolated in their homes, who lack family and social support networks, and who are exposed to serious and prolonged stress are more likely to experience a postpartum emotional disorder (see also Gjerdingen et al., 1990; Taylor, 1996). In addition, women who experience a traumatic labor, who are unprepared for the level of pain and discomfort they experience, and who undergo unexpected surgery may also be at high risk for postpartum emotional disorders. Oakley (1980) has argued, in fact, that the increased medicalization of childbirth in the United States and Great Britain (see Chapter 11), coupled with the lack of preparation for mothering and the low level of support offered to mothers (see Chapter 6), have contributed to the rise in the incidence of post-partum emotional disorders in these countries. Sociologist Verta Taylor (1996), however, has found that women who have experienced post-partum depression and band together to form support networks can work together to resist subordination by both the medical establishment and society at large.

---

ity of studies have relied on subjects' self-reports in determining the onset of premenstrual symptoms (see, for example, Thys-Jacobs et al., 1995). However, this method is highly unreliable for several reasons. First, there is evidence that retrospective studies dependent on subjects' recall produce exaggerated results compared with prospective studies, which begin with a sample of women who subsequently chart their cycles over several months (Koeske, 1980; Sommer, 1983). Second, studies show that there is a tendency for women with random mood changes to selectively remember those changes happening during the premenstrual phase of the cycle or to label them PMS if they occurred during this phase of the cycle (Hardie, 1997; Widom & Ames, 1988). Third, Culpepper (1992) notes that many women perceive researchers as condescending toward them and, therefore, these women are reluctant to report information about how they feel and behave during their menstrual cycles. Fourth, several recent studies indicate that social and psychological factors have an influence on the experience of PMS symptoms. It has been argued, for example, that the attitudes toward menstruation prevalent in a particular culture may affect women's reactions to their monthly periods (Woods et al., 1982). In the United States, menstruation has long been viewed as a negative event in a woman's life—at best it is an inconvenience, at worst, a "curse." Women have also been led to believe that they are physically unattractive just prior to and during menstruation and that they should restrict their behavior during their periods; they should not swim, bathe, or have sexual relations during that time. Although these negative attitudes have diminished somewhat in recent years, research indicates that they still are not uncommon. In one study, for instance, nearly a third of the male and female respondents felt that women need to restrict their physical activities while menstruating; more than half felt that women should not have sexual intercourse while menstruating; and one quarter said that women look different when menstruating (Golub 1992; see also Jurgens & Powers, 1991; Markens, 1996).

Clarke and Ruble (1978) report that negative attitudes toward menstruation are learned by both girls and boys at an early age. These negative expectations may influence women's experience of PMS symptoms. One researcher, for instance, asked a group of students to evaluate the behaviors of several hypothetical female patients. Included with each case was information about the patient's menstrual cycle. When the students thought that the patient was in the premenstrual phase of her cycle, they attributed any hostile, aggressive, or negative behaviors to biological causes; interestingly, they attributed positive behaviors during the same period to nonbiological factors (Koeske 1980). In a second experiment, psychologist Diane Ruble (1977) told a group of female subjects that physical tests indicated that they were in the premenstrual phase of their cycles. In reality, all the women were in another cycle phase, but they began to report PMS symptoms (see also Hardie, 1997).

A second difficulty with regard to PMS is that if it is, in fact, a medical entity, there is little consensus regarding what causes it. One theory, proposed by Katharina Dalton, a major PMS proponent, is that the "syndrome" is a result of declining progesterone several days before menstruation. Progesterone is an adrenal hormone and, since the adrenal hormones regulate such body functions as fluid retention, allergic reactions, and blood-sugar level, a drop in progesterone may cause an imbalance relative to other adrenal hormones, and may provoke the physical and psychological symptoms some women experience premenstrually (Golub, 1992). Dalton recommends progesterone injections as a "cure," but there is no empirical evidence to support her theory (Blum, 1997; Reid & Yen, 1980). Other hypothesized causes of PMS are nerve irritability, an imbalance in electrolyte metabolism, vitamin B deficiency, and either rising or falling estrodial production. Again, though, empirical evidence on the role of each of these factors is limited and often contradictory (Blum, 1997; Golub, 1992).

Given these findings, what actual behavioral or personality changes have been found to be related to the menstrual cycle, especially the premenstrual phase? This question, too, is difficult to answer because the results of most studies are inconsistent. Some of the research on mood swings, for example, has found that women tend to feel less able to cope with everyday problems during the premenstrual phase of their cycles than during the ovulatory phase (Friedman et al., 1980). But others report that negative changes in mood, as well as physical changes, may have more to do with stressful external events (e.g., the triple burden of child care, housework, and work outside the home) than with the phase of the menstrual cycle (Golub, 1992; Hardie, 1997; Ripper, 1991). Interestingly, in two studies in which both men and women participated, men were equally likely to experience mood swings, problems at work, and physical discomfort (Hardie, 1997; Rossi & Rossi, 1977). Indeed, one researcher, noting that men are subject to a daily hormonal cycle in which testosterone levels peak at about 4 A.M. and are lowest at around 8 P.M., stated, "When people say women can't be trusted because they cycle every month, my response is that men cycle every day, so they should only be allowed to negotiate peace treaties in the evening" (quoted in Gorman, 1992, p. 51).

A few studies show improved task performance premenstrually, leading one researcher to suggest that perhaps we should study "premenstrual elation syndrome" (Parlee, 1983). There is no evidence to support the notion that women's academic or work performance declines during the premenstrual phase of their cycles. The majority of studies report no relationship between task performance and menstrual cycle at all (Chrisler, 1991; Morgan et al., 1996). Some researchers have observed a relationship between menstrual cycle phase and such psychophysiological functions as visual, auditory, and olfactory sensitivity; galvanic skin response; and spontaneous body movement. "However, the variations among findings are such that one could select studies to support almost any hypothesis one chose" (Sommer, 1983, p. 82).

It does appear that many women experience some physical discomfort around the time of menstruation, but the majority appear to accept this as normal and do not see menstruation as debilitating (Golub, 1992). Ripper (1991) hypothesizes, in fact, that one of the reasons that researchers frequently find negative attitudes toward menstruation is that the questionnaires most often used in such studies only ask about negative effects. In her research using a questionnaire from which the bias toward negativity had been eliminated, she found that "The menstrual cycle did have an impact on most of the moods and perceptions of performance [of the women studied]; however, it is more accurate to describe this variation as positive, rather than negative" (Ripper, 1991, p. 25; see also Culpepper, 1992).

Certainly, these studies neither prove nor disprove the existence of PMS, but, taken together, they do allow us to roughly gauge the current state of scientific knowledge about the problem. In a nutshell, there are few definitive findings on PMS as a medical entity. Nevertheless, thousands of women seek treatment for PMS symptoms each year, and research in this area indicates that the side effects of many treatment programs may be worse than the condition itself. The most common treatment for PMS is the administration of the hormone progesterone, usually throughout the premenstrual phase of the cycle. Clinical studies of progesterone supplements indicate that they are largely ineffective in relieving PMS symptoms (Blum, 1997), but they may have serious side effects, including chest pains, vaginal and rectal swelling, a lessened sex drive, and bleeding between periods. What concerns researchers even more are the long-term effects of progesterone treatments since laboratory tests have linked progesterone injections with increased rates of breast tumors and cervical cancer. In addition, progesterone may have addictive effects (Golub, 1992).

Among the other common PMS treatments is the administration of megadoses of vitamin B_6, but this, too, is not without side effects. High doses of vitamin B_6 have been shown to cause nerve damage, leading to a loss of feeling in the fingers and toes (Fausto-Sterling, 1985). Moreover, Dr. Judith Abplanalp (1983) discovered in her careful review of the research on treating PMS that placebos (inactive substances with no medicinal content) are just as successful in relieving PMS symptoms as are vitamins, hormones, and other drugs (see also Blum, 1997). This means that patients are as likely to report feeling better after taking sugar pills as they are after a dosage of vitamin B_6, progesterone, or even Prozac.

We must be careful not to interpret these findings to mean that what women experience during their menstrual cycles is "all in their heads." Nor is it to say that biological factors are insignificant in women's menstrual experiences; the menstrual cycle is clearly rooted in biology (Blum, 1997). Instead, the point we are trying to make is that, in light of our poor understanding of PMS and its effects, and given the impact of social factors on women's menstrual experiences, some caution should be exercised in pursuing a PMS "cure." Research on premenstrual syndrome has been conducted for more than fifty years, and scientists are still unsure of precisely what it is or what causes it. Meanwhile, thousands of women have been encouraged to seek treatment for PMS, using substances that are known to be detrimental to their health, while the structural factors that produce stress in their lives and may lead to depression—such as the difficulty of balancing work and family responsibilities—are ignored (Markens, 1996; see also Chapters 6, 7, and 11).

The Interaction of Biology and Culture

The issues we have discussed in this chapter highlight the interaction between the social and the biological. However, it behooves us at this point to consider more precisely what we mean by *interaction*. Lynda Birke (1992, p. 74) has argued that feminist critiques of biological theories of gender have tended to conceptualize biology as something that comes first—"the biological base *onto* which experience and the effects of the environment are added during our development as individuals" (author's emphasis). Birke maintains that the difficulty with such a position is that it portrays development as progressing along a simple linear path: A person's biological beginnings impose constraints on what she or he can learn from the cultural environment, but the individual has no role or active part in her or his own development. Birke emphasizes, in contrast, that continuous and transformative change occurs throughout a person's lifetime and that the person's behavior can alter not only his or her environment, but also his or her biology and physiology. Certainly, much of the research we have reviewed in this chapter confirms this.

Birke urges feminist scientists to move beyond critiques that simply replace biological determinism with social constructionism that denies the body altogether. She urges instead the formulation of a transformative account of gender development, and we echo her call. Social constructionist critiques have been central in challenging the oppressive aspects of many biological determinist theories, but they have tended to reinforce the dichotomous view of biology versus environment, rather than transcending it. To focus on only the biological or the social is to tell, at best, just half the story. As Birke (1992, p. 76) points out, "our bodies are social, too, and our experiences of, and engagement with, a gendered world is as *embodied* persons. Surely those bodies, and their (often messy) processes, must be part of any continuing construction of gender?"

A **transformative account of gender development**—one that examines how culture and individual behavior may impact biology and physiology as well as vice versa—underlines the pitfalls of using biological principles to justify gender inequality and also overcomes a longstanding preoccupation with sex differences. As Janet Sayers (1987, p. 68) has observed, "Preoccupation with sexual difference and inequality has tended to be particularly intense at those times when prevailing differences between the sexes seem most likely to be eroded" (see also Markens, 1996). We may only speculate on the motives that underlie some scientists' tenacious attempts to establish a biological basis for behavioral and personality differences between women and men. The existence of difference, even if biologically caused, does not imply a hierarchical ordering, nor does it imply that one behavior or trait is inherently superior to another. That women and men are different in many ways is an observable fact; however, that either is discriminated against on the basis of these differences is a social injustice.

KEY TERMS

adrenogenital syndrome (AGS)   a condition occurring prenatally that is caused by a malfunction in the mother's or the fetus's adrenal glands or from exposure of the mother to a substance that acts on the fetus like an androgen

androgen-insensitive syndrome   a genetic defect that causes an *XY* fetus to be unresponsive to the androgens its testes secrete

brain lateralization   the specialization of the right and left hemispheres of the brain for different tasks

DHT deficiency syndrome   a condition in which an individual has no or abnormally low 5-alpha-reductase, an enzyme responsible for converting testosterone into dihydrotestosterone

Klinefelter syndrome   a chromosomal abnormality in which an individual has three (*XXY*) sex chromosomes, rather than the normal two (*XX* or *XY*)

sex chromosomes   one of the twenty-three pairs of human chromosomes, which plays a primary role in determining whether a fertilized egg will develop into a female or a male fetus

transformative account of gender development a theory of gender development that recognizes the truly interactive nature of biology and environment as well as individual agency in the creation of gender by examining how culture and individual behavior may impact biology and physiology and vice versa

Turner syndrome   a chromosomal abnormality in which an individual has only one sex chromosome (an *X*), rather than the normal pair (*XX* or *XY*)

SUGGESTED READINGS

Bem, S. L. (1993). *The lenses of gender: Transforming the debate on sexual inequality*. New Haven: Yale University Press.

Blum, D. (1997). *Sex on the brain*. New York: Viking.

Tavris, C. (1992). *The mismeasure of woman*. New York: Simon and Schuster.

NOTES

1. It was later discovered that Richard Speck, who one night brutally murdered nine student nurses in their dormitory rooms, was not, in fact, *XYY.*

2. Individuals affected by these conditions often have some combination of male and female anatomy, so physicians and researchers refer to them as *intersexed.* Some intersexed individuals have one ovary and one testis. More common, however, are those who have testes and some female genitalia but not ovaries, and those who have ovaries and some male genitalia but not testes (Kelly, 1995). Traditionally, these individuals were called *hermaphrodites* and *pseudohermaphrodites*, but these terms are offensive to intersexed people, so they are no longer used.

3. Indeed, Hoyenga and Hoyenga (1993) note that were it not for illnesses that AGS males contract, they would most likely go undetected.

4. In the same study, however, Hines and Kaufman (1994) also report that AGS boys showed less interest in rough-and-tumble play than non-AGS boys.

5. Kessler (1996) states that it is impossible to get accurate statistics on the incidence of conditions such as androgen-insensitive syndrome because unlike chromosomal abnormalities, these conditions are not officially registered. In fact, the physicians she interviewed would not even guess at the incidence, although all agreed that such conditions are very rare.

6. Unfortunately, this positive evaluation of *berdaches* and broad conceptions of gender were virtually extinguished through contact with White society. Although *berdaches* certainly did not disappear, by the end of World War II the common attitudes toward them in Native American communities were shame and often hostility. However, Roscoe (1991) reports a rediscovery of the positive valuation of *berdachism* among some North American Indian societies, largely through the combined efforts of the Native American rights movements and the gay rights movement (see also Williams, 1986).

7. MRI is a procedure that produces high-resolution images of the living brain by measuring the waves that hydrogen atoms emit when they are activated by radio-frequency waves in a magnetic field (Pinel, 1997). Pinel (1997) also provides an excellent discussion of other technology researchers and physicians use to study the brain.

3 Early Childhood Gender Socialization

Peering at babies through the window of a hospital nursery, onlookers can usually tell with little difficulty which infants are girls and which are boys. This ability to discern the newborns' sex is not because of obvious physical differences between the female and male babies, but rather because hospital staff wrap the girls in pink blankets and the boys in blue, or write the girls' names on pink cards and the boys' names on blue ones. Interestingly, Rhode (1997) reports that at the beginning of the twentieth century, girls were dressed in blue because that color was associated with delicacy, while boys wore pink because that color implied manliness. The specific colors, of course, are irrelevant. What is important are the traits the colors are supposed to signify. From the moment they are born, girls are considered dainty and boys strong—popular gender stereotypes that translate into expectations of children's behavior.

In this chapter, we will discuss how gendered expectations are transmitted to children through socialization. **Socialization** is the process by which a society's values and norms, including those pertaining to gender, are taught and learned. Socialization is a lifelong process that we will examine throughout the text, but in this chapter, we will concentrate on the socialization that occurs mostly in the early childhood years. Gender socialization is sometimes a conscious effort in that expectations are reinforced with explicit rewards and punishments. Boys in particular receive explicit negative sanctions for engaging in what is considered gender-inappropriate behavior. Gender socialization may also be more subtle, however, with gender messages relayed implicitly through the ways adults interact with one another as well as with children, through children's clothing, and through their books and toys. In addition, children socialize one another, explicitly and more subtly, through their interactions in peer groups. However, before we discuss the research on the content of early childhood gender socialization, let's look at the socialization *process*. To begin, we'll consider some of the theories that have been developed to explain *how* young children acquire their gender identities.

ᐧ Learning Gender

Research indicates that children as young as eighteen months old show preferences for gender-stereotyped toys. By the age of two, they are aware of their own and others' gender, and between two and three years of age, they begin to identify specific traits and behaviors in gender-stereotyped ways (Golombok & Fivush, 1994). Obviously, children are presented with gender messages very early in their lives, but how do they come to adopt this information as part of their images of themselves and their understanding of the world around them? In other words, how do little girls learn that they are girls, and how do little boys learn that they are boys? Perhaps more importantly, how do both learn that only boys do certain (masculine) things, and only girls do other (feminine) things? A number of theories have been offered in response to such questions. We will discuss the three major categories of theories: psychoanalytic theories, social learning theories, and cognitive developmental theories.

Psychoanalytic Theories

Certainly, the most famous psychoanalytic theory of gender identity development was presented by the Austrian physician, Sigmund Freud (1856–1939). Freud's perspective is known as *identification theory.*

According to Freud, children pass through a series of stages in their personality development. During the first two stages, referred to respectively as the *oral* and *anal* stages, boys and girls are fairly similar in their behavior and experiences. For both boys and girls, their mother is the chief object of their emotions since she is their primary caretaker and gratifies most of their needs. It is around age four, however, that an important divergence occurs in the personality development of girls and boys. Then, children become aware both of their own genitals and of the fact that the genitals of boys and girls are different. This realization signals the start of the third stage of development, the *phallic* stage. It is during the phallic stage that **identification** takes place; that is, children begin to unconsciously model their behavior after that of their same-sex parent, thus learning how to behave in gender-appropriate ways. Significantly, identification does not occur for girls the same way it does for boys.

For boys, identification is motivated by what Freud called **castration anxiety.** At this age, a boy's love for his mother becomes more sexual and he tends to view his father as his rival (the *Oedipus complex*). What quickly cures him of this jealousy is a glimpse of the female genitalia. Seeing the clitoris, the little boy assumes that all girls have been castrated for some reason, and he fears that a similar fate may befall him if he continues to compete with his father. Boys perceive the formidable size and power of their fathers and conclude that their fathers have the ability to castrate competitors. Consequently, instead of competing with his father, the little boy tries to be more like him and ends up, in a sense, with the best of both worlds: He gets to keep his penis *and* he can have a sexual relationship with his mother vicariously through his father. The boy, therefore, comes to identify with his father, incorporating his father's traits and behaviors, including those pertaining to gender, into his own social repertoire.

In contrast, a girl's identification with her mother is motivated by what Freud called **penis envy.** Penis envy develops in girls on first sight of the male genitals. Seeing the male's "far superior equipment" as Freud put it (1983/1933, p. 88), the little girl also thinks she has been castrated. She becomes overwhelmed by her sense of incompleteness, her jealousy of boys, and her disdain for her mother and all women since they share her "deformity." Instead, she shifts her love to her father, who does possess the coveted penis, and begins to identify with her mother as a means to win him. Eventually, the girl realizes that she can have a penis in two ways: briefly through intercourse and symbolically by having a baby, especially a baby boy. In other words, her wish for a penis leads her to love and desire men (initially in the person of her father), since they have a penis and can also provide a baby (Frieze et al., 1978). However, a female never fully overcomes the feelings of inferiority and envy, which leave indelible marks on her personality:

> Thus, we attribute a larger amount of narcissism to femininity, which also affects women's choice of object, so that to be loved is a stronger need for them than to love.

The effect of penis envy has a share, further, in the physical vanity of women, since they are bound to value their charms more highly as a late compensation for their original sexual inferiority. Shame, which is considered to be a feminine characteristic par excellence but is far more a matter of convention than might be supposed, has as its purpose, we believe, concealment of genital deficiency. . . . The fact that women must be regarded as having little sense of justice is no doubt related to the predominance of envy in their mental life. (Freud, 1983/1933, pp. 90, 92)

Freud's work called attention to the importance of childhood experiences and forced the scientific community of his time to consider that children might have sexual feelings and that what happens during childhood can have a lasting impact on an individual's personality. But before you start looking askance at every four-year-old you meet, let us also point out that identification theory has received considerable criticism. For one thing, the theory maintains that identification is an unconscious process. As such, we have no objective means to verify it. Instead, we must rely on either the psychoanalyst's interpretation of an individual's behavior or the individual's memories of childhood. Even if we are willing to trust the memories of individuals, we are still left with the problem of observer bias. Because the methods of psychoanalysts are extremely subjective, we may question whether their interpretations of individuals' experiences are accurate or whether they simply reflect what the psychoanalyst expects to find in light of identification theory. Other than clinical reports of psychoanalysts themselves, there is little evidence of the existence of castration anxiety in boys or penis envy in girls (Frieze et al., 1978; Sherman, 1971).

Freud also portrayed the gendered behaviors acquired in early childhood as fixed and stable over time. In other words, the theory leaves little room for personal or social change. However, while it is certainly the case that gender is resilient, it is also true that learning continues throughout our lives and that we may modify our behavior and attitudes as we are exposed to new situations and models.

Finally, it is impossible to overlook the antifemale bias in Freudian identification theory. Females are defined as inadequate; they are jealous, passive, and masochistic. Freud defined women as "an inferior departure from the male standard" (Bem, 1993, p. 59). Femininity itself was seen as a pathology (Brennan, 1992). In short, identification theory asserts that women are clearly men's inferiors. At its best, the theory legitimates gender inequality; at its worst, it is misogynistic and harmful to women.[1]

In light of these serious weaknesses, it is not surprising that some of Freud's early supporters, as well as more contemporary theorists working within a psychoanalytic framework, have offered substantial revisions or reinterpretations of Freud's original argument. Karen Horney (1967), Erik Erikson (1968), and Melanie Klein (1975), for instance, felt that Freud's theory was too "phallocentric," although each theorist continued to focus on how innate differences between the sexes influenced their respective psychological development. Horney rejected the idea that penis envy played a central role in females' psychosexual development and offered the provocative suggestion that males harbor jealousy toward females for their unique ability to bear children, a phenomenon she referred to as *womb envy*. Erikson also claimed that women's reproductive capacity—the fact, as he put it, that women have an inner space in which to carry and nurture new life—causes them to develop a psychological commitment to caring for others. In contrast, men's reproductive organs are external and active, which in turn is reflected in the male psyche with its external focus and action orientation (Bem, 1993). And Klein argued that the primary relation in the development of gender identity was not the father-son or father-daughter relationship centering around the penis, but rather the mother-child relationship centering around the breast, especially in terms of the emotions and conflicts the breast evokes in children (e.g., goodness/plentitude, badness/destructiveness) (Chodorow, 1989; 1995).

Others utilizing a psychoanalytic perspective, including Clara Thompson (1964), Jacques Lacan (1977), and Juliet Mitchell (1974), have placed the notion of penis envy in a social context. That is, women are jealous of the male organ only in that it is a symbol of male power and privilege in a patriarchal society. From this point of view, then, women are actually envious of men's higher status and freedom.

Feminist theorist Nancy Chodorow (1989; 1978) also offers a revision of identification theory that places gender acquisition squarely in a social context. Her goal is to explain why females grow up to be the primary caretakers of children and why they develop stronger affective ties with children than males do. She suggests that identification is more difficult for boys since they must psychologically separate from their mothers and model themselves after a parent who is largely absent from home, their fathers. Consequently, boys become more emotionally detached and repressed than girls. Girls, in contrast, do not experience this psychological separation. Instead, mothers and daughters maintain an intense, ongoing relationship with one another. From this, daughters acquire the psychological capabilities for mothering, and "feminine personality comes to define itself in relation and connection to other people more than masculine personality does" (Chodorow, 1978, p. 44).

Chodorow's work is provocative, but, like other psychoanalytic theories, it has been criticized as largely untestable and, therefore, lacking supporting evidence (Lorber et al., 1990). Chodorow has responded that her theory is empirically derived and is supported by clinical observations (Chodorow, 1995). But the reliability of clinical psychoanalytic data remains a concern; while Chodorow may interpret her patients' statements as supportive of identification theory, another clinician—even one who shares a feminist psychoanalytic perspective—may interpret the patients' statements differently. Moreover, her data are obtained from individuals who have sought her help in resolving problems, crises, and conflicts, so they may not be representative of the nonclinical population.

Chodorow's work has also been criticized as ethnocentric. As we will learn in Chapter 6, the sexual division of labor in which only women care for infants is not present in all societies, yet children in all societies acquire gender, whatever its specific content. Thus, the developmental sequence described by Chodorow seems to apply only to Western families, and not all Western families at that (Lorber et al., 1981). Chodorow's model, for example, may describe best the process of gender acquisition in White, middle-class families, but as Joseph (1981) argues, it does not accurately reflect the experiences of most African American mothers and daughters. Similarly, Segura and Pierce (1993) maintain that certain features of Mexican American families, such as the presence of multiple mothering figures (grandmothers, godmothers, aunts), require extensions or modifications of Chodorow's model to account for racial, ethnic, and social class differences in gender acquisition. Recently, Chodorow (1995) has responded to this criticism by calling on feminist psychoanalysts to conceptualize gender identity development in nonuniversal and less essentialist terms, taking into account the diversity in people's backgrounds and experiences, including race, ethnicity, social class, and sexual orientation. According to Chodorow, each individual participates in the construction of her or his gendered self through emotional reactions to experiences and even through fantasies, so that in a sense, each person's gender identity is unique. "I suggest," writes Chodorow, "that each person's sense of gender—her [or his] gender identity or gendered subjectivity—is an inextricable fusion or melding of personally created (emotionally and through unconscious fantasy) and cultural meaning" (1995, p. 517).

Chodorow's elaboration of feminist psychoanalytic theory will undoubtedly generate debate, some of which will continue to focus on the issue of testability since the unconscious remains a central theme. However, psychoanalytic theories are not the only available explanations of gender acquisition. Let's consider the other theoretical perspectives.

Social Learning Theories

Social learning theories are more straightforward than psychoanalytic theories in that they focus on observable events and their consequences rather than on unconscious motives and drives (Bandura 1986). Although there are a number of social learning theories, they share several basic principles that derive from a particular school of thought in psychology known as *behaviorism*. You are probably somewhat familiar with at least one important idea of behaviorism, the notion of **reinforcement:** A behavior consistently followed by a reward will likely occur again, whereas a behavior followed by a punishment will rarely reoccur. So, for example, your dog will probably learn to play frisbee with you if you give it a biscuit every time it runs to you with the plastic disk in its mouth. Conversely, the dog will stop urinating on your houseplants if you put it outside each time it squats or lifts a leg near the indoor foliage. According to behaviorists, this same principle of reinforcement applies to the way people learn, including the way they learn gender.

More specifically, social learning theory posits that children acquire their respective gender identities by being rewarded for gender-appropriate behavior and punished for gender-inappropriate behavior. Often the rewards and punishments are direct and take the form of praise or admonishment. For instance, while waiting in a check-out line, one of the authors overheard a little girl asking her father to buy her a plastic truck. Looking at her with obvious displeasure, he said, "That's for boys. You're not a boy, are you?" Without answering, the little girl put the toy back on the shelf. [Interestingly, research indicates that boys actually receive harsher disapproval for cross-gender behavior than do girls (see, for example, Fagot, 1985; Martin, 1990), a point to which we will return later.] However, children also learn through indirect reinforcement. They may learn about the consequences of certain behaviors just by observing the actions of others (Bronstein, 1988). In one study, for example, parents did not explicitly tell their children to play with toys considered gender-appropriate, but when children chose cross-gender toys, their parents were less likely to play with them (Langlois & Downs, 1980).

This latter point raises a second important principle of social learning theories: Children learn not only through reinforcement, but also by imitating or **modeling** those around them. Of course, the two processes—reinforcement and modeling—go hand in hand. Children will be rewarded for imitating some behaviors and punished for imitating others. At the same time, children will most likely imitate those who positively reinforce their behavior. In fact, social learning theorists maintain that children most often model themselves after adults whom they perceive to be warm, friendly, and powerful (i.e., in control of resources or privileges that the child values). Moreover, these theorists predict that children will imitate individuals who are most like themselves (Bussey & Bandura, 1984). Obviously, this includes same-sex parents, older siblings, and peers, but as we will see in Chapters 4 and 5, teachers and media personalities also serve as effective models for children.

The social learning perspective is appealing. Chances are that most of us have seen reinforcement in practice, and we know that children can be great imitators (sometimes to the embarrassment of their parents). However, the social learning approach is not without difficulties. First, studies of same-sex modeling indicate that children do not consistently imitate same-sex models more than opposite-sex models (Raskin & Israel, 1981). Rather, sex may be less important in eliciting modeling than other variables, especially the perceived power of the model (Jacklin, 1989). Girls are more likely to imitate male models than boys are to imitate female models, which may be because females are considered less powerful than males. As Golombok and Fivush (1994) put it, boys have a lot to lose by emulating female models. In addition, children tend to imitate a same-sex model only if that model is engaged in gender-appropriate behavior (Jacklin, 1989; Perry & Bussey, 1979). This finding suggests that children have some knowledge of gender apart from what they acquire through modeling. Finally, social learning theorists depict children as passive recipients of socialization messages; "socialization is seen as a unilateral process with children shaped and molded by adults" (Corsaro & Eder, 1990, p. 198). There is evidence, though, that children actively seek out and evaluate information available in their social environment (Bem 1983).

One set of theories that attempts to address these criticisms is the cognitive-developmental perspective, the third explanatory framework of gender learning that we will examine in this chapter.

Cognitive Developmental Theories

Cognitive developmental theories derive from the work of psychologists Jean Piaget and Lawrence Kohlberg, who both studied the mental processes children use to understand their observations and experiences. The unifying principle of cognitive developmental theories is that children learn gender (and gender stereotypes) through their mental efforts to organize their social world. Think of a very young child who is literally new to the world. Life must certainly seem chaotic. Thus, one of the child's first developmental tasks is to try to make sense of all the information he or she receives through observations and interactions in the environment. According to cognitive developmental theorists, young children accomplish this by looking for patterns in the physical and social world. Children, they maintain, have a natural predilection for pattern seeking; "once they discover those categories or regularities, they spontaneously construct a self and a set of social rules consistent with them" (Bem, 1993, p. 112).

The organizing categories that children develop are called **schema.** Sex is a very useful schema for young children. Why sex? The answer lies in the second major principle of the cognitive developmental perspective: Children's interpretations of their world are limited by their level of mental maturity. Early on in their lives (from about eighteen months to seven years of age, according to Piaget), children's thinking tends to be concrete; that is, they rely on simple and obvious cues. In our society (and most others), women and men look different: They dress differently, have different hairstyles, do different jobs. So sex is a relatively stable and easily differentiated category with a variety of obvious physical cues attached to it (Bem, 1993). Children first use the category to label themselves and to organize their own identities. They then apply the schema to others in an effort to organize traits and behaviors into two classes, masculine or feminine, and they attach values to what they observe—either gender appropriate ("good") or gender inappropriate ("bad").

Cognitive developmental theory helps explain young children's strong preferences for sex-typed toys and activities and for same-sex friends, as well as why they express rigidly stereotyped ideas about gender (Cann & Palmer 1986; Cowan & Hoffman 1986). Two- to six-year-old children are in the early stage of development that Piaget called the *preoperational stage.* During this stage, children tend to see every regularity in their world as a kind of immutable moral law, and they are not yet capable of *conserving variance*—that is, they cannot understand that even if superficial aspects of an object change (e.g., the length of a man's hair), the basic identity of the object remains unchanged (e.g., the person is still a man even if his hair falls below his shoulders). Studies indicate that as children get older and their cognitive systems mature, they appear to become more flexible with regard to the activities that males and females pursue, at least until they reach adolescence (Bem, 1993; Golombok & Fivush, 1994; Stoddart & Turiel, 1985; for a contrasting view see Carter & McClosky, 1983).

Critics of the cognitive developmental perspective have raised several concerns. One issue centers around the question of the age at which children develop their own gender identities. Cognitive developmental theorists place this development between the ages of three and five, but research indicates that it occurs sooner—as young as two years old (Cowan & Hoffman, 1986; Fagot & Leinbach, 1983). In addition, recent research indicates that not everyone uses sex and gender as fundamental organizing categories or schemas; there are some individuals who may be considered gender "aschematic," although they themselves have developed gender identities (Skitka & Maslach, 1990). Girls, for example, tend to have more knowledge of gender than boys, but are more flexible in their views about cross-gender activities and behaviors. Thus, the process by which a child learns to use sex as an organizing schema and the intervening variables that may mediate this learning process need to be better understood. Unfortunately, most of the research has been conducted with White, middle-class children from two-parent, heterosexual families, so little is known about how race and ethnicity, social class, family structure, and the sexual orientation of parents might affect the salience of sex and gender as organizing schema for diverse groups of young children. There is some research that shows that Black children are not taught to perceive gender in completely bipolar terms (Hale-Benson, 1986; McAdoo, 1988) and that Black as well as Latino children are less gender-stereotyped than White children (Bardwell et al., 1986; Isaaks, 1980), but the findings are not consistent across studies (see, for example, Gonzalez, 1982; Price-Bonham & Skeen, 1982).

This latter criticism is related to another, more serious charge: By portraying gender learning as something children basically do themselves, and by presenting the male-female dichotomy as having perceptual and emotional primacy for young children because it is natural and easily recognizable, cognitive developmental theorists downplay the critical role of culture in gender socialization (Bem, 1993; Corsaro & Eder, 1990). We may agree that children actively seek to organize their social world, but that they use the concept of sex as a primary means for doing so probably has more to do with the gender-polarizing culture of the society in which they live than with their level of mental maturity. Moreover, the male-female dichotomy may have perceptual and emotional primacy for young children not because it is a *natural* division, but because members of the children's social world consistently interact with them on the underlying assumption that they are in some unitary and bipolar way male or female and, therefore, teach them to organize their own identities and the world around them according to this same gender-polarizing schema (Davies, 1989). Research shows, for instance, that children who are highly gender schematic typically have parents, especially fathers, who give them a lot of both positive and negative reinforcement when it comes to gender-related activities. This reinforcement not only teaches gender-typed behavior, it also encourages children to pay more attention to gender as a social organizing category (Golombok & Fivush, 1994; Fagot & Leinbach, 1989). There are other organizing categories available with obvious physical cues, but children use sex instead—not because it is natural, but because in the culture of their society sexual distinctions are emphasized.

Psychologist Sandra Bem, whose work has made significant contributions to the cognitive developmental perspective (see, for example, Bem, 1983), has formulated an alternative perspective on gender acquisition that takes these criticisms into account. Let's briefly consider her ideas.

Bem's Enculturated Lens Theory of Gender Formation   Bem (1993) begins with the observation that the culture of any society is composed of a set of hidden assumptions about how the members of that society should look, think, feel, and act. These assumptions are embedded in cultural discourses, social institutions, and individual psyches, so that in generation after generation, specific patterns of thought, behavior, and so on are invisibly, but systematically reproduced. Bem calls these assumptions *lenses*. Every culture contains a wide assortment of lenses; for example, one of the lenses of U.S. culture that Bem identifies is radical individualism—but she concentrates her analysis on the lenses of gender. There are three gender lenses in the United States and in most Western cultures: gender polarization, androcentrism, and biological essentialism. **Gender polarization** refers to the fact that not only are males and females in the society considered fundamentally different from one another, but also these differences constitute a central organizing principle for the social life of the society. Bem uses the term **androcentrism** to refer to both the notion that males are superior to females, and to the persistent idea that males and the male experience are the normative standard against which women are judged. And finally, **biological essentialism** is the lens that serves to rationalize and legitimate the first two by portraying them as the natural and inevitable products of the inherent biological differences between the sexes. Bem's chief concern is how these lenses operate to mold males and females into the sex-typed likenesses enshrined in our culture.

The process of gender acquisition, Bem tells us, is simply a special case of the process of *enculturation* or socialization in general. She discusses two processes that she considers critical to "successful" enculturation. First, the institutionalized social practices of a society preprogram individuals' daily experiences to fit the "default options" of that society's culture for that particular time and place. At the same time, individuals are constantly bombarded with implicit lessons—what Bem calls *metamessages*—about what is important, what is valued, and what differences between people are significant in that culture. It is through these two processes that the lenses of the culture are transmitted to the consciousness of the individual, and the processes are so thorough and complete that, within a fairly short period of time, the individual who has become a "cultural native" cannot distinguish between reality and the way his or her culture construes reality.

One gets some sense of this melding of realities when visiting a society where the culture is different from one's own; "their" way of doing things seems wrong, even shocking. However, Bem (1993, p. 140) argues that a true native consciousness is acquired through enculturation during childhood because children "learn about their culture's way of construing reality without yet being aware that alternative construals are possible. In contrast to the adult visiting from another culture, the child growing up within a culture is thus like the proverbial fish who is unaware that its environment is wet. After all, what else could it be?"

The lens of gender polarization, Bem observes, begins to organize children's daily lives from the moment they are born. Recall the example that opened this chapter: Pink or blue name tags are attached to their bassinets in the hospital, and children are wrapped in pink or blue blankets. As we will discuss later in the chapter, this gender polarization continues throughout childhood through clothing, hair styles, bedroom decor, and toys. Is it any wonder that by the age of two, children are aware that there are "boy things" and "girl things"?

We may recognize in Bem's theory aspects of the social learning perspective as well as the cognitive developmental perspective. Gender socialization may be explicit, but Bem focuses more on the metamessages about gender, how gender polarization is taught implicitly through the way we organize our everyday lives and the lives of our children. (A metamessage about gender is sent, for instance, every time children observe that although their mother can drive a car, their father is the one who drives when their parents or the family go out together.) However, Bem does not see children (or adults) as passive receptors of culture. "[A] gendered personality is both a product and a process" (Bem, 1993, p. 152). Like other cognitive developmental theorists, she argues that the child is ripe to receive the cultural transmission because she or he is an active, pattern-seeking human being. By the time people become adults, it is not just the culture that imposes boundaries on their definitions of gender appropriateness, it is their own willingness to conform to these boundaries and evaluate themselves and others in terms of them. Moreover, what they have internalized as children is a social/cultural definition of sex, not a biological one, so that the cues children use for distinguishing between the sexes—a significant task in a gender-polarized society such as ours—are also social/cultural (e.g., hair style, clothing) rather than biological (genitals).

Bem also extends the cognitive developmental perspective by emphasizing that the lens of androcentrism is superimposed onto the lens of gender polarization. Children learn not only that males and females are different, but also that males are better than females and that what males do is the standard, while what females do is some deviation from that standard. The inclusion of the lens of androcentrism "dramatically alters the consequences of internalizing the gender lenses. Whereas before, the individual has been nothing more than a carrier of the culture's gender polarization, now the individual is a deeply implicated—if unwitting—collaborator in the social reproduction of male power" (Bem, 1993, p. 139).

The implications of Bem's theory for social change are fairly obvious. All societies must enculturate new members, but at least with respect to gender, we must alter the cultural lenses that are transmitted. This will involve nothing less than eradicating both androcentrism and gender polarization. Bem notes that some may argue that the former is currently underway because antidiscrimination laws have been enacted in recent years. However, she points out—and we will provide ample evidence of this throughout the text—that our society is so thoroughly organized from a male perspective that even policies and practices that appear to be gender-neutral are, on closer examination, strongly androcentric. "[A]ndrocentrism so saturates the whole society that even institutions that do not discriminate against women explicitly . . . must be treated as inherently suspect" (Bem, 1993, p. 190; see also Rhode, 1997).

At first glance, it may seem that eradicating gender polarization might be easier than eradicating androcentrism. However, Bem cautions that dismantling gender polarization involves more than simply allowing males and females greater freedom to be more masculine, feminine, androgynous, heterosexual, homosexual, bisexual, or whatever they would choose to be. Rather, it involves a total transformation of cultural consciousness so that such concepts are absent from both the culture and individual psyches. A modest beginning to this project is for parents to retard their young child's knowledge of our culture's traditional messages about gender, while simultaneously teaching her or him that the only definitive differences between males and females are anatomical and reproductive. In addition, parents must provide their children with alternative lenses for organizing and comprehending information. She suggests that parents substitute an "individual differences" lens that emphasizes the "remarkable variability of individuals within groups" (Bem, 1983, p. 613).

Throughout her discussion, Bem (1993) presents a number of research studies that support parts of the theory, particularly the various effects of gender polarization (see, for instance, Bem, 1975; 1981; Bem & Lenney, 1976; Frable & Bem, 1985). Like Chodorow's (1995) revision of the psychoanalytic perspective, Bem's ideas are certainly provocative enough to generate extensive research, as well as debate. For one thing, providing children with alternative lenses for organizing and understanding information can be considerably more difficult than it sounds. Research indicates that even parents who deliberately try to socialize their children in nontraditional, non-gender-stereotyped ways often end up interacting differently with their sons and daughters and encouraging gender-typed play and behavior (Golombok & Fivush, 1994; Weisner & Wilson-Mitchell, 1990).

Table 3.1 summarizes Bem's theory and the other theories of gender socialization we have discussed. Let's turn our attention now to the ways in which parents socialize their young children with respect to gender.

TABLE 3.1   Theories of Gender Socialization

Theory	Key People	Central Principles
Psychoanalytic Theories (e.g., identification theory)	Sigmund Freud, Karen Horney, Erik Erikson, Melanie Klein, Clara Thompson, Jacques Lacan, Juliet Mitchell, Nancy Chodorow	Children pass through a series of stages in their personality development. Until around age four, these developmental experiences are similar for girls and boys. At age four, however, children unconsciously begin to model their behavior after that of their same-sex parent, thus learning how to behave in gender-appropriate ways. For boys, the motivation for identification is castration anxiety, whereas for girls, it is penis envy.
		Modifications of this basic argument include the notion of womb envy as well as a focus on the mother-child relationship rather than the father-son or father-daughter relationship centering around the penis. This latter revision includes the view that gender acquisition revolves around the fact that boys must psychologically separate from their mothers, while girls do not experience this separation.
Social Learning Theories	Albert Bandura	Children acquire gender in two ways: through reinforcement (i.e., by being rewarded for gender-appropriate behavior and punished for gender-inappropriate behavior); and through modeling.
Cognitive Developmental Theories (e.g., gender schema theory, enculturated lens theory)	Jean Piaget, Lawrence Kohlberg, Sandra Bem	Children learn gender and gender stereotypes through their mental efforts to organize their social world. To make sense of sensory information, children develop categories or schema, which allow them to organize their observations and experiences according to patterns or regularities. Sex is one of their first schemas because it is a relatively stable, easily differentiated category with obvious physical cues attached to it.
		In the enculturated lens theory of gender formation, which also incorporates elements of social learning theory, children are socialized to accept their society's gender lenses (i.e., assumptions about masculinity and femininity). This enculturation occurs through institutionalized social practices as well as implicit lessons or "metamessages" about values and significant differences, which organize children's daily lives from birth.

Growing Up Feminine or Masculine

If you ask expectant parents whether they want their baby to be a boy or a girl, most will say they don't have a preference (Steinbacher & Gilroy, 1985). The dominance of this attitude, though, is relatively recent; from the 1930s to the 1980s, most Americans expressed a preference for boys as only children and, in larger families, preferred sons to outnumber daughters (Coombs, 1977; Williamson, 1976). In some parts of the world today, boys are still strongly favored over girls. In fact, as Box 3.1 on page 70 shows, in some countries this preference has resulted in a population imbalance, with a disproportionate ratio of males to females.

Even though American parents do not express a strong sex preference, research shows that parents do have different expectations of their babies and treat them differently, simply on the basis of sex. It has even been argued by some researchers that gender socialization actually may begin in utero by those parents who know the sex of their child before it is born. As Kolker and Burke (1992, pp. 12–13) explain, "The knowledge of sex implies more than chromosomal or anatomical differences. It implies gender, and with it images of personality and social role expectations." Such a hypothesis is difficult, if not impossible to test, but what currently is known is that gender socialization gets underway almost immediately after a child is born. Research shows, for instance, that the vast majority of comments parents make about their babies immediately following birth concern the babies' sex (Woollett et al., 1982). Moreover, although there are few physiological or behavioral differences between males and females at birth, parents tend to respond differently to newborns on the basis of sex. For example, when asked to describe their babies shortly after birth, new parents frequently use gender stereotypes. Infant boys are described as tall, large, athletic, serious, and having broad, wide hands. In contrast, infant girls were described small and pretty, with fine, delicate features (Reid, 1994). These findings are quite similar to those obtained in a study conducted twenty years earlier (Rubin et al., 1974), indicating that there has been little change in parental gender stereotyping.

That parents associate their child's sex with specific personality and behavioral traits is further evidenced by the effort they put into ensuring that others identify their child's sex correctly. It's often difficult to determine whether a baby is a boy or a girl because there are no physical cues: Male and female infants overlap more than they differ in terms of weight, length, amount of hair, alertness, and activity level. Parents most often use clothing to avoid confusion (Shakin et al., 1985). Boys are typically dressed in dark or primary colors, such as red and blue. They wear overalls that are often decorated with sporting or military equipment, trucks and other vehicles, or superheros. Girls are typically dressed in pastels, especially pink and yellow. Their dresses and slacks sets are decorated with ruffles, bows, flowers, and hearts. Parents also often put satiny headbands on their baby daughters (despite their lack of hair) and have their ears pierced. Disposable diapers are even different for girls and boys, not only in the way they are constructed, which arguably might have a rational basis to it, but also in the way they are decorated: Girls' diapers often have pink flowers on them; boys' diapers are embellished with sailboats or cars and trucks. Thus, clothing usually provides a reliable clue for sex labeling, although mistakes do still occur, which often anger parents. As one new

BOX 3.1
Where Have All the Young Women Gone?
Sex Preference and Gendercide

In the United States and Europe, even among those who express a preference for male children over female children, there remains strong disapproval of the use of medical technology, such as ultrasound and amniocentesis, to select for sex (Kolker & Burke, 1992). In some countries, such as China and India, where son preference is exceptionally strong, technology is increasingly being used not only for diagnostic purposes, but to identify the sex of a fetus (Burns, 1994; Gargan, 1991). If the fetus is the "wrong" sex—that is, a female—the parents frequently opt for an abortion. A Chinese publication recently quoted a man from a rural community who said, "Ultrasound is really worthwhile, even though my wife had to go through four abortions to get a son" (quoted in Kristof, 1991, p. C12).

Under normal circumstances, the birth rate of boys and girls in a society is roughly equal, but in China, India, and a number of other countries (e.g., Pakistan, Bangladesh), the sex ratio is skewed toward males (Coale, 1991). This imbalance has been the case historically in these countries as well. Female infants were often killed by being left exposed to the elements, or else they died in early childhood from neglect or lack of food. With the introduction of medical technology, such as ultrasound and amniocentesis, female infanticide is being replaced by selective abortion of female fetuses. This sex selection is widening the sex imbalance in some countries' populations, leading observers to argue that couples are practicing systematic *gendercide* (Warren, 1985). Since the 1970s, in fact, the sex imbalance in China and

India has widened (Burns, 1994; Jeffrey et al., 1988; Kristof, 1991; Shenon, 1994).

In 1994, the Indian Parliament passed a law criminalizing the use of prenatal tests solely to determine the sex of a fetus. However, observers have little confidence that the measure will be effective. Infanticide was outlawed in India more than a century ago, yet it remains a common practice, particularly with baby girls. A 1993 survey, for example, found that about 300,000 female newborns die each year from "gender discrimination"; they are either killed outright or die from neglect (Burns, 1994). In fact, some analysts are concerned that the law criminalizing prenatal testing for sex selection will simply drive up the price of such tests, causing poor couples to return to the practice of infanticide to rid themselves of unwanted daughters (Burns, 1994).

Some analysts also predict, however, that as more advanced technologies make fetal sex identifiable as early as the ninth week of pregnancy, sex selection may become more popular in the United States and Europe, too. Surveys indicate a growing willingness on the part of the medical community to use fetal diagnostic tools solely for identifying fetal sex. For example, in 1972, only 1 percent of U.S. physicians said they were willing to use fetal diagnostic technology solely to determine fetal sex, but within just three years, 25 percent stated they were willing to do so. Similarly, in an international survey conducted in 1988, 24 percent of geneticists in Britain, 47 percent in Canada, and 60 percent in Hungary said sex selection is morally acceptable (Kolker & Burke, 1992).

mother recently told us in frustration, "I dress her in pink and she always wears earrings, but people still look at her and say, 'Hey, big fella.' What else can I do?"

Clothing, then, plays a significant part in gender socialization in two ways. First, as children become mobile, certain types of clothing encourage or discourage particular behaviors or activities. Girls in frilly dresses, for example, are discouraged from rough-and-tumble play, whereas boys' physical movement is rarely impeded by their clothing. Boys are expected to be more active than girls, and the styles of the clothing designed for them reflect this gender stereotype. Second, by informing others about the sex of the child, clothing sends implicit messages about how the child should be treated. "We know . . . that when someone interacts with a child and a sex label is available, the label functions to direct behavior along the lines of traditional [gender] roles" (Shakin et al., 1985, p. 956).

Clothing clearly serves as one of the most basic ways in which parents organize their children's world along gender-specific lines. But do parents' stereotyped perceptions of their babies translate into differential treatment of sons and daughters? If you ask parents whether they treat their children differently simply on the basis of sex, most would probably say "no." However, there is considerable evidence that what parents *say* they do and what they *actually* do are frequently not the same. Let's examine some of this research.

• Parent-Child Interactions

The word *interaction* denotes an ongoing exchange between people. This meaning is important to keep in mind when discussing parent-child interaction, for the relationship is not one-way—something parents do to their children—but rather two-way, a give-and-take between the parent and the child. Parents sometimes raise this point themselves when they are questioned about the style and content of their interactions with their children. Parents report that male infants and toddlers are "fussier" than female infants and toddlers; boys, they say, are more active and anger more easily than girls. Girls are better behaved and more easy going. So if we observe parents treating their sons and daughters differently, is it just because they are responding to biologically based sex differences in temperament? Perhaps, but research by psychologist Liz Connors (1996) indicates that girls may be better behaved than boys because their mothers expect them to be. In observing girls and boys three-and-half to fourteen months old, Connors found few differences in the children's behavior. However, she also found that the mothers of girls were more sensitive to their children, while the mothers of boys were more restrictive of their children. Connors reports that fourteen-month-old girls are more secure in their emotional attachment to their mothers than fourteen-month-old boys, and she attributes this difference to mothers' differential treatment of their children.

Additional research lends support to Connors's conclusion. For example, Fagot and her colleagues (1985) found that although thirteen- and fourteen-month-old children showed no sex differences in their attempts to communicate, adults tended to respond to boys when they "forced attention" by being aggressive, or by crying, whining, and screaming, whereas similar attempts by girls were usually ignored. Instead, adults were responsive to girls when they used gestures or gentle touching, or when they simply talked. Significantly, when Fagot and her colleagues observed these same children just eleven months later, they saw clear sex differences in their styles of communication; boys were more assertive, whereas girls were more talkative.

In studies with a related theme, researchers have found that parents communicate differently with sons and daughters. Parents use a greater number and variety of emotion words when talking with daughters than sons. They also talk more about sadness with daughters, whereas they talk more about anger with sons (Adams et al., 1995; Fivush, 1991; Kuebli et al., 1995). One outcome of this differential interaction is that by the age of six, girls use a greater number of and more specialized emotion words than boys (Adams et al., 1995; Kuebli et al., 1995). Researchers have found that pre-schoolers whose mothers engaged in frequent emotion talk with them are better able to understand others' emotions (Denham et al., 1994), and by first grade, girls are better at monitoring emotion and social behavior than boys (Davis, 1995). Certainly, it is not unreasonable to speculate that through these early socialization experiences, parents are teaching their daughters to be more attentive to others' feelings and to interpersonal relationships, while they are teaching boys to be assertive, but unemotional except when expressing anger. Is it any wonder that among adults, women are better able than men to interpret people's facial expressions and are more concerned about maintaining social connections (Erwin et al., 1992; Goleman, 1996; Schneider et al., 1994)?

Are there other ways in which parent-child interactions differ by sex of the child? Research indicates that parents tend to engage in rougher, more physical play with infant sons than with infant daughters (MacDonald & Parke, 1986). Interestingly, the sex of the parent also appears to be significant. Fathers usually play more interactive games with infant and toddler sons and also encourage more visual, fine-motor, and locomotor exploration with them, whereas they promote vocal interaction with their daughters. At the same time, fathers of toddler daughters appear to encourage closer parent-child physical proximity than fathers of toddler sons (Bronstein, 1988). Both fathers and mothers are more likely to believe—and to act on the belief—that daughters need more help than sons (Burns et al., 1989; Snow et al., 1983). In these ways, parents may be providing early training for their sons to be independent and their daughters dependent. Moreover, Weitzman and her colleagues (1985) found that mothers tend to teach and question boys more than girls, thereby providing their sons with more of the kind of verbal stimulation thought to foster cognitive development.

In their study, Weitzman and her colleagues included mothers who professed not to adhere to traditional gender stereotypes. Although the differential treatment of sons and daughters was less pronounced among these mothers, it was by no means absent. This is an important point because it speaks to the strength of gender bias in our culture, reminding us that gender stereotypes are such a taken-for-granted part of our everyday lives that we often discriminate on the basis of sex without intentionally trying. "Even when we don't think we are behaving in gender stereotyped ways, or are encouraging gender-typed behavior in our children, examination of our actual behavior indicates that we are" (Golombok & Fivush, 1994, p. 26; see also Lewis et al., 1992; Weisner et al., 1994).

Still, it is also important to keep in mind that, like the research we discussed earlier, these studies are based almost exclusively on White, middle-class, two-parent, heterosexual families. We must ask how the findings might be different if the samples were more diverse. There is evidence that Black parents stress heavily for both male and female children the importance of hard work, independence, and self-reliance. Available data also show that Black children, regardless of sex, are at an early age imbued with a sense of financial responsibility toward their families, and with racial pride and strategies for dealing with racism (Hale-Benson, 1986; Poussaint & Comer, 1993; Thornton, 1997). The nontraditional content of this gender socialization could contribute to less gender stereotyping among Black children, although Hale-Benson (1986) also points out that the socialization experiences of young Black males and females are not identical or equal. Other researchers report as much, if not more, gender stereotyping among Blacks as among Whites (Price-Bonham & Skeen, 1982).

Similarly, studies that have examined social class have found modest support for the hypothesis that gender-stereotyped interaction decreases as one moves up the social class hierarchy (Burns & Homel, 1989; Lackey, 1989; but for contradictory findings, see Bardwell et al., 1986). One study that looked at the interaction of social class with race and ethnicity showed that the latter is the more important variable; that is, race and ethnicity have a stronger influence on child-rearing practices than social class does, but this research did not focus on gender socialization specifically (Hale-Benson, 1986).

Finally, there is little research on gender socialization in gay and lesbian families, although available studies indicate that children reared in such families are no different in their gender role behavior than children reared in heterosexual families. However, most of these studies used samples of children who spent at least part of their early childhood in heterosexual families (Golombok & Fivush, 1994).

Clearly, much more research is needed to elucidate the rich diversity of parent-child interactions and their outcomes among not only gay and lesbian families, but also families of color and families of different social classes.

Toys and Gender Socialization

Say the word "toys" in the company of children and you are likely to generate a good deal of excitement. Children will eagerly tell you about their favorite toy or about a "cool" new toy they'd like to have. Toys are, without a doubt, a major preoccupation of most children because, as any child will tell you, they're fun. However, toys not only entertain children, they also teach them particular skills and encourage them to explore through play a variety of roles they may one day occupy as adults. Are there significant differences in the toys girls and boys play with? If so, are these different types of toys training girls and boys for separate (and unequal) roles as adults?

More than twenty years ago, two researchers actually went into middle-class homes and examined the contents of children's rooms in an effort to answer these questions (Rheingold & Cook, 1975). Their comparison of boys' and girls' rooms is a study of contrasts. Girls' rooms reflected traditional conceptions of femininity, especially in terms of domesticity and motherhood. They contained an abundance of baby dolls and related items (e.g., doll houses) as well as miniature appliances (e.g., toy stoves). Few of these items were found in boys' rooms, where, instead, there were military toys and athletic equipment. Boys also had building and vehicular toys (e.g., blocks, trucks, and wagons). In fact, boys had more toys overall as well as more types of toys, including those considered educational. The only items girls were as likely to have as boys were musical instruments and books.

A decade later, another group of researchers (Stoneman et al., 1986) replicated Rheingold and Cook's study and obtained similar findings: Toys for girls still revolved around the themes of domesticity and motherhood, while toys for boys focused on action and adventure. A quick perusal of most contemporary toy catalogs reveals that little has changed in this regard during the 1990s as well. The toys for sale in the catalogs are usually pictured with models, which can be taken as an indication of the gender appropriateness of the toy. In the catalogs we examined (Childcraft, 1997; F. A. O. Schwartz, 1997; and Just Pretend, 1997), most of the toys were obviously gender-linked. We found, for instance, that little girls were most frequently shown with dolls or household appliances. The "dolls" boys were pictured with were referred to as "action figures" and included superheros (Superman, Batman), G.I. Joe (in a variety of roles, such as General Patton and the Golden Knight army paratrooper), characters from the *Star Wars* film series, and monsters (Spawn Vandalizer, with "real jaw-chomping action," and Deathlock, who is "half-man and half-cyborg"). Costumes for dressing up were also gender-specific. Boys were shown modeling the "Bold and Brave Collection," for the child with "the soul of an explorer" and "the heart of a hero." The set included costumes for a knight, a ninja, a cyborg, a pirate, and even a vampire. Girls were shown modeling the "Satin and Lace Collection," which was "designed to honor those timeless fantasies of girls." This set contained costumes for a ballerina, a princess, a fairy, an angel, and a bride. Accessories for the bride's costume (sold separately, of course) included a "diamond-look ring" on a heart-shaped pillow, five fill-in-the-blank wedding announcements, and a gift bag with two champagne flutes. On other pages of the catalogs, a little girl was talking on a pink cordless telephone with the sound effects, "As if" and "Whatever" from the film, *Clueless*, while a boy dressed in black and wearing dark glasses talked on a black cordless "spy gear" phone that had a flashlight for "night operations." Girls were shown bathing a doll in an "infant care center," weaving hair extensions and attaching them with barettes, and serving tea from a "teatime treasures" picnic hamper. Boys drove tractors, a train, and a rocket ship; worked in a fix-it shop; built a "space training center" out of snap-together plastic parts; played hockey and electric football; and hunted dinosaurs. Boys were shown with scientific toys in all but one instance (the "Science in the Kitchen" set) and with athletic equipment—important points to which we will return in Chapters 4 and 11.[2]

Of course, it may be argued that toy catalogs are directed primarily to parents, and parents usually claim that they buy gender-typed toys because that's what their children prefer. Research does show that children express gender-typed toy preferences as early as one year of age, but their toy "choices" may have been inspired even earlier by parental encouragement. For example, when adults were given the opportunity to interact with a three-month-old infant dressed in a yellow gender-neutral jumpsuit, they usually used a doll for play when they thought the infant was a girl, but chose a football and a plastic ring when they thought the infant was a boy (Seavey et al., 1975; see also Caldera et al., 1989; Fisher-Thompson et al., 1995). Parental encouragement of gender-typed toy choices are further reinforced by the toy catalogs (which children themselves spend a considerable time looking at), by television commercials, by the pictures on toy packaging, and by the way toy stores often arrange their stock in separate sections for boys and girls (Schwartz & Markham 1985; Shapiro 1990).

In considering the toys we've described, it is not difficult to see that they foster different traits and abilities in children, depending on their sex. Toys for boys tend to encourage exploration, manipulation, invention, construction, competition, and aggression. In contrast, girls' toys typically rate high on manipulability, but also creativity, nurturance, and attractiveness (see also Bradbard, 1985; Miller, 1987; Peretti & Sydney, 1985). As one researcher concluded, "These data support the hypothesis that playing with girls' vs. boys' toys may be related to the development of differential cognitive and/or social skills in girls and boys" (Miller, 1987, p. 485). Certainly, the toy manufacturers think so; the director of public relations for Mattel, Inc. (which makes the Barbie doll) stated in an interview that, "Girls' play involves dressing and grooming and acting out their future—going on a date, getting married—and boys' play involves competition and conflict, good guys versus bad guys" (quoted in Lawson, 1989, p. C1).

This attitude remains a major premise of the $15 billion-a-year toy industry, as evidenced by the new toys introduced annually at the American International Toy Fair. Among the offerings at the 1996 and 1997 toy fairs were "Tub Warriors," floating action figures armed with water-propelled weapons such as a canon and missile launcher; and "Melanie's Mall," in which a doll with long, silky hair, dressed in a miniskirt goes shopping in stores ("Beauty World," "Glamour Gowns") that children collect. The stores have their own shopping bags and Melanie has her own gold credit card (Lawson, 1996; 1997). It is not difficult to figure out which of these toys is targeted at the male market and which is intended for the female market.

The most popular toy for girls continues to be Barbie, with annual sales of $1.7 billion. In recent years, Barbie has been given several nontraditional roles, including dentist and astronaut (although her space wardrobe includes silver lingerie). In 1997, Mattel introduced "Talk with Me Barbie," in which Barbie has her own computer work station that can be attached to a real personal computer with a CD-ROM. Although some observers might see this invention as progress since it at least encourages girls to use computers (see Chapter 4), the game still focuses on shopping, makeup, and parties. More progressive was Mattel's 1997 announcement that Barbie is being redesigned to have more realistic body proportions; for thirty-eight years, Barbie's figure has translated into proportions of 36–20–32 (that is, the bust of an adult woman, the waist of a child, and the hips of a teenager). In 1997, Mattel also introduced "Share a Smile Becky," Barbie's disabled friend in a wheelchair, although the new doll met with mixed reactions from disability groups ("New Friend for Barbie," 1997).

In short, with few exceptions, toys for young children tend to strongly reinforce gender stereotypes. The messages these toys—and the marketing and packaging for the toys—send to children is that what they *may* do, as well as what they *can* do, is largely determined and *limited* by their sex. Apart from toys, what other items are significant in early childhood gender socialization? You may recall from the Rheingold and Cook (1975) study that books are one of only two items that boys and girls are equally likely to have. Let's take a brief look, then, at children's literature.

• Gendered Images in Children's Literature

Traditionally, children's literature ignored females or portrayed males and females in a blatantly stereotyped fashion. In the early 1970s, for example, Lenore Weitzman and her colleagues (1972) found in an analysis of award-winning picture books for preschoolers that males were usually depicted as active adventurers and leaders, while females were shown as passive followers and helpers. Boys were typically rewarded for their accomplishments and for being smart; girls were rewarded for their good looks. Books that included adult characters showed men doing a wide range of jobs, but women were restricted largely to domestic roles. In about one third of the books they studied, however, there were no female characters at all.

Fifteen years later, Williams et al. (1987) replicated the Weitzman study and noted significant improvements in the visibility of females. Only 12.5 percent of the books published in the early 1980s that they examined had no females, while a third had females as central characters. Nevertheless, although males and females were about equal in their appearance in children's literature, the ways they were depicted remained largely unchanged. According to Williams et al. (1987, p. 155), "With respect to role portrayal and characterization, females do not appear to be so much stereotyped as simply colorless. No behavior was shared by a majority of females; while nearly all males were portrayed as independent, persistent, and active. Furthermore, differences in the way males and females are presented is entirely consistent with traditional culture."

In 1997, children's librarian Kathleen Odean reported that although over four thousand children's books are published each year, in the vast majority females are presented in supporting roles and very few female characters are brave, athletic, or independent. Out of the thousands of books available for children of all ages, from preschoolers to adolescents, she compiled a list of just six hundred that are about girls who go against feminine stereotypes: girls who take risks and face challenges without having to be rescued by a male, girls who solve problems rather than having the solutions given to them, and girls who make mistakes but learn from them. There are, she notes, few books about girls' sports teams, even though over 2 million girls play on such teams (see Chapter 11), and no animal fantasies analogous to the popular *Wind in the Willows* with female characters.

One recent study indicates that at least for children's picture books, the race of the illustrator might make a difference in the amount of gender stereotyping depicted. Roger Clark and his colleagues (1993) analyzed children's picture books that received awards during the years 1987 through 1991 and compared those illustrated by White illustrators with those illustrated by African American illustrators. Among their findings were that while all the recent children's picture books contained more female central characters who are depicted as more independent, creative, and assertive than those in the past, the books illustrated by African American artists (and written by African American authors) gave female characters the greatest visibility and were significantly more likely to depict these females as competitive, persistent, nurturant, aggressive, emotional, and active. Clark et al. (1993) argue that the recent books illustrated by White artists reflect the liberal feminist emphasis on more egalitarian depictions of female and male characters, whereas those illustrated by African American artists reflect the aims of Black feminist theorists who emphasize women's greater involvement in an ethic of care and an ethic of personal accountability.

There is no doubt, then, that children's literature is less sexist than it was when Weitzman carried out her research, but for the most part, the changes have been modest. But modest though they may be, the question remains as to what impact less stereotyped books have on children's thinking about gender. In one study that tried to answer this question, the researcher found that nontraditional gender messages may be lost on young children. Bronwyn Davies (1989) read storybooks with feminist themes to groups of preschool boys and girls from various racial and ethnic and social class backgrounds. She found that the majority of children expressed a dislike for and an inability to identify with storybook characters who were acting in nontraditional roles or engaged in cross-gender activities. By the time the children heard these stories (at the ages of four or five), "[t]he power of the pre-existing structure of the traditional narrative [prevented] a new form of narrative from being heard." There were no differences across racial, ethnic, or social class lines. What did emerge as significant was parents' early efforts to socialize their children in nonsexist, non-gender-polarizing ways. Thus, the two children in the study whose parents did not support polarized gender socialization did not see anything wrong with characters engaged in cross-gendered behaviors and had less difficulty identifying with these characters—an encouraging finding that not only offers support for Bem's theory of gender acquisition that we discussed earlier, but also shows that nonstereotyped gender socialization is possible with concerted effort.

This finding is also especially important in light of research that shows that when characters are depicted as genderless or gender-neutral, adults almost always label the characters in gender-specific ways. In 95 percent of these cases, the labeling is masculine (DeLoache et al., 1987). The only pictures that seem to prompt feminine labels are those showing an adult helping a child, an interpretation consistent with the gender stereotypes that females need more help than males and that females are more attentive to children. Based on this research, then, it appears that "picturing characters in a gender-neutral way is actually counterproductive, since the adult 'reading' the picture book with the child is likely to produce an even more gender-biased presentation than the average children's book does" (DeLoache et al., 1987, p. 176).

To summarize our discussion so far, we have seen that virtually every significant dimension of a child's environment—his or her clothing, toys, and, to a lesser extent, books—is structured according to cultural expectations of appropriate gendered behavior. If, as the cognitive developmental theorists maintain, young children actively try to organize all the information they receive daily, their parents and other adults are clearly providing them with the means. Despite their claims, even most parents who see themselves as egalitarian tend to provide their children with different experiences and opportunities and to respond to them differently on the basis of sex. Consequently, the children cannot help but conclude that sex is an important social category. By the time they are ready for school, they have already learned to view the world in terms of a dichotomy: his and hers.

Parents, though, are not the only socializers of young children. Research has also highlighted the importance of peers in early childhood socialization. To conclude this chapter, then, let's consider the ways young children help to socialize one another.

• Early Peer Group Socialization

As we noted previously, socialization is not a one-way process from adults to children. Rather, childhood socialization is a collective process in which "children creatively appropriate information from the adult world to produce their own unique peer cultures"

(Corsaro & Eder, 1990, p. 200). Indeed, according to Beverly Fagot (1985), children's same-sex peers are the most powerful agents of socialization.

Children socialize one another through their everyday interactions in the home and at play. Research indicates, for example, that one of young children's first attempts at social differentiation is through increasing sex segregation. Observations of young children at play show that they voluntarily segregate themselves into same-sex groups. This preference for play with same-sex peers emerges between the ages of two and three and grows stronger as children move from early to middle childhood (Feiring & Lewis, 1987; Serbin et al., 1991). Moreover, when compared with girls, boys tend to interact in larger groups, be more aggressive and competitive, and engage in more organized games and activities (Corsaro & Eder, 1990; Maccoby 1988; Sheldon, 1990).

Thorne (1993) is critical of much of this research for focusing solely on sex differences and ignoring sex similarities and cross-sex interaction. She gives a number of examples in which young children work cooperatively and amiably in sex-integrated groups (see also Goodenough, 1990). She also points out that children frequently engage in "borderwork"; that is, they attempt to cross over into the world of the other sex and participate in cross-gender activities. Nevertheless, there is considerable evidence that even very young children reward gender-appropriate behavior and show disapproval for cross-gender behavior in their peers (Fagot & Leinbach, 1983; Goodenough, 1990; Martin, 1989). In fact, research shows that preschoolers disapprove of gender-"inappropriate" behavior by their peers more so than by adults (Golombok & Fivush, 1994).

Both boys and girls who choose gender-appropriate toys are more liked by their peers and have a better chance of getting other children to play with them (Martin, 1989; Roopnarine 1984). However, boys are criticized more by their peers for cross-gender play, and boys who play with girls are rated unpopular by their peers (Lobel et al., 1993; Roopnarine, 1984). Fagot and Leinbach (1983) found that for boys, peers are often more powerful socializers than teachers. When boys in the day care center they observed received contradictory messages from peers and teachers about gender-typed play, the boys were more likely to respond to their peers; teachers' exhortations had little impact on their behavior.

Clearly, young children actively participate in the socialization process. We will return to this topic in Chapter 4, when we discuss children's interactions with one another in school. Here, however, we can say that available data show that young children should be considered partners with parents and other caregivers in socialization, including gender socialization.

By the Time a Child Is Five

In summary, during early childhood, boys and girls—at least those from White, middle-class, two-parent, heterosexual families—are socialized into separate and unequal genders. Little boys are taught independence, problem-solving abilities, assertiveness, and curiosity about their environment—skills that are highly valued in our society. In contrast, little girls are taught dependence, passivity, and domesticity—traits that our society devalues. Children themselves reinforce and respond to adults' socialization practices by socializing one another in peer groups.

May we conclude from all this that nonsexist socialization is impossible? Certainly not. Recall Davies's (1989) study showing that conscious efforts at nonsexist socialization by parents do have a positive impact on children's attitudes and behavior (see also Lorber, 1986). However, we must keep in mind that parents are not the only ones responsible for gender socialization. Indeed, as we will see in Chapters 4 and 5, schools and the media take up where parents leave off, and peers remain active socializers throughout our lives.

KEY TERMS

androcentrism   male-centered; the notion that males are superior to females and that males and the male experience are the normative standard against which women should be judged

biological essentialism   a cultural lens that rationalizes and legitimates both androcentrism and gender polarization by portraying them as the natural and inevitable products of the inherent biological differences between the sexes

castration anxiety   Freud's notion that boys fear their fathers will castrate them because of their sexual attraction to their mothers

gender polarization   the assumption that males and females are fundamentally different from one another, and the practice of using these differences as a central organizing principle for the social life of the society

identification   a central concept of the Freudian-based theory of gender socialization; the process by which boys and girls begin to unconsciously model their behavior after that of their same-sex parent in their efforts to resolve their respective gender identity complexes

modeling   the process by which children imitate the behavior of their same-sex parent, especially if the parent rewards their imitations or is perceived by them to be warm, friendly, or powerful; a central concept of the social learning perspective of gender socialization

penis envy   Freud's notion of girls' jealousy of the male sexual organ

reinforcement   a central principle of social learning theories of gender socialization, which states that a behavior consistently followed by a reward will likely occur again, whereas a behavior followed by a punishment will rarely reoccur

schema   a central concept of the cognitive developmental perspective of gender socialization; a category used to organize and make sense of information and experiences

socialization   the process by which a society's values and norms, including those pertaining to gender, are taught and learned

SUGGESTED READINGS

Bem, S. L. (1993). *The lenses of gender: Transforming the debate on sexual inequality.* New Haven: Yale University Press.

Davies, B. (1989). *Frogs and snails and feminist tales.* Sydney: Allen and Unwin.

Golombok, S., & Fivush, R. (1994). *Gender development.* New York: Cambridge University Press.

For toy catalogs that picture models engaged in cross-gender behavior, consult "Constructive Playthings," available from the company of the same name, 1227 East 119th Street, Grandview, Missouri 64030; "Hand in Hand," available from First Step, Ltd., 9180 LeSaint Drive, Fairfield, Ohio 45014; and "Toys to Grow On," available from Toys to Grow On, 2695 E. Dominguez

Street, P. O. Box 17, Long Beach, CA 90801. In addition, "Childswork, Childsplay" is a catalog with numerous games and toys designed to teach emotional and social skills, such as cooperation, empathy, and nonviolent conflict resolution. It is available from Genesis Direct, Inc., 100 Plaza Drive, Seacaucus, NJ 07094.

The Feminist Press at the City University of New York is a great source for nonsexist children's literature. We also highly recommend Kathleen Odean's *Great Books for Girls* (New York: Ballantine Books, 1997). Although as the subtitle states, this is a guide to 600 books that will "inspire today's girls and tomorrow's women," the author emphasizes that boys, too, will enjoy most of the books listed. As Odean (1997) notes, "Present the right book in the right way and most children will want to read it" (p. 7). Our sons enthusiastically agree.

NOTES

1. Nevertheless, see Chodorow, 1994, for a feminist defense of Freud. Chodorow acknowledges the weaknesses in Freud's theory and addresses feminist critiques of Freud as well as Freudian critiques of feminism. See especially Chapter 1, and also Chodorow, 1989.

2. Similar to our examination of toy catalogs in 1993, we found that the 1997 catalogs had racially and ethnically diverse models, but rarely showed children with disabilities.

Schools and Gender

In a speech before a group of educators in 1980, Florence Howe, herself an educator, began by quoting from the writings of Frederick Douglass, the famous abolitionist. In the passage she selected, Douglass recalls his childhood as a slave on a Southern plantation and relays a conversation he overheard between the slave owner and the slave owner's wife. Said the slave owner to his wife, "If you teach that . . . nigger how to read, there would be no keeping him. It would forever unfit him to be a slave. He would at once become unmanageable, and of no value to his master. As to himself, it could do him no good, but a great deal of harm. It would make him discontented and unhappy" (quoted in Howe, 1984, p. 247). Howe selected this passage because it aptly illustrates what she calls the "power of education." Both Douglass and his master recognized that education may enable us to understand our social position and thus empower us to act to change it.

To this observation we must add another: Education is powerful in the sense that it may also serve to keep us in our respective places. More specifically, schools are officially charged with the responsibility of equipping students with the knowledge and skills they need to fill various roles in their society. This is accomplished primarily by requiring students to study subjects (e.g., reading, writing, mathematics, and history), known collectively as the **formal curriculum.** But schools also teach students particular social, political, and economic values. This instruction, too, may be done explicitly (by punishing students for being late, for instance), but just as often, these value messages are implicit in the curriculum materials used to teach traditional academic subjects. They constitute, in other words, a kind of **hidden curriculum** that operates alongside the more formal one. However, the subtle nature of the hidden curriculum in no way lessens its significance. Through it, students learn to view the world in particular ways. More importantly, they learn what they can expect for themselves in that world and, for certain groups of students, this may result in very low aspirations.

In this chapter, we will examine the kinds of messages both the formal and informal curricula send about gender, and we will assess their impact on the aspirations and achievements of male and female students. In addition, we will explore some of the recent efforts to transform the educational experience into a richer, more equal one for all students, male and female, from diverse backgrounds. Before we examine the current relationship between schools and gender, however, let's begin with a brief discussion of how this relationship has developed and changed over time.

An Historical Overview of Women and Men in Education

The word *school* derives from an ancient Greek word that means "leisure." This makes sense when one considers that until relatively recent times, only the very wealthy had enough free time on their hands to pursue what may be considered a formal education. Literacy was not a necessity for the average person; most people acquired the knowledge they needed to be productive citizens either on their own, or from parents, other relatives, coworkers, or tradespeople. In the post-Revolutionary War period, formal education came to be seen as a means of instilling patriotism and "civic virtue" in citizens who would now be voting for political leaders. Keep in mind, however, that voting was restricted to White, male property holders, so formal education remained largely their privilege, too. However, even for these privileged few, education was still somewhat haphazard. The educated man—for formal education was not open to females until 1786—was schooled in the classics, moral philosophy, mathematics, and rhetoric, although he acquired this knowledge through private study, tutoring, and travel as well as in a classroom (Graham 1978). Those who went to college were trained in self-discipline and moral piety as much as in academic subjects, for upon graduation they were to take their places among the White "ruling class" as ministers, lawyers, and other professionals (Howe, 1984).

Upper-class White women, when educated, were taught at home, but what they learned was far more restricted than the knowledge imparted to men. Women learned music and were given "a taste" of literature and a foreign language. Their education was to prepare them not to assume public leadership positions, but rather to better fulfill their "natural" roles in life as demure, witty, well-groomed partners for their elite husbands and as the first teachers of sons who would grow up to be voting citizens (Schwager, 1987). Even when schools for girls began to open in America—the first, the Young Ladies Academy, established in Philadelphia in 1786—the rationale behind them centered on women's domestic roles. The Young Ladies Academy, like most of the schools attended by wealthy young women and men, was private, although public schools did exist for White children of all social classes. However, the public schools at that time charged tuition, which put them out of reach for most families. It was also illegal to educate slaves, so most African American children, regardless of sex, were denied formal schooling of any kind (Hellinger & Judd, 1991; Howe, 1984).

With increasing industrialization in the United States during the nineteenth century, basic literacy and numeracy skills became increasingly important. Such skills were not needed for the manual labor predominant in agricultural societies, but were necessary for many newly created industrial jobs, including operating machinery, marketing and selling products, and keeping track of inventory. Also, as work moved away from the home and into factories, so did responsibilities traditionally fulfilled by the family, including education. And as immigration from Europe increased, education came to be seen as a means of insuring that American values were not "corrupted" by foreign influences (Hellinger & Judd, 1991). In 1830, the first free public schools for girls and boys opened in Massachusetts, and by 1850, all the states had established government-supported elementary and secondary schools to educate White children of all social classes. Black children were excluded until after the Civil War and even then, schools were racially segregated.

Mass public education produced two major consequences. The first was that White female literacy rates, at least in the northeastern part of the country, rose to match White male literacy rates. Unfortunately, Black literacy rates for both males and females remained substantially lower because of the tremendous barriers African Americans faced in obtaining an education (Schwager, 1987).

Second, the proliferation of elementary schools provided women with new career opportunities as teachers. In the early 1800s, men dominated teaching and looked on it as a good sideline occupation that provided extra income. The school year was relatively short and was structured around the farm calendar, with classes held during the winter months when farm chores were light. However, with urbanization and growing demands for higher educational standards in an industrialized society, teaching became a full-time job, albeit one that carried a salary too low to support a family. As a result, educational administrators employed women as a cheap and efficient means to implement mass education (Strober & Lanford, 1986). Women were paid 40 percent less than their male counterparts on the (often false) assumption that they had only themselves to support (Schwager, 1987). Their "maternal instincts" made them naturally suited to work with young children, and if a disciplinary problem arose, they could enlist the aid of the school principal or superintendent, who invariably was a man. Valued, too, were their supposed docility and responsiveness to male authority since male-dominated school boards were handing down strict guidelines for instruction and a standardized curriculum (Strober & Lanford, 1986; Strober & Tyack, 1980).

Black women, such as Lucy C. Laney, Nannie Helen Burroughs, Charlotte Hawkins Brown, and Mary McLeod Bethune, founded schools for Black children. Teaching was a particularly attractive career choice for Black women. For economic reasons, most had to work outside the home, but their employment opportunities were often limited to domestic service (see Chapter 7). Teaching not only improved their status and standard of living, "but often shielded [Black] women from the sexual harassment that many of them confronted in White homes" (Giddings, 1984, p. 101).

Given these circumstances, it is not surprising that teaching had become a "female profession" before the turn of the twentieth century (Schwager, 1987). Most of the women who became teachers were trained in *normal schools* (precursors to teacher training colleges) or in female seminaries, such as the Troy Female Seminary established in 1821. It was not until 1832 that women were permitted to attend college with men. Oberlin College in Ohio was the first coeducational college in the United States; it was, incidentally, also the first White college to admit Black students. Lawrence College in Wisconsin followed suit in 1847, and by 1872, there were ninety-seven coeducational American colleges (Leach, 1980). Still, the more prestigious institutions, such as Harvard, Yale, and Princeton, continued to deny women admission on a number of grounds. It was widely believed, for example, that women were naturally less intelligent than men, so that their admission would lower academic standards. A second popular argument was that women were physically more delicate than men and that the rigors of higher education might disturb their uterine development to such an extent that they would become sterile or bear unhealthy babies. Others argued that women would distract men from their studies, or that college would make women more like men: loud, coarse, and vulgar (Howe, 1984).[1]

Even at coeducational colleges, however, women and men had very different educational experiences. At liberal Oberlin, for instance, female students were expected to remain silent at public assemblies; in addition, they were required to care not only for themselves, but also for the male students by doing their laundry, cleaning their rooms, and serving them their meals (Flexner, 1971). Moreover, there, and at virtually every other coeducational college, women and men were channeled into different areas of study. Men specialized in fields such as engineering, the physical and natural sciences, business, law, and medicine. Women, in contrast, studied home economics, nursing, and, of course, elementary education (Howe, 1984). In fact, a teaching degree or certificate remained one of the few avenues of upward mobility for White, Black, and immigrant women well into the twentieth century (Giddings, 1984).

Nevertheless, some women did earn degrees in nontraditional or male-dominated fields, and many of them graduated from women's colleges. Wheaton College, in Norton, Massachusetts, was established in 1834 as the first women's college. In the late 1880s, the elite "Seven Sisters" colleges (Mount Holyoke, Vassar, Wellesley, Smith, Radcliffe, Bryn Mawr, and Barnard) were opened. What is perhaps most significant about these institutions is that they offered women the traditional men's curriculum in a highly supportive environment that fostered their ambitions and encouraged achievement. Consequently, "these institutions produced an exceptional generation of women during the 1890s who, nurtured by the collective female life of the women's college, emerged with aspirations to use their educations outside the confines of women's domestic sphere as it was narrowly defined in marriage" (Schwager, 1987, p. 362). Many of these women became leaders of the various social reform movements, including the suffrage movement, that grew during the early 1900s. A substantial percentage pursued further training or entered the professions. Even midway through the twentieth century when, as we will soon see, the overall percentage of female Ph.D.s dropped considerably, the women's colleges continued to graduate exceptional female students who often went on to graduate and professional schools (Tidball, 1980).

Women and Men in Education during the Twentieth Century

The emphasis on mass education did not diminish during the early decades of the twentieth century, fueled in large part by widespread concern over the influx of European immigrants into the United States. Special efforts were made to teach immigrants English and basic literacy skills, for according to many social reformers, education would help solve the social problems associated with immigrant life (e.g., poverty, alcoholism, and juvenile delinquency). This, coupled with continuing industrialization, promoted a steady rise in elementary and secondary school enrollments throughout the first half of the century.

Still, as Table 4.1 on page 86 indicates, an education gap between males and females persisted, especially at the higher educational levels. To some extent, this was because of the popular belief that education was less important for females. Although Tyack and Hansot (1990) maintain that gender was rarely a major factor in the development of educational policy, there is evidence that in the often overcrowded public schools, administrators appeared quite willing to let girls drop out, since their departure would open more spaces for boys.[2] In the 1930s, however, many states enacted laws that made school attendance until age sixteen mandatory. This, in turn, narrowed the gap at the secondary school level, but other factors operated to preserve it in colleges and graduate programs.

TABLE 4.1   The Education Gap between the Sexes, 1870–1995

Year	Percentage of Population Enrolled in Elementary and Secondary School (M/F)	Females as Undergrads (%)	Females as Bachelor's Degree Recipients (%)*	Females as Master's Degree Recipients (%)	Females as Doctorates (%)
1870	49.8/46.9	21	15	n.a.	0
1880	59.2/56.5	32	19	n.a.	6
1890	54.7/53.8	35	17	n.a.	1
1900	50.1/50.9	35	19	n.a.	6
1910	59.1/59.4	39	25	n.a.	11
1920	64.1/64.5	47	34	n.a.	15
1930	70.2/69.7	43	40	n.a	18
1940	74.9/69.7	40	41	n.a.	13
1950	79.1/78.4	31	24	29.3	10
1960	84.9/83.8	36	35	32	10
1970	88.5/87.2	41	41	39.7	13
1980	95.5/95.5	52.3	47.3	49.3	29.8
1990	96.3/95.9	54.5	53.2	52.5	36.2
1995	96.9/96.8	55.5	55.1	51.9	37.2

*Includes first professional degrees from 1870 to 1970.

Sources: Commission on Professionals in Science and Technology, 1992; Graham, 1978; U.S. Department of Commerce, Bureau of the Census, 1976, 1985, 1991, and 1997.

Looking again at Table 4.1, we see that, until the 1980s, women consistently comprised less than half the undergraduate student body in the United States, despite the fact that they make up slightly more than 50 percent of the country's population. Interestingly, in 1920, they did approach the 50 percent mark, but by 1930, their numbers had dwindled, continuing to fall until 1960. A similar pattern can be seen with regard to graduate school as measured by the percentage of doctoral degrees awarded to women. The percentage of female recipients of doctorates peaked in 1930, but then dropped considerably until 1970, when it began to rise once again.

How can we account for this kind of roller coaster pattern in women's representation in higher education? As we mentioned previously, a number of factors appear to be involved. The early growth in female college and graduate school enrollments was probably due, at least in part, to the first feminist movement and the struggle for women's rights (see Chapter 1). In addition, with males off fighting World War I, colleges may have looked to (tuition-paying) females to take their places (Graham, 1978). The Great Depression of the 1930s dashed many young people's hopes of attending college, but it is likely that women more often sacrificed further schooling, given the old belief that education (particularly a college education) was less important for them.

World War II sent men abroad again to fight, while women were recruited for wartime production jobs (see Chapter 7). After the war ended, an unprecedented number of men entered college, thanks to the GI bill. For women, though, the dominant postwar ideology idealized marriage and motherhood and promoted a standard of femininity by which women were judged according to how well they cared for their families, their homes, and their appearance. During the late forties and throughout the fifties, the number of women entering the professions declined substantially, while marriage and birth rates rose dramatically. The birth rate peaked in 1957; that same year, the average age for a first marriage for women was about twenty (Graham, 1978, p. 772).

Not all women bought into the postwar feminine ideal, and some pursued a college education with plans for a professional career. However, women who went to college during the forties, fifties, and even in the early sixties were often accused of pursuing an *Mrs.* instead of a *B.S.*, for the college campus came to be seen as the perfect setting for meeting a promising (i.e., upwardly mobile) mate. Sometimes, women dropped out of school to take jobs to help support their student-husbands.

This pattern appears applicable only with regard to the educational history of White women, however. When race is taken into account, a different historical overview emerges. According to Giddings (1984), for example, during the time that White women began to drop out of or not attend college, the number of Black women in college, especially in Black colleges, increased:

> By 1940, more Black women received B.A. degrees from Black colleges than Black men (3,244 and 2,463 respectively). By 1952–53, the surge of Black women had increased significantly. They received 62.4 percent of all degrees from Black colleges when, in all colleges, the percentage of women graduates was 33.4 percent. The percentage of Black women graduates was in fact just a little below that of male graduates in all schools (66.6 percent) and substantially higher than that of Black men (35.6 percent). An important dimension of this was that a large proportion of these women were the first in their families to receive college degrees. (p. 245)

Also significant is the fact that many of these women went on to graduate school. By the early 1950s, the number of Black women with master's degrees exceeded the number of Black men with this level of education. However, Black male Ph.D.s and M.D.s still outnumbered their female counterparts by a considerable margin (Giddings, 1984). Interestingly, Smith (1982) reports that Black females' educational aspirations are higher than those of Black males until college, when they begin to decline. This is a point to which we will return shortly.

Since the 1970s, the percentage of women and minority undergraduates and graduate students has risen substantially, and considerable attention has been given to the problems of sexism and racism at every level of schooling. Undoubtedly, the Civil Rights movement and the resurgence of the feminist movement during the sixties and seventies played a major part in bringing about these changes. With respect to sex discrimination, in particular, feminist lobbying efforts were instrumental in the passage of the Education Amendments Act of 1972, which contains the important provisions known as **Title IX.** Simply stated, Title IX forbids sex discrimination in any educational program or activity that receives federal funding. This law has resulted in a number of beneficial reforms in education, including gender equitable access to school athletic programs (see Chapter 11), standardized testing, and career advising and planning programs. Nevertheless, the educational experiences of males and females remain quite different and, more significantly, unequal. In the remainder of this chapter, we will examine the various structural factors that serve to perpetuate this inequality, from elementary school through graduate school.

Educating Girls and Boys: The Elementary Schools

When elementary school teachers are asked about the way they treat their students, they respond in the same way that parents do and state that they treat all their students fairly, regardless of their sex. Research indicates, however, that in practice, teachers typically interact differently (and often inequitably) with their male and female students. The interactions differ in at least two ways: the frequency of teacher-student interactions and the content of those interactions.

With respect to frequency of teachers' interactions with their students, studies show that regardless of the sex of the teacher, male students interact more with their teachers than female students do (American Association of University Women [AAUW] 1992). Boys receive more teacher attention and more instructional time than girls do. Of course, this may be due to the fact that boys are more demanding than girls. Boys, for instance, are more likely than girls to call out answers in class, thus directing teachers' attention to them more often. Interestingly, research also shows that when boys call out comments in class without raising their hands, teachers usually accept their answers, whereas teachers typically correct girls who call out answers by telling them the behavior is "inappropriate." But even when boys do not voluntarily participate in class, teachers are more likely to solicit information from them than from girls (Sadker & Sadker, 1994).

Apart from the frequency of teacher-student interactions, education specialists Myra and David Sadker (1994) reported that the content of teacher-student interactions also differs, depending on the sex of the student. By observing teacher-student interactions in the classroom over many years, the Sadkers found that teachers provided boys with more remediation; for instance, more often, they helped boys find and correct errors (see also Box 4.1). In addition, they posed more academic challenges to boys, encouraging them to think through their answers to arrive at the best possible academic response (see also Good & Brophy, 1987).

Other studies support these findings. For example, teachers' comments to boys are more precise than their comments to girls (AAUW, 1992). Even at very young ages, boys get more praise for the intellectual quality of their work, whereas girls are praised more often for being congenial and neat. For example, at a recent kindergarten graduation ceremony, one parent noticed marked differences in the awards given to boys and girls. Boys received awards for "very best thinker," "most eager learner," and "most scientific." Girls received awards for "all-around sweetheart," "cutest personality," and "best manners" ("Chart of Kindergarten Awards," 1994).

Gender and Special Education

Boys significantly outnumber girls in special education programs. Looking at the table below, we see that boys make up the majority of students labeled mentally retarded, seriously emotionally disturbed, and learning disabled. In trying to explain these gender differences, some analysts have argued that more boys than girls are born with disabling conditions. However, the findings of recent research cast doubt on this theory. According to medical reports, for example, the sex distribution of learning disabilities and attention deficit disorder is nearly equal. According to the American Association of University Women (1992), however, schools invariably identify more boys than girls as learning disabled. Yet, these boys test higher than girls on standardized intelligence tests. As the AAUW points out, school personnel may not be accurately identifying learning problems; they may be misidentifying behavioral problems in boys. This may be because girls are quieter, so they are more easily ignored. Boys are more likely to act out, so they are placed in special education programs that may not address their specific problems and needs.

At the same time, there is evidence that non-White children are disproportionately referred by school personnel for special education classes. For example, according to a 1998 report on special education in Connecticut, race and the school district in which a student lived were better predictors of whether the student would be labeled in need of special education than an actual diagnosis of a learning disability (Lambeck, 1998).

Placement in a special education program imposes a negative label on a student that severely limits the student's educational opportunities and, ultimately, his or her employment potential. Consequently, it is critical that those who are referred to such programs be accurately identified. Such identification must be based on medical diagnosis, not on the students' sex, race or ethnicity.

Elementary and Secondary School Students Identified with Learning Problems, by Race/Ethnicity and Sex, 1994

Race/Ethnicity and Sex	*Learning Problem*		
	Mental Retardation	Serious Emotional Disturbance	Specific Learning Disability
White			
Male	33.34	51.85	46.55
Female	24.43	13.69	20.50
African American			
Male	19.05	19.32	11.94
Female	12.39	5.20	5.28
Hispanic American			
Male	4.78	6.20	8.77
Female	3.47	1.60	4.24
Asian American/Pacific Islander			
Male	0.77	0.68	0.93
Female	0.58	0.17	0.42
American Indian			
Male	0.68	1.00	0.94
Female	0.50	0.29	0.43

Source: U.S. Department of Education, 1997, p. 1.

At the same time, however, while boys generally engage in more positive intellectual interactions with teachers, they are also more likely than girls to incur their teachers' wrath. Boys are subject to more disciplinary action in elementary school classrooms, and their punishments are harsher and more public than those handed out to girls. Perhaps boys misbehave more than girls; after all, as we learned in Chapter 3, preschool boys are encouraged to be active and aggressive, while preschool girls are rewarded for quiet play and passivity. It may be that the early childhood socialization of girls better prepares them for the behavioral requirements of elementary school. As Golombok and Fivush (1994) point out, much teacher-student interaction in the early grades is focused on behavior management, but by the time children reach fourth or fifth grade, they are well versed in classroom norms and attention turns primarily to academics. At this age, though, 90 percent of the positive feedback boys receive is for academic performance, while less than 80 percent of positive feedback girls receive is for academic performance. Less than 33 percent of the negative feedback boys receive is related to academic performance, but more than 66 percent of the negative feedback girls receive is related to academic performance. Golombok and Fivush (1994) conclude that, "From this pattern of praise and criticism, boys may be learning that they are smart, even if not very well behaved. Girls, on the other hand, are learning that they may not be very smart, but that they can get rewards by being 'good'" (p. 173; see also Jordan & Cowan, 1995).

The AAUW (1992) argues that the sex inequities embedded in teacher-student interactions lower female students' academic self-esteem and confidence. This relationship is complicated, however, by the factors of social class and race. For instance, recent research indicates that regardless of race, middle-class children receive more favorable evaluations from teachers than lower-class children (Brantlinger, 1993). Nevertheless, sex and race appear to have a powerful influence on the quality and quantity of teacher-student interactions. Interestingly, just as teachers maintain that they are gender-blind, they also declare themselves color-blind; however, one observer noted, "The teacher's color-blind view of the world, in reality, translates into a view of the world in which everyone is white" (Rush, 1998, p. 6).

Regardless of teachers' claims of not "seeing" the sex of a child or the color of a child's skin, sex and race intersect to produce differential teacher-student interactions. For example, Black students, regardless of their sex, are more likely to be reinforced for their social behavior, whereas White students are more likely to receive teacher reinforcement for their academic achievements (AAUW, 1992). Black girls in particular, though, are rewarded for nurturing, mediating, and keeping order (Cox, 1998). Black girls and boys with high academic ability are often ignored more that those with less ability, a finding that some researchers interpret as an indication that teachers expect Black children to have limited academic success (Fordham, 1996; Reid, 1982). Black boys receive significantly more qualified praise (e.g., "That's good, but . . .") than do other students, and they interact with their teachers less than other students do. Black girls interact with their teachers less than White girls, but try to initiate more teacher-student interaction than do White girls and Black and White boys; unfortunately, teachers often rebuff these students (AAUW, 1992; Cox, 1998). In fact, one researcher found that Black girls received the least reinforcement of any group of children (Reid, 1982). When Black girls perform as well as White boys in school, teachers tend to attribute their success to the Black girls' effort, but at the same time assume that the White boys must not be working up to their full potential. Clearly, social class and racial prejudices interact with sexism to have an especially pernicious effect on some students' educational experiences. We will return to this point shortly.

The gender messages that teachers send to students are often reinforced by the traditional curricular materials available in elementary schools. We noted at the outset of this chapter that students learn not only the academic subjects of their school's formal curriculum, but also a set of values and expectations known as the hidden curriculum. We can see the hidden curriculum at work in the selective content of textbooks and other educational materials. Studies conducted during the 1970s (see, for example, Weitzman & Rizzo, 1976) showed that, although the United States is a country with citizens of both sexes who share a rich and varied racial and ethnic heritage, racial minorities and women were conspicuously absent from elementary school textbooks and readers. During the 1980s and throughout the 1990s, researchers have found some improvements, but according to the AAUW (1992, p. 62), "the problems persist . . . in terms of what is considered important enough to study."

Regardless of the subject—English, math, reading, science—females and minorities continue to be underrepresented in textbooks. In history texts, for example, Native Americans and Chicanos are rarely mentioned apart from such events as Custer's last stand or the Alamo, and in both cases, it is made extremely clear who the "bad guys" were. African Americans and women are more likely to be included, but their representation is still relatively low. In one content analysis of eleven history texts, for instance, the one that devoted the most space to women still only allocated a total of 3.75 pages (.01 percent of the text) (Davis, 1995). The presentation of women and African Americans is usually limited to a few "famous women" or "famous Blacks"; or they are mentioned only in traditional historical contexts (slavery, the Civil War, and the Civil Rights movement for Blacks; the suffrage movement for women) or in terms of traditional roles (e.g., women who were married to famous men). The material is also sometimes belittling and at other times, inaccurate. In one text, for example, aviator Amelia Earhart is referred to as a stewardess; in other books, women's struggle for equal rights is discussed as the fight for equal rights for wives. Rarely is mention made of women's role in the westward expansion of the United States or in the Vietnam War (Davis, 1995). That there is a heterosexist bias in the texts goes without saying.

Most publishers today issue guidelines to textbook authors to assist them in avoiding sexist language, but the extent to which the guidelines are actually followed is uneven, and such guidelines do little to increase the representation of women and minorities in the texts nor to expand the content of the texts to include the perspectives of women and minorities on their own terms (AAUW, 1992; Sadker & Sadker, 1994). For example, there is evidence that children's readers have improved significantly with respect to the use of gender-neutral language and the inclusion of females. However, there continue to be imbalances in favor of males with regard to rate of portrayal and types of roles assigned to males and females in the stories (e.g., girls need to be rescued more than boys; boys are more adventurous than girls; women work for men, but not vice versa) (Odean, 1997; Purcell & Stewart, 1990).

The AAUW (1992) notes that the major curriculum reform projects that have been undertaken in the United States since the early 1980s have not been effective in addressing the issue of gender equity. However, since 1990, several state and local boards or commissions on education, such as those in New York and Pennsylvania, have re-evaluated the formal curriculum of their schools and undertaken revisions to make the curriculum more gender-fair, multicultural, and inclusive of lesbians and gay men. Needless to say, such efforts have generated considerable controversy, and most changes in schools' curricula regarding sex, race and ethnicity, sexual orientation, and social justice have occurred at the local level in only a handful of school districts (see, for example, Celis, 1993; Dunlap, 1995; "Schools' Books on Gay Families," 1997). The importance of using nonbiased, multicultural curriculum materials, however, is exemplified by evidence that indicates that children learn their lessons quite well. Consider, for instance, the results of recent studies of school children showing that the vast majority of boys see no advantage and numerous disadvantages to being female, while many girls feel it is better to be male. For example, the majority of youngsters in one survey believed that only males can be president (Rush, 1998; Sadker & Sadker, 1994; Snow, 1992).

The organization of school activities also gives children messages about gender. For example, many teachers continue to use various forms of *sex separation* in their classrooms: They may ask girls and boys to form separate lines, or they may organize teams for a spelling or math competition according to students' sex. Teachers also sometimes assign girls and boys different classroom chores; for instance, girls may be asked to dust or water the plants, whereas boys are asked to carry books, rearrange desks, or run equipment. In one observational study, a teacher's aide showed boys how to play a videotape on the classroom VCR and subsequently allowed them to perform the task themselves, but when girls wanted to play a tape, the aide set it up for them (Sadker & Sadker, 1994). Sociologist Barrie Thorne (1993), who has made extensive observations of elementary school classrooms, points out that teachers engage in contradictory practices: Sometimes they reinforce sex separation, but other times they challenge or disrupt it. She notes that teachers more often mix boys and girls than separate them, but that separating girls and boys in lines or seating arrangements, as well as pitting them against one another in classroom contests, is not uncommon. Moreover, this physical separation is reinforced by a verbal separation, in that teachers routinely use gender labels as terms of address to the students and invariably put "boys" first in speaking to the children, as in "boys and girls." Thorne observed that girls and boys typically separate themselves in school lunchrooms and on school playgrounds—probably much more than they do in their home neighborhoods—and teachers and aides often ratify this division by seeing certain areas as "girls' territory" and other areas as "boys' territory." When children are on the school playground, boys use more space than girls and more often invade girls' space and disrupt their play. When girls and boys do play cooperatively on school playgrounds, it is typically on terms set by the boys (Voss, 1997).

Trivial though they may appear to be, these kinds of interactions have at least three interrelated consequences. First, sex separation in and of itself prevents boys and girls from working together cooperatively, thus denying children of both sexes valuable opportunities to learn about and sample one another's interests and activities. Second, sex separation makes working in same-sex groups more comfortable than working in mixed-sex groups—a feeling that children may carry with them into adulthood and that may become problematic when they enter the labor force (see Chapter 7). Third, sex separation reinforces gender stereotypes, especially if it involves differential work assignments (Sadker & Sadker, 1994).

Thorne (1993) found that in a classroom activity with a central focus, such as the collective making of a map or taking turns reading aloud from a book, girls and boys participated together. Similar observations have prompted some educators to advocate that classroom activities be reorganized to facilitate *cooperative learning*. Cooperative learning involves students working together in small, mixed-sex, mixed-race/ethnic groups on a group project or toward a group goal (e.g., solving a problem, writing a report). The cooperative learning approach is designed to lessen classroom competition, maximize cooperation, foster group solidarity and interdependence, and promote understanding among members of diverse groups of children. Research indicates that cooperative learning does have a number of benefits: It appears to increase interracial friendships, it raises the self-esteem of students of all races and ethnicities, and it is especially helpful in mainstreaming students with disabilities (AAUW, 1992; Aronson & Gonzalez, 1988). Unfortunately, it appears to be less successful in fostering positive relationships between boys and girls in school. Similar to what occurs on school playgrounds, the use of small, unstructured work groups in the classroom, especially if it is infrequent, gives boys, but not girls leadership opportunities that can raise their self-esteem. Girls end up taking direction from boys, a pattern that reinforces gender stereotypes and lowers girls' self-esteem and their academic achievement (AAUW, 1992). More fundamental changes than simply providing mixed-group learning activities are necessary to bring gender equity to elementary school classrooms.

Finally, children receive messages about gender simply by the way adult jobs are distributed in their schools. Although approximately 87 percent of elementary school teachers and 83 percent of teachers' aides are women, women are underrepresented in the upper management of school administrations. For example, 40 percent of school officials and administrators are women; 43 percent of principals and assistant principals are women (U.S. Department of Commerce, Bureau of the Census, 1997). Research indicates that the sex of a school administrator can have a measurable effect on children's gender-role perceptions. According to one study of first graders, for instance, children who attended a school headed by a female principal held fewer gender stereotypes than those who went to a school with a male principal (Paradise & Wall, 1986).

In light of our discussion so far, it may be somewhat surprising to learn that girls on average earn higher grades than boys throughout their elementary school years (AAUW, 1992). However, girls' achievement test scores, as well as their self-confidence, decline as they progress through elementary school and high school (AAUW, 1992; Gilligan et al., 1990; Sadker & Sadker, 1994). Let's examine girls' and boys' educational experiences in high school in order to better understand these findings.

Educating Teenage Girls and Boys:
The Secondary Schools

Both parents and teenagers will attest that adolescence is one of the more stressful periods of the life cycle. As one's body changes and matures, so do one's interests, and the opinions of friends take on greater significance in the formation of one's self-concept. Young men and women both feel the need to be popular with their peers, but the means and measures of their success at this are somewhat different.

For teenage boys, the single most important source of prestige and popularity is athletic achievement. Related sources of social acceptance and self-esteem include physical and verbal fighting skills, a good sense of humor, and a willingness to take risks and defy norms of politeness (Eder, 1995; see also Adler et al., 1992 regarding the emergence of these factors as sources of popularity among preadolescents). The "nonjock" is at a serious disadvantage, socially and psychologically, in high school. It is the athlete, tough and "cool," who is looked to as a leader, not only by his peers, but also by teachers and parents. Moreover, on the court or on the playing field, boys are taught a variety of stereotypically masculine skills and values: aggression (including sexual aggression and the objectification of women), endurance, competitiveness, stoic invulnerability, self-confidence, and teamwork (Eder, 1995; Messner, 1989).

What about girls? For one thing, physical prowess and athletic ability are not girls' chief sources of prestige and popularity. Indeed, most teenage girls learn that to be athletic is to be unfeminine and, as we will discuss in Chapter 11, school officials reinforce this message by underresourcing girls' sports programs. Instead, what contributes most to a teenage girl's prestige and popularity is physical attractiveness. Girls' attractiveness may be enhanced when they wear stylish clothes and make-up, but too much make-up and too obvious an attempt to appear sexually alluring can result in negative labels, such as "whore" and "slut." Teenage girls must walk a fine line by demonstrating that they are sexually knowledgable, but not sexually aggressive. Unlike boys, girls are supposed to be sexually passive, the objects of boys' sexual advances, but not sexual initiators themselves (Eder, 1995).

Obviously, teenagers, both female and male, who are not heterosexual face tremendous difficulties in high school and, as Box 4.2 on page 96 shows, frequently experience isolation and ostracism from their peers as well as from adults. Also frequent targets of ridicule in high school are students who are overweight, who have physical disabilities, or who are in special education programs (Eder, 1995). Eder argues that the status hierarchies that emerge in high school are to some extent influenced by students' race and social class as well. In particular, when students of color are a numerical minority in a school environment, they are more easily socially isolated. Lower-class students are often regarded as deviant because of their clothing and appearance, although they may view wealthier students as "stuck-up." Social class intersects with gender in significant ways. For girls who are poor, opportunities to participate in activities that increase popularity are fewer because of their limited financial resources. Their families cannot afford name-brand clothes or summer cheerleading camp, for example. For lower-class boys, however, athletics is a primary vehicle for overcoming the obstacles to popularity that poverty imposes (Eder, 1995; see also Bernstein, 1995; and Chapter 11).

It is also in high school that young men and women are expected to formulate their career goals. Until the late 1960s, studies showed that high school boys had higher academic and career aspirations than high school girls. However, more recent research has found no sex differences in either the educational or occupational aspirations of young women and men, and some studies show girls as having higher aspirations than boys (Dennehy & Mortimer, 1992; Orenstein, 1994). Despite their raised aspirations, though, teenage girls still tend to underestimate their academic abilities (Dennehy & Mortimer, 1992; Eccles, 1985) and their self-confidence drops dramatically beginning around the age of ten (Bernstein, 1995; Brody, 1997; Orenstein, 1994). In their recent studies of adolescent girls, for example, psychologist Carol Gilligan and her colleagues have found that by age fifteen or sixteen, girls who had earlier exuded confidence become less outspoken and more doubtful about their abilities. Gilligan's initial research was with girls attending the Emma Willard School, an elite, private, single-sex school in New York (Gilligan et al., 1990). More recently, Gilligan and her colleagues have studied girls from poorer backgrounds in less privileged schools, including twenty-six racially and ethnically diverse teenage girls considered at high risk of dropping out of school and becoming unmarried mothers (Gilligan, et al., 1995). These researchers' findings once again highlight the intersection of gender with race/ethnicity and social class.

Gilligan and her colleagues (1995) report that at adolescence, regardless of race/ethnicity or social class, girls increasingly find that their experiences are devalued or ignored in patriarchal culture. The desirable or idealized woman in this culture often does not match their experience or their sense of themselves. Their socialization experiences have taught them to see themselves *relationally* (i.e., in connection to others), so in order to maintain and preserve the relationships they value, adolescent girls learn to be silent and, in the process, lose their energy and vitality to succeed on their own terms. They come to "absent themselves in order to be with other people" (Gilligan et al., 1995, p. 5). Girls from privileged backgrounds change or moderate their voices so they are more "acceptable" to those who show interest in them (e.g., boys, teachers, parents). In this way, they don't jeopardize the relationships that promise them honor, riches, and marriage in the future. Poor girls, who are disproportionately racial and ethnic minorities, don't live under such constraints. Their experience, however, tells them that while they can speak, nobody really cares about what they have to say; they are irrelevant, invisible. When they do speak up, their "big mouths" frequently get them into trouble. These girls become socially and psychologically isolated, which Gilligan and her colleagues (1995) see as the precursors to problems such as dropping out of school and early single motherhood (see also Fordham, 1996).

Although Gilligan's theory of females' "connectedness" and relationality has been criticized for various reasons (see, for instance, Hirsch & Keller, 1990; Kerber et al., 1986) and her research uses small convenience samples, her work does offer a provocative counterpoint to earlier theorists who argued that females' self-confidence and self-efficacy decline during adolescence because women fear success. During the

BOX 4.2
The High School Experiences of Lesbian and Gay Youth

Adolescence is a period of tremendous physical and emotional change. It is a time when most young women and men begin to actively explore their sexuality and sexual identities. Historically, our schools have been woefully remiss in educating young people about sex, but they have been most neglectful with respect to lesbian and gay youth. Although recent surveys indicate a willingness on the part of most teachers and school administrators to treat homosexual students in a nonjudgmental way and to attend school-sponsored workshops related to homosexual students, there also remains among most an unwillingness to proactively address the special needs of homosexual students or to openly affirm their sexual identities (Sears, 1992). The majority of school personnel, in fact, continue to assume the heterosexuality of their students and never raise the issue of sexual orientation.

With the exception of responding to especially blatant or heinous forms of harassment against homosexual students, most school personnel do not seriously confront the problem of **homophobia**—an unreasonable fear of or hostility toward homosexuals—in their classrooms or on school grounds (AAUW, 1992; Sears, 1992). "The absence of visible support from educators conveys to *all* students the legitimacy and desirability of the heterosexual standard" (Sears, 1992, p. 74, author's emphasis). Indeed, some school personnel are themselves openly homophobic, and their attitudes and behavior promote homophobia among students. In 1996, for example, the Utah state senate passed a bill prohibiting teachers from "encouraging, condoning or supporting illegal conduct." In Utah, sodomy is illegal, and promoters of the bill argued that it was designed to keep homosexuals out of the state's schools. At the same time, The Salt Lake City Board of Education banned all extracurricular clubs from the city's high schools in an effort to rid the schools of gay/lesbian/bisexual student groups. Students took to the streets in protest, but most were not sympathetic to their homosexual peers. Instead, the ban generated more hostility toward gays and lesbians as heterosexual students argued for a "ban on homosexuality, not clubs" (Brooke, 1996). At least eight other states are considering legislation similar to Utah's in order to stop discussion of homosexuality in school ("School Program," 1996).

What are the consequences of homophobia for lesbian and gay high school students? Research shows that lesbian and gay adolescents have a disproportionately high rate of substance abuse, sexual abuse, parental rejection, homelessness, academic problems, and risk-taking behavior (Lock & Kleis, 1998; Uribe & Harbeck, 1992; Voelker, 1998). They are nearly five times more likely than heterosexual students to miss school because they fear for their safety (Voelker, 1998). In one study, 80 percent of the gay and lesbian students reported having been verbally insulted at school, 44 percent were threatened with violence, 31 percent were chased or followed, and 17 percent were physically assaulted (Lock & Kleis, 1998). Not surprisingly, lesbian and gay adolescents are at an especially high risk of dropping out of school (Uribe & Harbeck, 1992).

The social rejection and violence that gay and lesbian students often receive from their non-homosexual peers and, not infrequently, from their parents, lead to low self-esteem, feelings of isolation, and a sense of inadequacy. Those who hide their sexual orientation may escape some of the physical and verbal harassment, but their secretiveness is likely to increase their feelings of loneliness and alienation. According to recent studies, one consequence of the low self-esteem and isolation is a disproportionately high rate of suicide and attempted suicide among gay and lesbian youth (Lock & Kleis, 1998). By some estimates, more than 30 percent of the approximately 5,000 suicides committed each year by young women and men between the ages of fifteen and twenty-four are related to emotional trauma resulting from sexual orientation issues and from societal prejudices about same-sex relationships (Harbeck, 1992).

In response to these disturbing statistics, organizations have been established throughout the United States to specifically meet the special needs of lesbian and gay youth (Woog, 1995). These include schools for gay, lesbian, and bisexual students or the children of gays, lesbians, and bisexuals. The first such school, the Harvey Milk School in New York, was founded in 1985 and now has about 80 students. There are also three public schools in Los Angeles and a private school in Dallas (Lambert, 1998). Most organizations, however, do not provide direct schooling, but rather offer other services, such as counseling, tutoring, meals, and sometimes shelter for homosexual and bisexual youth who have been kicked out of their homes after coming out to (or being found out by) their parents. Some organizations also offer programs, such as peer trainings at local schools to help foster acceptance of homosexual and bisexual youth and to help prevent harassment and violence. A number of organizations lobby school boards and state departments of education to make school activities and curriculum more inclusive of gay and lesbian youth (Green, 1993; Uribe & Harbeck, 1992; Woog, 1995). A national directory of organizations serving sexual minority youth is available from the Hetrick-Martin Institute, 401 West Street, New York, NY 10014.

There is evidence that these organizations are often successful in raising the self-esteem and, consequently, the academic achievement of the young women and men they serve, while also lowering rates of destructive behaviors. However, they have been somewhat less successful in getting school boards and education departments to respond (for exceptions, see Rimer, 1993; "School Program," 1996). As the AAUW (1992, p. 80) concludes, until the mainstream education system effectively addresses homophobia among its staff, students, and students' parents, it is abdicating its "responsibility not only to serve adolescents who are questioning their individual sexual orientation but to all students."

1970s, for example, psychologist Matina Horner (1972) argued that her research, which showed that women tended to perform better on word-game tasks when they worked alone rather than in mixed-sex groups, indicated that women are uncomfortable competing with men. Horner hypothesized that women may deliberately, although perhaps unconsciously, underachieve because they fear the consequences that success in high-achievement situations might bring—specifically, that they will appear unfeminine and, therefore, be rejected socially.

There is evidence that girls tend to feel uneasy and embarrassed about academic success (Orenstein, 1994; Sherman 1982), and some avoid subjects defined as masculine because they fear rejection by their peers (Tobias & Weissbrod, 1980). There is also evidence that their concerns are not unfounded: Girls who behave in ways defined by their peers as gender-inappropriate are likely to be unpopular and ostracized (Eder, 1995; Pfost & Fiore, 1990). Boys who behave in gender-inappropriate ways are also ridiculed and ostracized by their peers, but they do not consistently lower their academic or career aspirations as a result. Why?

One answer is that girls face a number of obstacles imposed by others that inhibit the realization of their academic and occupational goals. These obstacles are sometimes collectively called the *invisible* or *glass ceiling* (see also Chapter 7). One element of the invisible ceiling is the widespread belief that girls are not as intellectually gifted as boys and, therefore, cannot be expected to do as well in school. Research reveals, for example, that teachers, parents, and students themselves usually attribute boys' academic achievements to ability, whereas girls' achievements are attributed to effort or hard work, the implication being that those with lesser ability must expend greater effort to succeed (see Golombok & Fivush, 1994 for a summary of the attribution of academic success research). In addition, high school teachers, like their elementary school counterparts, tend to offer male students more encouragement, publicly praise their scholastic abilities, and be friendlier toward them than they are toward female students (Bush, 1987; Jones & Wheatley, 1990; Orenstein, 1994). As Bush (1987, p. 15) notes, "These findings are analogous to those for teacher expectations linked to class and/or race" in which teachers respond more positively to middle- and upper-class students than to working-class and poor students or to White students relative to minority students. There is evidence that students internalize these beliefs, which, if one is female (and poor and non-White), could reasonably lead to lowered self-confidence and self-efficacy—not for fear of success, but for fear of failure (AAUW, 1992, Bush, 1987; Fordham, 1996; Gilligan et al., 1995; Orenstein, 1994).

Another element of the invisible ceiling imposed on girls in secondary schools can be found in curriculum materials, which often send girls the message that they are unlikely to realize their ambitions. Recent reviews of high school textbooks, for instance, found both subtle and blatant gender biases, including language bias and gender stereotypes, omission of women and a focus on "great men," and neglect of scholarship by women (AAUW, 1992; Davis, 1995; "Where French Course," 1990). As in elementary school, research indicates that the type of curriculum materials used in the schools clearly has an impact on students' attitudes and behaviors. According to the authors of a review of more than 100 studies of gender-fair curriculum materials, "Pupils who are exposed to sex-equitable materials are more likely than others to (1) have gender-balanced knowledge of people in society, (2) develop more flexible attitudes and more accurate sex-role knowledge, and (3) imitate role behaviors contained in the material" (Scott & Schau, 1985, p. 228). The gender bias common in high school curriculum materials is compounded by the lack of attention to racial and ethnic diversity and differences in sexual orientation. As one young Latina recently commented in frustration about her high school history class, "'When are we going to get to talk about the Martin Luther King movement?' or stuff like that. And the teacher is like, 'We're getting there,' but they never do. . . . And we argue, 'Okay, when are we going to talk about us? When are we going to get to say what we want to say?' And they never get to it. It never happens" ("A Dialogue," 1998, p. 15).

School personnel may also contribute to making girls feel that they will be unable to fulfill their aspirations. For example, research indicates that school counselors provide little useful career information to girls; in one recent survey, more than 70 percent of the 600 female students questioned said that the career advice provided to them at school was either inadequate or not helpful (Miles, 1995). Studies also indicate that school personnel may channel male and female students into different (i.e., gender-stereotyped) fields and activities, with female students in particular being discouraged from pursuing such fields as mathematics, engineering, construction, and pharmaceuticals (AAUW, 1992; Marini & Brinton, 1984; Miles, 1995; Petro & Putnam, 1979; see also Box 4.3 on page 99).

BOX **4.3**

Gender, Mathematics, and Computers

For many years, much has been made of the fact that boys score higher than girls do on the Scholastic Assessment Test (S.A.T., formerly the Scholastic Aptitude Test) and that the differences between boys' and girls' scores historically has been largest on the math portion of the exam. In 1998, the gender gap in S.A.T. scores narrowed somewhat, largely because the test had been revised following charges of gender bias. Nevertheless, the gender gap in math scores on the test remained (Arenson, 1998).

Some observers have argued that the gender gap in math is biologically or genetically caused—that males, for example, have a genetic predisposition to excel at math or that the organization of their brains favors math achievement (see Chapter 2). Despite widespread attention to such claims in the popular media, there is little scientific data to support them. There is evidence that boys do better at math because they have better spatial skills, but the research indicates that these better spatial skills may be as much, if not more, a product of experience than of biology. The development of spatial skills as well as problem-solving ability, for instance, are tied to participation in competitive sports, which boys do more than girls. They are also associated with greater independence from parents, outdoor play, willingness to take risks, and neighborhood exploration—all activities more likely experienced by boys than by girls while growing up (Casey et al., 1997; Entwisle et al., 1994; Ramos & Lambating, 1996; see also Chapter 3).

Several other social factors also appear to be related to the gender gap in mathematics. One factor is the extent to which math and math-related activities are oriented to males rather than females. Observers have noted, for instance, that math word problems are often framed in terms of traditionally masculine-typed areas and interests (Rosser, 1989). Much computer software, especially computer games, is also masculine in its orientation (Crawford, 1990). Mathematics software programs typically center around male themes of adventure and violence. Research shows game covers depict males thirteen times more than they show females. Moreover, one-third of the females depicted in the best-selling video games in 1994 were victims of violence (Meyer, 1996). Consequently, girls may come to see math and computers as masculine—a perception that may affect not only their performance, but also their career aspirations. However, one study found that 85 percent of girls said they would find computer games fun to play if the games were oriented more to their interests than to those of boys, and at least one technology firm, Girl Games, is developing computer software and video games specifically for girls (Meyers, 1996). Still, research indicates that girls who are computer proficient sometimes pay a heavy social price. When interviewing adolescents, for example, Crawford (1990, p. 25) heard many stories from female achievers in computer courses "of boys being 'jealous' of [the girls'] knowledge of electronics and of 'hassling' the girls in class." The boys confirmed their view. As a result, some educators have recommended voluntary single-sex math classes for girls ("Math Theory Gains Ground," 1994; see also Kalinowski & Buerk, 1995).

In their classic study of gender and mathematics performance, Fennema and Sherman (1977) discovered that the major difference between males and females with regard to mathematics is not math ability per se, but rather extent of exposure to mathematics. Throughout elementary school, when boys and girls take the same math classes, there is little, if any, difference in math achievement. It is not until around seventh grade that the gap begins to appear (Entwisle et al., 1994). As the years progress, girls become less likely than boys to take any math courses beyond those required by their school for graduation. Yet, among girls and boys with identical math backgrounds, there is little difference in performance on math tests (see, for example, Cherian & Siweya, 1996).

(continued)

Two factors appear to be critical in influencing girls' and boys' decisions to enroll in math courses: their interactions with teachers and encouragement of their parents (Crawford, 1990). Research on teacher-student interaction indicates that there are various ways that teachers differentially reinforce math achievement in male and female students: by perceiving and conveying the belief that math is more important for boys than for girls, by encouraging girls to become more proficient at computational math and boys at problem-solving, and by calling on boys more than girls to solve problems in class (AAUW, 1992; Koehler, 1990; Leder & Fennema, 1990; Leung, 1990). Not surprisingly, few parents nowadays openly discourage their daughters from studying math or math-related subjects, but the message may be communicated indirectly. For instance, parents are more likely to enroll sons than daughters in computer camps (Hess & Muira, 1985). Girls and boys both recognize that computers will have a significant impact on their personal futures. However, boys are more likely to report having access to computers at home, although there is evidence that the difference is declining (Crawford, 1990; Mannix et al., 1996).

In summary, the weight of the evidence points to a variety of social factors as being responsible for observed gender differences in math and computer usage. In one sense, this is encouraging since, as we have argued previously, socially induced conditions are more easily changed than biologically caused conditions. The solution, in fact, seems obvious: Educators and parents must commit themselves to providing gender-equitable learning opportunities for girls and boys, starting with giving girls more freedom and encouragement to explore their neighborhoods and to participate in competitive sports (see Chapter 11). Until such steps are taken, math and computer proficiency will probably remain "critical filters" that block females' advancement into many lucrative and prestigious professions (Chesterman, 1990; Leder & Fennema, 1990; The McClintock Collective, 1990).

Finally, although elementary school girls can identify with their teachers, who are almost always women, it becomes more difficult to do so in high school, where about 43 percent of the teachers are men (U.S. Department of Commerce, Bureau of the Census, 1997). In vocational courses, female teachers are concentrated in subjects traditionally considered feminine: occupational home economics (92 percent), health (90 percent), and office occupations (69 percent). They are rarely found in industrial arts (4 percent), agriculture (6 percent), and trade and industry (9 percent). High school students are especially likely to have a male teacher for their math courses (57.7 percent) and science courses (65.4 percent). Teachers of these subjects also are usually White: Only 11 percent of math teachers, 10 percent of biology teachers, and 7 percent of chemistry teachers in grades nine through twelve are people of color (Commission on Professionals in Science and Technology, 1992).

Although there is no research that shows a clear cause-and-effect relationship, it is not unlikely that the rather discouraging nature of girls' high school experience, more than their fear of success, is what weakens their self-confidence and self-efficacy. Nevertheless, a high number of female high school graduates attend college. In fact, as Table 4.1 shows, they now constitute a slight majority of college students. Unfortunately, the education they receive continues to differ from that of their male peers in many important respects.

Educating Women and Men: Colleges and Graduate Schools

"What's your major?" is certainly a question college students get asked a lot. The next time you are in a group and that question comes up, compare the responses of the male students with those of the female students. Chances are, you will discover an interesting sex-specific pattern, for as Table 4.2 shows, men and women continue to be concentrated in very different fields of study. More male students pursue degrees in engineering, computer science, philosophy and religion, architecture, and the physical sciences (e.g., astronomy, chemistry, geology, physics). Female students are heavily concentrated in nursing, library science, social work, psychology, home economics, and education.

This imbalance persists and, in fact, worsens at the graduate level. Again, looking at Table 4.2 on page 102 we find that the graduate degrees of men and women tend to be concentrated in different fields. For example, men earn about 88 percent of the Ph.D.s in physics, but less than 7 percent of the Ph.D.s in nursing. Conversely, women earn nearly 75 percent of the doctorates in home economics, but just 11 percent of the doctorates in engineering.

An even more disturbing trend emerges at the highest graduate level: The number of female degree recipients declines dramatically. Consider that although women represent more than half of all bachelor's and master's degree recipients, they constitute slightly more than one-third of all doctorate recipients. More importantly, male Ph.D.s outnumber female Ph.D.s in several fields that have either a higher concentration of women undergraduates or a relative balance between the sexes at the undergraduate level. International relations is a good example. As Table 4.2 shows, men receive 43.5 percent of the bachelor's degrees in international relations, but about 79 percent of the doctorates. Similarly, in music, men are awarded about 49 percent of bachelor's degrees and 62 percent of doctorates; in political science, 57.5 percent of bachelor's degrees and 71 percent of doctorates; and in mathematics, 54 percent of bachelor's degrees and 78 percent of doctorates.

If we consider race as well as sex, we find that the overwhelming majority of all degrees are awarded to Whites of both sexes (78.5 percent in 1994). As we see in Table 4.3 on page 103, the higher up we go on the education ladder, the poorer the representation of non-White racial and ethnic groups. Moreover, this underrepresentation of women and men of color in higher education is expected to worsen in coming years as states dismantle affirmative action programs. In California and Texas, for example, enrollments of African American and Latino students at the states' colleges and universities declined significantly following decisions in both states in 1996 to repeal their affirmative action plans ("Segregation Anew," 1997; see also Bronner, 1997).

An important point that must be made with regard to race/ethnicity and sex is that these figures actually represent improvements for people of color and women in higher education. In 1977, for example, people of color received only about 13 percent of all higher education degrees awarded compared with more than 21 percent in 1994 (U.S. National Center for Education Statistics, 1996). Overall, however, women as a group have fared better. For instance, in 1970, women constituted only 13 percent of

TABLE 4.2   Percentage of Bachelor's, Master's, and Doctor's Degrees Conferred by U.S. Institutions of Higher Education to Women in Selected Fields of Study, 1993–1994

Major Field of Study	% Bachelor's Degrees Conferred to Women	% Master's Degrees Conferred to Women	% Doctor's Degrees Conferred to Women
Accounting	55.1	45.7	46.0
Agriculture & Natural Resources	35.0	38.9	23.2
Anthropology	63.5	61.4	53.3
Architecture	29.6	32.3	20.1
Art History	78.7	78.6	60.1
Astronomy	29.5	26.9	14.9
Banking & Finance	32.0	29.2	17.2
Biological & Life Sciences	52.1	52.6	41.1
Business Management	47.2	35.2	25.1
Chemistry	40.7	41.3	30.3
Communications	58.9	62.3	48.9
Computer & Information Sciences	28.4	25.8	15.4
Criminal Justice	38.8	38.0	44.0
Economics	29.5	32.7	24.1
Education	77.3	76.7	60.8
Engineering	16.4	15.4	11.1
English	65.8	65.6	57.7
Foreign Languages	70.1	66.9	59.9
Geology	33.9	31.2	17.7
Health Sciences	82.4	79.2	58.5
History	37.2	39.4	37.2
Home Economics	87.5	83.3	74.5
International Relations	56.5	45.1	21.2
Library Science	91.9	79.7	68.9
Mathematics	46.3	38.1	21.9
Music	51.7	51.6	37.9
Nursing	90.4	93.3	93.7
Philosophy	31.4	30.1	27.9
Physics	17.7	15.2	12.3
Political Science & Government	42.5	37.2	28.9
Psychology	73.1	72.1	62.2
Public Administration	48.7	48.9	33.8
Religion & Religious Studies	42.7	44.0	26.7
Social Work	85.8	82.9	69.5
Sociology	68.2	61.2	50.1
Visual & Performing Arts	57.0	60.1	44.4

Source: U.S. National Center for Education Statistics, 1996, pp. 258–265.

TABLE 4.3   Percentage of Bachelor's, Master's, and Doctor's Degrees Conferred by U.S. Institutions of Higher Education, by Race/Ethnicity and Sex, 1993–1994

| | *Racial/Ethnic Group & Sex** | | | | | | | | | |
| | *White* | | *Black* | | *Hispanic* | | *Asian/Pacific Islander* | | *American Indian/ Alaskan Native* | |
	Women	Men	Women	Men	Women	Men	Women	Men	Women	Men
*Degree Conferred***										
Bachelor's Degrees (Total = 1,131,893)	44.8	37.9	4.7	2.7	2.5	1.9	2.5	2.4	0.3	0.2
Master's Degrees (Total = 339,102)	48.5	36.5	4.3	2.2	2.0	1.5	2.1	2.4	0.3	0.2
Doctor's Degrees (Total = 31,611)	38.1	47.9	2.4	2.0	1.4	1.5	2.1	4.3	0.2	0.2

*Percentages do not add to 100 due to rounding.

**Total does not include degrees awarded to nonresident aliens.

Source: U.S. National Center for Education Statistics, 1996, pp. 286, 289, 292.

the doctoral recipients in the United States, up from 10 percent in 1960 (U.S. Department of Commerce, Bureau of the Census, 1985). It is especially noteworthy that women have made some of their greatest gains in fields that have had the fewest female students, such as the physical sciences and engineering. Although still small, the number of doctorates earned by women in engineering increased significantly in recent years (U.S. National Center for Education Statistics, 1996; see also Clewell & Anderson, 1991). Still, some nagging questions remain: Why does sex segregation in particular fields persist, and why is the education gap between the sexes still fairly wide?

In addressing the first question, we must consider not only why women are largely absent from certain fields, but also why there are so few men in fields such as nursing, home economics, social work, and library science. We can say with some certainty that the scarcity of men in the female-dominated fields has less to do with discrimination against them than with their unwillingness to pursue careers in areas that typically have lower prestige and lower salaries than the male-dominated fields. We have already noted that activities and topics deemed feminine are systematically devalued in our society. Until fields such as nursing and home economics are considered as important as business administration or geology—and are rewarded with comparable salaries—it will remain difficult to attract men to major in them (see also Chapter 7). However, in solving the puzzle of women's relative absence from the more prestigious and higher paying male-dominated fields, the issue of discrimination is central.

It is widely thought that sex discrimination in education has virtually disappeared, thanks to Title IX. You may recall that Title IX is the provision of the 1972 Education

Amendments Act that forbids discrimination in any educational program or activity that receives federal funding. However, Title IX has not eliminated sex discrimination in education. One important reason for the less than total success of Title IX is that, while the law abolished most overtly discriminatory policies and practices, it left more subtle forms of sex discrimination intact (Sandler & Hall, 1986). Sandler and Hall (1986, p. 3) refer to these subtle, everyday types of discrimination as **micro-inequities.** Micro-inequities single out, ignore, or in some way discount individuals and their work or ideas simply on the basis of an ascribed trait, such as sex. "Often the behaviors themselves are small, and individually might even be termed 'trivial' or minor annoyances, but when they happen again and again, they can have a major cumulative impact because they express underlying limited expectations and a certain discomfort in dealing with women" (Sandler & Hall, 1986, p. 3).

Hall and Sandler (1985) have documented more than thirty-five different kinds of micro-inequities experienced by female undergraduate and graduate students, including the following:

■ Male students are called on more than female students, are interrupted less when they are speaking, and, in general, their comments are taken more seriously by the professor (see also Guinier et al., 1995; Lewis & Simon, 1986; Myers & Dugan, 1996).

■ Professors may use sex-stereotyped examples when discussing men's and women's social or professional roles (e.g., always referring to physicians as "he" and nurses as "she").

■ References are made to males as "men" but to females as "girls" or "gals," or the generic "he" or "man" is used to refer to both men and women (see Chapter 5).

■ Comments are made about a female student's physical attributes or appearance, especially while she is discussing an academic matter or an idea (e.g., "Did anyone ever tell you how big your eyes get when you're excited about something?").

■ Comments are made that disparage women in general (e.g., references to single, middle-aged women as "old maids"), that disparage women's intellectual abilities (e.g., "You girls probably won't understand this"), or that disparage women's academic commitment and seriousness (e.g., "You're so cute; why would you ever want to be an engineer?").

It is difficult to imagine such comments being made to or about men or male students, but they are not infrequently made to or about women. Granted, "these behaviors do not happen in *every class*, nor do they happen all the time. But they happen often enough that they contribute to a pattern—a pattern of behavior that dampens women's ambition, lessens their class participation, and diminishes their self-confidence" (Hall & Sandler, 1985, p. 506, authors' emphasis; see also Myers & Dugan, 1996). More importantly, it appears that these inequities are more common in courses and fields of study traditionally dominated by men, and that they intensify in graduate school (Hall & Sandler, 1985; Rayman, 1993; Turner & Thompson, 1993). Clearly, this helps to explain the relative absence of women in the sciences and business and also at the doctoral level.

There are at least two other major barriers to equality for women in higher education: the lack of mentors and role models, and the incidence of sexual harassment. Before we discuss each of these, it is important to note that college peer culture may interact with structural variables, as well as with students' views of school formed earlier in their lives, to diminish young women's ambitions. Eisenhart and Holland (1992), for example, note that when young people go to college, they are often struck by the fact that they must study harder than they did in high school to achieve comparable grades. However, competing with study time, especially at residential colleges, is time for socializing with peers. Although a peer culture might help stimulate the development of high-achievement, career-related identities among college students—as we suspect it often does for male students—Eisenhart and Holland's research indicates that for women in college, the peer culture emphasizes involvement in romantic relationships and a concern with being physically attractive to men (see also Holland & Eisenhart, 1991; Stombler & Martin, 1994). The majority of women in Eisenhart and Holland's study spent most of their time with their peers discussing boyfriends or potential boyfriends, their own and others' physical appearances (with an emphasis on weight), and social activities. In contrast, most seemed to know little about their peers' schoolwork or career interests. Only the relatively few women who came to college with the view of higher education as a setting in which they could learn from "experts," especially those in their field of interest, did not succumb to the social pressures of the campus peer culture. African American female college students were found to be as sexually exploited and caught up in romance as White female college students were, but the African American students placed less emphasis on the goal of "finding a man" in college and were also less likely to believe that a man would be their source of economic support in the future (see also Stombler & Padavic, 1994). Thus, peer culture must be added to young women's socialization experiences in elementary and secondary school as well as at home as an important influence on their academic and career decisions.

We may ask, however, what it is about the university environment that allows such a peer culture to flourish for female students, and what makes it more attractive than the academic life of the institution? To answer these questions, we must return to the structural barriers that confront women in higher education.

Women Faculty and Administrators: Still Too Few

Despite the gains that women have made in the percentage of advanced degrees awarded to them, they are still underrepresented among university administrators and faculty. Women are 40 percent of administrators at U.S. colleges and universities; 84 percent of these women, however, are White (Ottinger & Sikula, 1993). The number of women college and university presidents has significantly increased over the past two decades; in 1995, there were 453 women heading U.S. colleges and universities, tripling the percentage of women college and university CEOs since 1975. However, this means that women are still just 16 percent of the chief executives of the approximately 2,900

TABLE 4.4   **Percent Distribution of Faculty by Academic Rank and Sex, 1996–1997**

Academic Rank	Sex	
	Women	**Men**
Professor	6.6	30.3
Associate Professor	9.6	19.1
Assistant Professor	11.8	13.6
Instructor	3.3	2.3
Lecturer	1.4	1.4
No Rank	0.3	0.4
All Combined	33.2	66.8

Source: Academe, March–April, 1997, p. 34.

regionally accredited institutions of higher education in the United States. Only 72 (16 percent) of women college and university CEOs are women of color (American Council of Education, 1995).

Women represent just 33.2 percent of full-time college and university faculty (American Association of University Professors [AAUP] 1997). In general, the more prestigious the institution or department, the fewer the women. For example, at doctoral granting institutions, women are 27.4 percent of the faculty, whereas at two-year colleges, women are 45.9 percent of the faculty (AAUP, 1997). Similarly, the higher the academic rank, the fewer the women. In the Ivy League—an elite group of eight universities—women hold only a small fraction of tenured professorships: For example, women are 9.4 percent of tenured professors at Yale, just over 11 percent at Harvard, 12 percent at Princeton, and 13 percent at Columbia (McLarin, 1996). Looking at Table 4.4, we see that college and university faculties are dominated by male full professors, but just 6.6 percent of college and university faculty are female full professors. The U.S. National Council on Education Statistics (1996) reports that 17 percent of full professors and 30 percent of associate professors are women, but women are 42.1 percent of assistant professors and 49.3 percent of instructors. One might expect the percentage of women in higher ranks to increase as more women enter academic employment and, in fact, the greatest increases in the representation of women in the professorial ranks has occurred at the associate professor and full professor levels (AAUP, 1997). Nevertheless, given that the tenure rate for women is 58 percent compared to 75 percent for men, one wonders if these gains will be sustained in the future (Ottinger & Sikula, 1993). Moreover, Table 4.5 shows that few college and university faculty are people of color, but women of color are most underrepresented.

Regardless of rank or tenure status, women faculty are paid less than men and, as Table 4.6 shows, the gap is widest at the highest academic rank. Indeed, even though the number of faculty who are women has increased substantially during the last fifteen years, there has been little change in the ratio of female faculty salaries to male faculty

TABLE 4.5   Full-time Instructional Faculty in Institutions of Higher Education, by Sex and Race, Fall 1993

	Sex (%)*	
Racial/Ethnic Group	**Women**	**Men**
White	28.4	57.4
Black	2.2	2.5
Hispanic	0.8	1.4
Asian/Pacific Islander	1.2	3.5
American Indian/Alaskan Native	0.14	0.23
Nonresident Alien	0.45	1.5
Race/Ethnicity Unknown	0.06	0.14

*Percentages do not add to 100 due to rounding.

Source: U.S. National Center for Education Statistics, 1996, p. 231.

salaries (AAUP, 1993). The gender gap in faculty salaries has remained fairly stable in the last ten years.

Female faculty and administrators, like female students, confront innumerable inequities—some subtle, some overt—on the campuses where they work (Bagilhole, 1993; Sandler & Hall, 1986). They may find, for example, that some male colleagues feel free to address them as "honey" or "dear," or that students consistently address male faculty as "Dr." while they are "Miss" or "Mrs." At department or committee meetings, they may be expected to record the minutes or, as the "token woman," to provide the "women's point of view" as if one woman can speak for all. Their personal

TABLE 4.6   Average Salary for Men and Women Faculty and Women's Salaries as a Percentage of Men's Salaries, 1996–1997

	Sex		Women's Salaries as a Percentage
Academic Rank	**Women**	**Men**	**of Men's Salaries**
Professor	$60,702	$68,884	88.1
Associate Professor	47,284	50,910	92.9
Assistant Professor	39,643	42,256	93.8
Instructor	31,242	32,489	96.2
Lecturer	32,945	37,006	89.0
No Rank	33,833	39,057	86.6

Source: Academe, March–April, 1997, p. 26.

lives may be scrutinized (e.g., "Who takes care of her kids?") and their appearance commented on (e.g., "Your pretty face certainly makes coming to work more pleasant"). But perhaps most frustrating and damaging of all, their work may be devalued by both colleagues and students, even when it is equal or superior to that of a man (Kolodny, 1993; Moore, 1997; Wennards & Wold, 1997).

Discrimination such as this effectively keeps women out of academia and prevents those already there from moving up. Once again, the problem is most acute in the academic disciplines traditionally dominated by men, but it has its greatest impact on women of color regardless of department. This is because women of color typically face double discrimination—discrimination on the basis of both race or ethnicity and sex—that is often perpetrated by White women as well as by men (Carty, 1992; Nieves-Squires, 1991; Pollard, 1990; Sandler & Hall, 1986). This discrimination helps to account for the even greater absence of women of color from academe that we saw earlier.

A net result of the imbalance of university faculty is a lack of mentors for female students and students of color. A **mentor** is a role model and more—usually an older, established member of a profession, who shows young, new members "the ropes" by giving advice and providing valuable contacts with others in the field. However, since mentors tend to choose protégés who are most like themselves, and since there are so few women in the upper echelons of the academic hierarchy, female students and junior faculty may have fewer opportunities to establish mentoring relationships and thereby lose out on the benefits such relationships provide (Nevels, 1990; Turner & Thompson, 1993). Some women have responded to this problem by establishing *peer* mentoring programs, in which women junior faculty as well as staff meet on a regular basis to provide one another with advice and support and to share ideas, information, and resources (Limbert, 1995).

Although some have questioned the necessity of a mentor for individual success (Speizer, 1981) and others have pointed to problems with the senior female-junior female mentoring model (Limbert, 1995), we maintain that at the very least, the presence of senior female faculty and administrators communicates to students and other members of the campus community that women are as capable, productive, and serious professionally as their male counterparts. Recent research also indicates that the presence of female faculty on campus may benefit male as well as female students in a number of significant ways. For instance, one recent study (Statham et al., 1991) has shown that the teaching emphases of male and female faculty differ; female faculty focus more on the student as the locus of learning, whereas male faculty focus more on themselves. Female faculty also tend to use a more interactive style in the classroom, making greater efforts than male faculty to get students to participate in class. In fact, this study showed that female faculty report that their teaching satisfaction derives from "students relating to each other, developing their own ideas, and coming prepared to participate in class discussions," while male faculty tended to see students' class participation as either a requirement or a waste of class time (Statham et al., 1991, p. 126; see also Deats & Lenker, 1994; Maher & Tetrault, 1994; McCormick, 1994). Female faculty also interact more with students outside of class than male faculty do. They are more involved in campus "quality-of-life" programs (e.g., the women's center, rape crisis hotlines). They chat with students more and provide them with more counseling than do male faculty. In contrast, male faculty report negotiating more with students about their course grades (Kolodny, 1993; Statham et al., 1991). In short, what these data indicate is that female university faculty may utilize a kind of instructional and interactional style that is more conducive to learning and more beneficial to both male and female students.

This is not to say that male faculty cannot be mentors or role models for female students; in fact, they often are. However, there is abundant evidence that male faculty typically interact differently with male and female students; we have already discussed some of these findings. Male faculty sometimes feel uncomfortable with female students, or they may relate to them paternalistically rather than professionally (Limbert, 1995). Worse still, they may view their female students as potential sexual partners and use their positions of power and authority to coerce sexual favors. As we will see next, this is not an uncommon experience for college women.

Sexual Harassment

Sexual harassment involves any unwanted leers, comments, suggestions, or physical contact of a sexual nature, as well as unwelcome requests for sexual favors. There are actually two types of sexual harassment. If the harassment is directly tied to the granting or denial of a benefit or privilege, such as a course grade or the chance to work on an important research project, it is called *quid pro quo* harassment. The second type of harassment involves creating a *hostile environment* by, for example, telling sexual jokes, using sexual innuendo, spreading sexual rumors, or publicly displaying sexually explicit material.

Studies conducted on campuses throughout the country indicate that between 20 and 49 percent of female faculty have experienced some form of sexual harassment along with 20 to 30 percent of female students (Dzeich & Weiner, 1990). A recent investigation by the General Accounting Office found that 97 percent of female students at U.S. military academies had experienced sexual harassment ("Schoolyard Teasing," 1994). However, sexual harassment is not a problem only on college and university campuses; it occurs in elementary and secondary schools as well. For example, in one nationwide survey of 1,632 public school students in grades eight through eleven, 85 percent of the girls and 76 percent of the boys reported experiences of sexual harassment (AAUW, 1993). Although only a small percentage of harassment victims experience quid pro quo harassment, a substantial percentage experience unwanted touching and verbal harassment that make for a hostile learning or working environment (AAUW, 1993; Loredo et al., 1995; Reilly et al., 1986). Unfortunately, few studies of sexual harassment have examined how race and ethnicity, social class, and sexual orientation interact with gender in sexual harassment incidents to produce particular outcomes for victims as well as perpetrators (DeFour, 1991; Desole, 1997; but see also Rospenda et al., 1998).

Despite the widespread nature of sexual harassment, most incidents go unreported to school or campus authorities. Instead, victims try to "manage" the problem (usually by simply avoiding the harasser whenever possible), or they tell only family members and friends about it (AAUW, 1993; Stanko, 1992). Neither of these tactics may be helpful, however. For example, attempts to avoid the harasser often are not easy; sometimes such efforts mean having to withdraw from a required course or other academic activity that may have been necessary or beneficial to the student's school achievement or career plans. In addition, family and friends sometimes blame the victim or, more often, simply advise her to ignore the harassment (AAUW, 1993; Reilly et al., 1986).

Even when victims choose to report incidents of sexual harassment, administrators may downplay it and, despite the fears of overly harsh sanctions that are frequently voiced by faculty, harassers usually are dealt with informally, with the most common sanction being a verbal warning from a superior (Mitchell, 1997; Robertson et al., 1988). Few universities have dismissed perpetrators, especially tenured faculty members, in response to sexual harassment complaints (Carroll, 1993; Clark, 1997). Moreover, despite widespread concerns among faculty regarding the possibility of false accusations, evidence indicates that these are rare. In fact, in their survey of 668 U.S. colleges and universities, Robertson and her colleagues found among the 256 administrators who responded to a question about how many false complaints of sexual harassment they had ever received, only 64 complaints were identified as proven to have been intentionally fabricated, compared with 425 documented incidents of sexual harassment and 760 estimated complaints of sexual harassment made at these institutions. "A rough extrapolation from the numbers given would make the false complaints less than 1 percent of annual complaints. This is a maximum estimate that does not take into account that some complaints listed as false by administrators may actually have been genuine according to our definition" (Robertson et al., 1988, p. 800).

A recent court ruling may have an important impact on the likelihood that victims will report sexual harassment. In 1992, the U.S. Supreme Court ruled that sexual harassment in school is a form of educational discrimination and that schools that fail to address the problem may be held liable for damages to victims. Nevertheless, while some victims have received monetary compensation as a result of this decision (see, for example, "Female Professor Receives $230,000," 1998; "Girl, 14, Wins Case," 1996), lower courts throughout the country have disagreed over the standard for determining a school's liability. In 1998, the U.S. Supreme Court severely narrowed the circumstances under which schools may be held liable for sexual harassment of students by teachers. In a 5 to 4 decision, the Court ruled that students who are sexually harassed by a teacher may sue their school district for monetary damages only if they can demonstrate that school district officials knew about the harassment and deliberately did nothing to stop it (Biskupic, 1998).

Court decisions have certainly played a role in prompting most school districts as well as colleges and universities to enact policies that prohibit sexual harassment and establish formal procedures for handling complaints (Chamberlain, 1997; Hawkesworth, 1997). Individuals who oppose such policies argue that they are unenforceable in practice, that they attempt to "legislate morality," and that they violate free speech protected by the First Amendment ("Schoolyard Teasing," 1994). Universities have already found that their attempts to regulate sexist and racist verbal harassment have not stood up well to court challenges. The courts have struck down a number of institutions' "speech codes," ruling that such regulations do violate the First Amendment (Bernstein, 1993). Some schools have also found that their handling of particular cases have led to angry charges of "overreaction" and "excessive political correctness." Such was the case in 1996 following the school suspensions of two boys, one six years old and the other seven, for kissing classmates on the cheek (Nossiter, 1996; Onishi, 1996). In 1997, the Department of Education's Office of Civil Rights issued guidelines to assist educational institutions in defining, preventing, and responding to sexual harassment. According to the guidelines, it is acceptable for a professor to assign reading material that is sexually explicit and even derogatory of women, but it is unacceptable for a group of students to target a peer for sexual taunting or to write sexually explicit graffiti about her or him. The guidelines emphasize that education officials must take into account the alleged harasser's age, level of maturity, and relationship to the victim. In addition, the guidelines stress that in order for a behavior to constitute sexual harassment, it must be severe and repetitive; a single, inappropriate act is not considered sexual harassment (Lewin, 1997a).

Most sexual harassment in educational settings is perpetrated by peers. However, at least 20 percent of cases involve a perpetrator who holds some formal authority or power over the victim (AAUW, 1993). Research indicates that harassment of a subordinate by an authority figure (e.g., harassment of a student by a teacher) is judged by most observers to be more serious than peer harassment. However, women judge sexual harassment in general to be more problematic than men do (Katz et al., 1996; Loredo et al., 1995). Perhaps this is because women are more likely to be victimized than men.[3]

Not all sexual harassment involves peers or a perpetrator who has formal authority over the victim. Researchers have also documented *contrapower sexual harassment* which "occurs when the target of harassment possesses greater formal organizational power than the perpetrator" (Rospenda et al., 1998, p. 40). According to Rospenda and her colleagues (1998), although contrapower sexual harassment has received less attention than peer and subordinate target/superior perpetrator harassment, it nonetheless occurs at an alarming rate. About one third of female faculty report that they have been harassed by students, most of whom were men (see Benson, 1984; Reilly et. al., 1986). In Rospenda et al.'s (1998) research, cases of contrapower harassment involved not only faculty harassed by students, but also a Black male faculty member who was harassed by a male secretary (race unspecified), a female faculty member who was harassed by a male secretary (race unspecified), and a Black female clerical worker who was harassed by a Middle Eastern male student worker. Rospenda and her colleagues emphasize in their analysis of these cases that gender interacts with other social factors such as race, class, and sexual orientation, increasing the likelihood that members of particular groups will be targets and also affecting the outcome of the incidents.

We will discuss the impact of sexual harassment on employees in Chapter 7. Here, however, let's examine the impact of sexual harassment on victims' educational experience. Research findings indicate that sexual harassment has serious negative consequences for student victims, especially females. Female students who have been sexually harassed are more likely than male sexual harassment victims to report that the incidents frightened them or had a negative impact on their school work (AAUW, 1993). Victims report declines in their academic performance, discouragement about studying a particular field, lowered self-esteem, emotional disturbance, and physical illness (AAUW, 1993; Bagley et al., 1997; Koss, 1991; Stanko, 1992). At the very least, sexual harassment fosters tension-filled relationships rather than mentoring relationships between students and faculty or other authority figures. Students consciously avoid certain teachers, and some teachers, afraid that their interest may be misinterpreted, distance themselves from students, particularly female students. The outcome is "limitations on students whose academic success often counts on developing a close working relationship with their instructors" (McCormack, 1985, p. 30). In short, sexual harassment creates an unpleasant and intimidating learning environment for students, especially female students, which, in turn, affects their performance, their personal and professional growth, and ultimately, their future careers.

Structuring More Positive Learning Environments

It seems clear that female students are shortchanged in their educational experiences, but the question of how to redress the inequities continues to be debated by educators. Interestingly, some observers advocate sex-segregated schools as a solution. This is not to say that these educators favor channeling girls and boys into "gender-appropriate" fields. To the contrary, their position is that single-sex institutions make it easier for both women and men to pursue fields of study not traditionally dominated by members of their sex (Estrich, 1994; Ruhlman, 1997). There is little research, however, on the advantages and disadvantages for boys in attending all-male schools, but studies do show that for girls, single-sex education is highly beneficial. Girls who attend single-sex schools have, on average, higher levels of self-confidence and greater success in obtaining high-status, high-paying jobs after graduation (Dobrzynski, 1995; Saltzman, 1996a). At all-female schools, for example, young women can major in such traditionally male-dominated fields as physics, engineering, and business without the discomfort of being in the minority and without discouragement from male peers and faculty (see, for example, Rayman, 1993).

Opponents of sex-segregated schooling point out that while it may help girls learn more and better, it does not address the problems of gender inequality and discrimination that characterize the institutions of our society. They argue that our goal should be restructuring social institutions so that males and females can work together under equitable conditions with an equitable distribution of resources and rewards (AAUW, 1998).

Such restructuring was a major rationale for the enactment of Title IX. Under Title IX, any sex segregation in public education must be justified by compelling educational reasons.[4] However, the Supreme Court, in interpreting Title IX and the equal protection clause of the Fourteenth Amendment as it pertains to education, has left open the possibility of single-sex public education by ruling in 1997 that states could offer diverse school options as long as these serve to break down rather than preserve traditional gender classifications. According to its founders, this was indeed the purpose of the Young Women's Leadership School, a public all-girls school opened in East Harlem, New York, in 1996, for girls in grades seven through nine (and by the fall of 2000, through grade twelve). The school, however, may be forced by the U.S. Department of Education to either admit boys or establish a separate, but equal boys' school nearby (Steinberg, 1997). This latter approach has been undertaken in California, where at least six school districts since 1997 have established all-boys and all-girls academies with equal facilities. It remains to be seen whether these schools will survive constitutional challenges in court brought by civil rights activists, who point out that separate-but-equal educational facilities for racial and ethnic groups were outlawed by the U.S. Supreme Court in 1954. They argue that sex should be viewed similarly (Lewin, 1997b).[5]

At the post-secondary level, the number of private, single-sex institutions has dramatically declined since the 1960s. By 1994, there were only three private men's colleges and eighty-four private women's colleges in the United States (Allen, 1996). One reason for this was the emphasis on equal educational opportunity, but financial concerns also played a part. During the past two decades, the college-age population declined, forcing many single-sex institutions to become coeducational in the hopes of attracting more new students—and more revenue. However, it was a court ruling more than finances that caused the only two public men's colleges in the United States—the Virginia Military Academy and the Citadel—to open their doors to women in 1996. The U.S. Supreme Court ruled in *United States* v. *Virginia*, that the state of Virginia could not deny to women the unique educational opportunities offered to men at VMI (Allen, 1996).[6]

Although the debate over single-sex education has received considerable attention recently, there are other methods for balancing the educational experiences of the sexes. One method is to develop a gender-fair curriculum by integrating learning materials about women, as well as people of color and gays and lesbians, into the curricula of educational institutions. At the university level, this has been accomplished in part through women's studies programs. By 1990, there were more than 600 such programs at U.S. institutions of higher learning.

One of the original goals of women's studies was to add women to the traditionally "womanless" curriculum (McIntosh, 1984). This resulted in numerous "special subject" courses or seminars—such as Women in History, Women in Literature, Women in Economics, and so on—not only in women's studies programs, but in other departments as well. Although this was an important step in increasing knowledge by and about women by making the invisible visible, these courses tended to focus on only those women who succeeded according to a male standard. Only "deserving" women were discussed—those women who behaved like men, who have done what men do. As a number of researchers have pointed out, such courses may actually have a negative impact on students, especially female students, because they may reinforce gender stereotypes and label women who cannot or will not behave like men "failures" (Goodstein, 1992; Koser, 1992).

Most women's studies and gender-based courses in other departments have moved well beyond this approach to one that considers how current knowledge bases, policies, and practices would be transformed if they were structured and organized from women's perspectives. This newer approach, for example, asks questions such as: How would the inclusion of women's unpaid labor in the home modify traditional analyses of the economy? and What are women's standpoints on various economic issues?

Of course, there are many different answers to such questions, since there are many different women's perspectives, which, as we noted in Chapter 1, are not only gendered, but also reflect the position holder's race, social class, sexual orientation, age, and physical ability/disability. According to a number of recent analyses, however, the challenge of diversity is one that remains unmet in the majority of women's studies courses. One recent examination of 100 women's studies course syllabi found that the incorporation of material from women of color and lesbians was limited at best (Cramer & Russo, 1992). Two-thirds of the syllabi had very little material on women of color; 20 percent had none at all; 50 percent used material only on African American women to cover all issues of race. According to the researchers, the most underrepresented groups of women in women's studies syllabi are Jewish women and women with disabilities. As the authors conclude, "the syllabi indicated a need for more self-education about diverse groups of women and a more consistent effort to decenter White, middle-class hetero-sexual women so that women of color do not only appear under discussions of racism, or lesbians only under discussions of sexuality, but throughout" (Cramer & Russo, 1992, p. 103; see also Bannerji et al., 1992; Watt & Cook, 1991).

Feminist educators have also been working diligently to transform the traditional curriculum so that women's experiences and perspectives are not the material of just women's studies courses, but are taught as knowledge in their own right—as half the human experience studied in all courses. Unfortunately, both women's studies and curriculum revision or transformation projects are being threatened by policy makers, administrators, and faculty who see them as academically weak, narrow in focus, and politically biased (Luebke & Reilly, 1995; Martin, 1994). Alan Bloom (1987), E. D. Hirsch (1987), and Roger Kimball (1990) were among the first and perhaps most vitriolic complainants against feminist education, women's studies, and similar programs on these grounds, but they were joined by female faculty (some of whom consider themselves feminists), journalists, and students (see, for example, Lehrman, 1993; Lutz, 1991; Paglia, 1992; Sommers, 1994). Their charges are frequently heard in institutional debates over the distribution of limited resources and the programs that should be cut as university budgets are trimmed. There are those who claim that university funds should not be spent frivolously on "marginal" (read "feminist") programs, but rather that money should be invested in the "essential" (read "traditional, Eurocentric, male-centered") curriculum.

Curriculum revision or transformation projects also are often derailed by faculty who resist being told what to cover in their courses or who simply refuse to undertake the work that revising their courses would entail (Aiken et al., 1988). Others claim that they already include women or "women's issues" in their courses, so there is no need to change anything. And still others continue to see the issue of gender (as well as race, class, sexual orientation, age, and disability) as unimportant or peripheral to what they teach (Garrison et al., 1992). This latter attitude is typified in the answers one of the authors received when she surveyed the faculty at her institution about whether they incorporate women's experiences and perspectives into their courses. The near-unanimous response was, "Only when they're relevant." When, we may ask, are the ideas and experiences of half of humanity not relevant?

There is evidence that women's studies courses and feminist education have a positive impact on students by diminishing stereotyped attitudes about women, increasing self-esteem, developing critical thinking skills, expanding students' sense of their options and goals in life, and helping students acquire a greater ability to understand their personal experiences in a broader social context (Howe, 1985; Luebke & Reilly, 1995). Nevertheless, the current threats to the future of women's studies and feminist education are quite real. A number of observers have warned that some of the most dangerous threats are more subtle than the ones we have discussed so far. Cramer and Russo (1992), for instance, argue that the renaming of women's studies as "gender studies" may serve to neutralize or dilute the emphasis on gender and sexual inequalities that constitutes the core of feminist analyses. Similarly, they argue that the establishment of men's studies programs by profeminist men can jeopardize the autonomy and strength of women's studies. Men's studies actually grew out of women's studies during the late 1970s and 1980s (Kimmel & Messner, 1998; Robinson, 1992). By the late 1980s, men's studies was offered on almost 200 college campuses in the United States (Project on the Status and Education of Women, 1986). Leaders in the area of men's studies maintain that it is complementary to women's studies and informed by feminist scholarship (see, for example, Brod, 1987). Although male attitudes and behavior have been the almost exclusive focus of the academic canon historically—resulting, we might add, in no charges of narrowness from those who see women's studies as too narrow—the role of gender in shaping these attitudes and behaviors was not critically examined until the formation of men's studies. However, Cramer and Russo (1992, p. 106) warn that men's studies can be positive only when "truly feminist and committed to challenging male power, but too often it focuses on how sex differences limit all of us equally, rather than on sexual inequality and the social significance of men's subordination of women." In addition, although advocates claim that one of the goals of men's studies is to revise the traditional view of men's experience as homogeneous and to elucidate the diversity of men's lives, particularly in terms of race and ethnicity, social class, and sexual orientation, recent reviews charge that for the most part, men's studies has simply paid lip service to diversity (Robinson, 1992; for a different view, however, see Kimmel & Messner, 1998).

Courses in gay and lesbian studies have also emerged, partly in response to the failure of the traditional curriculum to examine the intersection of gender inequality and heterosexual privilege, and also in response to political and cultural events of the 1970s and 1980s (Escoffier, 1992; Zimmerman & McNaron, 1996). For the most part, gay and lesbian studies courses have been housed in traditional academic departments or offered through research centers, such as the Lesbian/Gay Studies Center at Yale (established in 1986) and the City University of New York Center for Lesbian and Gay Studies (established in 1990). The City College of San Francisco was the first U.S. institution to establish a department of gay and lesbian studies in the United States (Collins 1992). In Canada, a number of lesbian studies programs have been initiated, although most appear to be sponsored by or housed in women's studies departments (Gammon, 1992). Today, lesbian and gay studies programs can be found throughout the world (see, for example, Hekma & van der Meer, 1992; Lindeqvist, 1996; Minton, 1992; Munt, 1996; Sayer, 1996).

Escoffier (1992, p. 8) argues that one of the most significant consequences of the growth of lesbian and gay studies is that it sets the stage for a major "historical shift in the intellectual life of lesbian and gay communities—the entry of the university into the communities' cultural development." Nevertheless, there is concern by some that divisions within gay and lesbian studies, particularly between lesbian feminists and queer theorists (see Chapter 1), will undermine the strength and stability of some programs, making them easier targets for budget cuts. At the same time, there are also concerns that as lesbian and gay studies becomes institutionalized in academia, it may lose its ties to the lesbian and gay political movements (Minton, 1992). This has been a concern for women's studies advocates and feminist educators as well. Indeed, Cramer and Russo (1992) argue that one of the most important challenges for women's studies and feminist scholarship in the next decade is to strengthen connections with political and social movements. These movements are sources of new ideas, diverse perspectives, and dynamic energy—all of which are vital in the continuing struggle against backlash and retrenchment.

Gender, Education, and Power

In this chapter we have examined how the educational experiences of female and male students—from elementary school through graduate school—are different and, more importantly, unequal. Although females now constitute a slight majority of students, they continue to confront a number of structural barriers. We have seen, for example, that women are underrepresented in textbooks and course material. They are interrupted and silenced in classroom discussions. They are channeled into relatively low-paying, low-prestige fields that have been devalued simply because they are female-dominated. They lack mentors and role models and, not infrequently, they are sexually harassed. This is not to say that males do not experience sexual harassment and are never subject to gender-based discrimination in education, but rather that when all dimensions of education are considered together, it is clearly girls and women who are disadvantaged. Indeed, given the rather dismal educational environment provided to most female students, we may begin to marvel at the many who do succeed in spite of the disadvantages.

We also discussed some of the means to remedy these inequities, such as increasing the number of feminist educators throughout the educational system; offering women's studies, feminist-based men's studies, and lesbian and gay studies programs; and initiating curriculum revision or transformation projects on an institution-wide basis. Although there continues to be resistance to and backlash against such efforts, their thrust has been to insure that the educational process is a democratic one that is not "merely technical and task-oriented [but also addresses] the facts of a multiracial and multicultural world that includes both women and men" (Andersen, 1987, p. 233). It is only when this vision becomes reality that we may speak of education as an empowering agent of social change rather than as a preserver of the status quo.

KEY TERMS

formal curriculum   the set of subjects officially and explicitly taught to students in school

hidden curriculum   the value preferences children are taught in school that are not an explicit part of the formal curriculum, but rather are hidden or implicit in it

homophobia   an unreasonable fear of and hostility toward homosexuals

mentor   usually an older, established member of a profession who serves as a kind of sponsor for a younger, new member by providing advice and valuable contacts with others in the field

micro-inequities   subtle, everyday forms of discrimination that single out, ignore, or in some way discount individuals and their work or ideas simply on the basis of an ascribed trait, such as sex

sexual harassment   any unwanted leers, comments, suggestions, or physical contact of a sexual nature, as well as unwelcome requests for sexual favors

Title IX   the provisions of the Education Amendments Act of 1972 that forbid sex discrimination in any educational programs or activities that receive federal funding

SUGGESTED READINGS

Eder, D. (1995). *School talk: Gender and adolescent culture.* New Brunswick, NJ: Rutgers University Press.

Luebke, B. F., & Reilly, M. E. (1994). *Women's studies graduates: The first generation.* New York: Teachers College Press.

Rittner, B., & Trudeau, P. (1997). *The women's guide to surviving graduate school.* Thousand Oaks, CA: Sage.

Sadker, M., & Sadker, D. (1994). *Failing at fairness: How America's schools cheat girls.* New York: Scribners.

Taylor, J. M., Gilligan, C., & Sullivan, A. M. (1995). *Between voice and silence: Women and girls, race and relationship.* Cambridge, MA: Harvard University Press.

Woog, D. (1995). *School's out: The impact of gay and lesbian issues on America's schools.* Los Angeles: Alyson Publications.

Zimmerman, B., & McNaron, T. A. H. (1996). *The new lesbian studies: Into the twenty-first century.* New York: The Feminist Press.

NOTES

1. Yale and Princeton did not admit women as undergraduate students until 1969. Harvard abandoned its practice of awarding separate degrees to Radcliffe graduates in 1963 and began awarding them Harvard degrees. However, the diplomas of male Harvard graduates bear the signatures of the President of Harvard and the Dean of the College, while the diplomas of female Harvard graduates are signed by the Presidents of Harvard and Radcliffe. This practice was still being debated in 1998.

2. This still occurs in some countries that have laws mandating more spaces for boys in schools. It was the case in South Korea until 1996, when 400 mothers of female students who had been denied admission to high school successfully protested that country's policy of admitting thirteen boys for every ten girls (Yoon, 1996).

3. Women are as sympathetic to male victims as female victims, at least when the harassment is perpetrated by a member of the opposite sex (Katz et al., 1996; Loredo et al., 1995). Little is known about reactions to same-sex sexual harassment, although Rospenda and her colleagues (1998) found considerable reluctance on the part of their research participants to discuss the subject. It certainly seems reasonable to speculate that homophobia inhibits the reporting of same-sex sexual harassment.

4. Private schools are exempt from this Title IX provision.

5. In the early 1990s, some African American leaders, concerned that the traditional U.S. education system had historically failed to meet the needs of minority youth, putting African American boys especially at high

risk of school failure, established public Afrocentric academies for elementary school children in a number of large U.S. cities. The schools in Detroit and Milwaukee were originally open only to boys, but court challenges resulted in rulings that the schools must also provide girls with an equal education (Wilkerson, 1991a). As we noted earlier, a school for homosexual students and the children of homosexual parents opened in Dallas in 1997, but because this school is private, its admissions policy is not likely to be challenged.

6. In an attempt to avoid becoming coed, alumni and officials of VMI tried to raise $100 million to buy the school from the state of Virginia, but were unsuccessful.

5 The Great Communicators: Language and the Media

Each year, American consumers spend more than $145 billion on media. About $46.5 billion is spent on books, newspapers, and magazines, while much of the remainder goes to audiovisual media, such as CDs, tapes, and movies. Without a doubt, one of the most popular forms of media is television. More than 98 percent of U.S. households have at least one television set (4 percent more than have telephone service). About 81 percent of households with televisions also have videocassette recorders, and more than 63 percent subscribe to cable television (U.S. Department of Commerce, Bureau of the Census, 1997). Television viewing consumes from 26 percent to 33 percent of adult Americans' leisure hours, and in the average U.S. home, the television is on six hours a day (Gerbner, 1993; Staples & Jones, 1985).

Obviously, the mass media are an important part of our everyday lives. Through them, we are both entertained and informed. In either case, however, we are mistaken if we think that the media are simply transmitting neutral or objective information and messages. Rather, as we will learn in this chapter, much of what is conveyed to us through the mass media is infused with particular values and norms, including many about gender. In other words, the media serve as gender socializers. Our focus in this chapter will be on what various media communicate about gender and how they communicate it. We will examine the gender images depicted in print media (newspapers and magazines) and an audiovisual medium (television), as well as a communication form common to both (advertisements). Although we will not discuss music, film, or theater, much of our analysis is applicable to those media too.

Before we look at the content of specific media, however, it's important for us to examine the primary means by which media messages are conveyed—that is, through language. While "a picture paints a thousand words," the English language itself expresses our culture's underlying values and expectations about gender. Let's see how.

Sexism and Language: What's in a Word?

"Sticks and stones may break my bones, but words will never hurt me!" How many times did you recite that chant as a child? In response to jeers or name-calling, we tried to tell our taunters that what they said had no effect on us. Yet, as we have grown older, we have come to realize that although words do not have the same sting as sticks and stones, they can indeed inflict as much harm. That is because words are symbols with meaning; they define, describe, and *evaluate* us and the world in which we live. The power of words lies in the fact that the members of a culture share those meanings and valuations. It is their common language that allows the members of a society to communicate and understand one another, and thus makes for order in society.

Language is a medium of socialization. Essentially, as a child learns the language of his or her culture, he or she is also learning how to think and behave as a member of that culture. What gender socialization messages, then, are conveyed through our contemporary language? Let's consider some of them.

To begin, consider the first group of word pairs in Part A of Box 5.1 on page 121. In each case, a word associated with men appears on the left and a word associated with

BOX **5.1**

Sexism and Language

A. Connotations

governor—governess
master—mistress
patron—matron
sir—madam
bachelor—spinster

Word Pairs

brothers and sisters
husband and wife
boys and girls
hostess and host
queen and king
Eve and Adam

B. Generic He/Man

policeman
spokesman
manpower
Social Man
mankind
workman's compensation
"Man the oars!"
he, him, his

Source: Compiled from Smith 1985; Strauss-Noll 1984.

women appears on the right. What does each word connote to you? The words associated with men have very different connotations than those associated with women, and the latter are uniformly negative or demeaning. The male words connote power, authority, or a positively valued status, while most of the female words have sexual connotations. Interestingly, many of these words originally had neutral connotations; *spinster*, for example, meant simply "tender of a spinning wheel." Over time, though, these words were debased, a process known as **semantic derogation.** "[L]exicographers have noted that once a word or term becomes associated with women, it often acquires semantic characteristics that are congruent with social stereotypes and evaluations of women as a group" (Smith, 1985, p. 48).

Reflecting on the words we have been discussing, what do their contemporary connotations tell us about the status of women in our society? In general, we see that women are associated with negative things, and men with positive things. Additional examples are abundant. Linguist Alleen Pace Nilsen (1991, p. 267), for instance, points out that the word *shrew*, taken from the name of a small, but vicious, animal is defined in most dictionaries as "an ill-tempered scolding woman." The word *shrewd*, however, has the same root, but is defined as "marked by clever, discerning awareness." In the dictionary Nilsen analyzed, the meaning of *shrewd* was illustrated with the phrase "a shrewd businessman." Consider also *patron* and *matron*, both Middle English words for father and mother. Today, *patron* signifies a supporter, champion, or benefactor, such as a "patron of the arts." A *matron*, in contrast, is someone who supervises a public institution, such as a prison, or is simply an old woman.[1] And which would you rather be: an old *master* (someone who has achieved consummate ability in your field), or an old *mistress* (an elderly paramour) (Lakoff, 1991)? It is important to note that many of the most unflattering and derogatory words for women are reserved for old women (Nilsen, 1991). Ageism often combines with sexism to doubly disadvantage women in our society.

Another form of semantic derogation is illustrated by the second group of word pairs in Part A of Box 5.1. When you read each word pair, chances are that the word pairs in which the female term precedes the male term sound awkward or incorrect. The tradition of placing the female term after the male term further signifies women's secondary status and is hardly accidental. Eighteenth-century grammarians established the rule precisely to assert that, "the supreme Being . . . is in all languages Masculine, in as much as the masculine Sex is the superior and more excellent" (quoted in Baron, 1986, p. 3). Thus, according to them, to place women before men was to violate the natural order. The masculine word also serves as the base from which compounds are made (e.g., from *king-queen* we get *kingdom*, but not *queendom*) (Nilsen, 1991). The exceptions to this usage rule are few (for instance, "ladies and gentlemen" and "bride and groom"), and most contemporary speakers of English perpetuate it—and its traditional connotation—in their everyday communications.

Semantic derogation is just one dimension of the larger problem of **linguistic sexism.** Linguistic sexism refers to ways in which a language devalues members of one sex, almost invariably women. In addition to derogating women, linguistic sexism involves defining women's "place" in society unequally and also ignoring women altogether. With respect to the former, for example, we may consider the commonly used titles of respect for men and women in our society. Men are addressed as *Mr.*, which reveals nothing about their relationship to women. But how are women typically addressed? The titles *Miss* and *Mrs.* define women in terms of their relationships to men. Even when a woman has earned a higher status title, such as *Dr.*, she is still likely to be addressed as *Miss* or *Mrs.* A couple we know, both Ph.D's, often get mail from friends and relatives addressed to Dr. and Mrs. To a large extent, a woman's identity is subsumed by that of her husband, particularly if she adheres to the custom of adopting her husband's family name when she marries. She will find that she not only acquires a new surname, but also a new given name, since etiquette calls for her to be addressed as, for instance, Mrs. John Jones rather than Mrs. Mary Jones (Miller & Swift, 1991b; Smith, 1985).

Another way that our language ignores or excludes women is through the use of the supposedly generic *he* and *man.* Traditional rules of grammar hold that these two terms should be used to refer not only to males specifically, but also to human beings generally. However, empirical research raises serious doubts as to whether this he/man approach is really neutral or generic (e.g., Gastil, 1990; Hamilton, 1988).

To understand the issue better, read the words in Part B of Box 5.1. What image comes to mind with each word? Do you visualize women, women and men together, or men alone? If you are like a majority of people, these words conjure up images only of men (Silveira, 1980; Treichler & Frank, 1989a; Wilson & Ng, 1988). Of course, it could be argued that these words lack context; provided with a context, it would be easier to distinguish whether their referents are specifically masculine or simply generic. Perhaps, but research indicates that context is rarely unambiguously generic and, consequently, the use of "he/man" language frequently results in "cognitive confusion" or misunderstanding. Miller and Swift (1991a, p. 256), for instance, cite the case of an eight-year-old member of a Brownie Scout troop who, after viewing a museum exhibit on environmental pollution and overpopulation called "Can Man Survive?", thoughtfully responded to the question by saying, "I don't know about him, but we're working on it in Brownies." Similarly, Adams and Ware (1989, p. 481) recount an incident that occurred at the conclusion of a popular television series on human evolution: The host of the program questioned the guest anthropologist about "what women were doing during this early period in the ascent of man."

There are those who feel that this emphasis on language is trivial or misplaced. Some maintain, for example, that a focus on language obscures the more serious issues of gender inequality, such as the physical and economic oppression of women. [Blaubergs (1980) provides an excellent summary of this and other, less compelling arguments against changing sexist language.] But we should keep in mind that "one of the really important functions of language is to be constantly declaring to society the psychological place held by all of its members" (quoted in Martyna, 1980, p. 493; Treichler & Frank, 1989a). Given that women are denigrated, unequally defined, and often ignored by the English language, it serves not only to reflect their secondary status relative to men in our society, but also to reinforce it. Changing sexist language, then, is one of the most basic steps we can take toward increasing awareness of sexism and working to eliminate it.

How can sexist language be changed? Various simple, but effective, usage changes have been implemented by individuals and organizations. Substituting the title *Ms.* for *Miss* and *Mrs.* is one example.[2] Alternating the order of feminine and masculine nouns and pronouns is another. Perhaps most controversial has been the effort to eliminate the generic *he/man*. Instead of *he*, one may use *she/he*, or *he and she*, or simply *they* as a singular pronoun. Nouns with the supposedly generic *man* are also easily neutralized— for example, *police officer*, rather than *policeman*; *spokesperson*, rather than *spokesman*. *Humanity* and *humankind* are both sex-neutral substitutes for *man* and *mankind* (Baron, 1986; Frank, 1989; Treichler & Frank, 1989b). These kinds of changes are not difficult to make (see, for example, McMinn, Troyer, Hannum, & Foster, 1991; McMinn, Williams, & McMinn, 1994). Try your hand at eliminating linguistic sexism by completing the quiz in Box 5.2 on page 124.

Because of the ease with which linguistic sexism can be overcome when the effort is genuinely made, we share Baron's (1986, p. 219) optimism "that if enough people become sensitized to sex-related language questions, such forms as generic *he* and *man* will give way no matter what arguments are advanced in their defense." Nevertheless, the way words and ideas are conveyed may be as important as the words and ideas themselves. Consequently, it is important that we also consider the issue of communication styles.

Do Women and Men Speak Different Languages?

Linguist Deborah Tannen (1990; 1994a; 1994b) argues that women and men are members of different speech communities. According to Tannen, women and men have different communication styles and different communication goals. Just as people from

BOX 5.2

Recognizing and Correcting Linguistic Sexism

Mark McMinn, Paul Williams, and Lisa McMinn (1994) have developed a scale to measure recognition of sexist language. They call it the *Gender-Specific Language Scale* (*GSLS*). The scale is administered as the quiz that appears below. Complete the quiz to see how good you are at recognizing and correcting sexist language. The correct answers appear at the end of the quiz.

Written Language Quiz

Read each of the following statements carefully and circle every problem you find, including problems with grammar, spelling, punctuation, and discriminatory language. Work quickly as you will have only five to ten minutes to complete this task.

1. Each persons' alertness was measured by the difference between his obtained relaxation score and his obtained arousal score.
2. The use of experiments in psychology presupposes the mechanistic nature of man.
3. The business executive's learned about domestic tasks from the homemakers.
4. When making an important decision one must first determine how other's will be affected and if the outcome is worth the cost.
5. The chairman of the board precided over the meeting.
6. The mailman wasn't never late, no matter how bad the whether.
7. She said she would ask her husband if she could go on the weekend trip with us.
8. The supervisor talked individually with the employees who were to be layed off.
9. The fire fighters' maintained composure when comfronted by the large dog.

10. First the individual becomes aroused by violations of personal space and then he attributes the cause of this arosal to other people in his environment.
11. Evolutionary theory proposes that the human species is evolving through a process of survival of the fittest.
12. Much has been written about the effect that a child's position among his siblings has on his intellectual development.

Answers

1. persons' (person's); his obtained (his or her obtained)—this latter error occurs twice in this sentence.
2. mechanistic nature of man (mechanistic nature of humans)
3. executive's (executives)
4. When making an important decision (When making an important decision,); other's (others)
5. chairman (chairperson); precided (presided)
6. mailman (letter carrier); wasn't never (was never); whether (weather)
7. There are no errors in this sentence.
8. layed off (laid off)
9. fire fighters' (fire fighters); comfronted (confronted)
10. First the individual (First, the individual); personal space (personal space.); and then (Then,); he (the individual); arosal (arousal); in his environment (in his or her environment)
11. There are no errors in this sentence.
12. his siblings (his or her siblings); his intellectual development (the child's intellectual development)

---

different cultures speak different dialects, women and men speak different *genderlects*. Women, maintains Tannen, speak and hear a language of intimacy and connection, whereas men speak and hear a language of status and independence. As a result, conversations between women and men are often like conversations between two people from different cultures and produce a similar result: a great deal of misunderstanding. But while Tannen's stories about miscommunications between women and men frequently bring smiles of recognition to people's faces, there are other researchers who question the extent to which women and men communicate differently. For example, Smythe and Meyer (1994) found few communication differences between women and men whom they studied. Instead, they found that for both women and men, communication patterns and styles were influenced by a number of situational factors, including the sex of the person with whom they were speaking and the context of the conversation. Similarly, in a study of listeners' reactions to friends' self-disclosures, Leaper and colleagues (1995) found few differences between female and male listeners, with the exception that female listeners gave more "active understanding" responses (e.g., explicit acknowledgment of the speaker's feelings or opinions) when the speaker was a female friend. Findings such as these remind us that communication is an *interactive* process affected by a variety of factors, of which gender is only one.

Nevertheless, researchers have observed that gender inequality characterizes much everyday communication, reflecting differences in men's and women's life experiences, social status, and power (Henley et al., 1985; Lakeoff, 1990; Nichols, 1986). For example, in cross-sex conversations, researchers have found that men often do more of the talking, which is a direct result of the fact that in many situations (e.g., business meetings), they have more opportunity to express their opinions. Men also interrupt women more than women interrupt them, and they have more success than women in getting a conversation focused on topics they introduce. Moreover, when men speak, listeners of both sexes more actively attend to them than to women speakers (McConnell-Ginet, 1989). The nonverbal communication of men in cross-sex interaction can also best be described as dominant. For instance, men control more space than women and they invade women's personal space more than women invade men's by standing closer to them, and by touching and staring at them more. Women, in contrast, tend to avert their eyes when stared at by men, but they also smile more than men whether they are happy or not, a gesture that can be viewed as both social and submissive (Henley et al., 1985).

These findings fly in the face of the common stereotype that women are more talkative than men. Research on same-sex conversation, however, does show that in all-female groups, women talk more than men do in all-male groups. While men prefer to talk to one another about work, sports, or activities they have in common, women tend to prefer to talk to one another about more personal topics (Bischoping, 1993). In addition, studies of same-sex talk indicate that women's conversations are less individualistic and more dynamic than men's conversations, with participants "enlarging on and acknowledging one another's contributions, responding to conversationalists' attempts to introduce topics, and signaling active listening by nods and *mmhmms* during a partner's turn" (McConnell-Ginet, 1989, p. 42). Interestingly, interruptions are frequent in women's conversations, but researchers have found that these interruptions are typically supportive rather than aggressive or hostile and often function to help the speaker put into words something she is having difficulty expressing (DeVault, 1986; Hayden, 1994).

Unfortunately, women's conversations have traditionally been negatively stereotyped and parodied. It is commonly believed, for example, that women devote the majority of their communications with one another to gossip and other frivolous matters, whereas men's communications with one another are more serious and, therefore, "important." Indeed, any negative traits and consequences of communication differences have been associated almost exclusively with women, in large part because men have had greater power to define acceptable standards of communication. In this way, women's communications have been considered not only different from men's, but also typically inferior (Lakoff, 1990).

There is some evidence that this situation may be changing. For example, Berryman-Fink (1994) found no differences in how women and men—be they superiors, peers, or subordinates—rated the communication competency of women in the workplace. Interestingly, however, Berryman-Fink also reports that in their self-evaluations, women rated their communication competency *lower* than others rated them. Some linguistic therapists would likely interpret this outcome as evidence that women need to develop greater self-confidence in certain communication settings. But an emphasis on personal change overlooks the fact that self-perceptions, as well as others' perceptions of us, are shaped not only by direct interaction, but also by other communication media. We are, in fact, bombarded daily with media images of gender. Let's turn our attention, then, to the mass media and their role as a gender socializer.

Gender and the Media

Raise the question of media portrayals of men and women, and someone will invariably argue that the media only give the public what it expects, wants, or demands. This popular view is known in technical terms as the **reflection hypothesis.** Simply stated, the reflection hypothesis holds that media content mirrors the behaviors and relationships, and values and norms most prevalent in a society. There is certainly some truth to this position. After all, commercial sponsors (the media's most important paying customers) want to attract the largest audience possible, and providing what everyone wants or expects seems like a logical way to do this. However, media analysts also point out that, far from just passively reflecting culture, the media actively shape and create culture. How?

Consider the network news. In a brief twenty-two minutes (accounting for commercials), these programs purport to highlight for us the most significant events that took place throughout the world on a given day. Obviously, decisions must be made by the program staff as to what gets reported, and that is precisely one of the ways the media shape our ideas and expectations. "The media select items for attention and provide rankings of what is and is not important—in other words they 'set an agenda' for public opinion. . . . The way the media choose themes, structure the dialogue and control the debate—a process which involves crucial omissions—is a major aspect of their influence" (Baehr, 1980, p. 30; see also Phillips, 1998).

In addition to their role as definers of the important, the media are the chief sources of information for most people, as well as the focus of their leisure activity. There is considerable evidence indicating that many media consumers, particularly heavy television viewers, tend to uncritically accept media content as fact. Although there are intervening variables, such as the kinds of shows one watches and the behavior of the real-life role models in one's immediate environment, the media do appear to influence our worldview, including our personal aspirations and expectations for achievement, as well as our perceptions of others (Gross, 1991). Not surprisingly, therefore, feminist researchers have been especially concerned with media portrayals of gender. If these depictions are negative and sexist, or if they distort the reality of contemporary gender relations, they may nevertheless be accepted as accurate by a large segment of the general public.

It has been argued that with respect to their treatment of women, the media are guilty of **symbolic annihilation** (Tuchman et al., 1978). That is, the media traditionally have ignored, trivialized, or condemned women. In the sections that follow, we will examine this charge more carefully. In addition, however, we will discuss the ways in which men have been exploited and denigrated by media portrayals. Although they typically fare better than women, men's media roles are also limited by stereotypes that are not always positive or flattering. Moreover, we will consider how symbolic annihilation occurs not only in terms of gender, but also in terms of race and ethnicity, social class, age, sexual orientation, and physical ability.

The Written Word: Gender Messages in Newspapers and Magazines

Researchers have recently found that regular reading of daily newspapers in the United States has declined significantly since the mid-1980s. They have also identified a gender gap in daily newspaper readership. In 1986, 65 percent of men and 61 percent of women were regular readers of daily newspapers; by 1997, 53 percent of men and just 49 percent of women said they read daily newspapers on a regular basis (Media Report to Women [MRTW], 1997a). One of the main reasons for the overall decline in regular newspaper readership is that more people are turning to televised news and information programs and newsmagazine programs (e.g., *20/20* and *Dateline*) for news (MRTW, 1996a). How can we explain the gender gap in regular newspaper reading?

A number of explanations have been offered to account for the difference. One researcher, for example, reports that the women who are least likely to read a newspaper every day are those who are young (between the ages of eighteen and thirty-four), unemployed, or who have children under the age of six. In fact, among women with all three of these characteristics, daily newspaper readership is only 40 percent. Readership is lower, then, among women who lack the time and financial resources that permit daily readership (MRTW, 1993a). But a second reason for the gender gap in newspaper reading is the fact that newspapers often do not speak to women, or if they do, they do so in a denigrating or patronizing way.

A quick perusal of just about any news daily gives one the impression that it is surely a man's world. News of women-centered activities and events, or of particular women (with the exception of female heads of state, women who have died or been killed, and women notable for their association with famous men) is usually reported as *soft* news and relegated to a secondary, "non-news" section of the paper. For instance, a 1996 study of twenty U.S. newspapers (ten large market and ten small-to-medium market) found that just 15 percent of front-page news references were of females and only 33 percent of front-page photos included women. These figures represent a decline to 1990 levels after a sharp rise in 1994. This study also found that women were largely absent from key local news pages (24 percent of references) and key business pages (14 percent of references). Moreover, men wrote 65 percent of front-page, local news, and business news articles and opinion pieces that appeared in the papers studied. Women received better coverage in the small and medium market papers than in the large market metropolitan papers (e.g., the *Chicago Tribune, Los Angeles Times, New York Times*, and *Washington Post*) (MRTW, 1996b; see also Dale, 1997; First & Shaw, 1996; MRTW, 1997b; Zoch, 1997). Women fare about the same in news magazines (e.g., *Time, Newsweek*, and *U.S. News and World Report*), where in 1993 they were 14 percent of references and 34 percent of bylines and photos (MRTW, 1993b).[3]

Perhaps more telling, though, is the way news about women is treated when it is reported as hard news. A 1980 study by Karen Foreit and her colleagues is enlightening on this point. These researchers found that in female-centered news stories, reporters were likely to mention an individual's sex (e.g., "the female attorney"), physical appearance (e.g., "the petite blonde"), and marital status or parenthood (e.g., "Dr. Smith is the wife of" or "the feisty grandmother"). Such details were rarely provided in male-centered stories. More than a decade after this study was conducted, examples of the trivialization of women remain plentiful (see, however, Hardenbergh, 1996). Consider, for example, that in December 1992, the Associated Press ran brief profiles of eight appointees to the Clinton Cabinet. There was one woman—Madeleine Albright, later confirmed as Ambassador to the United Nations—who was described as "a mother of three," but there was no mention of parental status in the male appointees' profiles (MRTW, 1993c). In the 1996 congressional elections, successful candidate Carol Mosley-Braun (D-IL) was described as "a den mother with a cheerleader's smile," while her opponent was described as "all business, like the corporate lawyer he is" (MRTW, 1996c). In general, coverage of strong, outspoken women is largely hostile. For instance, one study of newspapers found that 60 percent of articles about First Lady Hillary Rodham Clinton were negative ("A Survey Finds Bias," 1996; see also Thorson & Mendelson, 1996).

Feminists both here and abroad have long complained about media portrayals of themselves, as well as negative reporting of the women's movement. According to Faludi (1991), for example, the media depict feminists as a small, but vocal radical fringe group that most members of the general public dislike. Feminists are divisive, and the women's movement is portrayed as the root cause for contemporary women's problems. Faludi presents numerous examples from newspapers and news magazines in which, she argues, the message reflects a backlash against feminism—that is, women who pursue true equality with men in our society will ultimately sacrifice true happiness.

In attempting to explain the symbolic annihilation of women by newspapers, many analysts have emphasized that most of the staff at the nation's 1,500 daily newspapers are men. Of the approximately 54,000 people who work for daily circulation newspapers, 37 percent are women, a two percentage point increase since 1988.[4] Women are 31 percent of newsroom supervisors, but are significantly underrepresented in top executive and management positions. For example, only 19.4 percent of newspapers have female executive editors and just 8 percent are headed by women publishers (Voakes, 1997). A 1995 survey of staffers who had voluntarily left newspapers for other jobs found that women were significantly more likely than men to report negative experiences from working for newspapers, including lack of advancement opportunities, low levels of respect, and being inhibited from freely expressing their opinions (MRTW, 1996).

There does appear to be some effort being made, at least at the largest newspapers throughout the country, to increase the diversity of newsroom staffs and newspaper management. For instance, since 1993, leading papers such as the *Los Angeles Times*, the *Miami Herald*, the *Washington Post*, and the *New York Times* have sent representatives to the annual meetings of the National Lesbian and Gay Journalists Association to recruit staff (see Glaberson, 1993). However, it is impossible to determine how many lesbians and gay men work for newspapers in this country, since many remain closeted because of the intense stigma still attached to homosexuality. It is clear, though, that despite recent gains, racial and ethnic minorities, especially women of color, continue to be underrepresented on newsrooms staffs, particularly in high-level positions. In 1978, racial and ethnic minorities made up just 4 percent of newsroom employees; by 1997, 11.4 percent of newsroom staff were people of color. A substantial number of newspapers (45.5 percent) have no people of color on their staffs. Among racial and ethnic minorities working for newspapers, 5 percent are African American, 3 percent are Latino, 3 percent are Asian Americans, and less than 0.5 percent are Native Americans. (Voakes, 1997).

The question remains however, as to whether having more women—or people of color, or gay men and lesbians—on newspaper staffs actually decreases sexism—or racism or homophobia—in the papers. We know of no studies that have looked at the relationship between racial and ethnic representation or gay and lesbian representation on newspaper staffs and racism or homophobia in the papers (but see Glaberson, 1993). However, studies examining the relationship between sex of reporter and sexist reporting or news coverage have produced contradictory findings. One recent study, for instance, found that although female journalists quote women as sources more frequently than male journalists do, they tend to define expertise the same way male journalists do and, consequently, seek out the same types of experts that male journalists seek (Buresh et al., 1991; see also MRTW, 1996d; 1996e). According to one sociologist of the media, this is because women journalists' judgments about general news resemble those of men (Tuchman, 1979). Others, however, dispute this claim, arguing that the presence of women on newsroom staffs usually results in an expanded definition of what is newsworthy and the introduction of new topics not traditionally covered in the papers (Hardenbergh, 1996; Marzolf, 1993). Dorsher (1997) found that women write about women more than men do, but the number of stories about women written by men increases with the number of women in the newsroom.

Gender and Magazines.   Magazines are different from newspapers in many ways. Of particular interest to us is the fact that while newspapers seek a broad, general readership, magazines try to appeal to specific segments of the population. There are magazines that target specific racial and ethnic groups (e.g., *Latina*, *Ebony*, and *Black*

Enterprise). There are magazines that focus on particular interests or life experiences (e.g., *Byte, Track and Field, Divorce, Parents Magazine, Black Child*). And there are women's magazines (e.g., *Redbook, Working Woman, Seventeen*), and men's magazines (e.g., *Esquire, Sports Illustrated, Playboy*).[5] Even within these two large groups, there are various subgroups that specialty magazines target as potential readers. Subscribers to *Ms.: The World of Women*, for instance, are likely to have very different attitudes and interests than subscribers to *Cosmopolitan*, although both groups are almost exclusively female and both may see themselves as "liberated."[6]

Generally speaking, then, how do magazines expressly designed for women differ from those for men? Traditionally, women's magazines have promoted a "cult of femininity," that is, a definition of femininity as a narcissistic absorption with oneself—with one's physical appearance ("the business of becoming more beautiful"), with occupational success, and with success in affairs of the heart ("getting and keeping your man") (Ferguson, 1983; McCracken, 1993; Murphy, 1994). Although editors of many popular women's magazines say they think their readers today are more self-confident and accomplished, and have a wider range of interests than readers of the past, researchers have found few substantial changes in most women's magazines (Pogrebin, 1997a). McRobbie (1996) found, for instance, that in both adult and teen magazines for female readers, there has been an intensified focus on sex in recent years. She sees this as a reconstruction of female sexual identities that promotes boldness in women's behavior, "a determination to meet their male counterparts on equal grounds" (McRobbie, 1996, p. 178). Nevertheless, this new boldness puts its own constraints on what it means to be a woman: "Editors, design professionals and advertising departments are continually describing their ideal girl or woman through a language of consumer choices, career choices, lifestyle and outlook" (McRobbie, 1996, p. 181). Achieving the ideal still requires readers to buy particular clothes and cosmetics, to style their hair in particular ways, to say and do certain things in particular situations (in bed, on the job)—in short, to be *made over*, a theme (with instructions) found in nearly every issue of women's and girls' fashion magazines. The ultimate goal remains getting and keeping a man, even if the strategy is no longer romance, but rather aggressive sex appeal. Although some women's fashion and "service" magazines have recently done articles on formerly taboo subjects, such as lesbian relationships and bisexuality, they all remain firmly heterosexual in focus and exclude women who deviate from "normative, recognizable femininity" (McRobbie, 1996, p. 182; see also Murphy, 1994; Pogrebin, 1997a).

In previous editions of this text, we have undertaken our own unscientific analysis of women's magazines. In the first (1989) and second (1992) editions, we examined the contents of two issues of three of the most popular U.S. women's magazines: *Cosmopolitan* and *Glamour* (targeted primarily to White women) and *Essence* (designed for Black women). On both occasions, we found that relationships with men was clearly the dominant theme in all three magazines, with becoming beautiful the second most prevalent theme. Although each of the magazines had articles and features about careers and occupational success, achievement in the work world was often presented as being dependent on physical attractiveness (e.g., "dressing for success," applying the right makeup, or fixing one's hair a particular way). Advertisements reinforced these messages.

In preparing the third edition of the text (1995), we noticed some interesting differences among the three magazines. In *Cosmopolitan*, the focus on relationships with men seemed even stronger than in the past, and romance and sex were emphasized throughout the magazine. In contrast, both *Glamour* and *Essence* appeared to have increased their focus on health issues, family (as opposed to sexual) relationships, careers, and financial matters. However, despite the diversity in themes of the magazines' articles and columns, we found little change in the advertising. Making oneself beautiful in order to attract men remained the dominant message in the ads in all three magazines.

For this edition of *Women, Men and Society*, we again examined *Cosmopolitan*, *Glamour*, and *Essence*. Our findings are similar to those in 1995, with the exception that *Glamour* appeared to have returned to an emphasis on sex and relationships with men, especially on the magazine's cover. Indeed, the covers of *Cosmopolitan* and *Glamour* were hardly distinguishable from each other. *Cosmopolitan* promised to help readers "sexify" themselves with "new miracle hair goos" and makeover makeup tips. Readers would also be treated to "his top 20 *sex*planations," in which men advise readers about whether they should reveal their sexual history to their partners, play hard to get, or sleep with new partners fast. The cover of *Glamour* asked, "How many men have you slept with? What your number says about you," along with "42 little lies he might be telling you."

Inside the magazines, the emphasis on sex and relationships continued in a number of ways. One issue of *Cosmopolitan*, for example, had fourteen articles explicitly on sex and relationships, including "7 little things that make good sex great" (e.g., doing a strip-tease act for your partner or grabbing his crotch in public). But the sexual theme carried over into virtually all sections of the magazine: There was a quiz so readers could determine how "lusty" they are, a fashion page on "fun-derwear" ("as much fun for you to put on as for him to take off"), a beauty article on making a "hands-on home spa" ("You, him, a little mud, and plenty of steam make for a sexy stay-at-home weekend"), an article on ten skills a woman should master (e.g., asking a man out on a first date, developing a fabulous flirting technique), and *Cosmo* confessions in which readers "share their most shocking stories and steamiest secrets." Even an article on a serious health problem—polycystic ovarian syndrome—emphasized the effects on beauty and sex and was illustrated with photos of a woman, nude from the waist down, curled up on a sheet. While *Glamour* was a bit more tame, it nonetheless had eleven articles explicitly on sex and relationships as well as numerous tips on how to "manage" relationships and how to be alluring.

In contrast, *Essence* continued to focus primarily on careers, financial success, and health, although there was also a strong emphasis on beauty. For example, one of the cover stories, "Working Smart," had the subtitles, "Beat-the-Clock Beauty," "Give Your Wardrobe a Raise," and "Go from Employee to Entrepreneur." Inside, there were no articles on sex and only two on relationships with men ("Couples Growing Closer," and "Ask Him Out"). Overall, the articles covered serious, timely topics, such as race relations ("Black and White Women: What Still Divides Us"), suicide ("Death of a Superwoman"), and a profile of labor secretary Alexis Herman.

As in 1995, the advertising in all three magazines emphasized making oneself beautiful to attract men. Advertisements for cosmetics and perfumes remained the single most frequent category of ads overall, with hair care and personal hygiene second.[7] *Essence* had the fewest advertisements (see Pogrebin, 1997b) and, not surprisingly, most of the models in both the ads and the features were Black (77 out of 86). Nearly all the models in *Cosmopolitan* and *Glamour* were White (173 of 190 in *Cosmopolitan*, 180 of 204 in *Glamour*).

Men's magazines provide some glaring contrasts to women's periodicals. Historically, men's magazines have been more specialized, although recent analyses indicate that target audiences for women's magazines may also be getting narrower (Pogrebin, 1997a). Nevertheless, most men's magazines can still be placed in one of three categories: finance/business/technology, sports/hobbies, and sex. Sex, which we have seen is by no means absent from women's magazines, is still typically discussed in women's periodicals in terms of interpersonal relationships, whereas men's sex-oriented magazines objectify and depersonalize sex (see Chapter 8).

Apart from these three types of magazines, however, what are the dominant themes in more general periodicals designed for men? In the three previous editions of the text, we examined two men's magazines—*Esquire* ("Man at His Best") and *Gentleman's Quarterly*—which we felt were especially comparable to *Cosmopolitan* and *Glamour*.[8] In addition, for this fourth edition, we examined two other men's magazines, *Details* (which we included in 1995) and *Maxim* (which premiered in 1996) because they target a male audience somewhat younger than that of *Esquire* and *GQ*.

Overall, the predominant theme in *Esquire* and *GQ* has not changed over the ten years of our informal survey; it remains living a leisurely lifestyle that is made possible by one's financial success. Articles about music, art, film, travel, and sophisticated or famous men continue to be common. *GQ* devotes about thirty pages to men's fashion, *Esquire* about twenty-five pages. Still conspicuous by their absence are articles about male/female relationships. In our most recent perusal, we found only one article on this topic in *GQ* (an article on how extramarital affairs can upset a marriage) and two in *Esquire* (one by a regular columnist known as "the perfect man," who wrote about his experience at a sex clinic, and one in the "Dept. of Good News," on how frequent sex makes men healthier). There is also a monthly advice column in *GQ* called "Dr. Sooth," where readers' letters are answered. Here, we found the good doctor responded to readers' queries about how to tell if they are good kissers and if being stoned on marijuana during sex affects fertility. There were other features on women: one about actress Uma Therman (pictured on the cover of *Esquire*); two paragraphs on Madeleine Stowe accompanied by one black and white nude photo of the actress straddling a tree limb and another color photo of her dressed in a black lace see-through body stocking (*Esquire*'s "Women We Love" feature); and a fashion section on *men's* swimsuits featuring *female* model, Daniela Pestova, sometimes in a bikini, but usually topless, lounging with a male model (*GQ*).

Details and *Maxim*, which target men in their twenties and thirties, both featured women on their covers. On the *Details* cover, which folded out into three sections, actress Heather Graham was shown lying on a sheet, wearing only roller blades; the caption read, "Hollywood Golden Girl Heather Graham Opens Up." On the *Maxim* cover, actress Alyssa Milano, with a sultry smile, is shown removing a camisole; her lace-up leather slacks are untied. *Maxim*'s cover tells readers its focus is on "sex, sports, beer, gadgets, clothes, fitness" and promises articles that teach readers "how to score like a celebrity, rule at bar pool, beat a lie detector, scam a free gym workout." Apart from features about two actresses, *Details* had no articles on interpersonal relationships; the magazine had two articles about sex. Most of the articles in *Details* were on entertainment. In *Maxim*, articles ranged from a rundown of the "100 best guy movies" (the majority of which were about cowboys, war, sports, or crime) to an article on four archeologists beaten and robbed in the Mexican jungle to a "bar-crawl diary" (a writer "hangs out with celebrities") to an interview with four women about why they cheat on their boyfriends. Interestingly, *Maxim* also featured an article on women's magazines under its feature title, "Babe Management." The article asked, "Why is the woman you love so paranoid, neurotic, and just plain psycho?" The answer provided: "She's being coached by the loony magazines she reads." Readers are comforted by the fact that this article tells them "how to stay on top of her game." Although it might be argued that of the four men's magazines we reviewed, *Maxim* focused considerably more attention on male/female relationships, a closer look reveals that the common theme is how men can manipulate women into having sex with them and how they can better control or "manage" the women in their lives.

The low priority that men's magazines give to interpersonal relationships is reinforced by the advertisements that dominate their pages. Judging only by the ads, one might easily conclude that men spend the majority of their time playing sports with other men or alone, working out on exercise equipment, listening to music, buying sunglasses, drinking alcohol and smoking, much to the neglect of their personal hygiene. Apart from clothing advertisements in *GQ* and *Details*, the most common ads in all four magazines we looked at were for alcohol, cigarettes, and sunglasses. Equipment was second, especially athletic gear and exercise machines, as well as stereo equipment and cell phones. However, ads for cosmetics and personal hygiene products were relatively few (zero in *Maxim*, one in *Details*, three in *Esquire*, and five in *GQ*). Advertisements for various drugs were not uncommon, especially those to treat baldness. Like the women's magazines, most of the models in these ads were White.

Similar to women's magazines, then, periodicals intended for men generate their own gender images and ideals. Normative masculinity according to these magazines does not include establishing a long-term relationship with a woman. Instead, the real man is free and adventurous. He is a risk taker who pursues his work and his hobbies—including in this latter category relationships with women—with vigor. He is concerned about his personal appearance, but not in an all-consuming sense as women seem to be.[9] The magazines, of course, promise to help their readers achieve these goals, and in this respect, they are not at all unlike the magazines for women.

Despite their continuing appeal, magazines like those we have been discussing have shown declines in sales in recent years (Pogrebin, 1997a). Media analysts report that consumers appear to be turning away somewhat from print media and utilizing more electronic, audiovisual media. Television remains the most popular form of electronic media, especially since the advent of the cable networks, which now claim more than 63 million subscribers (U.S. Department of Commerce, Bureau of the Census, 1997). A critical question that arises, therefore, is whether the gender messages of television programming are any less sexist or exploitative than those we have found in the print media. Or do television programs simply reinforce the norms of femininity and masculinity promoted by the popular women's and men's magazines? These are questions that we will address next.

Television: The Ubiquitous Media Socializer

It can be argued that television is the most important media socializer. If we consider the number of televisions in the United States, as well as television's unique characteristics, this claim is easy to understand. Research documents the central place that television holds in the lives of most Americans. On any given day, the average American spends about 33 percent of his or her leisure time watching television—more time than is spent on any other leisure activity, including socializing with other people (7 percent), reading (6 percent), and engaging in outdoor activities (2 percent) ("At Leisure," 1993). Women watch television more than men do, and adults watch more than children do, although for children, watching television occupies more time than any other out-of-school activity (Comstock, 1991).[10] A recent national poll found that 68 percent of teenagers have their own televisions in their rooms (Goodstein & Connelly, 1998).

Television also has special characteristics that add to its potency as an agent of socialization. For instance, it is free, it is available to just about everyone, and it does not even require viewers to leave the privacy of their homes, as movies and theater do. It requires no special skills, such as literacy, to watch, and everyone, regardless of sex, race, age, social class, sexual orientation, and often, geographic location, gets the same visual and verbal messages. Research shows, however, that these factors (sex, race, etc.) may influence how members of various groups interpret or relate to program content (Berry, 1992; Comstock, 1991; Gross, 1991; Press, 1991). What sorts of socialization messages are television programs conveying?

One prominent message is that women are less important than men. Consider, for example, that there are fewer women than men on prime-time television. A recent study conducted over a ten-year period by a research team from the Annenberg School of Communication at the University of Pennsylvania found that on prime-time television, women play only about one out of every three roles—a figure, it should be added, that has not changed since 1954 (Gerbner, 1993; see also Metzger, 1992). This study, noteworthy for its magnitude as well as its findings, analyzed 19,645 speaking parts in 1,371 television programs on the three national networks, Fox Television, and eleven major cable networks.[11] Other studies, using significantly smaller samples of television programs and characters, have found an increase in the number of female characters on prime-time programs, although these women are more likely than men to play minor roles (Elasmar & Brain, 1997; Signorielli, 1997).

Not only do women have fewer roles on television, but the characters played by women tend to be younger and less mature than male characters and, therefore, less authoritative (Fejes, 1992). In a study conducted for the American Association of Retired Persons, for example, researchers found that in 1994, only 15 percent of female characters on prime-time television were aged forty-five and older; just 3 percent of major characters were identified as middle-aged. This study analyzed twenty-two years of television programming and found that during this period only three of every 100 major characters was sixty-five or older; less than one in 100 was a woman, aged sixty-five or older (MRTW, 1996f). Women on television age faster than men, and the older they are, the more likely they are to be portrayed as unsuccessful or without clearly defined occupational roles (Gerbner, 1993; MRTW, 1996f). As Condry (1989, p. 73) notes, "It is especially bad to be old on television, and it is terrible to be an old woman."

Young female characters are typically thin and physically attractive. Signorielli (1997) found, for instance, that 46 percent of women on television compared with just 16 percent of men are thin or very thin. Women are also more likely than men to make or receive comments about their physical appearance and to be shown grooming or "preening." Female characters are more likely to wear sexy clothes and be shown scantily dressed (e.g., wearing just underwear), and they are more physically fit than male characters (see also Metzger, 1992; MRTW, 1998a). In general, male television characters are given more leeway in terms of their appearance.

·This is not to say that the portrayal of women on television has not changed over the history of the medium. A number of researchers have documented important changes in the portrayal of women *and* men in recent years. For example, female prime-time characters today are more likely to work outside the home, and to be strong and independent women who depend on themselves to solve problems and achieve their goals; they also are more likely than male characters to be shown interacting with others in an honest and direct way (Dow, 1996; Press, 1991; Signorielli, 1997). Their male partners are nowadays depicted as idealized family men, who are sensitive to and supportive of their wives. These male characters are portrayed as quite willing to do more than an equal share of housework and child care. However, men on television are rarely shown doing housework (1 to 3 percent compared to 20 to 27 percent of women) (Metzger, 1992; Signorielli, 1997).

• Indeed, gender stereotypes are still prominent on television. Although more female characters have careers outside the home, only 28 percent are shown on the job compared with 41 percent of male characters. Women on television are still depicted as being preoccupied with romantic relationships; while male characters tend to talk about work, female characters tend to talk about romantic relationships. Women are more likely than men to use sex or romantic charm to get what they want, and they are more likely to cry and whine. Men, in contrast, are more likely than women to use physical force (Condry, 1989; Fejes, 1992; Signorielli, 1997).

One of the most significant changes on prime-time programming since the 1970s has been the incorporation of women's rights and gender equality themes, often presented from what could be considered a feminist perspective (Dow, 1996). In addition, a number of prime-time programs and made-for-television movies have sensitively addressed such topics as sexual assault, spouse abuse, and incest. Nevertheless, strong or serious feminists are usually portrayed negatively. "Strident feminists are usually seen as loners or disconnected souls" (Press, 1991, p. 39) and feminism is portrayed as "a combination of power dressing, economic success, belligerence, self-confidence, and female chromosomes" (Dow, 1996, p. 210; see also Japp, 1991). Feminist politics are typically avoided and political feminists are often punished for what is depicted as an unnecessary overcommitment to the feminist "party line."

Gender stereotypes frequently intersect with racial and ethnic stereotypes on television. Female or male, racial and ethnic minorities continue to be underrepresented on television (Condry, 1989; Rhodes, 1991). According to the Annenberg study, in a single week, the typical prime-time viewer sees an average of 355 characters with speaking parts on network television. Of these, only four are African Americans. The typical viewer will see only one Hispanic American every two weeks, one Asian American every three weeks, and one Native American every ten weeks (Gerbner, 1993). The newer networks—Fox, WB, and UPN—have increased the number of African Americans on television by developing more than twelve new situation comedies in which all the central characters are Black (e.g., *Between Brothers; Sister, Sister; Moesha*). Nevertheless, on the larger networks—ABC, NBC, and CBS—only a few dramas (e.g., *E.R., N.Y.P.D. Blue*) have racially and ethnically diverse casts. Most programs—particularly the sitcoms—remain "racially segregated" with a minor character of a race or ethnicity different from the core cast appearing only occasionally (Hass, 1998). Critics contend that major network programming that does include racial and ethnic minorities portrays them through White eyes and ignores racial conflicts (DeMott, 1996).

In addition to racial and ethnic minorities, other groups have been rendered invisible or negatively stereotyped in television programming. People with physical disabilities, for example, are just 1.5 percent of prime-time characters (Gerbner, 1993). Lesbian and gay characters are more likely to be found in made-for-television movies, particularly since the television industry has begun to address the problem of AIDS, but as Gross (1991) points out, the focus typically is on the reaction of family and friends to the disclosure that someone they know is gay. In 1997, the lead character on the television sitcom *Ellen* came out as a lesbian to more than 36 million viewers in one of the most widely watched episodes in television history.[12] By 1997, there were eighteen regular gay or lesbian characters on prime-time television programs, all on situation comedies. These characters included Carter Heywood on *Spin City*, who is also television's only African American gay character, and Susan Bunch and Carol Wylick on *Friends*, the first lesbian couple on TV to become parents ("Since Coming Out Is In," 1997). According to one observer, gay and lesbian characters are becoming more common on prime-time television, so that the fact that they are homosexual "is no longer a novelty and sufficiently interesting in and of itself" (quoted in Bruni, 1996).

If we turn from prime-time entertainment programming to news programming, we find that some groups have made progress in their portrayals on television. Indeed, the greatest move toward equality of the sexes in broadcasting has taken place in local television newsrooms. By 1997, 98 percent of local television news stations had women on their staffs; women were 37 percent of the local television news workforce (Papper & Gerhard, 1997). All-male news desks are rare on local televised news programs, where the trend has been toward male-female anchor teams. Unfortunately, female co-anchors often confront a double standard on the job. Higher standards of physical attractiveness and dress are sometimes set for them compared to their male colleagues, and they may be expected to look younger and act friendlier than male anchors (Craft, 1988; MRTW, 1993d). Most, in fact, are younger. More than a third of local television news anchors are women, but just 3 percent of them are over age forty; 50 percent of male local television news anchors are over forty and 16 percent are over fifty years old (Sanders & Rock, 1988). On national news programs, women are also younger than their male peers. With few exceptions (e.g., Barbara Walters), on national news programs, viewers do not see women who are in their late fifties or sixties. Consider, however, the ages of some of the most respected men on national news programs: Hugh Downs, for example, is in his seventies.

Overall, women have made fewer inroads on national network newscasts than local ones. The weeknight news on ABC, CBS, and NBC is anchored by men, although women do anchor weekend newscasts and co-anchor prime-time news programs. Research indicates, however, that the percentage of female correspondents reporting news on the three major networks has risen considerably since the mid-1970s, although in 1997, women were still just 19 percent of network news staffs and the percentage of network news stories filed by women was less than 20 percent (MRTW, 1997c).

Still, minority men and women remain dramatically underrepresented on the network news, with only slight improvements in recent years. In 1995, minority correspondents filed 12 percent of the news stories aired by the major networks, up from 7 percent in 1990 (MRTW, 1996g). According to the Annenberg study, only 0.2 percent of men and women on newscasts are people with disabilities (Gerbner, 1993). No figures are available regarding the number of lesbian and gay newscasters, who are virtually invisible on the networks.

Off-camera, people of color and women have also fared poorly. Nationally, just 8 percent of television news directors are people of color (5 percent African American, 1 percent Hispanic American, 1 percent Asian American, 1 percent Native American). Most non-White television news directors work at independent stations rather than network affiliates; only 4 percent of news directors at affiliate stations are not White. Women are 14 percent of television news directors (down from 18.5 percent in 1988). They are four times more likely to be news directors at independent stations than at network affiliates; 13 percent of news directors at affiliate stations are women (Papper & Gerhard, 1997). It is expected that the broadcast industry will become even less diverse over the next several years, since in 1998 a federal court struck down a Federal Communications Commission requirement that television stations actively recruit, hire, and train minority job applicants (Holmes, 1998).

Finally, before we close this section on television, we want to briefly discuss a relatively recent genre of television programming: the music video. Recent research analyzing videos on MTV and Black Entertainment Television (BET) shows that women are largely absent from music videos. Signorielli (1997) reports that 78 percent of music video performers are male. Alexander (1996) found that 55 percent of the 123 music videos she studied showed no women or showed women only in the background. Most women in music videos are White, whereas African American men are nearly as likely as White men to be in music videos. Other racial and ethnic minorities are rarely shown (Signorielli, 1997).

What concerns many observers is not so much the lack of women performers in music videos, but the portrayals of women when they are included. Women are often depicted as passive sex objects who are easily aroused sexually. They are often demeaned and abused by the men in the videos (Alexander, 1996; Media Education Foundation, 1995; Roland, 1993). Importantly, Roland (1993) reports male viewers are more likely than female viewers to see forced sex depicted in music videos as justified if mutual sexual attraction between the male and female performers was implied.

Roland's study suggests that men and women are likely to react to music videos differently. Additional studies lend support to this point. For example, Lewis (1990) notes that there is a male style of address that appears in most music videos, but that there is also a female style of address that comes across in many videos made by female musicians. Lewis argues that by the mid-1980s, female artists were taking on the privileged roles and experiences of males portrayed in most music videos, often depicting a dramatic reversal of gender roles or a rejection of traditional gender stereotypes. At the same time, the women in the videos began depicting female modes of cultural expression and experience in a celebratory rather than a deprecating way. While sex remained a central theme in many women's music videos, the message was often one of women in control of their sexuality, acting in their own interests rather than in the interests of men. Alexander (1996), too, has identified a category of music videos in which women are depicted as strong, self-reliant, and dominant in sexual relationships (see also McClary, 1991).

The question remains whether such depictions represent "progress" for women in music videos. It may certainly be argued that recent videos showing scantily dressed, sexually dominant young women are hardly less exploitative than earlier videos extolling the "chauvinism of rock culture" (Sherman & Dominick, 1986; see also Brown & Campbell, 1986). Still, the impact of these various types of videos on different viewing audiences is not well understood, and more research in this area is clearly needed.

We will return to the issue of the effects of television in general, but for now let's look at gender portrayals in advertising.

Gender Messages in Advertisements: Does Sexism Sell?

- An attractive young woman rushes home, removes her clothes, and gets into the shower. We hear her moaning, then shouting passionately, "Yes, yes!" Surely she is having a sexual experience. No, we quickly discover that she has washed her hair and the shampoo she used inspired her outburst.
- A young man wearing a business suit sits down on a bench near a busy city street corner and begins to unwrap the hamburger he has bought for lunch. A beautiful young woman crosses the street and strides purposefully yet seductively toward him. Soon it becomes clear that it is not the man she wants, but rather the hamburger.

These scenarios are quite familiar to us. They come, of course, from the contrived world of advertising and, like most advertisements, they are selling us more than a specific product; they are peddling needs and desires. In the first example, the implicit message is that every woman can experience orgasmic ecstasy every day by using the advertised product which, realistically, is designed only to clean her hair. In the second, men are told that regardless of what they look like or how socially inept they are, they too can attract beautiful women if they buy the advertised food, the real purpose of which is just to provide them nourishment. Just about everyone wants to be successful, physically attractive, even sexy. What advertisers often do is play on these desires by implying that their products not only serve their intended purposes, but also offer bonuses as well. In this way, "advertisements portray an image that represents the interpretation of those cultural values which are profitable to propagate" (Courtney & Whipple, 1983, p. 192).

Advertisements also portray images of gender that the advertising industry deems profitable. According to advertising analysts, for male consumers the message is typically to buy a particular product and get the "sweet young thing" associated with it, whereas for female consumers the message is to buy the product in order to be the sweet young thing (Masse & Rosenblum, 1988; McCracken, 1993; Strate, 1992). The dominant philosophy of the advertising industry has traditionally been that "sexism sells" (Courtney & Whipple, 1983; Drewniany, 1996; Lazier-Smith, 1989; Synder, 1997).

Sexism in advertising can be quite subtle. Consider, for example, the way models are posed. In a study that compared the ways women and men are depicted in magazine advertisements, Masse and Rosenblum (1988) found that female models are significantly more likely than male models to be depicted in subordinate poses. Female models are more frequently solitary and also appear more often as "partials," that is, only a part of their bodies, such as their legs or their lips, is shown. Models are also sometimes diminished in advertisements, although this is more common in men's magazines. Masse and Rosenblum found that almost a quarter of the female figures were not full-sized in men's magazines compared with less than 7 percent of the male figures. In women's magazines, 6.5 percent of female models and 7 percent of male models were diminished. Overall, 27 percent of the female models, but just 3.8 percent of the male models, in the magazine ads studied were subordinated in some way.

Besides the subtle sexism in advertisements, though, gender stereotyping is prevalent. What are some of the common gender stereotypes in print and television advertising? One set of stereotypes revolves around the occupations depicted. Although there has been minor improvement in recent years, occupational stereotyping by sex still pervades advertisements. Men hold positions of authority—they are the so-called experts—while women receive advice, usually from men, or are shown in traditional female occupations and roles (e.g., nurse, secretary, homemaker, mother) (Fejes, 1992). Suppose we told you that we were about to show you ten advertisements featuring male models, and we asked you to guess what jobs they would most likely be doing. You would probably have little difficulty coming up with a long list of answers because men in advertisements are shown in a wide range of roles—from white-collar professionals such as scientists, physicians, and business executives, to blue-collar workers such as plumbers, electricians, and exterminators. Less often, they are shown in family roles as husbands and fathers. But what if we asked the same question using ads with female models? Chances are your list would be considerably shorter. Although nontraditional roles for women are appearing more often than in the past, women's traditional roles, especially homemaker and mother, continue to far outnumber nontraditional portrayals. Women are less likely than men to be shown "on the job" in commercials. Instead, they are more likely to be shown in activities related to romance and relationships (e.g., dating, consoling children) (Drewniany, 1996; Signorielli, 1997). In fact, women are twice as likely as men to appear in television commercials as spouses or parents with no other occupation (Metzger, 1992).

In television commercials, women most often demonstrate household cleaning products, personal care items, and food, although since 1978, men have become three times more likely to sell domestic products (Metzger, 1992). Yet the announcers and background voices (known as voice-overs) in these ads are usually male. Research indicates that 75 percent of commercials have male voice-overs (MRTW, 1997d; see also Drewniany, 1996). The rationale of the advertising industry is that female voices are neither authoritative nor believable. Consumers, they maintain, trust a male voice; "the male voice is the voice of authority" (quoted in Courtney & Whipple, 1983, p. 136). But marketing research casts some doubt on this argument. For instance, studies show no differences in the persuasiveness of female and male voice-overs (Courtney & Whipple, 1983), and researchers have also found that female spokespersons are more trusted by the public than male spokespersons (Steenland, 1987). Such findings may help to account for the fact that female voice-overs have increased in recent years and they are no longer heard selling just cosmetics, food and toys, but a wider range of products, including cars, telecommunications and banking services, and airlines (MRTW, 1997d). Hopefully, this trend will continue.

At the same time, however, studies show that the sexually exploitative use of women in advertising has increased since 1970 (Lanis & Covell, 1995). In such advertisements, the female model has a purely decorative role; in other words, she has no clear relationship to the product and is shown simply because of her physical attractiveness and sex appeal. Typically, models are scantily dressed (e.g., in bathing suits or lingerie) and provocatively posed. While many consumers have come to expect these portrayals in personal care or cosmetics ads—indeed, they dominate such advertisements—they are also prevalent in nonappearance-related advertising. For instance, in a 1997 newspaper ad for Epson color printers, a woman is shown apparently clothed in a bathing suit. The ad copy tells the reader to look more closely: At 360 DPI, the woman is wearing the bathing suit, but at 720 DPI, the bathing suit appears to be wet. At 1440 DPI, the reader can see that the bathing suit is "painted on." Thus, Epson used a full-page ad with a nude model to demonstrate the superior quality of their printers (MRTW, 1997e; see also Walsh-Childers, 1996).

Researchers have found that the percentage of advertisements depicting men in decorative roles has also increased in recent years. As Patterson (1996, p. 94) puts it, "The image of men in advertising is either that of a 'Rambo,' solo conqueror of all he sees, or a 'Himbo,' a male bimbo." Accompanying this trend has been an increase in advertisements in which women are shown ogling or demeaning men—what Patterson (1996) calls the new "power babe" genre of advertising. Consider, for instance, the now famous Diet Coke commercial in which women at work in an office building time their daily break to coincide with the moment a handsome, athletic construction worker takes off his shirt. The women pop open their cans of Diet Coke to cool off from the sexual heat produced by watching the man "strip" (see Patterson, 1996 for other examples). It appears that the response of the advertising industry to complaints of sexism in ads using decorative female models has not been to eliminate such ads, but rather to demean men by portraying them as sex objects, too. This approach reflects the industry's confusion of gender equality with sexual permissiveness and exploitation.

The advertising industry is also increasingly using children, especially girls, in sexually exploitative ways, a trend referred to as the *Lolita syndrome* after a 1962 film that depicted a twelve-year-old girl seducing an elderly man. Such advertisements show the children in make-up and posed seductively, giving the impression that they are sexually available. According to critics, the trend has become so popular that adult models who have child-like bodies are often favored by advertisers (McKee, 1996). Of course, the emphasis on youth in advertisements corresponds with the denigration of the elderly. However, this denigration is usually reserved for elderly women. Older models, male or female, are rare in advertisements for products other than health aids, vitamins, and insurance. But when older male models are used, they have a better chance than older female models of being portrayed as authority figures. Older female models usually play the roles of loving grandmother or "feisty old lady" (Drewniany, 1996; Symthe, 1996).

Other groups, too, are nearly invisible in advertising. Although African American models are now seen more often in advertisements, especially on television, other racial and ethnic groups, including Hispanic Americans, Asian Americans, and Native Americans are rarely seen. With the exception of the furniture store chain, Ikea, which ran a television ad about a gay male couple who decided to live together, advertisements that depict models in gay and lesbian relationships are even more rare.[13] And how many advertisements—other than those for health care and charitable organizations—have you seen that use models with physical disabilities?

Despite industry claims that sexism sells, research provides only qualified support for this position. Advertisements that use women's sexuality to sell products to men do appear to be appealing to and effective with that constituency. Ads emphasizing sex also often appeal to teenagers of both sexes. However, such ads are ineffective with a large segment of adult female consumers (deYoung & Crane, 1992; Grigsby, 1992; Lanis & Covell, 1995). Other studies have shown that while consumers in general do like to see attractive models of both sexes in advertisements, the use of nudity, seminudity, and sexual innuendo may inhibit consumers' ability to recall the products and the advertisements in which they appeared (Courtney & Whipple, 1983).

It is estimated that the average American sees more than 37,000 advertisements annually just on television (Lanis & Covell, 1995). Moreover, there is evidence that this figure may be going up, since the number of minutes per hour that television devotes to commercials has been increasing, accounting for 25 to 33 percent of viewing time in 1996 (MRTW, 1997f). Print advertising is also increasing and can now be found on tiny stickers attached to fruits and vegetables, on bathroom stall doors and the walls over urinals, and on gasoline pumps (Cropper, 1998). Given the pervasive—some would say *invasive*—nature of advertisements, it makes sense to consider their potential effects on our attitudes and behavior. To conclude this chapter, then, let's look at the research on media effects.

Images of Gender in the Media: What Are Their Effects?

Defenders of the media sometimes argue that while media portrayals are often sexist, their effects are benign. "That only happens on television," they say. "People don't really believe that stuff." There is evidence, though, that contradicts their argument; many people, it seems, do believe that stuff.

The majority of research on media effects has focused on television largely because of its popularity, particularly with children, and because of its unique characteristics that we outlined earlier. A central issue has been the effects of violent television programming, an issue that we examine more closely in Box 5.3 on pages 142–143. With regard

BOX 5.3
Violence and the Media

In 1993, the Canadian Radio-Television and Tele-communications Commission issued strict rules regulating the broadcast of violent programming. These rules include a ban on the depiction of gratuitous violence, a limitation of the time that adult programming (including ads and promotions) containing violence can be broadcast (between 9 P.M. and 6 A.M.), and a total ban on any violent depictions in children's programs that minimize the effects of violence or that encourage or promote imitation of violence (MRTW, 1993f).

In contrast, in the United States, although concern has been expressed for many years over the social and psychological impact of escalating violence on television and in films, little action has been taken to curb it. In 1993, for instance, the chief executives of the major national networks, faced with threats that the federal government would enact legislation to limit violent television programming, agreed to air parental advisories before programs the networks consider violent. In addition, in 1997, the networks instituted a six-category ratings system to advise viewers fifteen seconds before the start of a program as to appropriate viewer ages for the program. The ratings system, however, has been widely criticized for being too vague (MRTW, 1997h). And despite the concerns about violent programming that prompted the development of the ratings system, research indicates that the number of violent programs increased in 1998. Sixty-one percent of programs contained some violence, and, in almost 75 percent of violent scenes, there was no remorse, criticism, or penalty for the violence shown (Mifflin, 1998).

The debate among representatives of the entertainment industry, psychologists and sociologists, legislators and attorneys, and worried parents regarding the effect of viewing violence is an old one. It is periodically fueled by incidents involving viewers acting out what they have seen in a program or film. In one case, for example, a five-year-old Ohio boy set fire to his family's mobile home after watching the MTV cartoon *Beavis and Butthead*, in which the central characters depicted setting fires as fun. The boy's two-year-old sister died in the fire. Following the release of the film *Money Train* in 1995, at least three New York city subway token booths were firebombed, mimicking a token booth firebombing depicted in the film (McFadden, 1995; Sudetic, 1995). The films *Natural Born Killers*, *The Program*, *Colors*, and *Taxi Driver* have also been implicated in murders and other violent crimes (Mifflin, 1998). Still, despite literally thousands of studies examining the question, "Does violent viewing *cause* violent behavior in viewers?" a precise answer remains elusive. There is a strong correlation between violent viewing and violent behavior, but researchers—and representatives of the entertainment industry—are quick to point out that a *correlation* between two variables does not necessarily mean that one *causes* the other.

There are three major theories about the relationship between violent viewing and violent behavior (Vivian, 1993). One emphasizes the *cathartic effect* of violent viewing. This perspective says that viewing violence can actually reduce the violent drives of viewers because watching allows viewers to fantasize about violence, thereby releasing the tensions that may lead to real-life aggression. It has also been argued that this catharsis may lead viewers to take positive rather than violent action to remedy the problem. For instance, Vivian (1993) reports that following the broadcast of the television movie, *The Burning Bed*, in which a severely abused woman ultimately kills her batterer-husband by setting fire to his bed while he sleeps, domestic violence agency hotlines were flooded with calls from battered women seeking help.

Vivian also notes, however, that *The Burning Bed* appears to have inspired others to take violent action. One man set his estranged wife on fire and another severely beat his wife, both claiming they were motivated by the movie. Such acts of direct imitation are at the heart of a second theory that focuses on the *modeling effect* of violent viewing. Put simply, this perspective maintains that media violence teaches viewers to behave violently through imitation or modeling. Critics, though, point out that despite the sensationalism surrounding individual acts of direct imitation, they are very rare. Moreover, studies of social learning, as we found in Chapter 3, indicate that there are several intervening factors that play a role in determining whether a specific act will be modeled by others. These include the model's and the learner's relative age and sex, the model's objective status and her or his status in the eyes of the learner, and whether or not the model is rewarded or punished for engaging in the behavior in question.

These and other factors are analyzed by researchers who propose a third theory that emphasizes the *catalytic effect* of violent viewing. This position maintains that if certain conditions are present, viewing violence *may* prompt real-life violence. These researchers talk about violent viewing in terms of *probabilistic causation* rather than direct causation. The violent viewing "primes" the viewer for violent behavior; it increases the risk of violent behavior, just like smoking cigarettes increases the risk of developing cancer. If the violence is portrayed as realistic or exciting, if the violence succeeds in righting a wrong, if the program or film contains characters or situations that are similar to those the viewer actually knows or has experienced, and if the viewer's media exposure is heavy, the probability of the viewer behaving violently increases (Bok, 1998; Mifflin, 1998; Vivian, 1993).

It is doubtful that the federal government will enact legislation to curb violent programming any time soon. Previous government attempts to regulate broadcast hours in order to prevent children from viewing programs or films with adult themes have been struck down by the courts as a violation of the First Amendment (see, for example, Lewis, 1993). What is more certain, however, is that the majority of U.S. households will continue to fulfill the last condition of the catalytic effect: frequency of viewing. It is estimated that by the time a child leaves elementary school, he or she will have watched 8,000 murders and more than 100,000 violent acts on television (Bok, 1998). Such figures hardly inspire optimism with respect to the inhibition of violence in our society.

to violent behavior, television's impact hardly seems benign. Is there a similar relationship between television viewing and perception of appropriate roles for women and men?

Recent research indicates that, at least among children, there is a keen awareness of gender stereotypes on television. One national survey found that both girls and boys aged ten to seventeen recognized the emphasis placed on physical attractiveness for females on television. They reported that female television characters tend to worry about their weight and appearance, whine and cry, and flirt, whereas male television characters act as leaders, play sports, and want to be kissed or have sex. Significantly more girls (69 percent) than boys (40 percent), however, responded that they want to look like a character on television, and 31 percent of girls, but just 22 percent of boys, actually changed something about their appearance to look more like a television character (Children Now, 1997).

This research suggests that television viewing may affect an individual's self-evaluation as well as more general perceptions about gender. There are, though, several factors that mediate the effects of television on viewers' perceptions. One factor is the viewer's age. For example, the ability to correctly judge whether a program is fact or fiction increases with age; by about ten or eleven, most children can distinguish fact from fiction in television programming. However, judgments about the plausibility of a program's content (that is, whether the characters and their activities are similar to real life even if the program is fiction) are unrelated to viewer age. Instead, plausibility is related to viewing frequency: Heavy television viewers tend to judge programs as more realistic than light viewers do (Wright et al., 1995; see also Comstock, 1991). Thus, a person who watches television a lot is more likely to consider the gender portrayals he or she sees as realistic. This does not mean that viewers just passively accept what they see and hear on television. Interestingly, though, young women appear to be more critical of television than young men are, and their dissatisfaction stems from the lack of programs about "important and serious issues" as well as the lack of female characters in the programs (MRTW, 1995).

Some have argued that an observed relationship between television viewing and gender stereotyping does not necessarily mean that the television viewing causes the stereotyping. It may be that those who tend to stereotype also tend to watch more television (Courtney & Whipple, 1983). There is research that shows that children tend to choose programs that conform to gender stereotypes they have already learned. In other words, the media reinforce gender stereotypes that children are taught both by their parents and in school because children will select those media presentations that conform to what they have previously learned (Liebert et al., 1992; Morgan, 1982).

Research on advertising has also generated interesting findings. In a now-classic study, Geis and her colleagues (1984) showed groups of students a series of television ads, some of which were gender-stereotyped and others that portrayed gender-role reversals. They then asked the students to write a short essay about how they pictured their lives ten years into the future. Women who saw the stereotyped ads tended to stereotype their futures; they emphasized homemaking and expressed few aspirations for achievement outside the home. In contrast, women who saw the role-reversed ads wrote essays similar to those of male subjects; their essays were achievement-oriented and had few homemaking themes. The researchers concluded that gender depictions in television advertising may be understood as gender prescriptions by female viewers and may affect their real-life aspirations (see also Baran & Blasko, 1984; but see Martin & Kennedy, 1996 for a somewhat different view regarding the effects of print advertisements). In a more recent study, Lanis and Covell (1995) found that advertising portrayals of women affect sexual attitudes and beliefs. They showed one group of men and women advertisements depicting female models as sex objects, whereas another group was shown advertisements with female models competently performing various nontraditional roles. Lanis and Covell found that the men who saw the sexist advertisements increased their tendency to gender stereotype and also scored higher than other research participants on a scale measuring attitudes supportive of rape and sexual aggression. Interestingly, though, seeing the progressive advertisements had no effect on men's attitudes. Women who saw the progressive ads scored lowest on the scale of rape-supportive attitudes, but women who saw the sexist ads also scored low on this scale and decreased their tendency to gender stereotype (see also Rosenwasser et al., 1987; Wroblewski & Huston, 1987).

Clearly, this research points to the detrimental effects of sexist media portrayals, but it is also significant because it indicates that gender-fair media images can have a positive impact. The media, especially television, are teaching tools; what is taught depends on what is shown. The evidence indicates when the media, and television in particular, provide "pro-social" content, they can effectively reduce gender stereotypes and other forms of prejudice. The positive effects of pro-social media content are strongest for young children (Condry, 1989; Mares, 1996). This suggests that one vehicle for reducing sexism is children's programming. The Federal Communications Commission has taken steps to improve the quality of children's programming; for example, the FCC requires television stations to provide three hours of educational programming to children each week. It remains to be seen whether such efforts are sufficient for achieving the task at hand.

Language and Media as Shapers of Gender

In this chapter we have examined the gender images communicated by the primary means by which we give and receive information: language and the mass media. Far from simply reflecting the values and norms of our culture, we have learned here how language and media shape and recreate culture. In this way, language and the media socialize us, and with respect to gender, much of this socialization takes place through *symbolic annihilation:* symbolically ignoring, trivializing, or demeaning a particular group, which in this case has traditionally been women. We have found, for example, that language "tells a woman she is an afterthought, a linguistic variant, an 'et cetera'" (Butler & Paisley, 1980, p. 50). Newspapers convey a similar message, and magazines, television, and the advertisements that dominate both, promote stereotypes of femininity and masculinity.

We have discussed evidence in this chapter indicating that such depictions do have a negative impact on men's and women's behaviors and self-concepts. But we have also reviewed research that shows that the media, particularly television, can be a powerful force in breaking down sexist stereotypes by sensitively and realistically portraying women and men in nontraditional roles. Some observers have argued that reducing sexism in the media will occur only if more women are hired for policy-making posts at newspapers, television stations, and advertising agencies. We, too, advocate a balanced representation of the sexes in these jobs, as well as a more diversified work force in terms of race and ethnicity, age, sexual orientation, and physical ability. In addition, however, a concerned public must take action. At the very least, we must use nonsexist language in our own communication. Other strategies include letter-writing campaigns to newspapers and television stations, and boycotts of products promoted in sexist advertisements. And, as Box 5.4 on page 146 shows, some women are using computer technology to develop alternative communications systems. Indeed, if language and the media help construct what comes to be defined as reality, we must act to insure that the reality constructed is a nonsexist one.

BOX **5.4**

Are Computers Becoming the Communication Medium of Choice for Women?

Although women watch television more than men, network television viewing by women decreased 3 percent in 1997 and 6 percent by female teens (Allen, 1997). At the same time, daily readership of newspapers was an average 5 percentage points lower for women than men (MRTW, 1998d). What information sources are women utilizing in place of these traditional communications media? According to media analyst Donna Allen, women are increasingly turning to the Internet not only to receive information, but also to communicate ideas, experiences, agendas, and news (Allen, 1997). Eaton (1997) reports that women are using the Internet to bypass traditional journalistic reporting. In this way, women can research an issue

that the mainstream press does not deem newsworthy and discuss the issue with others online throughout the world. On the Internet, an individual has potential access to about 70 million other people (Allen, 1997).

Currently, about 36 percent of women are Internet users. The younger a woman is, the more likely she is to use the Internet. In fact, among eleven- to twenty-year-olds, more girls than boys are on the Internet (Allen, 1997). These figures are evidence, suggests Allen (1997, p. 9), that "[w]omen worldwide are ... building their own communications systems, to speak their information for themselves."

KEY TERMS

linguistic sexism   ways in which language devalues members of one sex

reflection hypothesis   the belief that media content mirrors the behaviors, relationships, values, and norms most prevalent or dominant in a society

semantic derogation   the process by which the meaning or connotations of words are debased over time

symbolic annihilation   symbolically ignoring, trivializing, or condemning individuals or groups in the media

SUGGESTED READINGS

Bok, S. (1998). *Mayhem: Violence as public entertainment*. Reading, MA: A Merloyd Lawrence Book/ Addison-Wesley.

Dow, B. J. (1996). *Prime-time feminism*. Philadelphia: University of Pennsylvania Press.

Flanders, L. (1997). *Real majority, media minority: The cost of sidelining women in reporting*. Monroe, ME: Common Courage Press.

Green, K., & Taormino, T. (Eds.) (1997). *A girl's guide to taking over the world: Writings from the girl zine revolution*. New York: St. Martin's Press.

Lester, P. M. (Ed.) (1996). *Images that injure: Pictorial stereotypes in the media*. Westport, CT: Praeger.

In addition, Communications Research Associates publishes a quarterly newsletter, *Media Report to Women*, from which we have drawn heavily in this chapter. The newsletter provides summaries and often reprints excerpts from reports and articles covering virtually every dimension of the topic of gender and the media. Subscriptions or single copies may be ordered from Communications Research Associates, Inc., 10606 Mantz Road, Silver Spring, MD 20903-1228.

NOTES

1. It may be argued by some that a woman supporter of the arts could be called a *patroness* (which literally means "female father"). There are numerous other words like this: poetess, authoress, aviatrix, bachelorette. Miller and Swift (1991a) refer to these as "Adam-ribbisms." In each case, a neutral word is gendered in such a way that the base becomes male and the female is a diminutive. A similar effect is rendered when a gendered word is used to describe an otherwise neutral word. For instance, one often hears "woman judge" or worse, "lady doctor," but rarely, if ever, "man judge" or "gentleman doctor." In fact, it has been argued that unless the job holder's sex is identified as female with the adjective *woman*, most people simply assume the job holder is a man. Putting *woman* in front of another noun creates a kind of "sub-species nomenclature" (Miller & Swift, 1991a). Using *woman* as an adjective is also sometimes meant to convey negative images of the competencies or abilities of a person; consider, for instance, the negative stereotypes attached to "woman driver." Fortunately, both diminutives and the use of *woman* have become less frequent in public writing and speech (e.g., newspaper articles), although they remain a common feature of routine informal conversation.

2. Lakeoff (1990) notes that *Ms.* as a replacement for *Miss* or *Mrs.* has not been as widely accepted as its proponents had hoped, perhaps because it has been derogatorily labeled a "feminist word." It is most often used in place of *Miss*, and it is typically listed along with *Miss* and *Mrs.* as a form an individual may choose for her title of address if she wishes.

3. Analyses of the covers of the three largest news magazines (*Time, Newsweek,* and *U.S. News and World Report*) yielded similar findings: In 1995, seventy-two men made the covers of these magazines compared with just three women (model Claudia Schiffer; Susan Smith, who murdered her two sons; and Princess Diana) (MRTW, 1996h).

4. According to statistics compiled by the United Nations Department of Public Information (Gallagher, 1995), the United States ranks highly relative to other countries in terms of women's representation on press staffs. Only Namibia, where 46.6 percent of the press staff is female, and Luxembourg, where women's representation is 37.1 percent, rank higher. In most countries, only one fifth to one quarter of the press staff is female, and in some countries, such as India (7.9 percent), Japan (6.8 percent), and Germany (3.0), women's representation is below 10 percent.

5. In 1996 alone, 993 new magazines were launched. For the twelve years prior to 1996, the largest number of new periodicals were sex magazines. But in 1996, the largest number were classified as sports magazines (111), and sex dropped to fifth place (51) (Husni, 1997). Among the new sports magazines launched recently are several specifically designed for women (e.g., *Conde Nast Sports for Women, Sports Illustrated Women/Sport* (Pogrebin, 1997a).

6. Indeed, *Cosmopolitan* has attempted to capitalize on its image of the "liberated" woman. In February 1997, for example, *Cosmo* celebrated "the *Cosmo* Girl—past, present and future." Who is the *Cosmo* girl? She is the "fun, fearless female."

7. McCracken (1993) points out that in addition to overt advertisements, magazines also contain covert advertisements, that is, advertisements camouflaged by the magazine's cover or stories. For instance, an article on how to prevent wrinkles in one's skin typically suggests or mentions various products one can use for this purpose. About 95 percent of the pages of women's magazines are devoted to overt advertising, but no estimate is available on how much space goes to covert advertising. Given the prominence of the ads, however, we must agree with McCracken that women's magazines should be considered "advertising magazines for women."

8. We could not find a magazine similar to *Essence* that targets a primarily Black male audience.

9. However, a recent analysis of the magazine, *Men's Health*, found that male readers are increasingly being encouraged to obsess about their body image and sexual attractiveness. The author of the study concluded that the magazine is "peddling a standard of male beauty as unforgiving and unrealistic as the female version sold by those dewy-eyed preteen waifs draped across the covers of *Glamour* and *Elle*" (quoted in MRTW, 1998b, p. 6).

10. Comstock (1991) notes, however, that viewing time does vary by such factors as race, social class, and education. For example, African American children tend to watch more television than White children, but children who are poor, regardless of race, watch more TV than more affluent children and say that watching TV is important to them (MRTW, 1995). Given the relationship between social class and educational attainment, it is not surprising that the fewer the number of years of education completed by adults in a household, the more television watched in the household (Comstock, 1991).

11. This study also found that on children's programs, women have even fewer roles—one out of four—and that on no daytime serials, for which the audience is overwhelmingly female, do women make up a majority of the characters portrayed (Gerbner, 1993).

12. The coming-out episode of *Ellen* also won a number of prestigious awards, and ABC nearly doubled the advertising rate charged to sponsors of the show (MRTW, 1997g). In 1998, however, ABC cancelled *Ellen*. A number of observers suggested that the show was cancelled because of negative reactions to its pro-lesbian/gay content, but ABC executives denied the charge, citing declines in viewer ratings since the coming-out episode (MRTW, 1998c).

13. Elliott (1994) reports, however, that advertisers are beginning to take a greater interest in gay and lesbian consumers, so we may anticipate seeing more openly gay and lesbian models in advertisements. It is likely that this change will occur in print media before it occurs on television. For example, in 1996, Macy's, a department store chain, published a holiday catalog of men's clothing and accessories that featured on one page a picture of two men (one bare-chested), obviously fond of one another, exchanging gifts (Dunlap, 1996).

6

Gender and Intimate Relationships

What do you think of when you hear the words "family" or "intimate relationship"? Maybe the image of someone you love dearly comes to mind. Or perhaps you remember a special event—or just everyday routines that when viewed nostalgically seem special— that you shared with your parents, grandparents, siblings, other relatives, or close friends. Usually, when we think of families and intimate relationships, we think of people and places set apart, emotionally distinct from, public life. The intimate environment of home is often thought of as a haven from the more public institutions of our society, such as the economy, the government, and the legal system. For many of us, home is a place where we "let down our hair"; we can be ourselves and still be accepted lovingly by those around us.

If we look carefully at our daily lives, we can easily see that reality is far different from this idealistic view of family life and intimate relationships. We know well from our personal experiences that what happens at home frequently affects our performance on the job and at school, and problems at work or school usually come home with us. For some people, too, home is hardly a protective haven. As we will discuss later in this chapter, domestic violence is a serious social problem in our society—one that disproportionately affects women and children—but is masked by the notion of family privacy.

On a structural level, too, we can see the intersection of the public and private realms of our lives, and this intersection is gendered. The word *family*, in fact, reveals much about the impact of gendered institutional arrangements on our private lives. *Family* derives from the Latin word *famulus*, which means "household servant or slave." Historically, a man's family—his wife, children, and slaves—along with his material possessions, were defined by law as his property, and it was his wife's and children's legal duty to serve him in exchange for his economic support. Although few of us think of the family in this way any more, the legal system still exercises considerable control over the family by defining the members' rights and obligations to one another, albeit in somewhat more liberal, but no less gendered terms.

There are many other ways that the "private" world of the home is intertwined with the public world. For example, the type of jobs adult family members hold outside the home—or their lack of paid employment—affects the family's economic survival, where the family lives, how much time family members have to spend together, and what family members do for recreation (Thorne, 1992). As we will discuss in Chapter 7, the type of job a person is likely to hold, as well as that person's income, is related to gender. At the same time, families are in constant interaction with other institutions in society. For instance, poor families, especially poor women with children, must frequently interact with the state through social service agencies and the welfare system, whereas middle-class and wealthier families may utilize banks, stock brokerage firms, and similar organizations to handle their financial concerns (Thorne, 1992).

In this chapter, we will take a closer look at how the nonfamilial institutions and dominant norms of a society impinge on home life and intimate relationships, especially in terms of gender. At the same time, we'll examine how relations of production and reproduction in the home reinforce or undermine gender relations in society. These are by no means easy tasks, not only because the relationships between families and other institutions are complex, but also because much of our thinking about families is colored by our own familial experiences as well as by the culturally prescribed ideals of our society. In fact, sociology, as both a product and a reproducer of culture, has played a major role in the social construction of cultural images of families and intimate relationships. To begin, let's look at what sociology has traditionally had to say about the family and then review feminists' critiques of this perspective.

Sociology Constructs *The* Family

Aulette (1994) identifies the sociologist Ernest Burgess as the founder of family sociology, but it was the work of Talcott Parsons that essentially shaped this subfield of the discipline from the 1940s to the 1960s.[1] As we discussed in Chapter 1, Parsons was a *structural functional* theorist, and he applied this perspective to his writings on families and home life, as well as gender. His focus was on the **isolated nuclear family**, composed of a husband, wife, and their dependent children. When we say this type of family is isolated, we mean first, that family members live apart from other relatives (e.g., spouses' parents or siblings). Second, each family unit is isolated in that it is also financially independent of other relatives. Third, the family no longer performs many of its earlier functions—education, care of the sick, production of food and clothing—since these have largely been taken over by public institutions. Instead, the contemporary family has just two vital functions: "first, the primary socialization of children so that they can truly become members of the society in which they have been born; second, the stabilization of the adult personalities of the population of the society" (Parsons, 1955, p. 16).

In the isolated nuclear family, the two adults accomplish these tasks by following distinct and specialized roles: one expressive, the other instrumental. The **instrumental family role** includes leadership and decision-making responsibilities. It is filled by the spouse who is the economic provider for the family, traditionally the husband/father. The wife/mother assumes the **expressive family role,** which means that she does the housework, cares for the children, and sees to it that the emotional needs of family members are met. Although Parsons and other functionalists acknowledged that some married women, even a few with small children, were employed outside the home, even in the 1950s, they maintained that these women held jobs in the lowest occupational categories so as not to compete with or displace their husbands as chief "status-givers" and wage earners.

Of course, we might ask why this particular role differentiation came about. Why can't men sometimes be expressive and women sometimes be instrumental leaders? Recall from Chapter 1 that functionalists see these gender roles as rooted in the biological, especially the reproductive, differences between men and women. This role differentiation, they maintain, emerged among early humans as they adapted to physical as well as environmental changes. Because this role differentiation was functional, it was institutionalized over time.

Although much of the functionalist literature on the family was written in the 1950s, it warrants our examination for two reasons: first, because much of the sociological writing on families that followed it bears its imprint; and second, because we still hear these ideas echoed today in the "family values" rhetoric of the political right wing. Not surprisingly, this perspective has also had its critics, including feminist sociologists. We noted in Chapter 1 that feminists have questioned functionalists' rendering of gender relations in prehistory, offering an alternative interpretation of the fossil record. Let's consider some other problems inherent in this depiction of the family.

Evaluating the Functionalist Perspective of the Family

Critics of the functionalist perspective of the family question the extent to which the contemporary nuclear family is truly isolated from other kin. For one thing, functionalists juxtapose the contemporary family with the preindustrial family, implying that prior to industrialization, families enjoyed an extended structure—that is, grandparents, parents, children and perhaps other relatives shared a common household. Although cross-cultural research indicates that such arrangements are common in many non-Western preindustrial societies, historical evidence shows that in preindustrial Western societies, extended families were rare, except perhaps among the aristocracy. A short life expectancy precluded the possibility of even a three-generation family for most people. Rather, it is more likely that "three-generation families actually developed as a consequence of industrialization rather than being destroyed by it" (Allan, 1985, p. 6). Moreover, recent research indicates that many contemporary families are not isolated from extended kin. For example, most senior citizens live near family members, including their adult children and grandchildren. About half see a family member daily; more than 85 percent have at least weekly contact with their children (Taeuber, 1992). Family members continue to turn first to kin for advice, emotional support, and financial help. Among non-White families, including African Americans, Hispanic Americans, and Asian Americans, and among the working class and the poor, researchers have found extensive kin and friendship networks in which resources are pooled so families can survive hard times (Jayakody & Chatters, 1997; Neighbors, 1997; Segura & Pierce, 1993; Stacey, 1990; Taylor et al., 1997).

Harsher criticism has been leveled at functionalists' rigid differentiation of roles between the sexes. In Chapter 1, we critiqued the role concept itself for depoliticizing the analysis of gender relations. However, there are other problematic aspects of depicting men's and women's roles as instrumental and expressive, respectively. First, this role differentiation erroneously separates public life—what functionalists and others see as the masculine world of work, government, and so on—from the private, feminine world of the family. As we noted at the outset of this chapter, the idea of home as a separate domain from the public world—an idea that sociologists call the **public/private split**—is simply false. In their everyday lives, families do not experience these spheres as separate; they experience the public and private interdependently.

Another major problem with functionalists' rigid role differentiation is that it portrays instrumental and expressive activities as being mutually exclusive, and assumes their assignment on the basis of sex is natural. In other words, we are offered *the* male role and *the* female role, which are biologically based, and from this it follows that this arrangement is both normal and unchanging. We challenged this idea in Chapter 1, but we raise it again here because it extends to family forms and thus constructs *the* family as well. However, gender and family arrangements are not biologically given, but rather culturally prescribed and socially learned. In Chapter 2, we examined anthropological research that demonstrates the fluidity of gender. There is also considerable anthropological data that show tremendous cross-cultural variation in family forms as well as in the division of labor within families.

Every known society, for example, has a division of labor by sex (and also by age). However, what is considered men's work versus what is considered women's work varies dramatically from society to society. In some cultures, women build the houses; in others, this is men's work. In most societies, women usually do the cooking, but there are societies in which this is typically men's responsibility. In fact, research indicates that there are no tasks from which men are totally excluded, and the only tasks from which women are totally excluded appear to be the hunting of large sea animals (e.g., whaling) and the smelting of ores. There are very few societies in which women participate in metalworking, lumbering, and hunting large land animals, but there are exceptions (Murdock & Provost, 1973; O'Kelly & Carney, 1986). For example, among the Agta of the Philippines, women and men hunt deer and wild pigs with knives and bows and arrows. They fish with spears while swimming underwater, an activity that requires not only great skill, but also physical stamina. Women and men also gather vegetation together and share childcare (Estioko-Griffin, 1986). Families in this society can best be described as *egalitarian* rather than *patriarchal* (male-headed).

We need not look to faraway societies for alternatives to the traditional isolated nuclear family. In the United States, there are many variations in family structure and composition. What are these different family forms? Let's consider them briefly.

Contemporary Families: Diversity and Change

The number of traditional isolated nuclear families in the United States has declined dramatically during the past forty years. In fact, this type of family represents a minority of households in the United States today. In 1960, for example, less than 7 percent of married women with children worked outside the home and about 90 percent of family households had two parents present. By 1996, 70 percent of married women with children worked outside the home and 68 percent of family households had two parents (U.S. Department of Commerce, Bureau of the Census, 1997). Indeed, as we will see shortly, the most prevalent types of families today are **two-earner families** in which both adult partners are in the paid labor force, and **single-parent families,** families with children but only one adult who has financial responsibility for the household.

Looking at Figure 6.1 on page 154, we get a sense of the diversity of households in the United States today. Many of these households certainly consider themselves families. For example, the category "other male- or female-headed family households" includes **domestic partnerships:** unmarried heterosexual, gay, and lesbian couples who live together. The percentage of domestic partnerships is quite likely an underestimate, especially of gay and lesbian domestic partners, since concern about the consequences of

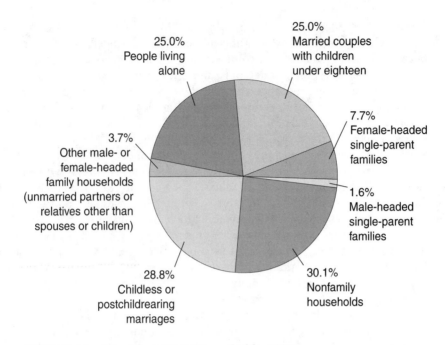

FIGURE 6.1   Diversity of U.S. Households, 1996*

*Percentages do not add to 100 because some households were counted in more than one category.

Source: Compiled from U.S. Department of Commerce, Bureau of the Census, 1997.

homophobia inhibits many from publicly identifying as intimates. The category "non-family households" may include what Kath Weston (1991) calls **chosen families,** which are composed of people unrelated by ancestry, marriage, or adoption, but who are nonetheless considered members of the family. Weston studied the chosen families that gay men and lesbians formed with close friends and sometimes ex-lovers after they were shunned by their parents, siblings, and other relatives because of their sexual orientation. She found that chosen families meet many of the same needs for their members as other families do: intimacy, companionship, and financial support. Researchers report, in fact, that these traits are among the hallmarks of a successful family—that is, a family whose members manage the stresses and strains of life together and who resolve their conflicts fairly (Cox, 1993).

We will take a closer look at each of these types of families shortly. For now, however, our point is that diversity rather than uniformity is the best way to characterize family composition in the United States today. In fact, the family forms we have mentioned so far do not even cover all the family forms and kinship networks that researchers have recently identified. *Blended families,* for example, are increasingly common. Blended families form when a couple with children divorces and one or both partners remarry someone who also has children, or the new couples have children of their own, or both. Similarly, sociologist Judith Stacey (1990) discovered what she calls *accordion households.*

In her study of working-class families in California's Silicon Valley, she found households that expand and contract as the needs of various kin, including "ex-familia" (e.g., siblings or parents of divorced spouses), change over time. In accordion households, as kin are taken in and leave, resources are pooled and distributed both as a survival strategy and as a demonstration of caring and love.

It appears, then, that the defining characteristics of a family are not official markers, such as marriage licenses, but rather emotional and financial ties. This definition is even being used increasingly by the courts in determining the rights and responsibilities of family members. For example, in a landmark case in 1989, the New York Court of Appeals ruled that a homosexual couple who had lived together for ten years could be considered a family under New York City's rent control regulations. The court reasoned that families are signified not only by signed marriage licenses, but also by long-term, exclusive relationships with the emotional and financial commitment of those involved (Gutis, 1989; see also Dunlap, 1994).

The diversity that characterizes families today is also characteristic of a related behavior, *sexual behavior*. Therefore, before we continue our discussion of diversity in families, let's look at several issues relating to sexuality and sexual behavior.

Sexuality and Reproductive Freedom

"I'm a virgin and proud of it," proclaimed a seventeen-year-old to a reporter recently ("'True Love Waits,'" 1993, p. A12). This teenager was one of several hundred young women and men who had signed "chastity pledges"—index cards bearing the promise to remain "sexually pure" until marriage. Recent research indicates, however, that these young people are a numerical minority. A majority of young women and men engage in premarital sex, and even teens who are virgins are often sexually active. Although they do not engage in sexual intercourse, research indicates that they do engage in other types of genital sexual activities, including oral sex and masturbation with a partner (Schuster et al., 1996).

Attitudes toward premarital sex have become more liberal. For example, in 1972, 37 percent of respondents to a national survey said that premarital sex is "always wrong," compared with just 26 percent who gave that response in 1988. By the early 1990s, only 19.7 percent felt that premarital sex is always wrong (Kain, 1990; Michael et al., 1994). We see these attitudinal changes reflected in behavior. According to the Children's Defense Fund (CDF) (1997), four out of five young men and women have sexual intercourse before age twenty. The average age of first intercourse is sixteen for boys and seventeen for girls. A 1998 study by the Kaiser Family Foundation found that although almost three-quarters of the teens surveyed said that their friends think it is a good thing to remain a virgin, nearly half also said they have felt pressured to have sex. Younger teens, aged thirteen to fifteen, were as likely as older teens, aged sixteen to eighteen, to say they had felt sexual pressure, but older teens were more likely to have succumbed to this pressure.

The Kaiser Family Foundation study (1998) also found that the gap in sexual experience between boys and girls had closed completely. In this study, age at first intercourse for boys and girls was fifteen. According to Carol Darling and her colleagues (1992), findings such as this indicate that the sexual double standard is, for the most part, a thing of the past. The **sexual double standard** refers to the tradition in our society, and in many others, of permitting young men to engage in sexual activity—or at least ignoring, overlooking, or forgiving their sexual escapades—while simultaneously condemning and punishing the same behavior by girls. Despite the liberalization of attitudes toward premarital sex, however, a considerable amount of research indicates that the sexual double standard is still alive and well. It continues to be common practice, for instance, for young men to brag about their sexual conquests and to win approval as "studs" for being sexually active. Although young women may engage in sexual activity more freely than in the past, they are still expected to do so within a committed relationship, a romance. Girls with multiple partners are regarded as "easy" or as "sluts" (Rubin, 1991).

There also appears to be a gender difference in young people's assessments of sexual intercourse. Both Rubin (1991) and Thompson (1984) report that the majority of young women they interviewed did not find sexual intercourse very pleasurable or satisfying. In fact, the young women preferred foreplay or sexual petting over intercourse. Most young women expressed disappointment after first intercourse, a finding that helps to explain why, after first intercourse, their rates of sexual activity are low relative to those of boys.

We have focused our discussion so far on heterosexual sex. We will discuss homosexuality shortly. First, however, let's consider one potential outcome of teen heterosexual sex: pregnancy and childbearing.

Teen Pregnancy and Childbearing

The rate of teen births in the United States declined steadily from 62.1 births per 1,000 girls aged fifteen to nineteen in 1991 to 54.7 births for every 1,000 girls aged fifteen to nineteen in 1996. In 1996, about 500,000 babies were born to mothers aged fifteen to nineteen, about 75 percent of whom were unmarried, and an additional 11,000 were born to mothers aged fourteen or younger, virtually all of whom were unmarried (Lewin, 1998a). In fact, despite the decline in the teen birth rate overall, the percentage of teen births to unmarried young women continues to grow (CDF, 1997). The birth rate for unmarried African American teens did decline during the early 1990s (to 91.7 births per 1,000 Black girls aged fifteen to nineteen), while the birth rate for unmarried Latina teens rose slightly (to 101.6 births per 1,000 Latina girls aged fifteen to nineteen). The birth rate for unmarried White teens remained fairly stable during this period (at 48.4 per 1,000 White girls aged fifteen to nineteen). Thus, the birth rate for unmarried African American and Latina teens continues to be twice as high as the birth rate for unmarried White teens and, overall, the United States still has the highest rate of teen births of any industrialized country in the world (CDF, 1997; Lewin, 1998a).

The disproportionately high rate of births to African American and Latina teens has been linked to the higher rates of poverty and lower levels of academic success among these populations. According to the Children's Defense Fund (1997), teens who are least likely to get pregnant and give birth are those who: (1) live in financially stable or affluent families; (2) are academically successful; and (3) have high aspirations with opportunities available to fulfill those aspirations (see also Brewster, 1992; Gilligan et al., 1995; Luker, 1996; Williams, 1991).

Another factor contributing to teen pregnancy is *sexual coercion*. Research indicates that as many as 50 to 70 percent of babies born to girls aged eleven to eighteen are fathered by males four to seven years older than the babies' mothers (Children's Defense Fund, 1997; Landry & Forrest, 1995; Robinson, 1996; Vobejda, 1997a). "The typical adolescent girl simply is not sufficiently empowered to negotiate sex and contraception with a male partner four or more years older than she is" (Children's Defense Fund, 1997, p. 85).

What are the consequences of teen pregnancy and childbearing? On a societal level, analysts have been primarily concerned with the economic consequences. These have been estimated to be between $13 billion and $19 billion a year and include increased medical expenses, lost tax revenue, and increased welfare payments. However, it is important to keep in mind that these statistics derive from the devastating impact that pregnancy and childbearing have on the lives of teens themselves—especially teenage girls, on whom the burden of the pregnancy and childrearing falls disproportionately—and their children. For teen parents, and in particular, teen mothers, the consequences include lowered chances of furthering their education, the financial burdens of raising a family, and fewer job opportunities. Babies born to teens are more likely than babies born to older women to be premature or low birthweight, largely because teen mothers are less likely than older mothers to receive adequate prenatal care. These children are also more likely to grow up in poverty or near-poverty, to have various health problems as they grow up, to have difficulty in school, and to become teen parents themselves (Children's Defense Fund, 1997; Luker, 1996).

A widespread myth is that generous welfare benefits encourage teen pregnancy and childbearing. However, research indicates that the rate of nonmarital teen births is highest in states with the lowest welfare benefits (Children's Defense Fund, 1997). Withdrawing social and financial supports from teen mothers, therefore, is not a viable solution to the problems of teen pregnancy and childbearing. One response has been to make contraceptives more available to teens through their school health programs, and studies are showing that an increasing number of sexually active teens are using contraception, although not consistently (Children's Defense Fund, 1997; Kaiser Family Foundation, 1998). Making contraceptives available, then, is simply not enough. Adolescents must be motivated to use the contraceptives, and this motivation appears to be spurred by the availability of other opportunities for achieving status and self-esteem—such as academic success and sports achievement—instead of becoming a parent (Gilligan et al., 1995; Luker, 1996).

The problems of teen pregnancy and childbearing raise the issue of **reproductive freedom,** an individual's ability to freely choose whether or not to have a child. The issue of reproductive freedom has been surrounded by controversy, so let's take some time to examine it more carefully.

Reproductive Freedom

Most discussions of reproductive freedom center on an individual's desire *not* to have a child. We will start our discussion with this point, but as we will soon see, the issue of reproductive freedom is not unidimensional and includes concerns that arise as a result of the desire to *have* children.

Contraception and Abortion.   The desires to prevent pregnancy and to control family size are not new. Historical and archeological evidence provide abundant proof that contraceptive methods and abortive techniques have been known and widely practiced for thousands of years. In the United States, though, most methods of contraception, along with abortion, were made illegal by 1850. There are various explanations of why such legislation was enacted. One is that the new laws were the result of efforts by professionally trained physicians to take control of the provision of health care by displacing midwives, who had performed and assisted with abortions as well as births (see Chapter 11). Another explanation is that the laws were an attempt by racist legislators and lobbyists to get White women to reproduce so that Whites would not be outnumbered by foreign immigrants and African Americans, whose populations were growing (Gordon, 1976; Luker, 1984; Mohr, 1978).

Whatever the reasons, it is women who have taken—some would say, have been forced to take—responsibility for birth control, so it is hardly surprising that they have led the social movements for planned parenthood and the legalization of contraception and abortion. Many women became active on these issues because they or someone close to them had experienced the stigma of illegitimacy or had suffered the painful, often tragic, consequences of illegal abortions. Minority women, in particular, frequently contributed to these causes with their health and their lives as the knowing or unwitting subjects in early medical research on the Pill, the IUD, and other contraceptive devices (see Chapter 11).

Abortion and certain forms of contraception remained illegal in this country until the 1970s, when the U.S. Supreme Court issued a series of rulings that made the decision to bear a child part of an individual's constitutionally protected right to privacy. The Court's landmark ruling in *Griswold* v. *Connecticut* (1971) served as a precedent for later cases. In *Griswold*, the Court invoked the right to privacy by invalidating laws that prohibit the use of contraceptives by married couples. One year later, the Court applied this principle in a case involving the distribution of contraceptives to unmarried adults (*Eisenstadt* v. *Baird*). Finally, in 1977, the Court ruled in *Carey* v. *Population Services International* that minors are protected by the same constitutional right to privacy. Therefore, the state cannot interfere in their decision not to bear children by denying them access to contraceptives.

Many young people now find it hard to believe that the distribution and use of contraceptives in the United States were illegal only about thirty years ago, and relatively few would like to see these decisions reversed. However, other Supreme Court rulings have generated more controversy, especially those dealing with abortion. In 1973, the Court ruled seven to two in the landmark case *Roe* v. *Wade* that women have a constitutionally protected right to choose abortion and that the state cannot unduly interfere with or prohibit that right. In this much misunderstood and hotly debated case, the Court actually made three rulings, one for each trimester of pregnancy. Specifically, the Court ruled that during the first trimester, the decision to abort is a strictly private one to be made by a woman in consultation with a physician; the state has no authority or compelling reason to interfere at this point. During the second trimester, abortion involves more health risks to women, so the state may impose some restrictions, but only to safeguard women's health. It is in the third trimester that the state's role is greatest; the Court ruled that the state may prohibit third-trimester abortions (except when an abortion is necessary to preserve a woman's life or health) because of the *viability* of the fetus—that is, the ability of the fetus to survive outside a woman's body. Importantly, though, in a companion case—*Doe* v. *Bolton*—the Court ruled that any restrictions imposed by the state must be reasonable and cannot inhibit a physician's duty to provide medical care according to his or her professional judgment. Thus, in *Doe* v. *Bolton*, the Court invalidated a number of state restrictions, including those that required two doctors to concur with the woman's decision to abort and committee approval of the decision.

Since 1973, the Court has consistently reaffirmed the basic principles underlying *Roe* v. *Wade* and has refused to overturn that decision. Nevertheless, in subsequent cases, the Court has made rulings that have placed limits on abortion, making it more difficult for some women—especially teens, poor women, and women who live in rural areas—to obtain abortions. These restrictions include, for example, allowing states to require parental notification and consent when minors seek an abortion; providing women seeking abortions with counseling on alternatives such as adoption; imposing waiting periods on women seeking abortions; denying Medicaid funds to pay for abortions; and prohibiting abortions in public hospitals. In upholding these restrictions, the Court maintains that it is permitting the states to discourage women from obtaining abortions, although it will not allow the states to obstruct women's choice of abortion (Risen & Thomas, 1998).[2]

These restrictions, along with increased use of contraceptives and a slight decrease in the number of women of childbearing age, have contributed to a drop in the rate and overall number of abortions performed in the United States. Since 1980, the number of abortions per 1,000 women aged fifteen to forty-four has declined about 20 percent, falling from 25 per 1,000 women to 20 per 1,000 women in 1995 (Vobejda, 1997b).[3] Another major factor contributing to this decline has been a decrease in the number of abortion providers. The Supreme Court has ruled that states can require that all abortions be performed by physicians (Carelli, 1997). Fewer obstetrics and gynecology residents are being trained to perform even first trimester abortions: 70 percent in 1992 compared with 92 percent in 1976. Although the number of clinics and doctors' offices providing abortions has declined only slightly since the mid-1980s, the number of hospitals performing abortions decreased by 18 percent (Cronin, 1996). Some of this decline is due to recent mergers of Catholic hospitals with secular hospitals, a growing trend that is not only eliminating abortion services, but also access to contraception, voluntary sterilization, and similar services (Kong, 1998). Meanwhile, the number of counties with an abortion provider also decreased significantly from 714 in 1978 to 495 in 1992, a 31 percent decline (Clark, 1995).

Another reason for the decline in abortion providers is the growing unwillingness of physicians to subject themselves to the threats and harassment of anti-abortion activists (Henshaw, 1995). Although the overall number of harassing incidents of abortion providers has decreased somewhat since the enactment of the federal Freedom of

Access to Clinic Entrances (FACE) Act in 1994, physicians and clinic workers continue to report that they are targets of stalking, threats, and other forms of harassment and violence by radical anti-abortion protestors. The activities of anti-abortion groups have included putting glue in clinic locks, releasing noxious butyric acid inside clinics, picketing abortion providers' homes, harassing their children, and even firebombing clinics and shooting doctors and clinic workers (Clark, 1995; Henshaw, 1995; Navarro, 1996).

Public opinion polls show that the majority of Americans believe that abortion should be legal under most circumstances. Only 15 to 20 percent of the population favors outlawing abortion completely; most people simply feel that abortion should be discouraged (Clark, 1995; Saletan, 1998; Stolberg, 1998; U.S. Department of Justice, Bureau of Justice Statistics, 1996). In particular, the overwhelming majority of the public continues to support legally available abortions during the first trimester of pregnancy; a much smaller percentage supports late-term abortions. Medical technology now makes it possible for fetuses born at 23 to 24 weeks to survive (although only about 42 percent of fetuses born at 24 weeks actually survive past the first year of life) (Stolberg, 1997a). However, late-term abortions (abortions performed more than twenty weeks into pregnancy) account for just 1.1 percent of all abortions; 52.2 percent are performed at less than nine weeks gestation and nearly 89 percent are performed at less than thirteen weeks gestation (Henshaw, 1995).

As we noted earlier, though, reproductive freedom is not only about abortion and contraception. Perhaps as controversial as abortion are some of the new reproductive technologies that are designed to assist women in becoming pregnant rather than preventing pregnancy.

New Reproductive Technologies

It is estimated that of the 60.2 million women of reproductive age in the United States, 10 to 13 percent are unable to conceive or maintain a pregnancy (Altman, 1998; Stolberg, 1997b). In addition, there are women, married and unmarried, who wish to have children but for whom pregnancy and childbirth pose severe health risks because of various physical disabilities (Asch, 1989). Postmenopausal women who want to have a child are unable to become pregnant by conventional means. Physically able single women and men may also wish to have children but not to marry or even enter into an intimate relationship to conceive a child. Furthermore, an increasing number of lesbian and gay couples are expressing a desire to become parents. For members of these groups, the **new reproductive technologies** (NRTs) represent a potential solution to what was, less than two decades ago, an all but unsolvable problem.

After the birth of the first "test tube" baby in 1978, reproductive technology developed rapidly. Today, an array of options is available: in vitro ("test tube") fertilization (IVF), in which eggs are fertilized in a laboratory dish and then the embryos are implanted in the uterus; gamete intrafallopian transfer (GIFT), in which eggs and sperm are injected into the fallopian tubes with the goal that they will unite and produce embryos; zygote intrafallopian transfer (ZIFT), in which embryos fertilized in vitro are transplanted to the fallopian tubes; intracytoplasmic sperm injection (ICSI), in which doctors screen a man's sperm to find the strongest one and inject it into a woman's egg;

egg donation, in which one woman's eggs are "harvested" and given to another woman; and surrogacy, in which a woman, through in vitro fertilization, serves as the "gestational host" for another couple's baby, relinquishing the baby and all parental rights and responsibilities to that couple when the baby is born.

If all of this sounds complicated, be assured that the ethical and legal questions the NRTs raise are far more complex than the procedures themselves. For instance, in vitro fertilization yields not one, but several embryos. Embryos not implanted are frozen for possible future use. Who decides the fate of these frozen embryos? What if one partner dies or a couple divorces? Who has "custody" of the frozen embryos (see, for example, Becker et al., 1994)? In surrogacy and egg donation cases, do surrogates and donors have any parental rights or responsibilities (see Becker et al., 1994; Hoffman, 1996; Shanley, 1993)? And what about the children born as a result of the NRTs? Do the children have a right to know about their unconventional origins and who their true biological parents are? How do we even define *parent* in these circumstances (see Altman, 1998; Hoffman, 1996; Kolata, 1993)?

While ethicists and legal scholars debate these and many other thorny issues posed by the new reproductive technologies, doctors, donors, and those seeking to have children are currently bound by relatively few regulations. The federal government for the most part has taken a hands-off approach toward regulating NRTs, with the exception of issuing standards for fertility clinics in terms of their success rates (Cowan, 1992). However, the clinics have been criticized for using methods—such as implanting four, five, even ten embryos at a time into a woman's uterus—to drive up their success rates (Kolata, 1998). Multiple implantations increase the chances of multiple fetuses (e.g., triplets, quadruplets, quintuplets). In fact, multiple births occur in one in every three births resulting from NRTs. These babies, though, are at greater risk of being premature, having low birth weight, and having serious disabilities. To avoid these problems, women found to be pregnant with multiple fetuses are often asked to undergo "fetal reduction"—that is, the selective abortion of one or more of the fetuses—a difficult, heartwrenching decision for most women, even those who are pro-choice, especially when they went to extraordinary lengths to get pregnant in the first place (Altman, 1998; Kolata, 1998).

Clearly, the issues surrounding the new reproductive technologies pose some difficult dilemmas, not only for legislators, physicians, and ethicists, but also for the individuals who are using these technologies to have children. However, for many people who wish to have a baby but cannot, these issues are moot; they simply cannot *afford* any of the alternatives. None of the procedures is inexpensive, and they are rarely covered by insurance. A single attempted in vitro fertilization costs on average $7,800, and only twelve states require that insurance companies cover this expense. Most couples make multiple attempts, but the overall success rate of the procedure is only about 22 percent (Stolberg, 1997b). Egg donation has a higher success rate—about 47 percent —but a single attempt costs between $14,000 and $20,000 (Hoffman, 1996; Stolberg, 1997b). The high price of the procedures makes them prohibitively expensive for many individuals and couples, even though their desire for a child is as strong as those who can afford the NRTs. Surrogates and egg donors are paid for their services and are usually recruited through advertisements placed by fertility clinics or "donor brokers" (private entrepreneurs who are paid a finder's fee for locating donors). Surrogates and egg donors are typically younger and less financially secure than those who pay for these services, raising the possibility that women in need of income will be vulnerable to exploitation by wealthier couples seeking to have children (Shanley, 1993; but see also Hoffman, 1996). And then there is the issue of the "marketplace": Given the rising demand for eggs and reproductive services, as well as the rising costs, there is concern that our reproductive material, as well as babies themselves, are increasingly being seen as commodities to be bought and sold.

In short, social class plays a major role in determining who will and who will not bear children. It is sadly ironic that poor women and women of color are one and a half times more likely to experience infertility, but because of the expense, are the least likely to be able to use any of the NRTs we have discussed (Rothman, 1992). Although some feminists see the new reproductive technologies as potentially liberating for women by giving them greater control over the reproductive process, others are deeply concerned that such technologies turn children into products and may also give rise to a "breeder class" of women composed primarily of poor women who rent their bodies or sell their eggs to the wealthy (Diamond, 1988; Raymond, 1990; Rothman, 1989; Shanley, 1993). The controversy is not likely to be resolved soon, even among feminists.

What is certain is that the new reproductive technologies are contributing to the growing diversity of family forms in this country. Let's discuss, then, various types of families and intimate relationships.

Varieties of Intimate Relationships

Heterosexual Marriages

Although most of us think of marriage in romantic rather than legalistic terms, a marriage is a legally binding contractual agreement. Unlike most contractual agreements, though, the conditions of the marriage contract cannot be changed or negotiated by the two parties involved. Only the state has the right to set the terms of the marriage contract. In fact, the contracting parties in a marriage rarely even review the conditions of their agreement before entering into it.

Historically, a marriage contract specified an exchange relationship between husband and wife. A wife's obligations included housework and complying with her husband's requests for sex. In return, the husband was obliged to financially support his wife, although he could determine the level of financial support he considered appropriate. The law granted husbands all decision-making authority in the family (Lindgren & Taub, 1993).

Nowadays, when we think of marriages, we think of partnerships, not exchanges. However, as we have already noted, marriages are still subject to government regulation, which defines the rights and responsibilities of spouses and specifies who may marry in terms of age, sex, and health requirements. There is tremendous variation among the fifty states as to the specific conditions of their marriage contracts, but most share several underlying assumptions, which bear some resemblance to marriage contracts historically. For example, most states continue to assume that the husband is the head of the family. Although a number of U.S. Supreme Court decisions during the 1970s and 1980s overturned state laws that impose the sex-based hierarchy in marriage implied by this assumption, rules remain in most states that imply a lesser status for women in marriage. For instance, in most states, the husband continues to retain the right to decide domicile (place of residence). In fact, in the majority of states, women are automatically assigned their husbands' domicile upon marriage, even if they live apart from their husbands because of their careers or to attend school. There are several consequences for a woman if her husband's domicile is different from her premarital domicile: She must reregister to vote; she may lose her right to attend a university in her own state as a resident student and, thus, have to pay higher tuition as an out-of-state student; and she may be unable to run for public office in her home state (Lindgren & Taub, 1993). Exceptions have been made by some courts and state legislatures, but most courts still do not recognize the right of married women to choose their own domicile.

Marital relations, then, are fundamentally power relations—usually the power of husbands over wives. As we saw in Chapter 1, power is essentially the ability to get others to do what we want them to do whether they want to do it or not. It is the ability to get one's own way. Again, however, many of us resist the idea of marriages as power struggles because we like to think that spouses are equal and if they disagree, they try to compromise. Does research support this view?

The answer to this question depends on how we measure power in marriage. Traditionally, sociologists measured marital power in terms of decision making. This strategy was developed in 1960 by Robert Blood and Donald Wolfe, who asked more than 900 wives who had the final say in such decisions as where to go on vacation, what car to buy, how much money to spend on food, where to live, and what doctor to consult. In general, their findings showed husbands to be more powerful than wives because they made most family decisions even though they usually talked matters over with their wives. Nevertheless, there were conditions under which this pattern varied. Blood and Wolfe found that the spouse who brought more "resources" to the marriage—for example, income, status, or education—was likely to be more powerful. Typically, this was the husband, but the greater a wife's resources, the more leverage she gained in decision making relative to her husband.

Although Blood and Wolfe's study was conducted nearly forty years ago, their findings have been substantiated by more recent research that has also found that, in most cases, the partner who earns more money tends to be the more powerful partner as measured by decision making. The more women earn relative to their husbands, the more power they accrue in the marriage; full-time homemakers, it seems, have little power (Blumstein & Schwartz, 1983). Nevertheless, there are also important exceptions. For instance, among couples who adhere to the belief that men should be the primary family breadwinners, husbands are more powerful regardless of either partner's earnings. The prevailing logic in such marriages is that if it is the man's role to be the family provider, then he should have the final say in most decisions (Thompson & Walker, 1989).

Pyke (1994) argues that a significant intervening variable in determining a couple's relative power in marriage is the *meaning* couples give to women's paid employment and unpaid household labor. For example, in her study of women in second marriages,

Pyke found that some women, upon remarriage, moved out of the paid labor force into the role of full-time homemaker, but simultaneously increased their marital power. This is because during their first marriages, the women were employed in low-paying, low-status jobs and the economic resources they brought to the marriage were devalued by their husbands. Their paid employment was not a source of marital power, but rather a source of exploitation and domination by their first husbands. They viewed their withdrawal from the labor market on remarriage as a sign of their greater marital power and of the increased support of their new spouses. The value their second husbands attached to their unpaid work in the home was evidenced in their husbands' expressions of gratitude for this work and by power-sharing between the partners.

Such findings alert us to the fact that there is more to marital power than we can discern just by asking questions about family decision making. For one thing, not all decisions carry equal weight; some are more significant in their consequences than others (Allan, 1985). In addition, power includes not only the authority to make decisions, but also the right to *delegate* responsibility for certain decisions to others (Blumstein & Schwartz, 1983). Finally, the old adage, "Actions speak louder than words" applies here. Some social practices are so taken-for-granted, so deeply embedded in ideology and family structure, that decisions do not have to be made about them; they are automatically carried out and rarely questioned (Allan, 1985).

Perhaps, then, we can learn more about power in heterosexual marriages by observing who *does* what—that is, the division of household labor—and who benefits from it, rather than asking who decides what. Let's consider the division of household labor among heterosexual couples.

Gender and Housework: Who Does What?   When it comes to housework, research consistently shows that wives spend more time on these chores than husbands do—as much as five times more hours per week, in fact (Shelton & John, 1993). Of course, this may not seem unfair if spouses are exchanging services according to the traditional marriage contract: She does the housework and he works in the paid labor force for their financial support. However, as we noted earlier in the chapter, this arrangement applies to only a small percentage of couples today. Most married women, like their husbands, are employed outside the home, and although husbands in two-earner families spend more time on housework than men who are sole breadwinners, they still do less than their wives. Husbands typically express a willingness to "help" their wives with the housework, but even among two-earner couples, the commonly held belief of both men and women is that housework is primarily "women's work" no matter what other demands wives have on their time (Shelton, 1992; Wilkie, 1993). Interestingly, men are less tolerant of gender inequality in the workplace than in their own homes (Kane & Sanchez, 1992). Consequently, employed wives end up working what sociologist Arlie Hochschild (1989) calls the "second shift": They are wage earners for part of the day and then come home to still more, albeit unpaid, work.

In fact, if you ask full-time homemakers what kind of work they do, they typically reply, "I don't work; I'm a housewife." What is so striking in such a response is that despite the fact that housework is socially and economically necessary work, it is not considered real work, not even by the women who have primary responsibility for doing it. One reason housework is not considered real work is that it is unspecialized, covering by some estimates more than eighty different tasks. It is also repetitive in that, in a sense, it is never fully finished: No sooner is a chore completed than it must be done again. This is because housework involves production for immediate consumption.

Another reason housework is not thought of as "real" work is that unlike work in the paid labor force, there is no fixed work schedule for housework. Homemakers rarely get time off, not even holidays—who, for instance, cooks those large holiday meals? Housework also differs from what we usually think of as "real" work in that it is intertwined with love and feelings of care. It is also privatized. We see people leaving their houses *to go to work;* we see them in public on the job. But housework is done in isolation in the home, and much of it is done when other family members are elsewhere (e.g., in the labor force or at school). And of course, one of the main reasons housework is not considered "real" work is that it is *unpaid.* In a society such as ours, individuals' status—how much people are valued by others as well as by themselves—often is measured by how much money they make.

Usually, when complaints about doing housework are raised, someone quickly points out how much easier it is today than in the past; after all, contemporary homemakers have so many labor-saving appliances at their disposal. Interestingly, however, research indicates that today's homemaker spends about as much time on household chores as a homemaker in the 1790s did (Cowan, 1984; Ogden, 1986). This is due in part to the fact that over the past two hundred years, as our standard of living has risen dramatically, so have our expectations of comfort and cleanliness at home. In addition, the average house is larger than it was two centuries ago, so there are more rooms to clean, and these rooms are filled with many more personal possessions.

Our intent here is not to romanticize the past, nor to suggest that homemakers would be better off if we turned back the clock. Rather, our point is that housework, despite technological advances and modern convenience, continues to be arduous and time-consuming work, and in most households, more of women's time than men's time is consumed by it.

Apart from the amount of time wives and husbands spend on housework, there are also differences in the kind of work they do around the house. Wives usually do most of the daily chores, such as cleaning and cooking. Men do less regular and less repetitive chores. So, for example, most wives prepare their families' meals, which must be done at least once or twice a day, every day. Husbands, though, usually mow the lawn and make minor repairs around the house, chores that need to be done only occasionally. Wives experience more time constraints because of the types of household chores they do, whereas husbands have more control over when they will do their chores (Hochschild, 1989; Shelton, 1992). Working the "second shift" means that wives have less leisure time. Wives also must balance home and employment responsibilities in ways that most husbands are not required to do. Husbands' relative freedom from housework lets them pursue employment opportunities, while wives may face restrictions on their employment opportunities because of their household responsibilities (Shelton, 1992; but for a different view, see Hochschild, 1997).

There is no denying that many couples today do strive to be more egalitarian, especially early on in their marriages, with a more equal division of labor between spouses. However, even couples who wish to be egalitarian often find that their effort toward an equal division of labor breaks down when they become parents. Let's consider, then, the caregiving responsibilities of two-parent, heterosexual families.

Caregiving. Despite the widespread belief that the birth of a child brings marriage partners closer together, sociologists as well as marriage and family counselors have learned that the addition of children to a household increases stress and lowers marital satisfaction (Cox, 1985; Larson, 1988). This observation is not really so puzzling. Although new parents are typically excited about the birth of their baby, they are rarely prepared for the level of disruption that a baby causes in their lives. For example, their sleep is frequently interrupted and lessened. There is, by necessity, less spontaneity in the relationship and less time to pursue outside interests. Financial pressures increase, as do household chores, and as the couple becomes immersed in parental roles, the partner/lover roles get squeezed out (Cowan & Cowan, 1992).

Nevertheless, these stresses do not affect mothers and fathers equally. Although most men today are present at the birth of their children, they typically are significantly less involved than women in primary child care (e.g., bathing, changing clothes, feeding). Although men's involvement in child care has increased during the past twenty-five years, especially in households in which both spouses are employed, evidence indicates that the so-called "new fathers," who are as involved as their wives in the care of their children, are still relatively rare (DeVault, 1991; Snarey, 1993; Walzer, 1996).

In general, research shows that fathers tend to be least involved in primary child care when their children are infants. They become more involved when the children are around eighteen months old and walking and talking. Their greatest level of involvement occurs during the middle childhood period, when the children are five to fifteen years old. Even then, the time fathers spend with their children is more oriented to recreation or academics—playing, reading to them, teaching them something, coaching them—than to primary caregiving (Snarey, 1993; Thompson & Walker, 1989). Mothers, even those who are employed full-time, still provide the majority of primary care of their children in addition to caring for their husbands and their homes. Studies show that the pattern is consistently found in relatively egalitarian households as well as in traditional ones. In fact, even in households where husbands report that they and their wives share tasks equally, observations of their behavior and their own words contradict them. Their wives usually must ask them to help and tell them specifically what to do (Walzer, 1996). Not only do women do more of the primary child care, but they also do more of the "mental work"—worrying, seeking advice and information—involved in rearing children (Walzer, 1996).

Some men say they would welcome greater involvement in the care of their children, but that their chief responsibility as a husband/father is as breadwinner and the structure of work in our society makes it difficult, if not impossible, for them to do more at home (Shelton, 1992; Snarey, 1993; Walzer, 1996; Weisner et al., 1994). As we discuss in Chapter 7, the occupational structure of our society has traditionally operated under the assumption that men are the economic providers of families and women are the caretakers. Men are expected to invest time and energy in their jobs; women are expected to do so in their families. So even though the federal Family and Medical Leave Act now requires companies with more than fifty employees to provide women *and* men with up to twelve weeks unpaid family leave with no loss of seniority, many employers still say that male employees should not take family leave (Chira, 1993). Indeed, if one accepts the traditional gendered model of employment and parenting, there is no need for family leave, childcare facilities, or equal pay for women and men.

Recent research has shown that men who hold white-collar professional, technical, and managerial positions are more likely than men in municipal and service jobs to be subjected to this sort of pressure. Men in lower-paid, blue-collar jobs have greater flexibility in their work schedules. Because of economic necessity, most of their wives also work outside the home, many in municipal and service jobs, too. These couples are less likely than white-collar professional couples to be able to afford paid child care, so the men have assumed a greater share of this responsibility. According to the U.S. Bureau of the Census, about 25 percent of fathers of children under age five living in two-earner families care for the children while their wives are working. However, 42 percent of fathers with service jobs provide this care compared with about 20 percent of white-collar professional and managerial fathers (Lawlor, 1998). One study found that working fathers of children under eighteen spent about 2.3 hours each working day with those children (up from 1.8 hours in 1977), while mothers spent 3.0 hours (down from 3.3 hours in 1977). On non-workdays, fathers spent about 6.4 hours with the children (up from 5.2 hours in 1977), while mothers spent 8.3 hours (up from 7.3 hours in 1977). Despite the increase in fathers' involvement, 56 percent of the working mothers in this study said they wished the fathers spent more time with the children (Bond et al., 1998).

This gendered division of caregiving has advantages and disadvantages for both women and men. On the one hand, women reap the benefits of developing close bonds with their children and of watching and contributing to their children's growth and development. These are experiences that most mothers find gratifying and emotionally fulfilling. At the same time, through their ties to their children and to their own parents and siblings, women are also *kinkeepers* in families; that is, they link the generations within the families and therefore are instrumental in preserving family cohesion. Kranichfeld (1987, p. 48) has identified this kinkeeping role as a source of family power in that as kinkeepers, "women do not just change the behavior of others, they shape whole generations of families" (see also Collins, 1990; Stacey, 1990).

This almost exclusive responsibility for caregiving denies women much personal autonomy, however. Housework can at least be postponed, but a child's needs must be met immediately. Child rearing, then, imposes severe limits on a mother's time and ability to pursue other interests, such as paid employment (Walzer, 1996). Fathers who have assumed an equal or near-equal role in child care have been quick to recognize these time constraints and the frustration they can entail (Lawlor, 1998).

The kinkeeper role can also be very stressful. For instance, women's midlife options may be constrained because their adult children need assistance with their own households or families or because elderly parents need care (Gerson et al., 1984). Ninety-five percent of the elderly and 90 percent of the disabled elderly live at home and rely on family members to provide virtually all of their care. Women traditionally have been the majority of caregivers to elderly family members. More than half of these women are between the ages of thirty-five and sixty-four, with a median age of forty-five. More important perhaps, 42 percent of them are employed full time, and an additional 13 percent are employed part time; 39 percent still have their own children in their households. This responsibility adds significantly to women's caregiving burden. As one study pointed out, women now spend an average of seventeen years of their lives caring for their children and eighteen years assisting their elderly parents (Montgomery & Datwyler, 1990; Older Women's League, 1989). At least one recent study, however, has found that men are assuming more responsibility for elder care, too. According to Bond and colleagues (1998) as many employed men as employed women (over one-third) report cutting back their work hours to care for an elderly relative.

Nevertheless, the research indicates that most men still escape many of the burdens of family care. They are relieved of the drudgery and the time constraints so that they may join the labor force to financially support their families. But if men have more freedom to give their time and energy to their jobs, the trade-off is social and emotional distance from their children. One study reported that 50 percent of the preschoolers questioned said that they would rather watch television than be with their fathers. Among seven- to eleven-year-olds, one in ten told researchers that their father is the person they fear the most (Pogrebin, 1982). Although we are speaking here of intact two-parent families, there is a sense in which such families are "father-absent." The loss for men can perhaps best be found in the words of fathers who have taken responsibility for the care of their children. These men say that child care has made them more sensitive, less self-centered, and more complete as human beings (Coltrane, 1989; Greif, 1985; Lawlor, 1998; Levine, 1997; Snarey, 1993).

Single-Parent Families

The issue of shared parenting is irrelevant in single-parent families, where only one parent is present to meet all the children's needs. Although the percentage of dependent children living only with their fathers has more than doubled since 1970, 86 percent of children living in single-parent households live with their mothers only: 83 percent of White children in single-parent families, 92 percent of African American children in single-parent families, and 88 percent of Latino children in single-parent families (U.S. Department of Commerce, Bureau of the Census, 1997).

The number of single-parent families has increased dramatically over the last two decades, rising from 13 percent of families with dependent children in 1970, to 29 percent of families with dependent children in 1993 (U.S. Department of Commerce, Bureau of the Census, 1997). Part of the increase reflects the growing number of women who have children, but remain unmarried. In 1970, unmarried mothers were only 0.8 percent of families with dependent children, but in 1996, they were almost 10 percent. Some of these women had children as a result of unintended or unwanted pregnancies, and many of these women (about 30 percent) are teenagers (U.S. Department of Commerce, Bureau of the Census, 1997). Some, however, are well-educated, gainfully employed, financially secure heterosexual or lesbian women who use one of the NRTs we discussed earlier, adopt a child, or choose to have a child but not marry the father. For these women, single parenthood represents a viable alternative to marriage because they have the financial resources, but they must still juggle career and caregiving responsibilities like married women do (Miller, 1992).

Both women and men may become single parents by being widowed, although the percentage of single-parent families in which the parent is widowed has declined since 1970. The most common way women and men become single parents is through divorce. Today, 50 percent of couples divorce within 7.2 years of pronouncing their wedding vows (U.S. Department of Commerce, Bureau of the Census, 1997).

Before the Industrial Revolution, fathers were usually awarded legal custody of their children, not only because they had the economic means to support them, but also because children were considered their father's property and the father was entitled to any products of their labor during their minority. As the Industrial Revolution progressed and production and education moved away from home, dominant ideas about childhood changed. Instead of being viewed as miniature adults, children came to be seen as helpless dependents in need of nurturing. Child-rearing experts advised that mothers were better caregivers than fathers. By the turn of the twentieth century, the courts had adopted the *tender years presumption*—the idea that a young child needs to be with his or her mother—which produced a dramatic shift in custody decisions in favor of mothers and against fathers (Lindgren & Taub, 1993). Today, although most courts favor joint custody awards that give both parents equal decision-making authority in rearing their children, the mother is still more likely to be awarded physical custody. Nevertheless, many joint custody arrangements include joint physical custody of the children, in which, if possible, the children spend equal amounts of time living in the home of each of their parents. There is little research on the impact of joint custody on either parents or children, but some analysts say that the arrangement works best if divorced parents are able to maintain a high level of cooperation with one another and live near each other so the children's schooling is not disrupted. It is also important that both agree to joint custody rather than having it imposed by the courts (Lindgren & Taub, 1993).

Researchers have found that the single-parenting experiences of men and women are different. For one thing, single fathers are more likely than single mothers to be well-educated, employed full time, and at least middle class. As a result, financial difficulty is not one of their common complaints about rearing children alone (although it may be of solo fathers who are widowed). In addition, single fathers usually receive considerable support from friends, relatives, and neighbors, who view them as somewhat extraordinary for parenting alone, but as needy when it comes to handling housework, cooking, and childcare (Teltsch, 1992). In fact, single fathers' most frequent complaints are that others treat them as incompetent parents (for example, teachers may ask to meet with their ex-wives instead of them) and they feel their social lives and careers are restricted because of the demands of parenting (Greif, 1985; Hanson, 1988).

Single mothers, however, tend to receive less support from others, and many report feeling isolated (Kamerman & Kahn, 1988). Most single mothers, like single fathers, struggle to fulfill employment responsibilities without sacrificing the well-being of their children. Some of these women face career dilemmas that are similar to those of single fathers, but because women are less likely than men to have high-status, high-income jobs (see Chapter 7), their employment constraints are more often inflexible work schedules, inadequate salaries, and unaffordable or inadequate childcare facilities. Simply finding a job may be difficult for a single mother, particularly if she has been out of the labor force for a number of years and has little work experience, or has little education and few marketable skills. Not surprisingly, then, the biggest problem of most single mothers is money (Holden & Smock, 1991; Kurz, 1995; Quinn & Allen, 1989).

Table 6.1 gives us a good indication of the financial problems of single-parent, female-headed families. Here we see that the median income of married-couple families is more than $17,000 greater than single-parent, male-headed families, but more than double that of single-parent, female-headed families. Moreover, Table 6.1 shows that the financial resources of minority single-parent, female-headed families are even more limited. More than 50 percent of children in single-parent, female-headed families are living in poverty (U.S. Department of Commerce, Bureau of the Census, 1997).

Some observers blame no-fault divorce laws for the poverty of female-headed households. Under no-fault statutes, either husband or wife may file for divorce on the grounds of "irreconcilable differences" and, unlike traditional divorce laws, neither has to prove that the other is to blame for the failure of the marriage. The elimination of fault has made divorce somewhat easier and maybe a bit less painful, but what worries some analysts is that it has also changed the economic outcome. Prior to no-fault divorce, the wronged or offended spouse—usually the wife—was compensated. Now, financial awards, such as alimony and child support, are determined primarily by need, by the spouse's ability to work and be self-supporting, and by the spouse's relative ability to pay. Alimony awards, in particular, are frowned on by the courts. In short, the courts try to treat divorcing husbands and wives as equals, even though, in reality, they rarely are equals, especially financially (Becker et al., 1994; Lindgren & Taub, 1993).

Researchers tell us that women, not men, are hurt economically by no-fault divorce, and because they are most likely to have custody of their children, the children also suffer the economic consequences. How do no-fault settlements add up in dollars and cents? One researcher found that within the first year after a divorce, women and their dependent children suffer a 73 percent drop in their standard of living, while men

TABLE 6.1 Median Family Income by Type of Family and Race/Ethnicity, 1994

Type of Family	Median Income ($)			
	All Families	White	Black	Hispanic
Married couple families	44,959	45,474	40,432	29,621
Wife in paid labor force	53,309	53,977	47,235	38,559
Wife not in paid labor force	31,176	31,747	25,396	20,676
Male householder, wife absent	27,751	29,460	20,977	21,787
Female householder, husband absent	18,236	20,795	13,943	12,117

Source: U.S. Department of Commerce, Bureau of the Census, 1997, p. 471.

enjoy a 42 percent rise (Weitzman, 1985). Others estimate the decline in income for women following divorce to be between 30 percent and 50 percent (Holden & Smock, 1991). One reason for this decline is that women's salaries, even if they work full time, are rarely equal to men's salaries. If a woman has been out of the labor force for an extended period of time, her ability to support herself and her children will be further impaired. Adding to the financial problems of divorce for women and children is the fact that in dividing marital property, the courts usually consider only tangible assets, such as the family's house, car(s), and furniture. Given that most divorcing couples have mortgages and other debts, by the time the bills are paid, there may be little left to divide. The equal division of property may even force the sale of the family home. However, there are other types of assets—for example, pensions and retirement benefits, licenses to practice a profession, medical insurance, or the value of a business—that only infrequently figure into property settlements. This means that one spouse (usually the husband) retains control of some of the family's most valuable assets (Becker et al., 1994; Lindgren & Taub, 1993).

Researchers also blame inadequate child support laws and lack of enforcement of these laws for contributing to the poverty of female-headed households (Jacob, 1989; Kamerman & Kahn, 1988). Child support payments usually do little to offset the financial decline that women and children experience after divorce. For one thing, just slightly more than half (56 percent) of divorced mothers are awarded child support by the courts. Second, average awards are relatively small—less than $3,000 per year—representing less than 12 percent of the average earnings of men aged twenty-five and older. Even among those who are awarded child support, about 24 percent never actually receive a payment and an additional 24 percent receive only partial payment (Children's Defense Fund, 1997; Kurz, 1995; U.S. Department of Commerce, Bureau of the Census, 1997). Despite the fact that the federal government has teamed up with state governments to implement a child support enforcement program, research indicates that there has been little overall improvement in compliance with child support orders (Children's Defense Fund, 1997).

Some analysts believe that both no-fault divorce and lack of child support enforcement are major contributing factors to the *feminization of poverty*, that is, the increasing percentage of the total poverty population composed of women and their children (see Chapter 7). Swelling the ranks of the poverty population are the *new poor:* people, many of whom are women, who were not born into poverty but who have been forced into it by recent events in their lives. According to researchers, a change in family composition, such as separation, divorce, marriage, remarriage, or becoming a parent, is the single most important factor affecting the economic well-being of families; the second most important factor is the labor market participation of family members, that is, who works outside the home (Holden & Smock, 1991; Kamerman & Kahn, 1988). Consequently, Bane (1986) refers to the poverty of many recently divorced women and their children as *event-driven poverty.*

The feminization of poverty and the concept of the new poor are important for understanding the consequences of gender inequality in marriage and divorce. Nevertheless, these concepts have been criticized for being both color-blind and class-blind. There are important economic differences among female-headed households of different social classes, races, and ethnicities. Upper middle-class and wealthy women who divorce may experience a drop in income and standard of living, but they are more likely than lower middle-class, working-class, and already poor women to own property and other assets independent of their husbands and to have the skills and educational background to help them to continue to live comfortably. We need only revisit Table 6.1 to see the economic differences between White and non-White female-headed households. Consequently, the poverty experienced by non-White women and their children after divorce is likely to be what Bane calls *reshuffled poverty*. In other words, poor families dissolve and the women and children form new, but still poor families. "Reshuffled poverty as opposed to event-caused poverty for [racial and ethnic minorities] challenges the assumption that changes in family structure have created ghetto poverty. This underscores the importance of considering the ways that race produces different paths to poverty" (Bane, 1986, p. 277).

Sociologists and others have traditionally equated female-headed families in general, and minority female-headed families in particular, with pathology (Smith, 1993). The female-headed family has been seen as a cause of not only poverty, but also a variety of other social problems, including juvenile delinquency, drug abuse, and alcoholism. This view, which also informs much of the debate over welfare "reform," holds that it is the "deviant" subcultural values of racial and ethnic minorities that cause the high percentage of female-headed families in these groups. But research has failed to uncover anything inherently "pathological" or "abnormal" in the female-headed family structure. In fact, researchers have argued that the Black female-headed family has historically been a source of strength and resistance to oppression (Collins, 1990; Height, 1989; Jewell, 1988; Ladner, 1971; McAdoo, 1986). If we are going to understand and help solve the problems of single-parent families, then, we have to take into account how gender inequality intersects with social class and racial and ethnic inequalities. The kinds and levels of stress experienced by single-parent families, and the families' methods and chances of success in dealing with them, are strongly influenced by these factors (Brewer, 1988; Jayakody & Chatters, 1997; McAdoo, 1986; Neighbors, 1997).

Intertwined with the financial consequences of divorce are the emotional consequences. As in the financial consequences of divorce, the emotional consequences differ for women and men. However, analyses of gender differences in the divorce experience are complicated by several factors. First, a person's feelings are likely to vary depending on who initiated the divorce and the reasons underlying the divorce. Feelings also change during the divorce process. For example, research indicates that for a majority of women, the most difficult emotional period occurs prior to the couple's separation. During this time, many women try hard to hold the marriage together, whereas men show a much lower level of awareness of marital difficulties. Following separation and divorce, though, women generally adjust better than men, a point to which we will return shortly (Diedrick, 1991).

A second problem in identifying gender differences in the divorce experience is that many studies use large aggregate samples, but the relative impact of divorce on the divorcing partners varies across subgroups of women and men. Research indicates that those who experience the greatest difficulty in adjusting to divorce are women with dependent children, especially those with children under six years old (Maudlin, 1991). These women experience higher levels of depression than childless women or women with grown children, and this depression is often related to their financial circumstances.[4] In fact, one of the best predictors of the relative well-being of divorced wives and husbands is the economic independence of the individual spouses (Holden & Smock, 1991). It is not surprising, therefore, that divorced women who are middle-aged, with a professional career, and either childless or without dependent children exhibit the highest level of post-divorce well-being (Gross, 1992).

Race and ethnicity also intersect with gender to influence individuals' adjustment during and after divorce. For example, Song (1991) points out that Asian-American women who strongly identify with their traditional ethnic community experience serious difficulty adjusting to divorce. This difficulty is an outgrowth of traditional Asian gender norms that label adult women who are unattached to men as "social nonpersons." These women may receive little emotional and financial support from others because they are blamed for the failure of their marriages. They also often become socially dislocated from community activities and friendships because other married women see them as potential seducers of their husbands, and married men worry that the behavior of these women might encourage their wives to divorce. It is not surprising, then, that these women tend to experience severe depression and other forms of distress following divorce (Song, 1991).

Although men almost always fare better than women economically following divorce, they often do not do as well emotionally or psychologically. One indication of this is the higher remarriage rate of divorced men compared with that of divorced women. Although women's best chances of improving their financial status after divorce is to remarry, they are more reluctant to do so than divorced men are. The remarriage rates of both divorced men and women have declined since 1970, but divorced men are about one and a half times more likely to remarry than divorced women (Gross, 1992; U.S. Department of Commerce, Bureau of the Census, 1997). Some men remarry rather quickly after they divorce; indeed, a relationship with another woman may have been the reason for the divorce. In addition, because divorced men are less likely to have custody of their children, it is easier for them to participate in social activities where they may meet potential remarriage partners. It is also the case that because of traditional gender norms in our society, men have more to gain from remarriage than women do. For instance, given the typical division of household labor in heterosexual marriages, one benefit of remarriage for men should be obvious. As one divorced man stated in a recent interview, what he missed most about marriage was "having a wife to 'keep the social life running' and to tend to 'certain little touches' that make a house a home" (quoted in Gross, 1992, p. A14). It is also the case that husbands are more likely than wives to rely on their spouses as their sole confidants (see Chapter 11).[5]

As Box 6.1 on page 174 shows, many of the findings on adjustment to widowhood parallel those obtained in the divorce research. Let's turn now to a discussion of other types of families and intimate relationships.

Singles and Domestic Partnerships

When we think of singles, most of us probably think of young heterosexual women and men who have not yet married. However, the single population in the United States is far more diverse. In addition to never-married heterosexuals, the single population

BOX **6.1**

Gender Differences in Adjusting to Widowhood

Psychologists tell us that the death of one's spouse is one of life's most emotionally traumatic experiences. Research shows, however, that women and men adjust differently to widowhood.

A crucial determinant of well-being for those who are widowed is the economic status of the individual spouses. Men are far less likely than women to experience financial difficulties during widowhood, primarily because men traditionally have had longer and more stable employment histories than women, earn more on average than women do, and are more likely than women to be employed in occupations that carry benefits such as pensions (Holden & Smock, 1991; see also Chapter 7). But not all women experience negative financial consequences from being widowed. Women who had low incomes before widowhood are likely to sink further into poverty after their husbands die. Since non-White couples are at greater risk of living in poverty, becoming a widow is more likely to have a detrimental economic impact on women of color (Davis et al., 1990; Holden & Smock, 1991).

As we will see in Chapter 11, men have higher mortality rates than women, even at middle age, so the majority of those widowed are women. In fact, widowed women outnumber widowed men five to one. Similar to those who divorce, widowed men are more likely to remarry than widowed women. For one thing, widowed men have a larger pool of potential partners available to them, especially since men often marry women who are several years younger than themselves. Second, men who are widowed, like men who are divorced, have more to gain from remarriage in terms of having their daily household needs met (Bedard, 1992). Many women —especially those who have established careers,

individual identities, and financial independence —do not find widowhood debilitating. This is not to say that they do not experience tremendous sorrow when their husbands die. Rather, it appears that widowed women adjust better to life alone than widowed men, particularly if they have been involved in activities outside the marriage and are financially secure (Nemy, 1992).

Unfortunately, many married couples do not have adequate life insurance or personal savings to guarantee financial security in widowhood, and Social Security and other government assistance programs, though helpful, are not sufficient. Consequently, widowhood doubles the poverty rate of women and substantially lowers women's standard of living in most socioeconomic groups (Holden & Smock, 1991). Young widows without children often experience the greatest financial difficulties, since they typically have little financial protection. They are not eligible for Social Security, and although their husbands may have had pensions at work, they may not have worked long enough to be vested. Moreover, some pensions do not pay benefits to the widow until the year in which her deceased husband would have been eligible for retirement benefits. Most young couples have little or no savings, and few have mortgage insurance that pays for their home if one spouse dies. Even though younger women are more likely than older women to have income from their own jobs, their salaries may not be sufficient to meet all the expenses that were incurred during the marriage. Still, while young widows, like older widows, experience a significant decline in their standard of living immediately following their husbands' deaths, their long-term prospects for improved financial circumstances are better than those of older widows (Holden & Smock, 1991).

includes gay men and lesbians who are not involved in a committed relationship; women and men, heterosexual and homosexual, who are not married but living with an intimate partner in what is called a *domestic partnership;* and separated, divorced, and widowed women and men with or without dependent children. We have already discussed divorce, widowhood, and single parenting, so let's look now at heterosexual and homosexual never-married singles and domestic partners.

Heterosexual Singles and Domestic Partners.   There are several common stereotypes about never-married heterosexuals. One stereotype is the swinging bachelor who "plays the field" and cherishes his independence. Another is the unmarried woman or "old maid," who struggles with loneliness and is desperate to find a man to marry before her "biological clock" stops ticking. Of course, in this case like most others, real life is quite different from stereotypes.

For most heterosexual young adults, singlehood is a temporary status. The vast majority eventually marry, but they are delaying marriage longer than in the past. In 1970, for example, the median age at first marriage was 20.6 for women and 22.5 for men; by 1990, it was 24.0 for women and 25.9 for men. However, the number of people who have never married has increased across all age groups, rising from 18.9 percent of males in 1970 to 26.8 percent in 1996 and from 13.7 percent of females to 19.9 percent during the same period (U.S. Department of Commerce, Bureau of the Census, 1997).

Singles delay and postpone marriage for several reasons, including more positive social attitudes toward singlehood; greater reluctance to marry given high divorce rates and growing awareness of domestic violence; and more widespread use of contraceptives, which means fewer marriages because of unwanted pregnancies. However, one of the most important reasons young adults give for delaying marriage is financial constraints (Bedard, 1992). For many young adults, delaying marriage is an economic necessity. Over the past three decades, there was a decline in the number of jobs that pay a wage adequate to establish an independent household, and unemployment rates were high. Housing prices have also increased substantially, with the median price of new and existing single-family homes more than doubling since 1980. Consequently, in contrast to the image of the swinging single's "pad," a substantial percentage of young adults—53 percent of those aged eighteen to twenty-four and 12 percent of those aged twenty-five to thirty-four—are living with their parents (U.S. Department of Commerce, Bureau of the Census, 1997). Between 1990 and 1996, marriage rates in the United States declined by 10 percent. In 1997, marriage rates went up by 3 percent, the largest increase since the 1970s. Sociologists attributed the increase to the strength of the economy, particularly the fact that the unemployment rate was the lowest it had been in ten years. Nevertheless, a recent survey of 9,100 college students found that although most expect to marry some day, their primary concern at present is finishing their education, establishing themselves in a professional career, and paying off debts. They appear to be rejecting long-term committed relationships, temporarily at least, in favor of casual short-term partnering (Levine & Cureton, 1998).

Some people also have difficulty finding a suitable marriage partner. Women and men who are physically or mentally disabled, for example, need intimacy and sexual gratification the same as other people, but their needs may go unfulfilled because others see them as unattractive or sexless (Hall, 1992; Kelly, 1995). African American women face some difficulty finding marriage partners for several reasons. One reason is the high mortality rate of young African American men (see Chapter 11). The death rate of

African American men aged fifteen to twenty-four is 693 per 100,000, whereas for White men the same age, the death rate is 308 per 100,000 (U.S. Department of Health, National Center for Health Statistics, 1998). A second reason is the disproportionate number of young African American men who are in prison. Although African American men make up only about 6 percent of the U.S. population, they are nearly 47 percent of the prison population (U.S. Department of Justice, Bureau of Justice Statistics, 1996; see also Chapter 8). A third reason fewer African American than White women marry is that African American men have poorer economic prospects, which make them less desirable partners (Lloyd & South, 1996; Tucker & Mitchell-Kernan, 1995; Wilson, 1987).

Instead of marrying, some heterosexual singles choose a domestic partnership, which we defined earlier as a cohabiting relationship between intimate partners not married to each other. Domestic partnerships appear to be an increasingly appealing lifestyle choice. In 1996, there were nearly 4 million unmarried heterosexual couples living together in the United States, an increase of more than 2 million since 1980 and more than 3 million since 1970 (U.S. Department of Commerce, Bureau of the Census, 1997). The actual number of couples is still small—just over 6 percent of all couples—compared with the number of married couples and the number of domestic partnerships in countries such as Sweden and Norway, where 12 percent of heterosexual couples live in domestic partnerships (Blanc, 1987; Kammeyer, 1987). Still, the increase over the past thirty years has been substantial, and the current number is probably an undercount, since many people do not report their cohabitation status to census takers and some partners maintain separate addresses even though they live together (Bedard, 1992).

What we know about heterosexual domestic partnerships is limited by the fact that most research has focused on college students or other young people, even though only 20.1 percent of domestic partners are couples under twenty-five years old. Most domestic partners (58.5 percent) are aged twenty-five to forty-four (U.S. Department of Commerce, Bureau of the Census, 1997). Domestic partnerships are likely to be different for couples at different stages of life, but sociologists have identified several trends that characterize most domestic partnerships.

First, researchers have found that most domestic partnerships are relatively short, typically lasting two years or less (Bumpass & Sweet, 1991; London, 1991). Within this time, most domestic partners either break up or marry; very few adopt cohabitation as a permanent lifestyle. Second, most heterosexual domestic partners are childless, although either partner may have children from a previous marriage. Only 36 percent of domestic partners have children under fifteen years old living with them (U.S. Department of Commerce, Bureau of the Census, 1994). It appears that when domestic partners want to add children to their household, they typically decide to marry first (Blumstein & Schwartz, 1983). Third, most domestic partners (56 percent) have never been married, and many have divorced parents (U.S. Department of Commerce, Bureau of the Census, 1991). Young adults whose parents are divorced express greater support for cohabitation than those whose parents are married (Black & Sprenkle, 1991).

Some local governments allow domestic partners to officially register their relationships, but in most cases registration has little legal significance. Many attorneys advise domestic partners to draw up contracts, but some courts have been reluctant to enforce them because they see the agreements as potentially undermining the institution of marriage. Other court rulings have been inconsistent. Consequently, if a domestic partnership breaks up, one partner may lose out financially, or a battle may ensue over the division of assets. Even if the relationship endures, other difficulties may surface. For instance, if one partner becomes ill, that partner's family may shut out the mate, preventing him or her from participating in decisions about the partner's care, or they may even bar the mate from hospital visits. In addition, if one partner dies without a will, his or her property may be inherited by family members instead of the mate (Rankin, 1987).

Although heterosexual domestic partners sometimes confront these problems, they at least have the option to legally marry. Gay and lesbian partners do not have that option; for them the dilemmas posed by domestic partnerships in general are often made worse by the social stigma attached to gay and lesbian relationships.

Gay and Lesbian Singles and Domestic Partners.   There is no way to precisely determine how many lesbians and gay men live in the United States. Because of the social stigma attached to homosexuality, many hide or "closet" their sexual orientation at least from some people or in certain situations, such as at work. Sexual orientation is usually measured through survey questions that ask about a person's sexual partners over a given period of time (e.g., within the past year, the past three years, or the past ten years). Given the extent of homophobia in our society, it is not surprising that gay men and lesbians would be reluctant to disclose their sexual orientation when asked by strangers in interviews or on questionnaires (Robson, 1992).

A second difficulty in determining the size of the nonheterosexual population derives from how we have traditionally conceptualized sexual orientation. We tend to think of sexual orientation the way we think of sex and gender: in dichotomous terms (that is, one is *either* heterosexual *or* homosexual). However, research conducted over many years indicates that sexuality is far more diverse and fluid. For one thing, there are individuals who are sexually and affectionally attracted to both women and men. Such individuals are *bisexual*, and they may express their sexual orientation in various ways. For example, bisexuals may have sexual relationships with women and men simultaneously, or their relationships may be sequential (at one time, with someone of the same sex; at another time, with someone of the opposite sex) (Kelly, 1995; Tucker, 1995).

Research also shows that a sizable percentage of the population that self-identifies as heterosexual reports having engaged in sexual activities with someone of the same sex, and many self-identified homosexuals report having had sex with someone of the opposite sex. However, more people express sexual attraction to members of their same sex or both sexes than apparently act on that attraction (Laumann et al., 1994). And people may change their sexual behavior throughout their lives, making it difficult at best to pin specific sexual orientation labels on them (Michael et al., 1994). In fact, the longer the time period researchers ask about in their surveys, the less likely the respondent is to be exclusively homosexual or heterosexual.

Not surprisingly, then, the size of the homosexual population is a controversial issue. The surveys, with all their methodological problems, indicate that only a small percentage of the population self-identifies as exclusively homosexual. Since the 1940s, the accepted figure was 10 percent, although some reports place the estimate as high as 20 percent. Research in the 1990s placed the figure considerably lower—in some studies as low as 1 percent, in others as high as 5 percent, but in most slightly above 3 percent for women and 4 percent for men (Barringer, 1993; Blum, 1997). Research in Great Britain and France shows similar findings (Waite, 1992).

Regardless of the numbers, accurate knowledge and genuine appreciation of gay and lesbian relationships are still goals rather than achievements largely because social science research itself has traditionally been heterosexist and homophobic. Much of what was written before the 1960s was written by heterosexuals and discussed from a psychoanalytic or psychiatric perspective, which until recently assumed that homosexuality is pathological and that homosexuals are "sick" or "abnormal" (Krieger, 1982). A lot of the research that is now being done on gay and lesbian relationships is conducted by gay and lesbian social scientists, and the findings indicate that there is as much diversity as there is among heterosexual men and women. In other word, there is no "homosexual lifestyle."

The results of this research also refute many other common myths about gay and lesbian relationships. For example, it is widely believed that gays and lesbians are sexually promiscuous and unable or unwilling to form committed intimate relationships. However, studies show that although gay men do have more partners on average than straight men, most also establish enduring intimate relationships (Kelly, 1995; Meredith, 1986). Research even indicates that lesbian couples generally have more stable relationships than either heterosexual couples or gay male couples (Blumstein & Schwartz, 1983). However, just as there is no distinct homosexual lifestyle, there is also no distinct homosexual value orientation toward love relationships. Instead, what appears to be more important than sexual orientation is one's sex—being male or female—and one's background. "Women's goals in intimate partnerships are similar whether the partner is male or female. The same is true of men" (Peplau, 1986, p. 118). Women typically place a higher value on emotional expressiveness in their intimate relationships (see also Blum, 1997). In gay male relationships, but even more so in lesbian relationships, equality between partners is also highly valued (Peplau, 1986). This is not to say that egalitarianism is always achieved in these relationships (see, for example, Caldwell & Peplau, 1984; Renzetti, 1992), but a significantly higher percentage of lesbians than heterosexual women report being treated as equals by their intimate partners (Hite, 1987).

Some researchers feel that gay and lesbian relationships are held to a higher standard than heterosexual relationships. After all, about half of all heterosexual marriages end in divorce within seven years, a statistic that hardly indicates relationship stability. In contrast, sociologist Kath Weston (1991) found in her research on gay and lesbian families that when gay and lesbian partners break up, they frequently maintain a close relationship with one another by making a transition from being lovers to being friends. Consequently, Weston argues, "one could make a good case that gay relationships endure longer on average than ties established through heterosexual marriage. If two people cease being lovers after six years but remain friends and family for another forty, they have indeed achieved a relationship of long standing" (p. 120). What is perhaps surprising to many observers is that gay and lesbian relationships can be so longlasting, given how destructive the discrimination against them must be.

Attitudes toward homosexuality have changed in recent years, and much of this change is a direct result of gay and lesbian rights activism (see Box 6.2 on page 180). However, studies indicate that most people in our society still consider homosexuality deviant or abnormal. Prejudice against gays and lesbians appears to be especially strong among middle-class people living in suburbia (Wolfe, 1998) and among men (Blum, 1997). These attitudes are tempered somewhat by beliefs that homosexuality is inborn, rather than chosen. Those who believe homosexuality is biologically determined—that homosexuals do not freely choose their sexual orientation—tend to support more civil rights and legal protections for gays and lesbians (Blum, 1997; Wolfe, 1998). Young people appear to be more liberal in their attitudes toward homosexuality than older adults. For instance, 33.5 percent of college students questioned in a national survey in 1996 favored laws prohibiting homosexual relationships. In 1976, 47 percent of college students favored such laws. Among adults surveyed nationally in 1996, however, 47 percent felt that homosexual relations between consenting adults should be illegal, and the older the age group, the higher the percentage of respondents favoring the prohibition (U.S. Department of Justice, Bureau of Justice Statistics, 1996).

Although homosexual relationships are not illegal per se, the United States Supreme Court ruled in 1986 in the case of *Bowers* v. *Hardwick* that states may criminalize homosexual acts such as sodomy even if they are engaged in by consenting adults in the privacy of their own homes. Gay and lesbian partners also may not legally marry in the United States.[6] Hawaii may soon become the first state to allow same-sex marriage. In 1993, a lesbian couple challenged the state's ban on homosexual marriage, arguing that it is unconstitutional. The state Supreme Court ordered the government to demonstrate a compelling interest to support the ban. In 1996, a Circuit Court judge ruled that no compelling reason had been provided and ordered the state to grant marriage licenses to same-sex couples. The state is appealing the decision, but even if Hawaii ends up allowing same-sex marriage, a new federal law, the Defense of Marriage Act, relieves other states from the legal obligation of recognizing same-sex marriages performed elsewhere (Goldberg, 1996a).

In the meantime, an increasing number of municipal governments, universities, and large corporations (including Lotus Development Corporation and Disney) are openly recognizing gay and lesbian domestic partnerships. Certain cities and municipalities allow gay and lesbian couples to officially register their domestic partnerships. Some people think registration is important because such public recognition lends legitimacy to the relationship. Registration may also have practical benefits, including insurance coverage for partners, family leaves, family membership rates, and inheritance protection. The AIDS epidemic has heightened concern over the need for legal recognition of domestic partnerships. Many gay men have had their dying partners removed from their care by an estranged and angry parent; have been excluded from decisions regarding their partner's care or even where the partner will be buried; and, in the absence of a will, have seen their deceased partner's belongings inherited by estranged parents or siblings.

The case of Sharon Kowalski and Karen Thompson also drew attention to this issue. Kowalski and Thompson had exchanged rings and pledged to be life partners, but because they were not—could not be—legally married, they were, as Robson (1992) put

BOX **6.2**
The Gay and Lesbian Rights Movement

Much of the progress in changing attitudes toward homosexuality and winning civil rights protections for gays and lesbians is a direct result of social activism on the part of gay and lesbian organizations that together make up the gay and lesbian rights movement. Not all of these activities are recent. Carrigan et al. (1987), for example, have documented efforts to "emancipate homosexuals" dating to the early nineteenth century during the first wave of feminism in Europe (see Chapter 1). Cruikshank (1992), Faderman (1991), and others have researched the histories of numerous organizations established in the United States as early as the 1920s to combat prejudice and discrimination against gays and lesbians, although their memberships were small and they did not identify homosexuals as an oppressed minority group. Such an identity began emerging after 1945 when new groups, such as the Mattachine Society for gay men and Daughters of Bilitis for lesbians, formed. The goals of these groups were modest by today's standards, but radical for their time: to provide support for homosexuals, to correct widespread inaccuracies about homosexuals and homosexual relationships, and to promote tolerance of homosexuals by heterosexuals (Cruikshank, 1992; Murray, 1996).

During the 1960s, as other social liberation movements gained momentum, so did the gay and lesbian rights movement. Like the feminist movement, the gay and lesbian rights movement was influenced by the Civil Rights struggle and anti-war activism (Cruikshank, 1992). The Stonewall Riots of 1969 are considered by most to be the political spark that galvanized the gay liberation movement. On June 27, 1969, New York police raided the Stonewall Inn, a Greenwich Village bar whose patrons were mostly lesbians and gay men. Tired of harassment and brutality at the hands of the police and the heterosexual public, the bar's patrons, joined by a crowd of about 2,000 others, fought back with two nights of street rioting.

Following Stonewall, a number of new, highly political and activist groups emerged, including the Gay Liberation Front and the Gay Activist Alliance, whose goal was to overthrow the sex/gender hierarchy (Murray, 1996). This was a time of gay pride, but it was also a time of heightened activism that included demonstrations, fundraising, the publication of newsletters and journals, lobbying for the passage of equal rights laws and the rescinding of discriminatory ones, as well as myriad other activities.

We note in this chapter and throughout this book the numerous successes of gay and lesbian rights activism. At the same time, however, we are witnessing setbacks and opposition to gay and lesbian rights, including continued denial of parenting opportunities and rights to gay men and lesbians, a rise in hate crimes (see Chapter 8), the continuing controversy over gays and lesbians in the military (see Chapter 9), the crusade against homosexuals and homosexuality being pursued by religious conservatives (see Chapter 10), and the underfunding of AIDS research (see Chapter 11). In 1998, Maine became the first state to repeal its gay rights law, which prohibited discrimination against gays and lesbians in employment, credit, housing, and public accommodations, even though public opinion polls showed a two-thirds statewide majority in favor of the law (Quinn, 1998). Currently, only nine states have such laws; five are in New England.

These setbacks have not re-silenced the gay and lesbian communities, but rather have often spurred greater political awareness and activism. More gays and lesbians are willing to be out about their sexual orientation and to demand that their rights be protected. Indeed, some observers predict increased social conflict on gay and lesbian rights issues as we move through the early decades of the twenty-first century (Murray, 1996).

it, legally strangers. When Kowalski was severely disabled in a car accident in 1983, her parents removed her from the home she shared with Thompson, put her in a nursing home, and barred Thompson from even visiting her. Thompson subsequently went to court asking to be made Kowalski's legal guardian. A lower court ruled in favor of the parents, but in 1991, an appeals court ruled that the medical testimony indicated that Kowalski was able to express a preference as to where and with whom she wanted to live, and she had consistently chosen to live at home with her partner. In addition, the appeals court stated that Kowalski and Thompson were a "family of affinity," a relationship that deserves to be respected.

Although such decisions have been regarded as victories by gay and lesbian rights advocates, critics of domestic partnership registration—and same-sex marriage as well —worry about the consequences for those who choose not to "legitimate" their relationships. Robson (1992), for instance, argues that historically, marriage has been a repressive institution that subjects intimate relationships to the rule of law. She also believes that state-approved registration and marriage divides gays and lesbians into those who are good—that is, those who are monogamous and restrict their sexuality to the marital bed—and those who are deviant. Will a certificate of registration—or a marriage certificate—become evidence of a committed relationship so that those who do not register or marry are denied rights and benefits? For example, if a couple who chose not to register or marry tried to adopt a child, someone who opposed the adoption might use this choice as evidence that they did not have a serious relationship (Bennet, 1993, p. B3).

It is in the area of parental rights that lesbian and gay domestic partners continue to encounter the greatest hostility and resistance. For instance, while opinion polls consistently show that over three-quarters of the general public thinks homosexuals should have equal employment rights and opportunities, this endorsement is qualified when the jobs in question involve physical contact (e.g., a physician) or contact with children (e.g., an elementary school teacher). In a 1993 *New York Times*/CBS poll, for instance, 55 percent of respondents said that they would object to their child having a homosexual elementary school teacher. More than half said that they would not permit their child to watch a prime-time television comedy that had homosexual characters in it, read a book about a homosexual couple, or play at the home of a friend whose parent is homosexual (Schmalz, 1993).

To a large extent, negative attitudes toward gays and lesbians as parents stem from widespread myths about relationships between homosexuals and children. For example, many heterosexuals believe that gay men try to seduce young boys, but the data on child molesters show that about 90 percent are heterosexual men (Greenfeld, 1996; Prentky et al., 1997). Many heterosexuals also think that homosexuals try to "recruit" children to their "lifestyle," and that simply seeing homosexual couples leads children into immorality. Such beliefs have been used repeatedly to prevent lesbians and gay men from becoming foster or adoptive parents and to deny them custody or visitation rights to their own children (Ayres, 1993; Robson, 1992). In 1996, for example, an appeals court in Florida upheld a lower court's ruling denying a lesbian mother custody of her daughter and awarding custody to her ex-husband who had been imprisoned for killing his first wife. The judge who originally decided the case said he wanted to give the child a chance to live in a "non-lesbian world" (Epstein, 1996).

Currently, only six states permit adoptions by same-sex couples, raising serious legal problems if a partner has custody of children from a previous marriage, has adopted children as a single parent, or has given birth to children using an NRT (Bruni, 1995; Robson, 1992). Despite the persistent myths, however, research consistently shows that children raised by gay and lesbian parents are emotionally healthy and well-adjusted (Bozett, 1988; Patterson, 1992; Recer, 1997). Moreover, growing up in a household with same-sex parents appears to have little effect on a child's sexual orientation. Research shows that most children grow up to be heterosexual, regardless of their parents' sexual orientation. Interestingly, this research also shows that children who grow up with lesbian parents tend to be more relaxed and more experimental than children who grow up in other households; they experience no confusion about their own sexual orientation (Golombok & Tasker, 1996). These findings underline a point that many lesbian and gay parents already know well: It is love that makes a family.

Violence in Families and Intimate Relationships

The image of the family as a haven from the harshness of the public world is tarnished by reports of widespread family violence. According to the U.S. Department of Justice's Bureau of Justice Statistics (1995), about 450,000 incidents of family violence occur in the United States each year. About 57 percent of these cases involve married couples or ex-spouses. Many victims, however, are reluctant to report the abuse. One national survey, for instance, found that only 6.7 percent of women assaulted by an intimate reported the assault to the police (Straus & Gelles, 1990). Thus, the official statistics probably underestimate the problem. To conclude this chapter, we'll discuss three forms of violence in intimate relationships: partner abuse, child abuse, and elder abuse.

Partner Abuse in Heterosexual Relationships

National surveys using random samples of married and cohabiting heterosexual couples show that each year, about 12 percent of adult intimates experience at least one incident of physical abuse at the hands of their partners. In one of the best known studies, sociologist Murray Straus found that for every 1,000 couples in the United States, there are 122 assaults by husbands and 124 assaults by wives each year (Straus, 1993).

On the surface, Straus's findings suggest that far from being a one-sided attack, partner abuse is usually *mutual abuse*, an exchange of physical and psychological abuse between partners (Straus, 1993). The mutual abuse perspective is not new (see, for example, Steinmetz, 1978), but it has gotten more attention lately. Newspaper articles and television talk shows have featured men's rights advocates who call for equal protection of battered men, citing findings that appear to show that women assault their male partners as much as men assault women (see, for example, Lewin, 1992).

Does scientific research support such a claim? Women do report using violence against their husbands or boyfriends at about the same or even a slightly higher rate than men report using violence against their wives or girlfriends. However, research also shows that men are more likely than women to underreport both the frequency and the severity of their violence (Crowell & Burgess, 1996; Dobash et al., 1998). A second problem with simply using self-reported incidence statistics is that it is impossible to determine from these figures whether a partner is acting in self-defense or retaliating against an abusive intimate. For instance, studies show that husbands typically initiate violence to control or punish their wives (Barnett et al., 1997). However, an even more serious problem with the incidence data is that they do not tell us anything about the consequences of the violence. Research consistently shows women are more often and more seriously injured by intimate partners than men are (Dobash et al., 1998). Women are also more likely to be killed by male intimates than men are. About one third of female homicide victims are killed by husbands, ex-husbands, or boyfriends, whereas only about 3 percent of male homicide victims are killed by wives, ex-wives, or girlfriends (Crowell & Burgess, 1996; Greenfeld, 1998). Clearly, then, intimate violence, like other behavior, is gendered; women's and men's violence against their intimate partners differs in both quantity and quality.

In trying to determine what causes partner abuse, some researchers have focused on the personal characteristics of batterers, asking, "What makes this person violent?" Answers to this question have ranged from evolutionary explanations to hormonal and neurological factors to personality traits and mental disorders. Other researchers have looked at socialization experiences, especially the experience of witnessing or being victimized by violence as a child. And still other researchers have examined institutional factors, including the influence of the media, religious traditions, and gender norms. What the research taken together suggests, however, is that partner abuse is not caused by any single factor, but by multiple factors, individual as well as structural (Crowell & Burgess, 1996).

Many people believe that alcohol and drug abuse cause intimate violence. Researchers have found a high incidence of alcohol and drug use associated with battering incidents (see, for example, Brookoff, 1997), but the relationship between substance abuse and battering is complex and not yet well understood. For example, the likelihood of violent behavior increases with excessive alcohol and drug use, but it is not certain if this outcome is because alcohol and drugs lower inhibitions, cloud judgment, or have some other physiological effects on the brain and nervous system (Crowell & Burgess, 1996). It is also sometimes the case that drinking and drug use do not *cause* battering, but instead are offered to *justify* or *excuse* such behavior: "I didn't know what I was doing; I was drunk" (Gelles, 1993). Most batterers, however, are not alcoholics or drug addicts (Edleson et al., 1985; Gelles, 1993; Herman, 1988).

Another common belief is that partner abuse only occurs among working class and poor couples or among non-White couples. Research demonstrates, however, that domestic violence is far more widespread and cuts across social class as well as racial and ethnic boundaries. Nevertheless, research also shows that battering is not evenly distributed among social classes or racial or ethnic groups. Battering is more frequent in low-income families (Moore, 1997; Schwartz, 1988), although when race and ethnicity are taken into account, the results are less consistent. Some studies report that the incidence of intimate violence is about the same for middle-class White, African American, and Latino couples, but higher for non-White low-income couples (Cazenave & Straus, 1990; Straus & Smith, 1990). Lockhart (1991), however, found a higher incidence of partner abuse among middle-class African American couples than middle-class White couples. Additional research shows that intimate violence is the leading cause of death for young, African American women (Stark, 1990).

Low income and poverty, then, seem to place women at higher risk of violent victimization by an intimate partner. These factors also help keep abused women trapped in violent relationships. Some people are unsympathetic to abused women because they believe that women should leave a relationship as soon as it becomes abusive. "If it's so bad," they ask, "why does she stay?" Research indicates that abused women typically do leave their partners, sometimes more than once, but leaving is more difficult than most people think (Brown, 1997). For one thing, they must have someplace to go. They may not have relatives or friends they can count on, and battered women's shelters may be full or unable to accommodate their needs (Dobash & Dobash, 1992). For many low-income battered women, leaving their abusive partners means becoming homeless (Browne & Bassuk, 1997). Second, these women must be able to support themselves and their children if they leave. In Chapter 7 we will discuss how various forms of employment and wage discrimination keep women in low-paying, low-status jobs. And we noted earlier in this chapter that women experience a substantial drop in their standard of living when they separate from their husbands. Economic dependence, therefore, keeps some women trapped in violent family relationships. For some women, leaving an abusive partner means having to go on welfare (Brandwein, 1999). In fact, women who are quick to leave an abusive relationship tend to be gainfully employed or to have good chances for employment, possess above-average resources, and have relatives nearby who are willing and able to help them (Pagelow, 1981). It is also important to keep in mind that leaving an abuser does not guarantee that the abuse will stop. In fact, research shows that abuse often escalates when a woman tries to leave or after she has left (DeKeseredy, 1997; Kurz, 1995).

Partner abuse takes place in the context of a violent society. Some people consider violence a normal part of everyday life, and a sizable minority of the population believes that under certain circumstances, men are justified in hitting their wives or girlfriends (DeKeseredy & MacLeod, 1997). In one national survey, more than one-quarter of the respondents (27.6 percent) indicated that slapping a spouse is necessary, normal, or good (Dibble & Straus, 1990). Other studies have found that one of ten high school students and two to three of ten college students experience courtship violence, but 29 to 36 percent of them interpret the abuse as love and as helping to improve their relationships (Flynn, 1987; see also DeKeseredy & Kelly, 1993, but for a different view see O'Leary, 1993). These attitudes are also sometimes reflected in court decisions. Consider, for example, a 1994 case in which a Maryland judge sentenced a defendant, a man who had killed his wife after he found her in bed with another man, to just eighteen months probation, stating that most men would have felt compelled to "punish" their partners under such circumstances ("Punishment is 18 Months," 1994).

Many advocates for battered women have criticized the legal system for not treating domestic violence as a serious problem and not responding to it effectively. Since the late 1970s, however, important legal changes have occurred, including passage of the federal Violence Against Women Act in 1994. This legislation includes increased funding for battered women's shelters and programs, a mandate for harsher penalties for batterers, and a provision that makes crossing state lines in pursuit of a fleeing partner a federal offense. The impact of the new law remains to be seen, but the hope is that it will help turn the tables on batterers who historically have been afforded more legal protection in our society than those they victimize.

Partner Abuse in Gay and Lesbian Relationships

Much less is known about partner abuse in lesbian and gay relationships. For one thing, we cannot do studies using large, national samples of gay and lesbian couples because many gay men and lesbians are not open about their sexual orientation. Therefore, it is impossible to establish with much accuracy the incidence of violence in same-sex relationships. Some researchers argue that it occurs at about the same rate as violence in heterosexual relationships (Brand & Kidd, 1986; Island & Letellier, 1991). However, these claims are based on studies of lesbians and gay men who volunteer for the research and who therefore may not be representative of the general lesbian and gay population. While we do not have very good estimates of the incidence of same-sex domestic violence, the limited research available shows that it does occur and, like heterosexual domestic violence, it is not a one-time situational event. Once it occurs, it is likely to recur and to grow more severe over time (Renzetti, 1992).

Many people assume that it is easier for abused lesbians and gay men to leave their partners because they are not married. However, research shows that gay men and lesbians have a high level of closeness and attachment to their partners; they have difficulty leaving abusive partners because they have a deep personal commitment to them and to the relationship. A second problem in leaving is that many lesbians and gay men are involved in domestic partnerships in which they share housing with their partners and have made joint purchases. Leaving an abusive partner may result in a substantial financial loss that may or may not be recoverable through legal action should the abused partner choose to take such action. Most, though, do not feel comfortable turning to the courts for help (Renzetti, 1992). Third, there are few shelters and services specifically for victims of same-sex domestic violence, and many lesbians and gay men do not feel welcome at shelters and services designed for heterosexual women (Renzetti, 1996). While many abused heterosexual women turn to their relatives for help, this isn't an option for some abused lesbians and gay men because they have not come out to their relatives about their sexual orientation or they have severed ties with their relatives (Renzetti, 1992). And finally, among gay men, HIV/AIDS increases abuse victims' reluctance to leave abusive partners. An abuse victim whose batterer has AIDS may feel tremendous guilt about leaving a dying partner with no one else to care for him. Conversely, an abuse victim who has AIDS may be so dependent on his batterer for financial support and physical assistance that he prefers to remain in the relationship rather than risk living alone (Letellier, 1996). In short, lesbian and gay victims of domestic violence are inhibited from leaving abusive partners not only because of their personal circumstances, but also because the homophobia that is prevalent in our society cuts them off from most alternatives.

Child Abuse

We often tell children to be wary of strangers, but the fact is that they are more likely to be harmed by someone they know, especially a family member. Estimates of child abuse and neglect range from about 1 million to nearly 3 million cases per year (U.S. Department of Health and Human Services, 1998). As many as one-third of all child abuse and neglect cases go unreported or undetected. Nevertheless, the incidence and severity of child abuse appears to be increasing. Between 1986 and 1993, for example, the number of children seriously injured rose almost 400 percent (Children's Defense Fund, 1997).

Recent research indicates that while there are no significant differences in the incidence of abuse across racial and ethnic groups, there are differences across age groups, with younger children at greater risk than older children. Children living in poor families also appear to be at greater risk than children living in more financially secure families (Children's Defense Fund, 1997). Girls are slightly more likely than boys to be abused; girls are 52 percent of child abuse victims. However, when type of abuse is taken into account, there are significant gender differences. Boys are more likely than girls to be physically abused and neglected. Girls are more likely to be emotionally abused, and they are three times more likely than boys to be sexually abused (U.S. Department of Health and Human Services, 1998; see also Box 6.3). Sexual exploitation of children may be perpetrated by strangers, but most victims know their abusers. The abuser is usually a relative, stepparent, family friend, or close neighbor. Accurate estimates of child sexual abuse are difficult to calculate, but research indicates that about 19 percent of girls and 9 percent of boys have been sexually abused by the time they turn eighteen, and about 40 percent are abused by a relative (Hodson & Skeen, 1987; Russell, 1986). The effects of sexual abuse on children include suicide attempts, risk-taking behavior (e.g., having sex during adolescence without using condoms or contraception and having multiple sex partners), fighting, and eating disorders. Interestingly, Shrier and her colleagues (1998) found that girls who have been sexually abused tend to act out more in adolescence, whereas boys who have been sexually abused tend to internalize their feelings and engage in more self-harm (see also Chapter 11).

In addition to poverty and gender inequality, several other factors have been identified as contributing to child abuse and neglect. There is evidence, for instance, that children from unwanted or unplanned pregnancies are at high risk of abuse and neglect (Cron, 1986; Zuravin, 1987). Most studies also show that mothers are more likely than fathers to abuse children (U.S. Department of Health and Human Services, 1998), although it is unclear whether this finding simply reflects the greater time that mothers spend with their children. It may also be caused in part by the greater social isolation of mothers that we discussed earlier. Parents who are socially isolated are more likely to abuse their children (Straus & Smith, 1990). But while mothers more often than biological fathers abuse their children, stepfathers and boyfriends of single mothers are also frequent abusers, especially sexual abusers (Gordon & Creighton, 1988; Hodson & Skeen, 1987). Finally, child abuse, like partner abuse, occurs in a specific social context. Most people approve of parents exercising strict control over their children and physically punishing children for misbehavior (Dibble & Straus, 1990), and there is a strong belief that what parents do in the privacy of their homes is their own business. As Box 6.3 shows, throughout most of the world, children are still viewed as the "property" of

BOX **6.3**

The Sexual Exploitation of Children: Child Prostitution

One of the byproducts of the grinding poverty that characterizes life for most families in Asia and Latin America is a dramatic rise in the number of child prostitutes. According to children's rights advocates, an increasing number of children in countries such as Brazil, the Philippines, and Cambodia are being kidnapped and forced into prostitution or sold to brothels by their parents, most of whom are desperate for income. The children may be locked in the brothels if they are considered likely to try to escape, but usually such measures are unnecessary; beatings and threats are typically enough to convince the children to stay. Accurate estimates of the number of child prostitutes are difficult to come by, with some experts setting the lower limit in the tens of thousands and others maintaining it is at least one million. The children involved are as young as six and as old as fifteen (the age of consent in most countries is sixteen). Most are girls (Goering, 1996; Kristof, 1996; Sherry et al., 1995).

Who are the customers of child prostitutes? Some are local men, neighbors of the children, to whom the children are rented out by their parents. Some are foreign businessmen and tourists. Some of the men are individual travelers, but others travel on organized sex tours. The tours, which first began in Japan, are now sold in such countries as Great Britain, South Korea, and Taiwan. If the girl is a virgin, the fee may be as much as $500, but immediately following the loss of her virginity, a young girl may be hired for anywhere from $2 to $10, depending on her age and experience (Kristof, 1996; Sherry et al., 1995).

Many customers justify their behavior by claiming that they are actually helping the children, providing them with much-needed money for their families and preventing them from having to work at even more dangerous or menial occupations. The customers also often rationalize that children from impoverished countries become sexually active at early ages anyway.

Another motivation for seeking young children, however, is the belief that they are less likely than adult prostitutes to be infected with HIV, the virus that causes AIDS (Sherry et al., 1995). According to international health experts, AIDS is spreading among prostitutes in many countries, especially in Asia. It is also spreading country to country because of international trafficking in prostitutes and because of travelers who contract the disease abroad and bring it home with them. Prostitutes report that few of their customers use condoms, and the younger the prostitute, the more powerless she or he is to insist that a condom be worn. The fact is, however, that child prostitutes are at greatest risk of contracting HIV because of their age: A child's vagina and anus are more easily torn from intercourse, causing open cuts, sores, and bleeding that facilitate HIV transmission (Kristof, 1996). Consequently, world health experts expect the incidence of AIDS in Asia and Latin America to continue to rise, with children making up an increasing percentage of those who become infected and eventually die from the disease (see also Chapter 11).

their parents, an idea that gives parents considerable leeway in terms of how they treat their children and one that helps perpetuate child abuse and neglect.

Elder Abuse

Elder abuse refers to the physical, psychological, or financial maltreatment, neglect, or exploitation of a senior citizen by an adult caretaker. Obviously, such abuse can be inflicted by anyone entrusted with the care of an elderly person, such as nurses, physicians, home health aides, bankers, or lawyers. However, research shows that the typical abuser is a family member (Kosberg, 1988; Mates, 1997; Pillemer & Finkelhor, 1988). It is estimated that 300,000 to 1 million elderly people are abused in the United States each year. Since the 1980s, the number of reported cases of elder abuse has increased 300 percent (Griffin et al., 1998; Pillemer & Finkelhor, 1988).

Although research into elder abuse did not really begin until the 1980s, the work that has been done suggests that those at greatest risk of being victimized are women who are aged seventy-five and older, infirm, and physically or financially dependent on others for meeting their basic daily needs (Kosberg, 1988; Pillemer & Finkelhor, 1988). Women may have higher rates of victimization because they outnumber elderly men, but also because they are more vulnerable to sexual assault and they have lower social status than elderly men. However, one study reported little difference in the victimization rates of women and men, but found that women suffered more serious physical and psychological harm from the abuse (Pillemer & Finkelhor, 1988).

Research on abusers shows that they are sometimes the elderly person's spouse, continuing a pattern of abuse in the marriage or taking revenge for previous abuse by the now-impaired partner (Kosberg, 1988; Pillemer & Finkelhor, 1988). However, more elderly people live with a spouse than with an adult child; when this fact is taken into account, the data show that adult children are more likely to abuse than spouses are (Pillemer & Finkelhor, 1988). Some of these adult children were abused by their parents when they were growing up and learned that violence toward intimates is acceptable behavior. Some may be retaliating against their abusive parents (Kosberg, 1988). Often, though, the abusers are adult daughters who have brought severely impaired aged parents into their home to care for them. The daughters continue to care for their own families and often work outside the home as well. They typically receive little or no outside help in caring for their parents, and eventually the psychological and financial stress become so great that they use violence to control their parents or to express resentment about the situation (Mates, 1997; Steinmetz, 1993).

At least thirty-seven states have enacted laws making reporting of incidents of abuse or neglect of senior citizens mandatory. Some analysts, however, question the effectiveness of such laws because they address the problem *after* abuse occurs. Also, the programs created by the laws are usually too underfunded to meet the needs of elderly victims (Callahan, 1988; Kosberg, 1988). Many advocates for the elderly believe that the best approach is prevention by, for example, providing adult children with greater professional assistance and support in caring for their parents. In addition, if elder abuse is a continuation of earlier family violence, then it must be addressed along with partner abuse and child abuse.

Families and Other Intimates: The Ideal and the Real Revisited

Our discussion in this chapter highlights the disparity between traditional images of ideal intimate relationships and their reality in everyday life. We have discussed how the social construction of *The Family*—that is, the isolated nuclear family of husband/breadwinner, wife/homemaker, and dependent children—is not an accurate description of the majority of families in the United States today. Unfortunately, this idealization creates another false idea: that other family arrangements and relationships, including single-parent families and gay and lesbian relationships, are inherently deviant or abnormal.

Another myth generated by the idealization of the isolated nuclear family is the notion of the family as a private retreat from the harsh public world. We have learned that while the family is, for many of us, a place where we can be our "real" selves and still be loved, it is also a place at the center of gendered struggles. Within the family, the gender inequality of the larger society is often replicated and preserved in a variety of ways: through the power imbalance between intimate partners, an inequitable division of household labor and caregiving responsibilities, the economic difficulties of female-headed households, and domestic violence. Many of these problems are made worse by racism, ageism, heterosexism, and social class inequality.

The idea of family privacy also overlooks the many ways in which other social institutions, such as government, impinge on intimate relationships. A recurring theme in this chapter has been the intersection of family life and employment. We have argued, in fact, that family relations cannot be understood in isolation from employment issues. In the next chapter, we turn to the topic of gender and the occupational work world, but because of the intersection of family life and work, many of the points we raised here will come up again.

KEY TERMS

chosen families families made up people unrelated by ancestry, marriage, or adoption, but who are nonetheless considered family members

domestic partnership a cohabiting relationship between intimate partners not married to each other

expressive family role the role of housekeeper and caregiver in the family, a role held by the wife/mother in a traditional isolated nuclear family

instrumental family role the role of providing financial support for the family and making key decisions, a role held by the husband/father in the traditional isolated nuclear family

isolated nuclear family a family in which the husband/father, wife/mother, and their dependent children establish a household geographically and financially separate from other kin and the adults carry out distinct, specialized roles

new reproductive technologies a variety of laboratory techniques that allow people who are infertile, physically unable to conceive or sustain a pregnancy, do not have a partner, or do not wish to enter into a committed relationship to become parents

public/private split the idea that home is a separate domain from the public world

reproductive freedom an individual's ability to freely choose whether or not to have a child

sexual double standard the tradition of permitting young men to engage in sexual activity while simultaneously condemning and punishing the same behavior by young women

single-parent family a family with children but only one adult who has financial responsibility for the household

two-earner family a family in which both adult partners are in the paid labor force

SUGGESTED READINGS

Bergen, R. (Ed.) (1998). *Issues in intimate violence.* Thousand Oaks, CA: Sage.

Horowitz, R. (1995). *Teen mothers: Citizens or dependents?* Chicago: University of Chicago Press.

Murray, S. O. (1996). *American gay.* Chicago: University of Chicago Press.

Risen, J., and Thomas, J. L. (1998). *Wrath of angels: The American abortion war.* New York: Basic Books.

Schwartz, P., & Rutter, V. (1998). *The gender of sexuality.* Thousand Oaks, CA: Pine Forge Press.

United Nations. (1996). *Family: Challenges for the future.* New York: United Nations Publications.

Weston, K. (1991). *Families we choose: Lesbians, gays, kinship.* New York: Columbia University Press.

NOTES

1. Certainly Parsons was not the only significant family sociologist of this period, but he is considered by many to be the most preeminent. Aulette (1994, p. 11), for example, quotes D. H. Morgan, who wrote, "It would not be too much of an exaggeration to state that Parsons represents *the* modern theorist on the family" (original emphasis).

2. According to a 1998 report by the World Health Organization, there are approximately 75 million unwanted pregnancies worldwide each year. Of these, 20 million women, 95 percent of whom live in developing countries, obtain illegal abortions that are performed by unqualified providers using unclean tools and unsafe methods. The methods include overdoses of drugs, applying heavy weights to the woman's abdomen, and inserting a stick or needle into the cervix. Between 10 and 50 percent of women who undergo an illegal abortion experience complications, including infections, hemorrhages, punctures and tears of the uterus, chronic pelvic pain, and tubal blockage. Sometimes, the complications result in the woman's death. In fact, the report notes that anti-abortion laws increase the rate of unsafe abortions which, in turn, leads to higher rates of maternal death (Bulman, 1998).

3. A 1997 study commissioned by the New Jersey Department of Human Services found that while abortion rates in New Jersey and across the United States declined between 1991 and 1996, abortion rates among welfare recipients in New Jersey increased substantially. The study found a relationship between the abortion rate and the state's welfare "reforms," in particular, the "family cap" provision enacted in 1992 that prohibits additional welfare benefits to recipients who have more children (Lewin, 1998c). In Chapter 7, we will explore further the impact of recent welfare "reforms."

4. A number of recent studies have focused on the emotional consequences of divorce for children. Some studies show that children of divorced parents have low academic achievement, elevated high school drop-out rates, high rates of single parenthood, low self-esteem, high rates of admission to psychiatric hospitals, and high teen suicide rates (Nicholi, 1991). Other researchers, however, caution that many of these studies do not make clear whether such problems emerge after the divorce or during the marriage. When children of divorced parents are compared with children from intact marriages, the differences in emotional and behavioral problems are actually small (Amato, 1994; Furstenberg & Cherlin, 1991). Some researchers maintain that children living in homes with high levels of conflict between the parents suffer as many, if not more, negative consequences as children of divorced parents (Kurz, 1995). It appears that the best indicators of a child's level of emotional adjustment are the child's relationship with his or her mother and the level of conflict between the child's parents (Furstenberg & Cherlin, 1991).

5. Although all fifty states have some form of no-fault divorce, some state legislatures are considering bills to eliminate the no-fault option, at least for couples with children, reasoning that no-fault divorce has made marital dissolution too easy and has hurt women and children. Such bills have been proposed in Colorado, Georgia, Iowa, Michigan, and Pennsylvania (Johnson, 1996).

6. In 1989, Denmark became the first country in the world to legalize homosexual marital unions by extending to officially registered homosexual couples all but a few of the rights and responsibilities of legally married heterosexual couples.

Gender, Employment, and the Economy

When we speak of a society's **economy,** we are referring to its system of managing and developing its resources, both human and material. The human resources of the economy constitute the **labor force.** Sociologists have long emphasized the significance of work in people's lives. At the most basic level, work is necessary to meet survival needs. Most work, though, is not done by individuals in isolation, but rather entails the coordination of the activities of a group. Work, in other words, is *social* as well as *economic,* and in the United States, as in other industrialized capitalist societies, the social organization of work is hierarchical. People do different jobs that are differentially valued and rewarded. Ideally, the value and rewards attached to a particular job should reflect its intrinsic characteristics—for example, the degree of skill required, the amount of effort expended, the level of responsibility involved, and the conditions under which it is performed. In practice, however, the value and rewards of a job often have more to do with the ascribed traits of workers—their race and ethnicity, for instance, and/or their sex.

Our focus in this chapter is on the different economic and employment experiences of women and men and the differential values and rewards that have been attached to their work. Both men and women have always worked, but the kinds of work opportunities available to them and the rewards they have received have typically depended less on their talents as individuals than on culturally prescribed and enforced notions of "women's work" and "men's work." These prescriptions vary from society to society, and they vary historically within a single society. We will begin our discussion here, then, with a brief historical overview of men's and women's labor force participation in the United States.

U.S. Working Women and Men in Historical Perspective

Men's and women's participation in the wage labor force has been shaped by a number of factors, not the least of which have been changes in production and demographic changes. These, too, have influenced prevailing gender ideologies of men's and women's appropriate work roles.

Undeniably, one of the most important changes occurred during the nineteenth century when the American economy shifted from being predominantly agricultural to becoming industrialized, moving production off the farms and into factories. Interestingly, industrialization is frequently discussed only in terms of its effects on male workers, the common assumption being that women did not accompany men into the factories, but instead remained at home as family caretakers. This was true only in certain households, however. Overall, men entered the paid labor force in significantly greater numbers than women. At the same time, dominant middle-class ideology dictated that the so-called true woman stayed at home and supposedly did not work. But among particular groups of women—women in poor and working class families, women rearing children alone, women of color, and immigrant women—few could afford to stay at home. The exigencies of survival required that they find paid employment, and the harsh reality of their work world stood sharply juxtaposed to the prosperous middle-class image of genteel womanhood (Cott, 1987; Glenn, 1992; Stansell, 1986).

In 1800, only about 5 percent of women worked outside the home, but by 1900, about 30 percent of women living in large U.S. cities were employed and a substantial number were factory workers (Dublin, 1994). In the New England textile mills, for instance, most of the labor force was female by 1850 (Dublin, 1994; Werthheimer, 1979). In cities such as Boston and New York, women were heavily concentrated in the garment industry as seamstresses (Glenn, 1990; Stansell, 1986). Other women did piece work, such as folding books, rolling cigars, or making flowers for wealthier ladies' hats. They labored fourteen to eighteen hours a day under extraordinarily unsafe conditions for a daily wage of 10 to 18 cents. While for some even these wages gave them independence from their families, many others turned most or all of their wages over to their parents to help support the household (Dublin, 1994).

Of course, factory work was unpleasant and dangerous for male as well as female workers, but from the outset men and women were largely segregated into different jobs with the more skilled—and better paid—work open only to men. Widespread stereotypes about women's innate passivity and physical weakness and their greater tolerance for tedium legitimated offering women work that was usually the most boring and repetitive. And despite the fact that many women's wages were crucial to their families' welfare, the belief that women worked only temporarily until they married was used to justify their lower wage rates (Kessler-Harris, 1990; Reskin & Hartmann, 1986). Labor organizers and male workers themselves capitalized on the notion that paid work was "unladylike" and argued that no woman would have to work if men were provided a "family wage." Trade unions systematically excluded women or organized them into separate unions. Far fewer women than men were unionized. Even in unions with large numbers of female members, the union leadership typically was male, although several recent historical analyses show that in some unions women did gain valuable organizing and leadership experience (Gabin, 1990; Glenn, 1990). Nevertheless, until the 1930s, most unions were racially segregated as well as sex segregated (Gabin, 1990; Hine, 1989).

Jobs in manufacturing, however, were available primarily to White women. Women of color, though more likely than White women to be in the paid labor force, historically have found their employment opportunities largely limited to agricultural work (e.g., fruit and vegetable harvesters), domestic work (e.g., house maids), and laundry work (Amott & Matthaei, 1991). For instance, in 1890, 38.7 percent of Black female workers held agricultural jobs, 30.8 percent were domestics, 15.6 percent were laundresses, but only 2.8 percent worked in manufacturing. Three decades later, agriculture, domestic service, and laundries still employed 75 percent of Black female workers and, although more Black women were in manufacturing, they faced widespread segregation and discrimination in the factories: "White women were sometimes able to start work one hour later, and when amenities such as lunchrooms, fresh drinking water, and clean toilets were available, they were available primarily to White women" (Sidel, 1986, p. 60; see also Glenn, 1992).

The experiences of Asian and Latina workers were similar to those of Black women with the important exception, of course, that Black women had also been enslaved in the United States (Glenn, 1992; Romero, 1992; Zavella, 1987). It is true, too, that the dirtiest, most menial, and lowest paying jobs went to minority men as well as minority women, but while minority men received considerably lower wages than White men, they were paid more than minority women (see, for example, Zavella, 1987). Historically, women of color have been the lowest paid members of the labor force.

Ironically, the social disorganization that many groups experienced as a result of industrialization, urbanization, and immigration during the nineteenth century actually created new job opportunities for White middle-class women, especially those who had a college education. Extending their domestic roles to the larger society, they took up "civic housekeeping" and lobbied for a variety of social welfare reforms, including wages and hours laws, child labor prohibitions, improved housing for the poor, and public health measures. Some supported these causes by forming or joining voluntary organizations, but others made a career of it by entering the "female professions" of nursing, teaching, and social work (Cott, 1987; Evans, 1987). Such jobs were not considered a threat to genteel womanhood since women were expected to perform good works and care for others. Other gender stereotypes were used to justify hiring women for secretarial and other clerical positions when production expanded and the need for service workers grew. It was argued, for instance, that women's natural dexterity and compliant personalities made them ideally suited for office work (Kessler-Harris, 1982). The idea that women's work was temporary or secondary to men's remained intact and helped to keep jobs sex segregated and women's wages depressed.

Table 7.1 shows men's and women's labor force participation rates from 1900 to 1998. The early decennial statistics, however, mask some important changes in the labor force during the first half of this century, especially during the Great Depression. You will notice in Table 7.1 that between 1920 and 1930, men's labor force participation rate declined slightly, whereas women's rose slightly. During the Depression, many married women entered the paid labor force to support their families when their husbands were out of work. Unfortunately, these women were often accused of stealing jobs from men, although "in reality, the pervasive sex segregation of the labor force meant that women and men rarely competed for the same jobs" (Evans, 1987, p. 46). In fact, the clerical and service jobs in which these women were concentrated have traditionally been less sensitive to economic downturns than male blue-collar jobs in manufacturing and the building trades (Reskin & Hartmann, 1986). Nevertheless, "numerous states, cities, and school boards passed laws prohibiting or limiting the employment of married women. And since cultural norms still ascribed the breadwinner's role to men, those women who lost paid jobs, or were unable to find paid work, found that relief programs for the unemployed consistently discriminated against them" (Evans, 1987, p. 47).

With the outbreak of World War II, the U.S. economy reversed itself, and the wartime production boom created jobs for millions of Americans, but especially for women. The enlistment of a large percentage of men into the military resulted in critical labor shortages and forced employers to recruit women to take men's places. Women entered the labor force in unprecedented numbers between 1940 and 1945 but, more importantly, they were given jobs previously held only by men—for example, welding, riveting, ship fitting, and tool making. Women of color, though still severely

TABLE 7.1   Labor Force Participation Rates by Sex, 1900–1998 (% population 16 and older)*

Year	Male	Female
1900	53.7	20.0
1920	54.3	22.7
1930	53.2	23.6
1940	55.2	27.9
1945	61.6	35.8
1950	59.9	33.9
1955	60.4	35.7
1960	60.2	37.8
1965	59.7	39.3
1970	61.3	43.4
1975	78.4	46.4
1980	77.8	51.6
1985	76.3	54.5
1990	69.0	56.8
1998	74.9	59.9

*Prior to 1947, the Census Bureau included in these figures all persons 14 years and older in the labor force.

Sources: Taeuber & Valdisera, 1986; U.S. Department of Commerce, Bureau of the Census, 1997; 1990; 1976; U.S. Department of Labor, 1998a.

discriminated against, also had new job opportunities opened to them during the war, not only in blue-collar work, but in clerical fields and in nursing as well (Glenn, 1992). For the duration of the war, the federal government campaigned aggressively to recruit women for the labor force by appealing to their sense of patriotism, but the government also urged employers to pay women the same wages men would have received and sponsored public day care centers, both of which were important practical incentives to women (Bergmann, 1986; Gluck, 1987; Milkman, 1987).

Once the war ended, women were laid off to make room in the labor force for returning servicemen. Federal war programs, such as public child care facilities, were discontinued, and new government-issued propaganda told women to return to their "normal" roles as wives and mothers at home. Some women did quit their jobs, and marriage and birth rates soared in the early postwar years. But public opinion polls showed that as many as 80 percent of the women who held jobs during the war wished to keep them, and a substantial number simply moved into the traditionally female-dominated—and lower paying—service sector rather than leave the labor force (Evans, 1987; Kesselman, 1990; Milkman, 1987).

As we see in Table 7.1, women's labor force participation rate never returned to its prewar level. In fact, since 1950, even though men's labor force participation rate has fluctuated in response to dips in the economy and calls to service during military conflicts, women's labor force participation rate has risen steadily. The greatest increase, however, occurred after 1965. To some extent, this was due to an important demographic change: Women's life expectancy increased and their fertility rate (even during the baby boom years) decreased compared with earlier generations. This meant that middle-class women who had been full-time homemakers could expect to spend fewer years rearing children and, therefore, they had greater freedom to pursue other activities including paid employment, although in recent years this freedom has been tempered for some who have taken on the responsibility of caring for aging parents in their homes (see Chapter 6).

The rising divorce rate since the 1960s, coupled with changes in divorce laws discussed in the previous chapter, also resulted in more women entering the labor force to support themselves and their children without the financial help of a spouse. Recent economic changes have played a major part, too. For one thing, the service sector of the economy expanded rapidly after the war and much of the job growth occurred in fields labeled "women's work"—primarily clerical work, but also health care and education (Glenn, 1992; Macdonald & Sirianni, 1996; Webster, 1996). Later economic recessions fueled women's labor force participation as two incomes became a necessity to make ends meet in many families (Smith, 1987). One of the most dramatic increases in labor force participation, in fact, has been among married women with children under the age of six; only 12 percent of such women were employed in 1950 compared with 62.7 percent in 1996 (U.S. Department of Commerce, Bureau of the Census, 1997). Finally, political and social changes were important, particularly those prompted by the feminist movement. The feminist movement itself called into question traditional notions of women's "proper place" and encouraged women to redefine their roles and to seek paid employment. Moreover, feminist activists were instrumental in securing the passage of legislation, which we will discuss later in this chapter, that facilitated women's greater participation in the labor force.

Today, the typical woman, like the typical man, is in the paid labor force and is working full time, year-round. However, there are significant differences between women's and men's employment experiences. One important difference is the kinds of jobs women and men typically do. Women and men remain largely segregated in different occupations, which are considered women's work and men's work respectively. This segregation has serious consequences for both female and male workers, so let's examine it more closely.

Sex Segregation in the Workplace

Occupational sex segregation refers to the degree to which men and women are concentrated in occupations in which workers of one sex predominate. A commonly used measure of occupational sex segregation is the **dissimilarity index,** also called the **segregation index** and sometimes simply **D.** Its value is reported as a percentage that tells us the proportion of workers of one sex that would have to change to jobs in which members of their sex are underrepresented in order for the occupational distribution between the sexes to be fully balanced (Reskin & Hartmann, 1986).

Using the index of dissimilarity in Table 7.2, we see the extent of occupational sex segregation in the United States and sixteen other industrialized countries. First, we find that the United States ranks fifth on the list, with a dissimilarity index of 38.4. This means that about 38 percent of the female labor force in the United States would have to change jobs in order to equalize their representation across occupations. Jacobs and Lim (1995) report that while occupational sex segregation was stable during most of the twentieth century, it has declined steadily since 1970. In fact, decreasing occupational sex segregation has been a trend in most industrialized countries if the dissimilarity index is used as an indicator. Nevertheless, segregation remains high in these countries, with few exceptions. The low level of sex segregation in Italy and Japan, though, may simply be a function of how the occupations are classified there. Japan, for example, uses very broad occupational categories (such as professional, technical, and managerial), while the other countries use more detailed ones (such as physician or nurse) (Roos, 1985). Recent reports indicate that sex discrimination in employment has been increasing in Japan following downturns in the country's economy (Sanger, 1994).

This point highlights a major weakness of the index of dissimilarity: its sensitivity to types of occupational classifications. The broader the occupational categories, the lower the index tends to be (Jacobs & Lim, 1995; Reskin, 1993; Sokoloff, 1992). Thus, in one study of the United States, the dissimilarity index was 40 when ten broad occupational

TABLE 7.2 Occupational Sex Segregation in Seventeen Industrialized Countries

Country	Index of Dissimilarity (D)
Italy	24.6
Japan	25.1
Germany	36.4
France	38.3
United States	38.4
Switzerland	39.2
Austria	39.2
The Netherlands	39.9
New Zealand	41.9
Canada	42.4
Sweden	43.2
United Kingdom	44.4
Australia	47.1
Ireland	47.6
Norway	47.9
Luxembourg	48.9
Denmark	49.7

Source: Jacobs & Lim, 1995, p. 276.

categories were used, but rose to 62.7 when 426 detailed occupational categories were examined (Jacobs, 1983). A second serious problem with the index of dissimilarity is that it masks both industry-wide and establishment sex segregation, a point to which we will return later (Carlson, 1992; Reskin, 1993).

Another way to gauge occupational sex segregation is simply to look at the percentage of workers of each sex that holds a specific job. Table 7.3 provides us with such information by showing the ten occupations employing the largest numbers of men and women. One of the most striking features of this table is the lack of overlap in the jobs held by men and women. Men, we find, are concentrated in the skilled trades and operative jobs. Women, in contrast, are primarily in teaching, clerical, and other service occupations. About one of every four full-time working women holds a clerical position and, as was the case just after World War II, the service sector continues to be an area of

TABLE 7.3   Top Ten Occupations for Men and Women, 1997

Men	# Employed	% Occupation Male
Construction worker (e.g., carpenter, dry wall installer)	3,365,000	98.3
Machine operator & tender, except precision	2,976,000	64.2
Truck driver	2,383,000	95.9
Sales supervisor or proprietor	1,836,000	60.3
Engineer	1,716,000	90.7
Protective service worker (e.g., police officer, detective, guard)	1,654,000	84.3
Vehicle/mobile equipment mechanic or repairer	1,504,000	98.6
Sales worker, retail & personal services	1,427,000	42.4
Janitor or cleaner	1,117,000	73.9
Material moving equipment operator (e.g., crane operator, bulldozer operator)	1,004,000	95.4

Women	# Employed	% Occupation Female
Teacher, except college & university	2,830,000	74.3
Secretary	2,220,000	98.7
Miscellaneous administrative support worker (e.g., office clerk, bank teller)	2,111,000	82.8
Sales worker, retail & personal services	1,939,000	57.6
Machine operator & tender, except precision	1,658,000	35.8
Registered nurse	1,351,000	92.5
Sales supervisor or proprietor	1,210,000	39.7
Nursing aide	1,148,000	88.6
Sales counter clerk	1,034,000	77.1
Health technologist or technician (e.g., laboratory technician)	1,002,000	76.7

Source: U.S. Department of Labor, 1998b, pp. 209–214.

high job growth for women as well as racial minorities (Glenn, 1992; U.S. Department of Commerce, Bureau of the Cenus, 1997; U.S. Department of Labor, 1998b).

A second significant feature of Table 7.3 is the extent to which the jobs listed employ one sex relative to the other. Of the ten largest occupations for women, six were more than 75 percent female, compared with a total civilian labor force in 1997 that was 43.1 percent female. Of the ten largest occupations for men, six were more than 75 percent male and five were more than 90 percent male. Men also tend to be concentrated in supervisory positions, even in areas that otherwise are predominantly female, such as sales and clerical work. As Table 7.3 shows, in sales, 60.3 percent of supervisors and proprietors are male. About 40 percent of clerical supervisors are male, although 98.2 percent of clerical staff (secretaries, typists, and stenographers) are female (U.S. Department of Labor, 1998b).

This is not to say that there has been no improvement in occupational sex segregation in recent years. As we noted previously, researchers have found that occupational sex segregation has been declining since 1970 (Jacobs, 1995). Looking again at Table 7.3, we see further evidence of reduced occupational sex segregation. Sales jobs, in particular, appear to be relatively well balanced in terms of their sex distribution. We also see that in the top female occupations, there appears to be less sex segregation than in the top male occupations. More men have entered traditionally female-dominated jobs such as teaching and nursing during the past ten years, thus slightly lowering sex segregation in these fields. Studies of long-term trends in occupational sex segregation also indicate that women have had modest success in moving into a small number of male-dominated occupations, especially in the professions, which do not appear in Table 7.3. This, too, helped to erode occupational sex segregation.

However, while small numbers of men and women entered sex-atypical occupations, many more men and women entered sex-typical jobs. Therefore, as Jacobs (1995) points out, the increase in women's labor force participation has to an appreciable extent offset the decrease in occupational sex segregation. Thus, although occupational sex segregation overall has clearly declined, women's chances of sharing the same job as men has simultaneously declined. There is also evidence that workers who hold sex-atypical jobs leave them at a disproportionate rate (see, for example, Wright, 1996) and, as we will discuss shortly, some jobs that had been fairly balanced, have recently become more sex segregated (Reskin, 1993). In short, these factors have tempered the gains made in reducing occupational sex segregation.

Consequently, the labor market in the United States continues to be a **dual labor market,** characterized by one set of jobs employing almost exclusively men and another set of jobs, typically viewed as secondary, employing almost exclusively women. This conclusion may come as a surprise to some readers in light of the extensive media coverage that has been given to "the new professional women" and to women now holding nontraditional blue-collar jobs (e.g., carpenters, miners). Certainly, we are not suggesting here that women have not made inroads into the high-status, high-paying professions as well as the skilled trades. To the contrary, available data indicate that they have. For instance, between 1962 and 1997, a twenty-five year period, the percentage of female engineers increased from 1 percent to 9.4 percent, the percentage of female physicians from 6 percent to 30.1 percent, and the percentage of female college and university teachers from 19 percent to 36.4 percent (Sidel, 1986; U.S. Department of Labor, 1998b). One of the most dramatic gains for women workers has been in underground mining. In 1978, 1 in every 10,000 underground miners was a woman; by 1990, owing largely to lawsuits and pressure on mine operators from the federal Equal Employment Opportunity Commission, 1 in every 20 craft workers, operatives, and laborers in the mining industry was a woman (Equal Employment Opportunity Commission [EEOC], 1991).

So, while there have been widely acclaimed improvements, occupational sex segregation remains a feature of the U.S. labor market and labor markets throughout most of the world (Jacobs, 1995). Getting a precise reading of occupational sex segregation is complicated by several factors. First, the number of women in many occupations historically has been so low that to say it doubled, tripled, or even increased tenfold does not mean that large numbers of women now hold these jobs or that the jobs are no longer male-dominated. For example, in 1974, women were just 3 percent of lawyers; in 1997, women were 31 percent of lawyers, but that translated into fewer than 160,000 female lawyers in the United States (U.S. Department of Commerce, Bureau of the Census, 1993; U.S. Department of Labor, 1998b). Even though the number of women employed in skilled trades increased by almost 80 percent between 1960 and 1970, by 1997, women were only 1.3 percent of carpenters, 1.3 percent of plumbers, 1.5 percent of auto mechanics, 2.2 percent of electricians, and 3.5 percent of painters (Sidel, 1986; U.S. Department of Labor, 1998b).

A second factor that complicates the full picture of occupational sex segregation is the fact that in recent years, several female-dominated occupations grew even more female dominated. For instance, women went from being 56.8 percent of food counter and fountain workers in 1970 to being 69.3 percent of such workers in 1997. Women were 77.7 percent of bookkeepers in 1950, but 90.6 percent in 1997 (Reskin & Hartmann, 1986; U.S. Department of Labor, 1998b).

Occupational sex segregation is also complicated by differences across various groups of workers. For example, the ages of workers are significant. Young workers, aged twenty to twenty-four, who are new to the full-time labor force show a moderately lower dissimilarity index than older workers. It is young women, in particular, who appear most likely to enter the male-dominated fields of engineering, science, management, and administration (Commission on Professionals in Science and Technology, 1992; Reskin and Hartmann, 1986; however, see also Wright, 1996). Education is also an intervening variable. Women's level of education is negatively correlated with level of occupational sex segregation (Reskin, 1993). Moreover, Reskin (1993) reports that although higher education does not appear to be related to female high school graduates' movement between sex-typical and sex-atypical jobs, it does seem to have an influence on whether or not they remain in a male-dominated occupation once they have entered one.

Another factor to be considered is race and ethnicity. As Carlson (1992, p. 271) points out, "Sex and race *simultaneously* structure individuals' labor market experiences and their concrete material outcomes" (author's emphasis). Dramatic drops in the dissimilarity index were reported for women of color, especially for Latinas and Asian American women, during the 1970s, but gains eroded somewhat during the 1980s (Carlson, 1992). Unlike the experiences of White women, only a small part of the decline in occupational sex segregation for racial and ethnic minorities appears to be due to women of color moving into professional occupations, "indicating that much of the increase in integration by sex for non-Whites occurred at the lower end of the occupational distribution" (Reskin & Hartmann, 1986, p. 23; see also Glenn, 1992; Lewis & Nice, 1994).

Although there are important differences between specific racial and ethnic groups within the broader categories—for example, between Japanese Americans and Vietnamese Americans—a good deal of the occupational shifting among minority women workers in recent years has been from one female-dominated service job to another. For instance, while Latinas remain concentrated in poorly paying, female-dominated jobs in food processing, electronics, garment manufacturing (sewing and stitching), and domestic service, their numbers have increased in female-dominated white-collar work, especially in secretarial and clerical jobs (EEOC, 1991; U.S. Department of Commerce, Bureau of the Census, 1997; Zavella, 1987). Such shifts have also occurred among African American women who went from being 70 percent of domestics in 1940 to about 30 percent of such workers in 1997, and from 1 percent of clerical workers to 12.5 percent during the same time frame. However, women of color have made substantially less progress than White women in moving into the professions traditionally dominated by White men. In business, for example, Black, Hispanic, and Asian women hold just 5 percent of the management positions. Among female managers, 86 percent are White, 7 percent are Black, 5 percent are Hispanic, and 2.5 percent are Asian ("Minority Women Lag," 1997).

Still, minority men also have not fared well in the professions. As one federal investigative body reported, race is a tougher barrier than sex in the workplace (U.S. Department of Labor, 1997). Overall, only 7.9 percent of African American workers and 4.3 percent of Hispanic workers, female and male, held jobs classified as professional specialties in 1996 (U.S. Department of Commerce, Bureau of the Census, 1997).

Sokoloff (1992) reports that during the period 1960 to 1980, some professions did become more integrated in terms of both the sex and race of the job holders, but the majority did not. In fact, her research shows that the employment of White men in most of the professions increased at a faster rate during this period than did the employment of women and minorities, so that White men's dominance of the professions has actually increased. Sokoloff found that although African American men made greater inroads into the professions than African American and White women, their success was mitigated by the fact that during this period they experienced a drop in their labor force participation rate by more than 10 percent. Collins (1989) further cautions that the limited gains of African Americans in the business professions have been concentrated in such fields as personnel and public or urban relations, making these executives especially vulnerable during periods of economic recessions (see also Johnson, 1997; Lewis & Nice, 1994; Zate, 1996).

Besides workers' age, education, and race and ethnicity, another factor that complicates the analysis of occupational sex segregation is the trend toward **occupational resegregation.** As Reskin and Hartmann (1986, p. 31) explain, "Perhaps after reaching some 'tipping point' integrated occupations become resegregated with members of one sex replaced by members of the other" (see also Reskin & Roos, 1990). This often occurs when a shortage of male employees leads employers to seek out female employees. The shortage of male employees may be the result of rapid growth of the field, which causes a high demand for workers, but it is often the result of men deliberately leaving an occupation because they perceive it as declining in skill, prestige, and salary (Wright & Jacobs, 1995). Strober and Arnold (1987) report that bank telling shifted from a male to a female occupation as men were lured to other jobs by higher salaries and as bank telling was deskilled to entail fewer responsibilities and thus less prestige. We also saw an example of this in Chapter 4, where we discussed the transition of teaching from a male-dominated to a female-dominated profession. Interestingly, the professionalization of teaching during the nineteenth century helped raise wage rates for teachers even though the profession was increasingly feminized. However, men benefitted more from these wage increases than women did, especially as they assumed the higher-status positions of school administration (Preston, 1995). Other occupations that currently appear to be undergoing resegregation include bartender and psychologist (Roberts, 1995; see also Reskin, 1993).

Finally, any beneficial effects on workers from declines in occupational sex segregation may be undermined by other forms of workplace sex segregation, in particular industry sex segregation and establishment sex segregation. **Industry sex segregation** occurs when women and men hold the same job title in a particular field or industry, but actually perform different jobs. Women are typically concentrated in the lower-paying, lower-prestige specialties within the occupation. Tallichet (1995), for example, studied the integration of women into underground coal mining. You'll recall that earlier in the chapter we noted that coal mining is an occupation that showed a high influx of women workers in the 1970s following sex discrimination lawsuits that prompted mine operators to recruit more women. However, despite the hiring of more women in this occupation, Tallichet found that the majority are concentrated in laboring jobs, the lowest level of mining, which usually involves mine maintenance. Similarly, Wright and Jacobs (1995, p. 339) point out that "in the case of bakers, women mostly work in supermarkets baking prepackaged dough, while men continue to monopolize the more skilled positions in bakeries."

Establishment sex segregation occurs when women and men hold the same job title at an individual establishment or company, but actually do different jobs. Again, women's jobs are usually lower paying and less prestigious. For instance, it is not uncommon in a law firm for women to be concentrated in the family law division, while men dominate the more lucrative corporate and commercial law department (Kay & Hagan, 1995). In a department store, men typically sell "big ticket" items like large appliances and furniture, while women sell clothing, cosmetics, and housewares (Hartmann, 1987; Reskin, 1993; Reskin & Hartmann, 1986).

In sum, although occupational sex segregation has declined in recent years, it has declined more for certain groups than for others; for the majority of workers, it remains a fact of everyday work life. Moreover, the gains that have been made are tempered by resegregation, industry-wide sex segregation, and establishment sex segregation. At this point, you are probably wondering why this is the case, especially since so much public attention has been given to policies such as affirmative action that are supposed to remedy employment discrimination. However, before we explore the reasons behind the persistence of occupational sex segregation, let's examine some of its most serious consequences.

Consequences of Occupational Sex Segregation

One serious consequence of occupational sex segregation is that it limits employment opportunities. Occupational sex segregation limits the employment opportunities of both sexes, but as we have already noted, it disadvantages women workers most because what is typically labeled "women's work" has some very negative features associated with it. Many women's jobs—such as librarian and elementary or kindergarten teacher—are considered by many people to be boring and tedious jobs. Women's jobs are generally thought to have less autonomy than men's jobs and to require less skill or intelligence. And, perhaps most important, women's jobs typically offer few rewards in the forms of compensation, mobility, union protection, benefits, or prestige. Occupational sex segregation keeps more women than men locked into such jobs (Burris, 1989; Doyal, 1990a; Williams, 1992; 1995).

One interesting way to examine how occupational sex segregation affects employment opportunities is to consider the experiences of workers who obtain employment in jobs nontraditional for their sex. In her classic study of women and men in corporate management, Rosabeth Moss Kanter (1977, p. 209) discussed this problem in terms of **tokenism,** the marginal status of a category of workers who are relatively few in number in the workplace. Tokens, according to Kanter, are "often treated as representatives of their category, as symbols rather than as individuals."

Kanter identified a number of serious consequences for token workers. For instance, because of their conspicuousness in the workplace, they are more closely scrutinized by others. This places intense pressure on them to perform successfully, creating a work situation that is highly stressful. In addition, tokens experience what Kanter calls *boundary heightening;* that is, dominant workers tend to exaggerate the differences between themselves and the tokens and to treat the tokens as outsiders. Thus, researchers have noted that women workers sometimes find themselves excluded from formal information networks that help them do their jobs, but more often they are shut out of informal social networks that may be just as crucial for their job performance and advancement. As male workers are well aware, important business is conducted not only in board rooms or at union meetings, but also on golf courses and in local taverns. However, it is these sorts of informal social/business activities in which women workers are least likely to be included by their male coworkers or supervisors (Couric, 1989; Davies-Netzley, 1998; Scott, 1996; U.S. Department of Labor, 1997).[1]

Kanter makes the argument that tokenism is a problem of numbers and, therefore, the employment experiences of women in sex-atypical occupations should become more positive as more women enter such positions. However, Zimmer (1988, p. 72) and others (e.g., Blum & Smith, 1988; Franklin & Sweeney, 1988; Williams, 1995) maintain that "men's negative behavior toward women in the workplace . . . seems to be much less motivated by women's presence in a numerical minority than by men's evaluation of women as a social minority—an opinion based on notions of inferiority rather than scarcity." In other words, "the crucial factor" that determines employment experiences "is the social status of the token's group—not their numerical rarity" (Williams, 1992, p. 263). Consequently, although women and men in sex-atypical jobs encounter discrimination, its forms and consequences differ significantly depending on the job holder's sex.

Sociologist Christine Williams's (1992; 1995) fascinating study of men in female-dominated occupations strongly supports this argument. Researchers who have studied women in sex-atypical occupations report that they are usually disadvantaged in hiring and promotions and that they encounter a "glass ceiling" as they attempt to navigate their way up the occupational hierarchy. The **glass ceiling** refers to the invisible barriers that limit workers'—typically women workers' and racial and ethnic minority workers'—upward occupational mobility. One of Williams's most intriguing findings is that men in sex-atypical occupations receive preferential treatment in hiring and, instead of encountering a glass ceiling, often ride a *glass escalator* up the hierarchy of these professions. According to Williams (1995), men in sex-atypical jobs frequently encounter invisible and sometimes less subtle pressures to move up in their professions. "Like being on an invisible 'up' escalator, men must struggle to remain in the lower (i.e., 'feminine') levels of their professions." These pressures may take quite positive forms, such as close mentoring and encouragement from supervisors (who, as we have already noted, are often men even though the field is female-dominated), but they may also be the result of prejudicial attitudes by those outside the profession, including the general public and clients, who question the masculinity of men in a traditionally female occupation. One male librarian whom Williams interviewed, for example, was transferred from the children's collection to the adult reference section of the library because some people complained about a man working with children. The underlying assumption here is that "only men who are child molesters or sexual perverts would be drawn to [this] specialty" (Williams, 1995, p. 13). But for this man, like many others in sex-atypical jobs, the prejudice worked to his advantage: He was transferred to a more prestigious department, to a job that carried more authority.

Williams (1995) reports that the men she interviewed indicated that their supervisors were more likely to discriminate against female employees than against them. An important exception, however, was men who were openly gay; gay men did not receive the favorable treatment afforded their straight male colleagues. For instance, Williams relates the experience of a male nurse who worked in a hospital where one of the physicians preferred to staff the operating room exclusively with male nurses as long as they were not gay.[2]

Another difference between men's and women's experiences of tokenism that Williams (1992; 1995) discovered was that men reported feeling "in control" in a female-dominated work environment. In contrast, women in male-dominated work environments report feeling intimidated and controlled. These differential experiences are further reflected in the incidence of sexual harassment in the workplace.

Sexual Harassment in the Workplace

You may recall that in Chapter 4 we defined sexual harassment as any unwanted leers, comments, suggestions, or physical contact of a sexual nature, as well as unwelcome requests for sexual favors. Men rarely experience sexual harassment from women in the workplace; there were no incidents of sexual harassment, for example, reported by the men in Williams's study. Women, on the other hand, routinely experience sexual harassment from men in the workplace. Studies in the United States and Great Britain reveal that from 42 percent to as many as 88 percent of women workers experience sexual harassment at some point during their work lives (Ragins & Scandura, 1995). In a 1989 study of 918 female attorneys in the United States, among whom one-third earned more than $100,000 a year, 60 percent reported that they had experienced unwanted sexual attention at work. Thirteen of these respondents stated that they had been victims of rape, attempted rape, or assault while at work; the assailants in most cases were their supervisors (Couric, 1989). In a 1992 survey of 640 women journalists working at 19 small, medium, and large newsrooms throughout the United States, 1 of every 3 respondents reported having been sexually harassed at work (MRTW, 1993e). And in a 1993 survey of 417 female family practitioners in Ontario, Canada, 75 percent said they had been sexually harassed by patients: Slightly more than half reported that the harassment took the form of suggestive looks and sexual remarks; about 25 percent reported suggestive gestures, offers of dates, and inappropriate gifts (e.g., g-strings, tapes of love songs); almost one-third reported patients had exposed themselves in sexually suggestive ways; and 4 percent reported that patients touched them inappropriately (Phillips & Schneider, 1993). Other studies have documented widespread sexual harassment of women workers in fields as disparate as coal mining (Tallichet, 1995) and investment banking (Meier, 1996).

Perhaps no other recent incident did more to highlight the problem of sexual harassment for women than the testimony of Anita Hill to the Senate Judiciary Committee during the confirmation hearings for Clarence Thomas's nomination to the U.S. Supreme Court in 1991. Although Thomas was ultimately confirmed as a U.S. Supreme Court Justice, Hill's recounting of his harassment of her raised public awareness of the seriousness of the problem and encouraged more women to report harassment incidents. Between 1991 and 1995, the number of sexual harassment charges filed each year more than doubled, reaching 15,549 cases in 1995 ("Sexual Harassment," 1996). More recent cases involving top political figures, including Senator Bob Packwood (R-OR) and President Bill Clinton, have also served to keep the problem of sexual harassment in the public's consciousness and have encouraged women to bring formal charges.[3]

Although women in all types of occupations confront sexual harassment, some observers claim that it is especially pervasive in male-dominated jobs to which women are new hires, since it may serve as a means for male workers to assert dominance and control over women who otherwise would be their equals (Gruber & Bjorn, 1982; Tallichet, 1995; Westley, 1982). Gruber (1998), for example, found that women who work in nontraditional jobs in a male-dominated work environment experience more sexual harassment than women who work in traditional female jobs. However, Gruber reports that women who work in female-dominated jobs that entail a high degree of contact with men also experience high rates of sexual harassment. In fact, in Gruber's study, level of contact between men and women in the workplace was one of the strongest predictors of sexual harassment, leading him to conclude that *where* a woman does her job is more important than the type of job she does in affecting her chances of being harassed. Ragins and Scandura (1995) also found that type of job was unimportant: They found no significant differences in reports of sexual harassment among women in male-typed occupations, female-typed occupations, and gender-integrated occupations, although within male-typed occupations, women who held blue-collar jobs reported more harassment than women who held white-collar jobs. Importantly, Rogers and Henson's (1997) study of a highly sex-segregated, feminized job—temporary clerical work—revealed other job characteristics that are significant. They found that the transitory nature of this type of employment increases women's vulnerability to all types of abuse, including sexual harassment. "[T]emporary workers are objectified and stripped of their personhood, paving the way for poor treatment, including sexual harassment" (Rogers & Henson, 1997, p. 217).

Regardless of the types of jobs in which it occurs, the consequences of sexual harassment for female workers are serious and harmful. Harassed women report a number of physical responses to the harassment, including chronic neck and back pain, upset stomach, colitis and other gastrointestinal disorders, and eating and sleeping disorders. Harassed women also become nervous, irritable, and depressed (Saltzman, 1996b; Stanko, 1985).

Despite the significant increase in reports of sexual harassment recently, most women still do not make official complaints. Instead, many women quit their jobs in order to end the harassment, although given the extent of the problem, this is no guarantee that they will not encounter a similar situation at another work site. Employers have responded to sexual harassment claims in a variety of ways. There is evidence that employers increasingly prefer to handle complaints quietly, through private mediation (Fine, 1997), although research also shows that employers who take a visible, proactive approach to addressing sexual harassment are more successful in lowering incidents of harassment than employers who just provide information about the problem to their employees (Gruber, 1998). Some employers have simply banned sexual relationships between coworkers, even if they are consensual, and a few require coworkers who wish to become intimate to sign "consensual relationship agreements" to protect against sexual harassment suits ("For Water Cooler Paramours," 1998; Robinson & Gosselin, 1998). Nevertheless, in 1998, the U.S. Supreme Court ruled that employers are always potentially liable for a supervisor's sexual misconduct toward an employee. To successfully defend against this liability, employers must show that they made reasonable efforts to prevent or promptly stop sexual harassment and that the employee unreasonably failed to take advantage of these efforts.

This decision is the latest in a series by the Court that has made it easier for employees to file—and win—sexual harassment suits.[4] For example, in 1986 and in a subsequent decision in 1993, the Court ruled that sexual harassment so severe and pervasive as to alter the conditions of the victim's employment constitutes a form of sex discrimination. The Court broadened the definition of sexual harassment to include any action that creates a work environment that would be reasonably perceived as hostile and abusive. Moreover, the Court held in 1993 that workers do not have to prove that the harassment caused them severe psychological injury in order to win a suit for damages. And finally, in 1998, the Court unanimously agreed that federal law protects people in the workplace from being harassed by coworkers or supervisors of the same sex.[5]

Sexual harassment is undoubtedly one of the most serious consequences of occupational sex segregation. However, there is one additional consequence that deserves special attention because of the harm it produces. This is the economic impact of sex segregation, or what is perhaps better known as the *wage gap*.

The Male/Female Earnings Gap

In their longitudinal analysis of the economic well-being of women and children, Corcoran et al. (1984, pp. 233–234) quote a biblical verse in which God, speaking to Moses, said, "When a man makes a special vow to the Lord which requires your valuation of living persons, a male between twenty and sixty years old shall be valued at fifty silver sheckels. If it is a female, she shall be valued at thirty sheckels." As Corcoran and her colleagues subsequently note, this biblical custom of valuing women's labor at three-fifths that of a man appears to have carried over into the contemporary work world. From 1960 to 1990, year-round female workers earned on average between 59 and 70 percent of what males workers earned. In other words, for every dollar a male worker made, a female worker made on average between 59 and 70 cents. For more than three decades, this ratio fluctuated within these boundaries (Taeuber & Valdisera, 1986; U.S. Department of Commerce, Bureau of the Census, 1991). In 1993, however, the earnings gap closed to 77 percent, a figure not worth celebrating, but an indication of progress.[6] For the next four years, the gap widened a bit. By 1997, it was 74.8 percent. Some observers attributed the widening to changes in welfare eligibility that sent many young, unskilled women into the labor force, a point to which we will return shortly. But others pointed out that much of the narrowing of the gap in previous years was the result not of women's wages rising, but of men's real wages falling so that they were closer to women's wages (Lewin, 1997c). In the first quarter of 1998, the wage gap narrowed once again—to 76 percent—which analysts believe reflects an increase in the minimum wage from $4.25 per hour to $5.15 per hour. Since more women than men are minimum wage workers, an increase in the minimum wage would help close the earnings gap (Love, 1998).

Of course, race and ethnicity are important intervening variables. Looking at Table 7.4 on page 208, we see that, in 1997, the earnings gap by sex was significantly wider for White workers (74.6 percent) than for either African American (86.8 percent) or Hispanic American (85.7 percent) workers. If we were to look only at the earnings gap by race and ethnicity, we would find that, in 1997, African Americans earned 77 percent of what Whites earn, while Hispanic Americans earned only 67.6 percent of what Whites earn. However, by making within-sex comparisons by race and ethnicity, we get a better picture of how race and ethnicity intersect with sex to depress wages. Using the data in Table 7.4, we can determine that, in 1997, African American women earned 84.5 percent of what White women earned, whereas Hispanic American women earned just 71.6 percent of what White women earn. For African American and Hispanic American men, the wage gap relative to White men is 72.6 percent and 62.4 percent respectively. Thus, although Hispanic American women have the lowest median weekly earnings of all groups, the gap between their earnings and those of women in

TABLE 7.4   Median Weekly Earnings of Full-Time Wage and Salary Workers
by Race/Ethnicity and Sex, 1997

Race/Ethnicity & Sex	Median Weekly Earnings	Female/Male Wage Gap
White	$519	
Male	595	
Female	444	74.6%
African American	400	
Male	432	
Female	375	86.8%
Hispanic American	351	
Male	371	
Female	318	85.7%

Source: U.S. Department of Labor, 1998b, p. 208.

other racial groups is actually narrower than the earnings gap between minority men and White men.

An individual's earnings, of course, are affected by the type of work she or he does. As we have already noted, women and minorities continue to experience widespread occupational segregation. The jobs in which they predominate tend not only to be less prestigious than those dominated by White men, but also to pay less. Recent statistics also indicate that minorities and women are more likely than Whites and men to be hired as contingent workers, temporary employees, on-call workers, and day laborers. Contingent workers do not have continuous ongoing employment, but rather work at a job for a fixed period of time, usually less than a year; their employment is contingent on employers' needs for their services. Temporary workers usually obtain employment through a temp agency; they typically work sporadically throughout the year and move from job site to job site as demand requires. On-call and day laborers work even less regularly, going to a job only when called. According to the Department of Labor (1995), the typical worker who holds one of these atypical work arrangements is young, female, and Black. Finally, as we have already noted, women are more likely than men to be employed in minimum wage jobs than in salaried occupations. In 1996, 49.9 percent of hourly wage workers were male; 5.1 percent earned the minimum wage or less. In contrast, 50.1 percent of hourly wage workers in 1996 were women and of these, 9.1 percent earned the minimum wage or less. Men's median hourly wage in 1996 was $9.81, whereas women's median hourly wage was $7.81. People of color are also disproportionately represented among minimum wage workers: 6.9 percent of White workers earned the minimum wage or less compared to 8.5 percent of African American workers and 9.7 percent of Hispanic American workers (U.S. Department of Commerce, Bureau of the Census, 1997).

The monetary rewards to the employers of these workers are obvious; not only do contingent, temporary, on-call, day labor, and minimum-wage employees receive lower wages than employees in traditional work arrangements and salaried occupations, but they also typically are not entitled to costly employment benefits such as medical and disability insurance, pensions, and paid vacations, and these workers are rarely unionized. Regardless of the economic benefits for employers, the effects on female and minority workers are overwhelmingly negative. Indeed, given these data, it is hardly surprising that women and racial and ethnic minorities are disproportionately represented among the poor.

The Earnings Gap, Poverty, and Welfare Policy

Approximately 11 percent of the White population in the United States is officially poor, whereas 14.6 percent of the Asian American population, 29 percent of the Black population, 30.6 percent of the Latino population, and 31.2 percent of the Native American population are officially living below the poverty line (U.S. Department of Commerce, Bureau of the Census, 1997).[7] As we learned in Chapter 6, female-headed households also are disproportionately represented among the poverty population, with a poverty rate more than double that of male-headed households (49.3 percent versus 22.8 percent); just 10.1 percent of married couple families live below the poverty line (Children's Defense Fund, 1998). When the race of female-headed households is taken into account, the figures are even more alarming: Nearly one in every two White female-headed households live below the poverty line, more than two of three African American and seven of ten Hispanic female-headed families are officially poor (U.S. Department of Commerce, Bureau of the Census, 1993).

When we think of poverty, we often think of unemployment. Unemployment rates, like the other statistics we have examined, vary by sex and race and ethnicity, although race and ethnicity have a greater impact on unemployment than sex does.[8] In 1998, the overall unemployment rates of both men and women, aged twenty and over, were quite low, although women's unemployment rate was slightly higher than the men's rate (4.4 percent and 3.8 percent respectively). However, the unemployment rates of African American male and female workers were more than double those of White workers, and the unemployment rates of Hispanic male and female workers were more than 50 percent higher than those of White workers (U.S. Department of Labor, 1998a). Thus, even when the economy is strong, as it was in 1998, racial and ethnic minorities reap fewer benefits than Whites.

What the unemployment rates also tell us, however, is that the majority of those living in poverty, including the majority of women who head households, are working. Some work only part time year-round or sporadically throughout the year, but most work full time. Of course, being unemployed significantly increases one's chances of falling into poverty, but employment does not necessarily lift an individual and her or his family above the poverty threshold. Consider, for example, that in 1994, the median weekly earnings of women who maintained families was just $350, which amounts to $18,236 per year (U.S. Department of Commerce, Bureau of the Census, 1997). If we take into account deductions for Social Security and employment-related expenses (e.g., child care, transportation, food, clothing), disposable income is reduced considerably. These families are thus placed precariously close to, if not below the official poverty line, which in 1994 was $11,821 for a family of three. It is important to emphasize, too, that we are speaking here of median earnings, which means that half of all females who head households and work full time, year-round earn less than $18,236 per year. Race and ethnicity are again intervening variables: Families maintained by Black women have annual median earnings of about $6,852 less than families maintained by White women, while families maintained by Latinas have median annual earnings of about $8,678 less than families maintained by White women (U.S. Department of Commerce, Bureau of the Census, 1997).

Let's compare the median earnings of women who maintain families with those of other heads of households. In 1994, married couple families earned $865 per week or $44,959 per year, and men who maintained families earned $534 per week or $27,751 per year (U.S. Department of Commerce, Bureau of the Census, 1997). Married-couple families and families maintained by men have median earnings higher than those of families maintained by women regardless of race or ethnicity, but the median annual earnings of African American and Hispanic married-couple families are respectively $5,042 and $15,853 less than those of White married-couple families. Families maintained by African American and Hispanic men have median annual earnings respectively of $8,483 and $7,673 less than families maintained by White men (U.S. Department of Commerce, Bureau of the Census, 1997). Nevertheless, in light of these data it is not difficult to see how employment is hardly a safeguard against poverty for women raising children alone, nor is it surprising that the inadequacy of their wages makes welfare benefits more appealing than jobs to some women who head households.

Sociologists Kathryn Edin and Laura Lein (1997), for example, found in their study of impoverished women that working mothers fared worse financially than mothers on welfare. Even though work seemed to bring in about 42 percent more income than welfare benefits, the gain was significantly diminished by employment-related expenses. Moreover, about 40 percent of the working mothers Edin and Lein interviewed lacked health insurance, while the women on welfare received Medicaid (federally financed health insurance), so the working mothers were more likely than the welfare recipients to forgo necessary medical care.

Edin and Lein's (1997) research is important because it debunks popular myths about welfare recipients and alerts us to the dangers inherent in the welfare "reforms" signed into law by President Clinton in 1996. One widespread myth about welfare recipients is that they can live quite well on the benefits they receive. Edin and Lein's study shows that welfare benefits are not sufficient to even make ends meet. The average welfare family spends about $300 more per month than what they receive in their welfare check and food stamp package. In other words, welfare and food stamps provide only about two-thirds the amount of money a welfare family needs to survive each month, and this is not because welfare recipients are spending their benefits frivolously or living the "good life" at taxpayers' expense. For example, Edin and Lein found that only 7 percent of a welfare recipient's income is spent on unnecessary items such as movies, a meal out, cigarettes, or alcohol, and Black women and Latinas spend less on these items than White women do. Rather, the inadequacy of welfare means that most of these women must find additional sources of income—legal or illegal—to make ends meet. It also means that most live in substandard housing and many cannot adequately feed and clothe their children. Indeed, Edin and Lein found that one in eight women in their study had kept their children home from school during the winter because they did not have sufficient clothing.

Champions of welfare "reform" have argued that welfare induces complacency in the face of hardship among single mothers and encourages them to have more children (Fineman, 1996; McCrate & Smith, 1998). Reflecting this argument, the Personal Responsibility and Work Opportunity Reconciliation Act, signed by President Clinton in 1996, contains among its provisions a mandatory work requirement after two years of assistance, a cap on the total time a family can receive assistance of five years, permission for the states to deny additional benefits to women who have more children while on welfare, the elimination of the bonus welfare mothers receive for helping the government collect child support from absent fathers, and significant reductions in the Food Stamp program (Kilborn, 1996; McCrate & Smith, 1998). Experts have no doubts that these "reforms" will succeed in reducing the number of welfare recipients in this country, but many warn that the new law is also likely to harm women and children unless "health insurance has been drastically reformed, wages raised, and job training, child care, and child support more scrupulously tended to" (McCrate & Smith, 1998, p. 62), and there is no evidence that any of this is taking place (Children's Defense Fund, 1998).

Gender, Poverty, and the Elderly.   While we have emphasized the intersection of sexism and racism in the generation and reproduction of poverty, it is also important to consider a third factor, age. Women are disproportionately represented among *individuals* living in poverty, but the statistics mask the fact that among these individuals, a large percentage are elderly women who live alone. Although the poverty rate of the elderly population has declined significantly since the late 1960s—from 28.5 percent or more than twice the rate of the general population in 1966, to 10.5 percent, somewhat less than the 13.8 percent rate for the general population, in 1995—improvement has been slower for elderly women (U.S. Department of Commerce, Bureau of the Census, 1997). About 58 percent of the population aged sixty-five and older is female, but females constitute more than 70 percent of the elderly poor and more than 80 percent of the elderly poor who live alone. Two-thirds of the elderly who live alone are widows and, in contrast with the stereotype of the "old, rich widow," most elderly widows are poor. Overall, the poverty rate of elders who live alone is 22 percent, compared with a 5.4 percent poverty rate for elders who live with a spouse and a 12 percent rate for elders who live with others. Importantly, however, race again intersects with sex to increase the risk of elderly poverty. For example, elderly Black men who live alone have a poverty rate more than double that of elderly White women who live alone; the poverty rate of elderly Black women who live alone is triple the poverty rate for elderly White women who live alone (U.S. Senate Special Committee on Aging, 1991). Thus, as Davis and her colleagues (1990) point out:

> As these figures suggest, elderly women living alone, often nonwhite widows of advanced age and declining health, are most vulnerable to poverty. . . . When elderly people living alone are categorized by sex, age, and race, the lowest poverty rate is for white men aged 65–74 . . . and the highest is for nonwhite women age 85 and above

... Even more troubling is evidence indicating that the concentration of poverty among elderly women living alone will worsen as we move into the next century. . . . While most of the older population will fare well economically over the next 30 years, the proportion of women with incomes below 150 percent of poverty will remain high: 45 percent in 1987, and 38 percent in 2020. . . . Among widows the situation is slightly worse, with the proportion who are poor or near-poor rising until the turn of the century. . . . [B]y 2020 poverty among the elderly will be almost exclusively a problem among elderly women. (pp. 43–45)

One of the reasons there are more women than men among the elderly poor is simply that there are more elderly women than elderly men; women, on average, live longer than men (see Chapter 11). Moreover, the longer they live, the greater their chances are of depleting their savings and slipping below the poverty line (Feldstein, 1998). The economic difficulties of elderly women are also directly related to their employment patterns, the wages they earned during their work lives, and their job benefits. For example, women are less likely than men to be employed in jobs that have private pension plans. According to one recent report, 25 million working women have no pension plans, and among those who do, most will receive about half the benefits men receive because their earnings are lower. About two-thirds of employed women work at jobs that have the lowest pension coverage rates ("25 Million Women," 1996). The average private pension benefit for women is $3,940 a year, compared with an average annual benefit of $7,468 for men (Lewin, 1995). In addition, since women earn less than men, their Social Security benefits will also be lower. In fact, only about 33 percent of retired women currently receive Social Security benefits based on their own work histories, since the benefits they receive as a spouse are about twice as much as what they are entitled to as individual retirees (Feldstein, 1998; Holden & Smock, 1991; Lewin, 1995). Women frequently interrupt their labor force participation because of caregiving responsibilities (see Chapter 6); in fact, women on average spend 11.5 years out of the paid labor force because of caregiving, whereas men spend an average of 1.3 years out for the same reason. Employment interruptions not only limit job opportunities, but also prevent women from accruing sufficient retirement benefits (Davis et al., 1990; Jacobsen & Levin, 1995). Although Supplemental Security Income (SSI) was designed to assist those not covered by Social Security or those for whom Social Security benefits are inadequate, the program has stringent eligibility requirements that disqualify many individuals even though they are poor. This, coupled with the fact that many eligible persons do not apply for SSI because they are unaware of the program or do not understand it, explains why less than one-third of the elderly poor who live alone—most of whom, we have seen, are women—receive SSI (Davis et al., 1990).

Another segment of the poverty population is made up of the homeless. As Box 7.1 shows, the homeless, like the poverty population as a whole, is diverse. Women's and men's experiences of homelessness, we learn, differ, as do those of single individuals and families.

At this point it is clear that the wage gap contributes to many pervasive and serious problems. A question that remains, however, is how the wage gap is related to occupational segregation. To answer this question, we need to examine explanations of the wage gap itself. In addressing this topic, we will concentrate primarily on the gender gap in wages, but we will also consider to some extent the racial/ethnic gap in wages.

BOX 7.1
Gender and Homelessness

In the minds of many of us with homes, myths rather than facts about homelessness predominate (Golden, 1992). So, the first question we need to address is: Who are the homeless?

Research indicates that the homeless are far more diverse than one might suppose. It is commonly believed that the homeless are unemployed single men and women who are alcoholics, drug addicts, or mental patients indiscriminately released from mental hospitals. Although it is certainly the case that some homeless fit into these categories, they are not the majority. Moreover, it is unclear whether substance abuse and symptoms of mental illness (e.g., hearing voices, "antisocial" behavior, hoarding) emerge before or after the individual becomes homeless—that is, whether these behaviors are adaptations to homelessness rather than causes of homelessness. Consider carefully for a moment what life on the streets or in public shelters might be like. The demoralization and disorientation that result from having to keep moving without having any place to go and having no structure to one's life are likely to psychologically weaken even the emotionally strong. As Golden (1992) discovered, however, most of the homeless are not severely mentally disturbed, nor do they have drug and alcohol problems.

Instead, research indicates that what all homeless people share in common is abject poverty. Since certain groups, such as racial and ethnic minorities, are disproportionately represented among the poor, they are also at greater risk of becoming homeless. Rossi (1989), for example, reports that nationally nearly 46 percent of the homeless are African Americans, almost 12 percent are Hispanic Americans, and about 5 percent are Native Americans. Additional research indicates that the majority of homeless adults are high school graduates and more than 24 percent have attended college. A considerable number of homeless adults hold full-time or part-time jobs, but these are typically minimum-wage jobs that do not provide enough income to obtain housing, especially in major metropolitan areas. However,

homelessness is not solely an urban problem; it is increasing in the nation's suburbs and rural regions as well (Kozol, 1988; Schmitt, 1988; Vanderstaay, 1992).

Importantly, the fastest growing segment of the homeless population is young families with children (Children's Defense Fund, 1998; Kolker, 1998; Kozol, 1988). "The average homeless family includes a parent with two or three children. The average child is six years old, the average parent is twenty-seven" (Kozol, 1988, p. 4). The vast majority of homeless families are women with children. For many, homelessness is an extension of the high rate of poverty among female-headed families. The primary reasons they are homeless are the rising cost of housing, the shortage of low-income housing units, and an inability to find an adequate-paying job (Children's Defense Fund, 1998). An increasing number of women and children are becoming homeless as a result of leaving an abusive husband/father. For abused women and children, living on the street is a survival strategy (Browne & Bassuk, 1997; Golden, 1992). But homelessness itself breaks up families; in many cities, for instance, women and children must stay in shelters separate from men (Kozol, 1988).

Golden (1992) emphasizes the gender differences in the causes of homelessness among single women and men. She points out, for instance, that the deinstitutionalization movement of the 1970s made more women than men homeless because more women than men were residents of psychiatric facilities during this period. More recently, however, Golden found that the primary reason for homelessness among women was loss of relationships. The majority of women Golden met as a shelter volunteer had adhered to a traditional feminine role of financial dependency on someone else, usually a husband, boyfriend, or father. When, because of death or some other reason, these relationships dissolved, the women simply could not fend for themselves.

Those women in Golden's study who had worked had no economic security. They held

(continued)

B O X **7.1**   **Continued**

marginal jobs that paid poorly and offered no benefits. Once they became homeless, they had greater difficulty than men getting work. Jobs open to women, even those in domestic service, typically required that they maintain a certain decorum in dress and appearance that was virtually impossible for homeless women. They found themselves excluded from many jobs for which references and appearances were irrelevant—day laborer, for example—because such jobs are not considered "women's work."

Although it certainly may not be said that life on the street is easy for men, it is nevertheless the case that street life is more difficult for women. For one thing, it is more dangerous in certain ways. Women are more vulnerable to physical assault, and researchers who have talked with homeless women report that rape and other sexual assaults are not uncommon (Golden, 1992; Vanderstaay, 1992). And only women run the risk of becoming pregnant as a result of a forced or consensual sexual encounter.

Even the most routine aspects of daily living are more difficult for homeless women than for homeless men. This largely results from the virtual absence of privacy afforded the homeless, and the fact that in our society women more than

men are socialized to value privacy, especially when carrying out basic hygienic functions. Thus, relieving oneself in public is not only physically, but also psychologically more difficult for women. Cleaning oneself in a public washroom or showering with others in a public shelter have a similar psychological effect on homeless women. And, as Golden (1992, p. 160) notes, "Any woman can imagine the potential for agonizing humiliation in having one's period on the street."

While it is true that many of those with homes tend to blame the homeless for their own plight, homeless women are especially stigmatized, and much of this stigma is sexually charged (Golden, 1992). It is assumed, for example, that homeless women are promiscuous and immoral. If they have children, they are stereotyped as "welfare mothers" who freeload off the system and promiscuously reproduce. If they are alone, they do not escape the label of promiscuity—in fact, they are frequent targets of sexual harassment because of it—but it is also assumed that their problems would be solved if they could just find a "good man." Ironically, what is overlooked in these cases is the fact that it was their relationships with men that often initially propelled these women into homelessness.

Explaining the Wage Gap

Table 7.5 shows median weekly earnings of selected occupations in 1997. The table contains a broad range of jobs that require different levels of training, skill, effort, and responsibility, but one consistent observation that can be made is that female-dominated occupations usually pay significantly less than male-dominated occupations. Recent research indicates, in fact, that occupational sex segregation alone accounts for about 20 to 40 percent of the difference in men's and women's earnings (Kay & Hagan, 1995; Sorensen, 1994). These studies document a strong inverse relationship between the extent to which women are represented in a specific job and that job's median earnings. "Earnings rise with the percentage of one's occupational co-workers who are men, whether or not the characteristics of workers and occupations are controlled . . . As women's share of an occupation rises, the pay of both men and women in that occupation appears to fall" (Lewis & Nice, 1994, pp. 393–394; see also Kay & Hagan, 1995; Reskin, 1993; Rosenfeld & Kalleberg, 1991).

TABLE 7.5   Median Weekly Earnings of Selected Male-Dominated and Female-Dominated Occupations, 1997

Occupation	Female (%)	Median Weekly Earnings ($)
Secretary	98.7	410
Receptionist	97.7	366
Child care worker	97.3	202
Dental assistant	96.4	366
Registered nurse	92.5	710
Bank teller	91.3	321
Nursing aide	88.6	300
Hairdresser or cosmetologist	87.7	311
Telephone operator	87.0	367
Elementary school teacher	83.4	662
Librarian	82.6	638
Textile sewing machine operator	79.7	263
Social worker	67.4	522
Mail carrier	28.6	677
Architect	18.4	822
Police officer or detective	11.3	697
Engineer	9.4	977
Welder	6.5	491
Truck driver	4.1	506
Logger	3.8	391
Airline engine mechanic	3.1	724
Fire fighter	3.0	707
Airplane pilot or navigator	1.1	1,079
Roofer	0.0	407

Source: U.S. Department of Labor, 1998b, pp. 209–214.

Many employers, economists, and public policy makers acknowledge that "women's work" almost always pays less than "men's work," but they maintain that the reason particular jobs have become female-dominated is because large numbers of women have freely chosen to enter them. Central to their argument is the assumption that women's primary allegiance is to home and family; thus, they seek undemanding jobs that require little personal investment in training or skills acquisition so that they can better tend to their household responsibilities. In other words, women choose to invest less than men in employment outside the home, so they get less in return. This explanation is called **human capital theory.**

In evaluating human capital theory, we will focus first on the issue of women's "choice" of occupations. It is certainly the case, as we learned in Chapter 6, that women bear primary responsibility for home and family care, but what is less clear is the extent to which this is voluntary. A major weakness in human capital theory is that it fails to distinguish between self-imposed job restrictions and structurally imposed ones. For instance, are nonemployed mothers who cannot find affordable and reliable child care really making a "free choice" to stay out of the labor market? Studies indicate that five of every six nonemployed women would enter the labor force if they could find adequate child care (Barrett, 1987; Reskin & Hartmann, 1986). The decision to remain at home or to accept low-paying jobs because the hours or work arrangements better suit one's child care responsibilities is most often a response to a structurally imposed constraint on women's occupational opportunities—that is, our government's failure to enact a national child care policy (see Box 7.2).

In fact, as we have already seen, the majority of women with very young children do work outside the home. Moreover, research shows that, contrary to the argument of human capital theorists, women's probability of working in a nontraditional occupation increases with the number of children they have. Although mothers of young children do try to avoid jobs with rotating shifts because of the child care difficulties they pose, having children has been positively correlated with women's efforts to leave female-dominated jobs for male-dominated ones (Reskin, 1993). The simple explanation for these findings is that the higher pay, better benefits, and greater opportunities for promotion found in male-dominated jobs make them especially attractive to women who make a major financial contribution to their families' support (Padevic, 1992; Padevic & Reskin, 1990; Rosenfeld & Spenner, 1992).

While women's marital and motherhood statuses do not appear to negatively influence their desire to work in male-dominated jobs, the choice to take such a job obviously is constrained by its availability. We use the term *availability* here to refer not only to a job opening, but also to the extent to which a job seeker perceives that she has a fair chance of being hired for the job, feeling welcome on the job, and succeeding in the job. Research shows that workers' decisions to take specific jobs reflect the occupational opportunities available to them. Historically, women have not been hired for jobs such as coal mining and shipbuilding, but evidence indicates that once employers began to open job opportunities in these fields, women responded by seeking such jobs (Kesselman, 1990; Reskin & Hartmann, 1986; Tallichet, 1995). However, the number of women already working in a particular job also has been shown to be important because such women serve as role models and mentors to other female job aspirants (Ferguson & Dunphy, 1992; U.S. Department of Labor, 1997; see also Chapter 4). If few or no women hold particular jobs, then women are likely to believe that these jobs are not really open to them, and they will rarely pursue them. The lack of women in an occupation or field sends a message to other women: You are unlikely to succeed here (Riger, 1988). Some women may choose not to enter certain occupations because they do not want to subject themselves to discrimination on the job and to a working environment that is hostile to women (Riger, 1988).

Research has documented male workers' efforts to exclude women from certain occupations by, for instance, deliberately excluding them from particular activities or even sabotaging their work (Reskin, 1993; Tallichet, 1995). Reskin and Roos (1990) found that the greater the power of male workers in the workplace—with power being measured in terms of male workers' average job tenure and the percentage of the male employees who are White, speak English, and are prime-age—the lower the presence

BOX 7.2
The Child Care Dilemma

Work in the United States is still organized under the assumption that workers are men who, if they have children, also have a wife at home to care for them (Shelton, 1992). As we have seen, however, this is not the case. The number of single-parent families in the United States has increased significantly during the last twenty-five years alone, and women with preschool-aged children have been one of the fastest growing segments of the labor force. Nevertheless, the federal government and most employers have responded ineffectively at best to these demographic changes. The United States, unlike at least 146 other countries, has no official government policy mandating *paid* parental leave, and we are one of the few advanced industrialized countries that lacks a government-mandated child care system (Haas, 1992; United Nations, 1998).

It was not until 1993 that the United States had any federal legislation mandating parental leave. Currently, the Family and Medical Leave Act requires employers with fifty or more employees to offer both women and men up to twelve weeks *unpaid* leave following the birth or adoption of a child or to care for a sick child or family member. This policy contrasts sharply with that of other countries. Sweden, for example, instituted a national policy of paid parental leave for both mothers and fathers in 1974; it was the first country to do so and continues to have one of the most comprehensive policies in the world. But even developing countries, such as the Sudan, Cameroon, and Nepal, have national paid maternity leave policies. Only Australia, New Zealand, Lesotho, Swaziland, and Papua New Guinea, besides the United States, do not (United Nations, 1998).

Research on the impact of the Family and Medical Leave Act in the United States indicates that men are far less likely than women to take the leave, primarily for two reasons. The first is money. As we have already learned, there is a substantial wage gap between women and men; few families can afford to have fathers, who typically earn more than mothers, stay at home on unpaid parental leave. Second, although employers are required to offer the leave to both male and female employees, studies show that men fear that their employers will view them as less dedicated to their careers and their companies if they take more than just a few days off following the birth of a child. The men worry that their employers may "punish" them for taking parental leave (Shelton, 1992). These perceptions are not unfounded, since studies also show that the majority of employers think that their male employees should take no parental leave (Chira, 1993; see also Lewin, 1997d).

The provisions of the Family and Medical Leave Act may also be unfeasible for many female workers as well, and again the reason is economic. Few single women who have babies can afford to take much unpaid time off from work. Among the working class and working poor, even in two-parent households, both partners' incomes are necessary for the economic survival of the family, thus making an unpaid leave for a woman, even in a low-paying job, financially unfeasible. Consequently, women in such circumstances, as well as workers in companies with fewer than fifty employees, must often return to work within days of their child's birth, arranging some form of child care for the infant.

It is not overstating the point to say that many working parents in the United States confront a child care crisis. According to the Children's Defense Fund (1998), 13 million preschool-aged children, including 6 million infants and toddlers, are in need of child care each year, and millions of older children are in need of after-school care. With the welfare law now mandating that beneficiaries go to work, the number of children in need of care is expected to skyrocket (Rimer, 1997; Swarns, 1998). But affordable, reliable, and high-quality child care is difficult to find, and for low-income families, the problem is especially acute. The cost of center-based care in an urban area ranges from $5,000 to $12,000 per year per infant and $4,000 to $8,000 per year per preschooler. Low-income families can apply for child care subsidies from their state governments, but most states have lengthy waiting lists for these subsidies: In Florida, the waiting list in 1997 contained the names of 21,000 children; in New Jersey, 15,000 children were on the waiting list; and in

(continued)

Texas, 37,000 families were waiting for state subsidies (Children's Defense Fund, 1998).

Some corporations and businesses have opened their own child care centers in recognition of the importance of family concerns and as means to attract and retain workers. Others provide child care referral services or a child care subsidy as a job benefit. Still others permit "flextime" (employees set their own work schedule as long as they work a requisite number of hours per day or week) and "flexplace" (i.e., employees work out of their homes at least part of the work day or week). Regardless of the advantages or disadvantages of any of these options, a more important point is that they remain exceptions. Most employers continue to view the parenting needs of their employees, female and male, as a "private" rather than a business matter. Moreover, none of these options is available to low-income workers and the working poor.

For many years, sociologists, child psychologists, pediatricians, and other experts debated the issue of whether day care is harmful to young children. After conducting literally hundreds of studies, their conclusion is really not surprising: The important question is not whether day care itself is good or bad; rather, the important issue is the quality of care provided. When caregiver-child ratios are low, children reap benefits: They have fewer behavior problems, are more proficient in language, engage in more complex play, and spend more time in learning activities (Lewin, 1998b). Especially important is the level of verbal interaction between caregivers and children; children who are provided with a high level of language stimulation during their first three years develop the verbal and cognitive skills they need to be school-ready ("Quality of Day Care," 1997). What is striking is the *lack* of day care providers who meet even minimal standards of care, let alone the high standards recommended by these studies.

Recent research shows that the quality of child care available in most communities throughout the United States, but especially in low-income communities, is mediocre at best. According to one study, six of seven child care centers provided care that ranges from mediocre to poor; one in eight potentially jeopardized the children's safety and development. Only 6 percent of child care centers nationally have high enough standards of care to be accredited by the National Association for the Education of Young Children. A study of home-based care—care provided by an individual in her private home—found that one in three provided care that could potentially inhibit a child's development (Children's Defense Fund, 1998).

One of the reasons for the poor quality of care offered by most child care providers is the poor pay providers themselves receive. As we have seen, "child care worker" is a low-paying position, with median weekly earnings of just $202. Many providers earn just slightly more than the minimum wage and receive no benefits.

A second reason for the poor quality of care offered by many child care providers is the failure of federal and state governments to adequately regulate child care. Thirty-nine states and the District of Columbia do not require home-based providers to have prior training, and thirty-two states require no prior training for center-based providers. Yet, as the Children's Defense Fund (1998) notes, most states require haircutters and manicurists to obtain 1,500 hours of training at an accredited school before they can be licensed.

The lack of affordable, reliable, and high-quality child care has led many observers in the United States to question, despite ideological claims to the contrary, whether we are a nation that truly cares about the well-being of our children. After all, other countries, such as France, whose taxes are higher, whose gross national product is lower, and whose government has cut spending in recent years, nevertheless provide high-quality child care and preschool education that are heavily subsidized by the government. In France, for example, 99 percent of children ages three, four, and five attend full-day preschools, where they receive the same educational program and level of services regardless of whether they come from poor families who pay the minimum $33 per child per month or from wealthy families who pay $800 per child per month (Greenhouse, 1993; Simons, 1997). Clearly, our nation's leaders and we as citizens must decide if our society is willing to provide at least adequate care for *all* our children and, if so, we must make the commitment of public funds necessary to make that goal a reality.

of women in the occupation (see also Kay & Hagan, 1995). Historical research has also shown how the actions of some unions have successfully excluded women from certain occupations, although the findings of more recent studies are mixed with regard to unions' positions on sex integration of particular jobs (see, for example, Cobble, 1991; Gabin, 1990). Interestingly, however, Reskin (1993) notes that one strategy used by unions to exclude women has been to demand that employers pay them wages equal to those of men for the same work, thereby making the hiring of women less financially attractive to employers.

Clearly the evidence we have discussed so far does not lend support to human capital theory, but for the sake of argument, let's assume for the moment that the theory is correct: Women choose jobs that involve fewer skills, fewer time demands, and less training than the jobs men choose. To what extent does this explain the difference in women's and men's wages? Based on the findings of recent studies, the answer is very little. For example, in one test of human capital theory, Kay and Hagan (1995) found that participation variables (e.g., weeks worked per year, hours per week invested in work, and hours per week devoted to child care responsibilities) accounted for practically none of the sizable wage gap they observed between male and female lawyers. Similarly, Corcoran and her colleagues (1984) calculated how much the differences in men's and women's education, work experience, work continuity, self-imposed restrictions on work hours and location, and rates of absenteeism contributed to differences in their salaries. Significantly, they, too, found that self-imposed restrictions on work hours and location explained almost none of the wage gap. Large differences in patterns of job tenure between male and female workers also explained little of the wage gap. "Although discontinuous employment [caused, for example, by temporary withdrawal from the labor force to bear and raise children] did reduce women's work experience, they apparently were not handicapped by having 'rusty' skills when they returned to the work force. After adjusting for the effects of lost experience, we found that labor force interruptions never significantly lowered wages for either women or white men" (Corcoran et al., 1984, p. 238; see, however, Jacobsen & Levin, 1995; Wellington, 1994). In fact, all of the factors they analyzed, taken together, accounted for less than a third of the wage gap between White men and White women and only about a quarter of the wage gap between White men and Black women.

Additional research indicates that sex differences in education have little to do with the wage gap. In a recent study of engineers, for instance, Robinson and McIlwee (1989) found that educational attainment, as well as experience in the work force and job tenure, failed to explain the lower status of the female engineers in their sample relative to the male engineers. With respect to education, the women and men in this study were virtually identical. In fact, Robinson and McIlwee note that female engineering students typically outperform male engineering students in their classes and have slightly higher grade point averages. Yet, for their sample, "[t]he educational achievements of these women . . . appear to yield fewer occupational rewards than do the men's" (Robinson & McIlwee, 1989, p. 463). Kay and Hagan (1995) made a similar observation in their study of lawyers. They found that men who had graduated from elite law schools earned on average $14,764 more than men who had not graduated from elite schools, but the status of the law schools attended by women made no difference in their earnings.

Reskin and Roos (1990) have argued that women seem to have to overqualify themselves in order to compete successfully with men in male-dominated jobs. Looking at Table 7.6, we find, in fact, that women's earnings are significantly lower than men's across educational levels. Women who have a Bachelor's degree can expect to earn on average slightly less than men with only high school diplomas. Race, though, is also a significant factor in wage differentials irrespective of employees' educational levels. White males at every level of education have higher incomes than Black men and both Black and White women (U.S. Department of Commerce, Bureau of the Census, 1996). Asian women have a higher educational attainment level than women in any other racial or ethnic group, but research indicates that they must work more hours than White women to attain comparable wages (Yamanaka & McClelland, 1994).

Another difficulty inherent in human capital theory is the assumption that women's work automatically entails lower skill, effort, and responsibility than traditional men's work. It fails to account for the fact that female-dominated jobs that require basically the same (and sometimes more) skill, effort, and responsibility as male-dominated jobs still pay less. To understand this point, return to the figures in Table 7.5. Here we find, for instance, that a child care worker earns $304 less per week than a truck driver and $475 less than a mail carrier. Additional examples are abundant. As Reskin (1993) points out, there are two significant issues that muddy our understanding of how training and skills affect the sex composition of jobs and the wage gap. One is that sex biases are built into the way *skill* is typically conceptualized and measured. As she and others (e.g., Steinberg, 1990) have found, male workers have had consistently greater success than female workers in promoting and enforcing the definition of their jobs as skilled. In addition, the job evaluation systems typically used to determine wages are highly subjective and often contain many gender stereotypes (Beatty & Beatty, 1984; Hartmann et al., 1985; Steinberg & Haignere, 1985). For

TABLE 7.6 Mean Monthly Income by Sex and Educational Attainment for Persons Age Eighteen and Older, 1993

Level of Educational Attainment	Earnings	
	Female Workers	**Male Workers**
Not a high school graduate	$ 621	$1,211
High school graduate	1,008	1,812
Some college, no degree	1,139	2,045
Vocational	1,373	2,318
Associate's Degree	1,544	2,561
Bachelor's Degree	1,809	3,430
Master's Degree	2,505	4,298
Professional Degree	3,530	6,312
Doctorate	4,020	4,421

Source: U.S. Department of Commerce, Bureau of the Census, 1996, p. 160.

example, skills that are utilized in predominantly female occupations, such as teaching, nursing, and social work, are frequently not recognized as compensable skills in job evaluation systems, at least in part because they are viewed as an extension of women's unpaid work in the home. As we learned in Chapter 6, most people do not think of housework and child care as "real" work—as work that requires any special skill, formal education, or training. Indeed, women are supposed to be nurturers "by nature." The incorporation of such stereotypes into job evaluation programs has caused the systematic devaluing of jobs traditionally held by women, while jobs traditionally held by men have often been overvalued, sometimes producing nonsensical results. A classic example is the study that found nursery school teachers' skills rated lower than dog trainers' skills (Briggs, 1975; see also Feldberg, 1984).

The second issue identified by Reskin (1993) is that a worker's sex as well as the sex composition of a particular occupation affects a worker's chances of acquiring specific job skills and of gaining access to jobs defined as skilled. Reskin points out, for instance, that in the crafts and the professions, men have controlled job training and this, in turn, has enabled them to prevent women from acquiring certain skills. Similarly, Tallichet (1995, p. 699) reports that male coal miners typically emphasize women's presumed inability to do masculine work, so they relegate them to mine jobs that require few skills and that serve and support male miners. Since there are still so few women in the mines, they are unable to successfully challenge this "gender-typed matching process."

In sum, what we have found here is that occupational sex segregation and the wage gap have little to do with the preferences or free choices of individual workers. A competing explanation of these problems focuses less on the choices and behaviors of workers (the "supply side" of the labor market) and more on the choices and behaviors of employers (the "demand side" of the labor market), including the employers' tendency toward sex discrimination as well as other forms of discrimination. We turn now to an evaluation of this alternative perspective, but as Reskin (1993) cautions, it must be kept in mind that in the everyday operations of workplaces, both demand-side and supply-side factors likely interact with one another to produce particular employment outcomes.

The Work World: Ideology and the Role of Law

A demand-side explanation for occupational sex segregation and the wage gap emphasizes how the actions of employers combine with structural aspects of the workplace to lessen the chances for sex integration and to widen sex differences in earnings. Among the factors considered crucial are the extent to which gender stereotypes come into play in hiring and promotion decisions as well as in the assignment of specific work tasks, in institutionalized recruitment and promotion procedures, and in pressures from regulatory agencies. Let's consider each of these.

Gender Stereotypes at Work

In our earlier discussion, we saw how beliefs about women's and men's "appropriate" roles historically helped give rise to a dual labor market. To review, the prevalent ideology was that a "proper lady" did not work unless she was unmarried or, if married, then child-less. A wide range of occupations were open to men, but women entered a limited number of jobs that supposedly matched their "natural" talents and simply extended their family roles into the public arena. These, as we have noted, were occupations in the "helping professions" and in blue-collar and low-level service fields (e.g., clerical work, sewing, assembling, and canning). This ideology gave rise to a corollary set of beliefs: that women did not need to work; that they worked only briefly until they married or had children (things all women should do); and that if they worked after marriage or the birth of children, it was only to buy "extras" for the family or to "help out" financially.

In short, employers and employees alike, women as well as men, came to see women's employment as secondary to that of men and to view women workers as less serious about or less committed to their jobs. The fact that such ideas stood in stark contrast with the reality of many women's everyday lives did not make these beliefs any less powerful or any less widely held. To the majority, it appeared that women deserved to be relegated to the lower rungs of the job hierarchy and to be paid less than men. What is more, the ideology of "true womanhood" was never extended to women of color. As Glenn (1987, pp. 359–360) notes, "Racist ideology triumphed over sexist ideology. Women of color were not deemed truly women, exempting them from the protective cloaks of feminine frailty or womanly morality."

Many readers probably think these ideas are "old-fashioned" and no longer prevalent in the work world. "People just don't think like that anymore," our students frequently tell us. However, research indicates that sexist and racist ideologies have not disappeared from the contemporary workplace. For example, in a recent survey by the Glass Ceiling Commission, a federal investigative committee within the Department of Labor, White male managers characterized women workers as "not tough enough" and "unwilling to relocate." They described Black men as "undisciplined, always late," and Hispanic men as "heavy drinkers and drug users who don't want to work," unless they are Cuban, in which case they are "brave exiles from Communism" (Kilborn, 1995). The objective evidence belies the stereotypes—women, for instance, miss fewer days of work than men do if we control for maternity leaves; Hispanic men work longer hours than White men work (Kilborn, 1995)—but the stereotypes were nevertheless prevalent and undoubtedly come into play, consciously or unconsciously, in managers' hiring decisions (see also Antilla, 1995).

Indeed, there remains in the minds of many employers and the general public a strong belief that there are certain jobs for which women and men are naturally unsuited (Reskin, 1993; Tallichet, 1995). Studies show that employers still often make hiring decisions on the basis of their beliefs about the kinds of jobs women like (see also Box 7.3). It is commonly believed, for example, that women like jobs that are clean and relatively easy. Consequently, employers considering applicants for a traditionally male job may justify their decision not to hire a woman on the grounds that she wouldn't like the job or wouldn't be happy in it because the work is dirty or difficult. However, such decisions are probably rationalizations, since the research indicates that while women do like clean working conditions—and so do men—the jobs in which women are concentrated are no cleaner than male-dominated jobs (Jacobs & Steinberg, 1990). Additional research shows that workers in male-dominated jobs are more likely than those

BOX **7.3**

The Gendered Division of Labor in the Global Marketplace

We have seen that the division of labor in the United States is gendered, with tasks sorted into "women's work" and "men's work." Importantly, these gender stereotypes permeate the production process worldwide, intersecting with other inequalities based on race and ethnicity, social class, and geographic location. To better understand this point, we need to examine how production typically takes place nowadays in the global marketplace.

Many of the goods we take for granted—clothing, for example, or VCRs, CD players, and computers—are largely manufactured outside the United States, in developing countries in Asia and Latin America. But these countries form just one link in a *commodity chain*, that is, a network of tasks that includes product design, marketing, and sales, in addition to product assembly. Each of the tasks in the commodity chain may be carried out in a different country, separated by thousands of miles, since there is no need for the tasks to be performed in close geographic proximity. Indeed, the corporations that make these products are called *multinationals* because they extend production and marketing throughout the world community. Consider, for instance, the production of electronics components, which is dominated by large corporations such as Motorola and Matsushita (which manufactures the brand names Panasonic, Technics, and JVC). Components are designed and fabricated in the corporation's host country—in this case, the United States and Japan. The components are then assembled in a developing country, such as Malaysia, where workers may be supervised by managers from another country, such as Korea. Once assembled, the components are shipped to their major markets—primarily Western industrialized countries—for final testing, packaging, advertising, and distribution.

Notice in this example that the tasks that require technical expertise in fields such as engineering and marketing are carried out in economically developed countries, whereas the low-skill

operations take place in poor, developing countries. There is a clear pecking order in the commodity chain, and the pecking order is differentiated not only by geographic location and the level of economic development of the country in which each task takes place, but also by the race/ethnicity, social class, and sex of the workers who perform each task. Design and fabrication, as well as marketing and distribution, are dominated by White men who are well-paid for their efforts. Supervision of assembly is dominated by Asian and Latino men, depending on the country in which assembly takes place. Although not as well paid as the designers, fabricators, advertisers, and distributors, indigenous supervisors are paid significantly more than assemblers, who are primarily young women. These women often work ten hours a day, six days a week, in unsafe manufacturing plants, for a wage of about $10 a week. "In Motorola in Malaysia, the work-force is mainly Malay or Indian, from lower classes or castes. Of the 4,500 people employed in the company there, 3,500 are women, concentrated in assembly and clerical work; the 1,000 men are employed as technicians, engineers, material handlers or administrators" (Webster, 1996, p. 48).

In their effort to drive profits up and production costs down, the multinationals are clearly taking advantage of the fact that resources—human as well as material—are far cheaper in developing countries than in industrialized ones. They are also capitalizing on the lack of health and safety regulations in these countries, which also helps to depress production costs. However, if these were the only reasons for basing assembly operations in the developing world, why don't the multinationals hire more men as assemblers? The answer to this question reflects not only gender stereotypes, but also the greater economic vulnerability of women in developing countries. According to Webster (1996), the multinationals hire mostly women for assembly because they believe women have the small, nimble fingers as

(continued)

BOX 7.3 **Continued**

well as the patience to perform the tedious, repetitive task of electronics assembly. Moreover, because of women's devalued status in many countries, they can be paid even less than indigenous men. Despite the low wages, however, the women workers are more productive than the men. They are also thought to be more docile and less likely to unionize, but just to be sure, the corporations keep them on short-term contracts; the prospect of losing the job because of labor unrest or changes in market demand is an ever-present threat.

Electronics is not the only industry to exploit the inequalities of international commodity chains. Consider also the Nike Corporation. In Indonesia and Vietnam, thousands of women, typically under the age of twenty-five, labor ten and a half hours a day, sixty-five hours a week, sewing Nike athletic shoes in manufacturing plants where exposure to carcinogens is 177 times higher than allowable by *local* standards and dust particles are eleven times higher (Greenhouse, 1997). The women earn about $2 a day. On such wages, most can only afford to live in bamboo or tin huts without running water. Many of the women are from rural areas and they cannot afford to bring their children with them to the cities. Indeed, it is the prospect of earning a better living that draws them to the Nike factories in the first place. But their wages are not sufficient to allow them to return to their villages to visit their children more than once a year. Meanwhile,

Nike's holdings in these countries are worth billions of dollars; holdings in Indonesia alone are estimated at more than $5 billion. Nike's president, Philip Knight, is one of the 400 wealthiest Americans, with a personal net worth of $5.3 billion ("The *Forbes* Four Hundred," 1996, p. 111; Herbert, 1996). The company also pays star athletes millions of dollars to endorse its products. Interestingly, while most of these athletes are men, they are also Black. Professional sports is one of the few fields in which Black men are expected to excel, showing once again the intersection of racism and sexism.

We can expect these trends in the international division of labor to continue as more and more companies move their production processes to developing countries. Recent research indicates that woman-centered development strategies—for example, providing women with micro-loans to start small businesses and training them in fields such as fish farming—can play a major role in reducing poverty and related social problems such as hunger in developing nations (Elson, 1995). Nevertheless, international agencies, such as the World Bank and the International Monetary Fund, are encouraging developing countries to build their economies on export-oriented industrialization—a strategy, as we have seen here, that reproduces inequalities between countries as well as between the women and men who work in those countries (Elson, 1995; Hsiung, 1996).

in female-dominated jobs to describe their own jobs as easy (Glass, 1990). Clean working conditions and how easy the job is simply do not rank highly among women workers' concerns. Instead, women workers' primary concerns are equal pay for equal work, affordable health insurance, paid sick leave, and pension and retirement benefits (U.S. Department of Labor, 1994).

When employers make employment decisions about an individual on the basis of characteristics thought to be typical of a group to which that individual belongs, the employers are engaging in what is called **statistical discrimination.** In other words, employers do not hire anyone who is a member of a group they think has low productivity. Statistical discrimination serves as a quick and inexpensive screening device (Reskin & Hartmann, 1986). On the face of it, statistical discrimination may not seem unfair; it certainly does not appear to be inherently sex-biased. However, as Reskin and

Hartmann (1986) convincingly demonstrate, it is often premised on gender stereotypes. For example, when making a choice between two job applicants with the same qualifications, one a young man and the other a young woman, employers still often favor hiring the young man, especially for a job requiring extensive training, because they think that many young women leave the labor force to have children. Notice, however, that their hiring decision is made irrespective of this individual applicant's child bearing or work intentions, of which the employer has no knowledge (Hartmann & Reskin, 1986). Notice, too, that employers also assume that men have little interest in or responsibility for childrearing—believing that men who have children also have a spouse to care for them. Although such assumptions may reflect the family lives of most men, they nevertheless disregard individual circumstances and work against single fathers and men who prefer an equal or primary parenting role (see Box 7.2 and Chapter 6). Interestingly, recent research shows that, all other factors being equal, men in traditional families, with wives at home caring for their children, earn higher salaries and get better pay raises than men in two-earner families (Schneer & Reitman, 1997). Perhaps the difference is due to employers' beliefs that men in traditional families, as sole breadwinners, work longer and harder than men whose wives also work and with whom they may need to share some childcare responsibilities.

Sexist workplace ideology also operates to preserve industry and establishment sex segregation. Because femaleness, as we noted previously, is a devalued trait in some workplaces, a concern over loss of prestige or status may prompt some firms or businesses to restrict their hiring of women (and racial minorities) either to "back office" jobs that have little contact with clientele (Glenn, 1992; Hartmann, 1987) or to a few "tokens" (Reskin & Hartmann, 1986). An example of this kind of thinking was provided by a colleague who works in a department of three men and three women at a small, private college. She recounted to us how one of her coworkers had objected to the hiring of another woman on the ground that the department would then be female-dominated and consequently lose status within the institution.

There is evidence that some work-related gender stereotypes have weakened in recent years and that women who have entered male-dominated occupations have positively changed many workplaces (see, for example, Lunneborg, 1990). Consequently, it is sometimes argued that sexist workplace ideology, although slow to change, will eventually break down as more women and men enter occupations nontraditional for their sex. However, there is also evidence that as particular gender stereotypes are refuted, new ones may develop to replace them. As Reskin and Hartmann (1986, pp. 65–66) explain, "A single woman worker who violates the stereotype can be explained as an exception; when the behavior of many women clearly belies a particular stereotype, a different one may emerge to maintain the gender homogeneity with which members of an occupation have become comfortable." Women, for example, sometimes feel they must adopt men's work styles in order to get ahead in their fields. Ironically, traits or behaviors admired in workers of one sex may be negatively redefined when exhibited by workers of the opposite sex so as to make the latter fit a stereotyped image. Thus, a male worker may be complimented for being aggressive in his work, while a female worker exhibiting the same behavior is likely to be derided for being "too pushy." Moreover, women who reach high-level positions may find it difficult to mentor women in the lower ranks because of institutional barriers, such as their boss's disapproval of all-female mentoring groups or fears that if their proteges do poorly, it will reflect negatively on them (Saltzman, 1996b; U.S. Department of Labor, 1997).

In addition to gender stereotyping, other factors having to do with the economics of the labor market and the organization of the workplace contribute to an increase or decline in occupational sex segregation and the wage gap. As we noted earlier, for example, an increased demand for workers, such as during wartime or a period of strong economic growth, can help to integrate traditionally segregated jobs. A rise in the demand for workers may also result from the rapid growth of a specific industry. Jacobs (1992) reports, for instance, that a 25 percent reduction occurred in overall occupational sex segregation during the two decades 1970 to 1990 simply as a result of the rapid growth of managerial jobs. With respect to organizational aspects of the workplace, Reskin (1993) points out that employers' reliance on informal networks to recruit new employees—that is, depending on current employees to tell people they know about specific job openings— usually preserves sex segregation, especially in already segregated workplaces, because such networks themselves tend to be composed of individuals of the same sex (see also Drentea, 1998; Tallichet, 1995). Research also shows that even when chief executives of companies support diversity in hiring in order to reach a more diverse clientele, the individuals who actually make the hires and who evaluate current employees can act to preserve occupational segregation. According to the Glass Ceiling Commission, for example, managers—the majority of whom were White men—stated that the most important factors in hiring and promotion decisions are "comfort, chemistry, relationships and collaboration." Of course, they feel most comfortable developing relationships and collaborating with employees most like themselves. Indeed, one manager actually said, "When we find minorities and women who think like we do, we snatch them up" (quoted in Kilborn, 1995, p. A14).

Various strategies have been suggested for reducing occupational segregation and narrowing the wage gap. They include integrating lower-level positions first so there is a diverse pool from which to promote internally; waiving seniority requirements for promotion for women and minority job holders; expanding job posting throughout a workplace so that workers will be made aware of position openings in areas that may not be closely related to the ones in which they are currently working; setting up mentoring programs; and establishing job "bridges" so that career paths in different areas (e.g., clerical, technical, administrative) may be connected (Reskin, 1993; U.S. Department of Labor, 1997; Williams, 1995). However, while such strategies may prove effective, a number of analysts maintain that many employers lack sufficient motivation to implement change. Employers, they argue, must be *forced* to change discriminatory policies and procedures. One important impetus for such changes has come from legislation. During the past three decades, several laws have been enacted in an effort to remedy occupational segregation and its consequences, especially the wage gap. However, as we shall learn next, there sometimes has been a disparity between the written law and the law in action, producing uneven results.

Legislation for Equality in the Workplace

Until the 1960s, the legal system functioned largely to reinforce gender discrimination in the workplace, rather than to remedy it. For the most part, law and judicial actions simply codified widespread gender stereotypes about men's toughness and women's innate weaknesses, which as Justice Bradley argued in 1872, "unfits [women] for many of the occupations of civil life" (*Bradwell* v. *Illinois*, 1872). Legislators and judges maintained that women were a "special class" of citizens in need of protection: "That her physical structure and a proper discharge of her maternal functions—having in view not merely her own health, but the well-being of the race—justify legislation to protect her from the greed as well as the passion of man" (*Muller* v. *Oregon*, 1908). Consequently, most states enacted laws restricting women's working hours and the kind of work women could do. In many states, for instance, women were prohibited from working at night or from performing a work task that involved lifting more than a prescribed maximum weight. Other states forbade employers from hiring women for jobs ruled dangerous or morally corrupting (e.g., bartending). Initially, a variety of reform groups, including suffrage and feminist organizations, endorsed protective labor laws in the belief that they would benefit women workers, but as the decades passed, it became clear that such legislation usually served to severely restrict women's employment (Christensen, 1988).

In the 1960s, owing in part to the efforts of the feminist and Civil Rights movements, the federal government acted to outlaw sex discrimination in employment.[9] The first important piece of legislation in this regard is **Title VII of the 1964 Civil Rights Act.** Title VII forbids discrimination in hiring, benefits, and other personnel decisions (such as promotions or layoffs) on the basis of sex, race, color, national origin, or religion, by employers of fifteen or more employees.[10] There are, however, a few exceptions permitted by the law. For instance, an employer may hire an employee on the basis of sex (or religion or national origin, but never race or color) if the employer can demonstrate that this is a *bona fide occupational qualification* (BFOQ), that is, a qualification "reasonably necessary to the normal operation of that particular business or enterprise." However, since the courts have interpreted the BFOQ exception narrowly, there are few occupations to which it applies (Christensen, 1988; Lindgren & Taub, 1993). According to guidelines issued with the law, for example, sex is considered a bona fide occupational qualification in those instances where authenticity and genuineness are required, such as roles for actors and actresses (Kay, 1988). Title VII has been implemented and enforced by the Equal Employment Opportunity Commission (EEOC), which can bring suit on behalf of an employee or class of employees who have been discriminated against by their employer. In 1995, more than 26,000 workers filed sex discrimination complaints, including sexual harassment complaints, with the EEOC (Saltzman, 1996).

A second important federal antidiscrimination policy is **Executive Order 11246,** better known as **Affirmative Action,** which was amended in 1968 to prohibit sex discrimination in addition to discrimination on the basis of race, color, national origin, and religion. Executive Order 11246 applies to employers who hold contracts with the federal government. It states that employers may be fined or their contracts may be terminated or they may be barred from future contracts if discrimination is found. But Executive Order 11246 goes beyond the mere prohibition of employment discrimination by requiring employers to take affirmative actions to recruit, train, and promote women and minorities. Since 1978, contractor compliance has been monitored by the Office of Federal Contract Compliance (OFCCP) in the Department of Labor. Besides this enforcement agency, the U.S. Department of Justice may also bring suit against discriminating employers, although it has rarely done so (Lindgren & Taub, 1993).

The impact of both Title VII and Executive Order 11246 is visible and far-reaching. Peruse the "want ads" of your local newspaper and you will see one result: Employers may no longer advertise sex-labeled or sex-specific jobs. Employers also may not use customer preference as a justification for sex discrimination. For instance, in *Diaz* v. *Pan American World Airways, Inc.* (1971), the Fifth Circuit Court ruled that men could not be denied employment as flight attendants on the ground that passengers expect and prefer women in this job. Today, nearly 30 percent of flight attendants are men (U.S. Department of Labor, 1998b). In addition, employers may not: use sex-based seniority lists; administer discriminatory pre-employment selection tests; set different retirement ages for workers of each sex; impose double standards of employment, such as policies requiring only female employees to remain unmarried; penalize women workers who have children; or discriminate on the basis of pregnancy (Christensen, 1988; Lindgren & Taub, 1993). Under these regulations, the courts have also struck down most state protective labor laws and, as we have learned, ruled that sexual harassment is a form of employment discrimination.

It is difficult to reconcile the clear evidence of persistent discrimination that we have presented in this chapter with the prohibitions stipulated by these laws and court decisions. Why, more than thirty years after the passage of this legislation, is occupational segregation still pervasive?

At least part of the answer rests with the limitations of the laws and the inconsistency with which they have been enforced. For one thing, Title VII and Executive Order 11246 define employment discrimination in limited, but complex terms, leading judges to arrive at varying interpretations of both these regulations and appropriate affirmative measures to remedy past discrimination (Blankenship, 1993; Greene, 1989; Lindgren & Taub, 1993). Moreover, since the mid-1980s, the U.S. Supreme Court has handed down rulings that have substantially increased the burden of employees in proving they have been discriminated against. For example, previously in cases in which an employee accused an employer of directly discriminating against her or him, the employee only had to provide *prima facie evidence* of discrimination in an employment decision (e.g., hiring, promotion, dismissal) and then demonstrate that the employer's argument that the decision was not discriminatory was not credible. Since 1993, however, employees have been required to provide *direct evidence* of discrimination (e.g., witnesses, or a letter or memo), which can be hard to come by, making it more difficult for employees to win their lawsuits (*St. Mary's Honor Center* v. *Hicks*, 1993).

Another factor influencing law enforcement is changes in government and political climate. The Republican administrations since 1980 have opposed large lawsuits against employers filed by a whole class of employees, favoring instead cases in which individual victims could be identified. They also opposed affirmative action and took steps to dismantle it. One strategy for doing so was to significantly reduce the budgets and staff of the EEOC and OFCCP. Less money and fewer staff attorneys meant that fewer cases could be processed and the number of cases dismissed by the compliance agencies rose significantly during the 1980s. Lax law enforcement sends employers the message that the government will tolerate a high degree of occupational sex segregation (Reskin, 1993).

Thus, while Title VII and Executive Order 11246 have made visible dents in our society's discriminatory work structure, the effects of these policies have been limited for at least two reasons. First, the inherent weaknesses and complexities of the laws themselves give judges considerable discretion, which frequently produces negative or contradictory outcomes for female and minority workers. Second, these policies, like all public policies, are vulnerable to political change. Given the antifeminism and hostility to affirmative action displayed by the Reagan/Bush administrations, it is not surprising that the modest, but hard-won employment gains of the 1960s and 1970s were eroded during the 1980s. Suits rose again during the Clinton administration, increasing 47 percent between 1990 and 1995. However, the future of Title VII and especially affirmative action depends to a large extent on rulings by the U.S. Supreme Court.

The wage gap has also been attacked directly by legislation that outlaws discriminatory pay policies. Perhaps the best known and most frequently used law of this type is the **Equal Pay Act of 1963.** The Equal Pay Act prohibits employers from paying employees of one sex more than employees of the opposite sex when these employees are engaged in work that requires equal skill, effort, and responsibility and that is performed under similar working conditions. This prohibition extends to other forms of discrimination in compensation, such as overtime. However, pay need not be equal if the difference is based on employees' relative seniority, merit, the quantity or quality of their production, or "any other factor other than sex" such as the profitability of their work (Christensen, 1988; Lindgren & Taub, 1993).

The courts have ruled that the work performed by employees of the opposite sex does not have to be identical to require equal pay, but need only be *substantially equal.* The courts have also ruled that employers may not justify unequal pay for their male and female workers by creating artificial job classifications that do not substantially differ in content (England, 1992). A major difficulty with the Equal Pay Act, however, is that it does not address the problem of sex-segregated employment, which, we have argued, is a root cause of the wage gap. The benefits of a law designed to provide equal pay for equal work are limited, therefore, if, as we have found, men and women are largely segregated into different jobs and predominantly female jobs are systematically devalued.

It is for this reason that women workers and others have increasingly called for **comparable worth,** that is, equal pay for different jobs of similar value in terms of factors such as skill, effort, responsibility, and working conditions. Comparable worth has been more popular in other countries, such as Australia, Great Britain, and Canada, than in the United States. Since 1985, a number of comparable worth cases have been brought on behalf of women workers in this country, but in general, the courts have not looked favorably on comparable worth as a means to remedy gender inequities in pay (England, 1992). Their reluctance is the result of two reasons: They do not wish "to punish employers who rely on the market in setting wages and who are not individually responsible for societal discrimination" and they do not wish "to become involved in trying to evaluate the worth of different jobs," which has proven to be a very difficult task (Christensen, 1988, p. 340). Nevertheless, at least twenty states and 1,700 local jurisdictions (e.g., city governments, school districts, public universities)— 1,300 of which are in Minnesota—have adopted comparable worth policies (England, 1992; Rhoads, 1994).

Although comparable worth might make a significant contribution to closing the gender gap in wages, the value of its broad use as an antidiscrimination strategy has been debated by many analysts, including feminists (England, 1992; Rhoads, 1994). Some researchers caution against seeing comparable worth, as well as Title VII and affirmative action, as panaceas for solving gender inequality in the workplace. Steinberg and Cook's (1988) conclusions in this regard are worth quoting at length:

> [E]qual employment requires more than guaranteeing the right to equal access, the right to equal opportunity for promotion, or the right to equal pay for equal, or even comparable worth. Additionally, it warrants a broader policy orientation encompassing social welfare laws that assume equality within the family; widespread use of alternative work arrangements that accommodate the complexities of family life within two-earner families; and a rejuvenated union movement, with female leadership more active at work sites in defending the rights of women workers. Social welfare laws, family policy, and government services must create incentives toward a more equal division of responsibilities for family and household tasks between men and women. Increasing child care facilities, as well as maintaining programs to care for the elderly, would help alleviate some of the more pressing demands made on adults in families. . . . This also means that tax policy, social security laws, and pension programs must be amended to make government incentives to family life consistent with a family structure in which husbands and wives are equal partners. (p. 326)

Few governments have even attempted such ambitious reforms, let alone been successful in implementing them.

The Intersection of Home and the Work World

A major theme of this chapter and the preceding chapter has been the interrelationship between family life and the work world. Men and women possess different levels of power in the family, with women typically being the less powerful partners. In Chapter 6, we learned that differences in power between intimate partners are related to differences in their income and other resources. The work women do in the home is unremunerated and, therefore, not even regarded as "real" work. As we saw in this chapter, however, women's jobs in the labor force are often seen as an extension of their work at home. Women's work is devalued and remunerated at a substantially lower rate than men's work.

Since employed women continue to bear primary responsibility for housework and child care, they shoulder a double work load compared with employed men, but receive fewer rewards. The unavailability of adequate and affordable child care, we have learned, is a major obstacle to employment for many women. But regardless of their objective circumstances, the widespread belief among employers and coworkers that women are physically and emotionally incapable of performing certain jobs serves to justify discrimination against them in hiring, promotion, and other employment-related opportunities and also constrains men from assuming equal caregiving responsibilities within families. The evidence discussed in this chapter shows that persistent stereotypes about women's and men's "appropriate" roles reinforce and perpetuate workplace sex segregation and its attendant consequences, including the male/female earnings gap. The prevailing assumption seems to remain that the public world of work is men's domain, whereas the private world of home belongs to women. If women are in the labor force, their employment is secondary to that of men. From our discussions in this chapter and Chapter 6, we know that these assumptions are patently false. We know, too, that both women and men suffer negative consequences from blind adherence to them.

Legislation such as Title VII, Executive Order 11246, and the Equal Pay Act is designed to protect workers of both sexes and racial and ethnic minorities from discriminatory employment practices. Although the legislation has fallen far short of equalizing the job opportunities and salaries available to female and male workers, and among workers of different racial and ethnic groups, there is evidence that when the laws are stringently enforced, they can help to lessen employment inequities. Still, this legislation was not designed to alter the gendered division of unpaid household labor. Since we know that this is directly tied to sex-based employment discrimination, we cannot expect women or men to be free to choose the work that best suits them as individuals unless the simultaneous elimination of both of these inequities becomes a central goal of our nation's public policy.

KEY TERMS

comparable worth   the policy of paying workers equally when they perform different jobs that have similar value in terms of such factors as skill, effort, responsibility, and working conditions

dissimilarity index (segregation index, D)   a measure of occupational sex segregation, reported in percent, that indicates the proportion of workers of one sex that would have to change to jobs in which members of their sex were underrepresented to achieve a balanced occupational distribution between the sexes

dual labor market   a labor market characterized by one set of jobs employing almost exclusively men and another set of jobs, typically lower paying with lower prestige, employing almost exclusively women

economy   the system for the management and development of a society's human and material resources

Equal Pay Act of 1963   forbids employers from paying employees of one sex more than employees of the opposite sex when these employees are engaged in work that requires equal skill, effort, and responsibility and is performed under similar working conditions, although exceptions, such as unequal pay based on seniority, merit, the quality or quantity of production, or any other factor besides sex, are allowed

establishment sex segregation   a form of occupational sex segregation in which women and men hold the same job title at an individual establishment or company, but actually do different jobs

Executive Order 11246 (Affirmative Action)   forbids federal contractors from discriminating in personnel decisions on the basis of sex, as well as race, color, national origin, and religion, and requires employers to take affirmative measures to recruit, train, and hire women and minorities; since 1978, implemented and enforced by the OFCCP

glass ceiling   invisible barriers that limit women workers' and minority workers' upward occupational mobility

human capital theory   explains occupational sex segregation in terms of women's free choice to work in jobs that make few demands on workers and require low personal investment in training or skills acquisition based on the assumption that women's primary responsibility is in the home

industry sex segregation   a form of occupational sex segregation in which women and men hold the same job title in a particular field or industry, but actually perform different jobs

labor force   the human resources of the economy

occupational resegregation   sex-integrated occupations become resegregated with members of one sex replaced by members of the opposite sex as the predominant workers

occupational sex segregation   the degree to which men and women are concentrated in occu-

pations that employ workers of predominantly one sex

statistical discrimination   employers do not hire anyone who is a member of a group they think has low productivity, regardless of an individual applicant's qualifications or intentions

Title VII of the 1964 Civil Rights Act   forbids discrimination in employment on the basis of sex, race, color, national origin, or religion, by employers of fifteen or more employees, although exceptions, such as the BFOQ, are allowed; implemented and enforced by the EEOC

tokenism   the marginal status of a category of workers who are relatively few in number in the workplace

SUGGESTED READINGS

Aslanbeigui, N., Pressman, S., & Summerfield, G. (Eds.) (1994). *Women in the age of economic transformation: Gender impact of reforms in post-socialist and developing countries.* London: Routledge.

Edin, K., & Lein, L. (1997). *Making ends meet: How single mothers survive welfare and low-wage work.* New York: Russell Sage Foundation.

Jacobs, J. A. (Ed.) (1995). *Gender inequality at work.* Thousand Oaks, CA: Sage.

Webster, J. (1996). *Shaping women's work: Gender, employment and information technology.* New York: Longman.

Williams, C. L. (1995). *Still a man's world: Men who do women's work.* Berkeley: University of California Press.

NOTES

1.   Another favorite site among men for conducting business is the strip club or topless bar, a venue in which most businesswomen feel uncomfortable at best. According to many businessmen, however, taking male clients to strip clubs and topless bars fosters "male bonding" that can produce lucrative business deals. As one businessman put it, "You get a bunch of guys in a room who don't know each other, you get drunk and look at naked women and the next day you're great friends" (quoted in Meredith, 1997, p. A1). This kind of attitude and behavior is the focus of two discrimination suits brought by businesswomen in Detroit and currently pending in the courts.

2.   The heterosexual men Williams interviewed also related some negative experiences of gender discrimination associated with gender stereotypes of masculinity, although these were rare. For example, male social workers and nurses reported that they were usu-

ally expected to handle aggressive or violent clients and patients. Similarly, a male librarian found himself transferred to the city's main library so he could double as a security guard. A male nurse also reported that during fire drills at the hospital where he worked, male nurses were required to go to the scene of the fire with the maintenance and housekeeping staff, presumably to help fight the fire, while female nurses were required to remain on the patient floors, closing doors and clearing the hallways (Williams, 1995).

3.   Some observers have criticized feminists and feminist organizations for what they call "selective outrage": being quick to condemn the behavior of Republicans such as Thomas and Packwood, but not speaking out against President Clinton because he has generally supported feminists and feminist positions (Mitchell, 1998).

4.   The 1998 decision by the Court holding employers potentially liable in all cases of workplace sex-

ual harassment is difficult to reconcile with another Court decision handed down just days earlier that immunized school districts from liability for the sexual abuse of students by teachers (see Chapter 4).

5. Prior to the Court's decision in this case, *Oncale* vs. *Sundowner Offshore Services*, most lower federal courts simply rejected same-sex harassment claims, arguing that Congress never intended same-sex harassment to be included as grounds for damages under Civil Rights law. Those courts that agreed to hear same-sex harassment claims usually limited them to cases involving heterosexual employees who filed complaints against homosexual coworkers (Greenhouse, 1998).

6. Our calculations of the earnings gap, unless otherwise noted, are based on *weekly* median earnings of full-time workers. The size of the gap varies depending on the type of wages one examines; the widest gap is found in annual wages because these figures usually include factors such as overtime and, therefore, reflect the differences in the total annual hours worked by women and men. We are grateful to Jane Hood for pointing out this variation to us.

7. The official government measure of poverty, known as the poverty line, is the amount of money an individual or family needs to purchase a minimally nutritional diet multiplied by three because it is assumed that the poor spend about one-third of their income on food. However, the measure has been widely criticized on a number of grounds, including the fact that the average family spends not one-third, but rather one-fifth of its income on food. Consequently, critics argue that the

official measure severely undercounts the poor (Porter, 1997).

8. The unemployment rate is officially defined as the percentage of the working-age population that is currently out of work, but actively looking for a job. This measure, though, undercounts the unemployed because it excludes "discouraged workers," that is, individuals who have given up hope of finding a job because they believe none is available or because they lack marketable skills. Discouraged workers are a subset of another group not counted in the unemployment rate, "persons marginally attached to the labor force." The marginally attached are people who want work, are available for work, and have looked for a job in the past year, but have not sought work in the past month. The Department of Labor (1998a) estimates that about 1.2 million people are marginally attached to the labor force; more than 260,000 are discouraged workers.

9. Our discussion of these laws is, by necessity, simplistic. For a more detailed and thorough discussion, see Blankenship, 1993; Deitch, 1993; and Lindgren and Taub, 1993.

10. Notice that sexual orientation is not a protected category under Title VII. In 1998, President Clinton signed an executive order to protect gay and lesbian *federal* employees from job discrimination. A bill has been pending in Congress for some time that would extend Title VII protection to gay and lesbian workers in the public and private sectors, but to date no action has been taken on the measure ("Clinton Grants Gay Workers Job Protection," 1998).

8

Gender, Crime, and Justice

Equality before the law is a constitutional guarantee in the United States. Yet, we know from our discussions so far that the laws of our land have allowed—indeed, even prescribed—discriminatory treatment of different groups of citizens. Women, for example, were historically defined by law as men's property and were systematically denied their civil rights, including the right to vote. In fact, in 1894, the U.S. Supreme Court ruled that women were not "persons" under the law. The case, *In re Lockwood*, was heard on appeal from the State of Virginia, where Belva A. Lockwood had been denied a license to practice as an attorney even though state law permitted any "person" licensed as an attorney in any other state to practice in Virginia. The Supreme Court upheld a lower court opinion that the word "person" meant "male." Consequently, "from 1894 until 1971 states could maintain that women were not legally 'persons' by virtue of this single Supreme Court decision" (Hoff-Wilson, 1987, p. 8; Sachs & Wilson, 1978).

Most of the court cases we discuss in this text fall within the realm of civil law, that is, the body of law that focuses on settling private disputes, such as divorces, contracts and private property issues, and conflicts in the workplace. In this chapter, however, we will focus on gender and *criminal law*. Criminal law encompasses behaviors that supposedly imperil the general welfare of the society and, consequently, it is the state that prosecutes the offender, not the individual citizen who has been harmed by the offending behavior. In other words, the violation of a criminal law is viewed, in theory at least, as a transgression against society as well as against an individual citizen.

What is defined in law as criminal, though, does not necessarily represent the interests of all segments of society. Rather, criminal law typically represents the interests of lawmakers. Historically, those who have had the power to make laws in the United States have been wealthy White men (see Chapter 9). Not surprisingly, therefore, the experiences of women and men in the criminal justice system tend to be different. Compounding these sex differences are differences in race, social class, age, and sexual orientation.

This chapter begins with a discussion of men and women as offenders. First, we will examine men's and women's relative crime rates. In addition, we will address their differential processing through the criminal justice system: from arrest to prosecution to conviction to sentencing to imprisonment. In studying the administration of justice, we will also have the opportunity to discuss issues pertaining to men's and women's roles as criminal justice professionals. Finally, we will conclude the chapter by examining differences in the criminal victimization of men and women, with special attention given to sexual assault and other violent crimes against women.

Women and Men as Offenders

Among the questions most often addressed by criminologists, two in particular seem most relevant to our present discussion: Who commits crime? and why? Traditionally, a common response to the first question has been men, especially young men. Indeed, a careful survey of criminological research conducted prior to the mid-1970s would probably lead you to conclude that women are rarely criminal. The little attention that was given to female offenders was largely limited to three contexts: (1) comparisons to underscore women's low crime rates relative to those of men; (2) studies of prostitution; and (3) analyses of the depravity of violent women, the rationale being that since "normal" women are passive, the few women who do commit violent crimes must be "sick" (Edwards, 1986). Clearly, in the minds of criminologists and the general public, "criminal" was equated with "male."

In 1975, however, this perception began to change, owing largely to the publication of two books—Freda Adler's *Sisters in Crime* and Rita James Simon's *Women and Crime*—each of which received widespread attention in both the academic and popular presses. A central theme in both books is that women's crime had begun to change both in its nature and in the number of offenses committed. In fact, according to Adler, the United States at that time was in the midst of a female crime wave. Although men were still committing a greater absolute number of offenses, the female crime rate was increasing more than the male crime rate. Thus, for example, Adler presented statistics from the F.B.I. *Uniform Crime Reports* (UCR) that show that between 1960 and 1972, women's arrest rates for robbery increased 277 percent compared with a 169 percent increase for men. Statistics on juvenile offenders revealed similar changes. What is more, Adler argued, females were not only engaged in more crime than previously, but also their criminal activity had assumed a more serious and violent character: women were committing crimes that traditionally had been committed by men. In this respect, Simon's work closely resembles Adler's, with the exception that Simon saw the increase in women's crime limited primarily to property offenses rather than violent crimes against persons. Still, she maintained that women were committing more crimes generally characterized as masculine, particularly white-collar and occupationally related offenses such as fraud and embezzlement.

These claims did not cause the greatest stir, however. Indeed, what received the most attention, especially from the popular media, were Adler's and Simon's explanations of their findings. Specifically, both argued that the changes they uncovered in the rate and character of female crime were logical outcomes of the women's liberation movement. As Adler (1975, p. 10) phrased it, "Is it any wonder that once women were armed with male opportunities they should strive for status, criminal as well as civil, through established male hierarchical channels?" Simon's position was a bit more complex. She argued that violent crimes by women had actually decreased because of feminism. "As women feel more liberated physically, emotionally, and legally, and less subjected to male power, their frustrations and anger decrease . . . [which results] in a decline in their desire to kill the usual objects of their anger or frustration: their husbands, lovers, and other men upon whom they are dependent, but insecure about" (Simon, 1975, p. 40). The down side, however, is that the feminist movement, by encouraging women's participation in the paid labor force, had also contributed to the rise in female property crime. "As women increase their participation in the labor force their opportunity to commit certain types of crime [e.g., white-collar and occupational crimes] also increases" (Simon, 1975, p. 40). Because of its emphasis on the women's movement, Adler's and Simon's perspective has become known as the **emancipation theory** (also called the **liberation theory**) of female crime.

Actually, this argument is not totally new; as Meda Chesney-Lind (1997) points out, during the first wave of feminism, criminologists and others warned that the emancipation of women would increase crime and immorality among women and girls. However, the greatest value of Adler's and Simon's work is that it forced a contemporary reassessment of the relationship between gender and participation in criminal activity. In critiquing Adler and Simon, subsequent analyses shed light on the extent to which female crime had actually changed and the degree to which the women's movement may have contributed to such a change. Let's consider some of these criticisms, and in doing so, examine what more recent studies tell us about the relationship between gender and crime.

One problem with both Adler's and Simon's work was their reliance on official crime statistics. These statistics represent only those crimes known to the police, which, it is estimated, are only about one-third of all crimes committed (U.S. Department of Justice, Bureau of Justice Statistics, 1994). A substantial amount of crime, however, goes undetected (see, for example, Inciardi et al., 1993), or is not reported by victims. And even when a crime is reported, the police exercise considerable discretion in deciding which complaints warrant their attention and which should be ignored, so not even all reported crimes are passed along to the F.B.I. But a more serious problem stems from the way Adler, in particular, used the UCR data. In comparing male and female rates of increase for specific crimes, she didn't control for the large difference in the absolute base numbers from which the rates of increase were calculated. If one base figure is small, even a slight rise will exaggerate the rate change. Conversely, a sizable increase in a large base figure is likely to appear as only a minor change (Smart, 1982; Terry, 1978). Take arrests for homicide, for example. Between 1965 and 1970, years included in Adler's analysis, the number of arrests of women for homicide increased almost 79 percent; during the same period, the number of homicide arrests for men increased 73 percent. However, in absolute terms, the number of homicides committed by women rose from 1,293 to 1,645, whereas for men, the figures were 6,533 and 8,858 respectively. If we look only at percent changes without taking into account these major absolute base differences, we end up with a very distorted picture of men's and women's involvement in crime.

A more accurate measure of changes in men's and women's criminal activity is to calculate sex-specific arrest rates, that is, the number of men arrested for a crime per 100,000 of the male population and the number of women arrested for the same crime per 100,000 of the female population. The sex differential in arrest rates can then be determined by calculating women's share of all arrests, male and female, for a specific offense. Researchers who have used this method to analyze the sex differential in arrest rates in recent years have found that there has been neither a significant widening nor a significant narrowing of the gender gap in arrests, with the important exception of certain types of property crimes—larceny theft, forgery/counterfeiting, fraud, and embezzlement—and drug offenses (Chesney-Lind, 1997; Simon & Landis, 1991; Steffensmeier, 1982; see also Table 8.1 on page 238). Box 8.1 on pages 239–240 discusses the complex relationship between drugs and crime, which is further complicated when gender, race/ethnicity, social class, and age are taken into account. Now let's take a closer look at the research on property crime. Do the research findings lend support to the

TABLE 8.1   Total Arrest Trends by Sex, 1987–1996

Offense Charged	Males			Females		
	1987	*1996*	*% Change*	*1987*	*1996*	*% Change*
Murder and nonnegligent manslaughter	12,247	12,062	–1.5	1,719	1,384	–19.5
Forcible rape	24,551	21,505	–12.4	299	247	–17.4
Robbery	93,885	101,998	+8.6	8,431	11,091	+31.6
Aggravated assault	209,782	284,004	+35.4	31,716	61,640	+94.3
Burglary	264,041	209,076	–20.8	24,442	27,190	+11.2
Larceny-theft	663,264	655,775	–1.1	297,624	337,434	+13.4
Motor vehicle theft	106,604	104,562	–1.9	11,454	16,427	+43.4
Arson	10,144	10,431	+2.8	1,603	1,860	+16.0
Crime Index total*	1,384,518	1,399,413	+1.1	377,288	457,273	+21.2
Other assaults	454,944	695,386	+52.9	81,583	177,644	+117.7
Forgery and counterfeiting	39,931	51,372	+28.7	21,056	28,105	+33.5
Fraud	127,472	168,385	+32.1	98,537	116,746	+18.5
Embezzlement	5,355	5,633	+5.2	3,329	4,619	+38.8
Stolen property: buying, receiving, possessing	86,771	84,867	–2.2	11,419	14,435	+26.4
Vandalism	160,482	182,709	+13.9	19,222	29,336	+52.6
Weapons: carrying, possessing	123,403	135,565	+9.9	10,177	11,637	+26.4
Prostitution and commercialized vice	29,335	30,657	+4.5	56,253	46,097	–18.1
Sex offenses (except forcible rape and prostitution)	62,263	59,062	–5.1	5,026	5,324	+5.9
Drug abuse violations	554,554	857,057	+54.5	99,872	173,831	+74.1
Gambling	16,811	13,834	–17.7	2,747	2,206	–19.7
Offenses against family and children	30,037	61,308	+104.1	6,493	19,263	+196.7
Driving under the influence	983,915	756,935	–23.1	127,476	130,246	+2.2
Liquor laws	320,504	352,456	+10.0	69,066	83,737	+21.2
Drunkenness	547,595	422,605	–22.8	54,833	57,656	+5.1
Disorderly conduct	389,340	437,824	+12.5	90,856	116,257	+28.0
Vagrancy	27,324	16,168	–40.8	3,439	4,135	+20.2
All other offenses (except traffic)	1,624,731	2,039,086	+25.5	297,922	465,210	+56.2
Total arrests	7,061,872	7,918,554	+12.1	1,512,860	2,056,390	+35.9

*The Index Crimes are the eight crimes considered most serious by the F.B.I.

Source: Federal Bureau of Investigation, 1997, p. 219.

BOX **8.1**

Drugs, Crime, and Gender

The arrest of women for drug offenses increased more than 74 percent between 1987 and 1996, leading some observers to conclude that the "war on drugs" is actually a war on women, particularly women of color (Bush-Baskette, 1998). Certainly, the war on drugs has emphasized making more arrests and imposing harsher punishments. Underlying this strategy is the assumption that taking drug offenders off the streets will dramatically lower the overall crime rate, since drug users and addicts regularly commit other crimes either because the drugs lower their inhibitions and distort their judgment, or because they are desperate for money to feed their habit. This view is reinforced by reports that a growing number of arrestees test positive for various drugs, including marijuana and cocaine, or admit to regular drug use during the month preceding their arrest (Innes, 1988). However, empirical research conducted in locations as diverse as Harlem, Miami, Chicago, and Honolulu indicate that the drugs/crime relationship is multidimensional and that gender is an important intervening variable.

Consider, for example, the findings of James Inciardi and his colleagues, who have done extensive research on street-addict lifestyles, in particular women's use of crack-cocaine. Inciardi et al. (1993) have found that involvement in both drugs and crime seem to begin at around the same time, usually during adolescence. Most adolescents eventually "age-out" of drug use and criminal activity, but for those who continue, escalation of both activities is likely. While increased crime to finance the drug use and simply to survive is one outcome, the relationship can also occur in the opposite direction—that is, a lucrative criminal career can make it financially easier to buy drugs, thus increasing drug use. "Over time, any single heroin or cocaine addict experiences many of these drug/crime interactions, leading to a sometimes chaotic existence. Anything that changes one factor—drug use or crime—will have an impact on the other" (Inciardi et al., 1993, p. 112).

In comparing male and female street addicts, researchers have found that in many ways they are similar. The greater their drug use, the more likely they are to be involved in other types of crime. They may commit a wide variety of offenses, but typically they engage in property crime and drug dealing, for which the probability of arrest is very low. Baskin and Sommers (1997) argue that female drug users are increasingly committing violent crimes, such as robbery, largely because conditions in impoverished inner-city neighborhoods encourage violence by both men and women. However, other researchers have not found a significant increase in violence among female drug users, although these women are frequent violent crime victims. Male drug users, it appears, are more likely to commit and to be victims of violent crime (Chesney-Lind, 1997; Inciardi et al., 1993). The research also shows that men who sell drugs are more likely than women to be "big-time dealers," perhaps increasing their risk of being involved in drug-related violence. Women who sell drugs are typically "small-time dealers," with each transaction averaging $10 or less. Because the financial payoff is so low, women dealers may make more transactions per day than men dealers, thus increasing their probability of being arrested (English, 1993).

Another significant gender difference in the drugs/crime relationship is that prostitution is often tied to drug use by women. It appears that many female drug users engaged in prostitution at least sporadically *before* they became heavy users, as a way to earn money to support themselves and their children. However, heavy drug use prompts many women to engage in prostitution to earn money for drugs; they may also exchange sex for drugs, and the sex-for-drugs phenomenon is especially high among female crack addicts (Chesney-Lind, 1997; Inciardi et al., 1993). The social and financial arrangements of most crack houses encourage prostitution. It is also the case that a female addict is more highly stigmatized than a male addict and is expected to prostitute herself. The

(continued)

BOX **8.1**   **Continued**

sex-for-drugs phenomenon, in fact, is so prevalent among female crack addicts that Inciardi and his colleagues (1993) concluded that this is the one way cocaine, relative to other drugs, has had a unique impact on women. Most importantly, they found that the exchange of sex for drugs, particularly in crack houses, routinely included extreme physical and psychological abuse of women "like nothing ever seen in the annals of drug use, street life, prostitution, or domestic violence" (Inciardi et al., 1993, p. 39). Indeed, Chesney-Lind (1997) notes that in light of findings such as these the question we should be asking is not are women becoming more violent, but rather, why do women use violence so rarely?

---

emancipation theory of female crime? Do the data show that these property crimes are occupationally related offenses committed by "liberated" women in the labor force?

Answers to these questions come from at least two sources. First, studies of female offenders reveal that they are "least likely to respond to ideologies of sex-role equality" (Sarri, 1986, p. 91). Rather, these women tend to be quite traditional in terms of gender (Campbell, 1984; Chesney-Lind & Rodriguez, 1983). In fact, Adler's (1975) own work indicated that female offenders often expressed a strong dislike of the women's movement and not infrequently considered feminists "kooks."

Second, as we saw in Chapter 7, although women's labor force participation has risen dramatically over the past twenty-five years, women remain segregated in low-prestige, low-paying clerical, sales, and service occupations. Simon and Landis (1991, p. 56) argue that the influx of women into these types of jobs affords them greater opportunities to embezzle, defraud, and forge: "They [are] not in a position to steal hundreds of thousands of dollars, but they [are] in a position to pocket smaller amounts." However, it is the low level of financial gain attached to these offenses, as well as characteristics of the offenders themselves, that have led others to maintain that to label them "white-collar" crimes is misleading. For instance, in her study of male and female white-collar offenders, Daly (1989a) found that the number of women involved in corporate crime (e.g., insider trading, advertising fraud) was low. Moreover, while the men had committed both serious and petty crimes, almost all of the women's crimes were petty offenses. The financial gains of the male offenders were ten times greater than the financial gains of the females offenders.

The types of offenses committed as well as the financial outcomes of these crimes were related to the relative employment status of the men and women. While more than half the male offenders held professional or managerial positions, most of the female offenders who had been employed were bank tellers and clerical workers. A higher percentage of the female offenders, though, had no ties to the paid labor force; they were involved in offenses that were not occupational, but instead included such activities as defrauding banks through loans or credit cards, or defrauding the government by obtaining benefits to which they were not legally entitled. The motives of the female and male offenders also differed, with the former more frequently citing family responsibilities rather than personal excesses or corporate profit-making as the underlying reasons for their behavior. Consequently, Daly (1989a, p. 790) concludes that, "The women's socioeconomic profile, coupled with the nature of their crimes, makes one wonder if 'white-collar' aptly describes them or their illegalities" (see also English, 1993). Certainly, they do not appear to be "liberated" women in any sense of the term.[1] As Crites (1976, p. 37) points out, "These women rather than being recipients of expanded rights and opportunities gained by the women's movement, are, instead, witnessing declining survival options."

Findings such as these suggest an alternative explanation for recent increases in the number of women involved in property crime and drug offenses, which is supported by the research of many feminist criminologists. This explanation centers on the economic marginalization of women, especially women of color, who are raising children alone (see Chapters 6 and 7). Significantly, research indicates that the typical female offender is young, nonwhite, poor, a high school dropout, and an unmarried mother (Arnold, 1990; Chesney-Lind, 1997; Gilfus, 1992). As we learned in Chapter 7, economic discrimination against women has the most impact on young, single, women of color, and recent welfare "reforms" are actually making the financial circumstances of these women and their children worse instead of better. There is ample evidence that these circumstances propel women into crime, primarily petty property crime and, increasingly, drug offenses. In other words, the rising rates of women in property crime are likely indicative of the increasingly difficult struggle for survival for some groups of women.

In sum, the claims of the emancipation theorists seem overstated at best. With the exception of a few types of property offenses, women have not made significant gains on male rates of crime, nor do they appear to be engaged in more violent, masculine, or serious offenses. Larceny-theft, which includes crimes traditionally committed by women (e.g., shoplifting) as well as forgery and counterfeiting (check forgery) and fraud (credit card fraud and welfare fraud) remain the crimes for which females are arrested most often. In 1996, these crimes combined accounted for nearly a quarter of all female arrests (Federal Bureau of Investigation, 1997). Returning to Table 8.1, we see that crime remains, for the most part, a male enterprise, virtually untouched by feminism and the women's movement. Over 79 percent of those arrested in the United States in 1996 were males; males accounted for 84.9 percent of those arrested for violent crimes and 71.9 percent of those arrested for property crimes (Federal Bureau of Investigation, 1997). Recent research indicates, in fact, that most of the increase in arrests between 1960 and 1996 can be accounted for by the rise in arrests of 15- to 29-year-old non-White males. Particularly in urban areas of the United States, it is this group that has for several decades dominated official arrest statistics, although the debate continues as to why this has been so. Is it because young Black males are engaged in more criminal behavior than members of other demographic groups (Byrne & Sampson, 1986; Wilbanks, 1987)? Or, are they more susceptible to arrest and criminal justice processing because of their race and sex? That is, do their higher arrest rates simply reflect the racism and sexism inherent in the American criminal justice system (Mann, 1993; Miller, 1996)? These are important questions that we will take up in the next section.

Given that women, poor and non-poor alike, are fairly law-abiding and that when they do offend, their crimes are relatively minor, one might expect that those women who are apprehended and processed through the criminal justice system would be treated relatively leniently. This position is known as the **chivalry** or **paternalism hypothesis.** To evaluate its accuracy, as well as the charge we raised earlier that the criminal justice system is racist as well as sexist, we need to turn our attention to the administration of justice in the United States.[2]

With Justice for All?

Criminologists point out that crime and criminals are, to a large extent, socially and legally produced or constructed. Edwin Schur (1984) explains:

> The production of "criminals" involves the creation of crime definitions by legislation, and the application of those definitions to particular persons through the various stages of criminal justice processing. At every stage decisions are being made by ordinary, fallible, and sometimes biased human beings. (p. 224)

Thus, in assessing the differential treatment of male and female offenders, we first need to examine some of the relevant characteristics of those charged with administering justice.

The Administration of Justice

One of the most salient features of the criminal justice system in the United States is male dominance. Historically, the overwhelming majority of police, attorneys, judges, corrections officers, and other law enforcement personnel have been White men. As Tables 8.2 and 8.3 show, the contemporary picture is much the same.

TABLE 8.2   Full-Time Sworn Personnel in Local Police Departments by Size of the Population Served, Race, and Sex, 1993

Population Served	Total	White M	White F	Black M	Black F	Hispanic M	Hispanic F	Other** M	Other** F
All sizes	100	75.2	5.7	9.1	2.2	5.5	0.7	1.4	0.1
1,000,000 or more	100	61.7	7.5	12.8	4.9	10.0	2.0	1.0	0.2
500,000–999,999	100	60.1	6.1	16.1	5.0	6.1	0.9	5.4	0.4
250,000–499,999	100	64.5	7.4	14.3	3.4	8.2	0.9	1.2	0.2
100,000–249,999	100	74.2	6.3	10.4	2.1	4.9	0.4	1.5	0.1
50,000–99,999	100	80.7	5.5	16.3	0.9	4.7	0.5	1.3	0.1
25,000–49,999	100	85.1	4.6	5.0	0.5	4.1	0.2	0.6	***
10,000–24,999	100	87.1	4.5	4.8	0.3	2.5	0.1	0.6	***
2,500–9,999	100	88.9	3.9	3.8	0.3	2.4	0.1	0.5	***
under 2,500	100	89.3	2.3	5.0	0.3	1.8	0.1	1.1	0.1

*Percentages may not add to 100 due to rounding.

**Includes Native Americans, Alaska Natives, Asian Americans, and Pacific Islanders.

***Less than 0.05 percent.

Source: U.S. Department of Justice 1997a, p. 39.

TABLE 8.3   Correctional Officers and Judges by Sex

Correctional Officers

Adult State Systems	
Total number of employees	309,361
Percent female, 1992	28.8
Juvenile State Systems	
Total number of employees	36,127
Percent female, 1992	36.6
Federal Bureau of Prisons[1]	
Total number of employees	23,333
Percent female, 1992	27.1

Judges (includes all judges in criminal and civil courts)

Federal	
Supreme Court, percent female, 1992	22.2[2]
Circuit Courts of Appeal, percent female, 1990	11.3
District Courts, percent female, 1990	9.2
U.S. Magistrates (full-time only), percent female, 1990	18.8
State	
Courts of Last Resort, percent female, 1991	9.8
Intermediate Appellate Courts, percent female, 1988	9.4

[1]The Federal Bureau of Prisons does not operate facilities for juveniles.

[2]Of a total of nine Supreme Court Justices, two are women, Sandra Day O'Connor and Ruth Bader Ginsburg (see chapter 10).

Sources: National Center for State Courts 1993; U.S. Department of Justice 1993, pp. 95–96; Ries and Stone 1992, p. 410.

Traditionally, a variety of reasons were offered to justify the exclusion of women from careers in law and law enforcement. It was said, for instance, that women were too weak and timid to enforce the law or to serve as corrections officers. Others maintained that women were too emotional and sentimental—easy "push-overs." Still others claimed that women were too "good" or righteous for such work; shortly before the turn of the century, one judge, in denying a woman admission to the bar, said, "Our profession has essentially and habitually to do with all that is selfish and extortionate, knavish and criminal, coarse and brutal, repulsive and obscene. Nature has tempered women as little for the judicial conflicts of the courtroom as for the physical conflicts of the battlefield" (quoted in Reid, 1987, p. 225). Of course, there were those who used similar arguments to promote women's involvement in law enforcement, the legal professions, and prison reform. It was argued, for example, that women would have a civilizing influence on the courtroom and the prison because of their "higher morality" and their innate need to help relieve the suffering of others. Interestingly, this notion of female morality and sentiment is still with us in scholarly as well as popular literature (Gilligan, 1982; Kerber et al., 1986). As Martin and Jurik (1996) point out, however, constructing women as different is problematic for several reasons. For instance, feminine virtues may be equated with incompetence if a job is defined in terms of traditional masculinity; such images ignore diversity among women, and if it turns out that women do not exhibit these supposed differences on the job, then there is no longer a valid reason to hire and promote them (see also Worden, 1993 for an excellent discussion of this debate).

Within police training academies, law enforcement agencies, and correctional facilities, assumptions about the supposed innate differences between women and men continue to be used to justify policies and practices that prevent the full integration of women into criminal justice and law-related occupations. Male coworkers and supervisors alike still tend to consider women to be physically and psychologically weaker than men, as manipulative and untrustworthy, as requiring and requesting special treatment, and as either "good" (supportive wives and mothers) or "bad" (seductresses and sex objects). Although Title VII successfully prohibited the exclusion of women from law enforcement and other occupations (see Chapter 7), ideas such as these continue to manifest themselves in behaviors that are nonetheless discriminatory against women and create at best an uncomfortable and at worst a hostile work environment for them. These behaviors include sexual harassment and other forms of harassment, differential assignment of duties, closer scrutinization of the work and appearance of women, and exclusion of women from informal activities (Heidensohn, 1992; Martin & Jurik, 1996; Morash & Haarr, 1995).

Consider police work, for example. Although women have constituted an increasing number of police recruits since the 1970s, they continue to be marginalized in training at many police academies (Pike, 1992). Instructors frequently use sexist (and typically sexual) humor to "liven up" the classes. They also commonly refer to female recruits as "girls" and "gals," while the male recruits are "men" and "guys." They tell recruits that female victims and suspects are more troublesome than male victims and suspects. Female victims are portrayed as helpless, but also unpredictable—they may turn on an officer. Special care must be taken with female suspects; for instance, they may act seductively in an encounter and then become violent, or they may unjustifiably claim they were molested during a search, although, recruits are told, male suspects do not seem to mind being searched by female officers. In her observations at two police academies, Pike (1992, p. 266) found that training films and slides often showed scantily dressed or nude women; one film listed the special groups officers must deal with as "drug addicts, the mentally ill, females, and suicides." Both male recruits and instructors routinely teased and flirted with female recruits, frequently quite aggressively, and although both felt there is a place for women in police work, they often did not think it could be equal to that of men.

Not surprisingly, these attitudes and behaviors carry over into police departments. As we see in Table 8.2, the number of female police officers in the United States remains small, but these figures represent significant increases since the 1970s. Martin (1992; 1990) credits this change to affirmative action programs, efforts to professionalize and unionize the police, an emphasis on community policing, legal limitations on the use of violence and physical force by officers, and the adoption of formal procedures for allocating assignments and promotions. In addition, the adoption of *commu-*

nity policing in many jurisdictions throughout the country may also help to improve the status of women in policing. Unlike the traditional policing orientation, which emphasizes "crime-fighting" as opposed to community service, community policing focuses on community service and requires officers to develop cooperative relationships with neighborhood residents. Proactive problem solving and relational skills (traditionally identified as feminine) are more important in community policing than toughness and physical aggression (traditionally identified as masculine) (Miller, 1998). Nevertheless, it is still unclear to what extent police departments have truly embraced community policing and reoriented the police role as opposed to simply paying lip service to community policing principles. Indeed, as Martin and Jurik (1996) point out, the Rodney King case gives us reason to be skeptical.

Researchers have also identified other serious problems that continue to disadvantage women and people of color in law enforcement. The belief in male superiority, for instance, is still strong within police departments. There are also double standards of behavior for women and men and different criteria for evaluation. When a female officer makes a mistake, for example, the consequences may be exaggerated. Department members also continue to make references to women's physical size and strength and to question the impact of these physical qualities on the effectiveness of female officers. Martin (1992) reports, however, that the physical appearance and conditioning of male officers receive considerably less attention from coworkers and supervisors. For example, she recounts an incident in which a female detective was removed from a case by her supervisor because she was overweight, whereas the weight of the male detectives was overlooked. Although she notes that most male officers no longer engage in blanket stereotyping or rejection of women in police work, they continue to view women's routine competence as exceptional. Moreover, female officers face a double bind: If they conform to the men's conceptions of "good" women, they will be viewed as too weak to do a competent job, but if they behave like the men, they will be labeled "bitches" and "dykes" (see also Johnston, 1995; Worden, 1993).[3]

This point raises one final way that male officers attempt to assert their superiority: by sexualizing the workplace. Sexual teasing, jokes, and innuendo are routine in police departments, and female officers typically join in this behavior. Sexual harassment, however, remains a serious problem, and it occurs not only in local and state departments, but in federal agencies, such as the F.B.I. as well ("Female Texas Ranger Quits," 1995; Johnston, 1993; Martin & Jurik, 1996; Mydans, 1994).[4]

Despite the prevalent stereotypes about female police officers, there is little evidence that they differ from their male colleagues in their attitudes toward police work and toward citizens. Experience, measured in years spent on the force, appears to be more important than an officer's sex in affecting her or his attitudes. Female officers do report lower levels of self-confidence than male officers (Worden, 1993), but this is hardly surprising; as we noted previously, a hostile environment contributes to lower self-confidence. More surprising, however, especially given the work environment we have described here, is the research finding that female police officers express greater job satisfaction than do male officers (Worden, 1993). Perhaps this is why lessened self-confidence does not appear to interfere with female officers' ability to perform their duties effectively. Price and her colleagues (1989) found that female officers seem to have a less aggressive style of policing than do their male counterparts, but the style used by an officer, female or male, is influenced by many factors, including the sex, race or ethnicity, and demeanor of suspects (Martin & Jurik, 1996). As Martin and Jurik (1996, pp. 92–93) point out, "Effective police officers of both genders are flexible, able to use both the crime fighter script (associated with masculinity) and the service script (associated with femininity), according to situation demands. . . . Ineffective officers may either too rigidly rely on their formal authority, and enact only the crime-fighting aspects of their role, or alternatively emphasize only the community service script and fail to maintain control of interactions when they are challenged."

Research indicates that female correctional officers have experiences similar to those of women in police work (Martin & Jurik, 1996; Zupan, 1992). As with other law enforcement occupations, the number of female correctional officers has increased since the 1970s (see also Table 8.3). While women have a shorter history of employment at all-male facilities than at all-female facilities, their numbers in men's prisons have risen in recent years. Still, women make up only about 13 percent of correctional officers at men's prisons, and often these women work in administrative or clerical positions rather than directly supervising inmates (Martin & Jurik, 1996). Moreover, in both men's and women's facilities, women comprise less than 10 percent of wardens and supervisors (Hunter, 1992).

A number of factors contributed to the increase in female correctional officers in recent years, including affirmative action programs, successful Title VII lawsuits brought by women seeking positions as correctional officers at all-male facilities, a decline in job applications by men, and the belief by policymakers that the addition of women staff would have a "calming effect" on inmates and promote more humane treatment (Martin & Jurik, 1996; Zupan, 1992).[5] These factors have also contributed to the high representation of women of color among correctional officers; depending on the facility, women of color may make up from one quarter to nearly one half of the corrections staff (Belknap, 1991; Maghan & McLeish-Blackwell, 1991).

Nevertheless, the increased presence of women in corrections has not led to their full integration in the workplace. Interestingly, female correctional officers appear to confront more resistance and harassment from male administrators and coworkers than from inmates (Martin & Jurik, 1996; Van Voorhies et al., 1991; Zimmer, 1986; Zupan, 1992).[6] Training and work assignments favor male correctional officers, and performance evaluations, which are supposedly based on objective criteria, disadvantage women for promotion (Britton, 1997; Martin & Jurik, 1996). Researchers, for example, have found that performance evaluations tend to focus on skills traditionally considered masculine (security functions), while ignoring skills traditionally considered feminine (communication and conflict diffusion skills) (Jurik, 1985; Zimmer, 1987).

Similar to police officers, female and male correctional officers show few differences in their attitudes toward their work and toward inmates. Female correctional personnel appear to value rules and structure more than their male coworkers do, and they experience more job-related stress; both of these findings are likely related to the pressure, criticism, and harassment they receive from their male colleagues (Jurik & Halemba, 1984; Lawrence & Johnson, 1991; Van Voorhis et al., 1991). Nevertheless, they do not express lower job satisfaction or less career commitment than male correctional officers (Jurik & Halemba, 1984; Zupan, 1992).

Women in more prestigious positions, female attorneys, for instance, are no less likely to escape such prejudices and discriminatory treatment. Recent research, in fact, demonstrates a pervasive bias against women in our nation's law firms and courtrooms (Bernat, 1992; Couric, 1989; Martin & Jurik, 1996; Morello, 1986; Padavic & Orcutt, 1997). A recent study in southern Arizona, for example, revealed that female attorneys are frequently subjected to disparaging and offensive remarks and behaviors by colleagues and judges, both inside and outside the courtroom. These may have the effect not only of making their work unpleasant and stressful, but also of lowering their credibility in the eyes of clients and the courts, which in turn might jeopardize their chances of winning their cases (MacCorquodale & Jensen, 1993). Such discrimination occurs not only in the lower courts, but at the federal level as well ("Court That Attacks Sex Bias," 1992; Riger et al., 1995; Weiser, 1997), and in private law firms as well as in public sector workplaces (Lentz & Laband, 1995; Rosenberg et al., 1993). Minority women often fare the worst. For example, they are sometimes mistaken as defendants (Bernat, 1992; Martin & Jurik, 1996). As one Black female attorney recounted, "I once appeared before a judge in Middlesex Superior Court [Massachusetts] who refused to address me until I showed proof that I was a lawyer, something not requested of any other attorney there that day" ("Massachusetts to Look at Sex Bias," 1986; see also MacCorquodale & Jensen, 1993).

To what extent, then, do such attitudes affect the disposition of cases? Do prejudices such as these disadvantage male offenders by affording their female counterparts greater leniency before the law? Or are male offenders advantaged by sexism in the criminal justice system? As a preliminary response, we can say that the sex of the offender does appear to play a part in the disposition of a case. However, a number of other factors interact with sex in producing specific outcomes. These include the offender's age and race or ethnicity as well as the offense with which he or she is charged and the number of previous criminal convictions. We can understand this better by comparing conviction rates and sentencing patterns for male and female offenders.

Do the Punishments Fit the Crimes?

More than two decades ago, criminologist Clayton Hartjen (1978, p. 108) observed that, "although a suspect's behavior is of primary importance in determining his or her chances of being arrested, in most cases the decision to arrest a person is based on factors that have little to do with the degree of a person's behavioral criminality. . . . It is not so much what a person does as what kind of person he [or she] is (or is seen by the police to be) that affects official labeling." Hartjen's argument can be extended to other stages of criminal justice processing that follow arrest, including the arraignment (at which time a plea is entered by the defendant), the trial (either by a judge—*which is known as a bench trial*—or by a jury), and sentencing. This treatment of defendants occurs because official actors within the criminal justice system—that is, the police, attorneys, and judges—exercise considerable discretion in deciding how particular cases, and, therefore, particular defendants, will be handled. This discretion may lead to widespread disparities in the treatment of offenders, which have less to do with the offenders' behavior than with their membership in specific groups, such as their social class, race and ethnicity, and sex.

Consider, for instance, the practice of *plea negotiation*, better known as *plea bargaining*. In a plea bargain, the prosecutor and the defense attorney work out an agreement whereby the defendant will plead guilty in exchange for some prosecutorial or judicial concession, usually a reduced charge (and, therefore, a reduced sentence), the reduction of multiple charges, or a recommendation of leniency by the prosecutor (which also has the effect of reducing the severity of the potential sentence) (Inciardi, 1993). It is estimated that about 89 percent of all criminal convictions are the result of negotiated guilty pleas (U.S. Department of Justice, 1997a). However, research indicates that plea bargaining may operate differently for different groups of offenders. Specifically, Mann (1993) points out that poor people and racial and ethnic minorities (who are disproportionately represented among the poor) experience greater pressure to enter a guilty plea because the public defenders assigned to them wish to dispose of as many cases in their overwhelming caseloads as quickly as possible. Whether they are guilty or not, Mann argues, these defendants are encouraged to enter a guilty plea so as not to run the risk of going to trial and being convicted of a more serious offense.[7] In addition, because the poor and racial and ethnic minorities are less likely to be able to post bail, they remain incarcerated in local jails until their trials, and thus may prefer to plead guilty in order to secure their release from what are typically deplorable conditions in these facilities.

Recent legal "reforms" enacted as part of the federal government's and state and local jurisdictions' renewed effort to "get tough" on crime have ruled out the possibility of plea bargaining for certain offenses and have also had a disparate impact on racial and ethnic minorities as well as women. Research shows that policies such as mandatory sentences for drug offenses and "three strikes and you're out" laws (i.e., a mandatory life sentence following a third felony conviction) have resulted in an increase in the number of racial and ethnic minorities sentenced to prison, but the most dramatic increase has been for Black women. According to Bush-Baskette (1998), during the 1980s, the number of Black females incarcerated in state or federal prisons increased by 278 percent, while the number of incarcerated Black males increased 186 percent and the overall prison population increased 168 percent. In fact, the increase for Black females was largest among all groups—Black, White, and Hispanic females and males.

For many years, researchers have documented differences in criminal sentencing based not only on offenders' sex and race or ethnicity, but also on their age, marital status, and a host of other nonlegal factors. This leads to **sentencing disparity,** the imposition of different sentences on offenders convicted of similar crimes. It is not difficult to understand why sentencing disparity is problematic; it results in unfair and inappropriate sentences that may be disproportionate to the severity of the crime or the offender's criminal history, and are based instead on irrelevant factors, such as the offender's sex and race or ethnicity.

Early studies of sentencing disparities between male and female offenders reported that women were given preferential treatment by the courts and were less likely than men to receive prison sentences for their crimes (Faine & Bohlander, 1976; Nagel & Weitzman, 1972). However, as Chesney-Lind (1986) points out, the difficulty with much of this early research is that it did not control for the less serious nature of most women's crimes. One recent study that took into account such factors as type of offense and prior convictions showed that offense severity and prior record have the largest effects on sentencing for both male and female offenders, and that when men and women appear in court under similar circumstances—that is, charged with similar crimes and coming from similar backgrounds—they are treated alike (Steffensmeier et al., 1993). But other researchers emphasize that it is an offender's background that often has the greatest influence on sentencing outcomes. For example, studies show that the perceived *respectability* of the offender—male or female—in terms of conformity to traditional gender norms influences sentencing. According to Miethe and Moore (1986), married, employed men with no prior offense record—that is, men who conform to the gender prescription of "respectable" masculinity—are sentenced more leniently than single, unemployed men with previous arrests or convictions. This is especially true for Black men; single Black men are sentenced more harshly than single White men (see also Daly, 1994; Myers & Talarico, 1986).

Similarly, women who conform to a traditional model of femininity—for instance, economic dependence on a man, no evidence of drug or alcohol use, no evidence of sexual deviance—may receive lighter sentences than women deemed less "respectable" by the courts.[8] Daly (1994) refers to this pattern of bias in judicial decision making as *familial-based justice*. She reports that defendants with family ties, especially those who are the primary caregivers of children, are treated more leniently by the courts than nonfamilied defendants. Based on interviews with court officials, she concluded that the protection of families and children, not the protection of women, influences much judicial decision making. However, judges are not inclined to give female drug offenders a "break" because they perceive them as being as likely as male drug offenders to get in trouble again (Steffensmeier et al., 1993). These findings help to explain why most incarcerated women are not only Black, but also young, poor, unmarried mothers, who are in prison for petty property crimes or drug offenses, usually drug possession rather than drug trafficking (Bush-Baskette, 1998; Chesney-Lind, 1997).

Another manifestation of "get tough" "lock 'em up" crime control policies is the imposition of longer sentences. Again, however, race and sex intersect to produce differential outcomes. Researchers have found that not only are non-White women more likely to be sentenced to prison, but the actual time served is longer for non-White women than for White women. Mann (1989) reports, for example, that although the White women in her study who were convicted of crimes against the person received sentences almost twice as long as those of the African American women convicted of the same crimes, the African American women actually stayed in prison longer than the White women (see also Bush-Baskette, 1998; Mann, 1995; Mauer & Huling, 1995).

Finally, the "get tough" approach to crime control, which emphasizes punishment over rehabilitation, has also resulted in a greater willingness to sentence offenders to death. Since 1980, the number of prisoners under sentence of death has increased more than 400 percent. Of the 3,054 prisoners awaiting execution in 1995, 43.4 percent were non-White, a figure far disproportionate to their representation in the general population; in 1995, only 17 percent of the U.S. population was non-White (U.S. Department of Commerce, Bureau of the Census, 1997). In 1998, the ratio of men to women on death row was 70:1, but there were strong indications that states were increasingly willing to execute women. Within the first three months of 1998, two women were executed, one in Texas by lethal injection and one in Florida by electrocution; prior to that time, only one woman had been executed in the United States since the death penalty was reinstated in 1977. Although these executions generated a storm of controversy, the dominant attitude among the general public appeared to be that an offender's sex should have no bearing on whether she or he is executed (Verhovek, 1998).

Thus, although there appears to be a widespread belief that women are treated chivalrously by the courts—being allowed, at times, to get away with murder (see, for example, Mansnerus, 1997)—the empirical research we have reviewed here hardly supports such a view. Rather, the "get tough" approach to crime characteristic of the current national climate and popular in the rhetoric of politicians has produced what Chesney-Lind (1997, p. 151) calls, " 'equality' for women with a vengeance when it comes to the punishment of crime."[9] And non-White women, in particular, are bearing the brunt of this growing punitiveness, a point to which we will return shortly.

Gender and Juvenile Offenders. Our focus so far has been on adult offenders, but research indicates that the age of the offender is also an important variable. Let's briefly consider how age intersects with sex as well as race and ethnicity to produce differential sentencing outcomes for juvenile offenders.

To begin, girls are more likely than boys to be charged with **status offenses,** that is, behavior which if engaged in by an adult would not be considered a violation of the law. These include, for example, running away from home, incorrigibility, truancy, being a "juvenile in need of supervision" (JINS), and being in danger of becoming "morally depraved." However, Chesney-Lind (1997) and others (see, for instance, Lees, 1989; Maquieira, 1989) point out, often these charges represent parents' attempts to adhere to and enforce the sexual double standard (see Chapter 6). Parents are significantly more likely to bring a daughter to court for her behavior than to bring a son for his (Chesney-Lind & Shelden, 1992; Feinman, 1992). Research shows that parents of adolescents at high risk for delinquent behavior—they live in economically marginalized, high-crime neighborhoods and have siblings who have been adjudicated delinquent— impose more restrictions on their daughters than on their sons. Boys have greater freedom to engage in activities outside the home, especially at night, whereas girls are often expected to help raise younger children in the household and their out-of-home activities are more closely monitored, particularly at night (Bottcher, 1995). Not surprisingly, then, boys typically engage in more delinquent behavior than girls and their offenses are more serious. Yet, the mere suspicion of sexual impropriety can result in more severe sentences for female juvenile offenders relative to their male counterparts (Bottcher, 1995; Chesney-Lind & Shelden, 1992).

Research also reveals that many young women charged as runaways are actually attempting to escape from physically and sexually abusive homes. Studies of young people entering the juvenile justice system show that girls are more likely than boys to have been abused and to have entered the juvenile justice system because of status offenses, while boys' entry was more often precipitated by involvement in more delinquent offenses (Chesney-Lind, 1997). Unfortunately, because of the juvenile courts' commitment to preserving parental authority, they frequently have forced these girls to return to their abusers, routinely ignoring girls' complaints about abuse (Arnold,

1990; Davis, 1993; Chesney-Lind, 1997). Ironically, then, "statutes that were originally placed in law to 'protect' young people have, in the case of some girls, criminalized their survival strategies" (Chesney-Lind, 1997, p. 28).

Females charged with status offenses are more harshly treated at every step of criminal justice processing and are more likely than males to be institutionalized for status offenses (Chesney-Lind & Shelden, 1992; Poe-Yamagata & Butts, 1996). Sentencing reforms to address these disparities have been enacted, but their effectiveness is questionable. For instance, one federal policy, the Juvenile Justice and Delinquency Prevention Act of 1974, required states receiving funds for delinquency prevention programs to divert status offenders away from juvenile correctional facilities. Since girls are more likely to be charged with status offenses, this policy at least initially helped to reduce their incarceration rates (Teilmann & Landry, 1981). However, in 1980, those rates again began to climb as a "get tough" attitude took hold with respect to juvenile offenders just as it did for adult offenders. In many jurisdictions, attempts were made to close what many viewed as loopholes permitted by the 1974 Act by reclassifying many status offenses as criminal offenses. Research indicates that this reclassification impacted more negatively on girls than on boys (Curran, 1984). Similarly, legal mandates that remove female status offenders from secure juvenile facilities—a practice that is undoubtedly beneficial to them—does not necessarily result in freedom from incarceration (Feinman, 1992). In fact, Chesney-Lind (1997, p. 75) argues that this "reform" has actually created a "two-track juvenile justice system—one track for girls of color and another for white girls." White girls are significantly more likely to be recommended for "treatment" (e.g., placement in a mental health facility), whereas girls of color are more likely to be recommended for a "detention-oriented" placement. Moreover, when institutional placements are examined, White girls are more likely to be placed in private facilities, while girls of color are more likely to be placed in public facilities (see also Bartollas, 1993; Miller, 1994).

To sum up our discussion so far, it appears that a number of extra-legal factors routinely come into play in the administration of justice. These include offenders' sex, race/ethnicity, age, and perceived respectability. "Taken together, [the] research findings suggest that the criminal justice system has been involved in the enforcement of traditional [and racialized] sex-role expectations as well as, and sometimes in place of, the law" (Chesney-Lind, 1986, p. 92). Let's turn our attention now to an examination of how these factors carry over from sentencing into corrections.

Gender and Corrections

The United States has one of the highest correctional populations in the world. In 1995, more than 5.3 million adult Americans were under some sort of correctional supervision: They were on probation, in jail or prison, or on parole. As we have already noted, incarceration rates have been rising at a dramatic rate, due largely to mandatory sentencing policies. The United States incarcerates over 1.2 million adults in state and federal prisons, a more than 300 percent increase since 1980. Nearly 500,000 adults are held in jails. Approximately 7,800 juveniles are also held in jails, many charged and awaiting trial as adults, and over 93,000 more juveniles are in custody in public and private juvenile detention facilities (Chesney-Lind, 1997; U.S. Department of Commerce, Bureau of the Census, 1997). According to Danner (1998), so great has been the increase in incarceration in recent years that most U.S. prisons are now operating at 114 percent to 126 percent capacity, and the federal government and many states are undertaking costly construction projects to build larger facilities. Indeed, Danner quotes an article from the magazine *The Nation*, which observed that prisons are "the only expanding public housing" in the United States (quoted in Danner, 1998, p. 2).

Historically, women have constituted only a small fraction of the U.S. prison and jail populations. For example, at the turn of the century, women were just 4 percent of the prison population in the United States; in 1970, they made up only 3 percent of this population. But the "lock 'em up" mentality of the 1980s and 1990s has swelled the total U.S. prison population and women's representation in it disproportionately to the increase in women's involvement in serious crime (Immarigeon & Chesney-Lind, 1990). A report by the U.S. Department of Justice (1991) states that the rate of growth in the incarceration of females has exceeded that of males every year since 1981. During the 1980s, the male inmate population increased by 112 percent, whereas the female inmate population increased by 202 percent. Women are now 6.1 percent of the state and federal prison population and 10.2 percent of the U.S. jail population (U.S. Department of Commerce, Bureau of the Census, 1997).[10] As Table 8.4 shows, and as we have already noted, women of color are disproportionately represented among the incarcerated.

Traditionally, the small numbers of incarcerated women have been offered as a rationale for paying little attention to them in both research and policy making. At the same time, the physical plant of women's prisons appeared less harsh than facilities that housed men and, therefore, less "problematic." The rapid rise in the number of female

TABLE 8.4   Prisoners under State, Federal, or Local Jurisdiction by Race and Sex, 1995

	Number of adults held in prisons or jails				Rate (per 100,000 adult residents) held in prisons or jails			
	White		*Black*		*White*		*Black*	
	Male	*Female*	*Male*	*Female*	*Male*	*Female*	*Male*	*Female*
1990	545,900	39,300	508,800	38,000	718	48	5,365	338
1991	588,800	42,200	551,000	40,800	740	51	5,717	356
1992	598,000	44,100	590,300	42,400	774	53	6,015	365
1993	627,100	48,500	624,100	47,500	805	56	6,259	403
1994	674,400	51,000	676,000	52,300	851	61	6,662	435
1995	728,500	57,800	711,600	55,300	919	66	6,926	456

Source: U. S. Department of Justice, Bureau of Justice Statistics, 1997.

prisoners and jail inmates, however, has brought increasing attention not only to the problems of incarceration in general, but also to the special problems faced by incarcerated women. For example, although some women's prisons are relatively more physically attractive than men's facilities and less secure—with minimum, medium, and maximum security inmates housed together—living conditions are not necessarily less harsh, less regimented, or less degrading (Baunach, 1992). Women's prisons, like men's prisons, have a paramilitary atmosphere, with rigid rules for behavior. In fact, research indicates that women in today's prisons are both overcontrolled and overpoliced (McClellan, 1994). For example, women are more likely than men to be cited for rules infractions, not because they are more unruly, but because they have more rules imposed on them. McClellan (1994) reports that these infractions include having too many family photos on display in their cells, not eating all the food on their plates, and possessing "contraband" (e.g., an extra bra or pillowcase, or candy). Moreover, McClellan found that women are punished more harshly than men for rules infractions.

Another difference between women's prisons and men's prisons is the availability of educational and vocational programming. Historically, these programs have been grossly underfunded in women's prisons, the rationale being that large numbers of programs for small numbers of women would not be cost-efficient. Traditionally, these programs reinforced gender stereotypes and conformity to the turn-of-the-century philosophy that the rehabilitative goal of women's prisons should be to teach "fallen women" how to be good wives and mothers. Consequently, these programs emphasized domestic "skills" over marketable job skills. Research indicates that women are more responsive to prison programs than men are, but women still have fewer opportunities to participate in such programs. Moreover, prison programs continue to ill-equip women for the contemporary work world and for successfully meeting the challenge of economic survival for themselves or as primary providers for their families. Unlike vocational programs in men's prisons, which at least focus on skilled trades such as carpentry, electronics, plumbing, and construction, most vocational programs in women's prisons train inmates for clerical work and garment manufacturing (Moyer, 1991; Simon & Landis, 1991).

Also inadequate in women's prisons are medical care and treatment programs. Although as Moyer (1991, p. 11) points out, "health care in all prisons tends to be disorganized and crisis oriented with a heavy reliance on part-time doctors and mental health personnel," there is evidence that fewer medical services are available in women's prisons even though women need more medical care than men. For example, more female inmates (3.9 percent) than male inmates (2.4 percent) are infected with HIV, the virus that causes AIDS, and the rate of HIV infection among female inmates has increased faster than the rate of infection among male inmates (69 percent vs. 22 percent) (Brien & Beck, 1996). However, Pollock-Byrne (1990) makes the important point that simply offering female inmates the same medical services as those offered to male inmates is an inappropriate solution to this problem, since the health care needs of women are different from those of men. Women, for instance, need gynecological and, not infrequently, obstetrical care while in prison; up to 6 percent of female inmates at any given time are pregnant. The mental health needs of female inmates are also different from those of men. For example, despite the fact that an increasing number of women are being imprisoned because of drug offenses, the drug treatment programs offered to female inmates are usually inadequate and ineffective. For one thing, they are often modeled on men's treatment programs even though, as we will see in Chapter 11, women abuse drugs and alcohol for reasons different from those of men. Moreover, the treatment of other medical complaints in prison can actually make women's drug problems worse. For instance, two of the most common medical complaints of female inmates are anxiety and depression, and they are frequently treated with psychotropic drugs such as tranquilizers. Such drugs are overprescribed for nonincarcerated women who seek medical help for these problems (see Chapter 11), but when this treatment is applied to incarcerated women, the majority of whom already have substance abuse problems, the result is often *transaddiction*—that is, addiction to different drugs (prescription drugs rather than street drugs), but addiction nonetheless.

Few institutions offer programs that effectively address the problems associated with physical and sexual abuse, despite the fact that more than 40 percent of women in prison report having been previously physically or sexually abused; about 12 percent of men in prison report a history of physical and sexual abuse (Chesney-Lind & Shelden, 1992; Snell & Morton, 1994). For about a third of female inmates, abuse began in childhood and continued into adulthood, but for many of these women, incarceration does not mean that the abuse will end. Recent investigations have documented widespread physical and sexual abuse of female inmates by male employees, including guards, at federal and state prisons as well as at local detention centers. Despite the fact that the number of female correctional officers has grown in recent years, most female inmates continue to be guarded by men, and some of these men use their authority to sexually exploit women prisoners. The abuse includes beatings, rape, and sexual coercion (e.g., withholding or bestowing privileges or goods to compel inmates to engage in sexual acts). Apart from blatant sexual abuse, the women also report repeated violations of their privacy, with guards entering rooms unannounced or strip-searches being conducted in the presence of male guards, an especially traumatic experience for a woman with a history of sexual abuse (Chesney-Lind, 1997; "Federal Lawsuit," 1997; Holmes, 1996; "U.S. Bureau of Prisons," 1998).[11]

Finally, the separation of inmates from their families presents acute problems for women. About 60 percent of male inmates have children (54.4 percent have children less than eighteen years old), and more than 76 percent of female inmates have children (67.5 percent have children under eighteen years old). Among male inmates with children under eighteen, about half report having lived with them before being incarcerated. In contrast, almost four out of five female inmates with children under eighteen lived with them before going to prison. As we learned in Chapter 6, few children live with their fathers only. If a man with children is sent to prison, it is likely that the mother of the children will retain custody of them and provide them with care; 88.5 percent of imprisoned men with children under eighteen report that the children are living with their mother. When a woman with children is sent to prison, however, it is often the case that the children's father played a small role in the children's lives and that their mother was their sole caretaker and provider. Consequently, rather than living with their father (22.1 percent), children of imprisoned mothers usually live with a grandparent (45.4 percent) or other relative (22.1 percent); about 10 percent are placed in foster homes or institutional care. Twenty-eight percent of incarcerated women with children under eighteen report that they lost legal custody of their children when they entered prison (U.S. Department of Justice, 1991).

The amount of time imprisoned mothers are permitted to visit with their children varies widely from institution to institution. A small number allow visitation seven days a week (Simon & Landis, 1991). Among these is the Bedford Hills Correctional Facility in New York, which established the first state prison nursery program that allows imprisoned mothers to care for their infants within the correctional facility until the infants are one year old or for eighteen months if the mother is to be paroled within that period. This program also provides incarcerated mothers with parenting classes and supplies child care for the infants while the mothers go to prison jobs or prison classes to earn high school diplomas (Harris, 1993; see also Snyder-Joy & Carlo, 1998). In contrast, most facilities allow visitation once a week, while a few allow it only once or twice a month. The length of the visits in these institutions also varies, but most institutions report that they do not have rooms equipped for the visits of very young children (e.g., high chairs, cribs) or even rooms to talk privately or perhaps to listen to music with older children (Simon & Landis, 1991). While a majority of institutions report that they have furlough programs that allow incarcerated mothers to visit with their children at home or in halfway houses, Simon and Landis (1991) found that most of these have stringent eligibility requirements.

Apart from the economic consequences of imprisoning women who are the sole economic providers for and caretakers of their children, incarceration also has serious psychological consequences for both the women and the children. The separation lowers the mothers' self-esteem and generates feelings of emptiness, helplessness, anger, bitterness, and guilt, as well as fears about the children's safety, of losing the children, or of being rejected by them (Baunach, 1992; Snyder-Joy & Carlo, 1998). The children, depending on their age, experience a sense of failure and a range of feelings of traumatic loss and abandonment, anger, guilt, and fear for their mother's safety (Huie, 1994; Snyder-Joy & Carlo, 1998).

The plight of imprisoned mothers and their children has fueled the debate over women's imprisonment in general. Given that most female inmates have committed relatively minor nonviolent crimes, a number of criminologists and advocates have questioned the appropriateness of imprisoning them in the first place. Immarigeon and Chesney-Lind (1990) identify several innovative programs designed to reduce women's imprisonment, but emphasize that these are rare. In most states, they note, systematic planning is atypical and female inmates continue to be neglected by policy makers. However, even when planning is involved, incarcerative policies still dominate (see also Chesney-Lind, 1997). Unfortunately, this is likely to remain the case, since most legislators appear to favor building more prisons and imposing longer prison terms on offenders rather than preventive or diversionary programs.

In sum, the picture with respect to law enforcement, sentencing, and corrections is a complex one. The "get-tough" crime control policies of the 1980s and 1990s have generated a rhetoric of equality—if you commit the crime, you do the time, no matter who you are—but in practice, as we have seen, a double standard of justice continues to operate, one that is particularly punitive for women, especially young, economically marginalized, non-White, single mothers. Does a double standard also come into play with respect to the treatment of male and female crime victims? We'll explore answers to this question in the next section.

Criminal Victimization: Gender, Power, and Violence

Concern about becoming a crime victim is a common fear among the general population in the United States. One national opinion poll, for example, found that more than a third of the respondents worried about themselves or a family member being sexually assaulted. More than a third also were worried about their homes being burglarized, and more than a quarter worried about being mugged. Fear of crime is higher among some segments of the population than others. Respondents living in urban areas expressed the highest levels of fear, and African Americans were more fearful than White Americans. Older people are more fearful than the young, and women are more fearful than men ("Perception," 1993). In general, fear of violent crime is stronger than fear of property crime.

There is, of course, a difference between fear of crime and the actual chances of becoming a crime victim. Looking at Table 8.5, we see data from the National Crime Survey showing rates of violent criminal victimization by sex, age, and race. The National Crime Survey is a semiannual federal study that questions a random sample of American households about their criminal victimization experiences. Looking only at the variable of sex, we see that men are significantly more likely than women to be victimized by violent crime. It is estimated, in fact, that 89 percent of all males now twelve years old will be the victim of a violent crime at least once during their lifetime, compared with 73 percent of females. However, this estimate is somewhat misleading since not all males have an equal likelihood of becoming a violent crime victim. Taking race and age into account, we see that it is young men of color—those between the ages of twelve and twenty-four—who have the highest victimization rates (see also Box 8.2 on pages 258–259).

Although the National Crime Survey is considered to be a fairly good indicator of the extent of criminal victimization in the United States and is the most widely utilized source of victimization statistics, there are several factors that make it problematic when considering the gendered nature of criminal victimization. As Gerber and Weeks (1992) point out, much of the crime—especially violent crime—of which women are the most likely victims goes unrecorded by the National Crime Survey. For example, the survey does not ask specifically about the crimes of spouse abuse and incest. In addition, although women report more crime to survey interviewers than to the police, they have difficulty reporting certain crimes, such as rape, to anyone. Consequently, analysts estimate that official victimization data represent perhaps only 10 to 30 percent of the rapes that actually occur (Gordon & Riger, 1991; Greenfeld, 1997). In fact, in a study financed by the federal government, researchers found that the number of completed sexual assaults in a given year may be more than five times as high as that reported in the National Crime Survey (Johnston, 1992).

TABLE 8.5   Violent Victimization Rates for Persons Age 12 and Older, by Race and Sex

Sex, Race, and Age of Victim	Total Population	Rate of Violent Victimization (per 1,000 persons)
White Males		
12–15 years	6,257,840	135.6
16–19 years	5,873,320	146.0
20–24 years	7,527,480	123.3
25–34 years	17,326,480	65.0
35–49 years	24,922,090	44.5
50–64 years	14,319,810	15.2
65 years & older	11,780,640	5.7
White Females		
12–15 years	5,948,580	88.2
16–19 years	5,576,340	102.4
20–24 years	7,375,450	78.1
25–34 years	17,135,720	57.9
35–49 years	24,903,460	33.6
50–64 years	15,282,970	14.3
65 years & older	16,311,340	2.8
Black Males		
12–15 years	1,234,310	141.6
16–19 years	1,138,680	124.8
20–24 years	1,111,420	71.1
25–34 years	2,539,490	66.9
35–49 years	3,199,810	49.9
50–64 years	1,499,080	28.5
65 years & older	973,190	33.7
Black Females		
12–15 years	1,234,480	129.8
16–19 years	1,100,140	109.3
20–24 years	1,419,040	97.5
25–34 years	2,983,380	59.0
35–49 years	3,750,950	40.5
50–64 years	1,855,770	13.5
65 years & older	1,590,380	6.7

Source: U.S. Department of Justice, 1997b, p. 15.

There are other ways, too, that women's criminal victimization is rendered invisible. For instance, Gerber and Weeks (1992) maintain that women have always been the victims of corporate crime—indeed, in cases such as the Dalkon Shield contraceptive device and silicone breast implants, women have been the only victims of such crimes—but most criminologists have overlooked the role of gender in their analyses of corporate criminality (for an exception, see Rynbrandt & Kramer, in press). Similarly,

BOX 8.2
Hate Crimes

Hate crimes, which are also called *bias crimes*, are crimes in which the offender's actions are motivated by hatred, bias, or prejudice, based on the actual or perceived race, ethnicity, national origin, religion, or sexual orientation of the victim. Hate crimes often take the form of slurs and vandalism, but not infrequently they involve violent physical attacks against individuals. In fact, victims of hate-motivated assaults typically suffer greater physical and psychological harm than victims of other assaults (National Institute Against Prejudice and Violence [NIAPV], 1990). For instance, they are four times more likely to require hospitalization than victims of other assaults (Goleman, 1990), and they also experience strong feelings of personal isolation (NIAPV, 1990).

Not everyone is at equal risk of hate crime victimization, however. Reports indicate that the most frequent victims are people of color and they are usually victimized by young, White males. Interracial couples also appear to be at especially high risk of victimization. Gay men and lesbians, too, are frequent targets of hate crimes. In recent surveys, as many as 92 percent of gay men and lesbians have indicated that they have been the targets of verbal abuse or threats because of their sexual orientation, and as many as 24 percent have reported physical attacks (Herek & Berrill, 1992). In 1995, hate crimes against gays and lesbians decreased about 8 percent over the previous year, but those that occurred were more violent ("Anti-Gay Crimes More Violent," 1996). Some analysts predict that the decrease will be shortlived because right-wing religious groups have vowed to intensify their crusade against homosexuals. Many conservative religious leaders portray homosexuals as evil, the "incarnation of Satan," and observers worry that such inflamatory rhetoric can motivate some zealots to try to eradicate gays and lesbians "in the name of God" (Liebman, 1995). However, such hate speech and crime is not unique to the United States. According to Amnesty International (1997, p. 7), "In countries all over the world, individuals are being targeted for

imprisonment, torture and even murder, simply on the grounds of their sexual orientation." Moreover, unlike the United States, which has antibias laws, there is no international protection for sexual minorities. Indeed, in many countries, government officials are the main perpetrators (Amnesty International, 1997; McNeil, 1995).

Notice, though, that in the official definition of hate crime codified in the United States as the federal Hate Crime Statistics Act of 1990, actions motivated by the *sex* of the victim are not included. In other words, specific acts or threats against women that are intended to intimidate, harass, induce fear, coerce, or punish them because of the perpetrators' misogynistic feelings or hostility toward them *as women* are not counted as hate crimes and, therefore, are outside the bounds of redress provided in hate crimes statutes (Miller, 1994). This glaring omission has led to considerable criticism by many feminists, who point out that much violence against women is *gender-motivated* and has the purpose of intimidating not just an individual woman, but women *as a group*, just as hate crimes directed against those covered by the law intimidate individuals because of their group affiliation (Center for Women Policy Studies, 1991b).

Consider, for example, one recent and particularly dramatic example: the shooting deaths of four female students and a female teacher in a schoolyard in Jonesboro, Arkansas in March, 1998, by a thirteen-year-old boy and his eleven-year-old friend. Although in the immediate aftermath of the shooting, the media focused on the problem of school violence, the motive for the killings offered by the thirteen-year-old was that he was angry at a girl who had broken up with him and he wanted revenge against her and other girls like her (Morello & Katel, 1998). In other words, four girls and one woman were killed and another nine girls and a woman were injured in that Jonesboro schoolyard *because they were female*. A similar incident occurred in Montreal in 1991, when fourteen female engineering students were shot to death in a university classroom by a man who left a note proclaiming his hatred of women and his desire to "kill the feminists."

Many people would argue that such incidents are rare and that, obviously, not all crimes involving female victims can be considered hate crimes. While we agree, it is also important to point out that in those instances when it is clear that women were victimized because of their sex, the advantage of having the category of sex included in hate crimes laws would be that offenders would be more severely punished for their actions. This is because offenses prosecuted as hate crimes carry additional penalties above those normally prescribed for a specific offense. More important, however, the inclusion of the category sex in hate crimes statutes would mandate funding for public education programs, victim services, prevention efforts, and special training for criminal justice personnel. Finally, women might be more willing to report incidents of harassment and violence if they believe that law enforcement officials recognize gender-motivated crime as a problem (Miller, 1994).

---

many criminologists who have studied homicide have focused largely on male victims as well as offenders, often including women only in discussions of crimes of passion. Yet the Department of Labor recently reported that while women account for only 8 percent of on-the-job deaths, 34 percent of women who die on the job are murder victims, compared with less than 15 percent of men who die at work. Homicide is the most frequent cause of on-the-job death for women, a finding that warrants further

7b).

eater fear of crime becomes more understand-
omen's greater fear of crime stems both from
rom the fact that their victimization is more
ialized relative to men's victimization. Con-
l images of crime and criminals. Regardless of
most women believe the typical criminal is a
o is mentally ill or addicted to drugs. Women
violent crime: Their common fear is of a psy-
attack them when they are simply going about
ves (Madriz, 1997). As Madriz (1997, p. 342)
e." Yet, all the available data show that women
stranger, but by someone they know. Women
e violent victimization at the hands of an ac-
ntimate than a stranger, whereas for men, the
a stranger are nearly the same as the chances of
they know (Craven, 1996). Let's explore this
e crime of rape, one of the crimes women fear
ciate with "stranger danger."

women fear the most (Gordon & Riger, 1991;
nong very young girls, as a recent survey of ele-
it asked the questions, "Would you rather be a

man or a woman? Why?" One ten-year-old girl responded, "The worst thing about being a woman is we get raped and killed. Women can get killed by their prettiness" (quoted in Snow, 1992, p. 1E). As this girl indicates, the fear of rape derives not only from the fact that rape is a serious crime but also because it is a crime associated with other serious offenses, such as robbery and homicide, and with gratuitous violence in addition to the rape itself (Gordon & Riger, 1991; Madriz, 1997). The fear of contracting AIDS through rape also adds to women's fear of this crime (Center for Women Policy Studies, 1991a).[12]

According to the F.B.I.'s "crime clock," one forcible rape is committed every six minutes in the United States (Federal Bureau of Investigation, 1997). During the 1980s, the rate of rape in the United States rose four times faster than the total crime rate (U.S. House of Representatives, 1990; see also DeKeseredy et al., 1993). However, during the first half of the 1990s, as the total violent crime rate decreased, the rate of rape also fell somewhat, declining by about 15 percent (Federal Bureau of Investigation, 1997). It is unclear whether the decline represents a real decrease in the number of rapes committed or a greater unwillingness on the part of victims to report the crime. Sexual assault is, in fact, one of the violent crimes *least* likely to be reported to the police (Center for Women Policy Studies, 1991a). Rape also has a relatively low conviction rate. About half of all reported rapes result in an arrest; only about 22 percent of those arrested are convicted (Federal Bureau of Investigation, 1997; Greenfeld, 1997). Of those convicted, about 66 percent receive prison sentences; the average prison sentence is slightly less than ten years, but most offenders actually serve less than five years (Greenfeld, 1997). One cannot help but ask what factors give rise to such startling statistics.

Rape legally occurs when a person uses force or the threat of force to have some form of sexual intercourse (vaginal, oral, or anal) with another person. This rather straightforward definition might lead us to conclude that the prosecution of rape cases is fairly simple, especially given current medical technology and modern evidence collection techniques. However, although at first it may appear that rape can be thought of in dichotomous terms (that is, a specific encounter is or is not a rape), research indicates that what is defined as rape differs widely among various groups, including victims and perpetrators (Bourque, 1989; Williams, 1985). Unfortunately, the crime of rape is still prevalently viewed in our society in terms of a collection of myths about both rapists and rape victims. These include the notions that some women enjoy "being taken" by force; that women initially say "no" to men's sexual advances to appear "respectable" and must be "persuaded" to give in; that many women provoke men by teasing them and therefore these women get what they deserve; and that most rapes are committed by strangers who attack lone women on isolated streets or in dark alleys. As a group of college students stated during a recent discussion about rape, if a woman is raped while she's walking alone late at night, what does she expect? She should have been more sensible, more cautious (see also Madriz, 1997). Thus, rape victims face a predicament unlike that of victims of any other crime; it is they who must prove their innocence rather than the state proving the guilt of the rapist (Estrich, 1987). To understand this better, let's examine several rape myths more closely.

One common rape myth is that rape victims have often done something to invite or precipitate the assault. Therefore, if they report the crime, rape victims must demonstrate that they are "real" or "worthy" victims. To do so successfully and thus have the complaint acted on by the criminal justice system, victims must report the assault promptly; a delay in reporting increases the probability the complaint will be *unfounded;* that is, the police officially declare that they do not believe the crime occurred or they consider it unprosecutable. Victims must also show emotional as well as physical trauma; an absence of cuts, bruises, and other injuries can cast doubt on the victim's credibility (see, for example, "Quebec to Appeal Rape Case," 1997). And, most importantly, victims must convince authorities that they were in no way responsible for the crime (Bourque, 1989). This last condition is an especially difficult one to fulfill since even the slightest deviation from "respectable behavior" may be taken as evidence of the victim's culpability. Men, for example, are even less likely than women to report that they have been raped—after all, men are supposed to be able to defend themselves. If they are gay, reporting the assault may do more harm than good. Gays are rarely deemed "worthy" rape victims by virtue of their choice of a "deviant" lifestyle, and reporting could lead to harassment by the authorities and others.

Only about 6 percent of rape victims, however, are men (U.S. Department of Justice, 1997b). Women, who are the vast majority of rape victims, are also most likely then to be retraumatized by reporting the crime. Because of the victim precipitation myth, female rape victims often find that if they have violated any of the stereotyped standards of respectable femininity—if they had been drinking or using drugs, walked alone at night, went home with the assailant or invited the assailant into their own home, went to a bar unescorted, or dressed "seductively"—the probability increases that their complaint will not be prosecuted or, if it is, that their assailant will be acquitted (see, for example, "Nature of Clothing," 1990). The police unfound four times as many rape cases reported to them as they do other reported index crimes (Federal Bureau of Investigation, 1997).

The victim precipitation myth also appears to render some groups of women, such as prostitutes and drug addicts, "unrapeable" in a sense. Rape complaints brought by prostitutes and addicts are routinely dismissed by police. "In New Haven [CT], faced with a prostitute dressed for work, the police have said, 'What do you expect? Look at you.' In Houston, officers have shut their notebooks after a victim said that she was raped in a crack house. In the Atlanta suburbs, victims have been told they will be given a lie detector test and sent to jail if any part of their story is untrue" (Gross, 1990, p. A14).

Historically, the myths that women enjoy forced sex, that they really mean "yes" when they say "no," and that they often falsely accuse men of rape out of shame or revenge, led to strict rules of evidence in rape cases that essentially placed the burden of proof on the victim. For instance, the victim's testimony had to be supported by other witnesses, and the state had to establish that she had tried sufficiently to resist her assailant. Today, many of these requirements have been revised or abolished both in the United States and abroad. But despite legal reforms, both judges and juries still seem reluctant to believe rape victims and to convict and punish accused rapists (Bourque, 1989; Herman, 1988). Consider, for example, the instructions that one judge in New Zealand gave to a jury just prior to its deliberation of a verdict in a 1996 rape trial: "The world," he said, "would be much less exciting if every man through history had stopped the first time a woman said 'no' " ("New Zealand Judge," 1996). The jury in this case, seven women and five men, deliberated only forty-five minutes before acquitting the defendant. Unfortunately, this case cannot be written off as an isolated incident in a far off place. Closer to home, in Great Britain, a judge told a thirteen-year-old rape victim, who was drunk at the time of the attack, that she should wait until she's older to drink, but if she can't wait, she should dilute the alcohol with lemonade (Gibb, 1998). Even closer to home, in New York, a judge ordered a fifteen-year-old sexual assault victim to demonstrate in open court how the defendant had grabbed her breasts (Kocieniewski, 1995). In North Carolina, a state representative stated at a hearing that a "real" rape victim cannot get pregnant because during a "real" rape, the woman's "juices don't flow, the body functions don't work" ("Lawmaker's Rape View," 1995). And in Michigan, the state supreme court ruled that rape victims' private counseling records can be used as evidence in the trials of their alleged attackers if a judge feels that the records are essential to the defense (Boyle, 1994).

These cases highlight the fact that in the majority of rape cases the central issue is not whether the complainant and the accused engaged in sexual intercourse, but rather whether the complainant *consented* to the act. As most prosecutors know quite well, it is the victim's consent that is most difficult to disprove, particularly in cases in which she and the accused know one another. A case involving a victim who knows or is familiar with her assailant is known as **acquaintance rape.** According to the U.S. Department of Justice (1994), at least 55 percent of rapes are acquaintance rapes. The younger the victim, the more likely she is to know her assailant; acquaintance rapes account for 90 percent of reported cases involving victims under the age of twelve (Greenfeld, 1996). Yet the vast majority of acquaintance rapes go unreported; women and girls raped by strangers are ten times more likely to report the crime than women raped by acquaintances (U.S. House of Representatives, 1990).

Acquaintance rapes are especially common on college campuses. Despite Roiphe's (1993) claims that the term "date rape" is being widely misapplied to cases involving boyfriends verbally coercing their girlfriends or to intercourse that occurs because the woman is intoxicated and becomes "sexually confused," empirical research indicates that the incidence of acquaintance or date rape on college campuses is hardly trivial. In an extensive three-year survey of college students, for example, Koss and her colleagues (1987) found that one in eight female college students reported being victimized during the preceding twelve-month period; 84 percent of those who had been victims of completed rapes knew their assailants. Other researchers have obtained comparable findings (see Schwartz & DeKeseredy, 1997, for a thorough review of college date rape studies).

So prevalent is acquaintance rape that some researchers argue that even if women do not go out alone at night and even if they stay away from certain parts of town, they are not necessarily well protected from the danger of being sexually assaulted (Gordon & Riger, 1991; Stanko, 1996). More than 33 percent of rapes take place at or in the victim's home; 21.3 percent occur at, in, or near the home of one of the victim's friends, relatives, or neighbors (U.S. Department of Justice, 1997).

One form of sexual assault that almost always occurs in the victim's home is **marital rape,** the sexual assault of a woman by her husband. Historically, a husband could not be charged with raping his wife even if he used physical violence to force her to have sex with him, or even if they were legally separated. For the most part, this was because a wife was legally regarded as the property of her husband; certainly no man could be prosecuted for a personal decision to use his property as he saw fit. It was not until 1977 that the Oregon state legislature repealed the marital exemption to its rape statute. Two years later, James K. Chretien became the first person in the United States to be convicted of marital rape (Reid, 1987).

Research indicates that marital rape often accompanies other forms of family violence. According to one study of 644 married women, 12 percent reported having been raped by their husbands (Russell, 1990). Finkelhor and Yllö (1985) found in their study of 393 randomly selected women that half their sample reported more than twenty incidents of marital rape and 48 percent indicated that rape was part of the common physical abuse their husbands inflicted on them. The most commonly cited statistic is that rape occurs in 9 to 14 percent of all U.S. marriages (Bergen, 1996). It is important to emphasize that what we are discussing here is not a situation in which one spouse wishes to have sex and the other does not, but gives in out of love or to please. Marital rape is a brutal physical assault that may have a graver impact on a victim than stranger rape, given that the assailant is a person whom she knows and, at least at one time, loved and trusted (Bergen, 1996; Finkelhor & Yllö, 1985).

Although all states now have criminal statutes prohibiting forced sex between a husband and wife, thirty-three states exempt husbands from prosecution for rape under certain circumstances, largely because of lingering doubts about the ability to prove nonconsent in a marital relationship. In some states, for instance, a woman may charge her husband with rape only if he used a weapon to force her to have sex. In a few states, a woman may charge her husband with rape only if they are not living together. Other states require that the partners be legally separated or have filed for divorce. In three states, exemption from prosecution for rape extends to unmarried cohabiting partners as well as married couples (Bergen, 1996; Small & Tetreault, 1990). Many wives are extremely reluctant to file rape charges against their husbands, especially if rape is part of an ongoing pattern of domestic violence. These women are fearful of retaliation by their husbands (see Chapter 6). Many women are also ashamed and do not want to make the problem public (Bergen, 1996).

Over the last two decades, the treatment of rape victims by the criminal justice system has improved considerably. Most police officers, for example, now receive special training to sensitize them to the trauma of victims, although judges are much less likely than police to receive such training (Kocieniewski, 1995). There are also innumerable victim support and advocate services available throughout the country. These are positive developments that should be applauded, but at the same time, they continue to focus attention on rape as primarily a "woman's problem," not as a problem of men's violence against women. When rapists are discussed, they are usually depicted as psychologically disturbed individuals who need special medical treatment (Madriz, 1997). Interestingly, however, researchers have been unable to uncover evidence of widespread psychological disturbance in rapists. Rapists are more likely than any other type of offender to have been physically or sexually abused as a child, but apart from this finding, psychological tests do not consistently discriminate between rapists and nonrapists (Greenfeld, 1997; Scully & Marolla, 1985). In fact, as Herman (1988, pp. 702–703) points out, "The most striking characteristic of sex offenders, from a diagnostic standpoint, is their apparent normality. Most do not qualify for any psychiatric diagnosis." An emphasis on the psychopathology of rapists preserves the common image of the rapist as a "monster," a "crazed animal"; after all, nice guys don't rape. Such images divert attention from both the cultural context and the power relations in which rape occurs (Madriz, 1997; Stanko, 1996; in press).

So, if most rapists are not mentally ill, why do they rape? Herman (1988) has argued that the propensity to commit sex offenses should be viewed as an addiction similar to alcoholism. Perhaps she is correct, but her explanation begs the questions of how one becomes an addict and why some individuals become addicted to committing sexual assaults and others do not. We think that an answer to the question of why rapists rape lies within the culture and social structure of a society. Consider, for instance, anthropological studies of societies that may be characterized as virtually "rape-free" (Lepowsky, Reiss, 1986; Sanday, 1981; 1996a; Sutlive, 1991). The most striking feature of these societies is their relatively egalitarian gender relations. Neither sex is viewed as more important or as more highly valued than the other, and both are considered powerful, although in different spheres of activity. Moreover, women in these societies are not socially and economically dependent on men; they control resources and act as autonomous decision makers. Finally, in most rape-free societies, nurturance and nonaggression are valued traits in individuals, and women typically are highly regarded not for their sexuality, but for their wisdom and skills.

Compare these societies with our own—one of the most "rape-prone" industrialized societies in the world (U.S. House of Representatives, 1990). The contrasts are glaring. First of all, we live in an extraordinarily violent society. Not only is the rape rate exceptionally high, but the United States also has the highest homicide rate relative to other industrialized countries. Yet we know that violence is not condoned for everyone; it is expected of, even encouraged among men, not women. This is just one dimension of unequal gender relations in our society. Men control greater resources and, therefore, are more powerful than women. Not infrequently, they use violence to further expand their power. One of the few "bargaining chips" women have in our society is their sexuality, and male violence can deprive them of personal control over even that. As one convicted rapist told an interviewer:

> Rape is a man's right. If a woman doesn't want to give it, the man should take it. Women have no right to say no. Women are made to have sex. It's all they are good for. Some women would rather take a beating, but they always give in; it's what they are for (quoted in Scully & Marolla, 1985, p. 261).

This quote also reveals the "conquest mentality" toward sex that is part of American culture in general, but which is particularly prominent in male peer group subcultures (Schwartz & DeKeseredy, 1997). Sex is something men get or take from women. Sometimes force is necessary to get women to "put out." It appears, then, that in the United States there is a very fine line between "normal" masculine sexual behavior and rape. Indeed, the rapist quoted here, like most rapists, did not think he had done anything wrong. But his attitude is not so unusual; consider, for example, the fact that large-scale studies of high school and college students have found that many young men and women believe that under some circumstances it is all right for a man to force a woman to have sex (Koss et al., 1987; Schwartz & DeKeseredy, 1997). Such findings demonstrate the extent to which sexual violence against women is an acceptable part of our culture. Schwartz and DeKeseredy (1997) and others (Benedict, 1997; Sanday, 1990; 1996) have found that among all-male social networks, especially those such as fraternities where heavy drinking is normative, as well as men's athletic teams, certain women, particularly those who are intoxicated, are considered "legitimate sexual targets." Such attitudes and behaviors are given tacit approval on campus because of the low probability that the complaints of victims deemed unworthy will be taken seriously and that assailants will be harshly punished (Schwartz & DeKeseredy, 1997; see also Benedict, 1997; Bernstein, 1996; Lipsyte, 1998).

Finally, the words of the rapist we have quoted reflect the degree to which women are sexually objectified in our society. Unlike women in rape-free societies, women in the United States and many other countries are viewed as sex objects, and female sexuality itself is treated as a commodity. Clearly the most common form of objectified, commoditized female sexuality is pornography. Let's briefly discuss pornography and its relationship to violence against women.

Pornography

In 1969, the President's Commission on the Causes and Prevention of Violence concluded in its report that media portrayals of violence can induce individuals to behave violently. In 1971, the Presidential Commission on Obscenity and Pornography concluded in its report that there is no causal relationship between exposure to pornography and subsequent sexual violence against women. Pornography, it said, is basically harmless. In 1986, the Attorney General's Commission on Pornography (also known as the Meese Commission) brought the issue full circle by concluding that violent pornography is causally related to both sexual violence and discrimination against women.

The inconsistency that characterizes these official reports reflects the general confusion that historically has clouded debates about pornography and its effects. Before we take up this issue, let's first define what we mean by *pornography*, since there are conflicting definitions of what is pornographic. Certainly, few people would be willing to argue that any pictured nude or any description of a sexual act is pornographic, but where does one draw the line? As Supreme Court Justice Douglas once noted in an obscenity trial, "What may be trash to me may be prized by others" (quoted in MacKinnon, 1986, p. 69).

Still, we can discern important objective differences between pornography and what may be called *erotica*. Gloria Steinem (1978) makes this distinction by pointing out that:

> "Pornography" begins with a root [*porne*] meaning "prostitution" or "female captives," thus letting us know that the subject is not mutual love, or love at all, but domination and violence against women. (Though, of course, homosexual pornography may imitate this violence by putting a man in the "feminine" role of victim.) It ends with a root [*graphos*] meaning "writing about" or "description of" which puts still more distance

between subject and object, and replaces a spontaneous yearning for closeness with objectification and a voyeur. (p. 54)

In contrast, Steinem tells us, *erotica* is derived from the root *eros* meaning "sensual love" and implying the mutual choice and pleasure of the sexual partners. We can see, then, at least two distinct features of pornography. First, it depersonalizes sex and objectifies women. Second, and more importantly, pornography is not even about sex, per se, but rather the degradation of women and often children through sex. In fact, the sex depicted in pornography is secondary to the violence, humiliation, and dominance it portrays (see also Mayall & Russell, 1993). To be sure, not all pornography is violent, but the objective of all pornography is the objectification and control of women—male dominance of the female body for the purpose of sexually arousing the male consumer —and often violence is one of the ways pornography accomplishes this goal (Dines et al., 1998).

Researchers have not been able to conclusively establish a direct causal link between viewing pornography and violence against women. However, there is substantial evidence that pornography, especially violent pornography, is a factor that *contributes to* violence against women. At its most extreme, violent pornography takes the form of "snuff" and "slasher" films in which women are tortured, disfigured, murdered, or dismembered for sexual pleasure (Russell 1993). However, a common theme in all forms of violent pornography is rape. "[N]ot only is rape presented as part of normal male/female relations, but the woman, despite her terror, is always depicted as sexually aroused to the point of cooperation. In the end, she is ashamed but physically gratified" (Scully & Marolla, 1985, p. 253; see also Dines et al., 1998). In laboratory studies, researchers have found that exposure to violent pornography increases men's sexual arousal and rape fantasies, lessens their sensitivity to rape and rape victims, increases their acceptance of rape myths, and most importantly, increases their self-reported possibility of raping (Allen et al., 1995; Donnerstein, 1983; Weaver, 1992). Experimental research, though, has been criticized for a number of reasons, not the least of which is that it is "unnatural" or "artificial" (Brannigan & Goldenberg, 1987; Donnerstein et al., 1987). However, research that relies on women's and men's accounts of the use of pornography and "real life" sexual violence shows a strong relationship between the two. Women who have been sexually abused frequently report that their abusers directed them to act out scenes the men had seen or read about in pornography, sometimes mentioning specific films (see Dines et al., 1998, for a detailed summary of this research). Research with men, including sex offenders, shows that pornography helps shape a male-dominant view of sexuality, contributes to a user's difficulty in distinguishing between fantasy and reality, and is often used to initiate victims and break down their resistance to particular types of sexual activity. As Jensen (in Dines et al., 1998, p. 119) describes it, pornography provides "a training manual for abusers" (see also Jensen, 1995; Norris & Kerr, 1991; Scully & Marolla, 1985).

Despite these findings, it is often argued that regulating or outlawing pornography infringes on the First Amendment right of free speech, and some observers fear that such regulations could be used to legitimate government censorship of any sexually explicit material including information on contraception, "safe sex," and so on. Recent government efforts to censor art exhibitions, such as the Robert Mapplethorpe photography exhibit, are frequently cited as examples. The First Amendment argument has prevailed in law; antipornography laws that were passed in Indianapolis, Minneapolis, Los Angeles, Cambridge (Massachusetts), and Bellingham (Washington) have been overturned by the courts on the ground that they violated First Amendment free speech guarantees. But to those who worry about encroachment on the First Amendment, antipornography activists ask if they would maintain the same position if the material in question was violently racist or anti-Semitic. As Russell (1993) argues:

> Indeed, there would be a public outcry—and rightly so—if there were special non-pornographic movie houses where viewers could see whites beating up people of color, or Christians beating up Jews, and where the victims were portrayed as enjoying or deserving such treatment. But if it's called pornography and women are the victims, then it is considered sex and those who object that it is harmful to women are regarded as prudes. (p. 11)

It is unlikely that the debate over pornography will be resolved soon. Feminists themselves are divided over the questions of whether pornography is harmful and should be outlawed (see Berger et al., 1991; Dines et al., 1998). There are those, for example, who maintain that pornography, even in portraying sadomasochism, is potentially liberating for women in that through it, women may become less puritanical and sexually passive and more open or aggressive about their sexual desires. This argument has not been lost on the porn industry, which has attempted to market more products, primarily videotapes, to women. The biggest market in pornography—about $1 billion a year—is in videotapes that can be rented or purchased in neighborhood general interest (as opposed to "adult") video stores. About 15 percent of pornographic videos are rented by women (Russell, 1993). Research indicates, however, that while women may go to the video store to rent the movie, the idea to watch it most often originated with their male partners. Women usually describe such films as boring, unimaginative, offensive, and exploitative of women (Rubin, 1991). Indeed, studies show that women do not react to pornography the same way men do and are more often upset and negatively affected by it (Senn, 1993).

The pornography industry is not grossing billions of dollars a year only from videotapes. In recent years, the industry has branched out into new areas. Phone pornography, or "phone sex" as it is sometimes called, is one new form (Russell, 1993), and as Box 8.3 on page 268 shows, the Internet is fast becoming a profitable international marketplace for pornography.

Institutionalized Violence against Women: Custom or Crime?

The historical accounts left by colonists and missionaries along with the ethnographies of anthropologists testify to the extent to which violence against women has been an institutionalized component of the cultures of many societies throughout the world (see also Box 8.4 on pages 269–270).

BOX **8.3**

Pornography on the Internet

The Internet is a revolutionary communications tool. Using the Internet, you can send a message that can reach literally millions of people throughout the world in a matter of seconds. Through the Usenet, which is distributed via the Internet, you can participate in an international electronic conferencing system, posting messages to and receiving messages from other people who have logged on to any one of the more than 17,000 Usenet groups currently available, each group specializing in a particular topic. On the World Wide Web, with its sophisticated multimedia technology, you can go shopping for specific items, send and receive photographs or even video and audio clips, and move from one computer site to another just by clicking the mouse on a "hot link." And you can do all these things in the privacy of your own home, conveniently, anonymously, and relatively inexpensively.

In light of these features and the more important fact that the Internet is largely unregulated, it is not surprising that the Internet is fast becoming an international marketplace for the sale and consumption of pornography. With the help of a search engine, an Internet user can find pornography to suit just about any taste, from bestiality to sadomasochism to pedophilia. What is more, the Internet user can meet and chat with others who share these interests, a fact that some observers find troubling. The Internet allows people with socially unacceptable interests, such as pedophiles, to find acceptability, which in turn

validates and reinforces their feelings and behavior. In fact, the Internet is becoming the most prevalent means for people with such interests to share pornography and even recruit partners, including children, for sexual activity (Fox, 1998).

A number of software makers and commercial online service providers are now offering filters to screen or block offensive transmissions and access to pornographic sites on the Internet, products that parents, in particular, are welcoming. But attempts to legislate broader restrictions have met with strong opposition and claims of First Amendment infringement. No one owns the Internet, and currently, no one controls the communications that come across it. Although law enforcement agencies have begun to initiate "cyberstings" to catch pedophiles transmitting child pornography and arranging in-person meetings with children, even this area of law is still largely undefined. Defense attorneys and civil libertarians charge that such policing techniques constitute entrapment, which is an illegal form of law enforcement, while prosecutors, the F.B.I., and Congress see it as an effective way to catch sexual predators and prevent crimes against children. We will no doubt see numerous cases challenging cyberstings and other Internet regulations as "cyberlaw" evolves in the early twenty-first century. In the meantime, there is also little doubt that the production and consumption of pornography via the Internet will continue to flourish.

From the tenth to the twentieth centuries, for example, the Chinese engaged in the practice of binding the feet of young girls. This was accomplished by bending all of the toes on each foot (except the big toes) under and into the sole, then wrapping the toes and the heel as tightly together as possible with a piece of cloth. Every two weeks or so the wrapped feet were squeezed into progressively smaller shoes until they were shrunk to the desirable size of just three inches. Typically, the feet would bleed and become infected, circulation was cut off, and eventually one or more toes might fall off. Needless to say, the process was extremely painful and countless women were crippled by it. Yet, they endured and perpetuated the custom—usually from mother to

BOX **8.4**

Violence against Women as Human Rights Violations

Historically, the physical and psychological abuse of women, though widespread in many societies throughout the world, has not been considered a human rights problem. According to Chapman (1990), there has been a high level of official and social tolerance of violence against women, with most governments and official agencies viewing the problem as an individual matter or simply as a consequence of being female. For example, when nineteen teenage girls were killed and seventy-one others were raped by male classmates during a protest over fees at a boarding school in Kenya in 1991, school officials told reporters that rapes of female students by males were not unusual at their school or others. The deaths were accidental, they claimed; as the deputy principal of the school explained, "The boys never meant any harm against the girls. They just wanted to rape" (quoted in Perlez, 1991, p. A7). However, officials have not only excused or ignored such violence, they also have participated in it. The rape and sexual abuse of female political prisoners while in official custody has been documented by human rights advocates (Amnesty International, 1991; Chapman, 1990; Sontag, 1993).

Violence against women as a human rights issue began to command greater public attention when, in 1993, media in the United States and Europe began to report on the systematic rape, sexual enslavement, torture, and murder of Bosnian Muslim women and children by Serbian military forces in the former Yugoslavia. According to a report by a team of European Community investigators, it is estimated that 20,000 Muslim women were raped by Serb soldiers since the campaign against Muslim communities in the former Yugoslavia was initiated (Riding, 1993). Rape, the investigators concluded, was being used as a weapon of war. It has served as a central element in the Serbian "ethnic cleansing" campaign; Bosnian men are murdered, while the women are raped with the goal of impregnating them to produce offspring with the "desirable" genetic material. At the same time, the rapes also are intended to de-moralize and terrorize the Muslim communities and to drive Muslims from their home regions. According to the European Community investigative team, rapes were often carried out in especially sadistic ways with the intent of inflicting the greatest humiliation on the victims. The investigators collected evidence that indicated that many Muslim women and children died during or after their rapes (Nikolic-Ristanovic, 1999; Riding, 1993).

Reports such as these rightfully have produced widespread calls in the United States and abroad for international sanctions against the Serbian military and for efforts to bring the perpetrators to trial as war criminals. It is important to note, however, that systematic violence against women is not unique to the former Yugoslavia, nor is it a new strategy. Two decades ago, Susan Brownmiller (1975) showed that throughout history, sexual abuse of "enemy" women has been a common state-supported warfare tactic. This abuse has most frequently involved rape, but it also has taken other forms, such as sexual enslavement. In 1993, for instance, the Japanese government issued a report in which it admitted that during World War II, it was involved in coercing women into prostitution to sexually service Imperial Army soldiers. Though in reality the women were sex slaves, they were euphemistically called "comfort women." It is estimated that from 100,000 to 300,000 women were enslaved. Most were from South Korea, but some were from Indonesia, China, Taiwan, the Philippines, and the Netherlands (McGregor & Lawnham, 1993).

More recently, attorneys assisting refugees seeking political asylum in the United States and Canada have documented extensive state-supported violence against women, including gang rape by police and military personnel, in numerous countries, including Haiti, Honduras, El Salvador, and Iran (Sontag, 1993). As a result, the United Nations High Commission on Refugees has issued special guidelines for government agencies to follow when evaluating women's applications for asylum. Canada has already adopted

(continued)

BOX **8.4**   **Continued**

a policy that allows women to be granted asylum if they can show persecution on the basis of their sex, but the United States has not yet followed suit (Sontag, 1993).* The United Nations has also issued a Convention on the Elimination of All Forms of Discrimination Against Women which, although it doesn't include a specific provision on violence, does include a number of provisions that in their effect impose sanctions for violence against women. Significantly, 101 countries as of 1990 had ratified this convention, but the United States was not one of them (Chapman, 1990). In 1994, however, the United States, for the first time, specifically addressed violence against women as human rights abuses in its annual human rights report, an indication perhaps that this problem is finally receiving some recognition in official government circles in the United States (U.S. Department of State, 1994).

*In 1994, however, a gay man was granted asylum in the United States on the ground that he was harassed and raped by police in his native country, Mexico, because he is homosexual. This case marked the first time that the U.S. Immigration and Naturalization Service has granted an individual asylum because of persecution stemming from the individual's sexual orientation.

---

daughter—for 1,000 years in the belief that it made them beautiful, and beauty ensured a good and lasting marriage (Dworkin, 1983). In a society in which all roles other than wife and mother, or prostitute, are closed to women, we may expect them to pursue whatever means are necessary for personal and economic security (Blake, 1994).

It was the case that men did not look favorably on natural-footed women. For one thing, they felt that tiny feet were feminine, so that binding helped differentiate women from men. In addition, the immobile woman was a status symbol, "a testimony to the wealth and privilege of the man who could afford to keep her" (Dworkin, 1983, p. 181). Aspirations to higher status, however, prompted the lower classes to copy the tradition which originated with the nobility. And finally, but perhaps most importantly, footbinding ensured chastity, fidelity, and the legitimacy of children in a society in which women literally could not "run around." It was believed that women were naturally lustful and lascivious; footbinding kept them morally in check (Dworkin, 1983).

A similar rationale was offered for *suttee* or widow burning, a custom practiced in India for approximately 400 years until it was officially outlawed in 1829. Suttee was a sacrificial ritual in which a widow climbed the funeral pyre of her deceased husband and set herself or was set on fire. Although the practice was supposed to be voluntary, records indicate that extreme measures were taken to prevent escape in case the widow changed her mind, such as "scaffolds constructed to tilt toward the fire pit, piles designed so that exits were blocked and the roof collapsed on the woman's head, tying her, weighting her down with firewood and bamboo poles. If all else failed and the woman escaped from the burning pile, she was often dragged back by force, sometimes by her own son" (Stein, 1978, p. 255). Since polygamy was also practiced and marriages between child-brides and men of fifty or older were not uncommon, some wives, still in their teens, were burnt alive with dead husbands they had rarely seen since their wedding day (Daly, 1983; Stein, 1978).

It appears that most women did not have to be coerced into suttee, especially in light of their alternatives. "Since their religion forbade remarriage [of widows] and at the same time taught that the husband's death was the fault of the widow (because of her sins in a previous incarnation if not in this one), everyone was free to despise and mistreat her for the rest of her life" (Daly, 1983, p. 190). Religious law required that unburnt widows live a life of extreme poverty, shaving their heads, wearing drab clothes, eating just one bland meal a day, performing the most menial tasks, never sleeping on a bed, and never leaving their houses except to go to the temple. Obviously, death might have seemed more appealing to many. Certainly, relatives and in-laws preferred it. Since it was widely believed that women were by nature lascivious, the widow was viewed as a possible source of embarrassment to her family and in-laws who feared she would become sexually involved with other men and perhaps even get pregnant. (The practices of a deceased husband's male relatives forcing his young widow to have sex with them were historically so common that the Hindi word for widow became synonymous with prostitute.) But suttee also had an economic motive: It ensured that the widow would make no claim to her husband's estate and his family would not have to support her. Thus, the Indian widow had to decide between a miserable life of poverty and harassment or an honorable but excruciatingly painful death that elevated her status in the community. For most, such a choice was no choice at all.

Although, as we have noted, suttee was outlawed in the early 1800s, there is evidence that the cultural view of widows has not changed much in some regions of India. Widows are still expected to abide by the old religious customs, living alone and in abject poverty, often homeless. In some areas, widows live at Hindu temples where they adopt the surname *Dasi*, which means *servant*, to demonstrate their religious devotion. Many spend eight hours a day—four hours in the morning and four in the evening—reciting religious chants to earn the equivalent of five cents along with a ration of rice or lentils. Some of these women were widowed when they were just fourteen years old and sought refuge in the temples to avoid a life of servitude to their in-laws (Burns, 1998).

Not surprisingly, there continue to be reports of Indian widows setting themselves on fire, either voluntarily or under pressure from in-laws or other relatives. According to Burns (1998), murders of widows are more common. A related problem in contemporary India is *dowry harassment* and murder, also known as bride-burning. Despite the Dowry Prohibition Act, made law in 1961, the practice of a bride's parents providing dowry for their daughters remains widespread. Daughters are considered an economic burden in India, so parents often try to marry them off at a young age and the promise of a dowry is seen as an incentive. However, expectations of the value of dowries have become inflated in recent years, and the groom's family, with whom the bride customarily lives, is sometimes so dissatisfied that they harass the new wife. The harassment may be only verbal, but frequently it is also physical. The abuse may drive the bride to suicide, but more commonly her husband or his family murder her, typically by dousing her with kerosene and setting her on fire. Accurate statistics on the number of dowry murders and attempted murders in India are difficult to come by, since these cases may be mislabeled "cooking accidents," but conservative estimates put the figure at 2,000 deaths per year (Bumiller, 1990; Chapman, 1990; Stone & James, 1995).

Another custom that has generated considerable controversy in recent years is *female circumcision*, which some observers prefer to call *female genital mutilation* (FGM) because the objective of the practice is to remove all or part of a woman's genitals. Female genital mutilation actually takes several forms, the mildest being *Sunna*, in which the hood of the clitoris is cut analogous to the practice of male circumcision, but this form is not commonly practiced. More widespread is infibulation, the most extreme form of FGM, which involves the removal of the clitoris, labia minora, and most of the labia majora, after which the vagina is stitched closed save for a tiny opening to allow for the passage of urine and menstrual blood. The most common form, however, is excision, whereby the clitoris as well as all or part of the labia minora are removed (Lightfoot-Klein, 1989). Currently, FGM is practiced in about forty countries, primarily in East and West Africa, and in many of these societies, it is not uncommon for as many as 90 to 98 percent of the female population to have had their genitals cut (Crossette, 1995; Ebomoyi, 1987; Renzetti & Curran, 1986).

In the Western world, publicity regarding female circumcision has triggered angry protests by feminists who have denounced the tradition as oppressive and barbaric, and who have insisted that governments immediately outlaw the practice (Walker & Parmar, 1993). Few African governments have passed laws prohibiting the practice, but the United States as well as France and Great Britain have outlawed it in response to the importation of the practice into their countries by African immigrants (Dugger, 1996). In Canada, the threat of FGM in one's home country is grounds for granting those fleeing the practice refugee status. In the United States, the courts have been less sympathetic, although some have granted asylum to women seeking to escape the practice (Crossette, 1995).

Given the way the operation is usually done and the serious medical problems that frequently result, the shock and indignation of Westerners is understandable. More specifically, the circumcision, excision, or infibulation is performed on young girls—sometimes as infants, but usually between the ages of six and fourteen—by an elder village woman or traditional birth attendant using various nonsurgical instruments such as a razor, a knife, or a piece of broken glass. Typically, no anesthetics are available. Once the operation is completed, dirt, ashes, herbs, or animal droppings may be applied to the wound in the belief that they will stop the bleeding and aid in healing. Not surprisingly, complications are common and include shock, hemorrhage, septicemia, and tetanus, which can result in the girl's death. At the very least, those who have undergone the procedure are unlikely to ever experience sexual pleasure; in fact, FGM typically makes sexual intercourse quite painful and increases the likelihood of maternal and infant mortality (Ebomoyi, 1987; Lightfoot-Klein, 1989; Rayner, 1997).

A small, but growing group of African women has been working to eliminate the practice in their own countries (MacFarquhar, 1996; Walker & Parmar, 1993). However, they are encountering considerable resistance from both women and men, who strongly object to having Western values imposed on them (Dugger, 1996b; French, 1997; Graham, 1986; MacFarquhar, 1996). The primary purpose of female genital mutilation is to protect a girl from sexual temptations and thereby preserve her marriageability. Among most practicing societies, there exist firmly entrenched beliefs about the insatiable nature of female sexual desire. The uncut are considered "dirty" and unmarriageable, making them unfit to fulfill what are considered in their societies to be women's two most valued roles, wife and mother (MacFarquhar, 1996; Renzetti & Curran, 1986). Many parents say that if they fail to have their daughters cut, no respectable men will associate with the girls, who will end up "running wild like American women" (Crossette, 1995; Dugger, 1996c; MacFarquhar, 1996). As one Ghanian activist explained, "To put it cynically, not to go through mutilation is to commit economic suicide" (quoted in Graham, 1986, p. 18). No wonder, then, that the majority of parents in practicing societies state that they will carry on the tradition with their daughters, and to circumvent the law banning FGM in the United States, many immigrants make tremendous sacrifices to save enough money to send their daughters back to their home country to have the operation performed (Dugger, 1996c).

In sum, female genital mutilation, like foot-binding and suttee, is a practice of institutionalized violence against women that many observers, particularly those in the West, have labeled criminal. Yet efforts to outlaw it rarely have been successful, and women themselves perpetuate this tradition. To most Westerners this appears irrational, but what we must consider is women's status in practicing societies. Female genital mutilation is one of the few means by which these women exercise power and achieve recognition. It is hardly surprising that women would cling to one of their only avenues of power and status, regardless of how damaging it may be. It may be argued, in fact, that their behavior is no less rational than that of Western women who very frequently seek harmful treatments or follow unhealthy diets for the sake of "beauty" (see Chapter 11).

If our goal, then, is the elimination of violence against women, laws banning particular practices are unlikely to be effective without simultaneous policies and programs to implement and ensure gender equality. In the final analysis, violence against women, whatever its form, is a direct outgrowth of the devaluation of women.

Power, Crime, and Justice

We have seen here that in societies that have accepted or condoned violence against women, whatever its form—rape, pornography, footbinding, suttee, or genital mutilation—women are viewed as innately inferior to men and are deprived of valued resources. Indeed, women may even participate in their own victimization as a means to exercise some power in their lives and to acquire a higher status.

Powerlessness, we have also suggested, may help to explain crime rates and the differential treatment of offenders by the criminal justice system. It is the relatively powerless—young, economically marginalized women and men of color—who are disproportionately represented in the official crime statistics and who receive the harshest treatment within the criminal justice system. They, too, are most likely to be victimized by crime.

We have emphasized in this chapter that the content of laws and the way they are enforced have a lot to do with the values and interests of the powerful. The vast majority of lawmakers and law enforcement personnel are White men. In the next chapter, we will explore this issue further by examining politics, government, and the military.

KEY TERMS

acquaintance rape   an incident of sexual assault in which the victim knows or is familiar with the assailant

chivalry hypothesis (paternalism hypothesis) the belief that female offenders are afforded greater leniency before the law than their male counterparts

emancipation theory (liberation theory)   the theory that female crime is increasing and/or becoming more masculine in character as a result of feminism or the women's movement

marital rape   the sexual assault of a woman by her husband

rape   when a person uses force or the threat of force to have some form of sexual intercourse (vaginal, oral, or anal) with another person

sentencing disparity   widely varying sentences imposed on offenders convicted of similar crimes, usually based on nonlegal factors, such as the offender's sex or race or ethnicity, or other inappropriate considerations

status offenses   behavior considered illegal if engaged in by a juvenile, but legal if engaged in by an adult

SUGGESTED READINGS

Bergen, R. K. (1996). *Wife rape: Understanding the response of survivors and service providers.* Thousand Oaks, CA: Sage.

Chesney-Lind, M. (1997). *The female offender: Girls, women, and crime.* Thousand Oaks, CA: Sage.

Dines, G., Jensen, R., & Russo, A. (1998). *Pornography: The production and consumption of inequality.* New York: Routledge.

Martin, S. E., & Jurik, N. C. (1996). *Doing justice, doing gender.* Thousand Oaks, CA: Sage.

Miller, S. L. (Ed.) (1998). *Crime control and women.* Thousand Oaks, CA: Sage.

Schwartz, M. D., & DeKeseredy, W. S. (1997). *Sexual assault on the college campus.* Thousand Oaks, CA: Sage.

NOTES

1. Women are also not well represented in blue-collar occupations such as truck driver, warehouse or dock worker, or delivery person, jobs that would provide them with opportunities for grand larceny, drug dealing, or the fencing of stolen merchandise (Steffensmeier, 1982).

2. The chivalry hypothesis has also been offered as an explanation for the rise in female arrest rates. Specifically, proponents of this position contend that historically police, attorneys, and judges have been reluctant to process women through the criminal justice system. Those women who were prosecuted were supposedly treated leniently or "chivalrously." However, the recent emphasis on gender equality in society could not help but penetrate the criminal justice system, with the result that male and female offenders are now more likely to be treated similarly. Thus, the rise in female arrest rates is simply an artifact of the increased willingness among criminal justice personnel to apprehend and prosecute women.

3. Despite recent reports that lesbians and gay men are finding greater acceptance in some police precincts in a few large cities (see, for example, Blumenthal, 1993; Egan, 1992), homophobia remains a predominant characteristic of most police departments (Leinen, 1993; Martin & Jurik, 1996). In addition, although there is evidence of less racism among White male officers toward minority male officers, minority female officers report experiences of both racism and sexism. As Martin (1989) points out, the impact of these experiences is more complex than what is conveyed by the term "double jeopardy," since these women confront racism on the part of White male and female officers and sexism on the part of White and non-White male officers (see also Martin & Jurik, 1996).

4. The F.B.I. only began to hire women as agents in 1972. Of the 11,548 agents in 1998, 16.2 percent were women (Federal Bureau of Investigation, 1998).

5. According to Zupan (1992), the 1977 U.S. Supreme Court ruling in *Dothard v. Rawlinson* jeopardized women's employment progress in male correctional facilities. In the *Dothard* case, the Court ruled (without supporting proof) that for security reasons women could be barred from jobs that required contact with inmates in maximum-security prisons. Nevertheless, most states continued the trend from earlier in the 1970s of increasing the employment of women at their male correctional facilities, although the *Dothard* ruling has often been used to justify restricting female correctional officers to clerical and nonsupervisory positions (Martin & Jurik, 1996; Zupan, 1992).

6. However, Martin and Jurik (1996) note that Black inmates sometimes show especially strong resentment toward Black women correctional officers because they see them as damaging racial unity and contributing to the emasculation of Black men.

7. Research has revealed what has come to be called the *jury trial penalty*. This refers to the fact that defendants who insist on a jury trial, if found guilty, are sentenced more harshly than defendants who plead guilty and thus avert a jury trial (see, for example, Spohn, 1990).

8. The female prostitute, of course, represents in many ways the antithesis of respectable femininity. She is independent and promiscuous, so, not surprisingly, she is the victim of routine harassment within the criminal justice system. But her customers, although guilty of breaking the law, are rarely prosecuted. Unfortunately, there is very little data available on male prostitution, to a large extent because researchers have focused on prostitution as exclusively a female crime (for exceptions, see Luckenbill, 1986; McNamara, 1994). However, given that male prostitutes violate our culture's gender prescriptions for men, they, too, may be treated more harshly than the average male offender.

9. One example of this "equality with a vengeance" can be found in Maricopa County, Arizona, where the sheriff, Joseph Arpaio, instituted female chain gangs in 1996, one year after he reinstated male chain gangs. The women, shackled at the ankles and wearing striped prison uniforms, pick up litter and paint over graffiti five days a week (Kim, 1996). Female chain gangs were also proposed in Alabama, but the governor vetoed the plan ("Chain Gangs for Women," 1996).

10. The U.S. Department of Justice also reports that women make up a growing percentage of adults on probation and parole. Between 1990 and 1996, for example, the proportion of probationers who were women increased from 18 percent to 21 percent, and the proportion of female parolees increased from 8 percent to 11 percent (Brown & Beck, 1997).

11. It interesting to note that male inmates have successfully brought suits to restrict access of female correctional officers to certain areas (e.g., showers) on the ground that the guards' presence infringed on their privacy rights (see, for instance, *Fort v. Ward*, 1979).

12. The statistical probability of contracting HIV/AIDS as a result of rape is unknown at this time. According to the Center for Women Policy Studies (1991a, p. 6), "in cases of sexual violence, research seems to assume that a rape survivor may already be infected with HIV, thus emphasizing the survivor's sexual history and deemphasizing the crime of rape." There is currently a debate over mandatory HIV testing of convicted rapists, with test results being provided to both rapists and their victims. In 1997, the Supreme Court of New Jersey ruled that a rape victim can demand that the rapist be tested for HIV/AIDS and the results be given to the victim. For a thorough discussion of the merits and disadvantages of HIV/AIDS testing of rapists, see Center for Women Policy Studies, 1991.

Gender, Politics, Government, and the Military

In the spring of 1776, Abigail Adams wrote to her husband John, "I long to hear that you have declared an independency—and by the way in the new Code of Laws which I suppose it will be necessary for you to make I desire you would Remember the Ladies, and be more generous and favourable to them than your ancestors." But his response revealed that the designers of the new republic had no intention of putting the sexes on an equal political footing. "As to your extraordinary Code of Laws," John Adams wrote back to his wife, "I cannot but laugh. . . . Depend upon it, We know better than to repeal our Masculine systems" (quoted in Rossi, 1973, pp. 10–11).

That Adams's sentiments were shared by his fellow revolutionaries is clear from their declaration that all men are created equal, although, at the same time, they considered some men (White property holders) more equal than others (Blacks, Native Americans, the propertyless). Of course, it has been argued that the Founding Fathers used the masculine noun in the generic sense, but the fact is that when the Constitution was ratified, women lost rights instead of gaining them. For instance, prior to ratification, women were permitted to vote in some areas, including Massachusetts and New Jersey, a right that was lost in the former state in 1780 and in the latter in 1807 (Simon & Danziger, 1991). As we saw in Chapter 1, ratification of the Constitution did not enfranchise women in the states; female citizens did not win the constitutional right to vote until 1920.

In this chapter, we will focus on some of the similarities and differences in women's and men's political roles and behavior historically and in contemporary society, primarily in the United States, but also elsewhere. As sociologists have repeatedly pointed out, when we speak about *politics*, we are essentially speaking about power—the power to distribute scarce resources, to institutionalize particular values, and to legitimately use force or violence. To the extent that men and women have different degrees of political power, they will have unequal input into political decision making and, consequently, their interests and experiences may be unequally represented in law and public policy. What is the political power differential between the sexes today? We will address that question on one level by assessing men's and women's relative success in winning public office and securing political appointments. In addition, we will examine the roles of men and women in defense and national security by discussing the issue of gender and military service. To begin our discussion, however, we will first take a look at differences in men's and women's political attitudes and participation, or what has become known in government circles as the *gender gap*.

The Gender Gap: Political Attitudes and Activities

There are few certainties for political candidates on election day, but from 1920, when women were granted full voting rights, until around 1980, there were two things they could count on: Fewer women than men would vote, and those women that did vote would vote similarly to men. Between 1920 and 1960, men's rate of voting exceeded women's rate by a considerable margin, although there was a gradual increase in women's voting rates over the four decades. During the 1960s, there was a sharp increase in women's voting rates and, by 1978, the margin of difference between women's and men's voting rates was just about 2 percent. Lake and Breglio (1992) attribute this change to the rise in women's level of educational attainment during this period as well as the rapid increase in the number of women working outside the home. Nevertheless, although more women were going to the polls during the 1960s and 1970s, their voting behavior continued to parallel that of men.[1]

In the 1980 presidential election, however, two significant changes occurred: More women than men cast ballots, and women voted significantly differently than men. Although 51 percent of the votes cast went to Ronald Reagan, we see in Table 9.1 that he got just 47 percent of women's votes compared with 55 percent of men's votes. This 8 percentage-point gap between women's and men's votes was the largest gap recorded since 1952 when such statistics began to be collected. (John Anderson, the third candidate in the 1980 presidential election received equal support from women and men, garnering just 7 percent of their votes.)

Political analysts were uncertain as to whether such differences were merely a fluke or represented a genuine shift in women's and men's voting patterns. Subsequent elections confirmed the existence of what has come to be known as the **gender gap**: differences in voting patterns and political attitudes of women and men. Looking again at Table 9.1, we see that in the 1984 presidential election, there also was a gender gap in voting, but it was smaller than in 1980—6 percentage points. In 1988, following the spring primaries, there was an unprecedented gender gap of 20 percent, with significantly more women than men favoring Michael Dukakis over George Bush. By November, however, Bush had successfully narrowed the gap to just 7 percent. In the 1992 presidential election, the gender gap remained and appeared not only in differences between men's and

TABLE 9.1   The Gender Gap in Presidential Elections, 1952–1996

Election Year	Candidate Elected	Percent Women Who Supported This Candidate	Percent Men Who Supported This Candidate
1952	Eisenhower	58	53
1956	Eisenhower	61	55
1960	Kennedy	49	52
1964	Johnson	62	60
1968	Nixon	43	43
1972	Nixon	62	63
1976	Carter	50	50
1980	Reagan	47	55
1984	Reagan	56	62
1988	Bush	50	57
1992	Clinton	46	41
1996	Clinton	54	43

Sources: "Portrait of the Electorate," 1992; 1996; CAWP, 1987.

women's support for Bill Clinton, but also their support for the third candidate, Ross Perot. While women and men supported Bush in relatively equal proportions (37 percent and 38 percent respectively), Clinton received 5 percent more of his votes from women, and Perot received 4 percent more of his votes from men. Finally, in the 1996 election, the gender gap was wider than it has ever been: 11 percentage points (54 percent of women voted for Clinton, while only 43 percent of men did).

In considering the gender gap, particularly in the 1980, 1984, and 1988 presidential elections, you may be wondering why the Republican candidates won, if more women than men were voting and more women than men supported the Democratic candidate. Lake and Breglio (1992) explain:

> The gender gap represents an important change in our political system, but has a direct impact on the outcome of an election only when the differences between men's and women's perceptions, priorities, and agendas are so pervasive and significant that they translate into a margin of support for a particular candidate among voters of one sex that more than offsets the margin of support the opposing candidate enjoys among voters of the other sex. (p. 199)

While this has occurred in several U.S. congressional elections since 1980, as well as a number of state senate and gubernatorial elections during the same period, it did not occur in a presidential election until 1996.

It is also the case that the gender gap is far more complex than it at first appears to be. The gender gap involves more than voting behavior; there are particular perspectives on political issues that underlie individuals' votes. Research consistently shows that at the heart of the gender gap are issues of economics, social welfare, foreign policy, and to a lesser extent environmental protection and public safety. Women, for example, feel—and rightfully so—more economically vulnerable than men (see Chapters 6 and 7). Women more than men express concern about health care (especially long-term care), child care, education, poverty, and homelessness. In contrast, men more than women express concern about the federal deficit, taxes, energy, defense, and foreign policy. Throughout the 1980s and 1990s, women have expressed greater pessimism about the economic condition of the country and have showed greater favor toward increased government activity in the form of programs to help families, even if such programs require increased taxes (Goldberg, 1996; Lake & Breglio 1992; Sciolino, 1996; see also Gidengil, 1995). It has been argued, in fact, that it was George Bush's emphasis on "family issues," education, improvements in child support collection, and economic empowerment for women—in short, his promise of a "kinder and gentler nation"—that helped him close what some called the "gender canyon" between himself and Dukakis during the 1988 campaign (Mueller, 1991). In 1996, many women who had voted for Bush in 1992 switched their support to Clinton because he displayed a sense of caring that was lacking in candidate Dole (Goldberg, 1996).

A strong and consistent gender gap also emerges with respect to issues of war and peace. This difference in the political opinions of women and men can be traced as far back as World War I. Women more than men considered the entry of the United States into both world wars to be mistakes and also voiced greater opposition to the

Korean and Vietnam Wars (Abzug, 1984; Baxter & Lansing, 1983). Similarly, in the wake of the 1983 terrorist attack in Beirut that killed more than 200 U.S. Marines, considerably more women (62 percent) than men (34 percent) favored the withdrawal of U.S. troops from Lebanon (Abzug, 1984). Following the U.S. invasion of Grenada, Ronald Reagan's popularity increased significantly, but only among men, 68 percent of whom approved of the military action compared with only 45 percent of women (Raines, 1983). In the last war in which the United States was directly involved, the war in the Persian Gulf, more women than men favored a negotiated settlement over military action, and fewer women than men felt that the loss of life—both military and civilian—was worth the victory (Dowd, 1990; Lake & Breglio, 1992).

However, while women favor peaceful solutions over military ones to international conflicts and prefer domestic social spending over military spending, they express greater distrust of other nations than men do and worry about how international relations might pose risks for the future security of the country. This concern is especially strong among women with children (Goldberg, 1996), and the concern carries over into issues of public safety, with women more than men expressing concern about crime and drugs (Lake & Breglio, 1992; Mueller, 1991; see also Chapter 8). Although support for the death penalty is high among both women and men—71 percent and 79 percent respectively in favor of the death penalty for persons convicted of murder—there is nevertheless a fairly large gender gap on this issue. Women are also more likely than men to favor gun control laws (Goldberg, 1996; U.S. Department of Justice, 1996).

Despite sex differences in these areas, on other topics, men's and women's political opinions are more likely to converge. For example, women and men share similar views on protecting the environment. Although more women than men express negative opinions about the use of nuclear energy and the safety of nuclear power plants, differences in their views on these topics have narrowed in recent years. Interestingly, women's and men's opinions on women's rights issues are more similar than one might predict, although there are important areas of difference. One such area is abortion and reproductive freedom; while a majority of both women and men support a woman's right to an abortion under at least some circumstances (see Chapter 6), more women than men report that the position of a political candidate on this issue would affect their vote. This holds for both pro-choice and anti-abortion women (Lake & Breglio, 1992; Sciolino, 1996).

Nevertheless, we should be cautious when making comparisons between women as a group and men as a group, for women and men, we have learned, are not homogeneous categories and frequently there are greater differences among groups of women and groups of men than between women and men. Other factors besides sex influence political attitudes and behavior. These factors include race and ethnicity, social class, age, education, and employment status (Gidengil, 1995; Lake & Breglio, 1992; Mueller, 1991; Poole & Zeigler, 1985). Looking at Table 9.2, for example, we can see that while more women than men supported Bill Clinton in the 1996 presidential election, race and ethnicity were more significant factors. More White women than White men supported Clinton, but both African American women *and* African American men overwhelmingly supported Clinton. African American women have increased their voting

TABLE 9.2   Voters in the 1996 Presidential Election

Voters	Percent of Total Vote	Percent Who Voted for		
		Clinton	Dole	Perot
Men	48	43	44	10
Women	52	54	38	7
White	83	43	46	9
African American	10	84	12	4
Hispanic American	5	72	21	6
Asian American	1	43	48	8
White men	40	38	49	11
White women	43	48	43	8
African American men	5	78	15	5
African American women	5	89	8	2
Family income was:				
< $15,000	11	59	28	11
$15,000–$29,999	23	53	36	9
$30,000–$49,999	27	48	40	10
> $50,000	39	44	48	7
> $75,000	18	41	51	7
> $100,000	9	38	54	6
18–29 years old	17	53	34	10
30–44 years old	33	48	41	9
45–59 years old	26	48	41	9
60 or older	24	48	44	7

Source: "Portrait of the electorate," 1996.

rates at a much faster pace than African American men and, since 1965, have been more likely than African American men to vote (Prestage, 1991). Age also intersected with race/ethnicity and sex in the 1996 election, but still race/ethnicity remains more significant.

Sexual orientation has also been significant in recent elections. In 1992, for the first time in U.S. history, lesbians and gay men were a visible and vocal political constituency. Lesbian and gay political organizations carried out successful voter registration drives and raised millions of dollars in campaign funds, not only for Bill Clinton, but also for U.S. congressional and state and local politicians whom they supported. It was estimated that between 4 million and 9 million lesbians and gay men voted in the 1992 election. This unprecedented open involvement in mainstream national politics by lesbians and gay men was prompted in large part by outrage over the federal government's response (or lack thereof) to the HIV/AIDS crisis (see Chapter 11) and the blatant homophobia expressed by speakers such as Pat Robertson at the 1992 Republican National Convention. While Mr. Bush distanced himself from the homosexual communities, Mr. Clinton promised to increase federal funding for HIV/AIDS research and treatment, to enact a national health insurance program, and to lift the ban on homosexuals serving in the U.S. military (Gross, 1994; Schmalz, 1992). Although Mr. Clinton largely failed to make good on these promises during his first term in office, lesbians and gay men continued to support him over Republican Dole in 1996, again influenced significantly by the homophobic rhetoric and anti-gay/lesbian policies promoted by Republican officeholders and candidates. General support of Democratic candidates by lesbians and gay men is expected to grow in the future as conservative Republican politicians continue their "assault on homosexuality" (Seelye, 1998).

The gender gap has sometimes been explained as an expression of fundamental—some would even argue inherent—differences between the sexes: women's greater focus on caring, community, and connectedness; men's greater focus on competition and individual rights (Gidengil, 1995; Lake & Breglio, 1992). However, the differences among various groups of women—for instance, differences between full-time homemakers and women in the labor force, between White women and women of color, between lesbians and straight women—indicate that differences in voting and political attitudes reflect the life circumstances of different groups of citizens. Constituencies vote in response to candidates' expressed positions on issues salient to their lives. Nevertheless, gender stereotypes die hard, and the notion that women's political views will be more moralistic or humanitarian than men's views is also typically applied to candidates seeking political office. We will turn our attention to public officeholders shortly. First, however, it is important that we consider whether the gender gap is found in political activities other than voting.

Gender and Political Activities

There are many other forms of political activity besides voting. According to political scientist Lester Millbrath (1965), there are basically three levels of political activism. The lowest level, **spectator activities,** include wearing campaign buttons or putting a bumper sticker on your car. Millbrath also considers voting a spectator activity because it requires minimal effort. In the middle are **transitional activities,** such as writing to public officials, making campaign contributions, and attending rallies or meetings. The highest level of political activity, what Millbrath calls **gladiator activities,** includes working on a political campaign, taking an active role in a political party, or running for public office. Gladiator activities require maximum effort and commitment.

Contrary to the popular myth that men are more interested and active in politics, there are actually few differences between the sexes in their level of political activism. In general, both women and men are fairly uninvolved in politics. Historically, women have been slightly more likely than men to engage in the spectator activities of wearing buttons and displaying bumper stickers, while men have been more involved in transitional activities, especially contributing money to political campaigns (Lynn, 1984). To a large extent, the gender difference in campaign contributions has been due to the fact that women have had significantly less discretionary income than men, but in recent years women's campaign contributions have increased substantially, an issue we will look at when we discuss the quest for political office.

However, it has also been the case that much of women's transitional political activism has been overlooked or devalued by researchers. Much of this activism has taken place at the grassroots community level by working-class women and women of color (Prestage, 1991). A substantial portion of this activism has focused on preserving and expanding government-funded services that the members of these communities depend on, but have seen diminished by budget cutbacks and retrenchment in recent years. Thus, working-class White women and women of color have organized and led rent strikes, tenant unions, school boycotts, and petition drives in efforts to save essential social services, welfare benefits, and health care programs (Bookman & Morgen, 1988; Seitz, 1995). However, because the study of political activism traditionally has been limited to lobbying, elections, and officeholding, these significant and sometimes successful political challenges have gone unnoticed by most scholars (Bookman & Morgen, 1988).

Indeed, a good deal of scholarly political research has focused on what Millbrath identified as the highest level of political activism, gladiator activities. Here the data are also mixed. Women, as Epstein (1983, p. 290) observed, have long served as political "footsoldiers": canvassing for votes door-to-door or by phone, stuffing envelopes, distributing campaign literature, and so on. They have been almost twice as likely as men to work for a political party or a campaign (Lynn, 1984). However, although women are well represented among campaign staff and volunteers, men have traditionally dominated party conventions. Male dominance at the conventions is noteworthy because:

> it is at party conventions that formal decisions are made about the major presidential candidates and the party platform, which spells out the party's positions on public issues. At conventions various factions come together to discuss common problems and to indulge in the bargaining and compromising that create the coalitions that comprise our national parties. At conventions party leaders interact with rank-and-file members to learn about concerns and potential troublespots in the coming election. For many party workers, a convention is viewed as a reward for years of faithful service. (Lynn, 1984, pp. 409–410)

As Table 9.3 on page 284 shows, until 1972, neither major party had ever had more than 17 percent female delegates at their national conventions. In 1972, however, the Democrats instituted affirmative action regulations that helped to dramatically increase the representation of female delegates to 40 percent. Although their numbers dropped in 1976, women finally achieved equal representation at the 1980 Democratic National Convention. In contrast, the Republicans, who have never adopted affirmative action rules for their conventions—opposition to affirmative action is included in the Republican Party platform—continue to have delegations with a majority of male members. However, at the 1996 Republican National Convention, women were better represented among delegates than were people of color; only 9 percent of the Republican delegates were non-White. At the 1996 Democratic National Convention, 32.2 percent of the delegates were people of color (Bennet, 1996; Democratic National Committee, 1997).

TABLE 9.3   Female Delegates to the National Political
Conventions, 1900–1996

Year	Democrats (%)*	Republicans (%)
1900	**	***
1904	**	***
1908	**	***
1912	**	***
1916	1	***
1920	6	3
1924	14	11
1928	10	6
1932	12	8
1936	15	6
1940	11	8
1944	11	10
1948	12	10
1952	12	11
1956	12	16
1960	11	15
1964	14	18
1968	13	17
1972	40	30
1976	34	31
1980	49	29
1984	50	44
1988	49	35
1992	50	41
1996	50	36

*Percentages do not necessarily reflect the proportion of convention votes held by female delegates; some Democratic delegates have held fractional votes.

**Less than 1 percent. Actual numbers: 1900, 1; 1904, 0; 1908, 2; 1912, 2.

***Less than 1 percent. Actual numbers: 1900, 1; 1904, 1; 1908, 2; 1912, 2; 1916, 5.

Sources: Benedetto, 1992; Bennet, 1996; CAWP, 1988; Democratic National Commitee, 1997; "Who Are the Delegates," 1992.

Gender and Public Office

Women and men, it seems, have a similar interest in politics if we use their voting rates and political activism as indicators. Yet, historically, men have had a virtual monopoly on public officeholding throughout the world. There are 191 countries in the world today; just four have female heads of government, ten have female foreign ministers, ten (including the United States) have female ambassadors to the United Nations, and seventeen have female speakers of parliament. Of the 179 countries with parliamentary governments, women hold just 11.7 percent of parliamentary seats. Although this number represents a nearly 400 percent increase since 1946, the number of parliaments has also grown (from 26 to 179) during that period. In fact, in the new post-socialist democracies of Eastern Europe, women have actually lost representation in government as a result of parliamentary elections. In Albania, for example, the number of women in parliament declined from 28 percent to 6 percent, and in Romania, from 33 percent to 4 percent, between 1987 and 1994. Nevertheless, in countries as diverse as India, France, and South Africa, women have made dramatic gains in political representation, and in the four Scandanavian countries—Sweden, Norway, Denmark, and Finland—women hold 33 percent to 40 percent of parliamentary seats, more than any other country worldwide (Inter-Parliamentary Union, 1997).

How well does the United States compare with other countries in terms of women's representation in national government? Out of 173 national legislatures studied by the Inter-Parliamentary Union (1997), the United States ranked thirty-ninth. The U.S. standing was certainly helped by the fact that during the 1980s and especially throughout the 1990s, women in this country made considerable progress in the political arena at all levels—federal, state, and local—although they remain grossly underrepresented, especially in the federal government. Before we examine the numbers more closely, however, let's discuss some of the factors that historically contributed to the disparity between the sexes in public officeholding.

One of the ways the gender gap in officeholding has traditionally been explained is in terms of boys' and girls' different socialization experiences. This argument maintains that dispositions toward politics are formed in childhood when boys are told they can grow up to be president some day; the best girls can hope for is to grow up to marry a man who may one day be a president. Consequently, children learn that politics is a masculine activity, and this is reflected in their adult behavior: Women rarely choose to run for public office.

This explanation has some appeal because, as we found in Chapter 3, early childhood socialization does have a powerful impact on the development of sex-typed attitudes and behaviors. Research, however, has found no sex differences in the political views of school-age children (Epstein, 1983). What is more, if differential socialization is at work, we would expect to find less similarity in men's and women's interest in politics than what we have seen here. Young women aspiring to political careers have had far fewer role models than their male counterparts, but this is changing as more women enter political races each election year. The availability of role models and mentors is important; many female officeholders state that they were inspired and assisted in their political careers by other women (Center for the American Woman and Politics, hereafter CAWP, 1984).

A second explanation for the small number of women officeholders is that women have greater difficulty meeting the demands of public life given their domestic responsibilities. Like most married employed women, female politicians who are married shoulder a double work load; their spouses, if they are married, do not usually assume primary responsibility for housekeeping or childcare. Particularly at the national level, the demands of public office take an extraordinary toll on the amount of time an officeholder can spend with her or his family. It is not surprising, therefore, that women typically enter politics at a later age than men (after their children are grown), and that female political elites are more likely than men to be single, widowed, or divorced, although they may still have children (Mandel & Dodson, 1992; Toner, 1996). In Europe, too, Lovenduski (1986) found that women in public office are less often married and have fewer children than their male colleagues. This does not mean that men do not experience conflict between their political careers and their family lives. Recent research indicates that they do and that the tension may be high. However, men are more likely to pursue their political ambitions despite the conflicts, whereas women frequently try to manage the conflict by delaying their political careers or by giving up one role for the other at least temporarily (Toner, 1996).

A third, although increasingly less frequent explanation is that men outnumber women in elected office because most women lack the necessary qualifications and credentials. It is certainly true that most female officeholders prior to World War II had inherited their seats and simply served out the terms of their deceased husbands or fathers. Even if they were elected, they usually had less education than the men, and because the legal and business professions were largely closed to them, they came to politics via different occupational backgrounds, typically teaching and social work. In recent years, however, this has changed. Female officeholders, in fact, are more likely than male officeholders to have attended college, and non-White female officeholders are more likely than female officeholders overall to have attended college (CAWP, 1985; Natividad, 1992; White, 1995). The number of women in public office who are lawyers and businesspeople has also risen, as has the number with previous elective experience (Clark, 1991). Although female officeholders still are less likely than their male colleagues to have held previous elective offices, they are more likely to have had other types of political experience. For example, female officeholders are more likely than their male counterparts to have held previous appointed government positions and to have worked on political campaigns before running for office themselves (CAWP, 1984; White, 1995; Witt et al., 1994). Consequently, the "qualifications and credentials argument" is less tenable today than in the past.

A fourth argument is that women may be relatively scarce in public office because of prejudice and discrimination against them that may occur on two levels: among the electorate and within political office. Studies of sexism among the electorate indicate that, in general, sexism has declined in recent years (Clark, 1991). In one recent national opinion poll in the United States, for example, a majority of respondents (51 percent) agreed that in a political race between a man and a woman with equal qualifications and skills, they would vote for the woman because the United States needs more women in high public office (41 percent disagreed and 8 percent were undecided). However, more women (57 percent) than men (45 percent) agreed with the statement ("Women Candidates," 1992). An international survey of 22,000 people in twenty-two countries found in 1996 that the majority of respondents in every country surveyed felt that government would be better if more women held political office. For example, 50 percent of respondents in India, 51 percent in Great Britain, and 59 percent in France expressed this opinion; 57 percent of respondents in the United States shared this view ("Poll," 1996).

The public has grown more accustomed to women running for political office and no longer considers it "unusual" or "unladylike." In an increasing number of political races, in fact, voters must choose between two female candidates (Belluck, 1998). However, research indicates that sex continues to be an important factor in many elections, since the electorate rarely views the skills and qualifications of female and male candidates in the same way, and gender stereotypes still dominate some voters' images of political candidates (Witt et al., 1994). For example, most voters still perceive female candidates, regardless of their individual qualifications and experience, to be better than male candidates at handling social issues, such as education, child care, health care, homelessness, welfare policy, and abortion. In contrast, voters typically believe that male candidates are more capable than female candidates in handling such matters as defense, foreign policy, economic issues, and large budgets. Such stereotypes may work in favor of or against both male and female candidates, depending on what types of issues happen to be most pressing on public awareness during an election campaign (Kahn & Goldenberg, 1991).

Of course, the media play a major role in shaping voters' perceptions of political candidates. Recent research shows that female and male candidates are covered differently by the media (see also Chapter 5). According to Kahn and Goldenberg (1991), media coverage of female candidates tends to focus on the viability of their campaign (i.e., their chances of winning given their resources), whereas media coverage of male candidates focuses more on campaign issues. Finally, regardless of the issues salient in a specific campaign, the media give greater coverage to female candidates' positions on what are typically considered female issues (e.g., education, drugs), and greater coverage to male candidates' positions on so-called male issues (e.g., national security, trade). This is not insignificant, since research shows that candidates, whether male or female, who receive female-typical media coverage are perceived as less viable than candidates who receive male-typical media coverage. In short, the media have traditionally disadvantaged female political candidates (see also Witt et al., 1994).

Prejudice and discrimination against female candidates can be found at a second level as well: within the political parties. Sexism within the political parties is well documented (Niven, 1998; Witt et al., 1994). The overwhelming majority of party leaders are men, many of whom still subscribe to traditional gender stereotypes; they often think male candidates have a better chance of winning and make better politicians than women (Niven, 1998). Such prejudice and discrimination is especially strong in the southern states and in states where a small party elite has a monopoly on decision making (Ayres, 1997a; Niven, 1998). It is estimated that this bias reduces the number of women nominated for state legislative seats by about one-third (Niven, 1998).[2]

Historically, when party leaders were confronted with women's increasing demands for greater political roles, they often responded by recruiting female candidates as "sacrificial lambs," that is, as candidates in races for which their party's nominee had virtually no chance of winning (Carroll, 1985). Recent research, however, indicates that this practice is now rare (Clark, 1991) and that party leaders in many states are actively recruiting female candidates because women *can* win by bridging the gender gap among the electorate (Belluck, 1998). Instead, research indicates that the more formidable obstacles for women seeking public office today are incumbency and access to campaign funds.

An **incumbent** is a person who holds political office and is seeking another term. Incumbents have several advantages during an election, not the least of which are high public visibility, recognition among voters, and the opportunity to campaign throughout their term in office. Because fewer women are in office, when they do run, it is more often as challengers rather than as incumbents and, not surprisingly, they lose more frequently when running against an incumbent than for an open seat. In 1992, for instance, it was expected that a large number of incumbents would lose reelection bids for the U.S. Senate and House because voters were expressing anger over disclosures of abuses in office such as the House banking scandal, and there appeared to be a strong voter sentiment for a change in government. It was thought that year that women and minority candidates would have their best chance ever at unseating incumbents in federal government. Nevertheless, out of 376 incumbents who won their primaries, 349 won reelection in November. Of the 48 women who won election to the U.S. House of Representatives in 1992, for instance, 24 were incumbents themselves and 22 ran for open seats (CAWP, 1993). Both female and minority candidates are still more likely to win if they are running for a seat vacated because of a resignation or retirement.[3]

Incumbent or not, all political candidates need money to run a campaign, and the more prestigious the office they seek, the more money they need. Traditionally, political campaigns have been financed through personal wealth subsidized by party funds. Since women and minorities have had fewer financial resources than White men, when they ran for office, their campaigns often did not have sufficient funds to be successful. And today, even more than in the past, money is essential to winning elections. Consider, for example, that in 1992 the average amount spent by U.S. senatorial candidates was over $9 million. In effect, this means that to run for the Senate, an individual had to raise about $30,000 a week for six years or be a multimillionaire (U.S. Department of Commerce, Bureau of the Census, 1994). Campaign spending for the 1996 presidential race was estimated to be a record $600 million (Wayne, 1996).

Where do such enormous sums come from? Certainly, most candidates for public office, especially at the national level, continue to be individuals with considerable personal wealth, but the lion's share of campaign funds today comes from private corporations and groups representing special interests. In fact, some special-interest groups dedicate themselves to fundraising and distributing contributions to the political campaigns of candidates who support the group's cause. These special interest groups are called **political action committees** or **PACs.** There are more 4,000 PACs in the United States today, representing corporations (e.g., Philip Morris, one of the largest tobacco, food and alcohol corporations in the United States), particular industries and professions (e.g., the American Medical Association, the American Bar Association), and specific issues (pro- or anti-abortion, pro- or anti-gun control). PACs contribute millions of dollars to campaigns, making them a powerful force on the political scene. In 1993–1994, for example, PACs contributed nearly $190 million to political candidates. Historically, however, female and minority candidates have received a relatively small percentage of these funds, with PAC representatives arguing that the reason is these candidates frequently do not solicit them ("Seeking Corporate PAC Money," 1986). This may be true to some extent, given that many PACs are parts of large corporations and professional associations in fields in which the percentage of women and minorities has been small, and women and minorities typically have not been members of the interlocking professional, social, and political networks through which large campaign contributions are frequently generated (Scott, 1994). Nevertheless, even when contributions are solicited, the funds received have tended to be smaller on average than those given to White male candidates (Carroll, 1985). As one female state officeholder recently explained, "[W]hen it comes to raising campaign money or cracking the state's big business establishment, which is a real power center, you can still run into a solid, male-dominated stone wall" (quoted in Ayres, 1997a, p. B8).

During the 1990s, however, even this dimension of the political arena began changing dramatically. For one thing, women's organizations successfully mobilized their memberships to support female or feminist candidates, not only "with their feet" by working on campaigns and voting, but also with their pocketbooks (CAWP, n.d.). In addition, women, racial and ethnic minorities, and lesbians and gay men established formal and informal political coalitions as well as their own PACs, such as the National Political Congress of Black Women's PAC, the Women's Campaign Fund, and Emily's List, which is widely considered to be one of the most powerful women's PACs, with over 24,000 members and more than $6 million in annual contributions (Friedman, 1993; Witt et al., 1994).[4] The gay and lesbian Victory Fund has raised hundreds of thousands of dollars in support of gay and lesbian political candidates (Gross, 1994). Thus, despite the many barriers that continue to hinder the political candidacies of women, racial and ethnic minorities, and gay men and lesbians, a steadily growing number of candidates from all of these constituencies are making successful bids for public office. Let's discuss now the relative numbers of women and men in specific elected and appointed offices and, when possible, look at race and ethnicity and sexual orientation as well.

Women and Men in State and Local Government

Table 9.4 on page 290 shows the number of women holding selected state and local offices. Clearly, men continue to dominate state and local government as they constitute the vast majority of officeholders in every category. Still, it is at the state level that women have made their greatest political gains in recent years.

Most important perhaps is the increase in the number of female state legislators. Although men continue to hold over 78 percent of all state legislative seats, the number of women legislators has increased more than fivefold since 1969, from just 4 percent to over 21 percent. In five states, women hold a third or more of the state legislative seats: Washington (39.5 percent), Arizona (37.8 percent), Colorado (35 percent), Nevada (33.3 percent), and Vermont (33.3 percent) (CAWP, 1998a). In New Hampshire, where 30.7 percent of the legislative seats are held by women, the house speaker and the governor are also women, but from opposing political parties (Goldberg, 1997).

Racial and ethnic minorities have made significant inroads at the state level, too. For example, in 1994, there were 199 Hispanic state executives and legislators, up from 110 in 1983. In 1993, there were 522 African American state legislators, an increase of 213 since 1981 (U.S. Department of Commerce, Bureau of the Census, 1997). Unfortunately, women of color are still grossly underrepresented in state legislatures. In 1998, women of color were just 3.1 percent of state legislators and 14.4 percent of female state legislators. African American women served in the legislatures of thirty-five states; they

TABLE 9.4   Women in State and Local Government,
Selected Offices, 1998

Public Office	Number of Women Officeholders
Governor	3
Lt. Governor	18 (of 42)
Secretary of State	12
Attorney General	8
State Treasurer	10
State Auditor or Comptroller	6
Chief State Education Official	11
Commissioner of Insurance	3
Commissioner of Labor	1
Railroad Commissioner	1
Commissioner of Public Lands	1
Corporation Commissioner	2
Public Service Commissioner	4
Public Utilities Commissioner	2
State Legislator	1,607 (21.6%)
Mayor (cities with populations over 30,000; n = 975 cities)	202 (20.7%)

Source: CAWP, 1998a.

were 2.3 percent of all state legislators, 10.5 percent of female state legislators, and 72.4 percent of minority female state legislators. Latinas served in the legislatures of fourteen states, holding a total of 45 seats and constituting 2.8 percent of female state legislators. Asian American women served in three states, held eleven seats, and were 0.7 percent of female legislators. Native American women served in six states, but held just eight seats total, thus constituting only 0.5 percent of female legislators. Respectively, Hispanic, Asian American and Native American women are 0.6 percent, 0.15 percent, and 0.11 percent of all state legislators nationwide (CAWP, 1998b).

Despite these low numbers, it is important to remember that they signify *gains* for racial and ethnic minorities, especially for women of color, in state elective office. Lesbians and gay men appear to have had less success at the state level, although they have made inroads in local elections. Tony Miller became the first openly gay candidate to run for statewide elective office in 1994, seeking the position of California secretary of state. Nationwide, fewer than 150 of the country's 450,000 elected officials are openly gay or lesbian (Gross, 1994; see also Ayres, 1997b).

Women and Men in the Federal Government

Looking at Table 9.5, we see the number of women in the U.S. Congress from 1949 to 1997. What is most striking about the figures in this table is not so much the small num-

TABLE 9.5   Women in the U.S. Congress, 1949–1997

Year	Congress	Senate	House
1949	81st	1	9
1951	82nd	1	10
1953	83rd	3	12
1955	84th	1	17
1957	85th	1	15
1959	86th	2	17
1961	87th	2	18
1963	88th	2	12
1965	89th	2	11
1967	90th	1	11
1969	91st	1	10
1971	92nd	2	13
1973	93rd	0	16
1975	94th	0	19
1977	95th	2	20
1979	96th	1	16
1981	97th	2	21
1983	98th	2	22
1985	99th	2	23
1987	100th	2	24
1989	101st	2	28
1991	102nd	2	28
1993	103rd	7	47
1995	104th	9	48
1997	105th	9	53*

*The tally for the 105th Congress does not include two Democratic delegates to the House from the Virgin Islands and Washington, DC, nor does it include Susan Molinari (R-NY) who resigned in August, 1997. However, it does include three representatives who joined Congress in 1998 as a result of special elections: Lois Capps (D-CA), Mary Bono (R-CA), and Barbara Lee (R-CA).

Source: CAWP, 1998c.

ber of women—most of you would probably predict that—but rather the lack of substantial improvement in these numbers over a four-decade period. Until 1993, it could hardly be said that there was a strong pattern of growth in the number of female elected officials at the federal level, particularly in the Senate. Although women have served in Congress since 1916, when Jeannette Rankin was elected to the House of Representatives, 45 percent of congresswomen prior to 1949 came to office through *widow's succession,* that is, they were appointed or elected to finish the terms of their husbands who were congressmen, but who died or became too ill to serve. Women who entered congressional office this way were sometimes reelected after their husband's term expired.

For female senators especially, this has been the primary means to office; it was not until 1983 (the 98th Congress) that two women served in the Senate simultaneously without either of them having gotten their seats through widow's succession (Lynn, 1984). In the 1992 elections—dubbed the "Year of the Woman" by some political analysts—women made significant progress in congressional officeholding. A record number of women were nominated for congressional seats in 1992: 11 for the Senate, 5 of whom won; and 108 for the House of Representatives, 48 of whom won. It was in this election that for the first time both senatorial seats for a state were held by women: Barbara Boxer and Diane Feinstein, both Democrats, were elected in California. In fact, California has elected more women to Congress than any other state.[5] The 1994 and 1996 congressional elections, as well as special elections in early 1998, brought even more female representation to Congress, especially the House of Representatives, and there is no reason to believe that the number of congresswomen will not continue to grow in the future. Despite these recent gains, it is important to keep in mind that if change continues at the present rate, it will take nearly 400 years more for women to achieve parity with men in Congress.

When race and ethnicity are taken into account, 1992 appears to have been a watershed election year for women and men of color as well. Although minority women and men, like White women, remain grossly underrepresented in both the Senate and the House, a record number of women and men of color were elected to Congress in 1992. Ben Nighthorse Campbell from Colorado (who was originally a Democrat, but later became a Republican), for example, became our country's first Native American senator, and Jay C. Kim, a Republican from California, became the first Korean American House representative. Still, by the 104th Congress, less than 12 percent of the seats were held by men and women of color; there were only four non-White senators and sixty-one non-White representatives (U.S. Department of Commerce, Bureau of the Census, 1997). In 1992, Carol Moseley Braun (a Democrat from Illinois) became the first African American female senator; in 1998, she remained the only woman of color in the U.S. Senate. In the House of Representatives, there were fifteen women of color in 1998: ten African American women, one Asian American woman, and four Latinas.[6] In all, women of color held just about 3 percent of all seats in the 105th U.S. Congress (CAWP, 1998c).

What happens to women after they get to Congress? In the past, women senators and representatives rarely held leadership positions. By 1993, there were only two women in high-ranking leadership positions (Senator Barbara Mikulski, a Democrat from Maryland, assistant floor leader; and Congresswoman Barbara Kennelly, a Democrat from Connecticut, chief deputy majority whip) and none chairing standing congressional committees. In fact, only six women have ever chaired standing congressional committees and they all served before 1977. It was not until the 104th Congress that a woman chaired a major Senate committee: Senator Nancy Kassebaum (a Republican from Kansas) chaired the Labor and Human Resources Committee. No woman has ever been majority or minority leader in the Senate. In the House of Representatives, to which women have had greater access than the Senate, no woman has served as House Speaker. Only three women have chaired House select committees. Instead, women most often hold secondary positions, and although they can now be found as members of most structured congressional groups (e.g., bipartisan caucuses), they still sometimes find themselves excluded from various unstructured groups (e.g., sporting groups). These latter groups have not been insignificant, for as we saw in Chapter 7, they may provide members with both an informal network and opportunities to build alliances with colleagues (CAWP, 1998d; Foerstel & Foerstel, 1996).

One of the reasons for women's exclusion from some positions and committees is their lack of seniority. For example, most analysts agree that it takes a minimum of five terms in the House before election or appointment to a powerful position is likely; floor leaders typically serve eighteen years before securing that spot (Gertzog, 1984; Lynn, 1984). Such findings, then, underline the importance of female incumbents seeking and winning reelection to consecutive terms; otherwise, although more women may fill congressional seats, their junior status will continue to cause them to be underrepresented in high-level positions.

We know that every chief executive of the United States has been male, as has every vice president. There has never been a female candidate for president from either of the major political parties, although former Senator Patricia Schroeder sought the Democratic nomination in 1988. It was not until 1984 that a woman was nominated by a major party for the office of vice president. However, in considering the executive branch of the federal government, we must keep in mind that those elected to office also have the privilege of making a variety of high-ranking appointments. As one report emphasized, presidential appointments, particularly for women and minorities, are critical for three major reasons:

1. They provide young professionals with valuable career experience.
2. They set an example for private employers to follow in hiring personnel.
3. They offer opportunities for input into policy making from individuals with diverse backgrounds and interests. (Pear, 1987)

There are 290 top government positions for which the president makes appointments, subject to senate confirmation. During Ronald Reagan's administration, support for women's rights was equivocal at best, but it was to Mr. Reagan's credit that he appointed women to about forty posts that had never before been held by a female, including several in nontraditional or stereotypically masculine areas. Nevertheless, Mr. Reagan had almost 300 federal judgeships to fill and appointed women to just 26 (8.7 percent) of them. This is important because federal judges have an impact on law beyond the administration that appointed them since their terms are for life. At the same time, the number of racial and ethnic minorities, male or female, who received political appointments declined significantly during the Reagan administration, from 44 to just 20 positions (Pear, 1987).

George Bush increased the number of presidential appointments to a level higher than any of his predecessors in the White House; 19.4 percent of Mr. Bush's appointments were women (a total of 185 women). Still, there were few women in his senior staff: nine women to forty men. Mr. Bush's most highly acclaimed female and minority appointment was that of Antonia Novello, a Latina, as Surgeon General. The seven women who were deputy assistants to the president, however, all worked in areas traditionally considered female fields. Bush, in fact, was described by those close to him as "a guy's guy" and his inner circle seemed to reflect this (Dowd, 1991).

President Clinton has shown a firm commitment to increasing diversity in the federal government through his presidential appointments. Although he was criticized during his first year in office for being too slow in naming appointments, members of the White House staff argued that this was due largely to President Clinton's determination to carefully scrutinize the lists of suggested appointees submitted by cabinet members so as to insure diversity (Jehl, 1993). For example, of the 486 people appointed to the President's cabinet since it was first established in 1789, only 22 have been women and 50 percent of these (11 women) were appointed by President Clinton (CAWP, 1998e). President Clinton also appointed the first openly gay man and lesbian to high-ranking federal posts: Bruce A. Lehman, Assistant Secretary of Commerce and Commissioner of Patents and Trademarks, and Roberta Achetenberg, Assistant Secretary of Housing and Urban Development (Riordan, 1994).[7]

Among the most important appointments the president may make are those to the U.S. Supreme Court, again because the impact of these appointments stretches well beyond the president's own administration, given that the justices hold life terms. Ronald Reagan nominated the first woman to the Supreme Court, Sandra Day O'Connor, in 1981. Historically, the all-male Court had done much to uphold and little to remedy sex discrimination. Well into the 1960s, the justices' decisions in sex discrimination cases reflected the opinion of Chief Justice Waite, who, in the 1875 case of *Minor* v. *Happersett*, declared that women, like children, are "a special category of citizens," in need of both discipline and protection. It was not until 1973 that the Court ruled that much of the discrimination against women was nothing more than "romantic paternalism" that, "in practical effect, put women not on a pedestal, but in a cage" (*Frontiero* v. *Richardson*). Nevertheless, as we have noted in other chapters, the Supreme Court did not subsequently strike down all forms of sex discrimination. With O'Connor's appointment, many feminists were hopeful that a woman on the Court would preserve the hard-won legal support of gender equality secured in earlier cases. However, O'Connor's record in this area has been mixed. Although typically she has supported equality in the area of employment, her opinions with respect to affirmative action have been uneven. In addition, she has not acted consistently to protect women's abortion rights; indeed, in her opinion in *Webster* v. *Reproductive Health Services* (1989), she explicitly called on the Court to reconsider its ruling in *Roe* v. *Wade* (see Chapter 6).[8]

George Bush made two appointments to the Supreme Court. In 1990, it was rumored that he would nominate Edith H. Jones to replace retiring Justice William Brennan, who had been considered by many to be the leading liberal voice on the Court. Instead, Mr. Bush chose David H. Souter, a White man. In 1991, Mr. Bush nominated Clarence Thomas, a Black man, to the Supreme Court. Justice Thomas's appointment, however, was not considered a victory for either racial and ethnic minorities or women because of his conservative record on affirmative action and the charges of sexual harassment leveled against him by Professor Anita Hill during his confirmation hearings.

In 1993, Ruth Bader Ginsburg, nominated by President Clinton, became the second female justice on the U.S. Supreme Court. Justice Ginsburg, who replaced retired Justice Byron R. White, had a strong record in support of gender equality and abortion rights. In 1994, a second Clinton nominee, Stephen G. Breyer, a White man whose lower court decisions were supportive of civil rights and reproductive freedom, replaced Justice Harry Blackmun on the Supreme Court.

The Justices have not done much to increase diversity in employment within the Court itself. Of the nine current justices, only Justice Breyer has hired the same number of female law clerks as male clerks. However, 88 percent of his clerks have been White. Justices O'Connor and Ginsburg have hired 43 percent and 40 percent female clerks respectively, but 91 percent and 90 percent of their clerks respectively have been White. Justice Stevens, who has been on the bench since 1975, has hired 28 percent female clerks and, with Justice Thomas, has the best record of hiring non-White clerks, 14 percent. All of the remaining justices have hired 17 percent or fewer female clerks and 10 percent or fewer non-White clerks. Chief Justice Rehnquist, on the Court since 1972, has hired only one non-White clerk, a Latino, while all of Justice Scalia's clerks have been White. As one observer put it, "Much of the power to shape race and gender relations in the USA rests mainly in the hands of White men" (Mauro, 1998, p. 12A).

In light of these statistics, we are reminded of an important point: The presence of a White woman or a person of color in a government post does not necessarily mean that women's or minorities' interests will be consistently and fairly represented or that gender and racial and ethnic equality will always be promoted. As observers of British politics during Margaret Thatcher's administration noted, a female leader may oppose women's rights and gender equality while some male leaders ardently support them. Indeed, the 1994 elections in the United States brought to Congress a number of ardently conservative Republican women who advocated drastic cuts in social spending and who opposed abortion rights (see, for example, Egan, 1996). It is also the case that most women in appointed government positions do not have an institutional mandate to actively work on gender-related issues, and even those who do must address them in the context of the administration's policy preferences (Boneparth & Stroper, 1988).

Still, research indicates that women in elected offices usually have a positive impact on the passage of women's rights legislation and are more likely than male legislators to give top priority to issues of particular concern to women (Ayres, 1997a; Carroll et al., 1991; Goldberg, 1997; Kelly et al., 1991; Mandel & Dodson, 1992). This finding is supported not only by analyses of legislators' activities while in office, but also by surveys of legislators' perceptions of the influence of female officeholders. In one such survey, for instance, 85 percent of female legislators and 74 percent of male legislators stated that the increased presence of women in public office affects the extent to which legislators consider how a particular bill will impact on women as a group (Mandel & Dodson, 1992).

According to Lovenduski (1986, p. 243), it appears that "a certain 'critical mass' of women"—and we would add, *feminist* women—"must exist to enable the development of a group identity and the resistance of socialization into male norms of behavior." This is also essential for breaking down gender stereotypes. However, the more sex segregated an institution is, the more difficult this is to achieve, as we will see next in our discussion of the military.

Women and Men in the Military

We noted earlier that women tend to express greater opposition to military intervention than men and, in general, they are thought to be more pacifistic. Clearly, this is not true for all women, nor has it ever been. Historical and cross-cultural research shows, in fact, that women have often supported militarism and have even engaged in combat and other military activities. Archeologists, for example, have discovered graves in Kazakhstan near the Russian border containing the remains of women warriors, who apparently defended their kin, land, and herds of animals while riding horseback, shooting with bows and arrows and wielding daggers (Davis-Kimball, 1997). During the nineteenth century, in the West African nation of Dahomey (now Benin), the king had an all-female fighting force of between 4,000 and 10,000 soldiers as part of his standing army (Sacks, 1979). More recently, Soviet women during World War II assumed combat roles as machine gunners and snipers, fighting with men in artillery and tank crews, and Israeli women fought in combat during the 1930s and 1940s, although their combat roles were not officially recognized. During the 1980s, 20,000 Eritrean women fought with men, driving tanks and firing heavy artillary, as members of the rebel army that liberated Eritrea from Ethiopian rule in 1991 (McKinley, 1996; for other recent examples, see MacDonald, 1992). In December 1986, Denmark became the first NATO country to allow women to join combat forces, with the exception of those on aircraft. Currently, women in Canada, Britain, the Netherlands, and Norway may assume jobs in every area of their country's armed forces, with few exceptions.[9]

In the United States, there are accounts of women who disguised themselves as men and fought at the front beside their husbands or brothers: Deborah Sampson, for instance, during the American Revolution; Lucy Brewer in the War of 1812; and Loretta Velasquez in the Civil War (Rustad, 1982). Although women have been officially prohibited from direct combat duty in the U.S. armed forces, they were employed during World War II in espionage and as saboteurs behind enemy lines. According to one researcher:

> The role of females was not trivial, and it certainly was in no way token. Indeed, this female role subjected women to risks of death or torture exactly parallel to those for males. . . . The meager evidence we have from the performance of women in espionage and sabotage suggests that women can be as brave and as coldly homicidal as men, whenever their patriotism calls for it. (Quester, 1982, pp. 226, 229)

For the most part, however, these American women were an exceptional few. Warmaking has been and, to a large extent, remains a male activity in the United States, and the military a male-dominated institution. This is not to deny the widespread involvement of men historically and in contemporary society in anti-war movements and peace activities. Throughout U.S. history, men have been pacifists and conscientious objectors, but as we noted earlier, in general, men tend to be much more favorably disposed to military solutions to international conflicts than women are, despite women's greater sense of distrust of other nations. As Cooke and Woollacott (1993) argue, war and the military are gendered and their gender is masculine; things that are feminine are derided in the military and consciously eliminated. Integration of the armed forces in the United States has been strongly resisted on the ground that women just don't have what it takes to be effective soldiers; they are too weak. For instance, Gen. Josiah Bunting 3d, superintendent of the Virginia Military Institute, which refused to admit women until ordered to do so by the U.S. Supreme Court in 1996, warned prospective female applicants to VMI that military training is not for the "faint of heart." "We teach what are called the vigorous virtues—determination, self-reliance, self-control, and courage," said Bunting. "This is achieved through the application of mental stress, physical rigor, minute regulations of behavior, pressures, hazards, and psychological bonding"—conditions that Bunting felt few, if any, women could endure (quoted in Allen, 1996, p. 18).

When American women were first recruited for military service during World War I, they were limited to nursing and clerical jobs that did not carry full military status and therefore none of the benefits to which male military personnel were entitled. During the Second World War, the Women's Army Corps (WAC) was established and granted women full military status with benefits throughout the war and for six months afterward. Other military corps for women were also begun and included the Women's Reserve of the Navy (WAVES) and the Women's Air Force Service Pilots (WASPS). Still, women's roles were strictly limited, and the War Department continued to adhere to a policy of recruiting men, no matter how uneducated, unskilled, or incompetent, before accepting women. Despite the fact that, especially as nurses, these women frequently faced dangerous and life-threatening conditions in war zones—some were wounded or killed—they were often derided by servicemen, civilians, and the press. Reporters seemed most interested in what the women were wearing, right down to whether they were issued girdles, whereas the general public and servicemen typically viewed them as whores or lesbians in search of partners (Rustad, 1982).

Until the late 1960s, women served as a reserve army in the truest sense for the military. Recruited as a cheap source of labor when manpower was low, they were dismissed as soon as men were available to replace them. Shortly after World War II, for instance, 98 percent of the Women's Army Corps was discharged, but because women had not been given the same civilian reemployment rights as men, they had greater difficulty finding work, and many were forced to take jobs well below their skill levels. For example, women who had been pilots during wartime found at the war's end that the only jobs they could obtain in the airline industry were as flight attendants or typists (Rustad, 1982). In addition, as Willentz (1991) has observed, the Veterans Administration has been (and remains) a system established by men for men, with the needs of female veterans largely overlooked (see also Palmer, 1993).

At the same time, women who joined the military had to meet higher enlistment standards than men; however, they were given fewer privileges and career opportunities and were subject to stricter regulations. For example, the 1948 Women's Armed Services Integration Act, while establishing a permanent place for women in the military, reserved 98 percent of the positions for men and placed a cap on the term of service and number of women who could be promoted to the rank of full colonel or Navy captain: one. No woman could become a general or an admiral. As part of their training, women were instructed in how to maintain a "ladylike" appearance, how to apply makeup, and how to get in and out of cars in their tight-fitting uniform skirts. Unlike male military personnel, they had to remain childless—pregnancy was grounds for discharge—and, if married, they had to prove that they were their husbands' primary source of financial support in order to receive dependents' benefits (Stiehm, 1985).

In the late 1960s and throughout the 1970s, a series of events took place that greatly expanded both the number and the roles of female military personnel. First, in 1967, Congress passed Public Law 90-30, which removed the limits on the number of enlisted women and the number of promotions for women officers. In addition, the women's movement was actively promoting the equal integration of women into all areas of life and, with the passage of the Equal Rights Amendment by Congress in 1972, many thought that this would extend to female military personnel as well. Also in 1972, congressional hearings were held on the role of women in the military, and the report that followed encouraged the Defense Department to recruit and utilize women on a more equal basis with men. In 1973, the military draft was replaced by the all-volunteer force, causing worried military planners to turn to the recruitment of women as a means to keep enlistments up. Adding to this were several court cases, such as *Frontiero* v. *Richardson* (1973), in which the Supreme Court, in fairly strong language that we have already quoted, overturned the military's policy of awarding dependents' benefits to female personnel using different standards from those applied to male personnel. Later in a federal court, the Navy's policy of barring women from sea duty was also struck down (*Owens* v. *Brown*, 1978). By 1976, ROTC was accepting women, as were the military academies, and Air Force women joined those in the Army and Navy in having flight schools open to them. Perhaps the most important change, though, occurred one year earlier in 1975, when the Defense Department lifted its ban on parenting for female personnel and made discharge for pregnancy available on a voluntary basis (Stiehm, 1985).

In light of this dramatic turn of events, it is hardly surprising that the number of women who entered the military rose substantially during the 1970s. Between 1972 and 1976, the number of military women tripled; by 1980, it had increased almost five-fold. Most of the increase occurred in the enlisted ranks, which, by 1980, accounted for 87 percent of female military personnel. However, like most men who enlisted, these women rarely stayed for more than one tour of duty and, in 1980, there were actually fewer women in the higher enlisted ranks (E-8 and above) than in 1972 (Stiehm, 1985).

During the Carter administration, there appeared to be a strong commitment to recruit women for the military, and the president even favored requiring women to register for the military draft when registration was reinstated. Interestingly, despite Ronald Reagan's more "hawkish" attitudes and his support of military buildup, he took a more conservative stance toward women in the military and, shortly after his election, the Defense Department scaled down their recruitment of female enlistees (Quester, 1982).

Following the end of the Cold War and the fall of socialism in the former Soviet Union and Eastern Europe, the Pentagon began to reduce the size of its active-duty troops and closed a number of military bases. One result of this military downsizing is reflected in Table 9.6, which shows a substantial decrease in active-duty military personnel at all levels during the 1990s. However, a second reason for the shrinkage is that enlistments also declined during the 1990s. In fact, in 1997, the army announced that it was lowering its education requirements to accept more recruits without high school diplomas so as to increase enlistments. Although the armed forces offer enlistment bonuses and money toward college to appeal to high school graduates, the low average salary of a recruit—about $769 a month—means that well-educated or highly skilled

TABLE 9.6 Men and Women on Active Military Duty by Race, 1985, 1990, and 1997

	1985	1990	1997
Men			
Officers	278,816	262,645	197,834
White	252,348	233,326	169,504
Black	16,054	16,366	13,892
Hispanic	4,222	5,427	6,311
Other*	6,192	7,526	8,127
Enlisted	1,649,233	1,623,714	1,031,231
White	1,261,842	1,138,985	781,701
Black	251,704	336,151	182,581
Hispanic	66,301	78,856	72,214
Other*	69,386	69,722	57,535
Women			
Officers	30,321	34,241	31,204
White	25,096	27,519	23,986
Black	3,728	4,602	4,349
Hispanic	546	753	988
Other*	951	1,367	1,881
Enlisted	179,049	108,700	163,317
White	114,421	136,219	79,204
Black	53,059	64,677	60,852
Hispanic	5,719	8,364	12,144
Other*	5,850	7,172	11,117

*Includes other races/ethnicities and those for whom racial/ethnic identification is unknown.

Source: U.S. Department of Defense, *Military manpower statistics,* 1997.

young people will look for better paying, more prestigious civilian jobs instead (U.S. Department of Commerce, Bureau of the Census, 1996).

Nevertheless, as Table 9.6 shows, today's military is more diverse than in the past. Women now make up about 13.7 percent of active-duty personnel. The proportion of military personnel who are racial and ethnic minorities has also increased. In fact, African Americans are overrepresented in the military: African Americans are 12.6 percent of the general population, but 18.4 percent of active-duty military personnel. The number of women of color, in particular, has grown most dramatically. These figures have some observers concerned that women and minorities, especially women of color, are entering the military in greater numbers not because they freely choose to, but because they are the most economically vulnerable segments of the population, with limited alternative opportunities open to them. The military may be especially appealing to members of these groups because it provides benefits they may have difficulty getting in the society at large, including a steady income, health insurance, education, and job training (Enloe, 1987; Wilkerson, 1991b).

With the growth in the proportion of women in the military, the jobs available to them have expanded somewhat as well. From the 1970s until 1994, the U.S. military utilized what was called the *risk rule* to determine the military jobs from which women would be barred. For the most part, these were ground combat and combat support jobs that entailed a substantial risk of being killed in action or captured as a prisoner of war. In 1993, then Secretary of Defense Les Aspin, on behalf of the Clinton administration, issued a directive ordering the armed services to permit women to fly aircraft in combat. In 1994, the Air Force and the Navy announced they had female pilots who were combat-ready. Also in 1994, the Army and Marine Corps opened some combat jobs to women, but continued to exclude them from direct combat, such as armor, infantry, and field artillery on the grounds that they lacked the physical strength needed for these jobs and their presence would disrupt morale (Schmitt, 1994a). However, despite several other exceptions—for example, women are prohibited from serving in units where the cost of renovations to accommodate them would be prohibitively expensive and in support jobs that operate and remain with direct ground combat troops—it is estimated that about 95 percent of military posts are now open to women. The exclusion of women from combat roles has historically had important consequences for female military personnel, since such positions command substantially higher salaries on average than support positions do. They are also critical for promotion to the highest military ranks; in fact, it has been argued that combat exclusion has been women's greatest impediment in achieving promotions (Enloe, 1987; Sciolino, 1990).

Many recent analysts have argued that the difference between many combat roles and combat support roles is more a matter of semantics than a reflection of the actual danger attached to the positions. For example, before women were permitted to fly combat aircraft, they regularly piloted the tanker aircraft that refuel fighters, making them targets for enemy fire (Lamar, 1988). Women also actively participated in the U.S. invasion of Panama and, for the first time, a female Army captain commanded U.S. soldiers in combat. One military official who reviewed the attack led by Capt. Linda Bray against Panamanian Defense Forces was quoted as saying that, "What has been demonstrated is the ability of women to lead, for men and women to work together as a team without distractions, and for women to react in an aggressive manner" (quoted in Gordon, 1990, p. A12). In 1990 and 1991, women accounted for more than 10 percent of the military troops deployed in the Persian Gulf crisis. Ironically, in this case, U.S. female military personnel risked their lives (five, in fact, were killed and two were taken prisoners of war) in defense of a country in which women are afforded few civil rights—where, in fact, they are still considered men's property. But it was women's involvement in the Gulf War that prompted Gen. Charles C. Krulak, Commandant of the Marine Corps, to order in 1995 that training of male and female marines be equalized, and to order in 1997 that female marines participate in the 17-day combat training program previously required only of male marines (Janofsky, 1997). Nevertheless, while the probability of women using this training increases with every military conflict that the United States enters, the *official* exclusion of women from direct ground combat remains in place.

Although many within the military and among the general public have praised the Defense Department's greater openness to women in recent years, other observers caution that simply permitting women to hold more military jobs does nothing to address the rampant sexism that continues to plague the military (see also Box 9.1 on page 302). One of the most serious manifestations of this problem is widespread sexual harassment of female military personnel. A survey of 47,000 women conducted by the Pentagon in 1996 found that 55 percent reported experiencing some form of sexual harassment, ranging from sexual assault to offensive remarks, during the previous year. Half of those reporting harassment said they were harassed by superior officers. Sixty percent of the women who were harassed did not file a formal complaint primarily because they felt nothing would be done, they would be blamed, or their superiors would retaliate against them. According to this report, most of the women believed that reporting the harassment would end their military careers (Egan, 1996).

The problem of sexual harassment in the military first got widespread media attention in 1991, when an official government investigation revealed widespread abuse of female naval officers by at least 175 male Navy pilots during their annual convention known as Tailhook (Gordon, 1993). More recently, in 1996, a military jury convicted an Army drill sergeant of raping six trainees, and he was sentenced to twenty-five years in prison and was dishonorably discharged. Eleven other staff members at the Army training center where these rapes occurred were also charged with sexual misconduct. However, the drill sergeant's conviction and the charges against the other staffers also raised concerns about racism, since all of the accused were African Americans and the majority of the accusers were White (Kilborn, 1997). Army investigators denied racist motives and widened their investigation of sexual harassment and abuse to all Army training facilities in the United States and abroad. The results of the investigation have not yet been released, but by April 1997, the Army had received over 1,200 sexual harassment complaints through calls to an emergency hotline it had established ("Sergeant Gets 25-Year Term," 1997).

In response to these recent sexual harassment scandals, a special panel appointed by Defense Secretary William Cohen recommended in 1997 that the Army, Navy, and Air Force segregate men's and women's core units of both basic and advanced training, although field and classroom training could remain coed (Myers, 1997). Interestingly, however, a second advisory committee, which inspected twelve military training schools and interviewed military personnel, found strong support for even greater sex integration than currently exists, since such conditions more accurately mirror the real-life conditions under which recruits eventually will work (Shenon, 1998). In March 1998, Defense Secretary Cohen announced that the armed forces training would not become sex segregated, but he also ordered increased supervision of recruits, especially in barracks, and an increase in the number of women serving as recruiters and drill sergeants. Cohen also called for the establishment of job incentives to attract better qualified individuals to the position of drill sergeant (Myers, 1998; see also, Johnson, 1998).

The impact of Cohen's orders remains to be seen, but the scandals themselves give us reason to seriously question the future role of women in the military. It has been argued that "the changing nature of warfare, which is based on technology rather than brute force, does not justify the exclusion of women" from any aspect of military duty

BOX 9.1

"Don't Ask, Don't Tell": Homosexuals in the U.S. Military

On February 5, 1994, the federal government implemented its new policy toward homosexuals in the military. The policy, known as "Don't Ask, Don't Tell," basically permits lesbians and gay men to serve in the military as long as they are not open about their sexual orientation and do not engage in homosexual acts. A homosexual act is defined broadly as human contact to satisfy sexual desires between members of the same sex as well as any bodily contact that a reasonable person would see as demonstrating a propensity toward homosexual behavior (such as holding hands with a person of the same sex). Under the new policy, men and women who join the military will no longer be asked if they are homosexuals, nor will they be discharged from the military if they admit to being homosexual. However, such an admission would be enough to allow military officials to begin investigating the individual to determine if he or she is engaging in homosexual acts.

Critics of the new policy say it is not significantly different from the old one (Directive No. 1332.14), which prohibited "persons who engaged in homosexual conduct," or who "demonstrate a propensity" to do so, from serving in the military. Under the old policy, military officials investigated individuals suspected of being homosexual, and suspects were often harassed, subjected to humiliating interrogations, and coerced into naming others in the military who might be homosexual. Such investigations resulted in about 1,400 women and men being discharged annually from military service without the benefit of judicial proceedings. Many of these women and men had outstanding service records and were decorated veterans (Cammermeyer, 1994; Shilts, 1993).

Supporters of the new policy maintain that it prevents the military from launching aggressive and arbitrary investigations to find homosexuals. Early evaluations of the new policy did show that the number of homosexuals discharged from the military declined in 1994: That year, 597 homosexuals were discharged compared with 682 in 1993 and 708 in 1992 (Schmitt, 1995). However, a more recent study showed that the number of service members discharged for homosexuality has actually increased since the new policy went into effect: 850 women and men were discharged in 1996, an 18 percent increase over 1995 and a 42 percent increase over 1994 (Shenon, 1997). Although the reasons for the increase are unclear at this point, homosexual service members report that many commanders do not fully understand the new policy or are intentionally misusing it. The new policy gives commanders greater discretion in handling reports of homosexual service personnel, and many commanders are homophobic. As a result, some commanders are still initiating aggressive investigations of individuals on the basis of unreliable information or accusations from coworkers. Some analysts also argue that the controversy generated over the policy itself caused a backlash against homosexuals in the military by focusing attention on them. (Schmitt, 1994b; Shenon, 1997).

The "Don't Ask, Don't Tell" policy survived its first legal challenge in 1996 when the U.S. Supreme Court refused to declare it unconstitutional. It remains to be seen, however, whether the policy will withstand future constitutional challenges if reports continue to show that it is raising rather than lowering the number of discharges for homosexuality.

(Rustad, 1982, p. 230), but in light of the widespread reports of sexual harassment of women in the military and given the onerous tasks that military personnel are often called on to perform, especially during wartime, some observers are wondering whether women's increased participation in the military is a positive development. Should we really want women to fully participate with men in all aspects of the military, including waging war? This question spotlights a feminist dilemma concerning women's and men's involvement in the military. As Rustad (1982, p. 5) phrased it, "Does the inclusion of women in martial roles mean greater opportunities or does it mean only that women will have the same rights as males to perform strenuous, dangerous, and obnoxious tasks?" There are those who maintain that if women want full equality with men, then they must accept the fact that that status entails obligations, including defending their country, as well as privileges. In fact, some people feel that this may be the only way for women to prove that they deserve equality. But opponents of these views emphasize feminism's goal is not to turn women into men, but rather to establish a new value system in which nurturing instead of aggression is rewarded for both women and men. As political scientist Cynthia Enloe (1993) argues, an increase in the number of women in the military should not be viewed as a feminist victory. Women in the military are pressured to fit in, to become "one of the boys," which in turn legitimates rather than changes the masculinization of the military.

Although it is unlikely that this debate will be settled soon, there are at least two important points that should be kept in mind. The first is that there are some women who wish to participate on an equal footing with men in the military, just as there are men who would welcome the combat exemption now afforded to women. Inasmuch as feminism encourages individuals to exercise control over their lives, one feminist approach to the dilemma is to lobby the government to allow both women and men the right to choose whether they will serve in the military as well as in what capacity they wish to serve.

At the same time, however, feminism does not mean adherence to total relativism. That is, feminists do not need to see every life choice as positive or beneficial simply because some individuals favor it. It is possible to oppose militarism, but also hold that while the military establishment remains a central institution in our society, those women and men who participate in it should have equal roles. While we work to change the masculinization of the military, to end mandatory registration for military service, and to prevent military solutions to international conflicts, we should not make a choice "between our daughters and our sons," a choice that "robs women as well as men. In the long and short run, it injures us all" (quoted in Rustad, 1982, p. 4).

The Politics of Gender

The purpose of this chapter was to examine the different political roles and attitudes of men and women primarily in the United States, but in other parts of the world too. We have seen that women have been neglected in most discussions of government and politics. Denied the right to vote until 1920 and denied equal protection of the laws until the 1970s, American women have long been excluded from the practice of politics on the grounds that they were too stupid, too frail, too emotional, and too irrational.

As we have seen in this chapter, this situation is finally beginning to change. Once it was documented that women are as interested and active in politics as men are and, more significantly, that they are more inclined than men to vote, political analysts and campaign strategists began to sit up and take notice of female constituents and candidates. Differences in the political opinions of men and women received more careful study, and a gender gap on certain issues—economics, social welfare, and foreign policy, in particular—was revealed. Currently, more women are running for and being elected to public office, and more are obtaining political appointments, than ever before. Along with White heterosexual women, women and men of color and lesbians and gay men are increasing their numbers in public officeholding and making themselves known as powerful political constituencies. Nevertheless, the percentage of women in general in government decision-making posts and in the military remains small. Even more underrepresented in government are women and men of color and lesbians and gay men. Indeed, it could take several centuries longer for parity among these groups to be achieved.

Historically, the exclusion of women as well as other oppressed groups from elected or appointed political and military leadership roles was justified on the ground of Divine will—that it was part of God's plan, in other words, and not "in the nature of things" for members of these groups to have authority over White, heterosexual men. Indeed, in the United States, despite the constitutionally established separation of church and state, sociologists have long recognized that religion and politics are highly interactive. In this chapter we have examined the role of government in perpetuating and often justifying inequality. In the next chapter, we will consider religion's role.

KEY TERMS

gender gap   differences in the voting patterns and political attitudes of women and men

gladiator activities   the highest level of political activism in Millbrath's typology; include working on a political campaign, taking an active role in a political party, or running for public office

incumbent   an individual who holds political office and seeks another term

political action committee (PACs)   special-interest groups that dedicate themselves to fundraising and distributing contributions to the political campaigns of candidates who support their cause

spectator activities   the lowest level of political activism in Millbrath's typology; include voting, wearing a campaign button, or displaying a political bumper sticker

transitional activities   the mid-range of political activism in Millbrath's typology; include writing to public officials, making campaign contributions, and attending rallies or political meetings

SUGGESTED READINGS

Moore, B. L. (1996). *To serve my country, to serve my race: The story of the only African American WACs stationed overseas during World War II*. New York: New York University Press.

Niven, D. (1998). *The missing majority: The recruitment of women as state legislative candidates*. Westport, CT: Greenwood.

Norton, M. B. (1996). *Founding mothers and fathers: Gendered power and the forming of American society*. New York: Vintage.

Rimmerman, C. A. (Ed.) (1996). *Gay rights, military wrongs: Political perspectives on lesbians and gays in the military*. New York: Garland.

Schroeder, P. (1998). *24 years of house work . . . and the place is still a mess: My life in politics.* Kansas City, MO: Andrews McMeel Publishing.

In addition, the Center for the American Woman and Politics (CAWP), National Information Bank on Women in Public Office (NIB), of the Eagleton Institute of Politics at Rutgers University (New Brunswick, NJ 08901), has available numerous fact sheets and other publications on gender-related issues in politics. The Center may be reached by phone at 908-828-2210, or on the World Wide Web at http://www.rci.rutgers.edu/~cawp

NOTES

1. It is important to note that much of the information available on women's political behavior and opinions dates only to the early 1950s. It was not until 1952 that polltakers began to analyze political opinion data by sex. To gauge women's political activities and opinions, historians and political scientists have relied on other data sources, such as the archives of women's organizations.

2. Women in other countries also report that the prejudice of party leaders, the majority of whom are men, is a significant obstacle for women seeking political office. Of the 418 political parties in eighty-six countries surveyed by the Inter-Parliamentary Union (1997), only 10.8 percent of party leaders were women and only one third of the positions in the parties' governing bodies were held by women.

3. As we will discuss shortly, a record number of minority candidates also won elections to the U.S. Senate and House in 1992. According to political analysts, a major factor in their success was a provision in the Voting Rights Act that required congressional redistricting in the states to more accurately reflect the racial composition of those districts. In 1993, however, the U.S. Supreme Court ruled in a 5–4 decision that such redistricting may be unconstitutional gerrymandering if in effect it denies White voters equal protection of the law (*Shaw* v. *Reno*). The ruling is expected to have an effect on redistricting nationwide and on the outcome of future elections (see, for example, Hicks, 1998).

4. In 1990, Emily's list had only 3,500 members, but membership nearly tripled in just two years. Emily's List supports pro-choice Democratic candidates.

5. In 1998, there were still seven states that had never elected a woman to the U.S. Congress: Alaska, Delaware, Iowa, Mississippi, New Hampshire, Vermont, and Wisconsin. The inclusion of New Hampshire in this list is surprising since it is among the ten states that have the highest percentage of female *state* legislators: 30.7 percent of New Hampshire's state legislators were women in 1998 (CAWP, 1998c; Goldberg, 1997). Worldwide, by 1997, only nine of the 173 countries with legislatures had no female representatives (Inter-Parliamentary Union, 1997).

6. In addition, two non-White women served as delegates to the House of Representatives: Donna Christian-Green (D-Virgin Islands) who is Caribbean American, and Eleanor Holmes Norton (D-District of Columbia), who is African American (CAWP, 1998c).

7. While presidential appointments usually generate political debate, several of President Clinton's nominations have drawn attention to gender-related and minority issues, in particular. For example, before nominating Janet Reno for Attorney General, Mr. Clinton nominated first Zoe Baird and then Judge Kimba M. Wood. Both women, however, eventually withdrew from the confirmation process when it was disclosed that they had hired illegal aliens as nannies for their children and had failed to pay Social Security and other taxes for these employees. The ensuing controversy focused attention, if only briefly, on the issue of wages for illegal immigrants, especially immigrant women, and on the child care problems of working women (Martin, 1993). Another controversial nomination was that of Lani Guinier as head of the Civil Rights Division of the U.S. Department of Justice. Guinier, an eminent Black female attorney whose nomination was supported by more than 400 law professors as well as the deans of twelve major law schools, was opposed by political conservatives because of her liberal position on affirmative action. President Clinton eventually withdrew her nomination and subsequently nominated a Black man for the position, but the incident served to reignite debates surrounding affirmative action as well as voting rights. Another Clinton appointee, Dr. Jocelyn Elders, an African American woman, was forced to resign as Surgeon General, largely because of her outspoken support of condom distribution in the nation's public high schools and her strong advocacy for better sex education in the schools. The controversy surrounding her resignation spotlighted concerns about adolescent pregnancy and questions about reproductive freedom for young people.

8. Mr. Reagan also appointed the most conservative member of the current Court, Justice Antonin Scalia. In his opinions since joining the Court in 1986,

Justice Scalia has shown himself to be vehemently opposed to abortion rights as well as affirmative action.

9. Although Norway permits women in all military jobs, Britain prohibits their participation in armored and infantry divisions, and the Netherlands and Canada do not permit women to serve on submarines. Canada, however, plans to install separate living quarters for women on submarines so that this restriction can be lifted. Each of these countries has far fewer women serving in its military than the United States does: 1.7 percent in the Netherlands, 2.4 percent in Norway, 3.4 percent in Denmark, 6.0 percent in Britain, and 10.9 percent in Canada, compared with 13.7 percent in the United States (U.S. Department of Defense, 1997; "Women in Combat," 1993).

There is no doubt that religion or religious teachings play an important part in most people's lives. Consider, for example, that in the United States alone, there are currently more than 1,300 different religious denominations, sects, and cults; 69 percent of the population are members of a church or synagogue, and about 96 percent profess beliefs in a personal God (Bedell, 1996; Princeton Religion Research Center, 1996; U.S. Department of Commerce, Bureau of the Census, 1997). Western religious beliefs differ significantly from those held by people in other parts of the world, but regardless of the specific content of religious teachings, religion appears to be a cultural universal. Every known society has some form of religion; archeologists have found what they think are religious artifacts dating back to the earliest cave-dwelling humans (Renzetti & Curran, 1998).

Why is religion so appealing? The answer lies in the fact that all religions, despite the tremendous variation among them, respond to particular human needs. First, virtually everyone seeks to understand the purpose of their existence as well as events in their lives and environments that seem unexplainable. Religion offers some answers to these puzzles, thus giving meaning to human existence and easing somewhat the psychological discomfort caused by life's uncertainties. Second, religion provides its followers with a sense of belonging, for it is not usually practiced alone, but rather, as the social theorist Emile Durkheim put it, in a "community of believers." And finally, religion lends order to social life by imposing on its adherents a set of behavioral standards. These include both prescriptions and proscriptions for how the faithful are to conduct themselves and relate to others. Importantly, however, religions typically establish different rules and often different rituals for men and women. These differences will be our main focus in this chapter.

Obviously, given the sheer number of religions, it's impossible for us to examine the gendered teachings of them all. Instead, we will limit our discussion to three of the major religious traditions in the world today: Judaism, Christianity, and Islam. Throughout our discussion, we will find that historically, despite women's often greater religious devotion, the major religious traditions have been overwhelmingly patriarchal, according men higher spiritual status and privileges and frequently legitimating the subordination of women, as well as various racial and ethnic groups and members of other religions. Although religion has contributed to the oppression of women and other minorities, religious principles have also inspired many to work for social change as well as spiritual liberation. Therefore, this chapter would not be complete without a look at the efforts of both religious feminists and nonfeminists to influence not only religious attitudes and practices, but also social policies and social structure. Let's begin with a general discussion of the relationship between gender and religion.

Gender and Religiosity

Sociologists use the term **religiosity** to describe an individual's or group's intensity of commitment to a religious belief system. We noted at the outset of this chapter that 69 percent of persons in the United States claim membership in a church or synagogue. However, church membership as well as one's level of commitment to a professed reli-

TABLE 10.1   Religious Identification by Sex, Race/Ethnicity, and Age, United States

| | Religious Identification (%) | | | |
	Protestant	Catholic	Jewish	Other
Sex*				
Men	56	27	2	1
Women	60	26	2	2
Race/Ethnicity				
White	58	27	2	2
Black	73	11	**	**
Hispanic	24	63	2	2
Age				
Under 30	45	32	1	2
30–49	57	26	2	1
50–64	64	26	2	1
65 & older	69	22	2	1

*These figures are for individuals who report church/synagogue affiliation. More women (73 percent) than men (64 percent) are affiliated.

**Less than 0.05 percent.

Source: Princeton Religion Research Center, 1996, pp. 41–42.

gion (i.e., one's religiosity) vary across social groups. Looking at Table 10.1, for example, we find that most people, regardless of sex or race, hold some religious identification. Additional research shows that among those who are unaffiliated with a specific religion, men outnumber women by a ratio of nearly 2:1 (Gallup & Castelli, 1989; U.S. Department of Commerce, Bureau of the Census, 1990). Race and ethnicity are also significant in terms of religious identification. As Table 10.1 shows, Black Protestants outnumber both White and Hispanic Protestants, whereas Hispanic Catholics outnumber both White and Black Catholics.

Religious identification is just one of the ways religiosity can be measured, and some sociologists believe it is not the best way, since simply identifying with a particular religion does not necessarily mean that a person *practices* the religion. Table 10.2 on page 310 shows differences between women and men on several other measures of religiosity commonly used by sociologists. Here we see that more women than men actually go to church or synagogue; that more women than men consider religion to be very important in their lives; and that considerably more women than men believe that religion can answer all or most of today's problems. Other studies show that women are more likely to pray and to read the Bible regularly (Miller & Hoffman, 1995). In short, women appear to be more religious than men. Moreover, additional research indicates that when race and ethnicity are also taken into account, women of color have especially high levels of religiosity. In some Black churches, for example, women make up from 70 to 90 percent of the congregations (Gallup & Castelli, 1989; Gilkes, 1985; Grant, 1986).

TABLE 10.2 Comparing Religiosity by Sex

Church Attendance

Question: Did you, yourself, happen to attend church or synagogue in the last seven days?

Women: 47% Yes
Men: 37% Yes

Importance of Religion

Question: How important would you say religion is in your life: very important, fairly important, or not very important?

Women 66% Very important
26% Fairly important
8% Not very important

Men 49% Very important
33% Fairly important
17% Not very important

Belief in an Afterlife

Question: Do you believe in heaven?

Women: 93%
Men: 86%

Belief in Religion as an Answer to Contemporary Problems

Question: Do you believe that religion can answer all or most of today's problems, or that religion is largely old-fashioned and out of date?

Women: 65% Can answer most of today's problems
17% Old-fashioned/out of date
18% No opinion/Other

Men: 56% Can answer most of today's problems
25% Old-fashioned/out of date
19% No opinion

Sources: Princeton Religion Research Center, 1996.

Several theories have been offered to explain sex differences in religiosity. One explanation, for instance, maintains that women are more submissive, passive, obedient, and nurturing than men, and these traits are related to high levels of religiosity. Proponents of this theory, however, disagree on at least two major points. One area of disagreement is whether these traits are "natural" or learned (see Chapter 3). A second area of dispute is the nature of the relationship between these personality traits and religiosity: Do these "feminine" traits precede a high level of religiosity and thus, perhaps, cause it, or does religiosity induce people to be more submissive, passive, obedient, and nurturing, regardless of sex? There is research that indicates that men who exhibit these characteristics are, like women, more religious than those who do not exhibit these characteristics, but this research still does not answer the temporal question of which comes first, the personality traits or the high level of religiosity (Thompson, 1991).

A second theory of sex differences in religiosity has focused on the division of labor, specifically women's primary responsibility for family well-being and child care. One version of this theory argues that religious activities such as church attendance are considered an extension of household responsibilities and, therefore, are more likely engaged in by women. A second version of this theory maintains that women simply have more time for religious activities. However, studies that have tested each version of this theory have obtained inconsistent findings (Cornwall, 1989). Clearly, more research is needed not only to clarify sex differences in religiosity, but also to pinpoint the source of these differences (see Miller & Hoffman, 1995).

Although women as a group show higher levels of religiosity than men, there is evidence that at least on some measures, such as church attendance, women's level of religiosity has been declining in recent years (McDonald, 1996). Some analysts believe that this decline reflects in part the growing number of women who say they are alienated from the mainstream religions because these religions are male-dominated and image God as male. One of our goals in this chapter is to evaluate this charge, and we begin in Box 10.1 on page 312 by considering various images of God. As the box shows, most people in Western religions image God as male. There is evidence, though, that in previous historical periods and in other cultures, images of God were feminine or androgynous. Let's briefly examine some of this evidence.

Goddesses and Witches

Astarte, Anat, Anahita, Asherah, Attoret, Attar, and Au are names few of us recognize today, but each name was intimately familiar to worshippers thousands of years ago. These are a few of the names in different languages and dialects for the Great Goddess, known also as the Queen of Heaven and the Divine Ancestress. Archeologists have discovered relics of worship to her among the cultural remains of peoples as disparate as the ancient Babylonians and pre-Christian Celts, at sites as distant as northern Iraq and southern France, and dating as far back as 25,000 B.C.E. (Carmody, 1989; Gadon, 1989; Stone, 1976). For example, at sites of what are thought to be "the earliest human-made dwellings on earth" belonging to the Aurignaican mammoth hunters (Upper Paleolithic period), archeologists have found stone, clay, and bone figurines of women they think were the idols of "a great mother cult" (Stone, 1976, p. 13). Similarly, among the ruins of later cultures, such as the Catal Huyak who, around 6000 B.C.E., inhabited part of what is now Turkey, excavators have recovered sculptures of women depicted in various life stages and forms, leading them to conclude that one of the principal deities was a goddess who was associated with creativity, fertility, death, and regeneration (Carmody, 1989; Stone, 1976). Of course, we must be cautious in interpreting archeological finds, since the artifacts themselves do not prove that there were widespread and flourishing goddess cultures. However, it is the case that representations of goddesses are

BOX 10.1

Imaging God

What does God look like? How you answer this question depends to a large extent on the dominant culture of your society. Most Western Christians and Jews image God as a White male. To envision God as Black or a female seems silly to some, heretical to others. Despite the fact that Jesus was a Middle Easterner and, therefore, probably dark-skinned with dark hair and eyes, he is typically depicted in the United States and other Western societies as White and often blond. Attempts to portray him otherwise are usually met with fierce opposition. In 1996, for example, when the director of a 600-year-old religious play to be staged in Canada announced that the part of God would be played by a woman, religious leaders denounced it as "paganism" (McDonald, 1996). So hostile are many White Christians to the idea of a Black Jesus that when, in 1997, a Catholic performing arts center in New Jersey announced that a Black man would portray Jesus in the annual Easter play, the center was flooded with complaints. Ironically, the same actor was also appearing as Lucifer in a play at a nearby theater, and he noted that no one had objected to a Black man playing the Devil (McQuiston, 1997). And in 1998, the play "Corpus Christi," which portrays a Christ-like gay hero, provoked so much hate mail that theaters installed metal detectors to screen for weapon-carrying ticket-holders (Brantley, 1998).

In many African American churches, we do find statues and portraits of God and Jesus as Black men. A number of denominations have also revised their prayer books and scripture readings to be more gender-inclusive, referring to God not only as Father, but also as "All-Holy Maker" and "She Who Dwells Within" (McDonald, 1996). Some women have also begun to pray to God personified as female, and they report a number of positive psychological effects, including a stronger sense of religious belonging and improved self-confidence (McDonald, 1996; Sausy, 1991; Steinfels, 1994). However, as the table shows, the number of people who image God as female remains small (Roof & Roof, 1984).

Gendered Images of God

Question: Which of the following images do you associate with God? (You may select more than one.)

Image	Percent Surveyed Who Image God This Way
Master	48.3
Father	46.8
Judge	36.5
Redeemer	36.2
Creator	29.5
Friend	26.6
King	20.6
Healer	8.3
Lover	7.3
Liberator	5.5
Mother	3.2
Spouse	2.6

Source: National Opinion Research Center, *General Social Survey,* 1989, pp. 156–159.

abundant in sites throughout the world, especially in some of the best preserved Old European caves (Carmody, 1989).

The goddesses we have described so far were associated with fertility and were typically invoked as mother. Researchers who have studied goddess-worshipping societies point out that this demonstrates the high value placed on motherhood in these societies. Even in societies that also worshipped male gods, researchers tell us, female gods were believed to wield as much and often more power than male gods, and were ascribed roles and traits, such as wisdom and courage, that only later were typed masculine. "Pre-Christian Celts, for example, worshipped Cerridwen as the Goddess of Intelligence and Knowledge. The Greek Demeter and the Egyptian Isis were lawgivers, wise dispensers of good counsel and justice. Egypt also celebrated Maat, the Goddess of Cosmic Order, while Mesopotamia's Ishtar was the Prophetess, the Lady of Vision and Directoress of the People" (Carmody, 1989, p. 20). In India, Ireland, and Sumer, goddesses were credited with the invention of the alphabet, language, and writing (Carmody, 1989).

Thus, evidence of goddess worship is abundant and convincing, but what is less clear is why and how male or father-centered religions came to displace it. To explain this change, some theorists draw on the factors that may have originally given rise to matriarchal religions. Matriarchal religions are thought to have emerged out of early humans' concern for survival as well as their desire to explain the generation of life and the phenomenon of death. Significantly, these early peoples did not understand the relationship between sexual intercourse and childbearing, and therefore assumed that women were the sole possessors of creative life forces. Women, then, were revered not only as producers of future generations, but also as the primal ancestor. What is more, since women alone were considered parents, children took the maternal name and traced descent along the mother's line. Although these theorists caution us not to romanticize or glorify this period as a golden matriarchal age, there is evidence that the status of women in these early human communities was high (Gimbutas, 1989; Stone, 1976).

Researchers speculate that as the male role in reproduction came to be better understood, the appeal of matriarchal religions diminished. Once it was certain that the reproductive process could not take place without the help of a man, the status of the father became significant. But as male generative power increased in value, women's status declined. Women came to be seen merely as the carriers and caretakers of future generations, whereas men provided the generative "seed," making them the true sources of life.

Another explanation of how patriarchal religions supplanted matriarchal ones begins with the observation that female-centered religions were just one of many religious orientations adhered to in ancient societies. Besides monotheistic matriarchal religions, there were polytheistic religions that worshipped male and female deities; other monotheistic religions that worshipped a male deity; and even religions that worshipped the "sacred androgyne," a deity that was simultaneously female and male (Carmody, 1989). It has been argued that the displacement of most of these religious traditions by one that favored the worship of a single male god may have been the result of ongoing political battles among various societies—for example, disputes over land or over who should rightfully rule, as well as military conquests aimed at empire building. The victors in these struggles would, in all likelihood, impose their own standards and traditions—including religious ones—on the vanquished (Christ, 1983; Gimbutas, 1989). Proponents of this theory believe that the goddess cultures were usually pacifistic, which could have made them especially vulnerable to aggression from other societies (Carmody, 1989; Gimbutas, 1989).

Regardless of whether both or neither of these theories is correct, it is perhaps more significant that attempts to eradicate worship of female gods have never been completely successful. Research indicates that throughout history, groups continued to pay homage to a variety of female deities and spirits, although they were frequently forced to practice their rites and rituals secretly because of violent persecutions by those of the dominant faith (Gimbutas, 1989). During early Christian times, for example, several groups claimed to be the disciples of Christ and wrote their own gospels of Christ's teachings. Among these were the gnostic Christian sects whose practices and beliefs were rich in female symbolism (Christ, 1983). Some gnostic groups described God as a divine Dyad: the Primal Father and the Mother of All Things. Others spoke of the Holy Spirit as Mother, or as Wisdom, the female element in God. Women in the gnostic sects also held positions of authority; they were preachers and prophets and even ordained priests (Pagels, 1979). However, other, more patriarchal sects, led by those who eventually established themselves as the Church Fathers, suppressed the gnostics and branded them heretics. Although researchers emphasize that the gnostics were not declared heretical simply because of the high status they accorded women, the practical effect of their suppression was the exclusion of much female symbolism and leadership from what became the recognized Christian Church (Christ, 1983).

Scholars have argued, too, that witchcraft was a carryover of the beliefs and traditions of the Great Goddess religions (Ginzburg, 1991). Although today most people associate witchcraft with evil spells and devil worship, the meaning of the word *witch*, "wise one," hints at the truer character of this practice. **Witchcraft** includes naturalistic practices that have religious significance, such as folk magic and medicine, as well as knowledge of farming, ceramics, metallurgy, and astrology. It was popular among plain, rural folk whose survival depended on good crops and healthy livestock. Because of women's long and close association with nature, fertility, and health, most witches were women. Their careful study of nature "enabled them to tame sheep and cattle, to breed wheat and corn from grasses and weeds, to forge ceramics from mud and metal from rock, and to track the movements of the moon, stars and sun" (Starhawk, 1979, p. 261). Appropriately, then, it was the witches who led the annual planting and harvesting celebrations. They also practiced folk magic and medicine, using herbs to cure the sick and relieve pain. Not surprisingly, many people sought their help and looked to them for comfort (Ehrenreich & English, 1973; Reis, 1998; Starhawk, 1979).

It appears that witchcraft peacefully coexisted with the established Christian churches for quite some time. Many people, it seems, elected to observe the traditions of both, and there is evidence that country priests were sometimes reprimanded by their superiors for participating in the seasonal "pagan" festivals (Starhawk, 1979). Nevertheless, witchcraft clearly posed a threat to Church authority. Carol Christ (1983) explains:

> The wise woman was summoned at the crises of the life cycle before the priest; she delivered the baby, while the priest was called later to perform the baptism. She was the first called upon to cure illness or treat the dying, while the priest was called in after other remedies had failed, to administer the last rites. Moreover, if the wise woman had knowledge of herbs which could aid or prevent conception or cause abortion, she had a power over the life process which clearly was superior to that of the priest, and which according to official theology made her a rival of God himself. If, moreover, she appealed

to pagan deities, some of them probably female, in the performance of divinations or blessings and spells used to promote healing and ward off evil, then it is not difficult to see why she was persecuted by an insecure misogynist Church which could not tolerate rival power, especially the power of women. (pp. 93–94)

Indeed, by the late fifteenth century, the Church had officially declared war on witches. The two Dominican theologians who were put in charge of routing out and prosecuting the witches, Heinrich Kramer and James Sprenger, actively promoted the notion of witchcraft as a Satanic cult. They maintained that women were more attracted to witchcraft because they were less intelligent, more impressionable, and more lascivious than men (Christ, 1983).[1] Tragically, in their zeal to rid the world of witches, Catholic and Protestant authorities tortured and killed between one half million and 9 million people during the fifteenth to eighteenth centuries, about 80 percent of whom were women (Barstow, 1992; Nelson, 1979; Reis, 1998; Starhawk, 1979).[2]

The worship of female deities survives today in some Native American religious rituals and in Aboriginal Australian and various African societies, although Western anthropologists have typically devalued these practices, labeling them "primitive" (Carmody, 1989). In addition, however, many feminists have revived or developed woman-centered spiritual traditions as part of their effort to make religion more responsive and relevant to female experience. Before we discuss feminist spirituality, however, let's examine the traditional teachings on gender espoused by the predominant patriarchal religions that we identified at the opening of this chapter.

Traditional Religious Teachings on Gender

In trying to summarize the gendered teachings of even three major religious traditions, we immediately confront a number of problems. For one thing, although many denominations and sects share a few basic tenets—for instance, all Christians believe Jesus was the Son of God—they tend to diverge considerably when it comes to more specific religious principles and practices, including those that concern appropriate roles for women and men. For instance, the Southern Baptist Convention, the largest Protestant denomination in the United States, takes a conservative stance regarding the proper role of women in religious and social life. In 1998, the Southern Baptist Convention amended its official statement of beliefs for the first time in thirty-five years to state that a wife should "submit graciously" to her husband, assuming her "God-given responsibility to respect her husband and to serve as his 'helper'" (quoted in "Southern Baptists," 1998, n.p.). In contrast, Quaker women have been called the "mothers of feminism," because of their social activism and the leadership roles they have historically held in their religious denomination (Bacon, 1986). Despite these clear differences, members of both groups are undeniably Christians. Similarly, the rules governing male and female behavior among Orthodox Jews are very different from those adhered to by Reform Jews, as we will see shortly.

We should also keep in mind that the beliefs, attitudes, and practices of individuals who claim membership in a particular religion often are quite diverse. Research, for example, shows that it is inaccurate to assume that all Catholics accept and respond to the official teachings of their church in the same way; Catholics, like those who identify with other religious traditions, are a heterogeneous group (Bohlen, 1995; Greeley, 1990; Princeton Religion Research Center, 1996; Steinfels, 1996).

Our brief discussion in this chapter, therefore, is intended merely as an overview of the general attitudes toward men and women expressed in the teachings of three very broad religious traditions. We cannot address all the fine distinctions among the many sects and denominations that identify with a particular tradition, but we will try to show within each some gradations in attitudes—conservative, moderate, and liberal—with respect to three main topics: (1) appropriate behavior and rituals for the male and female faithful; (2) the regulation of sexuality; and (3) the relative positions of men and women as church leaders or authorities.

Another problem arises, however, in interpreting scriptures and religious teachings. We will find that a single passage of sacred text may be translated or edited to legitimate gender oppression or to promote gender equality. As Virginia Sapiro (1986, p. 191) found, "The same Bible has proven to some people that women and men are equal and should take full leadership roles in religions and society, and it has proven to others that women are inferior, periodically unclean, dangerous, and subordinate to men." These contradictions are especially significant given that religious leaders cite scripture or other sacred texts as the source of their authority and as the foundation of church doctrine. Thus, in evaluating a particular religious teaching and the official rationale behind it, we must also consider alternative interpretations of the sacred writings on which church leaders claim it is based. These reinterpretations are often the products of feminist religious scholarship.

With these qualifiers in mind, then, let's examine the gendered teachings of Judaism, Christianity, and Islam.

Judaism

Jewish history spans more than 3,500 years. Throughout much of this period, Jewish women and men have been governed by a set of laws (*halakhah*) spelled out for them in the Talmud. The **Talmud,** thought to have been compiled around C.E. 200, records the oral interpretations of scripture by ancient rabbis and forms the crux of religious authority for traditional Judaism. However, in response to changing social conditions and political upheavals, such as diaspora and countless persecutions, Jewish leaders over the years have modified and reinterpreted Jewish law. In fact, as Paula Hyman (1979, p. 112) points out, "Much of the strength of the Jewish tradition has derived from its flexibility and responsiveness to the successive challenges of the environments in which it has been destined to live" (see also Adler, 1998).

Contemporary Judaism is largely congregational. That is, "public rituals [are] practiced in local synagogues whose congregations selected a mode of worship and expressed their preference for certain Jewish theological interpretations" (Pratt, 1980, pp. 207–208). There are three major types of congregations: Orthodox, Conservative, and Reform.[3] Orthodox Jews most strictly adhere to the traditional teachings of the Talmud, and we will begin our discussion with them. Then we will see how the teachings and practices of the Conservative and Reform congregations differ.

Orthodox men and women have separate and very clearly defined rights and obligations under Jewish law. Orthodoxy requires that men preserve and carry on Jewish tradition through communal worship and daily prayer at specified times, and especially through religious study. Traditionally, the scholarly and spiritual realms have been reserved for men. Women, in contrast, are exempt from these religious duties (*mitzvot*) on the ground that fulfilling them would interfere with their primary roles as wives, mothers, and homemakers. Women, then, control the domestic realm, where they tend to the needs of their husbands and children. It is essentially because of his wife's household labor that the Orthodox man is free to pursue religious study and to fulfill his other *mitzvot*. Women must also see to it that their children, especially their sons, receive sound religious training. Orthodox women have their own *mitzvot* to fulfill, including separating bread dough in preparation for the Sabbath, lighting the Sabbath and holiday candles, assuring that the dietary laws are followed, and observing the rules of modesty (*tznoit*) and female bodily cleanliness (Carmody, 1989; El-Or, 1993).

Significantly, most Orthodox Jews do not see this separation of roles as the relegation of women to an inherently unequal or inferior status. Rather, Orthodoxy maintains that in preserving the moral purity of their households, women engage in a form of religious expression comparable to that of men, and for this they are honored and respected both within the tradition and by their husbands and children (Kaufman, 1991). Nevertheless, critics have countered that women's exemptions in effect exclude them from public ritual—"the real heartland of Judaism"—and, therefore, from full participation in the religious community (Onishi, 1997; Umansky, 1985; Webber, 1983). Not surprisingly, women are not permitted to be ordained Orthodox rabbis. Besides their exemption from particular *mitzvot*, Orthodox women may not read the Torah during worship or in prayer groups. A woman may not lead a prayer service, and only men can be counted in a *minyan*, the quorum needed to hold a prayer service. Women are not permitted to sing in the Orthodox synagogue; "the ancient rabbis considered the female voice to be profane" (Pratt, 1980, p. 211). *Mehitzah* mandates a seating division between men and women in synagogues; Orthodox women are often seated in the back of the synagogue or in balconies, although this arrangement is considered an improvement over earlier practices whereby women were forced to sit behind a curtain, in a separate room, or even outside the building (Neuberger, 1983). In some Orthodox congregations today, women and men simply sit on opposite sides of the synagogue.

Non-Orthodox feminist Jews have been especially critical of the laws governing male-female relations within the Orthodox family. Both women and men are permitted to acquire and inherit property, but wives may not bequeath their property while they are married without their husbands' consent. Women may not formally initiate marriage, although once wed they are entitled to adequate support from their husbands (Webber, 1983). Perhaps the most disabling laws for women, however, are those regulating divorce and remarriage. Within Orthodoxy, divorce is unilateral: Only a husband may divorce his wife, not vice versa. A woman may institute divorce proceedings by charging her husband with "matrimonial offenses" before the religious court, which in turn can pressure the husband to grant his wife a *get* (a religious divorce). However, until the husband grants the *get*, the Orthodox woman is not free to remarry according to Jewish law, even if she has obtained a civil divorce.

Similar restrictions apply to the woman whose husband is "missing, presumed dead." According to Jewish law, an *agunah* (the "forsaken wife") cannot remarry unless a witness testifies to her husband's actual death. Under strict Jewish codes, such a witness must be a male Jew, but it has not been uncommon, especially during wartime and persecutions, for rabbis to bend the rules a bit by "accepting the testimony, for instance, of women, minors, slaves, and non-Jews in this matter" (Neuberger, 1983, pp. 136–137). Still, if the woman could not muster evidence of any sort, she remained married in the eyes of Orthodox authorities.

Despite these restrictions, however, Jewish law recognizes the rights of both women and men to sexual fulfillment in marriage. Religious scholars, in fact, often contrast what they consider to be a more positive attitude toward sexuality in Judaism with the more negative Christian view that we will discuss shortly. But others have argued that "it is precisely in this area that the second-class status of women within Judaism is highlighted," and they typically cite dress codes and the laws of family purity to illustrate this point. For example, regardless of the temperature, Orthodox women are expected to wear long skirts, stockings, sleeves below the elbow, and, if they are married, hats or head scarves. The laws of family purity include the rules of bodily cleanliness that we mentioned earlier, which revolve around a woman's menstrual cycle. For a two-week period each month, the Orthodox woman is considered impure. During this time, anything the *niddah* (menstruating woman) touches also becomes impure. Consequently, she must be physically segregated from men, and contact with her is permitted only after she has stopped menstruating for seven days and has been ritually purified in a *mikveh* (a special bath) (Webber, 1983).

Orthodox scholars and authorities justify the dress codes and purity laws on a number of grounds: For example, they promote modesty, they protect women's safety and health, they "spiritualize" sexual relations, and they help to "renew a marriage through a kind of monthly honeymoon" (Webber, 1983, p. 144). Less sympathetic observers have characterized them as the products of patriarchal religious leaders' fears and hatred of female sexuality. However, it may surprise you to learn that what appears to be repressive religious law to non-Orthodox and feminist observers is considered quite liberating in a sense by many Orthodox Jewish women. In her fascinating study of newly Orthodox Jewish women (or *ba'alot teshuvah*), for example, Kaufman (1991, p. 8) found that these women valued the family purity laws as well as other halakic prescriptions because such rituals "put them in touch with their own bodies, in control of their own sexuality, and in a position to value the so-called feminine virtues of nurturance, mutuality, family, and motherhood." Most of the women Kaufman interviewed were young and well educated with middle-class, non-Orthodox backgrounds. Prior to their conversion to Orthodoxy, some had been married, but all had experienced what might be called the downside of sexual freedom: frequent, casual, uncommitted sexual relationships with men. In Orthodoxy, they told Kaufman, they regained control over their sexuality, they felt an enhanced status as women and as mothers, and they considered the men in their lives more respectful, supportive, and committed to their relationships.

To some readers, the Orthodox women in Kaufman's (1991) study certainly sound like feminists. One of her most significant findings was that although the women said they rejected feminism as antifamily, the way they described their Orthodox lives had a great deal in common with many of the values espoused by radical feminists. Particularly interesting are Kaufman's analyses of sex-segregated living under Orthodoxy and of the *mikveh* as establishing a "women's community" and rituals that compose a "women's culture." While Kaufman makes clear that the women who participated in her study definitely were not radical feminists, her research highlights the importance of attempting to understand a group's behavior and experiences from the members' own perspective.

In contrast with the women in Kaufman's (1991) study, some Orthodox Jewish women, especially those who are well educated and have studied Torah, are less satisfied with various *halakic* proscriptions on women's religious participation and have tried to change them. Most of these women say that their reason for seeking change has nothing to do with gender equality or feminism, but rather with a personal need to enrich their religious experiences and thus deepen their spirituality. Among the recent changes are the presence of women lawyers in Orthodox religious courts and women officers on Orthodox synagogue boards. Some Orthodox women formed women-only *davening* (prayer) groups which, though not technically a *minyan*, bring women together to worship, to sing, and to read the Torah and the rabbinical commentaries in an effort to develop their own understanding of them. Such groups, however, have received strong negative reactions from many Orthodox rabbis and other members of the congregation. Although women's prayer groups are not in themselves a violation of Orthodox law, the public reading of Torah by the women is (Onishi, 1997). At times, women's attempts to pray as men do have been met by violence. In 1997, for example, when a group of Jewish women accompanied by Jewish men attempted to read a Torah scroll near the Western Wall in Jerusalem to commemorate the religious holiday *Shavuot*, they were pelted with rocks and bags of excrement, spat on, and physically attacked by angry Orthodox men (Kraft, 1997). Other women who have simply tried to pray at the Wall have also been physically attacked and have had chairs and benches thrown at them (Shapiro, 1997). Secular women in Jerusalem who are considered to be dressed immodestly by Orthodox men have had their car tires slashed, had rocks thrown at them, and been spat on ("Israel Orthodox Attack Skirts," 1996). As Kaufman (1991, p. 68) points out, "The inviolability of the Jewish code of law mitigates against the possibility of women challenging a legal system developed, defined, and continuously refined by males. Moreover, if women are not encouraged or given the opportunities to study the very texts . . . from which interpretations of those laws derive, there is no opportunity for them to challenge those laws in a manner the community will perceive as authentic or legitimate, or to develop female leadership" (see also Adler, 1998).

There are signs, though, that at least in the United States some Orthodox congregations are becoming more gender-inclusive. Two Orthodox synagogues in New York, for instance, recently hired women to assist the rabbis as paid interns, positions previously reserved for young men studying for the rabbinate. While the women perform some of the rabbis' duties, their roles remain fairly limited. Nevertheless, many Orthodox leaders have criticized the hiring of female interns and warn that opening more religious roles to women could eventually lead to a schism in Orthodox Judaism (Goodstein, 1998).

Reform Judaism stands in stark contrast to Orthodox Judaism. Reform Judaism was begun in the mid-1800s to make Judaism more "up-to-date." Reform Jews reject the authority of the Talmud and also the Judaic principle that God will send a Messiah to lead the Jews back to the promised land (Johnstone, 1988). They focus on the importance of developing a personal standard of ethics rather than following rabbinic laws. A hallmark of Reform Judaism is its emphasis on gender equality. As early as 1845, Reform Judaism recognized the need for equal and integrated roles for women and men and, by the turn of the century, it had made significant strides toward this goal (Neuberger, 1983). The *mehitzah* (seating division) was abolished; women were permitted to sing in synagogue choirs and to be counted in a *minyan;* girls were included in religious education programs and confirmed along with boys; and the prayerbook eliminated many of the blatantly sexist prayers, including men's daily thanksgiving that God had not made them women. The Reform Movement also established many social service and educational organizations in which women and men worked together. Women were even admitted to the rabbinical seminary, although when a woman first sought to become a Reform rabbi in 1922, authorities sternly rejected her (Briggs, 1987).

It was not until 1972 that Reform Judaism opened rabbinical ordination to women. Today, there are more than 100 women rabbis in the United States. Moreover, in 1990, Reform Judaism's Central Conference of American Rabbis voted to accept sexually active gay men and lesbians into the rabbinate (Goldman, 1990a), and in 1996, the Conference voted to endorse the legalization of gay and lesbian marriages ("Rabbi Group," 1996). Although the 1996 resolution states that rabbis would not be required to officiate at gay and lesbian weddings if they did not want to, observers note that an increasing number of Reform rabbis are willing to officiate at such ceremonies and recognize them as legitimate Jewish marriages.[4]

The third Jewish denomination, Conservative Judaism, was deliberately established as a middle-of-the-road alternative to Orthodoxy and Reform Judaism. Conservative Judaism originated in the United States in the 1880s, but gained members in the 1920s and 1930s as it appealed to European Jewish immigrants who had become "Americanized" and wished to "modernize" their worship (such as by praying in English), but did not want to abandon all their religious traditions (Cummings, 1986; Martin, 1978). It is understandable, then, that Conservative Judaism has moved more slowly than Reformism toward equality between the sexes.

Early on, Conservatism permitted women and men to sit together during worship, and women were encouraged to participate in the religious education of children and in the care and upkeep of the synagogue itself. Nevertheless, women were excluded from some of the most important parts of worship, including handling and reading the Torah (Pratt, 1980; Umansky, 1985). In 1973, these prohibitions were lifted and, by the mid-1980s, women were permitted in the Conservative rabbinate (Cummings, 1986; Umansky, 1985). An even more significant step was taken in 1990 when the leadership of the Cantors Assembly, the professional organization of 400 Conservative Jewish cantors, voted to admit women. Cantors chant liturgy on behalf of the congregation during religious services and so are considered to play a more central role in worship than rabbis, whose job it is to teach and preach (Goldman, 1990b).

Conservative Judaism, however, continues to prohibit the ordination of lesbians and gay men as rabbis. Conservative Jewish authorities welcome lesbians and gay men as individual members of Conservative congregations, but leave the decision of whether to hire homosexuals as teachers or youth leaders up to individual rabbis in each Conservative synagogue.

Within Conservative and Reform Judaism, as in other religious congregations, there are many believers who identify themselves as feminists and who attempt to integrate their feminist values into their religious practices. For example, Jewish feminists have rediscovered and begun to teach others about the Biblical heroines among the Israelites. These include Deborah, who was not only a ruler, judge, priestess, and prophetess, but also a military commander who led the Israelites to victory in a major battle against the Canaanites (Pogrebin, 1992). Jewish feminists are revising old rituals and developing new ones that emphasize the shared humanity and equal participation of women and men. For example, to mark Passover, women now hold Seders where they tell not only the story of Moses leading the Jews out of Egypt, but also the story of his sister Miriam, who saved his life by hiding him in the bullrushes. Some women have revived the ancient holiday of *Rosh Chodesh*, which celebrates the new moon each month (McDonald, 1996). Also important are rituals to solemnize significant stages in a girl's life just as those in boys' lives are solemnized: for example, celebrating a daughter's birth with a special blessing, giving gifts on the occasion of a girl's "redemption," and celebrating the transition from childhood to womanhood through *bat mitzvah* (Carmody, 1989; Pogrebin, 1992).

We will return to a discussion of feminist religious ritual at the conclusion of this chapter. Now, though, let's look at the gendered teachings of two other major religious traditions: Christianity and Islam.

Christianity

It is not uncommon for Christian church leaders and theologians to cite the teachings of St. Paul when delineating the proper roles of Christian women and men. In one frequently quoted passage, for example, Paul instructs the Christians of Ephesus:

> Let the wives be subject to their husbands as to the Lord; because a husband is head of the wife, just as Christ is head of the Church, being himself savior of the body. But just as the Church is subject to Christ, so also let wives be to their husbands in all things (Ephesians 5:22–24).

Elsewhere, Paul explains why women must cover their heads at religious gatherings, but men need not:

> A man indeed ought not to cover his head, because he is the image and glory of God. But woman is the glory of man. For man is not from woman, but woman from man. For man was not created for woman, but woman for man (I Corinthians, 11:7–9; the latter two lines appear to be references to the Genesis creation story).

The sexism in Paul's writings, although hotly debated, is perhaps less important than the fact that they have been repeatedly used by church fathers and Christian theologians to legitimate and even promote the subordination of women. Recall, for example, the amended statement of beliefs of the Southern Baptist Convention that we quoted earlier.

There is considerable evidence that the leadership of the early Christian movement was shared by men and women. Both served as missionaries spreading the "good news of salvation." Both sheltered the persecuted, studied and interpreted scriptures, and prophesied (Carmody, 1989; McNamara, 1998; Schussler Fiorenza, 1979). Within the first hundred years, however, an all-male hierarchical structure was firmly in place. Somewhere along the line, it seems, the example and teachings of their first leader, Jesus, were forgotten or ignored. Feminist Biblical scholars and theologians emphasize that there is no evidence that Jesus was in any way sexist. Instead, there is considerable evidence that he rejected the sexist norms of the society in which he lived by, for example, holding men and women to the same standard of morality and by not deriding women's nature or their abilities. It appears, in fact, that he related to women as he related to men: as individuals who needed his help, as colleagues, and as friends (Carmody, 1989; McNamara, 1996).

The rationale for the decision of male church authorities later to exclude women from leadership roles remains open to speculation. We have already discussed their efforts to suppress gnosticism, which could have been related to it. Soon we will examine some of the more recent arguments in favor of continuing this exclusion. What is clear at this point, however, is the effect of their choice: Women were relegated to a second-class citizenship within Christianity, a status that persists in many Christian denominations to this day.

Within the Christian tradition, both men and women have been characterized in contradictory ways. Men are supposed to be rational, authoritative, and in control, yet they are depicted as weak-willed when confronted with women's feminine charms. Indeed, women have often been portrayed as temptresses—"the devil's gateway" according to one church father—who cause men to sin much the same way Eve supposedly led Adam into the original sin in the Garden of Eden. At the same time, though, the virgin, pure of heart and body, has been extolled by Christianity, as has the good (i.e., docile, modest, and long-suffering) mother. Both are exemplified by Mary, the mother of Jesus, who is said to have been both virgin and mother simultaneously (McNamara, 1996).

Such images hint at the Christian church's traditional teachings on sexuality. Historically, sex was discussed as an activity to be avoided if possible, except for the purpose of procreation. Celibacy was regarded by many as a better way of life. For instance, "John Chrysostom, a very influential Eastern father, urged virginity because marriage was only for procreating, the world was already filled [he was writing about C.E. 382], and marriage therefore tended to function as a concession to sin" (Carmody, 1989, p. 171). Similarly, according to Augustine, a highly influential father of the Western church, sexual intercourse was the means by which original sin was transmitted across generations. The Protestant reformers, such as Luther and Calvin, were more temperate in their views of sex. While restricting sex to married couples, they recognized both husbands' and wives' needs for the "medicine for venereal desire," but they warned against "overindulgence" and reminded their followers that women could only attain salvation through childbearing (Carmody, 1989).

Today, Christian teachings on sexuality remain mixed. Virtually all sects and denominations continue to frown on nonmarital sex, although groups within various churches have recommended more open-minded discussion of sexuality. In 1992, for instance, a study group of the Evangelical Lutheran Church in America issued a report, "The Church and Human Sexuality: A Lutheran Perspective," in which the group urges the church to consider more carefully what it calls the "created goodness" of sexuality. The study group, not surprisingly, affirms marriage and committed love relationships; recommends that young people refrain from sex until they are ready to make a permanent commitment; and denounces adultery, promiscuity, pornography, sexual abuse, and media exploitation of sexuality. However, it also expresses the views that masturbation is healthy, that teenagers who are sexually active should use condoms, and that the church should consider affirming committed same-sex relationships by blessing them (Lewin, 1992b).

To some observers, the Lutheran study group's report is a signal that more positive attitudes toward sexuality are developing among the Christian leadership of at least some churches. Certainly, a report such as this is especially significant for homosexuals who have been openly condemned and often persecuted by Christianity. It is unlikely that the condemnation of homosexuals will soon disappear from the teachings of most Christian churches (Berliner, 1987; Heyward, 1987). In fact, despite the Lutheran Study Group's 1992 report, two Lutheran churches in San Francisco were expelled from the denomination in 1996 after hiring two gay clergy members as their pastors, an action that violates the denomination's rule against ordaining noncelibate homosexuals. Several Baptist churches have also been expelled from their regional religious organizations because they have welcomed homosexuals as church members without teaching that homosexual activity is sinful (Niebuhr, 1996a). The General Conference of the United Methodist Church, the second largest Protestant denomination in the United States, has voted to retain its official position that homosexuality is incompatible with Christian teaching (Niebuhr, 1996b). In fact, as we will discuss later in this chapter, some fundamentalist sects are calling for increased repression of homosexuals.

Nevertheless, recent actions within a few churches indicate that significant changes are in the making. In 1988, the United Church of Canada, that country's largest Protestant denomination, voted to admit homosexual men and women to its clergy, and in 1996, a court of the Episcopal Church ruled that gay men and lesbians could be ordained as both priests and bishops (Niebuhr, 1996c). There is also a greater willingness on the part of clergy in some Protestant denominations, including the Episcopal, United Methodist, and Lutheran Churches, to bless gay and lesbian couples in ceremonies of "holy union" (Niebuhr, 1998).

Even though a few Protestant churches appear open to reconsidering their official teachings on sexuality, the Catholic Church represents a denomination that has remained steadfastly resistant to change in this area. The Catholic Church, in fact, speaks as one of the most conservative denominations in this regard. It recently reiterated its strong disapproval of homosexuality, calling it a serious "disorder." Although the Catholic Church has said that parents of homosexuals should love their children, it has also argued that discrimination against homosexuals in the area of adoption, foster care placement, military service, and employment as teachers and coaches is not unjust, and it has directed its bishops to actively oppose any legislation that promotes public acceptance of homosexuality and homosexual relationships (Steinfels, 1992; Williams, 1987; however, see also Archdiocesan Gay/Lesbian Outreach, 1986).

In addition to its condemnation of homosexual relationships, the Catholic Church also continues to require celibacy on the part of clergy and nuns, and it prohibits the use of artificial contraception. Its opposition to abortion is well known, but the Vatican has also voiced objections to artificial insemination and *in vitro* fertilization, holding that it is "the right of every person to be conceived and to be born within marriage and from marriage" (The Congregation for the Doctrine of the Faith, 1987, p. 703). Medical intervention is acceptable only when it assists "the conjugal act," not when it replaces it (see, for example, Riding, 1992).

The Catholic Church has also stood firm in its opposition to the ordination of women to the priesthood, with the Pope saying that the issue is not even open to debate among the faithful (Cowell, 1994; Steinfels, 1995a). Church authorities argue that priests act in the name of Jesus and represent him physically; therefore, they must be men. They also point out that Jesus called twelve men to be his apostles, not twelve women, nor twelve men and women. Proponents of ordination to the priesthood counter with evidence that, in fact, many of the disciples of Jesus were women who held central leadership roles in the early Christian church. Junia, for example, is referred to in Romans 16:7 as apostle, and Phoebe was a missionary coworker with St. Paul (Hilkert, 1986; Schussler Fiorenza, 1983). In fact, a commission of biblical scholars appointed by the Pope more than two decades ago concluded that there is no scriptural prohibition of the ordination of women (Steinfels, 1995a). A 1995 *New York Times* poll found that 61 percent of U.S. Catholics favor the ordination of women to the priesthood (Steinfels, 1995a; see also Bohlen, 1995).

The issue of the ordination of women to the priesthood is without a doubt one of the most divisive issues in the Catholic Church today. Nevertheless, women's ministerial roles within the Catholic Church are increasing, largely as a result of a growing shortage of priests. From 1966 to 1993, for example, the number of men in Catholic seminaries declined 85 percent, and the number of graduate theology students in the final stages of ordination preparation declined by 59 percent. By 1994, more than 10 percent of the 20,000 Catholic parishes in the United States had no resident pastor, and many parishes, especially in rural and inner-city areas, had to rely on part-time or "circuit-rider" priests who pay periodic visits to administer the sacraments (Eckholm, 1994). Consequently, an increasing number of Catholic parishes are relying on women to lead them. By 1994, more than three hundred Catholic parishes in the United States without a resident priest were led by "pastoral administrators," 75 percent of whom are women, either laywomen or nuns, who perform all the duties of a pastor except administer the sacraments (Eckholm, 1994; Wallace 1992). Even in parishes with priests, much of the daily ministry, including counseling, preaching, and giving Communion, is done by laywomen and nuns. Still, the women in these positions report that their greatest source of job dissatisfaction stems from the stringent limits that are imposed on them by the church hierarchy, especially the church's prohibition against these women performing rituals performed by male clergy (Ebaugh, 1993; Eckholm, 1994; McNamara, 1996).

Historically, nuns were expected by church leaders to be silent and obedient help-mates of the bishops (McNamara, 1996; Weaver, 1995). At the same time, however, religious sisters played an active role in secular society, especially in Catholic schools and hospitals (Briggs, 1987; Ebaugh, 1993; McNamara, 1996). Since the mid-1960s, largely because of widening roles for laypeople within the church, but also as a result of a growing feminist consciousness, the number of women joining religious orders has dropped dramatically. Today, there are only slightly more than 100,000 nuns in the United States and their median age is 66 (Ebaugh, 1993). The women entering convents nowadays are, like the men entering seminaries, older on average than in previous decades. Many of these women have had professional careers and hold college and graduate degrees, and some are feminists who support the ordination of women and challenge the sexism of the church from within the organization itself—a point to which we will return momentarily (Ebaugh, 1993; Steinfels, 1995b; Wallace, 1992; Weaver, 1995).

Unlike the Catholic Church, virtually all the Protestant churches now ordain women to their ministries (Weaver, 1995). In 1989, the Episcopal Church consecrated its first female bishop, Barbara C. Harris, despite strong opposition from some Episcopal Church leaders, and in 1996, the World Methodist Council chose Frances Alguire as its first female and lay leader. The number of women priests and ministers has grown steadily since the early 1970s, and the number of women enrolled in seminaries and divinity schools rose from just 10.2 percent in 1972 to 31 percent in 1992 (Bedell, 1993).

Nevertheless, women ministers still confront sexism in their churches and denominations. They may experience discrimination in access to leadership positions, ministerial assignments and responsibilities, and salary, even if they have higher degrees and more seminary training than most male ministers (Briggs, 1987; Jacquet, 1988; Zoba & Lee, 1996). These gender disparities have led some observers to argue that women clergy encounter a "stained glass ceiling" within their churches. Although some women clergy are breaking through this ceiling (see, for example, Goldman, 1990c), most are finding that it is thicker, more opaque, and less permeable than the glass ceiling encountered by lay working women (Goldman, 1992; see Chapter 7).

The inequality that has historically characterized most Christian denominations leads one to wonder how church leaders can reconcile this discrimination with their professed concern for social justice. It has also caused many believers to question the relevance of organized Christianity to their own lives and to the contemporary world (McDonald, 1996; Welch, 1985). Consequently, some have abandoned the Christian faith altogether or at least have stopped practicing their religion in any formal sense (see, for example, Hout & Greeley, 1987). But, as we have noted, other church members have chosen to stay and work for change from within their religious institutions by challenging church teachings and "depatriarchalizing" religious language, symbols, and ritual. This latter group, of course, includes Christian feminists.

One of the most significant innovations of Christian feminism has been the establishment of the **Women-Church movement,** a coalition of feminist faith-sharing groups which, although ecumenical, is composed largely of Roman Catholic women. Women-Church offers a feminist critique of traditional Christianity while providing members with alternative, woman-centered rituals and forms of worship (Anderson & Hopkins, 1991; Farrell, 1992; Hunt, 1991; McPhillips, 1994). For example, there are liturgies for the celebration of a young woman's first menstrual period as well as other natural stages in a woman's life. And, like all religions, Women-Church practices rites of repentance and forgiveness, but Women-Church members pray that patriarchal church members will repent from the sins they commit against women (Ruether, 1988).

In addition to the woman-centered aspects of its rituals, Women-Church appeals to many Christian feminists because of its nonhierarchical organization and its emphasis on identifying with and serving all oppressed people in a "discipleship of equals" (Farrell, 1992; Hunt, 1991; McPhillips, 1994; Ruether, 1988; Schussler Fiorenza, 1983). Nevertheless, Women-Church has been criticized from within for being predominantly White and middle class and for failing to incorporate religious forms of worship valued by women of color (Erikson, 1992; Hunt, 1991). Women-Church has also disappointed some early supporters who feel that it has not had as great an effect on traditional religious traditions and hierarchy as they had hoped it would (Erikson, 1992).

We will come back to the topic of feminist spirituality shortly. First, let's examine the gendered teachings and practices of one other world religion, Islam.

Islam

Islam, which means submission to Allah (God), is the second largest religion in the world in terms of membership—Christianity is the largest—but it is the world's fastest-growing religion, adding 25 million new members each year (Marty & Appleby, 1992). Islam was founded by the prophet Muhammad. Muhammad was born in Mecca (now the capital of Saudi Arabia), but fled to Medina around C.E. 622. There he gathered followers and established himself as a powerful religious leader before returning to conquer Mecca in 630.

Muhammad is said to have received over the course of his lifetime a series of revelations from Allah, which he in turn passed on to his followers in the form of rules of behavior. These are compiled in the **Qur'an** (Koran), which Muslims accept literally as the word of God. Muhammad's teachings and those of his immediate successors are recorded in the *Hadith*, which along with the Qur'an, serves as the basis for *shari a* (Islamic law). Taken together, these three sources constitute a religious framework that governs every aspect of Muslims' daily lives, including interactions between women and men. Indeed, 80 percent of the Qur'an is devoted to prescriptive and proscriptive verses concerning proper relations between the sexes (Engineer, 1992; Haddad, 1985).

It is clear that Islam radically altered male-female relations, although whether for better or for worse is a point still disputed by religious scholars. It appears that in the days of Muhammad, a variety of sociosexual arrangements coexisted. Some groups were decidedly patriarchal, valuing males above females (female infanticide was common) and allowing men as many wives as they could buy or steal regardless of the women's consent or the men's ability to support them (Carmody, 1989). Within other groups, however, women enjoyed considerable independence and practiced polyandry (had more than one husband). By the seventh century, there was movement away from gender equality among even some of these groups, particularly the ones in Mecca, as commercial expansion provided increasing contacts with northern societies whose religions (Judaism and Christianity) were already strongly patriarchal. Islam, some scholars maintain, consolidated this trend toward patriarchy, although Muhammad did not totally divest women of their rights (Ahmed, 1986; Engineer, 1992; Hekmat, 1997).

Muhammad declared that a woman's consent had to be obtained before a marriage and that she be paid the brideprice instead of her father. He also recognized women's conjugal rights, their rights to ownership of their jewelry and earnings, their right to initiate divorce, and their right to inheritance (although their share was half that of male heirs). Women, like men, were expected to adhere to the Five Pillars of Islam, which include prayer five times a day and fasting during the holy month called *Ramadan*, and they worshipped with men in the mosques (Engineer, 1992; Hekmat, 1997).

Muhammad permitted men to have more than one wife, imposing a generous limit of four as long as they could be supported. He opposed female infanticide, but gave men unconditional custody rights to their children (boys at age two, girls at age seven). Moreover, despite the Qur'an's verses on the centrality of justice and the equal worth of all human beings, it declares men to be women's "guardians" and "a degree above" them (Ahmed, 1986, pp. 678–679). A wife's duties include obedience to her husband (Higgens, 1985). According to the Qur'an, "Men are in charge of women because God has made one to excel over the other and because they spend their wealth" [referring to men's financial support of women] (quoted in Haddad, 1985, p. 294). Unfortunately, Muhammad's successors took these words to heart and used them to justify the suspension of many rights the prophet had allowed women, so that "by the second and third centuries of Islam, 'the seclusion and degradation of women had progressed beyond anything known in the first decades of Islam'" (Ahmed, 1986, p. 690; see also Hekmat, 1997).

Today, many Islamic leaders maintain that men and women hold equal status, although they are quick to emphasize that this equality does not derive from sharing the same privileges and responsibilities, but rather from the *complementarity* of their roles. "In this world view men and women are equal before God, but they have somewhat different physical, mental, and emotional qualities, somewhat different responsibilities in the family and society, and therefore somewhat different rights and prerogatives" (Higgens, 1985, p. 491).

In Islamic societies today, men are the undisputed heads of both the sacred and secular realms, including the household. Theirs is the public sphere, where they conduct religious and worldly affairs and assume a variety of roles with few restrictions. In orthodox Islamic societies, women are largely confined to the private sphere, the home, but even there they are not in charge. Their duties are to serve their husbands, to keep house, to bear many children, and to instruct the children in the ways of Islam. "Not only is [the Muslim woman] created to be pregnant [she is an "envelope for conception" according to one Islamic leader], but more specifically all her roles are defined by her relations to the men in her life" (Haddad, 1985, p. 286). Prior to marriage, the Muslim woman is under the control of her father, brothers, and other male relatives. Her marriage is arranged for her, usually by these men, and she may be married while in her early teens to a man she has never met or has met only briefly in the presence of her male relatives, since Islamic law forbids any public contact between unmarried women and men (Kinzer, 1997).

Islamic law imposes a number of restrictions on men's behavior—for example, they may not drink alcohol or gamble, and they must dress modestly—but men are given considerably more freedom than women are. Because women are thought to possess an innate capacity for sexual allurement, extraordinary measures (by Western standards at least) are taken to prevent them from tempting men. The most obvious examples are *purdah* and the *chador*. Purdah refers to the practice in traditional Islamic societies of severely restricting women's access to public life by secluding them in their homes and permitting them to venture out only in cases of emergency or out of necessity.[5] In some Islamic societies, such as Saudi Arabia, women are prohibited from traveling alone and must be accompanied by their fathers, brothers, or a close male relative, unless they have written permission from one of these individuals that states they may travel alone (Ahmed, 1992; Goodwin, 1994; Hekmat, 1997). Iranian women may not ride a bicycle, jog, or swim, except in officially sanctioned, sex-segregated places (Sciolino, 1997). When a Muslim woman appears in public, she must dress modestly, that is, veiled and clothed in a loose-fitting garment (the *chador*) that covers her from head to toe. Originally, such restrictions were imposed only on Muhammad's wives, but after his death they were extended to all Muslim women, a practice that continues in most Islamic societies today (Ahmed, 1986; Haddad, 1985; Sciolino, 1997). Official penalties for violating the dress code can be very serious. In Iran, for instance, a woman who did not cover her head and body properly was traditionally subjected to as many as seventy-four lashes; today, she faces a jail term of ten days to two months (Sciolino, 1997).[6]

Of course, in all but the most traditional Islamic societies today, there are many women who go to school or work outside the home. Nevertheless, every effort is made to insure that they do not mingle with the opposite sex—that they are, in effect, invisible to men. There are female physicians, for instance, but they treat only female patients, just as female teachers instruct only female students. If a male teacher must instruct female students, he does so from behind a screen where he stations himself before the women enter the classroom (Darrow, 1985; Higgins, 1985; Sciolino, 1997). In Saudi Arabia, all banks have women's branches where only female tellers and lending officers work and attend to an all-female clientele (Goodwin, 1994). Women are also excluded from the mosques and from most religious rituals, although most women make regular visits to the sanctuaries of Islamic saints where men, though permitted, rarely go (Goodwin, 1994; Mernissi, 1977).

The level of orthodoxy practiced by Muslims does vary by country as well as by sect. Lebanon and Malaysia, for instance, are considerably more liberal than Saudi Arabia and Iran, which are themselves more liberal than Afghanistan and Algeria. And Islamic countries have not be left untouched by feminism, although it is a feminism developed in the context of deeply valued religious beliefs and does not mirror Western feminism (Crossette, 1996; Fernea, 1998; Mydans, 1996; Sciolino, 1997). Small groups of Muslim women have begun to organize and develop strategies on how to obtain more rights and freedom, including more job opportunities, the right to study the Qur'an at the mosque, and especially greater equality under family law (Ahmed, 1992; Miller, 1992). In most Islamic societies, for example, women may be beaten by their husbands without legal recourse. "Honor killings" still occur in some Islamic societies, where male relatives stone or stab to death a woman who has dishonored her family by, for instance, committing adultery, engaging in premarital sex, or simply just socializing with a man in public. Muslim women usually do not have the right to initiate divorce, although their husbands may divorce them simply by repudiating them, and fathers typi-cally receive sole custody of their children after a divorce (Hekmat, 1997; Mydans, 1996; Sciolino, 1997).

Despite efforts by Islamic feminists to improve women's status and opportuni-ties, the revolutions that have occurred in recent years in several Islamic countries have meant for many a return to orthodox practices after an interlude of modernization. Interestingly, while some women and men, especially the young and well-educated, have expressed their displeasure over this renewed orthodoxy, there has not been wide-spread resistance among the majority of the countries' populations. Many women, in fact, have donned the veil and *chador* with a willingness that puzzles many Western observers. Ironically, however, it appears that they are motivated by many of the same factors that prompted the women in Kaufman's (1991) study that we discussed earlier to convert to Orthodox Judaism. More specifically, many Muslim women explain their openness to orthodoxy in terms of institutional protection. A veiled woman is recog-nized by all as religiously devout and off limits to men. She may go about her business without fear of being molested or harassed; she feels safe (Ahmed, 1992; Crossette, 1998; El-Or, 1993; Miller, 1992).

It is also the case that for some women, donning the veil and *chador* is a political statement, an expression not just of religious devotion, but of militancy, rebellion, and protest against oppressive political regimes, secularism, and Western imperialism in their countries (Afshar, 1993; Ahmed, 1992; Darrow, 1985; Kinzer, 1998). To these women, the enemy is not male oppression, but rather outside forces that threaten to destroy the Islamic way of life. Through their devotion to Islam, as evidenced by their adherence to its laws and customs, some Muslim women see themselves on the front lines of the revolution (Haddad, 1985; however, see also Gole, 1996).

In some ways, then, the conservative politicization of Islamic women gives them more in common with Orthodox Jewish women and conservative American Christian women than would at first be thought (Gerami, 1996). Each of these groups embraces religious **fundamentalism,** a religious orientation that denounces secular modernity and attempts to restore traditional spirituality through selective retrieval of doctrines, beliefs, and practices from a sacred past (Marty, 1992). These groups have a particular vision of how their society should be structured and women's distinct place within that structure—a vision shaped by their religious beliefs. Jewish, Christian, and Islamic fun-damentalists integrate their religious beliefs into political activity in an effort to make their vision a reality. Let's consider this issue further by discussing the political activism of two religious movements in the United States: Christian fundamentalists, who are often referred to as the religious New Right, and the liberation theology of minority churches.

Religion, Politics, and Social Change

As we noted at the conclusion of Chapter 9, theoretically at least, the church and the gov-ernment in the United States are supposed to constitute separate spheres of influence. Yet, sociologists have long recognized that the ideology of the separation of church and state is largely a myth. In practice, the affairs of the state and the interests of organized religion are closely and intricately intertwined. Historians tell us, for example, that Christian fundamentalists or "evangelicals" as they are sometimes called, were active in the American Revolution, the abolitionist movement, the campaign for prison reform in the late 1700s, and a number of other political causes and social reforms (Pohli, 1983).

Today, evangelicals remain politically active, constituting what many refer to as the religious "New Right." It is estimated that the religious New Right has more than 40 million members, which, although small relative to the total U.S. population, is still a sizable number. More importantly, this group has taken a strong public stand on what it calls "family issues," such as women's rights, including abortion and reproductive freedom; sex education; and especially homosexual rights. Let's take a brief look, then, at this religious/political movement and its activism around these issues, which have been at the top of the feminist agenda as well.

Christian Fundamentalism and the Politics of Gender and Sexual Orientation

Fundamentalist Christians interpret the Bible literally, taking it to be truly God's word. The Bible, to fundamentalists, not only teaches religious doctrine and moral principles, but also renders an accurate account of history and science (Ammerman, 1991). A true believer unquestioningly accepts what is written in the Bible as Truth (Marty & Appleby, 1992). At the same time, fundamentalist Christians believe that a person can only attain eternal salvation by living in accordance with the teachings of the Bible and thus developing a personal relationship with Jesus Christ. They also believe that it is their responsibility to "save" or "rescue" others by evangelizing—that is, zealously preaching God's word—through books, television and radio broadcasts, door-to-door canvassing, and even political lobbying (Ammerman, 1991). Fundamentalist church leaders exhort their congregations to be "soldiers of Christ" by combatting the erosion of Christian values in the secular world. At the core of this erosion are feminism, the homosexual rights movement, and other liberal political and social movements (Klatch, 1988).

Not surprisingly, therefore, the fundamentalist Christian churches, along with other conservative Christian groups such as the predominantly Catholic Right to Life Movement, have been at the forefront of political opposition to feminist-supported policies and programs. For instance, they lobbied aggressively and successfully against the Equal Rights Amendment, and they spearheaded campaigns to remove feminist and other types of "objectionable" books and materials from school libraries and classrooms. Since 1973, they have lobbied Congress for a Human Life Amendment that would overturn *Roe* v. *Wade*, once again outlawing abortion. Groups such as Operation Rescue, led by Free Methodist minister Rev. Philip Benham, have picketed abortion clinics, harassed patients and abortion providers, and sometimes used violence to stop abortions (see Chapter 6). A primary target of the religious New Right is gay men and lesbians. In 1997, for example, the Southern Baptist Convention launched a boycott against the Walt Disney Company because of the entertainment corporation's "anti-family, pro-gay" policies and programming ("Baptists Boycott 'Pro-Gay' Disney,"

1997).[7] The Christian Coalition, founded by televangelist Pat Robertson, led congressional lobbying efforts for passage of the Defense of Marriage Act (see Chapter 6), and recently joined with fourteen other conservative groups to fund "The Truth in Love Campaign," a national advertising campaign depicting "former" homosexuals who experienced a deep religious transformation and "converted" to heterosexuality (Miller, 1998). And some fundamentalist groups have undertaken a "ministry of public pickets" to spread the message that "God hates fags" (Carelli, 1997; see also Rich, 1998).

What accounts for the religious New Right's open hostility toward feminism and gay and lesbian rights? Members of the religious New Right believe that feminists, gays and lesbians, and other "political liberals" undermine the Christian family by promoting lifestyles and values inimical to "God's plan" for men and women. More specifically, they define marriage as a sacred union that can only be entered by a man and a woman. They adhere strongly to the belief that a man's role is to provide for and protect his family. For example, one fundamentalist Christian men's group, the Promise Keepers, holds two-day rallies in sports stadiums and arenas, where speakers preach, pray, and lead hymns to encourage men to be more spiritual family providers. In contrast, God's plan for women puts them at home caring for their husbands and children, and just as men are subordinate to God, so are women subordinate to men (Klatch, 1988; "Southern Baptists," 1998).

The religious New Right has shown itself to be well organized and persuasive. Although sexual and financial scandals involving church leaders damaged the movement's credibility among some of its followers during the 1980s, the religious New Right enjoyed a resurgence during the 1990s. Some observers credit fundamentalists' masterful use of media and communication technology for this upswing in popularity. Computer-generated mailings, television and radio broadcasts, and use of the Internet and World Wide Web have helped New Right leaders not only promote their political agenda, but also raise money. Enrollments in fundamentalist Christian schools, which now number over 10,000, have also increased, and fundamentalist Christian political candidates have won about 40 percent of the elections they have entered (Ammerman, 1991; Marty & Appleby, 1992; Mydans, 1992). Although some analysts believe that the religious New Right's strength and popularity are overstated, most feminists and homosexual rights activists are responding to the fundamentalist Christian movement as a powerful political foe.

Still, while religion as represented by the New Right seeks to turn back the clock or at least preserve the status quo, religion can also inspire resistance to oppression and promote liberating social change. Let's briefly consider religion in this context.

Minority Churches: Resistance and Liberation

The religious New Right opposes liberal social change and social equality, but for racial and ethnic minorities, the church has historically been a source of inspiration and strength in their struggles to overcome discrimination and to secure equal rights and opportunities. The Black churches, for example, have produced many prominent and influential political leaders and social activists, such as the late Rev. Martin Luther King, Jr., and the Rev. Leon Sullivan. A number of Black politicians were first ministers in Black churches: the Rev. Jesse Jackson, for instance, and former Congressman William Gray of Pennsylvania. The Black churches, in particular, have provided an organizational center within the Black community where members can develop programs of action to overcome racial oppression; the Rev. King's strategy of nonviolent civil disobedience and direct action is an example (Lincoln & Mamiya, 1990).

Even before the Rev. King's leadership, however, minority churches were centers of social and political activism for women of color. As we noted earlier, for example, women have been the majority of members of many Black churches (Gilkes, 1985; Grant, 1986). As historian Evelyn Brooks Higginbotham (1993) has documented, African American churchwomen's activities have long been a means by which they nurtured the survival of their communities, articulated a group consciousness, and organized resistance to oppression. Hunt (1991, p. 32) refers to their "holy boldness" as religious agents in their community churches, and Natividad (1992) even attributes the contemporary predominance of African American women in politics relative to other women of color to their long-term experiences as community and church leaders (see also Prestage, 1991).

Despite their membership numbers, their level of church participation, and their strong support of their churches, Black women have encountered sexism and considerable resistance from Black male church leaders to their assuming leadership roles within the church. "Most often this takes the form of barring women from a formally defined ministerial office even when they may already be performing its functions. Hence, in some Afro-American Pentecostal Churches, the male ministers hold the title 'preacher' but women ministers are called 'teacher' although their tasks may be identical" (Briggs, 1987, p. 411; Grant, 1986; Lincoln & Mamiya, 1990). Fewer than 5 percent of Black churches have female pastors. Black women who do become pastors are usually charged with leading small or dwindling congregations, rather than large, thriving ones. Surprisingly, the Black female clergy who have risen highest in the religious ranks have been in predominantly White denominations or in churches established by women (Funk, 1996).

Among Black female clergy, there appears to be some optimism that this situation will improve over the next several decades. For one thing, more Black women say they are called to careers in ministry. The number of Black women in seminaries nearly doubled during the first half of the 1990s. Still, just 8.8 percent of students enrolled in theological schools are Black, and 25 percent of these Black students are women. Almost half of the Black female students are enrolled in only two-year programs. The numbers are similar for other people of color. Hispanic Americans are just 2.6 percent of theology students and Asian Americans 4.9 percent (Bedell, 1993; Briggs, 1987; Funk, 1996).

It appears, then, that while minority churches have served as catalysts for social action against racial oppression, this has not typically extended to the problem of gender inequality within society or within the churches themselves (Grant, 1986). This disparity has not lessened the bond women of color feel with their churches nor their community activism through their churches. In fact, minority churchwomen themselves have been reluctant to identify their activities and concerns as feminist, since they generally see feminism as a White, middle-class women's movement (Briggs, 1987; see also Chapter 1). Nevertheless, feminist theologians of color have joined with White feminist theologians in critiquing the sexism of the dominant religious traditions and in working to depatriarchalize these religions. To conclude our discussion, then, let's look at some of their efforts.

Challenges to Religious Patriarchy: Feminist Spirituality

It is really inaccurate to speak of **feminist spirituality** in the singular or to depict it as a unified religious movement, for within it one hears a plurality of voices professing different beliefs and advocating different strategies for change and reconstruction. Yet there are some common themes that feminist spiritualists share. Perhaps the most important theme that runs throughout feminist spirituality is the rejection of the *dualism* of patriarchal religions. That is, the major patriarchal religious traditions separate God and the world, the sacred and the profane, spirit and body (or nature), viewing them as distinct and placing human beings in tension between them. According to feminists, "This [dualistic model] is a model for domination, because [it divides reality] into two levels, one superior and one inferior" (Christ & Plaskow, 1979, p. 5; Erikson, 1993). In contrast, feminists emphasize the unity of spirit and nature and see *experience* as the source of spirituality. Experience includes the events of the life cycle (e.g., menarche, coupling or marriage, parenthood, menopause, and so on) as well as developing an awareness of one's location in the social structure: recognizing oppression, confronting it, and acting to bring about liberation (Anderson & Hopkins, 1991; McPhillips, 1994; Ruether, 1988). One of the goals of feminist spirituality is to *resacralize* (define as sacred) the ordinary, what has been defined as profane by patriarchal religious traditions (McPhillips, 1994). It is over the issue of how to implement this principle, however, that feminist spiritualists part company with one another.

There are those who feel that the Judeo-Christian traditions and other patriarchal religions are so hopelessly mired in sexism that they have abandoned these religions altogether. Instead, some feminists have turned to nature (see Box 10.2 on page 334), others are reviving the practice of witchcraft, and still others are rediscovering the ancient prebiblical goddess traditions. In fact, these ancient spiritual traditions are becoming so popular that the travel industry has begun offering pilgrimages to the shrines of ancient goddesses, and *Publisher's Weekly*, which monitors the publishing industry, reports that books on women's spirituality make up one of the fastest-growing segments of the market (McDonald, 1996).

While some feminist spiritualists advocate a complete break with men and all that is male-identified (e.g., Daly, 1978; 1984), many welcome both women and men into their traditions on the ground that patriarchal religions may oppress members of both sexes through heterosexism, racism, and class bias, for example. From this perspective, women's experiences may provide the foundation for a feminist spirituality; however, simply substituting female religious supremacy for male religious supremacy offers little potential for liberation for members of either sex (Anderson & Hopkins, 1991; Erikson, 1992).

BOX 10.2
Ecofeminism

Ecofeminism emerged during the 1970s as a branch of feminism that celebrates what its adherents see as innate personality traits of women—caring, nurturance, gentleness—and women's close association with nature. As Irene Diamond (1992, p. 371) explains, it is "an ethic and politics which sees a connection between the domination of women and the domination of nature" (see also Mies & Shiva, 1993). Ecofeminism is an earth-based spirituality movement that draws heavily on goddess imagery and ritual, which is not surprising given that, as we learned earlier, goddess worship celebrated many aspects of female biology, but especially women's sexuality and reproductive capacities. There is an emphasis on healing, ecological balance, an equality of all living beings (human and nonhuman), and regeneration (Griffin, 1995).

Ecofeminism combines its spiritual emphases with direct political action to bring about a more harmonious, ecologically balanced society. Because of women's biology—as reproducers and nurturers—they are seen as closer to the earth. Similarly, because women have been exploited and denigrated, they more fully understand the exploitation and denigration of the biosphere, as well as the exploitation and denigration of people in economically undeveloped societies because of Western imperialism and Western economic development models (Mies & Shiva, 1993). Consequently, it is women who are best suited to lead the ecology movement and to develop a nonhierarchical society based on respect for all living things. To be effective leaders, however, women must get back in touch with their bodies and discover the full power of their natural femaleness. Hence, the return to goddess spirituality.

It is hardly surprising that ecofeminism is a controversial movement, even among feminists.

While it has been praised for highlighting the dangers of environmental exploitation, it has been criticized for biologizing traditional Western femininity and glorifying the notion of a universal female nature. A number of feminist theorists see a serious danger in ecofeminists' emphasis on women's biologically based differences from men. As one feminist critic (Biehl, 1990, pp. 9, 11) explains:

> When sociobiological justifications of androcentrism build reproductive differences into elaborate theories of "female nature," feminists have traditionally shown that they unjustly shore up sexist institutions and ideologies. . . . When ecofeminists root women's personality traits in reproductive and sexual biology, they tend to give acceptance to those male-created images that define women as primarily biological beings. . . . Indeed, ecofeminism's healthy impulse to claim women's biology has in many cases become an acceptance of the same constricting stereotypes of "women's nature" that have long been used to oppress them.

Despite these objections to ecofeminism—and they are by no means insignificant—most feminists agree that this movement makes important contributions to both feminist spirituality and the political liberation of the oppressed. First, it provides women with another option for religious expression, one that accords them dignity and a special revered status. At the same time, and perhaps more importantly, it extends this dignity and status to the oppressed in developing countries. Consequently, it has succeeded in forging ties between Western feminists and people in developing societies—something mainstream feminism has long failed to do (see Chapter 1).

As we have noted throughout this chapter, however, not all feminists are completely disenchanted with the Judeo-Christian and Islamic traditions. Some, often called "reformers," have chosen instead to challenge patriarchal religious forms and to reclaim Judeo-Christian and Islamic history, language, symbols, and ritual as their own (Crossette, 1996; McDonald, 1996). To them, Judaism, Christianity, and Islam contain "the seeds of [their] own renewal" and, more importantly, "these feminists believe that the church [and synagogue and mosque are] worth renewing" (Weidman, 1984, p. 2, author's emphasis).

The first challenge that feminist reformers face is to *rename* the elements of their religions so that they speak to women as well as to men (Chopp, 1989). At the most basic level, this means divesting God-talk and religious symbolism of its he/man qualities by, for example, depicting the deity as both female and male, referring to God as She or Mother, or using gender-inclusive or gender-neutral language such as Mother and Father or simply Holy One.

Once God is no longer imaged solely as male, the next step is to rediscover women's contributions to religious heritage by critically rereading scriptures and sacred texts and examining other available evidence. From such careful study, for instance, we now know of the wealth of feminine imagery in the Old Testament and of the many ancient Hebrew heroines, wisewomen, and religious leaders; we have already mentioned Deborah, but there was also Vashti, Esther, Huldah, and Beruriah to name just a few examples (Brooten, 1982; Gendler, 1979; Pogrebin, 1992). We also noted Jesus's female disciples and their central leadership roles in the early Christian church. Feminist Islamic scholars have also begun reinterpreting sacred texts, arguing on the basis of their research that the Qur'an does not dictate a patriarchal society; rather, it has been interpretations of the Qur'an by patriarchal men that have produced such dictates (Ahmed, 1992; Crossette, 1996; Miller, 1992).

In addition to renaming and rediscovering, feminist reformers are restructuring religious ritual so that it is relevant to women as well as men. Jewish feminists, in particular, have been active in developing women's services and ceremonies for the Sabbath, Haggadah, Rosh Hodesh, Passover, and other holidays (Adler, 1998; Brozan, 1990; Pogrebin, 1992). Christian feminists have written women's prayers, organized women's prayer groups, and told women's stories and perspectives from church pulpits (Byrne, 1991). In some cases, their efforts have resulted in changes in mainstream religious practices, such as the adoption of gender-neutral language in church services (see, for example, Canadian Bishops' Pastoral Team, 1989; McDonald, 1996).

Like those who have broken with the patriarchal religious traditions, religious reformers disagree on the issue of whether feminist spirituality should be a women-only enterprise or a joint venture that includes members of both sexes. There are some who maintain that women need separate places and methods for worship, at least until they have fully reclaimed their religious heritage and reestablished a position of equal status and authority within the mainstream religions. Others are concerned that feminist spirituality is dominated by White heterosexual women, while the diverse traditions and spiritual needs of women and men of color along with lesbians and gay men are being overlooked. Consequently, there are those (e.g., Isasi-Diaz, 1991; Mollenkott, 1991) who are calling on members of these groups to rediscover or to construct new religious traditions and rituals that better express the spirituality of their life experiences. Still others, however, argue that separatism itself gives rise to and perpetuates inequality, and that the goal of feminist spirituality should be the building of a nonhierarchical human fellowship that unites groups historically excluded from mainstream churches because of their sex, race or ethnicity, social class, or sexual orientation (Erikson, 1992; Zappone, 1991).

Of course, it may be that this issue is unresolvable, but we do hope that through the struggle to come to grips with it, people will develop better ways to fulfill what appears to be a basic human need, religious expression. What we must keep in mind, however, is that a resurging religious fundamentalism threatens to negate even the most modest steps that have been taken toward gender equality and gay and lesbian rights. Despite the appeal that orthodoxy has for some women, it is nevertheless the case that religious fundamentalists vehemently oppose liberal trends, especially in gender relations and equal rights for sexual minorities, and fundamentalist groups have become more active politically in order to get their position represented in civil as well as religious law. Increasingly, feminism and gay and lesbian rights groups are being held up as devils to be defeated, rather than as movements for liberation. In Israel, religious leaders are arguing that orthodoxy is a unifying force central to national security. In the Islamic world, women's liberation is described as a Western imperialist plot to weaken Islamic nations and eventually overthrow them. In the United States, Christian fundamentalist leaders have urged their followers to "rid the nation of the disease-ridden homosexual lifestyle" (quoted in Liston, 1998, p. A2). Perhaps the underlying message in all of this is that more can be gained by feminist spiritualists working together—women and men, homosexuals and heterosexuals, all races and ethnicities and social classes—than by each group going its separate way.

KEY TERMS

ecofeminism an earth-based feminist spirituality movement that celebrates women's close association with nature and that sees a connection between the domination of women and the domination of nature

feminist spirituality a religious movement comprising diverse segments with differing beliefs and strategies for change, but unified in rejecting the dualism characteristic of traditional patriarchal religions; dualism is replaced with the theme of the unification of spirit and nature and the principle that human experience is the source of spirituality

fundamentalism a religious orientation that denounces secular modernity and attempts to restore traditional spirituality through selective retrieval of doctrines, beliefs, and practices from a sacred past

Qur'an (or Quran, variation of Koran) the book of sacred writings accepted by Muslims as revelations made to Muhammad by Allah; understood by Muslims to be literally the word of God

religiosity an individual's or group's intensity of commitment to a religious belief system

Talmud the foundation of religious authority for traditional Judaism

witchcraft naturalistic practices with religious significance usually engaged in by women; includes folk magic and medicine as well as knowledge of farming, ceramics, metallurgy, and astrology

Women-Church movement a coalition of feminist faith-sharing groups, which offers a feminist critique of traditional Christianity while providing members with alternative, woman-centered rituals and forms of worship

SUGGESTED READINGS

Adler, R. (1998). *Engendering Judaism*. New York: Jewish Publication Society.

Comstock, G. D. (1996). *Unrepentent, self-affirming, practicing: Lesbian/bisexual/gay people within organized religions*. New York: Continuum.

Gerami, S. (1996). *Women and fundamentalism: Islam and Christianity*. New York: Garland.

Higgenbotham, E. B. (1993). *Righteous discontent: The women's movement and the Black Baptist Church, 1880–1920*. Cambridge: Harvard University Press.

Kaufman, D. R. (1991). *Rachel's daughters: Newly Orthodox Jewish women*. New Brunswick: Rutgers University Press.

Reis, E. (Ed.) (1998). *Spellbound: Women and witchcraft in America*. Wilmington, DE: Scholarly Resources.

Sered, S. S. (1994). *Priestess, mother, sacred sister: Religions dominated by women*. New York: Oxford University Press.

NOTES

1. Men did not completely escape persecution for witchcraft, however. Even brother Dominicans were not immune from prosecution. For example, Giordano Bruno, a Dominican philosopher, was burned alive in 1600 because he used magic and gnosticism to defend Copernicus's theory of the solar system.

2. Recent reports indicate that the Vatican may soon publicly apologize for the Catholic Church's persecution of witches and heretics. The Vatican has invited academics who study the Counter-Reformation to report on the church's role in the persecution, with the possibility that it may include the persecution in a penitential rite planned for March, 2000 (Johnston, 1998).

3. A fourth congregation, Reconstructionist Judaism, was established in the 1960s. Reconstructionist Judaism rejects all the doctrines of traditional Judaism, including the Torah and Talmud; stories in the Bible are considered myths. Instead, Reconstructionist Jews emphasize humanistic values and the cultural heritage of Judaism. Reconstructionist Judaism is highly egalitarian and allows the fullest participation of women; about 20 percent of Reconstructionist rabbis are women. However, being new, it is still small compared with the other three Jewish denominations (Carmody, 1989).

4. Interestingly, while there appears to be an increasing willingness among Reform and Conservative rabbis to officiate at same-sex unions, there remains a reluctance to officiate at interfaith marriages. One recent survey of rabbis, for instance, found that none in the Orthodox or Conservative traditions had officiated at interfaith marriages, although 11 percent of Orthodox rabbis and 32 percent of Conservative rabbis said that they had referred interfaith couples to other rabbis who would marry them. Significantly more Reform and Reconstructionist rabbis had married interfaith couples: 36 percent of Reform rabbis and 62 percent of Reconstructionist rabbis had officiated at interfaith weddings; 69 percent of Reform rabbis and 100 percent of Reconstructionist rabbis said they also referred interfaith couples to other rabbis who would marry them (Niebuhr, 1997). This continued resistance to interfaith unions reminds us of a story a friend recently told us. Our friend, who is a Jewish lesbian, introduced her new lover, who happened to be Catholic, to her mother; "What," our friend's mother asked, "you couldn't find a nice Jewish girl?"

5. When the Taliban movement came to power in Afghanistan in 1996, the new government immediately imposed *purdah* on all females. Girls were denied schooling and women lost their jobs overnight. *Purdah* has imposed severe hardship on widows, in particular, since most were providing the sole economic support of their families; it is estimated that there are between 25,000 and 30,000 Afghani widows as a result of the war with the former Soviet Union and the rebellion against the former government led by the *mujahedeen*. But *purdah* has also imposed hardship on the entire population of Afghanistan, since most teachers and health care workers in that country were women. There are not enough male teachers to staff the schools that remain open for boys, and hospitals have been so understaffed that government officials had to call some women back to work (Crossette, 1998).

6. Women who violate the rules of modest dress or who engage in immodest activity may also be attacked by

angry citizens. In Iran, a woman was beaten for riding a bicycle on a path used by men. In Afghanistan, women have been whipped for leaving their homes unaccompanied by their husbands or a male relative. And in Algeria, four women were decapitated in July, 1996 when they appeared on Algiers beaches wearing bikinis ("Israel Orthodox Attack Skirts," 1996).

7. The Walt Disney Company offers health benefits to partners of gay and lesbian employees. The entertainment company has also opened its theme parks for "Gay Days" organized by gay and lesbian groups. The South-

ern Baptist Convention and other religious New Right groups were also angered when Disney-owned ABC television broadcast the coming-out episode of the sitcom, *Ellen* (see Chapter 5). *Ellen*, of course, was a program for an adult audience, but some groups have also accused Disney of promoting homosexuality in its children's animated films. The American Family Association, for example, denounced *The Lion King* because they believed that the film portrays a homosexual relationship between a meerkat and a wart hog.

11 Gender and Health

Health care and, in particular, access to health care, have been top priorities on the national agenda since the 1980s. As health care costs rose during the 1980s at an average rate of 8.3 percent a year (compared with an average increase of 5.6 percent for all items on the Consumer Price Index [CPI]), access to health care shrunk for large segments of the U.S. population. By 1989, 15.7 percent of the U.S. population (34.1 million people) were medically uninsured (U.S. Department of Commerce, Bureau of the Census, 1997; U.S. Department of Health and Human Services, 1991). During the first half of the 1990s, the average annual increase in the cost of health care dropped steadily to 4.5 percent in 1995, 1.7 percent above the average annual increase for all items on the CPI. Nevertheless, access to health care did not improve: In 1995, 16.5 percent of the U.S. population (39.1 million people) were medically uninsured (U.S. Department of Commerce, Bureau of the Census, 1997; U.S. Department of Health and Human Services, 1997).

At the same time that access to health care has been shrinking for specific segments of the population, there has been increasing interest in how diet and lifestyle choices contribute to health. In response to reports that diet, exercise, and other aspects of an individual's lifestyle affect her or his health, many Americans quit smoking, began eating low-fat, high-fiber foods, and spent millions of dollars on health club memberships and exercise equipment. Importantly, however, the individuals who make up the first group we have discussed—the uninsured—have little in common with those who make up the second group. About 14 percent of the uninsured are children under the age of fifteen who live with an unemployed parent or a parent who is working part time or full time in a job that provides no medical benefits. In fact, more than nine of ten medically uninsured children lives with at least one parent who is working. The number of workers who have employer-provided health insurance has been declining since 1982 (Children's Defense Fund, 1991; 1998; U.S. Department of Health and Human Services, 1997). More than 61 percent of the uninsured have annual family incomes of less than $25,000 per year; more than a third have incomes below $14,000 per year. And nearly 85 percent of the uninsured are women and men of color (U.S. Department of Health and Human Services, 1997). In contrast, the "health club set" is predominantly White, with middle-class or higher average annual incomes, and is between the ages of twenty-five and forty-four (National Demographics and Lifestyles, 1994).

In short, although research has established direct links between diet and lifestyle and health, what we eat and how we live is less of a choice for some people than for others. In fact, researchers have found that even if America's poor get more exercise, improve their eating habits, and cut down on smoking and drinking, their health will not improve substantially, since these factors account for only about 13 percent of the difference between the death rates of poor Americans and of more affluent Americans. Instead, researchers maintain that the health status of the poor is most affected by lack of medical care, the stress of poverty, working at dangerous jobs, and living in substandard homes and polluted neighborhoods (Lantz et al., 1998). In other words, a person's health and access to health care, along with his or her diet and lifestyle, are influenced to a considerable extent by a number of factors over which he or she has little control: most importantly, social class, race and ethnicity, age, and, as we will learn in this chapter, sex.

In this chapter, we will consider how sex and gender relations affect health status and how they interact with other factors—social class, race and ethnicity, age, sexual orientation—to shape not only health status, but also the physician-patient relationship and treatment by the health care system.

It is important to keep in mind, though, that when we talk about health, we're talking about more than simply the absence of illness. Health is, as the World Health Organization (1960, p. 1) has told us, multidimensional. It is "a complete state of physical, mental, and social well-being." Let's begin our discussion by looking first at physical health; then, later in the chapter we will take up the issue of mental health.

Gender and Mortality

One of the most consistent sex differences that can be observed across contemporary industrialized societies is that women, on average, live longer than men (see Box 11.1 on page 342 for a discussion of sex and life expectancy in developing countries). Looking at Table 11.1 on page 343, we see first that the United States ranks low relative to many other countries in terms of both female and male life expectancy. (**Life expectancy** refers to the average number of years an individual may be expected to live from a given age or from birth.) The United States ranks nineteenth in terms of female life expectancy and twenty-third for male life expectancy. (The U.S. rankings have declined since the 1980s.) However, in all the countries listed, women have a longer life expectancy than men. The gap is narrowest in Cuba, but even there, the difference is nearly four years.

As Table 11.2 on page 344 shows, even though life expectancy for both sexes has improved over the decades, women's advantage increased significantly from the turn of the century until 1975. In the United States, for example, there was only a two-year difference in female and male life expectancies in 1900. By 1970, the life expectancy gap between the sexes had widened to 7.7 years. Since 1975, the sex gap in life expectancy has narrowed, although it remained significant at 6.4 years in 1995 (U.S. Department of Health and Human Services, 1997).

We also see in Table 11.2 a consistent racial disparity in life expectancy. Whites enjoy almost a seven-year advantage over Blacks in terms of life expectancy. In fact, the life expectancy of Black males in 1995 was only slightly better than the life expectancy of White males in 1940. Similarly, the life expectancy of Black females in 1995 was little better than the life expectancy of White females in 1950. The gender gap in life expectancy has not narrowed as much for Blacks as it has for Whites, indicating that race is a more significant factor than sex in the life expectancies of African Americans. Nevertheless, a significant sex difference in life expectancy persists regardless of race.[1]

A number of theories have been offered to account for the sex differential in life expectancy. At least part of the difference appears to be caused by biological factors. Genetics, for instance, play a role. As we learned in Chapter 2, humans have twenty-three pairs of chromosomes, one of which determines sex. If an individual is male, his sex chromosomes are XY; a female has two X chromosomes. Scientists know that the X chromosome carries more genetic information than the Y, including some defects that

BOX 11.1
Sex and Life Expectancy in Economically Undeveloped Countries

In economically undeveloped countries, life expectancy in general is considerably lower than it is in developed and industrialized countries, and the gap between male and female life expectancies is narrower. Average male and female life expectancies in low-income (undeveloped) countries (excluding China and India) are fifty-four and fifty-six respectively, whereas in high-income (industrialized) countries they are seventy-three and seventy-nine respectively (World Bank, 1996).

Sex differences in life expectancies in low-income countries are related to gender norms and also to the feminization of poverty in these countries. This is not to say that men in undeveloped countries are not poor; poverty touches the lives of men as well as women in these countries. But as Doyal (1990b, p. 509) points out, "it is women who must manage the consequences of poverty for the whole family" and this impacts on their life expectancy as well as their general health.

Consider, for example, that women in low-income countries are responsible for securing water and daily fuel for their families. This usually means traveling long distances by foot and carrying back (typically on their heads) heavy loads while often holding babies or small children. Women are also involved in the production of food for their families, usually through subsistence agriculture, and because modern technology is rarely available to them, this means they must cultivate and harvest their crops by hand or by using crude tools, such as digging sticks (Messias et al., 1997). Grains must be husked and ground by hand, a process that takes many hours and is physically exhausting. Cooking the food exposes women to the hazards of inhaling wood smoke or emissions from biomass fuels, such as cattle dung. "Emissions from biomass fuels are major sources of air pollution in the home, and studies have shown that cooks inhale more smoke and pollutants than the inhabitants of the dirtiest cities" (Doyal, 1990b, p. 510).

Customs also contribute to sex differences in health and life expectancy. For instance, in some societies women are prohibited by religious and moral teachings from being seen defecating, so they must wait until dark to relieve themselves. This, though, can lead to constipation and other bowel and intestinal problems and also increases their risk of assault. In many countries, customs governing the distribution of food dictate that women and children will eat less than men. Among children, boys are usually fed better than girls, lowering girls' chances of surviving infancy. Among adults, men often eat first; when they are finished, the women and children can eat what is left. Consequently, women and children have higher rates of malnutrition than adult men (Doyal, 1990b).

In light of these data, it is hardly surprising that in some low-income countries, such as Bangladesh and Nepal, the sex difference in life expectancy is the reverse of that in industrialized countries; that is, in some low-income countries, men on average outlive women (World Bank, 1996; see also U.S. Department of State, 1994).

---

can lead to physical abnormalities, but instead of making females more vulnerable to X-linked disorders, this seems to give them a genetic advantage. A female typically needs two defective X chromosomes for most genetically linked disorders to manifest themselves; otherwise, one healthy X chromosome can override the abnormal one. On the other hand, a male who has a defective X chromosome will have the genetically linked

TABLE 11.1   Life Expectancy at Birth, by Sex for Selected Countries*

Country	Female Life Expectancy (in years)	Male Life Expectancy (in years)
Japan	83.1	76.5
France	82.3	73.8
Switzerland	81.7	75.0
Canada	81.4	74.9
Sweden	80.8	75.5
Australia	80.8	74.7
Spain	80.7	73.4
Norway	80.5	74.2
Netherlands	80.5	74.3
Italy	80.5	73.7
Greece	80.4	75.0
Finland	79.6	72.1
England & Wales	79.5	73.9
Austria	79.5	72.9
Germany	79.3	72.8
New Zealand	79.2	72.8
Puerto Rico	78.9	69.6
Singapore	78.9	73.2
United States	78.8	72.2
Northern Ireland	78.7	72.7
Israel	78.5	74.7
Ireland	78.2	72.6
Portugal	77.9	70.6
Denmark	77.9	72.7
Costa Rica	77.8	73.3
Slovakia	77.7	69.7
Scotland	77.4	71.7
Cuba	76.8	72.9
Czech Republic	76.5	69.3
Poland	76.0	67.4

*Data cover the period 1990–1993.

Source: U.S. Department of Health and Human Services, 1997, pp. 106–107.

disease because that is the only X chromosome he has. This is thought to account for the higher number of miscarriages of male fetuses and the greater ratio of male to female neonatal deaths (106:100) and infant deaths (Holden, 1987; Stillion, 1995). Hormonal differences between the sexes also contribute to the life expectancy gap. In particular, the female sex hormones, the estrogens, appear to give women some protection against heart disease, the number one cause of death in the United States (Waldron, 1995).

TABLE 11.2 Life Expectancy at Birth, by Sex and Race, 1900–1995

Year	All Races		White		Black*	
	Male	*Female*	*Male*	*Female*	*Male*	*Female*
1900	46.3	48.3	46.6	48.7	32.5	33.5
1920	53.6	54.6	54.4	55.6	45.5	45.2
1930	58.1	61.6	59.7	63.5	47.3	49.2
1940	60.8	65.2	62.1	66.6	51.5	54.9
1950	65.6	71.1	66.5	72.2	58.9	62.7
1960	66.6	73.1	67.4	74.1	60.7	65.9
1970	67.1	74.7	68.0	75.6	60.0	68.3
1975	68.8	76.6	69.5	77.3	62.4	71.3
1980	70.0	77.4	70.7	78.1	63.8	72.5
1985	71.1	78.2	71.8	78.7	65.0	73.4
1990	71.8	78.8	72.7	79.4	64.5	73.6
1995	72.5	78.9	73.4	79.6	65.2	73.9

*Data for the years 1920, 1930, and 1940 include other non-White populations in addition to the Black population.

Sources: U.S. Department of Commerce, 1987, p. 69; 1990, p. 72; U.S. Department of Health and Human Services, 1986, p. 84; 1993, p. 44; 1997, p. 108.

Marital status is also related to life expectancy, at least for men. In one recent study, for instance, researchers found that after controlling for crucial intervening variables, such as income, education, smoking, drinking, and obesity, men between the ages of forty-five and sixty-five who lived alone or with someone other than a spouse were twice as likely to die within ten years as men of the same age who lived with spouses. This relationship did not hold for women; women were more negatively affected by low income than by lack of a spouse (Davis et al., 1990; see also Hu & Goldman, 1990). Although researchers are not certain why marriage appears to be so important to the health of men, studies show that men rely almost totally on their spouses for social support. Not surprisingly, then, married men express a higher level of well-being than their nonmarried peers. There appears to be no difference, however, in the level of contentment expressed by married versus nonmarried women. Women have wider social support networks than men. When a woman's husband dies, she retains the social support of relatives and friends (Helgeson, 1995; see also Chapter 6).

We will return to the relationship between marital status and well-being later in this chapter. Importantly, though, this relationship may be an indicator of another major component of the gender gap in life expectancy: behavior differences between the sexes. More specifically, we can observe a relationship between life expectancy and conformity to traditional gender stereotypes. To understand this better, let's examine male and female mortality rates for particular causes. (A **mortality rate** is simply the number of deaths in proportion to a given population.) Table 11.3 provides sex- and race-specific mortality rates for various causes. Let's look at some of these more closely.

TABLE 11.3   Mortality Rates for Selected Causes of Death for White and Black Males and Females, 1993

Cause of Death	White Males	Black Males	White Females	Black Females
All causes	627.5	1,052.2	367.7	578.8
Natural causes	554.3	905.2	342.8	542.1
Diseases of the heart	190.3	267.9	99.2	165.3
Cerebrovascular diseases	26.8	51.9	22.7	39.9
Malignant neoplasms	156.4	238.9	110.1	135.3
Chronic obstructive pulmonary diseases	28.2	26.6	17.8	12.2
Pneumonia & influenza	16.6	25.9	10.4	13.5
Chronic liver disease & cirrhosis	10.8	16.1	4.6	6.6
Diabetes mellitus	12.2	26.3	10.0	26.9
Human immune deficiency virus	19.0	70.0	1.9	17.3
External causes	73.1	147.1	24.8	36.7
Unintentional injuries	42.9	59.8	16.6	20.1
Motor vehicle crashes	22.5	25.3	9.7	8.5
Suicide	19.7	12.9	4.6	2.1
Homicide and legal intervention	8.9	70.7	3.0	13.4
Drug-induced causes	6.2	13.0	2.8	4.4
Alcohol-induced causes	9.7	21.3	2.7	5.5

Source: U.S. Department of Health and Human Services, 1996, pp. 110–111.

Heart Disease

The male death rate from heart disease is about 84 percent higher than the female death rate from heart disease. In fact, the greatest single contributor to men's higher mortality rate overall is coronary heart disease, which includes heart attacks (Waldron, 1995). What accounts for this particular sex disparity in mortality? Scientists have found a number of behavioral and cultural factors that are contributors.

First, more men than women smoke, and men are more likely than women to be heavy smokers. Cigarette smoking has been shown to cause and worsen heart disease. It is estimated that sex differences in smoking account for about a third of the sex differences in heart disease mortality (Waldron, 1995). However, sex differences in smoking have been declining since the 1940s, as more women took up smoking, and more men than women have quit smoking. Because there is a lag time between when a person begins smoking and the appearance of detrimental effects of smoking on the person's health, including heart disease mortality, the impact of women's increased smoking during the 1940s, 1950s, and 1960s has only recently shown itself in a narrowing of the gender gap in heart disease mortality. In fact, although heart disease mortality has decreased for both women and men over the last decade, the male decrease has been higher than the female decrease (Thun et al., 1995; Waldron, 1995).

However, while cigarette smoking obviously plays a major role in the gender gap in heart disease mortality, other factors also contribute since the difference is substantial even among nonsmokers. Another factor that some researchers believe contributes to the gender gap in heart disease mortality is men's greater likelihood to adopt the Coronary Prone Behavior Pattern, or what many call the *Type A personality*. Research indicates that Type A individuals are more than twice as likely as laid-back Type B personalities to suffer heart attacks, regardless of whether or not they smoke. Interestingly, the characteristics of Type A closely parallel those typical of traditional masculinity: competitive, impatient, ambitious, aggressive, and unemotional (Helgeson, 1995; Spielberger & London, 1985). Not surprisingly, researchers have found that coronary patients who display strong or extreme masculinity in a negative sense do more poorly healthwise than other coronary patients (Helgeson, 1995).

Another configuration of personality traits recently associated with coronary heart disease is what researchers are calling the *Type D personality* (Lesperance & Frasure-Smith, 1996). Traditionally described as the "strong, silent type," the Type D personality has difficulty expressing negative emotions. They typically keep their feelings hidden and see talking about their worries as a sign of weakness. Research shows that this personality type is more common among men than women and is consistent with traditional masculinity. Men are less likely than women to disclose their needs and feelings of vulnerability (Helgeson, 1995). Yet, research indicates that Type D personalities have an increased risk of heart attacks and have poorer recovery rates following a heart attack (Lesperance & Frasure-Smith, 1996).

The findings with regard to Type A and Type D personalities are useful because they show the detrimental impact that adhering to a traditional masculine gender role can have on men's health. However, more research is needed with diverse groups of study subjects to more fully understand the relationship between gender roles and heart disease, especially since much previous research was based largely on samples of White men and was sometimes influenced by stereotypes. For example, early reports depicted heart disease as a health problem of executives, a middle- and upper-class disease, or as some referred to it, a "disease of affluence." Those most likely to be stricken were said to be hardworking, successful professional men—men striving to "keep up with the Joneses" and to get ahead. Blue-collar workers and housewives were thought to be less susceptible, supposedly because they were less pressured, although it was predicted that women's rates of coronary heart disease would rise as more women entered professional fields (Ehrenreich, 1983; House, 1986).

However, assumptions like these ignore the serious stressors that blue-collar workers confront: for example, speed-ups, little or no control over work, and low rewards. This may partially account for the higher coronary heart disease mortality rate among African American men who, as a group, are underrepresented among white-collar professionals and overrepresented among unskilled laborers. Many female-dominated jobs, especially in the service sector, may also be considered highly stressful for these same reasons (LaCroix & Haynes, 1987). Female heart attack patients report having experienced more stressful life events than male heart attack patients (Helgeson, 1990). One recent study has shown a strong correlation between living in neighborhoods with high concentrations of female-headed households and heart disease mortality among women

(LeClere et al., 1998). Obviously, poverty may be the underlying contributing factor here, since such neighborhoods have significantly lower median incomes than neighborhoods dominated by male-headed households (see Chapter 6). However, the researchers found that for older women, the relationship holds even when poverty is taken into account. This finding indicates that such neighborhoods may be more stressful environments for older women, perhaps because there are fewer social supports for them, given that younger single mothers must devote most, if not all, of their time attending to the immediate needs of their families.

It has also been argued that the traditional homemaker role can be highly stressful (Doyle, 1990a). Interestingly, while employed women face the doubly stressful burden of job responsibilities coupled with home and family care, they do not appear to be more likely than full-time homemakers to develop coronary heart disease. In fact, some studies indicate that just the opposite may be the case. In general, women employed outside the home appear to be healthier than nonemployed women, even when employed women must fulfill multiple roles, such as worker, parent, spouse, and homemaker. According to LaCroix and Haynes (1987, p. 103), "the employment role is the strongest correlate of good health for women," although it is unclear why. Again, more research is needed on diverse groups of women, comparing women employed in low-status, low-income jobs with women in high-prestige, well-paying jobs, since there is evidence that role *quality* may be more important for well-being than role occupancy per se (Barnett & Baruch, 1987; Messias et al., 1997). More research is also needed on sex differences in social support networks among coworkers, relationships between supervisors and their employees, the socioeconomic benefits of working outside the home, and sex differences in access to and use of health care services among employed and unemployed women and men.

Although the female mortality rate from heart disease is lower than the male mortality rate from heart disease, diseases of the heart are still the primary causes of death for women. In fact, when age is taken into account, more women than men die from heart disease and related disorders. In 1995, for example, 374,849 women died from diseases of the heart compared with 362,714 men (U.S. Department of Health and Human Services, 1997; see also Wenger, 1997). Although heart attacks are rare for premenopausal women under the age of fifty, the heart attack rate for postmenopausal women climbs quickly, soon equaling the heart attack rate for men over fifty years old. It appears that women actually develop heart disease at a rate similar to that of men, but six to ten years later in life, and that the symptomatic manifestation of heart disease in women may follow a different pattern than that in men (Henig, 1993). Women also constitute two-thirds of those who suffer a heart problem known as *Syndrome X*. Syndrome X appears to be caused by hypersensitivity in the nerves leading to the heart, esophagus, and chest, but it is still a poorly understood and underresearched problem (Cannon, 1993). In fact, some medical researchers have argued that far less is known about heart disease in women because, until quite recently, studies of heart disease focused exclusively on male subjects, thus perhaps erroneously generalizing from the findings on one sex to both sexes and reinforcing the false notion that women are unlikely to suffer from heart disease and its effects (Nechas & Foley, 1994).

Looking back at Table 11.3 for a moment, we see that African American men's and women's mortality rates from heart disease are considerably higher than those of White men and women, although the rate for African American women is still far below that of African American men. African Americans are twenty times more likely than Whites to suffer from high blood pressure, a condition that contributes to heart disease (see, however, Gillum et al., 1997). Research has linked elevated blood pressure in African Americans to the stress of dealing with racial discrimination in everyday life. In fact, one study found that stress induced by racial discrimination has as much or more of an impact on blood pressure as smoking, lack of exercise, and a high-fat, high-sodium diet (Kreiger & Sidney, 1996; see also Armstead et al., 1989; Klag et al., 1991). Once African Americans are diagnosed with heart disease, they are 40 percent less likely than Whites to undergo bypass surgery or angioplasty, a statistic that some researchers also attribute to racism: Most cardiologists are White, and they may have difficulty communicating effectively with Black patients, making it harder for the patients to trust them (Haney, 1996a).

We will discuss the patient-physician relationship in greater detail shortly, but first let's consider the gender gap in mortality for other causes of death.

Cancer

Men's death rate due to cancer is more than 58 percent higher than women's cancer death rate, excluding breast cancer, prostate cancer, and other sex-specific cancers (e.g., ovarian cancer) (U.S. Department of Health and Human Services, 1997). Again, men's smoking habits contribute to this difference. As we noted earlier, historically, more men than women have smoked, and men's smoking habits are riskier than women's (e.g., they smoke more of each cigarette they light) (Waldon, 1995). However, we have also noted that more men than women have quit smoking in recent years. In addition, as with coronary heart disease, the gender gap in mortality for lung cancer is narrowing because we are beginning to see the ill effects of smoking on women who took up the habit decades ago. From the 1960s through the 1980s, for example, women's mortality from lung cancer increased 600 percent, from 26 per 100,000 to 155 per 100,000. During the same period, men's lung cancer mortality doubled, from 187 per 100,000 to 341 per 100,000. However, there was no increase in the lung cancer mortality rate of nonsmokers, strong evidence of the major role smoking plays in the development of lung disease (Thun et al., 1995).

Adding to the risk of developing cancer are industrial hazards, especially the inhalation of particular dusts such as asbestos, and exposure to toxic fumes and chemicals. Men are more likely to experience toxic workplace exposures—another byproduct of occupational sex segregation (Waldron, 1995). However, certain female-dominated jobs—such as micro-chip and electronic component assembly, which is more than 90 percent female, a majority of whom are women of color—involve extensive exposure to toxic chemicals (Fox, 1991). Yet, less is known about occupationally related cancers and female mortality, since most research involving women's health and the workplace has focused on their reproductive health. There are, however, a variety of ways that the work environment can affect a person's health, so let's take a closer look at occupational health hazards.

Occupational Hazards to Male and Female Workers

There's a certain irony in the phrase, "to work for a living," given that many workplaces are quite hazardous, even deadly. Historically, a recognition of this led to the enactment of laws prohibiting the employment of women in particular occupations. The stated rationale for such measures was not simply that women are "the weaker sex," but also that their childbearing function warranted them special protection so as to insure the health and viability of future generations. In practice, "protective" legislation has had two major effects: (1) legitimation of employment discrimination against women; and (2) neglect of the potential risks posed by workplace hazards to male workers' health, including their reproductive health.

The Pregnancy Discrimination Act of 1981 forbids employment discrimination against women workers solely on the basis of pregnancy. If a hazard can be shown to affect a fetus through either the mother or the father, then excluding only women from the workplace is illegal. It is estimated that over 14 million U.S. workers each year are exposed to known or suspected reproductive hazards in the workplace. Not surprisingly, then, reproductive disorders are among the ten most frequent work-related injuries and illnesses in the United States. However, little is known about the effects of most workplace toxins and other occupational hazards on the reproductive health of either sex, and male workers in particular have been virtually ignored (Blakeslee, 1991; Paul et al., 1989). It is clear that workplace toxins can affect the female reproductive system in many different ways, particularly during pregnancy, but it is also plausible that these toxins could damage sperm or be transmitted through semen, causing visible congenital malformations as well as the possibility of childhood or adult cancer in the offspring (Bellin & Rubenstein, 1983; Hatch, 1984; Williams, 1988).

Unfortunately, many researchers, employers, and policy makers traditionally operated under the assumption that women are more important than men in the reproductive process. Until 1991, most employers simply excluded women from certain hazardous jobs or employed only infertile or surgically sterilized women in such jobs (Chavkin, 1984a; Samuels, 1995; Williams, 1988). In other words, employers have typically addressed the problem by removing women from the workplace instead of rendering the workplace safe for both female and male workers (Paul et al., 1989; Samuels, 1995). This is no solution at all, for the fact of the matter is that "toxic chemicals do not discriminate—they affect both female and male hearts, muscles, livers, and kidneys— and both female and male reproductive systems. . . . Men, women, and their offspring, are all at risk from toxic exposures; we do not know whether these risks are sufficiently different to justify the selection of one of them as needing more protection than the other" (Bellin & Rubenstein, 1983, pp. 87, 97).

We suspect that protection of women and their offspring was less a motivating factor in the adoption of exclusionary policies than employers' concern with corporate liability and the advantages they accrued from a sex-segregated labor force (see Chapter 7). For one thing, exclusion from the workplace does not necessarily protect women from exposure to toxins. Men may transport residues home on their hair, skin, and clothes, with women being exposed through their daily unpaid activities as housewives (Rosenberg, 1984).[2] Indeed, housework itself is hazardous, but it is rarely considered in discussions of occupational health and safety because it is not recognized as "real work" (Chavkin, 1984b; Messias et al., 1997; Rosenberg, 1984).

Second, exclusionary policies were common in male-dominated industries, but not in equally hazardous female-dominated occupations (Doyal, 1990a; Goldhaber et al., 1988). We know from our discussion in Chapter 7 that women, especially women of color, have always worked at dangerous jobs. In fact, racial discrimination in the workplace has meant that Black workers of both sexes are at significantly greater risk than White workers of suffering an occupational injury or illness. For example, approximately 89 percent of Black steel workers work at the coke ovens compared with about 32 percent of White steel workers; the coke ovens are the most dangerous work site in the steel industry (Staples, 1995; see also Fox, 1991).[3]

In 1991, sex-biased workplace exclusionary policies were successfully challenged when the United States Supreme Court reversed a lower court's decision that women could be barred from jobs that might potentially harm a fetus. The case, *United Automobile Workers* v. *Johnson Controls*, involved a battery company that prohibited fertile women, pregnant or not, from working at jobs that entail exposure to lead. The company argued that the exclusionary policy was not discriminatory because it is in the public's interest to protect the health of unborn children. However, the Supreme Court maintained that although employment late in pregnancy may sometimes pose a risk to the fetus, it is up to the woman to decide whether or not she will continue to work. Employers, ruled the Court, may not force a woman to choose between having a job and having a baby. Not surprisingly, most employers have complied with this decision not by making the workplace safer for the reproductive health of employees of both sexes, but rather by simply leaving it up to workers themselves to decide whether or not to risk working in an unsafe, unhealthy work environment. Such a choice is really no choice at all for most workers in toxic work environments, since they have few other job options.

Exposures to workplace toxins, however, are not the only hazards women and men face on the job. Accidents and homicides also claim workers' lives, although not surprisingly male and female workers face different levels of risk. For example, although men make up 54 percent of the labor force, they account for 92 percent of workers who die from job-related injuries. Most of these men die accidentally—for example, in vehicle accidents, from falls, and in fires or explosions. While women are far less likely than men to die in a work-related incident, the major cause of work-related death for women is homicide (see Chapter 8). Thirty-four percent of women who die on the job are murder victims. These deaths are largely a result of women being concentrated in retail trade and food service, which showed increases in job-related homicides in recent years, most of which were associated with robberies or robbery attempts. About 17 percent of female homicide victims killed at work were killed by husbands, ex-husbands, boyfriends, and ex-boyfriends, the end product of a history of domestic violence (U.S. Department of Labor, 1997).

Women and men also have significantly different rates of death from non-job-related accidents and homicides, a point that we will take up next.

Other Causes of Death

For the remaining causes of death listed in Table 11.3, only two—specifically, diabetes mellitus, and pneumonia and influenza—are not associated with behavioral differences between the sexes. For example, chronic liver disease and cirrhosis of the liver are frequently caused by excessive alcohol consumption and related malnutrition. Since men are more than four times more likely than women to drink heavily—an issue that we will discuss in greater detail later in the chapter—it is little wonder that their mortality rate from chronic liver disease and cirrhosis is more than twice as high as women's (U.S. Department of Health and Human Services, 1997; Waldron, 1995).

Men's drinking habits also contribute to their higher accidental death rate. Men are involved in nearly twice as many fatal car accidents in which the driver was intoxicated (Waldron, 1995). Even when not drinking, though, men drive more recklessly than women. Despite the unflattering stereotype of "the woman driver," women have fewer accidents than men, even when we control for the sex differences in the number of miles driven. The fatal vehicular accident rate for women is 17.5 per 100,000 licensed drivers, compared with the male rate of 53.2 per 100,000 licensed drivers. Women have also shown greater improvements in driving-related safety habits (e.g., wearing seat belts) than men have (Waldron, 1995). Females, of course, are socialized to act safely, to seek help, and to avoid risks. Males, in contrast, are encouraged at an early age to be adventurous, independent, and unafraid of taking risks (see Chapter 3). Consequently, they, more often than females, are involved in the kinds of dangerous situations that may lead to accidental death (Staples, 1995; Stillion, 1995).

Masculinity, we also know, is equated in many people's minds with aggressiveness. Men are expected, even encouraged, to behave violently, and this in turn is reflected in their higher suicide rate and their higher death rate due to homicide (Stillion, 1995). Although women make twice as many suicide attempts as men, they are less likely to succeed in killing themselves. Moreover, the gender gap in suicide has increased in recent years (Waldron, 1995). Some analysts have interpreted these findings to mean that most women who attempt suicide do not really wish to kill themselves, but rather to seek help, while more men actually kill themselves because they have difficulty seeking help or because they are simply more determined to kill themselves (Stillion, 1995). Others, however, have hypothesized that men are more successful in committing suicide because of the methods they use to accomplish the task. Women and men attempt suicide using items from their environment with which they are most familiar and to which they have easiest access. "Masculine" items, such as guns, tend to be more lethal than "feminine" items, such as pills (Kushner, 1985).

The mortality rates from homicide are particularly illuminating for they are products of the intersection of sexism, racism, and social class inequality. In general, men are nearly four times more likely than women to be murdered or to die from "legal intervention" (U.S. Department of Health and Human Services, 1997). Significantly, 89 percent of homicides involving male victims are committed by other men; 90 percent of female victims are murdered by men (Craven, 1996; see also Chapter 8). Looking carefully at Table 11.3, though, we see that race is a more important variable than sex. Although Black females are far less likely than Black males to be murdered, they have a higher rate of victimization than either White males or White females. Most of the excess of male mortality caused by homicide, however, is accounted for by Black male victimization. Indeed, since 1978, homicide has been a leading cause of death for young Black males aged fifteen to twenty-four (U.S. Department of Health and Human Services, 1997). About 20 percent of the difference in life expectancy between White and Black men is attributed to differences in the homicide rate between these two groups (Staples, 1995). The high homicide rate of Black males reflects to a large extent their residential concentration in urban, high-crime neighborhoods and their dis-advantaged economic position (Lee, 1989; Staples, 1995). To paraphrase one observer, there appears to be incestuous relationships between racism, sexism, poverty, crime, and ill health (Holloman, 1983).

Acquired Immune Deficiency Syndrome (AIDS)

The Centers for Disease Control reported the first cases of AIDS in the United States in June, 1981. By June 1996, more than 530,000 AIDS cases had been reported in this country, a rate of 26.7 per 100,000 people in the population. By 1993, AIDS was the second leading cause of death of Americans aged twenty-five to forty-four (U.S. Department of Health and Human Services, 1996; 1997). However, as with the other diseases we have discussed, not everyone is at equal risk of becoming infected with the human immunodeficiency virus (HIV, the virus that causes AIDS). Risk of HIV infection is influenced by sexual orientation, race and ethnicity, and gender, and the groups at greatest risk appear to be changing.

There are only a few ways that HIV is transmitted (see Box 11.2). HIV is carried through blood, semen, and vaginal secretions, so one of the most common ways for the disease to be transmitted is by sexual contact with an infected person. The riskiest form of sexual contact is anal intercourse because it frequently causes tears in the rectal lining and blood vessels, allowing the virus to pass from the semen of the infected partner into the blood of the other partner. Gay and bisexual men account for about 52 percent of total AIDS cases reported since 1985, but the percentage of people with AIDS who are gay or bisexual men has declined in recent years. In 1985, for example, 66.8 percent of people with AIDS were gay and bisexual men, but by 1995, the percentage had dropped to 43.5 (U.S. Department of Health and Human Services, 1997). Experts attribute this decline to successful education campaigns in the gay community about AIDS prevention.

A second common way of contracting HIV is by using contaminated needles to inject drugs. The disease can be transmitted if a drug user injects himself or herself with a used needle that has traces of blood containing HIV. People with AIDS who are injection drug users increased from 17.2 percent in 1985 to nearly 26 percent in 1995 (U.S. Department of Health and Human Services, 1995). Research indicates that impoverished racial and ethnic minorities are more likely than Whites to be injection drug users, so their risk of infection is greater. In 1995, for instance, 14 percent of Whites with AIDS had contracted the disease through injection drug use, compared with 36 percent of African Americans and 32.9 percent of Hispanic Americans (U.S. Department of Health and Human Services, 1997). AIDS is already the leading cause of death among African Americans aged twenty-five to forty-four. Shortly after the turn of the century, more than half of all people with AIDS will be African American; an African American will be nine times more likely to be diagnosed with AIDS than someone who is not African American (Rimer, 1996). Efforts to curb HIV transmission among injection drug users by establishing needle exchange programs have not been widely supported by federal, state, and local governments because some people believe that such programs encourage illegal drug use.

BOX **11.2**

AIDS Prevention

Health officials have given us clear and simple advice with regard to preventing AIDS: practice safe sex, and if you are an IV drug user, do not share needles or other injection devices. The following are some additional facts about AIDS and AIDS prevention:

- AIDS is transmitted primarily through sexual contact—homosexual and heterosexual. You can help prevent infection by practicing safe sex: use a condom during (from start to finish) every act of sexual intercourse (vaginal as well as anal). Currently, there is little evidence that AIDS can be contracted through oral sex. However, the Surgeon General advises that if you or your partner are at high risk for AIDS or either of you has sores or cuts in or around your mouth or genitals, oral sex should be avoided. There is no danger of contracting AIDS from kissing.
- Do not rely on a potential sexual partner's word as a safeguard against AIDS, especially if you are a woman. A recent study of sexually active eighteen- to twenty-five-year-olds in southern California found that 35 percent of the men surveyed admitted that they had lied to a woman in order to have sex with her. Twenty percent of the men said that they would lie to a woman who asked if they had been tested for AIDS; they would say they had been tested and that the results were negative (Cochran & Mays, 1988).
- Since the mid-1980s, a number of clubs and dating services have opened throughout the country for individuals who have tested negative for AIDS. This, however, is not a reliable indicator that a potential partner is not infected for at least three reasons: (1) a small percentage of AIDS tests turn out to be false-negatives (i.e., the individual actually has the AIDS antibodies in his or her

blood even though the test results are negative); (2) the individual may have been infected shortly before being tested, in which case the antibodies may not be detected, or he or she may become infected after the test; and (3) some individuals—no one knows how many—simply do not produce the AIDS antibodies detected by the tests even though they may have been infected.
- If you do not inject drugs, you have eliminated one of the main sources of AIDS infection. Anyone who does inject drugs should use only a clean, previously unused needle, syringe, or other injection device.
- There is no risk of contracting AIDS by donating blood. At the same time, the risk of infection from a blood transfusion is extremely low since all blood donors now are screened and blood donations are not accepted from members of high-risk groups. In fact, some health officials maintain that the blood supply is safer than it ever was because of the increased general screening.
- There is no risk of contracting AIDS through social contact, for example, hugging, shaking hands, crying, coughing or sneezing; sharing beds, cups, eating utensils, or other personal items; using toilets, telephones, swimming pools, furniture or equipment. In short, you cannot contract AIDS from any nonsexual contact, except intravenous drug use with an AIDS-contaminated needle.

Recent research indicates that factual knowledge about AIDS has increased significantly since the 1980s, especially within the general gay male population and among both heterosexual and homosexual college students. Nevertheless, studies also show that while safe sex practices among members of these groups have increased, there is still a high level of risk-taking behavior (Ames, et al., 1992; Bearden, 1992; Osmond, et al., 1993).

Vaginal intercourse, although less risky than anal intercourse and injection drug use, is also a means of HIV transmission. About 66 percent of those who have contracted HIV through heterosexual sex are women, and the majority of them through unprotected vaginal intercourse with an infected partner. Between 1985 and 1995, the percentage of people with AIDS who were women tripled, increasing from 6.5 percent to 18.6 percent (U.S. Department of Health and Human Services, 1997). Once again, however, race and ethnicity intersect with gender to affect risk. African American and Hispanic American women are especially at risk, since so many more African American and Hispanic American men are infected than White men. African American women, for instance, make up two-thirds of all women infected with HIV (Rimer, 1996).

The risk of HIV infection is also high for poor women, a disproportionate number of whom are women of color. For some poor women, sex is a source of income (Osmond et al., 1993). Health experts are also concerned that the growing use of crack cocaine and the rising incidence of other sexually transmitted diseases in poor urban areas contributed to HIV infection. Female crack users often engage in unprotected sex in exchange for money or drugs (Inciardi et al., 1993). And the presence of other sexually transmitted diseases, such as syphilis, can facilitate HIV transmission. The second most frequent means of HIV infection among women is injection drug use: 39.3 percent of women with AIDS were infected as a result of injecting drugs (U.S. Department of Health and Human Services, 1997).

The number of people infected with HIV continues to grow, but the number of AIDS deaths declined in 1997 for the first time since the epidemic began. The decline indicates that people who become infected with HIV are not developing AIDS as quickly as in the past and that people with AIDS are living longer. Most experts credit new HIV treatments, particularly drugs called protease inhibitors (Altman, 1997). It remains to be seen whether the drugs will lower AIDS mortality in the long term, since they are very expensive—well beyond the financial reach of the people who are most at risk of contracting HIV.

HIV infection and AIDS are severely stigmatized. To a large extent, the social stigma stems from people's misunderstandings about HIV transmission. Despite efforts to educate the general public, the level of misinformation is still high, and widespread myths and stereotypes often lead to prejudice and discrimination against people with HIV/AIDS (Herek & Glunt, 1997). Meanwhile, people with AIDS and those close to them must cope with not only the physical devastation wrought by the disease, but also in many cases the psychological trauma of devastated social networks and increased social isolation (see, for example, Turner et al., 1998; Weitz, 1991). Certainly, public anxiety about diseases such as HIV and AIDS is understandable, but discrimination against and isolation of people with AIDS and their families is an unacceptable response to this health crisis.

Women, Men, and Morbidity

We have seen that, on average, women outlive men by over six years. But interestingly, despite their longer life expectancy and lower mortality rates, women have higher **morbidity** (i.e., illness) **rates** than men. Women have higher rates of illness from acute conditions and nonfatal chronic conditions, and they are slightly more likely to report their health as fair to poor. They make more physician visits each year, and they have twice the number of surgical procedures performed on them as men do (Cleary, 1987; Doyal, 1990b; U.S. Department of Health and Human Services, 1997; Waldron, 1995). Cleary (1987, p. 55) reports that "Those differences are largest during women's reproductive years (ages seventeen to forty-four) but even when reproductive conditions are excluded, there is a residual gender difference in short-term disability."

The higher morbidity of women may be related to their longer life expectancy. The older one is, the more likely one is to suffer from a chronic illness that restricts one's activities. Women comprise 59 percent of the population over 65 and 72 percent of those 85 and older (U.S. Department of Commerce, Bureau of the Census, 1997). Low income adds to the health problems of the elderly, particularly elderly women (Davis et al., 1990). As we saw in Chapters 6 and 7, elderly women, especially women of color, are significantly more likely than elderly men to live below the poverty line. There is a direct relationship between poverty and ill health (Gornick et al., 1996; Schweder, 1997; Syme & Berkman, 1997). One recent study, in fact, found a strong relationship between women's experiences of gender inequality, including lower incomes and greater financial hardship, and poor health (Ross & Bird, 1994). Moreover, official measures of poverty miss a considerable number of the elderly poor who are housed in public institutions and nursing homes. Almost 75 percent of nursing home residents are female (U.S. Department of Commerce, Bureau of the Census, 1991).

A second explanation of women's higher morbidity is that it is simply an artifact of their greater use of medical services. That is, men may experience as many or more symptoms as women, but they ignore them. Such behavior is again compatible with traditional gender norms: Men are stoic and physically strong, while women are frail and need assistance (Helgeson, 1995). There is some evidence to support this hypothesis. For example, although women delay as long as men before getting medical attention for some disorders, men tend to underestimate the extent of their illness more than women do, and they utilize preventive services less often (Waldron, 1995). In addition, the medical community itself is not free of these gender stereotypes and may serve to reinforce them. Historical research, in fact, indicates that physicians have frequently equated normal femininity with the sick role (Ehrenreich & English, 1986). To understand this better, though, we need to look at the differences in the ways women and men are treated by the health care system.

Sexism in Health Care

Medical practitioners in the United States subscribe, for the most part, to a *functional model* of health, which sees the human body as analogous to a machine. Illness temporarily disrupts the normal functioning of this "machine," preventing its owner from fulfilling his or her usual responsibilities. Curative medicine specializes in the scientific repair (i.e., diagnosis, treatment, and cure) of the malfunctioning human machine. "Once 'fixed' the person can be returned to the community" (Rothman, 1984, p. 72).

Sociologist Barbara Katz Rothman (1984) argues that the functional model of health has traditionally made women more than men susceptible to "illness labeling" by the medical establishment. This is because historically, women in general have not been considered contributing members of society—"as people doing important things"—since their primary roles were performed outside the public sphere, in the home. "[W]omen were more easily *defined* as sick when they were not seen as functional social members" (1984, p. 72, author's emphasis). This was particularly significant during the nineteenth and early twentieth centuries when physicians were competing with other healers for patients. The "nonfunctional" woman was a status symbol as well as a symbol of femininity. This image, though, was class- and race-specific; only middle- and upper-class White women (physicians' best paying customers) were viewed as delicate and frail. Poor and working-class women, immigrant women, and women of color were thought to be more robust; it was argued that their less civilized nature made them strong and able to withstand pain. Of course, these women could hardly afford to be sick, even if their wealthy mistresses and employers had permitted it (Ehrenreich & English, 1986; Rothman, 1984).

At the same time, many women of that period did display symptoms of physical weakness, for example, fatigue, shortness of breath, fainting spells, and chest and abdominal pains. These symptoms, though, were probably the consequences of stylishness:

> A fashionable woman's corset exerted, on the average, twenty-one pounds of pressure on her internal organs, and extremes of up to eighty-five pounds had been measured. Add to this the fact that a well-dressed woman wore an average of thirty-seven pounds of street clothing in the winter months, of which nineteen pounds were suspended from her tortured waist. (Ehrenreich & English, 1986, p. 285)

Physicians at the time, however, overlooked the effects of clothing styles on women's health and took these symptoms instead as further evidence of women's inferior constitutions. It was obvious to them that women needed special care, and they responded with the medical specialties of obstetrics and gynecology. Essentially, these specialties medicalized the natural biological events in women's lives: menstruation, pregnancy and childbirth, lactation, and menopause.

There is substantial evidence that early on, physicians' services were often more detrimental than beneficial to women's health. Medical intervention in childbirth is an example. Prior to the nineteenth century, the birth of a child was looked on as a family event, not a medical one. Women gave birth in the presence of female friends, relatives, and midwives who took a noninterventionist approach, letting nature take its course. For the most part, their role was supportive, trying to ease the labor of the birthing woman by making her as comfortable as possible. But when competition for patients began to intensify during the nineteenth century, physicians, who were virtually all men, began to deride midwives as uneducated "quacks." Physicians claimed to have scientific expertise in the area of childbirth. Only they had access to the specialized knowledge and medical instruments that would make childbirth safer, easier, and quicker. Eager for relief from the birthing trauma, women who could afford it increasingly gave birth with a physician, rather than a midwife, in attendance. The physician, having made his claims, felt pressured to "perform," especially if witnesses were present. "The doctor could not appear to be indifferent or inattentive or useless. He had to establish his identity by doing something, preferably something to make the patient feel better" (Wertz & Wertz, 1986, p. 140). However, these were the days before asepsis (the germ theory of disease—that germs cause disease—wasn't proven until 1876), anesthesia, and other important medical developments. Medical schools in the early 1800s offered only a few courses and no clinical experience (Starr, 1982). Doctors' interventions were typically crude and harmful: for instance, bloodletting until the laboring patient fainted, the application of leeches to relieve abdominal and vaginal pain, the use of chloride of mercury to purge the intestines, and the administration of emetics to induce vomiting (Wertz & Wertz, 1986).

Given these techniques, it is hardly surprising that births attended by physicians had higher maternal and infant mortality rates than those attended by midwives for most of the 1800s (Rothman, 1984). Nevertheless, the physicians succeeded in convincing state legislators—men with socioeconomic backgrounds similar to their own—that midwifery and other types of "unscientific" medicine (e.g., herbal medicine) were dangerous. After 1910, the states enacted strict licensing laws that, in effect, drove midwives, herbalists, and other healers out of the business of birthing babies and the practice of medicine (Nechas & Foley, 1994; Starr, 1982). Between 1900 and 1957, the number of practicing midwives in the United States declined dramatically from about 3,000 to 2 (Barker-Benfield, 1976).

Today, obstetricians and gynecologists retain their virtual monopoly on women's health care. Women, in fact, are encouraged to obtain their general medical care from these specialists. Note that there are no comparable medical specialties devoted to "men's diseases" or men's reproductive health, but about 69 percent of obstetricians/gynecologists are men. The overwhelming majority are also White (American Medical Association, 1998).

Advances in medical science and technology have clearly benefitted women and saved many lives, but many analysts still question how much medical intervention into women's normal biological functioning is really necessary. Consider again medical intervention into pregnancy and childbirth. During pregnancy, women normally gain weight, retain fluids, and experience nausea. Doctors have sometimes responded to these changes by prescribing special diets and medications. These may prove helpful for some women, but there are well-documented and tragic examples of how various drugs, such as thalidomide and Bendectin, have produced severe fetal deformities and illness. The drug diethylstilbestrol (DES), a synthetic estrogen, was once widely prescribed to prevent miscarriages, but was taken off the market when it was found to cause cancer in the daughters of women who had taken it (Rothman, 1984).

Studies also show that doctors may intervene in pregnancy for the sake of convenience—their own and the mother's—as well as to reduce their chances of facing malpractice claims (Davis-Floyd, 1992). For example, the rate of caesarian deliveries in the United States has more than doubled since 1975, when it was just 10.4 births per 100 live births. During the first half of the 1990s, the rate of caesarean deliveries averaged 22 per 100 live births, although the Centers for Disease Control maintain that a rate of 15 caesarean births per 100 is more medically appropriate. Most caesarians are scheduled, rather than emergency deliveries, and the Centers for Disease Control maintain that about 36 percent of caesarean deliveries are medically unnecessary (Centers for Disease Control, 1993; U.S. Department of Commerce, Bureau of the Census, 1997). The federal government and health insurers have become more concerned about the high rate of caesarian deliveries because they raise health care costs; caesarians are almost twice as expensive as vaginal deliveries. Interestingly, the majority of caesarian deliveries are performed in for-profit hospitals on women covered by private medical insurance (Centers for Disease Control, 1993).

The increasingly widespread use of electronic fetal monitoring has also contributed to the rise in caesarian deliveries. Physicians, fearing malpractice suits, have taken to routinely using fetal monitors, even for low-risk deliveries. Increasingly common is the use of home fetal monitoring to detect early labor. Home fetal monitoring costs about $100 to $300 per day, an average of about $5,000 per pregnancy. Medical corporations that are offering the service encourage physicians' use of it by allowing them to be shareholders in the company. For the relatively small investment, physicians can receive a return of as much as 15 percent by prescribing the company's equipment. However, studies indicate that the use of electronic home fetal monitoring is no more beneficial or effective in preventing premature delivery than simple daily telephone contact between the pregnant woman and a nurse. Nevertheless, electronic home fetal monitoring is a thriving business—one in which a large number of physicians have invested (Meier, 1993).

The medicalization of pregnancy and childbirth is just one example of often unnecessary medical intervention into normal biological events in a woman's life; there are numerous others. Menopause, for instance, is still viewed as problematic by many physicians, who treat it as a hormone deficiency. Synthetic estrogens (known as estrogen replacement therapy) are frequently prescribed to help women overcome the side effects of menopause, such as hot flashes, depression, irritability, and vaginal inelasticity. Estrogen replacement therapy seems to have beneficial effects for some women, including protection from heart disease, but there are also negative effects as well, such as an increased risk of breast cancer. Moreover, these treatments are often touted in ageist as well as sexist terms, promising women eternal femininity and youthfulness (Greer, 1992).

However, it is poor women and women of color who have suffered most at the hands of the medical establishment. Historically, these women have been treated by physicians as little more than training and research material. In fact, gynecological surgery was developed by physicians who first practiced their techniques on Black and immigrant women. It has been documented, for example, that J. Marion Sims, the "father of gynecology" and one of the early presidents of the American Medical Association, kept a number of Black female slaves for the sole purpose of surgical experimentation. "He operated [without anesthesia] on one of them thirty times in four years. . . . After moving to New York, Sims continued his experimentation on indigent Irish women in the wards of New York Women's Hospital" (Ehrenreich & English, 1986, p. 291).

Researchers have also documented widespread sterilization abuse of poor women and women of color because of racial, ethnic, and social class discrimination (Ruzek, 1987). Davis (1981), for instance, found that as recently as 1972, 100,000 to 200,000 sterilizations took place that year under the auspices of federal programs. The majority of these sterilizations involved poor minority women who allegedly underwent the surgery voluntarily, although there is evidence that many were misled or coerced. "Women were sterilized without consent, or consent was obtained on the basis of false or misleading information—commonly that the operation was reversible or that it was free of problems and side-effects. Information was given in languages women did not understand; women were threatened with loss of welfare or medical benefits if they did not consent; consent was solicited during labor; and abortion was conditioned upon consent to sterilization" (Committee for Abortion Rights and Against Sterilization Abuse, 1988, pp. 27–28). In 1979, the federal government issued regulations to prevent involuntary sterilizations, but some analysts maintain that poor women are still coerced into sterilization in other, more subtle ways. One way, for instance, is the virtual elimination of federal funding for abortions. "The federal government assumes 90 percent of the cost of most sterilizations under Medicaid at the same time that it pays for only a minuscule number of abortions. This funding disparity amounts to a government policy of population control targeted at poor people and people of color" (Committee for Abortion Rights and Against Sterilization Abuse, 1988, p. 28). Not surprisingly, statistics continue to show that Black women are significantly more likely to be surgically sterilized than White women are (U.S. Department of Health and Human Services, 1997).[4]

Sexism is not unique to obstetrics and gynecology, however; research shows that sexism can be found in virtually all medical specialties. For instance, one recent study found that male physicians better understand and communicate more effectively with male patients than female patients. In this study, the researchers found that female patients were more than twice as likely as male patients to have the motivation for their office visit misunderstood by their male physicians (Boland et al., 1998). Cardiology provides another example. Cardiology is male-dominated in terms of both physicians and patients. We have already noted the widespread belief that women are at low risk for heart disease and its consequences, including heart attacks. Recent studies show that most physicians do not respond as quickly to female patients' symptoms of heart disease as they do to male patients' symptoms. For example, one study found that women with heart disease are not receiving aggressive treatment for dangerously high cholesterol levels, although 80 percent of the female patients studied could have achieved safe cholesterol levels if their doctors had prescribed the appropriate drugs—drugs that are routinely prescribed for men with heart disease (Schrott et al., 1997). Women must often prove that there is a genuine problem with their hearts by being significantly sicker (e.g., having a heart attack or congestive heart failure) in order for their complaints to be acted on aggressively by a physician (Nechas & Foley, 1994). This in large part helps to explain why women are less likely than men to survive heart bypass surgery. By the time they undergo the operation, they are usually much sicker and slightly older than the male patients (Kahn et al., 1990). Additional studies show, in fact, that when women go to emergency rooms with complaints about chest pains, they wait twice as long as men to see a doctor and twice as long for an electrocardiogram, and they are 50 percent less likely to be given medications that inhibit further damage to the heart and other parts of the body following a heart attack (Henig, 1993). After a heart attack, women make more visits to their doctors, but they receive fewer diagnostic tests and medical procedures during this period than male patients do (Schwartz et al., 1997).

Women are also less likely than men to receive the most sophisticated type of pace-maker, even when differences in their cardiac conditions are controlled for (Schuppel et al., 1998).

In short, research documents a legacy of negative and stereotypic attitudes among physicians toward women, especially poor women, women of color, and elderly women. Women's health concerns not infrequently are trivialized or misunderstood. This, in turn, leads to less than humane treatment and less effective health care for women (Nechas & Foley, 1994). As Box 11.3 shows, lesbians and gay men also receive less humane and effective treatment because of heterosexism in health care.

These prejudices—sexism, racism, ageism, classism, and heterosexism—are learned by physicians during their medical training. The role models available to medical students—medical school faculty and practicing physicians—are typically men who themselves have been steeped in this tradition, and it may appear in their teaching as well as their interactions with students, colleagues, and patients. Nechas and Foley (1994), for example, found that sexual remarks, jokes, and innuendo were common in medical schools. Another recent study found that nearly half of female physicians surveyed (47.7 percent of 4,501 female physicians) reported having been harassed by male colleagues and teachers simply because they are women. For instance, they were called "honey" in front of patients or other medical personnel, or they were told that medicine was not an appropriate field for women. In this same study, 36.9 percent of female physicians reported experiences of sexual harassment by male colleagues and teachers, including lewd remarks, groping, and kissing (Frank et al., 1998; see also Conley, 1998). Female physicians also report frequent harassment by male patients, who make suggestive remarks and gestures, expose themselves in sexually suggestive ways, and touch them inappropriately (Phillips & Schneider, 1993). However, patients may also be harassed and sexually abused by physicians: In one survey of 600 emergency room physicians in Canada, for instance, researchers found that 9 percent knew a colleague who had had sex with a patient, while 6 percent admitted they themselves had had sex with a patient (Ovens & Permaul-Wood, 1997). However, another study conducted in the United States found 40 percent of physicians who had been charged with sexual misconduct continue to practice medicine ("Sex Offender MDs Still Practicing," 1997).

Clearly, the traditional doctor-patient relationship itself appears to be unhealthy, especially for women seeking medical care. It has been argued, though, that this relationship will gradually change as more women enter the medical profession, since they will be better able to communicate with female patients and they have a better understanding of the female body (Fee, 1983; Klass, 1988). Others are skeptical of this argument and call for more radical changes in health care delivery. Before we consider these alternatives, let's take a closer look at the roles and experiences of women and men in the health care professions, especially in light of what we have already learned about the gender-based and sexual harassment of female physicians.

The Patriarchal Hierarchy of Health Care Work

In Chapter 6, we discussed how functionalist sociologists, such as Talcott Parsons, differentiate between male and female roles as instrumental and expressive, respectively.

BOX 11.3
Heterosexist Health Care

When choosing a physician, what characteristics do you look for? Most likely, you consider the physician's credentials: medical school attended, board certification, years practicing, perhaps even awards and honors. You may also ask around to see what kind of reputation the physician has. But if you are a lesbian or gay man, one of the most important characteristics to you as a patient is that the physician feel comfortable with homosexuals and be knowledgeable about the special health needs of gays and lesbians. Research indicates that homosexuals often do not disclose their sexual orientation to health care providers because they fear rejection, ridicule, and disrespect (Tiemann, et al., forthcoming). Many believe their care will be negatively affected if providers are aware of their sexual orientation (Johnson, et al., 1981).

Studies show that these fears are not unfounded. Consider, for example, the lesbian who went to a neurologist because she was having severe headaches and occasional memory loss. While taking this woman's medical history, the physician questioned why she did not use contraception. When she replied that she is a lesbian, the neurologist reassessed all her symptoms in light of this information and decided she should have psychological testing and be evaluated by a clinical psychologist. Her physical problem was redefined as a psychological disorder stemming from her sex-

ual orientation. Another lesbian, who disclosed her sexual orientation to her allergy specialist was told that her lesbianism might be caused by her allergies and that perhaps a series of injections would "cure" her (Tiemann et al., forthcoming). Other gay men and lesbians report that although their health care providers don't explicitly state their disapproval or discomfort with their patients' homosexuality, their behavior betrays their feelings: They are startled, become nervous, and can no longer maintain eye contact, preferring to look at the floor or past the patient. The providers may also stop talking with the patient or not engage in extensive questioning, which in turn, could result in misdiagnoses or inadequate treatment (Stevens, forthcoming).

Heterosexual physicians typically assume that their patients are also straight. A substantial number—40 percent in one study—admit that they are sometimes or often uncomfortable providing care to gay and lesbian patients (Matthews, et al., 1986). The heterosexism and homophobia that characterizes health care, however, has a negative impact on gays and lesbians. Some forego care altogether. Most, though, simply hide their sexual orientation from medical professionals even though their failure to disclose this information could mean that they do not get the care they need (White & Dull, forthcoming).

Within the traditional patriarchal family, men are the instrumental leaders of the household and command greater power in decision making primarily because they are the breadwinners. Women, in contrast, are housekeepers and nurturers. Interestingly, critics of traditional medical practice in the United States draw parallels between patriarchal relations in the family and the male-female relations dominant in the delivery of health care. "The doctor/father runs a family composed of the nurse (wife and mother) and the patient (the child). The doctor possesses the scientific and technical skills and the nurse performs the caring and comforting duties" (Fee, 1983, p. 24).

The sex distribution of workers across specific health care fields makes this parallel even sharper. Health care historically has been an area of high female employment because many health care jobs were viewed as an extension of women's roles in the home. Not surprisingly, therefore, women constitute more than 88 percent of health service workers today, although they make up only about a quarter (26.4 percent) of practicing physicians (U.S. Department of Commerce, Bureau of the Census, 1997). Women are concentrated in the "helping," "nurturing," and housekeeping jobs in health care. For example, they constitute 93.3 percent of registered nurses; 90.2 percent of dieticians and nutritionists; and 88.4 percent of nursing aides and attendants (U.S. Department of Commerce, Bureau of the Census, 1997). These positions have lower prestige and lower incomes than male-dominated health professions, such as physician, although the acute shortage of nurses during the 1980s did result in substantial pay raises and other benefits for members of the nursing profession. This, in turn, attracted more men to the field, although the profession has consistently remained more than 90 percent female.[5] The least prestigious and lowest paying jobs are filled largely by women of color (Doyal, 1990a; Glenn, 1992).

We have already seen how male physicians drove female health care providers, such as midwives, out of practice early in this century. In addition, women and racial and ethnic minorities historically were excluded from medical schools or discouraged from entering or completing medical training, either through blatant or, more recently, subtle forms of discrimination (Nechas & Foley, 1994). Since 1971, however, the number of female and minority medical school students and graduates has increased significantly (see Table 11.4). In 1971, for example, women were just 10.9 percent of medical school students; by 1994, their numbers had nearly quadrupled to 41.1 percent (U.S. Department of Health and Human Services, 1997). In 1975, women were just 13.4 percent of medical school graduates, whereas in 1993, they were 37.9 percent of medical school graduates (National Center for Education Statistics, 1996). As Table 11.4 also shows, racial and ethnic minorities have also increased their representation among medical school students and graduates, although in 1997, there was an 11 percent drop in minority medical school enrollments. Most experts attribute this decline to recent federal court decisions and state referenda that ended affirmative action programs in medical school admissions, discouraging some minorities from applying and causing school administrators to be overly cautious in admissions decisions so as to avoid a "reverse discrimination" lawsuit ("Minority Enrollment Drops," 1997).[6]

Although the greater presence of women and people of color in medical school classes is certainly a welcome trend, some observers question the extent to which these groups will be able to change the sexism and other inequalities that seem entrenched in our health care system. Some of this skepticism stems from the fact that female and minority medical students receive their training in the same sexist, racist, class-biased, and homophobic system of medical education that White males do. As we have already noted, they also have very few role models other than White men. The representation of women among medical school faculty has improved somewhat since 1975, from 15.1 percent to 24 percent in 1994 (Kirschstein, 1996). But while the number of minority faculty has increased considerably since 1975, the number of White faculty has also increased, thereby keeping the proportion of minority faculty fairly constant (between 19 and 21 percent) over the last two and a half decades (Commission on Professionals in Science and Technology, 1992).

We have already discussed the widespread gender discrimination, including sexual harassment, that female physicians experience. A rather discouraging finding of the

TABLE 11.4   Medical School Enrollments and Graduates by Sex and Race, Selected Years

Percent of first-year students enrolled in medical school who were:	1980–1981	1994–1995
Women	28.9	42.2
White (non-Hispanic)	82.9	66.3
Black (non-Hispanic)	7.9	8.9
Hispanic	4.8	6.8
Asian	3.3	17.2
American Indian	0.4	0.8

Percent of total students enrolled in medical school who were:	1980–1981	1994–1995
Women	26.5	41.1
White (non-Hispanic)	85.0	67.7
Black (non-Hispanic)	5.7	7.6
Hispanic	4.9	6.2
Asian	2.9	16.5
American Indian	0.3	0.6

Percent of medical school graduates (M.D.'s) who were:	1993–1994
Women	37.9
White (non-Hispanic)	73.4
Black (non-Hispanic)	6.1
Hispanic	4.0
Asian/Pacific Islander	14.8
American Indian/Alaskan Native	0.4

Sources: National Center for Education Statistics, 1996, p. 296; U.S. Department of Health and Human Services, 1997, p. 242.

Frank et al. study (1998) was that young women were the most likely to have these negative experiences, an indication that despite the greater presence of women in the medical profession, their situation is not significantly improving. Moreover, this study found that women in the male-dominated (and highest-paying) specialties, such as surgery, were more likely than other women to report harassment and discrimination. This finding helps to explain why these specialties remain male-dominated. As one recent medical school graduate explained, women interested in the male-dominated specialties are often treated so poorly during those rotations that they abandon their aspirations to pursue one of these specialties (Manning, 1998). Not surprisingly, women are concentrated in general medicine, pediatrics, and other lower-paying specialties (Kirschstein, 1996).

Recent research indicates that female physicians appear to care for female patients better than male physicians do. For example, female physicians have been found to perform more Pap tests on their patients and to order significantly more mammograms. This is especially true when the practices of younger female and male physicians are compared (Franks & Clancy, 1993; Lurie et al., 1993). Nevertheless, some observers continue to express concern that as long as medical students are socialized into a physician role that is paternalistic and authoritarian, the detrimental aspects of the physician-patient relationship, particularly for female and non-White patients, are not likely to improve. From this perspective, the solution to the inequities in health care is not simply to put more women and people of color in positions of power within the current medical system, but rather to change the system itself. As we will see next, this goal is a cornerstone of the feminist health care movement.

Feminist Health Care

The feminist health care movement emerged during the 1960s as an outgrowth of the broader feminist struggle against sexism and gender inequality (see Chapter 1). Women meeting in small consciousness-raising groups began to relate their individual medical experiences, which contained some common themes: "[the doctor-patient relationship] was all too often characterized by condescension and contempt on the part of the doctor, and feelings of humiliation on the part of the patient" (Marieskind & Ehrenreich, 1975, p. 39). Out of these discussions grew the realization that women needed to develop their own standards of health and normalcy by studying women's bodies, including their own. By 1975, these early efforts had produced more than 1,200 feminist health care groups in the United States alone.

The feminist health care movement combines self-help with political practice (Withorn, 1986). According to health education specialist Sheryl Ruzek (1987, p. 188), feminist health activists "educate themselves and other women about health issues, provide alternative services, and work to influence public policies affecting women's health." They accomplish these goals in diverse ways. With regard to education, for instance, feminists have produced a large and impressive body of literature covering diverse health and medical issues in a nontechnical, highly readable style and format. One of the first, and perhaps the best known, example is the Boston Women's Health Collective's book *Our Bodies, Ourselves*, published in 1973 and revised in 1992. A walk through the health section of any mainstream bookstore today will demonstrate the wide array of feminist health care publications currently available.

Feminist health activists have also organized "know-your-body courses," in which women not only learn about their bodies—thereby demystifying them—but also learn how to provide themselves with basic care through, for example, breast self-exams and pelvic self-exams. In the way of alternative medical care, women have opened their own clinics to provide a variety of services, such as gynecological care, pregnancy testing, counseling, and abortion services. There are two distinctive features of feminist clinics: (1) "the bulk of a patient's encounter, from initial intake to the final counseling, is with women like herself"; and (2) "the woman is not the object of care but an active participant" (Marieskind & Ehrenreich, 1975, p. 39).

Finally, in terms of influencing public policy, feminist health activists have formed organizations, such as the National Women's Health Network, which has more than

20,000 members. Such groups lobby local, national, and international decision makers regarding policies affecting women's health throughout the world (Ruzek, 1987).

The feminist health care movement has not been free of problems. For one thing, women's clinics often face severe staffing shortages and funding difficulties. Such clinics are among the first to lose during government budget cuts (Withorn, 1986). Not surprisingly, the clinics can usually provide only limited services, usually just obstetrical and gynecological care. In addition, the movement in general has sometimes been criticized for not posing a more serious challenge to the medical establishment. "Many health activists believe that it is virtually impossible to create a truly humane health care system for women in a capitalist society. Yet none of the strategies used directly attack the underlying economic organization of society" (Ruzek, 1987, p. 195). Most still focus on individual treatment, rather than institutional change. And there is the added danger that an emphasis on self-care may simply serve to relieve the state of any responsibility for insuring the health of its citizens, female and male (Ruzek, 1987; Withorn, 1986).

Despite these difficulties, the feminist health care movement is to be applauded for providing many women with safe, affordable, and affirming medical services. Equally important is the movement's central role in identifying and publicizing the inadequacies and inequities of our traditional health care system. Although the movement's focus has been on women, its analysis of the problems inherent in traditional health care delivery has also been beneficial to men, especially poor, working-class, and minority men who not infrequently are also subjected to inhumane and condescending treatment at the hands of an elitist medical establishment. Evidence of the movement's success can also be found in U.S. medical schools, which have adopted some of its ideas. For example, many medical schools now have genital teaching associate programs to teach aspiring physicians how to do a pelvic exam. Similar to the early "know-the-female-body" courses, genital teaching associate programs hire women to teach medical students how to more sensitively perform a pelvic examination. The focus of these programs is on developing interpersonal skills as much as medical techniques (Kelly, 1998).

Another contribution of the feminist health care movement has been to give women "a sense of pride and strength in their bodies" (Marieskind & Ehrenreich, 1975, p. 38). Let's continue to explore this issue by discussing gender, physical fitness, and athletic participation.

Gender, Sport, and Fitness

Knowing the particular strengths and weaknesses of one's body, feeling fit and energized, being comfortable with and appreciative of one's body are all empowering. What is more, developing one's physical potential instills a sense of achievement that encourages an individual to undertake other types of challenges (Lenskyj, 1986). A recognition of this underlies the much quoted phrase, "sports builds character." Unfortunately, the missing, but nevertheless understood adjective here has long been *masculine* character. Consider, for instance, the 1971 case of *Hollander* v. *Connecticut Conference, Inc.*, in which a female student was barred from competing on her high school's boys' cross country team, even though she had qualified, because the state interscholastic athletic conference prohibited coed sports. In deciding in favor of the athletic conference, the judge stated, "Athletic competition builds character in our boys. We do not need that kind of character in our girls, the women of tomorrow" (quoted in Lawrence, 1987, p. 222).

The judge's statement reflects the traditional belief that athletics is a masculine pursuit incompatible with our cultural standards of feminine beauty and female heterosexual attractiveness. In one sense, this is true; the ways in which sporting and fitness activities are typically organized and played out represent the antithesis of our culture's definition of femininity. The main ingredients of sport in our society are competition and domination, self-control and toughness, and violence and aggression. From their earliest encounters with sports, males are taught to develop a "killer instinct" on the playing field or court. Sport, they learn, is confrontation with an opponent; it entails a certain degree of sweat, exhaustion, and, most importantly, pain to be satisfying. Winning, of course, is "everything." Men and boys who don't play this way—who do not exhibit "forceful masculinity" in athletics—are ridiculed for playing "like girls" (Messner, 1992; White et al., 1995).

Females have not been excluded from sport and physical fitness activities altogether, but their participation historically has been limited. They have been encouraged to assume a supportive role as cheerleaders rather than as direct participants. Those who have participated directly have been channeled into "feminine sports," such as swimming and diving, skating, gymnastics, and aerobic dancing. Those women who seriously pursued sports often did so under great stress, being labeled "mannish" and "unfeminine" or inept by others (Blinde & Taub, 1992; Jarrat, 1990; Nelson, 1992). For instance, one recent study showed that in the minds of many people, a serious female athlete must be a lesbian, and this labeling, in turn, continues to control the number of women in sports and the behavior of female athletes. "Women athletes are seen as something less than 'real women' because they do not exemplify traditional female qualities (e.g., dependency, weakness, passivity)" (Blinde & Taub, 1992, p. 163). The exception, according to one writer, is the Black female athlete who, in the Black community, "can be strong and competent in sport and still not deny her womanliness" (Hart, 1980).

In the early 1970s, however, a number of developments began to transform both women's and men's participation in sport and fitness activities. Perhaps the most important event was passage in 1972 of Title IX of the Education Amendments Act. You may recall from Chapter 4 that Title IX prohibits sex discrimination in educational programs, including sports, that receive federal funding. In effect, Title IX forced most U.S. educational institutions to broaden their athletic programs for girls and women and to spend more money on girls' and women's sports. The effects have been significant: For example, at U.S. colleges and universities, the percentage of female varsity athletes rose from 16 percent in 1971 to 38 percent in 1997; the number of athletic scholarships awarded to women at the highly competitive National Collegiate Athletic Association (NCAA) Division I schools increased from 20 percent in 1977 to about 33 percent in 1997 ("Conference Report," 1997; Dunkle, 1987; Raiborn, 1990). But while there have clearly been significant improvements in women's athletics since the early 1970s, inequities remain. For instance, the average Division I NCAA-member school spends $849,130 per year on men's athletic scholarships and $372,800 per year on scholarships for female athletes.

The average base salary for a men's head basketball coach was $71,511 in 1991 compared with $39,177 for a women's head basketball coach (NCAA, 1992; see also Theberge 1993 for a discussion of sex disparities among coaches in Canada).

A similar pattern can be found throughout the sports world. Since the 1970s, women have made tremendous gains in athletic participation. In 1994, for instance, 328 young women played on their high school's boys' varsity football team. Although they were a minuscule 0.03 percent of all high school football players, they significantly increased girls' representation in this sport (Bloom, 1995). At the amateur level, ice hockey has been growing in popularity among women. Between 1988 and 1998, the number of women registered with USA Hockey, the national organization that governs amateur hockey, increased from about 5,500 to over 20,000. This number is expected to grow even more because of the gold medal win by the U.S. women's ice hockey team at the 1998 Winter Olympics (Kannapell, 1998; LaPointe, 1998 but see also Theberge, 1997). At the professional level, there are now two professional women's basketball leagues (the American Basketball League and the Women's NBA), and in 1997, two women were hired as referees in the Men's National Basketball Association (Wise, 1997).

Still, most people continue to devalue women's involvement in sports, regarding women as less serious athletes than men and questioning female athletes' physical and psychological strength and stamina. Consider, for example, that the average salary of a female professional basketball player in 1996 was about $70,000, while star players were paid as much as $125,000 (Smallwood, 1997). In 1996, Michael Jordan made over $300,000 *per game* and over $193 million in endorsements ("The Year of the Michaels," 1996). While Jordan was regarded by most as the best player in the NBA, even an average male player was paid an annual salary of $1.7 million (U.S. Department of Commerce, Bureau of the Census, 1997).

Of course, many people would argue that men's sports produce greater revenues than women's sports, and they would be right. However, this argument overlooks the fact that our culture trivializes women's sports and women athletes, while promoting sport as the epitome of masculinity and proof of the physical basis of gender difference (White et al., 1995). We can see this in the way the media report on men's and women's sports. First, women athletes and women's sporting events are underreported, except during the Olympic Games or other major international competitions (Messner et al., 1993). For example, Messner and his colleagues (1993) found that men's sports get 92 percent of televised sports news coverage in the United States, whereas women's sports get just 5 percent of such coverage; the remaining coverage is mixed or gender-neutral. Second, the media's sports reporting also emphasizes a certain type of "orthodox masculinity," particularly toughness and courage in the face of physical risk (Robinson, 1992; White et al., 1995). Women athletes not only do little to sell this kind of masculinity, but also they pose a serious challenge to it. Third, when women are highlighted in the media, it is often as sex objects or as victims. For example, in a content analysis of *Sports Illustrated* covers between February 1993 and February 1994, Ryan (1994) found that over the fifty-two-week period, only six women were featured. On one occasion, the women were not athletes, but models; this, of course, was the famous "swimsuit issue." Another issue also showed women who were not athletes; it showed the widows of two professional baseball players who had been killed in a boating accident. The other three women were athletes, but they were featured as victims rather than victors: Monica Seles, the professional tennis player, was shown with a knife protruding from her back after she had been stabbed by a spectator at a match; Mary Pierce, another tennis player, was featured in a special report on her father's abuse of her; and Nancy Kerrigan, the Olympic figure skater was featured after she had been attacked by associates of a rival skater. There are several sports magazines designed specifically for female audiences, including *Conde Naste Sports for Women* and *Sports Illustrated Women/Sport*, but they are published irregularly. One analysis of these magazines also found that they focus more on health and fitness rather than on sport per say, although they do profile competitive sportswomen (MRTW, 1998b; see also Messner et al., 1993).

Despite the continued gender stereotyping of athletes, considerable research has emerged from the fields of sports medicine and sports psychology that debunks many of the myths about the physical and emotional consequences of athletics for men and women. One of the first myths that was refuted, for instance, was the notion of "no pain, no gain" in exercise. Sports medicine specialists were quick to point out that by ignoring the signals their bodies send them through pain, athletes were likely to injure themselves, sometimes permanently (men are more likely to subscribe to this tenet than women) (White et al., 1995). Sports medicine researchers also demonstrated that participation in sports and vigorous exercise do not "androgenize" women's muscles, nor do they harm the female reproductive system. To the contrary, exercise may lessen menstrual discomfort and ease childbirth (Christensen, 1993; "Longer Menstrual Cycles," 1996). Third, the notion that men are naturally better athletes than women because of biological differences in their physical size and strength is also being called into question, especially for certain sports. Recent analyses, for example, show that in track, although men's running times have been improving since the turn of the century, women's running times have been improving at more than double the men's rate, so that if such trends continue, women's and men's track performances will be comparable in the near future (Whipp & Ward, 1992).

Meanwhile, sports psychologists have found while physical exercise and participation in sports can increase self-confidence as well as reduce the likelihood of developing various chronic illnesses such as coronary heart disease, a focus on winning at all costs can produce unhealthy outcomes, including serious illness and injury, as well as a sense of failure, especially in men, since so few ever reach the top of the athletic hierarchy (Klein, 1995; President's Council on Physical Fitness and Sports, 1997; White et al., 1995).[7] Sports sociologist Harry Edwards has highlighted the disproportionate impact these negative outcomes have had on young Black men, since they are typically channeled into sports, but rarely have a "social safety net" to protect them if they "fail." Indeed, Edwards and others have played a major part in uncovering both the exploitation of African American athletes and the racism that continues to permeate organized sports. As one writer expressed it, "In sports, as in the plantation system of the Old South, the overseers are white and the workers are black" (Runfola, 1980, p. 93; see also Messner, 1987).

There is evidence that although most female athletes are highly competitive, females in general tend to approach sports differently than males in general. Studies, for example, indicate that women and girls tend to be more flexible and cooperative players of team sports and have a greater concern for the fairness of the game rather than "winning at all costs" (Gilligan, 1982; Jarratt, 1990; Nelson, 1992). In a sense, then, women and girls actually have been freer to approach sports in the way that at least theoretically they are supposed to be approached: in the spirit of play and for the purpose of personal enjoyment and enrichment.

The growth in fitness activities and sports participation has not been lost on entrepreneurs. Selling everything from clothing to exercise equipment to "power" foods, they recognize the growing national interest in exercise and sports as big business, a business that yields more than $5.5 billion a year. Interestingly, however, their marketing strategy is often not significantly different for male and female consumers: Research shows that many of the fitness products and programs are being touted to women *and* men with promises of youthfulness, thinness, and sex appeal rather than health, well-being, and physical agility (Lenskyj, 1986; MRTW, 1998b). However, as we will discuss in the final section of this chapter, the commercial tendency to imbue women and, increasingly, men, with insecurity about their bodies and appearance often results in serious psychological as well as physical harm.

The Politics of Mental Health and Mental Illness

Up to this point, we have been discussing physical health and illness, but let's take some time to explore gender issues in mental health and illness. Gender provides a strong link between physical and mental health since physicians have tended to view women's physical complaints as psychosomatic, that is, as "all in their heads." Research shows that physicians often see women's use of medical services as one of the ways women typically cope with psychological problems. Consequently, physicians commonly prescribe psychotropic drugs for women who visit them with complaints of physical ailments. According to Nechas and Foley (1994), for example, women receive about 66 percent of psychoactive drug prescriptions. These prescriptions are typically written by internists, general practitioners, and obstetricians/gynecologists rather than psychiatrists.

Historically, it was also common for physicians to assume that "malfunctions" in women's reproductive systems caused psychological disturbances. Around the turn of the twentieth century, for instance, physicians maintained that ovarian dysfunctions caused "personality disorders" in women—specifically, troublesomeness, eating like a ploughman, masturbation, attempted suicide, erotic tendencies, persecution mania, simple "cussedness," and dysmenorrhea. The "cure" physicians devised was ovariotomy (i.e., removal of the ovaries, or "female castration"). Ehrenreich and English (1986) report that:

> In 1906 a leading gynecological surgeon estimated that there were 150,000 women in the United States who had lost their ovaries under the knife. Some doctors boasted that they had removed from fifteen hundred to two thousand ovaries apiece. . . . Patients were often brought in by their husbands, who complained of their unruly behavior. . . . The operation was judged successful if the woman was restored to a placid contentment with her domestic functions. (p. 290)

Today, many physicians believe that menstruation and menopause precipitate personality disorders in women, ranging from depression to violent behavior, even though there is little evidence to support this and much to refute it (Gitlin & Pasnau, 1990; see also Chapter 2). Drugs, such as synthetic hormones that have been linked to cancer, have superseded surgery as "treatment."

These examples highlight some of the difficulties we need to consider when discussing mental health and illness: the problems of definition, identification, and appropriate treatment. Psychiatrists themselves disagree as to what does and what does not constitute mental illness. At one extreme are those who claim that most mental disorders are objective conditions that have identifiable organic or genetic causes. At the other extreme are those who argue that mental illness is a political and moral label, not a medical one, and that mental institutions are not hospitals, but rather facilities to control those singled out as deviant.

Although most mental health specialists hold a position somewhere in between these two extremes, the disagreement itself makes it obvious that the identification of mental illness is a difficult enterprise at best. Just how difficult it is was demonstrated by D. L. Rosenhan and his colleagues in a classic experiment conducted in 1973. Rosenhan and seven associates were admitted to several different mental hospitals by claiming they were hearing voices. Their symptom, though, was contrived, as were the names and occupations they gave; however, they made no other changes in their life histories or regular behavior. Each of these pseudopatients expected to be identified quickly as an imposter by hospital personnel, but none was. Instead, the hospital staffs reinterpreted their normal behavior and previous life experiences to coincide with the mental illness diagnosis. They spent an average of nineteen days in the hospital, with all but one diagnosed schizophrenic.

The Rosenhan experiment illustrates that what is identified as mental illness "may be in the culturally filtered eye of the beholder rather than in the malfunction of the physiology or psyche of the person whose behavior is being judged" (Little, 1983, p. 345). Because mental health practitioners, like other human beings, are not immune from social conditioning and therefore cannot be completely objective, we may expect their clinical judgments to reflect, at least in part, aspects of the culture to which they belong. Throughout this text, we have identified a variety of cultural stereotypes regarding gender, sexual orientation, race and ethnicity, age, and social class. How do such stereotypes influence clinical assessments of mental health and illness? Let's consider this question now.

The Double Standard of Mental Health

Nearly thirty years ago, a group of social scientists asked seventy-nine mental health professionals (forty-six men and thirty-three women) to describe "a healthy, mature, socially competent (a) adult, sex unspecified, (b) a man, or (c) a woman" (Broverman et al., 1970, p. 1). What they discovered was that the characteristics of mental health in the responses differed according to the sex of the person being described. More importantly, however, they found that traits considered healthy for an adult *person* were almost identical to those judged healthy for *men*, including independence, a sense of adventure, and assertiveness. In contrast, the healthy, mature, socially competent adult woman was described as submissive, dependent, excitable in minor crises, and conceited about her appearance. As Broverman et al. (1970, p. 5) concluded, "This constellation seems a most unusual way of describing any mature, healthy individual."

Since 1970, this study has been replicated a number of times under a variety of circumstances and with different subjects (Brooks-Gunn & Fisch, 1980; Hansen & Reekie, 1990; Philips & Gilroy, 1985; Wise & Rafferty, 1982). These replications have yielded results that support Broverman et al.'s original findings. What we see here, then, is that stereotypical masculine behavior is assumed by many clinicians to be the norm or the ideal standard of mental health. This, in turn, puts women in a double bind. On the one hand, if they choose to behave as a healthy, mature adult, they risk being labeled abnormal (i.e., masculine women). On the other hand, women who follow the cultural script for the healthy, mature woman may find themselves unhappy, dissatisfied, and psychologically troubled (Gilbert & Scher, 1999; Tavris, 1992).

Robertson and Fitzgerald's (1990) research demonstrates how this stereotype may also work against men who choose to deviate from traditional norms of masculinity. Robertson and Fitzgerald showed one of two versions of a videotaped conversation between a male patient (in reality, an actor) and his therapist to forty-seven other therapists. In one of the tapes, the patient stated he was an engineer with a wife at home who cared for their children. In the other tape, he indicated that his wife was an engineer and he stayed home with the children. Therapists who viewed the first tape attributed the man's problems to job or marital pressures or to biological causes. However, those who saw the second tape typically diagnosed the man as severely depressed and attributed the depression to his adoption of the domestic role, even though he reported to his therapist in the tape that his staying at home had worked out well for the family. In addition, these therapists tended to focus on the man's adoption of the domestic role as something to be treated through therapy and some appeared hostile toward the patient, questioning his notion of what it means to be a man. In short, this study indicates that men who choose not to adhere to the traditionally prescribed masculine role are at risk of being labeled mentally ill (see also Gilbert & Scher, 1999; Hansen & Reekie, 1990; Tavris, 1992).

Besides sex, an individual's race or ethnicity may influence whether he or she is labeled mentally ill as well as the particular disorder that is diagnosed. Loring and Powell (1988), for example, found that mental health professionals were more likely to diagnose Blacks than Whites as violent, even though the cases they were evaluating were identical in all other respects (see also Fulani, 1988; Littlewood & Lipsedge, 1989).

Finally, it is also the case that definitions of mental illness and standards of mental health change over time as a behavior gains greater acceptance by the general public or as a result of successful lobbying on the part of a particular group. For instance, in its 1980 revision of the *Diagnostic and Statistical Manual for Mental Disorders*—the official psychiatric classification scheme—the American Psychiatric Association (APA) voted to delete homosexuality from the listing. Prior to this time, homosexuality was officially considered a mental illness and was sometimes "treated" with aversion therapy (e.g., the injection of drugs to induce vomiting while the "patient" looked at homosexual erotica) and electroshock therapy. The demedicalization of homosexuality in 1980 was chiefly the result of tireless campaigning and political confrontation between gay rights activists, such as the National Gay and Lesbian Task Force, and the APA (Busfield, 1986).

In the sections that follow, we will discuss several mental disorders that have a higher incidence among members of one sex than the other. We'll pay particular attention to how traditional gender relations may foster these disorders and how gender stereotypes may affect clinicians' diagnoses and treatments of patients. In addition, we will consider how other factors, including a patient's race and ethnicity, age, social class, and sexual orientation, may influence diagnosis and clinical outcomes.

Depression, Histrionic Personality, and Agoraphobia.   Each of us, at one time or another, has felt depressed. In everyday usage, *depression* refers to feeling down, "blue," or sad. Depression as a clinical syndrome, however, is more severe and prolonged. **Clinical depression** entails persistent feelings of discontent or displeasure accompanied by at least four of eight symptoms (poor appetite or weight loss, insomnia or increased sleep, psychomotor agitation or retardation, loss of interest in usual activities, loss of energy or fatigue, feelings of worthlessness, diminished concentration, and suicidal ideation) that are present daily for at least two weeks without evidence of any other disorder (Rothblum, 1982).

Women have consistently higher rates of depression than men, according to studies of both clinical populations and the general public. It is estimated that during the course of their lives, 15 percent of men, but 24 percent of women in the United States experience clinical depression (Hirschfield et al., 1997). Globally, it is estimated that 3.5 times more women than men become clinically depressed at some point in their lives (World Health Organization, 1996). What is more, this sex difference begins to emerge as early as puberty (Allgood-Merton et al., 1990).

The incidence of depression among men and women, however, also varies by race and ethnicity, social class, and marital status. Women of color and poor women who head households (among whom racial minorities are disproportionately represented) have the highest rates of depression of any group (Landrine & Klonoff, 1997; McGrath et al., 1990). Cannon and her colleagues (1989) report, though, that the interaction of race and social mobility affects rates of depression among middle-class women. In their study of 200 female professionals and managers employed full time, they found that Black women who had been raised in middle-class households and White women who had been raised in working-class households had the highest levels of depressive symptoms. Their study also shows that single women and women with children are more likely to be depressed than married women or childless women.

However, other researchers have found that married women are more susceptible to depression than both never-married women and married men. Interestingly, the reverse is true for men: Never-married men are more likely to suffer depression than married men. According to the American Psychological Association (1985, p. 8), "marriage is associated with a 71 percent reduction in illness for minority men, 63 percent for white men, 28 percent for white women, and 8 percent for minority women." Also of special interest is the observation that among divorced women and men, the former experienced more depression during the marriage, whereas the latter grew depressed during the marital separation (Rothblum, 1982; see also Helgeson, 1994; Chapter 6).

A number of theories have been developed to explain these differences. One is that the difference is merely a statistical artifact of women's greater likelihood to seek help for their problems. There is evidence of bias among psychiatrists, especially male psychiatrists, toward diagnosing depression in women (Loring & Powell, 1988), and there is also evidence of men's unwillingness to seek professional help for depression since such behavior is considered "unmanly" (Real, 1997). These findings, though, leave unexplained the higher rate of depression reported by women in general community surveys in which respondents, regardless of sex, have not usually sought help (Cleary, 1987; Joiner & Blalock, 1995; Landrine & Klonoff, 1997). It also cannot explain the variation in depression by age, race and ethnicity, social class, and marital status.

A second argument focuses on hormonal differences between the sexes, but evidence in support of this is sparse. There is a strong relationship between postpartum hormonal changes and depression (see Chapter 2), but this can account for only a small portion of the rate variation between the sexes, and it also does not explain the variation between White women and women of color.

It seems more likely that social factors are responsible for the differences in depression rates that we have observed. There are two major psychological explanations: the *learned helplessness hypothesis* and the *social status hypothesis*. According to the learned helplessness hypothesis, females are socialized to respond passively to stress, but males are taught to respond assertively. Consequently, when confronted with a stressful life event, men are more likely to take some kind of action, whereas women tend to become depressed. At first glance, this argument is appealing, but if we look at it closely, we see that it amounts to little more than victim blaming. "Many women find their situation depressing because real social discrimination [not faulty socialization] makes it difficult for them to achieve by direct action and self-assertion, further contributing to their psychological distress" (Weissman, 1980, p. 102; see also Miller & Kirsch, 1987). For instance, research indicates that an important contributing factor to women's increased risk of clinical depression is their greater vulnerability to physical and sexual abuse. According to Nechas and Foley (1994), if one controls for the incidence of physical and sexual abuse among depressed women, the rates of depression for women and men are equalized. The learned helplessness hypothesis also overlooks the fact that most women do take direct action to address the source of their depression, although in many instances their efforts are unsuccessful because of their limited resources (Davies et al., 1998). Thus, it appears that the social and economic conditions under which particular groups of women live, not certain inherent or learned feminine traits, put them at greater risk for clinical depression.

This is precisely the premise of the social status hypothesis, which also emphasizes that the traditional roles afforded to women (i.e., homemaker, mother) offer limited sources of personal satisfaction compared with the diversity of jobs available to men (Doyal, 1990b; World Health Organization, 1996). Given their double burden of housework and paid work, one would expect employed women to experience greater psychological distress than full-time homemakers, but interestingly, research shows that just the opposite is usually the case (Thoits, 1987). Moreover, women who have high-income, high-status jobs also have high levels of psychological well-being and few symptoms of psychological distress, irrespective of marital status (Golding, 1988; Horwitz, 1982). If we consider the stress and disadvantages imposed by poverty, sexism, and racial and ethnic discrimination, the depression so prevalent among low-income women and women of color is easy to understand. In fact, one recent study found that the single best predictor of women's depressive symptoms was personal experiences of sex discrimination and, since women of color were found to have more discriminatory experiences than White women, it was not surprising that sex discrimination had an even greater negative impact on their psychological well-being (Landrine & Klonoff, 1997).

These findings are not unrelated to those regarding the lower incidence of depression in married men compared with never-married men. Research suggests first of all that married men usually have someone available in whom to confide: their wives (Helgeson, 1995). Women, who are socially expected to give others emotional support, typically display a willingness to listen to their husbands' problems and try to help. Interestingly, husbands are not inclined to reciprocate when their wives are troubled (Lott, 1987). In addition, as we learned in Chapter 6, men's traditional roles as husbands and fathers place relatively fewer demands on them in the home and permit them considerable control over the demands that are made of them. In contrast, women's traditional roles as wives and mothers afford them fewer options, thereby combining high demands with little control, an inherently stressful situation that obviously could foster depression (Barnett & Baruch, 1987; Doyal, 1990b; World Health Organization, 1996). In short, a person's level of psychological well-being within a marriage is strongly affected by his or her marital power (Steil & Turetsky, 1987; see also Chapter 6).

Two other disorders that are more prevalent among women than men are histrionic personality and agoraphobia. *Histrionic personality* refers to what was formerly called *hysteria*. In ancient times, as well as more recent ones, hysteria was thought to be caused by the movement of the uterus through the body. Thus, by definition, all hysterics were women. According to available estimates, the ratio of females to males exhibiting histrionic personality today is between 2:1 and 4:1 (Chambless & Goldstein, 1980), although some psychologists maintain that the clinical description of histrionic personality in diagnostic manuals virtually guarantees that it will still be applied more often to women than to men (Tavris, 1992).

What are the characteristics of the histrionic personality? The **histrionic personality** is commonly described as demanding, dependent, manipulative, melodramatic, scatterbrained, and seductive but frigid. Hysterics may also exhibit a *conversion reaction*, that is, they exhibit a physical illness or disorder that has no apparent organic cause. Most frequently, this takes the form of pain, hyperventilation, fainting, violent fits and convulsions, and paralysis (Chambless & Goldstein, 1980).

Given the close resemblance of the histrionic personality to our culture's traditional conception of normal femininity, some analysts have argued that females are socialized into careers as hysterics. That is, because women have been taught to derive their sense of self-worth from others' reactions to them, some may resort to extreme measures, such as the histrionic traits we've described, to attract attention and win approval (Wolowitz, 1972). Although there is some support for this hypothesis, it is also possible that hysteria is a response to a highly stressful situation that an individual perceives to be extremely threatening, but that he or she feels powerless to change. In other words, hysteria may be a form of rebellion, especially when conversion reaction is taken into account (Ehrenreich & English, 1986). Consider, for example, that conversion reactions are common among men during wartime. For the married woman, conversion reaction renders her "incapable of carrying out her responsibilities and renders her dependent on her family. These behaviors as well are more easily tolerated in women and may cause less conflict for the hysteric and her family than would an overt rejection of onerous duties" (Chambless & Goldstein, 1980, pp. 116–117). In any event, care must be taken to insure that the terms histrionic personality and hysteria are accurately applied and not simply used to denigrate women or to dismiss their real physical symptoms as unfounded. One example of the latter is employers who maintain that the physical ailments of their female industrial workers are psychosomatic ("assembly-line hysteria") rather than products of an unhealthy working environment (Doyal, 1990a; Harris, 1983).

Agoraphobia is sometimes referred to as *anxiety hysteria*. **Agoraphobia** is commonly defined as fear of open spaces, but this may mean a fear of crowds, public places, expressways, being away from home, in short, "any situation in which escape to safe territory or to a trusted companion might be hindered; the more confining the situation, the more anxiety-provoking" (Chambless & Goldstein, 1980, p. 119). If agoraphobics perceive themselves to be in such a situation, they often experience a panic attack, that is, an episode of terror during which they may hyperventilate, experience tightness in the chest and a number of other symptoms that they interpret as evidence of "impending doom." In fact, Chambless and Goldstein (1980) hypothesize that agoraphobia is really not a fear of open spaces or of separation, but of panic attacks and the consequences. Thus, agoraphobics avoid places in which they think panic attacks will occur.

About 80 percent of agoraphobics are women, and it is estimated that more than one million women suffer from agoraphobia. Just why this is so remains open to speculation since systematic research on examining the gendered aspects of agoraphobia only began during the 1970s. It may be that since females are not typically encouraged to confront fear in the way males are, they become "helpless in the face of stress and more easily trapped in situations from which they see no escape" (Chambless & Goldstein, 1980, p. 123). Agoraphobics tend to be passive and dependent and have difficulty expressing their personal needs—traits traditionally fostered in females. In addition, researchers have noted that many agoraphobics are women in their twenties and thirties who are unhappily married and who have young children. Usually, these women have never been on their own, and their parents and husbands reinforce their dependency (see, for example, Hafner & Minge, 1989). Often, they are quite literally trapped in their marriages since they do not have the money or the skills to survive on their own. Even if the means to leave are available, the prospect of being alone—something they have never experienced—frightens them into remaining in their marriages. Agoraphobic symptoms may be caused by these particular circumstances (Chambless & Goldstein, 1980).

Although these hypotheses are provocative, further research is needed to deepen our understanding of both agoraphobia and histrionic personality. Even more important, this research must examine racial, ethnic, and social class differences, in addition to sex differences, among those who have these disorders.

Alcohol and Drug Addictions.   Some researchers, we have said, claim that in react-
ing to stress, women tend to be passive, whereas men typically take some sort of action.
In the extreme, males may respond by "acting out," for example, by fighting or becoming abusive, and by abusing alcohol or drugs. Men have consistently higher rates of
problem drinking and illicit drug use than do women.

With respect to alcohol use, men outnumber women among heavy drinkers,
regardless of race or ethnicity. In general, men are three times more likely than women
to be heavy drinkers (Robert Wood Johnson Foundation, 1993). Men do more public
drinking than women, so they are less likely to drink alone. They also engage in more
"binge drinking" or episodic heavy drinking (Ettore, 1997; Wechsler et al., 1995).

According to Morrissey (1986, p. 159), "The availability of and accessibility of
alcohol to specific groups is symbolic of the positions of those groups in a hierarchy."
She notes that at the turn of the century, the sociologist Thorstein Veblen observed
that the taboo against women drinking was one of the ways men in the United States
symbolically demonstrated their higher status. In other words, drinking for men historically has been a kind of status symbol, and male dominance in society affords men
greater access to alcohol, which, in turn, increases their likelihood of developing drinking problems.

Alcohol consumption certainly appears to be compatible with stereotyped masculinity (Lemle, 1984). Two researchers found, for instance, that males who exhibit
exaggerated masculinity ("hyper-masculinity") are more likely to be substance (i.e.,
alcohol and drug) abusers (Mosher & Sirkin, 1984).[8] Males also receive greater indirect social support for drinking. In general, there continues to be stronger social disapproval of heavy drinking by women than by men (Waldron, 1995). According to
Ettore (1997, p. 14), the gender norms regarding drinking can be summed up in the
phrases, "real men drink," but "nice girls don't." Parents monitor daughters' behavior
more than sons' behavior, thus giving sons more opportunities to drink (Barnes et al.,
1997). Wives are more tolerant of their husbands drinking than vice versa. About 90
percent of wives remain with alcoholic husbands compared with just 10 percent of husbands who stay with alcoholic wives (American Psychological Association, 1985).

In recent years, some observers have worried that the push for equality among
women would lead to a breakdown in traditional gender norms regarding drinking, thus
leading more women to drink more heavily (that is, to behave like men). Others were
concerned that as more women moved into the labor force, especially into male-dominated positions, they would experience greater stress that might lead to increased drinking. Such concerns have been fueled by liquor advertisements designed to appeal to
"liberated women" (Morrissey, 1986). There is, however, no empirical support for these
concerns, which together are often referred to as the *convergence hypothesis.* For one thing,
there has been a decrease in alcohol consumption by women over the past twenty years.
In fact, although there has been a decrease in heavy drinking by both women and men,
the decline has been greater for women, so that the gender gap in heavy drinking has
actually widened (Waldron, 1995). Second, although employed women are less likely
than unemployed women to be total abstainers, this does not mean that they engage in
more stress-related drinking. Their drinking habits may simply reflect their greater opportunity to drink socially or their greater exposure to alcohol in both work-related and

social settings (Biener, 1987). In fact, success-oriented women appear the least likely to become substance abusers in reaction to stress (Blum & Roman, 1987; Snell et al., 1987). As one writer put it, "If female drinking problems are increasing, it is most likely not because women's liberation has arrived but because it has not" (Sandmair, 1980, p. 242).

Of course, as with the other health-related behaviors we have discussed, sex is not the only important variable to consider. Research shows that a number of factors affect the sex-alcohol use relationship. One of these factors is sexual orientation. Although women are less likely than men to be heavy drinkers, studies indicate that lesbians are significantly more likely than heterosexual women to engage in heavy drinking, have drinking problems, or become alcoholic. Alcoholism is also considered a serious problem among gay men. This is thought to be due at least in part to the fact that because bars historically have been relatively safe havens for lesbians and gay men, they assumed a central role in gays' and lesbians' social lives and leisure activities. More important factors are likely to be societal homophobia and oppression of homosexuals, which generate feelings of alienation and isolation among lesbians and gay men; these feelings are associated with increased alcohol consumption (Ettore, 1997; Nicoloff & Stiglitz, 1987). However, estimating the incidence of problem drinking among lesbians and gay men is difficult; lesbians and gay men as well as problem drinkers (homosexual and heterosexual) are stigmatized in our society, so members of both groups sometimes closet themselves.

Race and ethnicity are also important factors to consider when looking at the sex-alcohol relationship. Research shows that Black women and men, for example, are more likely than White women and men to be abstainers from alcohol. Among Blacks and Whites who drink, rates of heavy drinking appear to be similar for women (about 7 percent), but higher for Black men (31 percent) compared with White men (23 percent). However, social class and age intersect with race and sex in influencing drinking patterns. For instance, if we use education as an indicator of social class, we find that Black men with less than a high school education drink three times as much as White males with the same educational background. As a general rule, the higher the men's educational attainment, the lower their rates of drinking, regardless of race. However, highly educated Black men who drink are more likely to develop a serious drinking problem than similarly educated White men who drink. It has been hypothesized that this may be due less to the fact that they are actually more likely to become alcoholic than it is to the fact that as high-status minorities, their behavior is more closely scrutinized and, therefore, any deviance is more easily detected. Finally, it has been found that heavy drinking by Black males increases as they grow older, in particular from young adulthood to middle age, whereas the reverse pattern is true for White males. This difference may be the result of White males' greater probability of increasing economic stability as they age compared with the cumulative effect of Black males' experiences of discrimination and economic marginalization (Bachman et al., 1997; Barr et al., 1993; Staples, 1995; see also Gilbert & Collins, 1997).

Once again, therefore, it appears that the social-structural conditions in which particular groups of women and men live affect the likelihood that they will develop drinking problems. It is important to note, however, that with regard to sex, there are physiological factors that also must be taken into account. More specifically, when women drink heavily, they suffer greater impairment than men who are heavy drinkers. Recent medical research has shown that females have less of a particular stomach enzyme that helps the digestion of alcohol before it passes into the bloodstream. Consequently, more alcohol goes into women's bloodstreams than into men's, even if women drink the same amount as men relative to body size. More importantly, heavy drinking further inhibits the production of the enzyme, so that alcoholic men lose some of their ability to digest alcohol, but alcoholic women lose this ability completely because their stomachs have virtually none of the enzyme. As a result, women are more susceptible to liver damage and other physical problems if they become alcoholic (Freeza et al., 1990).

Despite such findings, the fact that more males than females develop drinking problems has led to the view that alcoholism is a "male disease." Consequently, alcoholism treatment programs typically have been designed by men for men (Ettore, 1997; Walitzer & Connors, 1997). Moreover, women alcoholics suffer greater stigmatization than do male alcoholics at least in part because excessive drinking violates traditional gender norms for women. Not surprisingly, then, women alcoholics express greater reluctance than male alcoholics about entering treatment programs. The most frequent reason underlying this reluctance is fear of the adverse consequences—such as losing custody of their children—of being officially labeled alcoholic (Blume, 1997; Ettore, 1997).

Just as alcohol has been more readily available to men, so too have men had greater access to illicit drugs. Men, in fact, control the illicit drug trade in the United States and abroad, which is not surprising given their greater involvement in virtually all forms of criminal activity (see Chapter 8). Men use illicit drugs more than women and they are more likely to be regular or habitual users. As is the case with alcohol consumption, there is no evidence that male and female patterns of drug use are converging, although among twelve- to seventeen-year-olds there has only been a 1 to 2 percentage-point sex difference in marijuana and cocaine use since the 1980s. Moreover, men are involved in over 60 percent of all cocaine-related emergency room episodes, a figure that has shown little variation since 1985 (U.S. Department of Health and Human Services, 1997). Nevertheless, women's use of cocaine, especially crack cocaine, has received a good deal of publicity in recent years. Inciardi and his colleagues (1993, pp. 38–39) attribute this publicity to the application of a sexual double standard. "Women's cocaine use is seen as more alarming than men's because it is connected to both old ideas about women's drug use (but not men's) being a source of sexual corruption and newer ideas about women's workforce participation leading to new pressures and temptations for women—including drug use—because they are taking on male role characteristics." Thus, although there are no empirical data to support these claims, women's drug use, like their alcohol use, is more negatively stereotyped and more highly stigmatized than similar behavior by men (Inciardi et al., 1993).

This is further reflected in traditional analyses that have depicted female drug abusers as showing greater psychological maladjustment than their male counterparts; that is, they are considered sicker than male drug abusers. Recent research, however, fails to support this claim. Female and male drug abusers score similarly on tests of psychological adjustment and report similar routes to their introduction to drug use. Both males and females were typically introduced to drugs by a relative (including a parent or step-parent or a sibling) or by their peers (Chesney-Lind, 1997; Sutker et al., 1981). Both men and women are usually introduced to drugs by men: their fathers or stepfathers, uncles, brothers and, for women, boyfriends (Chesney-Lind, 1997; Inciardi et al., 1993). Once they have been initiated into illicit drug use, though, men's and women's reasons for continued use differ. Men are more likely to continue to use drugs for thrills or pleasure; women are more likely to continue to use drugs as a kind of self-medication. For example, women who abuse drugs are more likely than male abusers to have a long history of physical and sexual abuse. For women, then, drugs are often used "as a coping mechanism for dealing with situational factors, life events, or general psychological distress" (Inciardi et al., 1993, p. 25; see also Chesney-Lind, 1997; Fullilive et al., 1992).

These findings make clear that drug treatment programs for women must be designed to address women abusers' unique needs and concerns, but this is rarely the case. Consider, for instance, one response to female drug abusers that became increasingly popular during the 1980s: prosecuting pregnant drug users, usually on charges of delivering drugs to a minor (through the umbilical cord) or child abuse (under the assumption that a viable fetus is a person) (Green, 1993). By 1997, at least thirty states had attempted such prosecutions, but district attorneys failed in all but one: In 1996, the South Carolina Supreme Court ruled in a 3–2 decision that because a viable fetus is a person, its mother can be prosecuted under the state's child abuse laws for engaging in behavior, such as taking drugs, that endangers its health.

Needless to say, this approach to pregnant drug abusers generated immediate controversy. Prosecutors who supported it argued that they were motivated by a concern over the alarming increase in the number of drug-addicted babies being born in the United States (about one in ten live births in 1990). Criminal prosecution, they said, would be a way to force drug-addicted women to get help for their problem, while simultaneously protecting the unborn infant. But those who opposed criminal prosecution of pregnant drug abusers pointed out that apart from the constitutional issues, what the prosecutors overlooked is the lack of drug treatment programs for women, especially pregnant women. Out of approximately 7,000 drug treatment programs available nationwide, only about fifty provide female patients with obstetric and child care as well as special counseling (Diesenhouse, 1990). In one survey of New York City programs, 54 percent excluded all pregnant women, 67 percent excluded pregnant women on Medicaid, and 82 percent excluded crack-addicted pregnant women on Medicaid (Chavkin, 1990). It hardly seems just or even sensible, then, to prosecute female abusers on the grounds of getting them into treatment when the treatment is unlikely to exist.

It is also the case that, like alcohol treatment programs, drug treatment programs are usually designed to address the needs and concerns of male drug addicts (Fogel & Woods, 1995). These, we have noted, are typically different from those of female addicts. Inciardi and his colleagues (1993) explain:

> One problem is the subject matter included in therapy. An obvious example is that chemically dependent men often have a problem controlling their behavioral expression of anger, while women are much more likely to be troubled by not having ever learned to express anger in the first place. Or the type of therapy may need to be quite

different. Successful group therapy for chemically dependent men, for example, often involves confrontations with peers in order to help them recognize and admit their underlying problems, while women tend to react badly to confrontational techniques and instead benefit from intensive mutual support from peers. (p. 29; see also Ettore, 1997; Walitzer & Connors, 1997.)

It is support from peers as well as family members that women drug abusers are least likely to get. Research indicates that women who enter treatment encounter opposition and less support from their families and friends than men who enter treatment. Although female addicts may initially get help from extended family, such as shelter for themselves and their children or financial support, they experience increasing isolation as their addiction worsens (Chesney-Lind, 1997). They often end up alone. According to one researcher, only one woman in ten leaves her addicted male partner, whereas nine out of ten men leave addicted female partners (Hinds, 1990). In one study that asked addicts who among their family and friends would help them end their drug habits, the most common response for female addicts was no one; 50 percent more female addicts than male addicts reported that they had no friends or family members to provide them with that kind of support (Inciardi et al., 1993).

Significantly, the same reason that underlies women's dependence on illicit drugs—responding to a history of abuse as well as the depressed circumstances of their lives—also appears to be responsible for their dependence on prescription drugs. The one form of drug addiction more common among women than men involves the use of prescription drugs. Unlike illicit drugs, women have easy access to prescription drugs. We noted earlier that doctors often prescribe mood-altering psychotropic drugs to women. The most frequently prescribed drugs are minor tranquilizers and sedatives, such as benzodiazepines. Such drugs are highly addictive even when taken in normal therapeutic doses (Ettore, 1992). About half of all American women use psychotropic drugs; they are 70 percent of habitual tranquilizer users and 72 percent of antidepressant drug users (Gold, 1983; see also Inciardi et al., 1993).

One final note: Women are more likely than men to suffer *cross-addictions*—that is, simultaneous addiction to both alcohol and drugs (Ettore, 1997; Nechas & Foley, 1994). This appears to be due to women's greater likelihood to report alcohol-related problems to their physicians, who then may prescribe tranquilizers to help the women "cope" better and, therefore, stop drinking. Unfortunately, this frequently exacerbates the problem and may result in an overdose due to the combination of tranquilizers and alcohol, another tragic consequence of sexist health care.

Eating Disorders.   In considering eating disorders, it is useful to think in terms of a continuum (Wooley & Wooley, 1980). At one end is *obesity;* an individual is obese if he or she is 25 percent above the average weight for someone of his or her age and height. Americans in general have been gaining weight over the past three decades, so that by 1996, there were more overweight than normal or underweight men and women in the population. But while more men (59 percent) than women (49 percent) are overweight, more women (4 percent) than men (2 percent) are obese (Haney, 1996b). Moreover, poor women and African American women (whom we know are disproportionately represented among the poor) are more likely than more affluent and White women to be obese. Poor women are seven times more likely than nonpoor women to be obese, while 51 percent more African American women than White women are obese (Foster et al., 1997; Freedman, 1986; Gortmaker et al., 1993).

The obese are usually blamed for their condition. It is assumed that they lack self-control, are lazy, and engage in overeating. However, research indicates that often the obese eat no more than those who are thin; sometimes, they eat much less. It appears that for many, obesity is caused by factors over which they have little or no control: heredity, metabolism, and nutrition (which helps to account for the social class dimension of the problem) (Bouchard et al., 1990; Popkin et al., 1996; Stunkard, et al., 1990; Wadden et al., 1997). Nevertheless, tremendous pressure is put on the obese to lose weight. For example, they are discriminated against in the job market, made the brunt of jokes by the media and others, and judged by the general public to be sloppy, stupid, and ugly (Attie & Brooks-Gunn, 1987; Freedman, 1986). Women suffer more negative consequences from being obese than men do. According to one recent study, for example, obese women are more likely than obese men to lose socioeconomic status independently of their family's social status and income; they were also 20 percent less likely than nonobese women to marry. In contrast, the negative impact of obesity on men's socioeconomic status and chances of marrying were much smaller. This does not mean that men are not stigmatized for deviating from cultural norms of male physical attractiveness, but for men, short stature has a greater negative impact than obesity (Gortmaker et al., 1993; Sargent & Branchflower, 1994).

The findings of the Gortmaker et al. and Sargent and Branchflower studies are also important in understanding why the vast majority of people with other eating disorders are women. In the United States, fat is equated with ugliness, whereas thinness is associated with beauty and high social status. (Consider, for instance, the often-quoted adage, "You can never be too rich or too thin.") It also appears that our cultural standard has idealized an increasingly thinner body since the 1920s (Attie & Brooks-Gunn, 1987; Brumberg, 1998; Freedman, 1986; Silverstein et al., 1986; Tavris, 1992). This is true for men as well as women, but men, as we have already seen, are given considerably more leeway with regard to their weight. Moreover, women are frequently judged less by what they do than by how they look.

Not surprising, therefore, is the fact that women tend to evaluate their self-worth in terms of their appearance. Unfortunately, their estimates of themselves are often unrealistically negative. Women consistently express dissatisfaction with their bodies, and most frequently they couch this dissatisfaction in terms of weight. In fact, one national survey found that women's dissatisfaction with their bodies has intensified in recent years. This study showed that 48 percent of women between the ages of eighteen and seventy had negative global body evaluations compared with 30 percent in 1985. Most of these women were dissatisfied with their middle or lower torso, their weight, and their muscle tone (Cash & Henry, 1995). While this study surveyed *adult* women, however, other studies show that adolescent girls express even greater dissatisfaction with their bodies (Brumberg, 1998; Pliner et al., 1990). Young women, in particular, hold inaccurate perceptions about their bodies, especially their body weight. For example, they typically overestimate their weight, whereas young men tend to underestimate theirs. Mintz and Betz (1986) found in their study of college students that the majority of women felt that, on average, they were ten pounds overweight, whereas the majority of men considered themselves an average of three pounds underweight. The overweight men in this study perceived themselves to be thinner than they actually were, whereas the only women who judged themselves as being of normal weight were really slightly underweight. Similar findings were obtained by McCaulay et al. (1988). Significantly, more women than men, the research tells us, are obsessed with the desire to be thin (Hesse-Biber, 1989).

This cultural and personal obsession with weight can lead to eating disorders. One is *chronic dieting.* One of every two women reports being on a diet "most of the time" (Freedman, 1986). Although this may not appear to be serious, it can have severe physical and psychological consequences (Attie & Brooks-Gunn, 1987). Chronic dieters try dozens of different diet plans—many of which are dangerously unhealthy—over the course of many years, sometimes beginning when they are as young as ten or eleven years old. Ironically, the dieting may have the opposite effect of what they desired, since restricting food intake can lower one's metabolic rate which, in turn, requires that dieters eat even less to sustain further weight loss. This is why after a dieter stops following some diets, she (or he) often regains lost poundage quickly, prompting the start of another diet (Polivy & Herman, 1985). Thus, a vicious cycle ensues, with chronic dieters perpetually dissatisfied with their appearance and, in extreme cases, being thin becomes more important than other aspects of the self and other activities (Wooley & Wooley, 1980).

Some people turn to eating as a way to handle stress. Women are more likely than men to do this (Ettorre, 1992), perhaps because food shopping and preparation have been women's responsibilities and because women's magazines highlight food by presenting tempting recipes and advertisements (Silverstein et al., 1986). However, since women also tend to be preoccupied by the fear of weight gain, some may develop the disorder known as **bulimia.** Bulimics engage in binge eating, consuming large quantities of food (usually "junk" food) in a short period of time. Afterwards, fearful that they will gain weight, they purge themselves of the food by fasting, taking laxatives (sometimes a dozen or two dozen a day), exercising excessively, and most commonly, by inducing vomiting.

Bulimia is difficult to detect because bulimics usually do not show extreme weight loss. Bulimia, though, causes serious psychological and physical damage. The binge-purge cycle may take on the character of an addiction, like alcoholism (Ettorre, 1992). Frequently, the gastrointestinal tract is damaged due to the overuse of laxatives, and the esophagus is harmed by the effects of repeated vomiting. Reports indicate that bulimia is a widespread problem, particularly on college campuses, with estimates that from 4 to 20 percent of college students, virtually all of them women, are bulimic (Thompson, 1994).

Finally, at the other extreme end of the eating disorders continuum, opposite obesity, is **anorexia.** Anorectics have a compulsive fear of becoming fat and literally starve themselves to prevent weight gain or to lose more weight. Anorectics—an estimated 90 to 95 percent of whom are women—have an exceptionally distorted body image, feeling or considering themselves to be fat even when they are emaciated. The symptoms of anorexia include a 25 percent loss of original body weight with concomitant refusals to eat (Zerbe, 1993).

Until quite recently, most research on anorectics focused on young, White heterosexual women in their teens and twenties, from middle-class or wealthy families, since it was assumed that it is this group who is most likely to become anorectic. However, studies using more diverse samples are now finding this eating disorder among working-class women, women of color, and lesbians (Root, 1990; Rosen et al., 1988; Thompson, 1994) and among some groups of men (Carlat et al., 1997; Striegel-Moore et al., 1986). It is unclear whether these changes represent a true increase in anorexia among these populations, or whether the widespread stereotype of the anorectic as a young, wealthy, White heterosexual woman prevented clinicians from seeing anorexia in members of these groups. In any event, research now indicates that although rates of diagnosed anorexia are still higher among middle-class and wealthy White women, diagnoses of anorexia and related eating disorders are increasing among young, Black, Hispanic, and Native American women in rural and low-income areas (Root, 1990; Rosen et al., 1988; Snow & Harris, 1989; Thompson, 1994), as well as among gay men (Carlat et al., 1997; Gettleman & Thompson, 1993; Striegel-Moore et al., 1986).

Researchers and clinicians have found that anorectics often have difficulty expressing their personal needs and desires, and may feel they have little, if any, control over their lives. Their weight becomes the one thing they can control. Controlling their appearance is also a way to please others (Zerbe, 1993). It is not difficult to see how this theory could apply to anyone with low self-esteem—not only White women, but also women of color and lesbians and gay men. But in trying to explain why so many anorectics are women, regardless of race and ethnicity, social class, or sexual orientation, clinicians have often resorted to the psychoanalytic literature claiming that female anorectics want to deny their womanhood by making their bodies masculine (i.e., noncurvacious), that they are striking out against their mothers, or that they are confused about their sexuality. An alternative perspective sees anorectic women as actually embracing an exaggerated image of womanhood. "Anorectics are seeking beauty through body transformation (just as most 'healthy' women do). The goal is not to reject womanliness but to enact it by becoming thinner and lovelier than anyone else" (Freedman, 1986, p. 156).

Although cases of anorexia have been documented for at least a century, serious research on the disorder has only been underway for about four decades. Not surprisingly, then, there are no definitive findings with regard to causal factors, psychoanalytic or otherwise. Of course, a complex disorder such as anorexia is likely caused by multiple, intersecting factors. What concerns us here is that in studying anorexia and other eating disorders, clinicians and researchers have often focused on the pathologies of individuals rather than on the cultural and social environment in which they live. It is important not to lose sight of the fact that the predominance of eating disorders among women is a sociopolitical issue as well as a clinical one. To fully understand anorexia and other eating disorders, therefore, we need to examine not only women's personal backgrounds, but also our society's cultural constructions of femininity and the female body, food and appetite. Feminist researchers, for example, have argued that anorexia is not really about being thin, but about controlling female appetites, which include sexual desires as well as a desire for food. Feminists also hypothesize that anorexia may be a way for women not to reject being female, but rather to reject the stifling constraints of domesticity and traditional feminine roles. Unfortunately, however, anorexia produces effects that are the opposite of empowerment and independence: The physical weakness and frailty induced by anorexia eventually require the women to be cared for and their activities to be monitored by others (Bordo, 1993).

While feminists have moved the analysis of anorexia and other eating disorders beyond a singular focus on weight loss, they still recognize the cultural obsession with thinness as an important contributing factor to these problems. The desirability of a slender body, though, is just one of our society's beauty norms. In Box 11.4, we take a closer look at beauty norms to see their differential impact not only by sex, but by race and ethnicity as well.

Sexism and Mental Health Services

We noted at the outset of our discussion of mental health and illness that diagnosis and, therefore, treatment of psychological problems are often highly subjective processes. Clinicians, like everyone else, bring to their work particular biases that derive from their personal backgrounds and characteristics, as well as from their training in a specific institutional system. We have discussed that clinicians tend to use a masculine model of mental health. That this persists today is not surprising, given that the mental health professions, like medicine in general, are hierarchically structured and men predominate at the top of the hierarchy. For example, only about 28 percent of psychiatrists are women (American Medical Association, 1998). What are some of the other important features of traditional mental health care, and what are their implications for the treatment of female and male patients?

Critics of traditional mental health care have given special attention to what they see as its emphasis on conformity to dominant cultural standards and its corresponding intolerance of diversity or uniqueness (Ballou & Gabalac, 1985; Brown, 1994). More specifically, mental health practitioners, while claiming to be objective medical experts, often function simply as upholders of the status quo. Their judgment of what constitutes mental health is conformity to dominant (i.e., White, middle-class, heterosexual, male) expectations, although for many individuals these are oppressive. Conversely, any departure from these norms can be interpreted as a symptom of pathology or mental disorder. The traditional clinician, then, sees the source or cause of a problem as existing within the patient; the goal is to change the patient rather than the external conditions that may be affecting the patient. Treatment is considered successful when the patient "adjusts" to (i.e., uncritically accepts and conforms to) her or his circumstances. This can be accomplished with a variety of techniques, such as psychoanalysis, behavior modification, or drug therapy.

Critics acknowledge that this model is more progressive and humane than many treatment models popular in the past. It also seems to be a beneficial approach to the most severe cases of mental illness. According to the critics, however, it is not an appropriate treatment model for the majority of patients who seek therapy or mental health care (Ballou & Gabalac, 1985). Consider, for example, traditional clinical evaluations

BOX 11.4

Beauty Norms

What is beauty, and who is beautiful? Although it has been claimed that standards of beauty transcend culture (see, for example, Perrett et al., 1994), most research indicates that beauty norms vary cross-culturally as well as historically (Rooks, 1996; Wolf, 1991). Normative standards of beauty are also gendered and, in our society, women, more so than men, are valued by others and derive their self-worth from how well they match up to our culture's idealized image of the beautiful woman.

What does the beautiful woman in our society look like? As we have already discussed, she is thin. However, since the mid-1980s, the idealized female body has also become curvier; the beautiful woman is thin, but has large breasts. And, of course, beauty is equated with youth; as a woman grows old in our society, she does not grow more beautiful. Consider the supermodels of recent years. They possess what has been dubbed the "waif look": the look of the child-woman, who is infantile and unthreatening, but alluring and, therefore, sexually appealing to many men in an age when most women are striving to be strong, independent adults (Kaye, 1993). The appeal of the child-woman can also be seen in the growth of beauty pageants for children, where six-year-old girls are dressed in gowns and showgirl costumes; made up with eye shadow, blush, and lipstick; and encouraged to pose and perform with coquettish style. As one observer put it, this billion-dollar-a-year industry blurs "the lines between what is cute and what is sensual" (quoted in DeWitt, 1997, p. 4E).

In our society, where women have long been held to unrealistic standards of beauty—whatever the specific characteristics of the ideal happened to be at the time—young, physically attractive women have been prized by men of all ages. A beautiful woman many years younger than her male partner increases *his* prestige in the eyes of others; consider, for instance, that young, attractive women married to older men are often referred to as "trophy brides." Men, then, appear to benefit from the beauty norms imposed on women in our society, but what are the effects of these norms on women themselves?

As we have already noted, since body image is strongly linked to self-esteem, rigid, unattainable beauty norms cultivate in women anxiety about and dissatisfaction with their appearance, starting at an early age (Allgood-Merton et al., 1990; Ussher, 1989; Whitaker et al., 1990). They also induce women to engage in unhealthy—sometimes even life-threatening—practices, in order to try to attain the unrealistic ideal. Such practices include not only constant dieting, which may lead to more serious eating disorders as we have discussed, but also plastic surgery, typically to enlarge breasts, reduce or straighten noses, and remove wrinkles and body fat. Breast augmentation surgery, for example, is the second most common type of cosmetic surgery performed in the United States, with 75–85 percent of women undergoing the procedure for nonmedical reasons, usually because they want bigger breasts. The most common procedure is liposuction, in which a tube is inserted into the body through a tiny incision, usually in the thighs and abdomen, and fat is literally sucked out (Rynbrandt & Kramer, 1995; Williams, 1992). Of course, such procedures are available only to those who can afford them, since most cosmetic surgery is not covered by medical insurance. Moreover, although many of these procedures have negative effects, many women are not deterred. For example, following reports that leaky silicone breast implants had caused serious illness and disfigurement in thousands of women, the number of breast augmentation procedures declined briefly, but by 1998, they were increasing again.

Women of color are especially disadvantaged by the dominant culture's beauty norms, for a central component of idealized beauty is whiteness. Despite the positive impact of the "Black is beautiful" movement of the late 1960s, a number of analysts have observed a return to racist beauty standards within the African American community in recent years. As Sandler (1992) points out,

(continued)

BOX 11.4   Continued

historically in this country light-skinned Black people, especially Black women, have enjoyed higher status than dark-skinned Black people. In her interviews with African Americans, Sandler found that light-skinned Black people were considered privileged within the Black, as well as the White, communities. Light-skinned women were preferred as partners by Black men, regardless of the darkness of the color of the men's skin. Light-skinned Black women are preferred not only because of the skin color, but also because they often have narrower noses and "good hair," that is, hair that is not "nappy" (Rooks, 1996). Sandler (1992) and Rooks (1996) document the negative impact racist beauty norms have on women of color as well as the lengths to which some non-White women will go to more closely resemble the idealized image of White beauty. Creams for lightening skin and chemical treatments to straighten hair are two common "beauty techniques" Black women use, but cosmetic surgery to "Caucasianize" the nose (narrow the nostrils and build the bridge) is growing in popularity among middle-class Black women. Asian women, too, are turning to cosmetic surgery to "Caucasianize" their eyelids (Sandler, 1992).

It is the case that men are also increasingly using plastic surgery to better conform to our society's idealized image of male physical attractiveness. This image emphasizes the musculature of the body, so that a growing number of men are using cosmetic surgery to enhance their calves, chests, and buttocks with silicone implants. Youthfulness is also an important dimension of male physical attractiveness, so more men are now having face lifts and hair implant surgery, as well as liposuction to reduce stomach, chest, and breast fat. Men were 10 percent of cosmetic surgery patients in 1980, but by 1994 they were 26 percent of cosmetic surgery patients (Spindler, 1996).

But while men are increasingly buying products and undergoing treatments to make them look younger and more physically attractive, it is important to keep in mind that, unlike women, they are not consistently encouraged by their parents, peers, or the media to be obsessed with their appearance, nor do they usually consider their bodies a material resource. And while more men are becoming conscious of their body image, attractiveness norms for men are hardly as arbitrary, capricious, or *dangerous* as those for women. Few men die trying to be handsome; more than 70,000 women are thought to be seriously ill with infections, autoimmune reactions, and cancer from leaky breast implants alone (Rynbrandt & Kramer, 1995).

---

of homosexuals. Many gays and lesbians enter therapy because of low self-esteem and depression. Mental health practitioners often assess these troubles as resulting from homosexuality itself, rather than from societal discrimination against homosexuals. To them, the first sign of "healthy adjustment" is for the patient to acknowledge his or her sexual orientation as the problem or "disorder" to be treated.

Even more disturbing is the high incidence of sexual abuse of patients by their therapists. Research reveals that about 10 percent of male therapists and 3 percent of female therapists have been involved in at least one "incident of intimacy" with a patient; 80 percent of male therapists who have had intimate involvements have done so with more than one patient. In one study, half of the 1,320 clinical psychologists surveyed reported that they had treated patients who had had sexual relations with a previous therapist. These patients frequently experience emotional problems similar to those of incest victims. About 10 percent of these patients are so severely affected that they must be hospitalized; 1 percent commit suicide (Sonne & Pope, 1991). In about 90 percent of cases of sexual abuse by therapists, the patient/victim is a woman (Gilbert & Scher, 1999). Sometimes, though, victimized patients are children, and more than 50 percent of child patient/ victims are girls. Although the American Psychological Association considers sex between a therapist and client unethical, researchers have found that neither threats of malpractice nor felony convictions have been effective in deterring therapists from having sex with their patients. However, more victimized patients are choosing to sue their therapists, and the courts have ruled that consent of a patient to sexual relations is not an acceptable defense for therapists (Gilbert & Scher, 1999; Pope et al., 1993).

Feminist Therapy

More females than males make use of mental health services, and so the biases and problems inherent in the traditional system are especially detrimental to them. Recognizing this, some practitioners have sought to reform mental health care delivery through the adoption of *gender-aware* or *nonsexist counseling*. "Nonsexist counseling seeks to treat clients as human beings and actively to refute sex ascription in theory and in practice, that is, in options offered to the clients and in the values espoused by the therapist" (Ballou & Gabalac, 1985, p. 30). While nonsexist counseling clearly has advantages over the traditional model, some practitioners see it as only the first step in a series of necessary changes. These practitioners are striving to remodel mental health care along feminist lines. Let's briefly examine their work.

Feminist therapy is part of the broader feminist health care movement. Although there are actually a number of feminist therapies, we can identify several principles common among them that form the foundation of this approach to mental health care.

First, feminist therapists establish egalitarian relationships with their clients (Gilbert & Scher, 1999). Rather than being someone to whom something is done by an expert, the client takes an active part in therapy, and the therapist engages in self-disclosure with the client. The therapy, then, is viewed as a shared learning process. A corollary to this is that the feminist therapist accepts the client's knowledge and personal experiences as valid, rather than interpreting them as defensive strategies. In other words, to the feminist therapist, the client may be the best authority on her or his problem.

A second related principle is that feminist therapy assumes that external conditions, not individual interpersonal ones, generate most psychological difficulties, particularly those experienced by women and other marginalized groups (Brown, 1994). "The therapist facilitates the client's ability to understand, both generally and personally, the existence and impact of cultural conditioning and biased social/economic/cultural structures. . . . The goal is to build skills for coping and creating, to develop astute social analysis, and sophisticated consideration of the potential consequences of change" (Ballou & Gabalac, 1985, pp. 31, 33). A fundamental part of this process is the analysis of gender relations (Burstow, 1992; Gilbert & Scher, 1999).

Finally, feminist therapists are committed to working for broader social changes that benefit not only their individual clients, but all women and oppressed groups (Brown, 1994). For instance, they may lobby for adequate and affordable day care; for safe, sanitary, and low-cost housing; and for shelters for battered women and the sexually abused. In short, feminist therapists are advocates for social change that will empower the disadvantaged and provide them with social and economic autonomy—factors these therapists recognize as essential for mental health.

Although a goal of feminist therapy clearly is to assist members of oppressed groups, especially women, there is little empirical evidence so far that demonstrates its success in this regard. Future research should address this issue by determining to what extent feminist therapy is available to those most disadvantaged by the current social structure: poor women and women of color and their children (for steps in this direction, see Brown, 1994; Burstow, 1992). To date, however, the impact of feminist therapy is still largely unassessed.

Toward a Healthy Future

The data discussed in this chapter are disturbing. Taken together, they indicate, to paraphrase Harrison (1984), that traditional constructions of gender are hazardous to our health.

With regard to physical health, traditional masculinity appears to put men at greater risk for a variety of physical conditions, such as heart disease and stroke, various forms of cancer, and chronic liver disease. Their greater likelihood to smoke, drink alcohol, and engage in violence renders them more susceptible not only to these diseases, but also to accidents, homicide, successful suicide, and alcohol and illicit drug abuse. In fact, it seems that the more a man conforms to traditional masculinity, the greater is the risk to his health.

The same appears to be true with regard to women who firmly adhere to traditional femininity. For them, however, the greatest threat appears to be to their mental health. Those who embrace the traditional feminine role are more prone to depression and other psychological problems. Moreover, although women tend to live longer than men, there are indications that their quality of life may be poorer. This is evidenced by mental health statistics as well as their higher morbidity and greater likelihood of institutionalization.

With few exceptions, people of color and the economically disadvantaged have poorer health than White, middle-, and upper-class men and women. They also receive the poorest quality health care from a system that is sexist, racist, heterosexist, ageist, and class-biased. As we discussed in this chapter, this system of physical and mental health care has not infrequently done more harm than good, particularly to women, people of color, gay men and lesbians, and the poor, both historically and currently.

In response to the inadequacies and abuses of traditional health care, feminists have begun to offer alternative services. These have as their core principles: a nonhierarchical structure; an egalitarian and mutually educational relationship between patient and provider; a recognition of external (i.e., structural rather than personal) causes for individuals' physical and psychological troubles; and a commitment to advocacy and action to bring about social change. Although the feminist model of physical and mental health care is not without problems of its own, it does hold the promise of transforming our traditional medical services into "forces committed to undoing damage [and] achieving and maintaining health" (Ballou & Gabalac, 1985, p. 169). Let's hope it succeeds in fulfilling this promise, for the outcome is not insignificant. Indeed, it is a matter of life or death.

KEY TERMS

agoraphobia   commonly defined as a fear of open spaces because of the risk of being separated from a trusted companion, but more recently understood as possibly a fear of panic attacks and their consequences

anorexia   an eating disorder in which an individual, because of an obsessive fear of becoming overweight, literally starves; characterized by a distorted body image, a 25 percent loss of body weight, and refusal to eat; 90 to 95 percent of anorectics are females

bulimia   an abnormal and constant craving for food, also known as binge-purge syndrome, in which the individual consumes large quantities of food in short periods of time followed by fasting, use of laxatives, or induced vomiting to purge the food and prevent weight gain

clinical depression   severe and persistent feelings of discontent or displeasure accompanied by at least four of eight symptoms (poor appetite or weight loss, insomnia or increased sleep, psychomotor agitation or retardation, loss of interest in usual activities, loss of energy or fatigue, feelings of worthlessness, diminished concentration, and suicidal ideation) that are present daily for at least two weeks without evidence of any other disorder

histrionic personality   a personality disorder composed of a variety of symptoms that include dependency, manipulation, melodrama, and forgetfulness, as well as the exhibition of a physical illness or disorder (e.g., pain, hyperventilation, fainting, convulsions, paralysis) that has no apparent organic cause

life expectancy   the average number of years of life remaining to an individual at a given age

morbidity rate   the illness rate of a given population

mortality rate   the number of deaths in proportion to a given population

SUGGESTED READINGS

Brown, L. (1994). *Subversive dialogues: Theory in feminist therapy.* New York: Basic Books.

Messner, M. A., & Sabo, D. F. (1994). *Sex, violence and power in sports.* Freedom, CA: The Crossing Press.

Nechas, E., & Foley, D. (1994). *Unequal treatment.* New York: Simon and Schuster.

Rooks, N. M. (1996). *Hair raising: Beauty, culture, and African American women.* New Brunswick, NJ: Rutgers University Press.

Sabo, D., & Gordon, D. F. (Eds.) (1995). *Men's health and illness.* Thousand Oaks, CA: Sage.

Weitz, R. (1991). *Life with AIDS.* New Brunswick, NJ: Rutgers University Press.

NOTES

1. Life expectancy also varies significantly by the region of the country in which a person lives. In fact, scientists have found greater regional variation in life expectancy throughout the United States than in any other high-income industrialized country. In some parts of the United States, such as rural South Dakota, which is heavily populated by Native Americans, as well as in some inner city areas, male life expectancy is more than fifteen years less than the average male life expectancy for the country as a whole. In fact, male life expectancy in these areas is as low as male life expectancy in some developing countries ("Surprises in a Study," 1997).

2. One recent study has also found that husbands who are unfaithful to their wives may increase their wives' chances of developing cervical cancer. Researchers found that women whose husbands frequented prostitutes or who had many sexual partners were five to eleven times more likely to develop cervical cancer than women whose husbands were monogamous (Shah et al., 1996).

3. Staples (1995) also reports that over 75 percent of hazardous waste sites are located in predominantly Black communities, a factor that likely contributes to the high cancer mortality rate of Black Americans.

4. Minority men have also been subjected to abuses by the medical establishment. One especially egregious example is the "Tuskegee Study of Untreated Syphilis in the Negro Male," conducted from 1932 to 1972 in rural Alabama. In this study, more than 400 Black men diagnosed with syphilis were denied treatment for the disease so that researchers from the U.S. Public Health Service could observe the disease's effects on Black men over the course of their lifetimes. The study was conducted without the informed consent of the research subjects and resulted in not only intense pain and suffering for the men, but also for their wives and children, who also sometimes became infected. In 1997, President Clinton formally apologized to the remaining survivors and to the families of the deceased for the federal government's sponsorship of the study. For a thorough discussion of what has come to be called the "Tuskegee Experiment," see Jones, 1993.

5. In medically underserved areas as well as in large practices with a high managed care case load, the use of nurse practitioners to handle some of the physician's routine duties is growing. In fact, some nurse practitioners are opening their own practices in direct competition with physicians. Although some physicians welcome the help, others see independent nurse practitioners as a threat to their practices and, therefore, their incomes (Freudenheim, 1997). It remains to be seen whether the increase in independent nurse practi-

tioners will result in a professional "turf battle" like the one physicians waged against midwives, herbalists, and other healers in the nineteenth century.

6. Interestingly, a recent study shows that medical school graduates who were admitted to medical school with special consideration for race or ethnicity have the same graduation rate, get similar residency evaluations, choose their specialties in about the same percentages, and follow essentially equivalent career paths as graduates who were regularly admitted (Davidson & Lewis, 1998).

7. Messner (1987) notes, for instance, that only 6 to 7 percent of high school football players play in college and of those who do, about 8 percent are drafted into the pros, but only 2 percent eventually sign a professional contract. The odds are similar for basketball players. Moreover, even for those who reach the top, success may be shortlived: the average NFL career is four years, and the average NBA career is 3.4 years.

8. Interestingly, Wechsler and his colleagues (1995) found that female college students who adopted the masculine "animal house" values of fraternity members (e.g., viewing parties as a very important part of college life) were as likely as male college students to be heavy or binge drinkers. Moreover, Wechsler et al. found that male college athletes were more likely than nonathletes to be binge drinkers.

GLOSSARY

acquaintance rape an incident of sexual assault in which the victim knows or is familiar with the assailant

adrenogenital syndrome (AGS) a condition occurring prenatally that is caused by a malfunction in the mother's or the fetus's adrenal glands or from exposure of the mother to a substance that acts on the fetus like an androgen

agoraphobia commonly defined as a fear of open spaces because of the risk of being separated from a trusted companion, but more recently understood as possibly a fear of panic attacks and their consequences

androcentrism male-centered; the notion that males are superior to females and that males and the male experience are the normative standard against which women should be judged

androgen-insensitive syndrome a genetic defect that causes an *XY* fetus to be unresponsive to the androgens its testes secrete

anorexia an eating disorder in which an individual, because of an obsessive fear of becoming overweight, literally starves; characterized by a distorted body image, a 25 percent loss of body weight, and refusal to eat; 90 to 95 percent of anorectics are females

biological essentialism a cultural lens that rationalizes and legitimates both androcentrism and gender polarization by portraying them as the natural and inevitable products of the inherent biological differences between the sexes

brain lateralization the specialization of the right and left hemispheres of the brain for different tasks

bulimia an abnormal and constant craving for food, also known as binge-purge syndrome, in which the individual consumes large quantities of food in short periods of time followed by fasting, use of laxatives, or induced vomiting to purge the food and prevent weight gain

castration anxiety Freud's notion that boys fear their fathers will castrate them because of their sexual attraction to their mothers

chivalry hypothesis (paternalism hypothesis) the belief that female offenders are afforded greater leniency before the law than their male counterparts

chosen families families made up of people unrelated by ancestry, marriage, or adoption, but who are nonetheless considered family members

clinical depression severe and persistent feelings of discontent or displeasure accompanied by at least four of eight symptoms (poor appetite or weight loss, insomnia or increased sleep, psychomotor agitation or retardation, loss of interest in usual activities, loss of energy or fatigue, feelings of worthlessness, diminished concentration, and suicidal ideation) that are present daily for at least two weeks without evidence of any other disorder

comparable worth the policy of paying workers equally when they perform different jobs that have similar value in terms of such factors as skill, effort, responsibility, and working conditions

DHT deficiency syndrome a condition in which an individual has no or abnormally low 5-alpha-reductase, an enzyme responsible for converting testosterone into dihydrotestosterone

dissimilarity index (segregation index, D) a measure of occupational sex segregation, reported in percent, that indicates the proportion of workers of one sex that would have to change to jobs in which members of their sex were underrepresented to achieve a balanced occupational distribution between the sexes

domestic partnership a cohabiting relationship between intimate partners not married to each other

dual labor market a labor market characterized by one set of jobs employing almost exclusively men and another set of jobs, typically lower paying with lower prestige, employing almost exclusively women

ecofeminism an earth-based feminist spirituality movement that celebrates women's close association with nature and that sees a connection between the domination of women and the domination of nature

economy the system for the management and development of a society's human and material resources

emancipation theory (liberation theory) the theory that female crime is increasing and/or becoming more masculine in character as a result of feminism or the women's movement

Equal Pay Act of 1963   forbids employers from paying employees of one sex more than employees of the opposite sex when these employees are engaged in work that requires equal skill, effort, and responsibility and is performed under similar working conditions, although exceptions, such as unequal pay based on seniority, merit, the quality or quantity of production, or any other factor besides sex, are allowed

establishment sex segregation   a form of occupational sex segregation in which women and men hold the same job title at an individual establishment or company, but actually do different jobs

Executive Order 11246 (Affirmative Action)   forbids federal contractors from discriminating in personnel decisions on the basis of sex, as well as race, color, national origin, and religion, and requires employers to take affirmative measures to recruit, train, and hire women and minorities; since 1978, implemented and enforced by the OFCCP

expressive family role   the role of housekeeper and caregiver in the family, a role held by the wife/mother in a traditional isolated nuclear family

feminist movement (women's movement)   a social movement that spans more than a century of U.S. and European history and that is represented today in most countries of the developing world as well; it is composed of many diverse segments, each committed to eliminating gender oppression as well as other inequalities.

feminist paradigm   a school of thought that explains gender in terms of the political and socioeconomic structure in which it is constructed and emphasizes the importance of taking collective action to eradicate sexism in sociology as well as in society, and to reconstruct gender so that it is neither a harmful nor an oppressive social category

feminist spirituality   a religious movement comprising diverse segments with differing beliefs and strategies for change, but unified in rejecting the dualism characteristic of traditional patriarchal religions; dualism is replaced with the theme of the unification of spirit and nature and the principle that human experience is the source of spirituality

formal curriculum   the set of subjects officially and explicitly taught to students in school

fundamentalism   a religious orientation that denounces secular modernity and attempts to restore traditional spirituality through selective retrieval of doctrines, beliefs, and practices from a sacred past

gender gap   differences in the voting patterns and political attitudes of women and men

gender polarization   the assumption that males and females are fundamentally different from one another, and the practice of using these differences as a central organizing principle for the social life of the society

gender roles   social roles that are prescribed for a society's members, depending on their sex

gender stereotypes   summary descriptions of masculinity and femininity that are oversimplified and generalized

gender   socially generated attitudes and behaviors, usually organized dichotomously as masculinity and femininity

gladiator activities   the highest level of political activism in Millbrath's typology; include working on a political campaign, taking an active role in a political party, or running for public office

glass ceiling   invisible barriers that limit women workers' and minority workers' upward occupational mobility

hidden curriculum   the value preferences children are taught in school that are not an explicit part of the formal curriculum, but rather are hidden or implicit in it

histrionic personality   a personality disorder composed of a variety of symptoms that include dependency, manipulation, melodrama, and forgetfulness, as well as the exhibition of a physical illness or disorder (e.g., pain, hyperventilation, fainting, convulsions, paralysis) that has no apparent organic cause

homophobia   an unreasonable fear of and hostility toward homosexuals

human capital theory   explains occupational sex segregation in terms of women's free choice to work in jobs that make few demands on workers and require low personal investment in training or skills acquisition based on the assumption that women's primary responsibility is in the home

identification   a central concept of the Freudian-based theory of gender socialization; the process by which boys and girls begin to unconsciously model their behavior after that of their same-sex parent in their efforts to resolve their respective gender identity complexes

incumbent   an individual who holds political office and seeks another term

industry sex segregation a form of occupational sex segregation in which women and men hold the same job title in a particular field or industry, but actually perform different jobs

instrumental family role the role of providing financial support for the family and making key decisions, a role held by the husband/father in the traditional isolated nuclear family

isolated nuclear family a family in which the husband/father, wife/mother, and their dependent children establish a household geographically and financially separate from other kin and the adults carry out distinct, specialized roles

Klinefelter syndrome a chromosomal abnormality in which an individual has three (*XXY*) sex chromosomes, rather than the normal two (*XX* or *XY*)

labor force the human resources of the economy

life expectancy the average number of years of life remaining to an individual at a given age

linguistic sexism ways in which language devalues members of one sex

marital rape the sexual assault of a woman by her husband

mentor usually an older, established member of a profession who serves as a kind of sponsor for a younger, new member by providing advice and valuable contacts with others in the field

micro-inequities subtle, everyday forms of discrimination that single out, ignore, or in some way discount individuals and their work or ideas simply on the basis of an ascribed trait, such as sex

modeling the process by which children imitate the behavior of their same-sex parent, especially if the parent rewards their imitations or is perceived by them to be warm, friendly, or powerful; a central concept of the social learning perspective of gender socialization

morbidity rate the illness rate of a given population

mortality rate the number of deaths in proportion to a given population

new reproductive technologies a variety of laboratory techniques that allow people to become parents who are infertile, physically unable to conceive or sustain a pregnancy, do not have a partner, or do not wish to enter into a committed relationship

occupational resegregation sex-integrated occupations become resegregated with members of one sex replaced by members of the opposite sex as the predominant workers

occupational sex segregation the degree to which men and women are concentrated in occupations that employ workers of predominantly one sex

paradigm a school of thought that guides a scientist in choosing the problems to be studied, in selecting the methods for studying them, and in explaining what is found

patriarchy a sex/gender system in which men dominate women, and what is considered masculine is more highly valued than what is considered feminine

penis envy Freud's notion of girls' jealousy of the male sexual organ

political action committee (PACs) special-interest groups that dedicate themselves to fundraising and distributing contributions to the political campaigns of candidates who support their cause

power the ability to impose one's will on others

public/private split the idea that home is a separate domain from the public world

Qur'an (or Quran, variation of Koran) the book of sacred writings accepted by Muslims as revelations made to Muhammad by Allah; understood by Muslims to be literally the word of God

rape when a person uses force or the threat of force to have some form of sexual intercourse (vaginal, oral, or anal) with another person

reflection hypothesis the belief that media content mirrors the behaviors, relationships, values, and norms most prevalent or dominant in a society

reinforcement a central principle of social learning theories of gender socialization, which states that a behavior consistently followed by a reward will likely occur again, whereas a behavior followed by a punishment will rarely reoccur

religiosity an individual's or group's intensity of commitment to a religious belief system

reproductive freedom an individual's ability to freely choose whether or not to have a child

schema a central concept of the cognitive developmental perspective of gender socialization; a category used to organize and make sense of information and experiences

semantic derogation the process by which the meaning or connotations of words are debased over time

sentencing disparity widely varying sentences imposed on offenders convicted of similar crimes, usually based on nonlegal factors, such as the offender's sex or race or ethnicity, or other inappropriate considerations

sex chromosomes   one of the twenty-three pairs of human chromosomes, which plays a primary role in determining whether a fertilized egg will develop into a female or a male fetus

sex/gender system   the institutionalized traits, behaviors, and patterns of social interaction that are prescribed for a society's members based on sex; the system incorporates three interrelated components: (1) the social construction of two dichotomous genders on the basis of biological sex; (2) a sexual division of labor; and (3) the social regulation of sexuality

sex   the biologically determined physical distinctions between males and females

sexism   the differential valuing of one sex over the other

sexual double standard   the tradition of permitting young men to engage in sexual activity while simultaneously condemning and punishing the same behavior by young women

sexual harassment   any unwanted leers, comments, suggestions, or physical contact of a sexual nature, as well as unwelcome requests for sexual favors

sexual politics   analysis of gender inequality as rooted not only in the public sphere, but also in the supposedly private sphere of the family and intimate male/female relationships

single-parent family   a family with children but only one adult who has financial responsibility for the household

social movement   a group that has organized to promote a particular cause through social action

socialization   the process by which a society's values and norms, including those pertaining to gender, are taught and learned

sociology   the scientific study of human societies and cultures, and of social behavior

spectator activities   the lowest level of political activism in Millbrath's typology; include voting, wearing a campaign button, or displaying a political bumper sticker

statistical discrimination   employers do not hire anyone who is a member of a group they think has low productivity, regardless of an individual applicant's qualifications or intentions

status offenses   behavior considered illegal if engaged in by a juvenile, but legal if engaged in by an adult

structural functionalist paradigm   a school of thought that explains gender as being derived from the biological differences between the sexes, especially differences in reproductive functions

symbolic annihilation   symbolically ignoring, trivializing, or condemning individuals or groups in the media

Talmud   the foundation of religious authority for traditional Judaism

Title IX   the provisions of the Education Amendments Act of 1972 that forbid sex discrimination in any educational programs or activities that receive federal funding

Title VII of the 1964 Civil Rights Act   forbids discrimination in employment on the basis of sex, race, color, national origin, or religion, by employers of fifteen or more employees, although exceptions, such as the BFOQ, are allowed; implemented and enforced by the EEOC

tokenism   the marginal status of a category of workers who are relatively few in number in the workplace

transformative account of gender development   a theory of gender development that recognizes the truly interactive nature of biology and environment as well as individual agency in the creation of gender by examining how culture and individual behavior may impact biology and physiology and vice versa

transitional activities   the mid-range of political activism in Millbrath's typology; include writing to public officials, making campaign contributions, and attending rallies or political meetings

Turner syndrome   a chromosomal abnormality in which an individual has only one sex chromosome (an X), rather than the normal pair (XX or XY)

two-earner family   a family in which both adult partners are in the paid labor force

witchcraft   naturalistic practices with religious significance usually engaged in by women; includes folk magic and medicine as well as knowledge of farming, ceramics, metallurgy, and astrology

Women-Church movement   a coalition of feminist faith-sharing groups, which offers a feminist critique of traditional Christianity while providing members with alternative, woman-centered rituals and forms of worship

REFERENCES

Abbott, P. (1991). Feminist perspectives in sociology: The challenge to "mainstream" orthodoxy. In J. Aaron & S. Walby (Eds.), *Out of the margins: Women's studies in the nineties* (pp. 181–190). London: Falmer Press.

Abplanalp, J. M. (1983). Premenstrual syndrome: A selective review. In S. Golub (Ed.), *Lifting the curse of menstruation* (pp. 107–123). New York: Haworth Press.

Abzug, B. (1984). *Gender gap*. Boston: Houghton Mifflin.

Adams, K. L., &. Ware, N. C. (1989). Sexism and the English language: The linguistic implications of being a woman. In J. Freeman (Ed.), *Women: A feminist perspective* (pp.470–484). Mountain View, CA: Mayfield.

Adams, S., Kuebli, J., Boyle, P. A., & Fivush, R. (1995). Gender differences in parent-child conversations about past emotions: A longitudinal investigation. *Sex Roles, 33,* 309–323.

A dialogue about race and gender in school. (1998, Winter). *Outlook,* pp. 12–16.

Adler, F. (1975). *Sisters in crime.* New York: McGraw-Hill.

Adler, P. A., Kless, S. J., & Adler, P. (1992). Socialization to gender roles: Popularity among elementary school boys and girls. *Sociology of Education, 65,* 169–187.

Adler, R. (1997). *Engendering Judaism.* New York: Jewish Publication Society.

Afshar, H. (Ed.) (1993). *Women in the Middle East.* New York: St. Martin's Press.

Ahmed, L. (1986). Women and the advent of Islam. *Signs, 11,* 665–691.

Ahmed, L. (1992). *Women and gender in Islam.* New Haven: Yale University Press.

Aiken, S. H., Anderson, K., Dinnerstein, M., Lensink, J., & MacCorquodale, P. (1988). *Changing our minds: Feminist transformations of knowledge.* New York: State University of New York Press.

Alexander, S. (1996). *The gender role paradox in youth culture: An analysis of women in music videos.* Unpublished manuscript available from the author: St. Mary's College, Notre Dame, IN.

Allan, G. (1985). *Family life.* New York: Basil Blackwell.

Allen, D. (1997, Winter). Women are creating their own communications systems. *Media Report to Women,* p. 9.

Allen, L. S., & Gorski, R. A. (1992). Sexual orientation and the size of the anterior commissure in the human brain. *Proceedings of the National Academy of Sciences, 89,* 7199–7202.

Allen, M. (1996, September 22). Defiant V. M. I. to admit women, but they will face tough rules. *New York Times,* pp. 1, 18.

Allen, M., D'alessio, D., & Brezgel, K. (1995). A meta-analysis summarizing the effects of pornography II. *Human Communication Research, 22,* 258–283.

Allgood-Merten, B., Lewinsohn, P. M., & Hops, H. (1990). Sex differences and adolescent depression. *Journal of Abnormal Psychology, 99,* 55–63.

Altman, L. K. (1997, February 28). U.S. reporting sharp decrease in AIDS deaths. *New York Times,* pp. A1, 24.

Altman, L. K. (1998, April 29). Health panel seeks sweeping changes in fertility therapy. *New York Times,* pp. A1, 22.

Amato, P. (1994). Life-span adjustment of children to their parents' divorce. *The Future of Children: Children and Divorce, 1,* 149–152.

American Association of University Professors (AAUP). (1993, March–April). Treading water: The annual report on the economic status of the profession, 1992–1993. *Academe,* pp. 8–33.

American Association of University Professors (AAUP). (1997, March–April). The annual report on the economic status of the profession, 1996–1997. *Academe,* pp. 15–39

American Association of University Women (AAUW). (1992). *How schools shortchange girls.* Washington, DC: Author.

American Association of University Women (AAUW). (1993). *Hostile hallways: The AAUW survey on sexual harassment in America's schools.* Washington, DC: Author.

American Association of University Women (AAUW). (1998). *Separated by sex: A critical look at single-sex education for girls.* Washington, DC: Author.

American Council on Education (1995). *Women presidents of U.S. colleges and universities.* Washington, DC: Author.

American Medical Association. (1990). *Physician characteristics and distribution in the United States.* Chicago: Author.

American Medical Association. (1998). *Women in Medicine.* Washington, DC: Author.

American Psychological Association. (1985). *Developing a national agenda to address women's mental health needs.* Washington, DC: Author.

Ames, L. J., Atchinson, A. N., & Rose, D. T. (1992). *Love, lust, and fear: Safe sex decision making among gay men.* Paper presented at the Annual Meeting of the American Sociological Association, Pittsburgh, PA.

Ammerman, N. T. (1991). North American Protestant fundamentalism. In M. E. Marty & R. S. Appleby (Eds.), *Fundamentalisms observed* (pp. 1–65). Chicago: University of Chicago Press.

Amnesty International. (1991). *Women on the front lines.* New York: Amnesty International.

Amnesty International. (1997). *Breaking the silence: Human rights violations based on sexual orientation.* London: Amnesty International.

Amott T. L., & Matthaei, J. A. (1991). *Race, gender and work.* Boston: South End Press.

Andersen, M. L. (1987). Changing the curriculum in higher education. *Signs, 12,* 222–254.

Anderson, S. R., & Hopkins, P. (1991). *The feminine face of God.* New York: Bantam.

Angier, N. (1992, September 1). Hyenas' hormonal flow puts females in charge. *New York Times,* pp. C1, C10.

Angier, N. (1997, March 14). Sexual identity not pliable after all, report says. *New York Times,* pp. A1, A18.

Anti-gay crimes more violent. (1996, March 12). New York: Associated Press. (Internet).

Antilla, S. (1995, April 26). Young White men only, please. *New York Times,* pp. D1, 7.

Archdiocesan Gay/Lesbian Outreach (AGLO). (1986). *Homosexuality: A positive perspective.* Baltimore: Author.

Arenson, K. W. (1998, January 14). A revamped student test reduces the gap between sexes. *New York Times*, p. B7.

Armstead, C. A., Lawler, K. A., Gordon, G., Cross, J., & Gibbons, J. (1989). Relationship of social stressors to blood pressure responses and anger expression in Black college students. *Health Psychology, 8,* 541–556.

Arnold, R. A. (1990). Processes of victimization and criminalization of Black women. *Social Justice, 17,* 153–165.

Aronson, E., & Gonzalez, A. (1988). Desegregation, jigsaw, and the Mexican-American experience. In P. A. Katz & D. A. Taylor (Eds.), *Eliminating racism* (pp. 301–314). New York: Plenum.

Asch, A. (1989). Reproductive technology and disability. In S. Cohen & N. Taub (Eds.), *Reproductive laws for the 1990s* (pp. 69–124). Clifton, NJ: Humana Press.

A survey finds bias on the front page. (1996, April 17). *New York Times*, p. A17.

At leisure: Americans' use of downtime. (1993, May 9). *New York Times*, p. E2.

Attie, I., & Brooks-Gunn, J. (1987). Weight concerns as chronic stressors in women. In R. C. Barnett, L. Biener, & G. K. Baruch (Eds.), *Gender and stress* (pp. 218–254). New York: Free Press.

Aulette, J. R. (1994). *Changing families*. Belmont, CA: Wadsworth.

Ayres, B. D. (1993, September, 9). Judge's decision in custody case raises concerns. *New York Times*, p. A16.

Ayres, B. D. (1997a, April 14). Women in Washington statehouse lead U.S. tide. *New York Times*, pp. A1, B8.

Ayres, B. D. (1997b, October 26). Gay prosecutor reluctantly goes public. *New York Times*, p. 16.

Baca Zinn, M. (1992). Reframing the revisions: Inclusive thinking for family sociology. In C. Kramarae & D. Spender (Eds.), *The knowledge explosion: Generations of feminist scholarship* (pp. 473–479). New York: Teachers College Press.

Baca Zinn, M., & Dill, B. T. (1996). Theorizing difference from multiracial feminism. *Feminist Studies, 22,* 321–331.

Bachman, J. G., Wadsworth, K. N., O'Malley, P. M., Johnston, L. D., & Schulenberg, J. E. (1997). *Smoking, drinking and drug use in young adulthood: The impacts of new freedoms and new responsibilities*. Mahwah, NJ: Lawrence Erlbaum.

Bacon, M. H. (1986). *Mothers of feminism*. San Francisco: Harper and Row.

Bagilhole, B. (1993). How to keep a good woman down: An investigation of the role of institutional factors in the process of discrimination against women academics. *British Journal of Sociology of Education, 14,* 26–274.

Bagley, C., Bolitho, F., & Bertrand, L. (1997). Sexual assault in school, mental health and suicidal behaviors in adolescent women in Canada. *Adolescence, 32,* 341–366.

Bailey, J. M., & Pillard, R. C. (1991). A genetic study of male sexual orientation. *Archives of General Psychiatry, 48,* 1089–1096.

Bailey, J. M., Pillard, R. C., Neale, M. C., & Agyei, Y. (1993). Heritable factors influence sexual orientation in women. *Archives of General Psychiatry, 50,* 217–223.

Baker, S. W. (1980). Biological influences on human sex and gender. *Signs, 6,* 80–96.

Ballou, M., & Gabalac, N. W. (1985). *A feminist position on mental health*. Springfield, IL: Charles C. Thomas.

Bandura, A. (1986). *The social foundations of thought and action: A social cognitive theory*. Englewood Cliffs, NJ: Prentice-Hall.

Bane, M. J. (1986). Household composition and poverty. In S. H. Danzinger & D. H. Weinberg (Eds.), *Fighting poverty: What works and what doesn't* (pp. 209–231). Cambridge, MA: Harvard University Press.

Banner, L. (1984). *Women in modern America: A brief history*. San Diego: Harcourt, Brace, Jovanovich.

Banner, L. (1986). Act one. *Wilson Quarterly, 10,* 90–98.

Bannerji, H., Carty, L., Dehli, K., Heald, S., & McKenna, K. (Eds.) (1992). Unsettling relations: The university as a site of feminist struggles. Boston: South End Press.

Baran, S. J., &. Blasko, V. J. (1984). Social perceptions and the by-products of advertising. *Journal of Communication, 34,* 12–20.

Bardwell, J. R., Cochran, S. W., & Walker, S. (1986). Relationship of parental education, race, and gender to sex role stereotyping in five-year-old kindergartners. *Sex Roles, 15,* 275–281.

Barker-Benfield, G. J. (1976). *The horrors of the half-known life*. New York: Harper and Row.

Barnes, G. M., Farrell, M. P., & Dintcheff, B. A. (1997). Family socialization effects on alcohol abuse and related problem behaviors among female and male adolescents. In R. W. Wilsnack & S. C. Wilsnack (Eds.), *Gender and alcohol* (pp. 156–175). New Brunswick, NJ: Rutgers Center of Alcohol Studies.

Barnett, B. M. (1993). Invisible Southern Black women leaders in the Civil Rights movement: The triple constraints of gender, race, and class. *Gender & Society, 7,* 162–182.

Barnett, O. W., Lee, C. Y., & Thelan, R. (1997). Gender differences in attributions of self-defense and control in interpartner aggression. *Violence Against Women, 3,* 462–481.

Barnett, R. C., & Baruch, G. K. (1987). Social roles, gender, and psychological stress. In R. C. Barnett, L. Biener, & G. K. Baruch (Eds.), *Gender and stress* (pp. 122–143). New York: Free Press.

Baron, D. (1986). *Grammar and gender*. New Haven: Yale University Press.

Barr, K. E. M., Farrell, M. P., Barnes, G. M., & Welte, J. W. (1993). Race, class, and gender differences in substance abuse: Evidence of middle-class/underclass polarization among Black males. *Social Problems, 40,* 314–327.

Barrett, N. (1987). Women and the economy. In Sara E. Rix (Ed.), *The American woman, 1987–88* (pp. 67–99). New York: W. W. Norton.

Barringer, F. (1993, April 25). Measuring sexuality through polls can be shaky. *New York Times*, p. 28.

Barstow, A. L. (1992). *Witchcraze*. New York: Harper Collins.

Bartollas, C. (1993). Little girls grown up: The perils of institutionalization. In C. Culliver (Ed.), *Female criminality: The state of the art* (pp. 469–482). New York: Garland.

Bashevkin, S. (1996). Tough times in review: The British women's movement during the Thatcher years. *Comparative Political Studies, 28,* 525–552.

Baskin, D. R. & Sommers, I. B. (1997). *Casualties of community disorder: Female violent offenders*. Boulder, CO: Westview.

Baunach, P. J. (1992). Critical problems of women in prison. In I. L. Moyer (Ed.), *The changing roles of women in the criminal justice system* (pp. 99–112). Prospect Heights, IL: Waveland.

Baxter, S., & Lansing, M. (1983). *Women and politics* (revised edition). Ann Arbor: The University of Michigan Press.

Bearden, J. (1992). *Attitudes and knowledge about AIDS and college student sexual behavior.* Paper presented at the Annual Meeting of the Society for the Study of Social Problems, Pittsburgh, PA.

Beatty, R. W., & Beatty, J. R. (1984). Some problems with contemporary job evaluation systems. In H. Remick (Ed.), *Comparable worth and wage discrimination* (pp. 59–78). Philadelphia: Temple University Press.

Becker, M., Bowman, C. G., & Torrey, M. (1994). *Feminist jurisprudence.* Minneapolis: West.

Bedard, M. E. (1992). *Breaking with tradition.* Dix Hills, NY: General Hall.

Bedell, K. B. (Ed.). (1993). *Yearbook of American and Canadian churches.* New York: National Council of Churches.

Bedell, K. B. (Ed.) (1996). *Yearbook of American and Canadian churches.* New York: National Council of Churches.

Bellafante, G. (1998, June 29). Feminism: It's all about me! *Time*, pp. 54–62.

Bellin, J. S., & Rubenstein, R. (1983). Genes and gender in the workplace. In M. Fooden, S. Gordon, & B. Hughley (Eds.), *Genes and gender IV: The second X and women's health* (pp. 87–100). New York: Gordian Press.

Belluck, P. (1998, January 19). "Year of the Woman" senators in tough re-election races. *New York Times*, pp. A1, 12.

Belknap, J. (1991). Women in conflict: An analysis of women correctional officers. *Women and Criminal Justice*, 2, 89–116.

Bem, S. L. (1975). Sex role adaptability: One consequence of psychological androgyny. *Journal of Personality and Social Psychology*, 31, 634–643.

Bem, S. L. (1981). Gender schema theory: A cognitive account of sex typing. *Psychological Review*, 88, 354–364.

Bem, S. L. (1983). Gender schema theory and its implications for child development: Raising gender-aschematic children in a gender-schematic society. *Signs*, 8, 598–616.

Bem, S. L. (1993). *The lenses of gender: Transforming the debate on sexual inequality.* New Haven: Yale University Press.

Bem, S. L., & Lenney, E. (1976). Sex typing and the avoidance of cross-sex behavior. *Journal of Personality and Social Psychology*, 33, 48–54.

Benedetto, R. (1992, July 10). Delegates are a wealthy, liberal and loyal lot. *USA Today*, p. 9A.

Benedict, J. (1997). *Public heroes, private felons: Athletes and crimes against women.* Boston: Northeastern University Press.

Bennet, J. (1993, January 11). Registry for gay couples holds benefits and risks. *New York Times*, p. B3.

Bennet, J. (1996, August 12). The delegates: Where image meets reality. *New York Times*, p. A1.

Benson, K. A. (1984). Comment on Crocker's "An Analysis of University Definitions of Sexual Harassment." *Signs*, 9, 516–519.

Berenbaum, S. A., & Hines, M. (1992). Early androgens are related to childhood sex-typed toy preferences. *Psychological Science*, 3, 203–206.

Bergen, R. K. (1996). *Wife rape: Understanding the response of survivors and service providers.* Thousand Oaks, CA: Sage.

Berger, R. J., Searles, P., & Cottle, C. E. (1991). *Feminism and pornography.* New York: Praeger.

Bergman, B. R. (1986). *The economic emergence of women.* New York: Basic.

Berliner, A. K. (1987). Sex, sin, and the church: The dilemma of homosexuality. *Journal of Religion and Health*, 26, 137–142.

Bernat, F. P. (1992). Women in the legal profession. In I. L. Moyer (Ed.), *The changing role of women in the criminal justice system* (pp. 307–321). Prospect Heights, IL: Waveland Press.

Berstein, N. (1996, February 11). Civil rights lawsuit in rape case challenges integrity of a campus. *New York Times*, pp. 1, 32.

Bernstein, R. (1993, May 30). Cap, gown and gag: The struggle for control. *New York Times*, p. E3.

Bernstein, S. (1995). Feminist intentions: Race, gender, and power in a high school classroom. *NWSA Journal*, 7, 18–34.

Berry, V. (1992). From good times to the Cosby Show. In S. Craig (Ed.), *Men, masculinity and media* (pp. 111–123). Newbury Park, CA: Sage.

Berryman-Fink, C. (1994). Communication competencies of women employees: A comparison of self-ratings and other ratings. In L. H. Turner & H. M. Sterk (Eds.), *Differences that make a difference* (pp. 5–12). Westport, CT: Bergin and Garvey.

Bettencourt, B. A.,& Miller, N. (1996). Gender differences in aggression as a function of provocation: A meta-analysis. *Psychological Bulletin*, 119, 422–447.

Biehl, J. (1990). *Rethinking ecofeminist politics.* Boston: South End Press.

Biener, L. (1987). Gender differences in the use of substances for coping. In R. C. Barnett, L. Biener, & G. K. Baruch (Eds.), *Gender and stress* (pp. 330–349). New York: Free Press.

Birke, L. (1992). Transforming biology. In H. Crowley & S. Himmelweit (Eds.), *Knowing women: Feminism and knowledge* (pp. 66–77). Cambridge: Polity Press.

Bischoping, K. (1993). Gender differences in conversational topics, 1922–1990. *Sex Roles*, 28, 1–18.

Biskupic, J. (1998, June 23). High court limits schools' liability on harassment. *Washington Post*, p. A1.

Bjorkqvist, K. (1994). Sex differences in physical, verbal, and indirect aggression: A review of recent research. *Sex Roles*, 30, 177–188.

Black, L. E., & Sprenkle, D. H. (1991). Gender differences in college students' attitudes toward divorce and their willingness to marry. In S. S. Volgy (Ed.), *Women and divorce, men and divorce* (pp. 47–60). New York: Haworth.

Blake, C. F. (1994). Foot-binding in Neo-Confucian China and the appropriation of female labor. *Signs*, 19, 676–712.

Blakeslee, S. (1991, January 1). Research on birth defects turns to flaws in sperm. *New York Times*, pp. 1, 36.

Blanc, A. K. (1987). The formation and dissolution of second unions: Marriage and cohabitation in Sweden and Norway. *Journal of Marriage and the Family*, 49, 391–400.

Blankenship, K. M. (1993). Bringing gender and race in: U.S. employment discrimination policy. *Gender & Society*, 7, 204–226.

Blaubergs, M. S. (1980). An analysis of classic arguments against changing sexist language. *Women's Studies International Quarterly*, 3, 135–147.

Bleier, R. (1984). *Science and gender.* New York: Pergamon Press.

Blinde, E. M., & Taub, D. E. (1992). Homophobia and women's sport: The disempowerment of athletes. *Sociological Focus, 25,* 151–166.

Blood, R. O., & Wolfe, D. M. (1960). *Husbands and wives.* New York: Free Press.

Bloom, A. (1987). *The Closing of the American mind.* New York: Simon and Schuster.

Bloom, M. (1995, September 27). A show-stopper puts her best foot forward. *New York Times,* pp. B9, 14.

Blum, D. (1997). *Sex on the brain.* New York: Viking.

Blum, L., & Smith, V. (1988). Women's mobility in the corporation: A critique of the politics of optimism. *Signs, 13,* 528–545.

Blum, T. C., & Roman, P. M. (1997). Employment and drinking. In R. W. Wilsnack & S. C. Wilsnack (Eds.), *Gender and alcohol* (pp. 379–394). New Brunswick, NJ: Rutgers Center of Alcohol Studies.

Blume, E. (1983). Methodological difficulties plague PMS research. *Journal of the American Medical Association, 249,* 2864–2866.

Blume, S. B. (1997). Women and alcohol: Issues in social policy. In R. W. Wilsnack & S. C. Wilsnack (Eds.), *Gender and alcohol* (pp. 462–490). New Brunswick, NJ: Rutgers Center of Alcohol Studies.

Blumenthal, R. (1993, February 21). Gay officers find acceptance on New York's force. *New York Times,* pp. 1, 30.

Blumstein, P., & Schwartz, P. (1983). *American couples.* New York: William Morrow.

Bohlen, C. (1995, November 26). Catholics defying an infallible church. *New York Times,* p. E3.

Bok, S. (1998). *Mayhem: Violence as public entertainment.* Reading, MA: Addison-Wesley.

Boland, B. J., Scheitel, S. M., Wollan, P. C., Silverstein, M. D. (1998). Patient-physician agreement on reasons for ambulatory general medical examinations. *Mayo Clinic Proceedings, 73,* 109–117.

Bond, J. T., Golensky, E., & Swanberg, J. E. (1998). *The 1997 National Study of the Changing Workforce.* New York: Families and Work Institute.

Boneparth, E., & Stroper, E. (1988). Introduction: A framework for policy analysis. In E. Boneparth & E. Stroper (Eds.), *Women, power and policy: Toward the year 2000* (p. 119). New York: Pergamon.

Bookman, A., & Morgen, S. (Eds.) (1988). *Women and the politics of empowerment.* Philadelphia: Temple University Press.

Booth, A., Shelley, G., Mazur, A. Tharp, G.,and Kittock, R. (1989). Testosterone and winning and losing in human competition. *Hormones and Behavior, 23,* 556–571.

Bordo, S. (1993). *Unbearable weight: Feminism, Western culture, and the body.* Berkeley, CA: University of California Press.

Bosch, F. X., Castellsague, X., & Shah, K. V. (1997). Male sexual behavior and human papillomavirus DNA: Key risk factors for cervical cancer in Spain. *Obstetrical and Gynecological Survey, 52,* 106–107.

Boston Women's Health Book Collective. (1992). *Our bodies, ourselves.* New York: Simon and Schuster.

Bouchard, C., Tremblay, A., Despres, J., Nadeau, A., Lupien, P. J., Theriault, G., Dussault, J., Moojani, J., Pinault, S., & Fournier, G. (1990). The response to long-term overfeeding in identical twins. *The New England Journal of Medicine, 322,* 1477–1482.

Bourque, L. B. (1989). *Defining rape.* Durham, NC: Duke University Press.

Boxer, S. (1997, December 14). One casualty of the women's movement: Feminism. *New York Time,* p. WK3.

Boyle, J. (1994, August 31). Trials can use rape counseling files victims' statements are subject to scrutiny. *Detroit Free Press,* p. 1B.

Bozett, F. W. (1988). Gay fatherhood. In P. Bronstein & C. P. Cowan (Eds.), *Fatherhood today: Men's changing role in the family* (pp. 214–235). New York: John Wiley.

Bradbard, M. R. (1985). Sex differences in adults' gifts and children's toy requests at Christmas. *Psychological Reports, 56,* 969–970.

Brah, A. (1991). Questions of difference and international feminism. In J. Aaron & S. Walby (Eds.), *Out of the margins: Women's studies in the nineties* (pp. 168–176). London: The Falmer Press.

Brand, P. A., & Kidd, A. H. (1986). Frequency of physical aggression in heterosexual and female homosexual dyads. *Psychological Reports, 59,* 1307–1313.

Brandwein, R. (Ed.) (1999). *The ties that bind: Family violence, women, and welfare.* Thousand Oaks, CA: Sage.

Brannigan, A. & Goldenberg, S. (1987). The study of aggressive pornography: The vicissitudes of relevance. *Critical Studies in Mass Communication, 4,* 262–283.

Brantley, B. (1998, October 14). Nice young man and disciples appeal for tolerance. *New York Times,* pp. E1, E9.

Brantlinger, E. A. (1993). *The politics of social class in secondary school.* New York: Teachers College Press.

Brennan, T. (1992). *The interpretation of the flesh: Freud and femininity.* London: Routledge.

Brewer, R. M. (1988). Black women in poverty: Some comments on female-headed families. *Signs, 13,* 331–339.

Brewster, K. L. (1992). *Race differences in adolescent sexual activity: Another piece of the puzzle.* Paper presented at the Annual Meeting of the American Sociological Association, Pittsburgh, PA.

Brien, P. M. & Beck, A. (1996). *HIV in prisons, 1994.* Washington, DC: U.S. Department of Justice, Bureau of Justice Statistics.

Briggs, N. (1975). Guess who has the most complex job? In B. A. Babcock, A. E. Freedman, E. H. Norton, & S. C. Ross (Eds.), *Sex discrimination and the law: Causes and remedies* (pp. 203–205). Boston: Little Brown.

Briggs, S. (1987). Women and religion. In B. B. Hess & M. M. Ferree (Eds.), *Analyzing gender* (pp. 381–407). Newbury Park, CA: Sage.

Britton, D. M. (1997). Gendered organizational logic: Policy and practice in men's and women's prisons. *Gender & Society, 11,* 796–818.

Brod, H. (1987). The case for men's studies. In H. Brod (Ed.), *The making of masculinities* (pp. 39–62). Boston: Allen and Unwin.

Brody, J. E. (1997, November 4). Girls and puberty: The crisis years. *New York Times,* p. F9.

Bronner, E. (1997, October 14). Group suing U. of Michigan over diversity. *New York Times,* p. A24.

Bronstein, P. (1988). Father-child interaction. In P. Bronstein & C. P. Cowan (Eds.), *Fatherhood today: Men's changing role in the family* (pp. 107–124). New York: John Wiley.

Brooke, J. (1996, February 28). To be young, gay and going to high school in Utah. *New York Times,* p. B8.

Brookoff, D. (1997, October). *Drugs, alcohol, and domestic violence in Memphis.* Washington, DC: National Institute of Justice.

Brooks-Gunn, J., & Fisch, M. (1980). Psychological androgyny and college students' judgments of mental health. *Sex Roles, 6*, 575–580.

Brooks-Gunn, J., & Matthews, W. S. (1979). *He and she.* Englewood Cliffs, NJ: Prentice-Hall.

Brooten, B. J. (1982). *Women leaders in the ancient synagogue.* Chico, CA: Scholars Press.

Bottcher, J. (1995). Gender as social control: A qualitative study of incarcerated youths and their siblings in greater Sacramento. *Justice Quarterly, 12*, 33–57.

Broverman, I. K., Broverman, D. M., Clarkson, F. E., Rosenkrantz, P. S., & Vogel, S. R. (1970). Sex-role stereotypes and clinical judgments of mental health. *Journal of Clinical and Counseling Psychology, 34*, 1–7.

Brown, J. (1997). Working toward freedom from violence: The process of change in battered women. *Violence Against Women, 3*, 5–26.

Brown, J. D., & Campbell, K. (1986). Race and gender in music videos: The same beat but a different drummer. *Journal of Communication, 36*, 94–106.

Brown, J. M., & Beck, A. J. (1997). *Probation and parole populations, 1996.* Washington, DC: U.S. Department of Justice.

Brown, L. (1994). *Subversive dialogues: Theory in feminist therapy.* New York: Basic Books.

Browne, A. & Bassuk, S. S. (1997). Intimate violence in the lives of homeless and poor housed women. *American Journal of Orthopsychiatry, 67*, 261–278.

Brownmiller, S. (1975). *Against our will.* New York: Simon and Schuster.

Brozan, N. (1990, April 9). Telling the seder's story in the voice of a woman. *New York Times*, p. B4.

Brumberg, J. (1997). *The body project: An intimate history of American girls.* New York: Random House.

Bruni, F. (1995, November 5). For gay couples, ruling to cheer on adoption. *New York Times*, p. 41.

Bruni, F. (1996, October 13). It may be a closet door, but it's already open. *New York Times*, pp. H1, 40.

Buckley, S. (1997). *Broken silence: Voices of Japanese feminism.* Berkeley, CA: University of California Press.

Bulbeck, C. (1988). *One world women's movement.* London: Pluto Press.

Bulman, E. (1998, March 20). UN: Unsafe abortions kill thousands. *Atlanta Constitution*, p. 1.

Bumiller, E. (1990). *May you be the mother of a hundred sons: A journey among the women of India.* New York: Random House.

Bumpass, L. L., & Sweet, J. E. (1991). The role of cohabitation in declining rates of marriage. *Journal of Marriage and the Family, 53*, 913–927.

Buresh, B., Gordon, S., & Bell, N. (1991). Who counts in news coverage of health care? *Nursing Outlook, 39*, 204–208.

Burns, A., & Homel, R. (1989). Gender division of tasks by parents and their children. *Psychology of Women Quarterly, 13*, 113–125.

Burns, A. L., Mitchell, G., & Obradovich, S. (1989). Of sex roles and strollers: Female and male attention to toddlers at the zoo. *Sex Roles, 20*, 309–315.

Burns, J. F. (1994, August 27). India fights abortion of female fetuses. *New York Times*, A3.

Burns, J. F. (1998, March 29). Once widowed in India, twice scorned. *New York Times*, pp. 1–12.

Burris, B. H. (1989). Technocracy and gender in the workplace. *Social Problems, 36*, 165–180.

Burstow, B. (1992). *Radical feminist therapy: Working in the context of violence.* Newbury Park, CA: Sage.

Busfield, J. (1986). *Managing madness.* London: Hutchinson.

Bush, D. M. (1987). *The impact of family and school on adolescent girls' aspirations and expectations: The public-private split and the reproduction of gender inequality.* Paper presented at the Annual Meeting of the American Sociological Association, Chicago, IL.

Bush-Baskette, S. R. (1998). The war on drugs as a war against Black women. In S. L. Miller (Ed.), *Crime control and women* (pp. 113–129). Thousand Oaks, CA: Sage.

Bussey, K., & Bandura, A. (1984). Influence of gender constancy and social power on sex-linked modeling. *Journal of Personality and Social Psychology, 47*, 1292–1302.

Butler, M., & Paisley, W. (1980). *Women and the mass media: Sourcebook for research and action.* New York: Human Sciences Press.

Byrne, J. M., & R. J. Sampson, W. (Eds.) (1986). *The social ecology of crime.* New York: Springer-Verlag.

Byrne, L. (Ed.) (1991). *The hidden tradition: Women's spiritual writings rediscovered.* New York: Crossroad.

Caldera, Y. M., Huston, A. C., & O'Brien, M. (1989). Social interactions and play patterns of parents and toddlers with feminine, masculine, and neutral toys. *Child Development, 60*, 70–76.

Caldwell, M. A., & Peplau, L. A. (1984). The balance of power in lesbian relationships. *Sex Roles, 10*, 587–599.

Callahan, J. J. (1988). Elder abuse: Some questions for policymakers. *The Gerontologist, 28*, 453–458.

Cammermeyer, M. (1994). *Serving in silence: The story of Margarethe Cammermeyer.* New York: Penguin.

Campbell, A. (1984). *The girls in the gang.* Oxford: Basil Blackwell.

Canadian Bishops' Pastoral Team. (1989, September 21). Inclusive language: Overcoming discrimination. *Origins, 21, 1*, 259–260.

Cann, A., & Palmer, S. (1986). Children's assumptions about the generalizability of sex-typed abilities. *Sex Roles, 15*, 551–557.

Cannon, L. W., Higginbotham, E., & Guy, R. F. (1989). *Depression among women: Exploring the effects of race, class and gender.* Center for Research on Women, Memphis State University, Memphis, TN.

Cannon, R. O. (1993). Chest pain with normal coronary angiograms. *New England Journal of Medicine, 328*, 1706–1708.

Caplan, P. J., & Caplan, J. B. (1994). *Thinking critically about research on sex and gender.* Reading, MA: Addison-Wesley.

Caraway, N. (1991). *Segregated sisterhood: Racism and the politics of American feminism.* Knoxville: University of Tennessee Press.

Carelli, R. (1997a, June 16). *Supreme Court upholds abortion ban.* Washington, DC: Associated Press. (Internet).

Carelli, R. (1997b, January 21). *Church must limit anti-gay protests after losing court bid.* Washington, DC: Associate Press. (Internet).

Carlat, D. J., Camargo, C. A., Jr., & Herzog, D. B. (1997). Eating disorders in males: A report on 135 patients. *American Journal of Psychiatry, 154*, 1127–1132.

Carlson, S. M. (1992). Trends in race/sex occupational inequality: Conceptual and measurement issues. *Social Problems, 39*, 268–290.

Carmody, D. L. (1989). *Women and world religions.* Nashville: Abingdon.

Carrigan, T., Connell, B., & Lee, J. (1987). Toward a new sociology of masculinity. In H. Brod (Ed.), *The making of masculinities* (pp. 63–100). Boston: Allen and Unwin.

Carroll, C. M. (1993). Sexual harassment on campus: Enhancing awareness and promoting change. *Educational Record, (74)1*, 2126.

Carroll, S. J. (1985). *Women as candidates in American politics.* Bloomington, IN: Indiana University Press.

Carroll, S. J., Dodson, D. L., & Mandel, R. B. (1991). *The impact of women in public office: An overview.* New Brunswick, NJ: Center for the American Woman and Politics.

Carter, D. B., & McClosky, L. A. (1983). Peers and the maintenance of sex-typed behavior: The development of children's conceptions of cross-gender behavior in their peers. *Social Cognition, 4,* 294–314.

Carty, L. (1992). Black Women in academia: A statement from the periphery. In H. Bannerji, L. Carty, K. Dehli, S. Heald, & K. McKenna (Eds.), *Unsettling relations: The university as a site of feminist struggles* (pp. 13–44). Boston: South End Press.

Casey, M. B., Nuttall, R. L., & Pezais, E. (1997). Mediators of gender differences in mathematics college entrance test scores: A comparison of spatial skills with internalized beliefs and anxieties. *Developmental Psychology, 33,* 669–680.

Cash, T. F., & Henry, P. E. (1995). Women's body images: The results of a national survey in the U.S.A. *Sex Roles, 33,* 19–28.

Cazenave, N. A., & Straus, M. A. (1990). Race, class, network embeddedness and family violence: A search for potent support systems. In M. A. Straus & R. J. Gelles (Eds.), *Physical violence in American families: Risk factors and adaptations to violence in 8,145 families* (pp. 321–340). New Brunswick, NJ: Transaction.

Celis, W. (1993, January 6). Schools across U.S. cautiously adding lessons on gay life. *New York Times,* p. A19.

Center for the American Woman and Politics (CAWP) (n.d.). *Women make a difference: Women supporting women.* New Brunswick, NJ: Author.

Center for the American Woman and Politics (CAWP) (1984, June). *Women's routes to elective office.* New Brunswick, NJ: Author.

Center for the American Women and Politics (CAWP). (1985, May). *Black women office-holders.* New Brunswick, NJ: Author.

Center for the American Woman and Politics (CAWP). (1987, April). *Fact sheet: The gender gap in Presidential elections, 1952–1984.* New Brunswick, NJ: Author.

Center for the American Woman and Politics (CAWP). (1993, April). *Women in the U.S. Congress, 1993.* New Brunswick, NJ: Author.

Center for the American Woman and Politics (CAWP). (1998a, March). *Women in elective office, 1998.* New Brunswick, NJ: Author.

Center for the American Woman and Politics (CAWP). (1998b, March). *Women of color in elective office, 1998.* New Brunswick, NJ: Author.

Center for the American Woman and Politics (CAWP). (1998c, January). *Women in the U.S. Congress, 1998.* New Brunswick, NJ: Author.

Center for the American Woman and Politics (CAWP). (1998d, January). *Women in the U. S. Senate, 1922–1998.* New Brunswick, NJ: Author.

Center for Media and Public Affairs. (1993, January 7). 1992—The year in review. *Media Monitor,* p. 35.

Center for Women Policy Studies. (1991a). *More harm than help: The ramifications of mandatory HIV testing for rapists.* Washington, DC: Author.

Center for Women Policy Studies. (1991b). *Violence against women as bias motivated hate crime: Defining the issues.* Washington, DC: Author.

Centers for Disease Control. (1993, April 23). Rates of caesarian delivery—United States, 1991. *Morbidity and Mortality Weekly Report 42,* 285–289.

Chafetz, J. S. (1988). *Feminist sociology: An overview of contemporary theories.* Itasca, IL: F. E. Peacock.

Chafetz, J. S., & Dworkin, A. G. (1986). *Female revolt: Women's movements in world and historical perspective.* Totowa, NJ: Rowman and Allanheld.

Chafetz, J. S., Dworkin, A. G., & Swanson, S. (1990). Social change and social activism: First-wave women's movements around the world. In G. West & R. L. Blumberg (Eds.), *Women and social protest* (pp. 302–320). New York: Oxford University Press.

Chain gangs for women cause furor. (1996, April 28). *New York Times,* p. 30.

Chamberlain, E. M. (1997). Courtroom to classroom: There is more to sexual harassment. *NWSA Journal, 9,* 136–154.

Chambless, D. L., & Goldstein, A. J. (1980). Anxieties: Agoraphobia and hysteria. In A. M. Brodsky & R. Hare-Mustin (Eds.), *Women and psychotherapy* (pp. 113–134). New York: The Guilford Press.

Chapman, J. R. (1990). Violence against women as a violation of human rights. *Social Justice 17,* 54–70.

Chart of kindergarten awards. (1994, December 5). *Wall Street Journal,* p. B1.

Chavkin, W. (1984a). Walking a tightrope: Pregnancy, parenting, and work. In W. Chavkin (Ed.), *Double exposure* (pp. 196–213). New York: Monthly Review Press.

Chavkin, W. (1984b). Part 3, On the homefront: Women at home and in the community, introduction. In W. Chavkin (Ed.), *Double exposure* (pp. 215–217). New York: Monthly Review Press.

Chavkin, W. (1990). Drug addiction and pregnancy: Policy crossroads. *American Journal of Public Health, 80,* 483–487.

Cherian, V. I., & Siweya, J. (1996). Gender and achievement in mathematics by indigenous African students majoring in mathematics. *Psychological Reports, 78,* 27–34.

Chesler, E. (1994, February 6). No, the first priority is stop coercing women. *The New York Times Magazine,* pp. 31, 33.

Chesney-Lind, M. (1986). Women and crime: The female offender. *Signs, 12,* 78–96.

Chesney-Lind, M. (1997). *The female offender.* Thousand Oaks, CA: Sage.

Chesney-Lind, M., & Rodriquez, N. (1983). Women under lock and key. *The Prison Journal, 63,* 47–65.

Chesney-Lind, M., & Shelden, R. G. (1992). *Girls delinquency and juvenile justice.* Pacific Grove, CA: Brooks/ Cole.

Chesterman, C. (1990, May). Women, art, and technology. *Refractory Girl,* p. 27.

Children Now & the Kaiser Family Foundation. (1997). *A national survey of children: Reflections of girls in the media—A summary of findings and toplines.* Menlo Park, CA: Author.

Children's Defense Fund. (1988). *Teenage pregnancy: An advocate's guide to the numbers.* Washington, DC: Adolescent Pregnancy Prevention Clearinghouse.

Children's Defense Fund. (1991). *The state of America's children—1991.* Washington, DC: Author.

Children's Defense Fund. (1997). *The state of America's children—Yearbook 1997.* Washington, DC: Author.

Children's Defense Fund. (1998). *The state of America's children—Yearbook 1998.* Washington, DC: Author.

Childers, M. (1990). A conversation about race and class. In M. Hirsch & E. F. Keller (Eds.), *Conflicts in feminism* (pp. 60–81). New York: Routledge.

Chira, S. (1993, October 21). Fathers who want time off for families face uphill battle. *New York Times*, p. C6.

Chodorow, N. (1978). *The reproduction of mothering.* Berkeley: University of California Press.

Chodorow, N. (1989). *Feminism and psychoanalytic theory.* New Haven: Yale University Press.

Chodorow, N. J. (1994). *Feminities, masculinities, sexualities: Freud and beyond.* Lexington, KY: University of Kentucky Press.

Chodorow, N. (1995). Gender as a personal and cultural construction. *Signs, 20*, 516–544.

Chopp, R. S. (1989). *The power to speak: Feminism, language, and God.* New York: Crossroad/Continuum.

Chrisler, J. C. (1991). The effect of premenstrual symptoms on creative thinking. In D. L. Taylor & N. F. Woods (Eds.), *Menstruation, health, and illness* (pp. 73–83). New York: Hemisphere.

Chrisler, J. C., &. Levy, K. B. (1990). The media construct a menstrual monster: A content analysis of PMS articles in the popular press. *Women and Health, 16*, 89–104.

Christ, C. P. (1983). Heretics and outsiders: The struggle over female power in western religion. In L. Richardson & V. Taylor (Eds.), *Feminist frontiers* (pp. 87–94). Reading, MA: Addison-Wesley.

Christ, C. P., & Plaskow, J. (1979). Introduction: Womanspirit rising. In C. P. Christ & J. Plaskow (Eds.), *Womanspirit rising* (pp. 118). San Francisco: Harper and Row.

Christensen, A. S. (1988). Sex discrimination and the law. In A. H. Stromberg & S. Harkess (Eds.), *Women working* (pp. 329–347). Mountain View, CA: Mayfield.

Christensen, C. L. (1993). Basic exercise physiology: Myths and realities. In G. L. Cohen (Ed.), *Women in sport* (pp. 119–132). Newbury Park, CA: Sage.

Christian, H. (1994). *The making of anti-sexist men.* New York: Routledge.

Clark, C. S. (1995, April 7). Abortion clinic protests. *CQ Researcher*, pp. 299–308.

Clark, J. (1991). Getting there: Women in political office. *The Annals of the American Academy of Political and Social Science, 515*, 63–76.

Clark, M. M. (1997). The Silva case at the University of New Hampshire. *NWSA Journal, 9*, 77–93.

Clark, R., Lennon, R. & Morris, L. (1993). Of Caldecotts and kings: Gendered images in recent American children's books by Black and non-Black illustrators. *Sex Roles, 7*, 227–245.

Clarke, A., & Ruble, D. N. (1978). Young adolescents' beliefs concerning menstruation. *Child Development, 49*, 201–234.

Cleary, P. D. (1987). Gender differences in stress-related disorders. In R. C. Barnett, L. Biener, & G. K. Baruch (Eds.), *Gender and stress* (pp. 39–72). New York: Free Press.

Clewell, B. C., & Anderson, B. (1991). *Women of color in mathematics, science and engineering: A review of the literature.* Washington, DC: Center for Women Policy Studies.

Clinton grants gay workers job protection. (1998, May 29). *New York Times*, p. A16.

Coale, A. J. (1991). Excess female mortality and the balance of the sexes in the population: An estimate of the number of "missing females." *Population and Development Review, 17*, 517–523.

Cobble, D. S. (1991). *Dishing it out: Waitresses and their unions in the twentieth century.* Urbana: University of Illinois Press.

Cochran S. D., &. Mays, V. M. (1988). Issues in the perception of AIDS risk and risk reduction activities by Black and Hispanic/Latina women. *American Psychologist, 43*, 949–957.

Collins, P. H. (1986). Learning from the outsider within: The sociological significance of Black feminist thought. *Social Problems, 33*, S14–S32.

Collins, P. H. (1990). *Black feminist thought.* Cambridge, MA: Unwin and Hyman.

Coltrane, S. (1989). Household labor and the routine production of gender. *Social Problems, 36*, 473–490.

Commission on Professionals in Science and Technology. (1992). *Professional women and minorities.* Washington, DC: Author.

Committee for Abortion Rights and Against Sterilization Abuse. (1988). *Women under attack: Victories, backlash, and the fight for reproductive freedom.* Boston: South End Press.

Comstock, G. (1991). *Television and the American child.* San Diego: Academic Press.

Condry, J. C. (1989). *The psychology of television.* Hillsdale, NJ: Lawrence Erlbaum Associates.

Conference report. (1997, March 28). *Philadelphia Daily News*, p. 128.

The Congregation for the Doctrine of the Faith. (1987). Instruction on respect for human life in its origin and on the dignity of procreation. *Origins, 16*, 698–711.

Conkey, M. W., & Gero, J. M. (1991). Tensions, pluralities, and engendering archeology: An introduction to women and pre-history. In J. M. Gero & M. W. Conkey (Eds.), *Engendering archeology* (pp. 3–30). New York: Basil Blackwell.

Conley, F. K. (1998). *Walking out on the boys.* New York: Farrar, Straus & Giroux.

Connell, R. W. (1995). *Masculinities.* Berkeley, CA: University of California Press.

Connors, L. (1996). *Gender of infant differences in attachment: Associations with temperament and caregiving experiences.* Paper presented at the Annual Conference of the British Pyschological Society, Oxford, England.

Cooke, M., & Woollacott, A. (Eds.) (1993). *Gendering war talk.* Princeton, NJ: Princeton University Press.

Coombs, L. C. (1977). Preferences for sex of children among U.S. couples. *Family Planning Perspectives, 9*, 259–265.

Corcoran, M., Duncan, G. J., & Hill, M. S. (1984). The economic fortunes of women and children: Lessons from the panel study of income dynamics. *Signs, 10*, 232–248.

Cornwall, M. (1989). Faith development of men and women over the life span. In S. J. Bahr & E. T. Peterson (Eds.), *Aging and the family* (pp. 115–139). Lexington, MA: Lexington Books.

Corsaro, W. A., & Eder, D. (1990). Children's peer cultures. In W. R. Scott (Ed.), *Annual review of sociology, Volume 16* (pp. 197–220). Palo Alto, CA: Annual Reviews, Inc.

Cott, N. F. (1986). Feminist theory and feminist movements: The past before us. In J. Mitchell & A. Oakley

(Eds.), *What is feminism? A reexamination* (pp. 49–62). New York: Pantheon.

Cott, N. F. (1987). *The grounding of modern feminism.* New Haven: Yale University Press.

Couric, E. (1989, December 11). An NJL/West survey, women in the law: Awaiting their turn. *National Law Journal,* pp. S1, S12.

Courtney, A. E., & Whipple, T. W. (1983). *Sex stereotyping in advertising.* Lexington, MA: Lexington Books.

Court that attacks sex bias reported often guilty of it. (1992, August 7). *New York Times,* p. A17.

Cowan, A. L. (1992, June 1). Can a baby-making venture deliver? *New York Times,* pp. D1, D6.

Cowan, C. P., & Cowan, P. A. (1992). *When partners become parents.* New York: Basic Books.

Cowan, G., & Hoffman, C. D. (1986). Gender stereotyping in young children: Evidence to support a concept learning approach. *Sex Roles, 14,* 211–224.

Cowan, R. S. (1984). *More work for mother.* New York: Basic Books.

Cowell, A. (1994, May 31). Pope rules out debate on making women priests. *New York Times,* p. A8.

Cowell, P. E., Turetsky, B. I., Gur, R. C., Grossman, R. I., Shtasel, D. L. & Gur, R. E. (1994). Sex differences in aging of the human frontal and temporal lobes. *Journal of Neuroscience, 14,* 4748–4755.

Cox, F. D. (1993). *Human intimacy: Marriage, the family and its meaning.* Minneapolis: West.

Cox, M. J. (1985). Progress and continued challenges in understanding the transition to parenthood. *Journal of Family Issues, 6,* 395–408.

Cox, R. S. (1998, Winter). Speaking out for those "loud Black girls." *Outlook,* pp. 8–11.

Craft, C. (1988). *Too old, too ugly, and not deferential to men.* Rocklin, CA: Prime Publishing and Communications.

Cramer, P., & Russo, A. (1992). Toward a multicentered women's studies in the 1990s. In C. Kramarae & D. Spender (Eds.), *The knowledge explosion* (pp. 99–117). New York: Teachers College Press.

Craven, D. (1996). *Female victims of violent crime.* Washington, DC: U.S. Department of Justice, Bureau of Justice Statistics.

Crawford, K. (1990, May). Girls and computers. *Refractory Girl,* pp. 21–26.

Crenshaw, K. W. (1994). Mapping the margins: Intersectionality, identity politics, and violence against women of color. In M. A. Fineman & R. Myktiuk (Eds.), *The public nature of private violence* (pp. 93–118). New York: Routledge.

Crick, N. R., & Grotpeter, J. K. (1995). Relational aggression, gender, and social-psychological adjustment. *Child Development, 66,* 710–722.

Crites, L. (Ed.) (1976). *The female offender.* Lexington, MA: Lexington Books.

Cron, T. (1986). The Surgeon General's workshop on violence and public health: Review of the recommendations. *Public Health Reports, 101,* 8–14.

Cronin, A. (1996, February 25). Abortion: The rate vs. the debate. *New York Times,* p. 4E.

Cropper, C. M. (1998, February 26). Fruit to walls to floor, ads are on the march. *New York Times,* pp. A1, D8.

Crossette, B. (1995, December 10). Female genital mutilation by immigrants is becoming cause for concern in the U.S. *New York Times,* p. 18.

Crossette, B. (1996, May 12). Muslim women's movement gaining strength. *New York Times,* p. 3.

Crossette, B. (1998, April 6). Afghan women demanding end to their repression by militants. *New York Times,* pp. A1, 8.

Crowell, N. A., & Burgess, A. W. (1996). *Understanding violence against women.* Washington, DC: National Academy Press.

Cruikshank, M. (1992). *The gay and lesbian liberation movement.* New York: Routledge, Chapman and Hall.

Culpepper, E. E. (1992). Menstruation consciousness raising: A personal and pedagogical process. In A. J. Dan & L. L. Lewis (Eds.), *Menstrual health and women's lives* (pp. 274–284). Urbana: University of Illinois Press.

Cummings, J. (1986, August 3). Woman in conservative rabbi post. *New York Times,* p. 24.

Curran, D. J. (1984). The myth of the "new" female delinquent. *Crime and Delinquency, 30,* 386–399.

Curran, D. J., & Renzetti, C. M. (1993). *Social problems: Society in crisis.* Boston: Allyn and Bacon.

Dale, C. (1997). *Uncommon roles and common routes: Narrative in obituaries of prominent women, 1994–95.* Paper presented at the Annual Meeting of the Association for Education in Journalism and Mass Communication, Chicago, IL.

Daly, K. (1989a). Gender varieties in white-collar crime. *Criminology, 27,* 769–793.

Daly, K. (1989b). Neither conflict nor labeling nor paternalism will suffice: Intersections of race, ethnicity, gender, and family in criminal court decisions. *Crime and Delinquency, 35,* 136–168.

Daly, K. (1994). *Gender, crime, and punishment.* New Haven, CT: Yale University Press.

Daly, M. (1978). *Gyn/Ecology.* Boston: Beacon Press.

Daly, M. (1983). Indian suttee: The ultimate consummation of marriage. In L. Richardson & V. Taylor (Eds.), *Feminist frontiers* (pp. 189–190). Reading, MA: Addison-Wesley.

Daly, M. (1984). *Pure lust.* Boston: Beacon Press.

Danner, M. J. E. (1998). Three strikes and it's *women* who are out: The hidden consequences for women of criminal justice policy reforms. In S. L. Miller (Ed.), *Crime control and women* (pp. 1–14). Thousand Oaks, CA: Sage.

Darling, C., Kallen, D., & VanDusen, J. (1992). Sex in transition, 1900–1980. In A. Skolnick & J. Skolnick (Eds.), *Family in transition* (pp. 151–160). New York: Harper Collins.

Darrow, W. R. (1985). Woman's place and the place of women in the Iranian revolution. In Y. Y. Haddad & E. B. Findly (Eds.), *Women, religion and social change* (pp. 307–320). Albany: State University of New York Press.

Davidson, R. C., & Lewis, E. L. (1997). Affirmative action and other special consideration admissions at the University of California, Davis, School of Medicine. *Journal of the American Medical Association, 278,* 1153–1158.

Davies, B. (1989). *Frogs and snails and feminist tales.* Sydney: Allen and Unwin.

Davies, J., Lyon, E., & Monti-Catania, D. (1998). *Safety planning with battered women.* Thousand Oaks, CA: Sage.

Davies-Netzley, S. A. (1998). Women above the glass ceiling: Perceptions on corporate mobility and strategies for success. *Gender & Society, 12,* 339–355.

Davis, E. A. (1995). *Sex bias in United States history textbooks.* Paper presented at the Annual Meeting of the Eastern Sociological Society, Philadelphia, PA.

Davis, K., Grant, P., & Rowland, D. (1990, Summer). Alone and poor: The plight of elderly women. *Generations, 14,* 43–47.

Davis, M., Neuhaus, J. M.. Moritz, D.J., & Segal, M. R. (1990). *Living arrangement influences survival of middle-aged men.* Paper presented at the Annual Meeting of the American Public Health Association, Santa Barbara, CA.

Davis, N. J. (1993, Summer). Female youth homelessness —systematic gender control. *Socio-Legal Bulletin,* pp. 22–31.

Davis, T. L. (1995). Gender differences in masking negative emotions: Ability or motivation? *Developmental Psychology, 31,* 660–667.

Davis-Floyd, R. E. (1992). *Birth as an American rite of passage.* Berkeley: University of California Press.

Davis-Kimball, J. (1997). Warrior women of the Eurasian steppes. *Archeology, 50,* 44–48.

Deats, S. M., & Lenker, L. T. (1994). *Gender and academe: Feminist pedagogy and politics.* Lanham, MD: Rowman and Littlefield.

Deaux, K., & Kite, M. E. (1987). Thinking about gender. In B. B. Hess & M. M. Ferree (Eds.), *Analyzing gender* (pp. 92–117). Newbury Park, CA: Sage.

DeFour, D. C. (1991). The nterface of racism and sexism on college campuses. In M. A. Paludi (Ed.), *Ivory power: Sexual harassment on campus* (pp. 45–52). Albany: State University of New York Press.

Deitch, C. (1993). Gender, race and class politics and the inclusion of women in Title VII of the 1964 Civil Rights Act. *Gender & Society 7,* 183–203.

DeKeseredy, W. S. (Ed.). (1997). Post-separation woman abuse. A special issue of *Violence Against Women, 3* (6).

DeKeseredy, W. S., & Kelly, K. (1993). The incidence and prevalence of woman abuse in Canadian university and college dating relationships. *Canadian Journal of Sociology, 18,* 137–159.

DeKeseredy, W. S., & McLeod, L. (1997). *Woman abuse: A sociological story.* Toronto: Harcourt Brace Canada.

DeKeseredy, W. S., Schwartz, M. D., & Tait, K. (1993). Sexual assault and stranger aggression on a Canadian university campus. *Sex Roles, 28,* 263–277.

Delmar, R. (1986). What is feminism? In J. Mitchell & A. Oakley (Eds.), *What is feminism? A re-examination* (pp. 8–33). New York: Pantheon.

DeLoache, J. S., Cassidy, D. J., & Carpenter, C. J. (1987). The three bears are all boys: Mothers' gender labeling of neutral picture book characters. *Sex Roles, 17,* 163–178.

Democratic National Committee. (1997). Personal communication.

DeMott, B. (1996, January 7). Sure, we're all just one big happy family. *New York Times,* pp. H1, 31.

Denfeld, R. (1996). *The new victorians.* New York: Warner Books.

Denham, S. A., Zoller, D., & Couchoud, E. A. (1994). Socialization of preschoolers' emotional understanding. *Developmental Psychology, 30,* 928–938.

Dennehy, K., & Mortimer, J. T. (1992). *Work and family orientations of contemporary adolescent boys and girls in a context of social change.* Paper presented at the Annual Meeting of the American Sociological Association, Pittsburgh, PA.

Desole, G. (1997). Review essay: Sexual harassment. *NSWA Journal, 9,* 155–164.

DeVault, M. L. (1986). *Talking and listening from women's standpoint: Feminist strategies for analyzing interview data.* Paper presented at the Annual Meeting of the Society for Symbolic Interaction, New York, NY.

DeVault, M. L. (1991). *Feeding the family.* Chicago: University of Chicago Press.

DeWitt, K. (1996, February 5). New cause helps feminists appeal to younger women. *New York Times,* p. A10.

de Young, S., & Crane, F. G. (1992). Females' attitudes toward the portrayal of women in advertising: A Canadian study. *International Journal of Advertising, 11,* 249–255.

Diamond, I. (1988). Medical science and the transformation of motherhood: The promise of reproductive technologies. In E. Boneparth & E. Stroper (Eds.), *Women, power and policy: Toward the year 2000* (pp. 155–167). New York: Pergamon.

Diamond, I. (1992). Ecofeminist politics: The promise of common ground. In C. Kramarae & D. Spender (Eds.), *The knowledge explosion: Generations of feminist scholarship* (pp. 371–378). New York: Teachers College Press.

Diamond, M., & Sigmundson, K. H. (1997). Sex reassignment at birth: Long-term review and clinical implications. *Archives of Pediatrics and Adolescent Medicine, 151,* 298–305.

Dibble, U., & Straus, M. A. (1990). Some social structure determinants of inconsistency between attitudes and behavior: The case of family violence. In M. A. Straus & R. J. Gelles (Eds.), *Physical violence in families* (pp. 167–180). New Brunswick, NJ: Transaction Publishers.

Diedrick, P. (1991). Gender differences in adjustment to divorce. In S. S. Volgy (Ed.), *Women and divorce, men and divorce* (pp. 33–45). New York: Haworth.

Diesenhouse, S. (1990, January 7). Drug treatment is scarcer than ever for women. *New York Times,* p. 26E.

Dines, G., Jensen, R., & Russo, A. (1998). *Pornography: The production and consumption of inequality.* New York: Routledge.

Dittman, R. W., Kappes, M. H., Kappes, M. E., Borger, D., Meyer-Bahlburg, H. F. L., Stenger, H., Willig, R. H., & Wallis, H. (1990a). Congenital hyperplasia I: Gender-related behavior and attitudes in female patients and sisters. *Psychoneuroendocrinology, 15,* 401–420.

Dittman, R. W., Kappes, M. H., Kappes, M. E., Borger, D., Meyer-Bahlburg, H. F. L., Stenger, H., Willig, R. H., & Wallis, H. (1990b). Congenital hyperplasia II: Gender-related behavior and attitudes in female salt-wasting and simple-virilizing patients. *Psychoneuroendocrinology, 15,* 421–434.

Dobash, R. E., & Dobash, R.P. (1992). *Women, violence and social change.* London: Routledge.

Dobash, R. P., Dobash, R. E., Cavanagh, K., & Lewis, R. (1998). Separate and intersecting realities: A comparison of men's and women's accounts of violence against women. *Violence Against Women, 4,* 382–414.

Dobrzynski, J. H. (1995, October 29). How to succeed? Go to Wellesley. *New York Times,* pp. 1, 9.

Donnerstein, E. (1983). Erotica and human aggression. In R. G. Green & E. I. Donnerstein (Eds.), *Aggression: Theoretical and empirical reviews* (pp. 127–154). New York: Academic Press.

Donnerstein, E., Linz, D., & Penrod, S. (1987). *The question of pornography*. New York: Free Press.

Dorsher, M. (1997). *Women and 'all the news that fit to print.'* Paper presented at the Annual Meeting of the Association for Education in Journalism and Mass Communication, Chicago, IL.

Dow, B. J. (1996). *Prime-time feminism*. Philadelphia: University of Pennsylvania Press.

Dowd, M. (1990, November 20). Americans more wary of Gulf policy, poll finds. *New York Times*, p. A12.

Dowd, M. (1991, May 20). Bush appoints more women, but most top aides are men. *New York Times*, pp. A1, B6.

Doyal, L. (1990a). Waged work and women's well being. *Women's Studies International Forum, 13*, 587–604.

Doyal, L. (1990b). Hazards of hearth and home. *Women's Studies International Forum, 13*, 501–517.

Drakulic, S. (1991). *How we survived communism and even laughed*. New York: W. W. Norton.

Drentea, P. (1998). Consequences of women's formal and informal job search methods for employment in female-dominated jobs. *Gender & Society, 12*, 321–338.

Drewniany, B. (1996). Super Bowl commercials: The best a man can get (or is it?). In P. M. Lester (Ed.), *Images that injure* (pp. 87–92). Westport, CT: Praeger.

Dublin, T. (1994). *Transforming women's work*. Ithaca, NY: Cornell University Press.

Dugger, C. W. (1996a, October 12). New law bans genital cutting in United States. *New York Times*, p. 1, 28.

Dugger, C. W. (1996b, September 11). A refugee's body is intact but her family is torn. *New York Times*, pp. A1, B6–7.

Dugger, C. W. (1996c, December 28). Tug of taboos: African genital rite vs. U.S. law. *New York Times*, pp. 1, 9.

Dunkle, M. C. (1987). Women in intercollegiate sports. In S. E. Rix (Ed.), *The American woman, 1987–88* (pp. 228–231). New York: W. W. Norton.

Dunlap, D. W. (1994, November 17). End of co-op dispute hailed as victory for gay couples. *New York Times*, p. B3.

Dunlap, D. W. (1995, December 10). Hearing held on gay issues in the schools. *New York Times*, p. 31.

Dunlap, D. W. (1996, January 21). Gay images, once kept out, are out big time. *New York Times*, pp. 29, 32.

Dworkin, A. (1983). Gynocide: Chinese footbinding. In L. Richardson & V. Taylor (Eds.), *Feminist frontiers* (pp. 178–186). Reading, MA: Addison-Wesley.

Dzeich, B. W., & Weiner, L. (1990). *The lecherous professor: Sexual harassment on campus*. Boston: Beacon Press.

Eagly A. H. (1987). *Sex differences in social behavior: A social-role interpretation*. Hillsdale, NJ: Lawrence Erlbaum Associates.

Eagly, A. H., & Steffan, V. J. (1986). Gender and aggressive behavior: A meta-analytic review of the social psychological literature. *Psychological Bulletin, 100*, 309–330.

Eaton, B. C. (1997). *Cyber-wimmin: Co-opting the dominant discourse*. Paper presented at the Annual Meeting of the Association for Education in Journalism and Mass Communication, Chicago, IL.

Ebaugh, H. R. (1993). Patriarchal bargains and latent avenues of social mobility: Nuns in the Roman Catholic Church. *Gender & Society, 7*, 400–414.

Ebomoyi, E. (1987). Prevalence of female circumcision in two Nigerian communities. *Sex Roles, 17*, 139–151.

Eccles, J. (1985). Sex difference in achievement patterns. In T. B. Sonderegger (Ed.), *Nebraska symposium on motivation 1984: Psychology and gender* (pp. 97–132). Lincoln: University of Nebraska Press.

Eckholm, E. (1994, May 30). Wellspring of priests dries, forcing parishes to change. *New York Times*, pp. 1, 7.

Edelson, J. L., Eisikovits, Z., & Guttmann, E. (1985). Men who batter. *Journal of Family Issues, 6*, 229–247.

Eder, D. (1995). *School talk*. New Brunswick, NJ: Rutgers University Press.

Edin, K., & Lein, L. (1997). *Making ends meet*. New York: Russell Sage Foundation.

Edwards, S. S. M. (1986). Neither bad nor mad: The female violent offender reassessed. *Women's Studies International Forum, 9*, 79–87.

Egan, T. (1992, October 4). Police chief becomes target in anti-gay battle. *New York Times*, p. 22.

Egan, T. (1996, January 15). Idaho freshman embodies G.O.P.'s hope and fear in '96. *New York Times*, pp. A1, 12.

Ehrenreich, B. (1983). *The hearts of men: American dreams and the flight from commitment*. New York: Anchor-Doubleday.

Ehrenreich, B., & English, D. (1973). *Witches, nurses, and midwives: A history of women healers*. Old Westbury, NY: Feminist Press.

Ehrenreich, B., & English, D. (1986). The sexual politics of sickness. In P. Conrad & R. Kern (Eds.), *The sociology of health and illness* (pp. 281–296). New York: St. Martin's Press.

Ehrhardt, A. A., & Meyer-Bahlburg, H. F. L. (1981). Effects of prenatal sex hormones on gender-related behavior. *Science, 211*, 1312–1318.

Eicher, E. M., & Washburn, L. L. (1986). Genetic control of primary sex determination in mice. *Annual Review of Genetics, 20*, 327–360.

Eisenhart, M. A., & Holland, D. C. (1992). Gender constructs and career commitment: The influence of peer culture on women in college. In T. L. Whitehead & B. V. Reid (Eds.), *Gender constructs and social issues* (pp. 142–180). Urbana, IL: University of Illinois Press.

Eisenstein, H. (1991). *Gender shock*. Boston: Beacon Press.

Elasmar, M. G., & Brain, M. (1997). *The portrayal of women on prime-time TV programs broadcast in the United States*. Paper presented at the Annual Meeting of the Association for Education in Journalism and Mass Communication, Chicago, IL.

Elliott, S. (1994, June 9). A sharper view of gay consumers. *New York Times*, pp. D1, D19.

Ellis, L. (1982). Genetics and criminal behavior. *Criminology, 20*, 43–66.

El-Or, T. (1993). The length of the slits and the spread of luxury: Reconstructing the subordination of ultra-orthodox Jewish women through the patriarchy of men scholars. *Sex Roles, 29*, 585–598.

Elson, D. (1995). Male bias in the development process: An overview. In D. Elson (Ed.), *Male bias in the development process* (pp. 1–28). Manchester: Manchester University Press.

Engineer, A. A. (1992). *The rights of women in Islam*. New York: St. Martin's Press.

England, P. (1992). *Comparable worth: Theories and evidence*. New York: Aldine de Gruyter.

English, K. (1993). Self-reported crime rates of women prisoners. *Journal of Quantitative Criminology, 9*, 357–382.

Enloe, C. H. (1987). Feminist thinking about war, militarism, and peace. In B. B. Hess & M. M. Ferree (Eds.), *Analyzing gender* (pp. 536–548). Newbury Park, CA: Sage.

Enloe, C. H. (1993). *The morning after*. Berkeley: University of California Press.

Entwisle, D. R., Alexander, K. L., & Olson, L. S. (1994). The gender gap in math: Its possible origins in neighborhood effects. *American Sociological Review, 59*, 822–838.

Epstein, C. F. (1983). Women and power: The roles of women in politics in the United States. In L. Richardson & V. Taylor (Eds.), *Feminist frontiers* (pp. 288–304). Reading, MA: Addison-Wesley.

Epstein, G. A. (1996, August 31). Judges rule against lesbian mom. *Tampa Tribune.* p. 1

Equal Employment Opportunity Commission. (1991). *Job patterns for minorities and women in private industry 1990.* Washington, DC: Author.

Erikson, E. H. (1968). *Identity: Youth and crisis.* New York: Norton.

Erikson, V. L. (1992). Back to the basics: Feminist social theory, Durkheim and religion. *Journal of Feminist Studies in Religion, 8*, 35–46.

Erikson, V. L. (1993). *Where silence speaks: Feminism, social theory and religion.* Minneapolis: Fortress Press.

Erwin, R. J., Gur, R. C., Gur, R. E., Skolnick, B., Mawhinney-Hee, M.,& Smailis, J. (1992). Facial emotion discrimination: 1. Task construction and behavioral findings in normal subjects. *Psychiatry Research, 42*, 231–240.

Escoffier, J. (1992). Generations and paradigms: Mainstreams in lesbian and gay studies. In H. L. Minton (Ed.), *Gay and lesbian studies* (pp. 7–26). New York: Haworth Press.

Estioko-Griffin, A. (1986). Daughters of the forest. *Natural History, 95*, 5.

Estrich, S. (1987). *Real rape.* Boston: Harvard University Press.

Estrich, S. (1994, May 22). For girls' schools and women's colleges, separate is better. *New York Times Magazine*, pp. 38–39.

Ettorre, E. (1992). *Women and substance abuse.* New Brunswick, NJ: Rutgers University Press.

Ettorre, E. (1997). *Women and alcohol: A private pleasure or a public problem?* London: Women's Press.

Evans, S. M. (1979). *Personal politics: The roots of women's liberation in the Civil Rights movement and the new left.* New York: Knopf.

Evans, S. M. (1987). Women in twentieth century America: An overview. (pp. 33–66). In S. E. Rix (Ed.), *The American woman in 1987–88.* New York: W. W. Norton.

Faderman, L. (1991). *Odd girls and twilight lovers.* New York: Columbia University Press.

Fagot, B. I. (1985). Beyond the reinforcement principle: Another step toward understanding sex role development. *Developmental Psychology, 21*, 1097–1104.

Fagot, B. I., Hagan, R., Leinbach, M. D., & Kronsberg, S. (1985). Differential reactions to assertive and communicative acts of toddler boys and girls. *Child Development, 56*, 1499–1505.

Fagot, B. I., & Leinbach, M. D. (1983). Play styles in early childhood: Social consequences for boys and girls. In M. B. Liss (Ed.), *Social and cognitive skills: Sex roles and children's play* (pp. 93–116). New York: Academic Press.

Fagot, B. I., & Leinbach, M. D. (1989). The young child's gender schema: Environmental input, internal organization. *Child Development, 60*, 663–672.

Faine, J. R., & Bohlander, E. (1976). *Sentencing the female offender: The impact of legal and extra-legal considerations.* Paper presented at the Annual Meeting of the American Society of Criminology, Tucson, AZ.

Faludi, S. (1991). *Backlash: The undeclared war against American women.* New York: Anchor Books.

Farrell, S. A. (1992). *Women-church: A contradiction or the perfect feminist organization?* Paper presented at the Annual Meeting of the American Sociological Association, Pittsburgh, PA.

Farrell, W. (1993). *The myth of male power.* New York: Simon and Schuster.

Fausto-Sterling, A. (1985). *Myths of gender.* New York: Basic Books.

Federal Bureau of Investigation. (1997). *Crime in America.* Washington, DC: U.S. Government Printing Office.

Federal Bureau of Investigation (1998). *Employment.* At http://www.fedstats.gov.

Fee, E. (1983). Women and health care: A comparison of theories. In E. Fee (Ed.), *Women and health: The politics of sex in medicine* (pp. 17–34). Farmdale, NY: Baywood.

Feinman, C. (1992). Criminal codes, criminal justice and female offenders. In I. L. Moyer (Ed.), *The changing roles of women in the criminal justice system* (pp. 57–68). Prospect Heights, IL: Waveland Press.

Feiring, C., & Lewis, M. (1987). The child's social network: Sex differences from three to six years. *Sex Roles, 17*, 621–636.

Fejes, F. J. (1992). Masculinity as fact. In S. Craig (Ed.), *Men, masculinity and media* (pp. 9–22). Newbury Park, CA: Sage.

Feldberg, R. L. (1984). Comparable worth: Toward theory and practice in the United States. *Signs, 10*, 311–328.

Federal lawsuit says two states failed to protect female inmates. (1997, March 11). *New York Times*, p. A20.

Feldstein, K. (1998, April 13). Social Security's gender gap. *New York Times*, p. A27.

Female professor receives $230,000 to settle harassment lawsuit. (1998, February 10). Troy, NY: Associated Press. (Internet).

Female Texas ranger quits. (1995, May 23). Austin, TX: Associated Press. (Internet).

Fennema, E., & Sherman, J. (1977). Sex-related differences in mathematics achievement, spatial ability, and affective factors. *American Educational Research Journal, 14*, 51–71.

Ferguson, M. (1983). *Forever feminine: Women's magazines and the cult of femininity.* London: Heinemann.

Ferguson, T., & Dunphy, J. S. (1992). *Answers to the mommy track.* Far Hills, NJ: New Horizon Press.

Fernea, E. W. (1998). *In search of Islamic feminism.* New York: Doubleday.

Fine, L. (1990). *The souls of the skyscraper: Female clerical workers in Chicago, 1870–1930.* Philadelphia: Temple University Press.

Fine, S. (1997, September 15). Sexual harassment policies softening. *The Globe and Mail.*

Fineman, M. A. (1996). The nature of dependencies and welfare "reform." *Santa Clara Law Review, 36*, 1401–1425.

Finkelhor, D., & Yllö, K. (1985). *License to rape: Sexual abuse of wives.* Beverly Hills, CA: Sage.

First, A., & Shaw, D. (1996). *Not there yet: Coverage about and by women in foreign news—A 1995 multinational study.* Paper presented at the Annual Meeting of the Association for Education in Journalism and Mass Communication, Anaheim, CA.

Fisher-Thompson, D., Sausa, A. D., & Wright, T. F. (1995). Toy selection for children: Personality and toy request influences. *Sex Roles, 33*, 239–255.

Fivush, R. (1991). Gender and emotion in mother-child conversations about the past. *Journal of Narrative and Life History, 1*, 325–341.

Flexner, E. (1971). *Century of struggle*. Cambridge, MA: Belknap.

Flynn, C. P. (1987). Relationship violence: A model for family professionals. *Family Relations, 36*, 295–299.

Foerstel, K., & Foerstel, H. N. (1996). *Climbing the hill: Gender conflict in Congress*. Westport, CT: Praeger.

Fogel, C. I., & Woods, N. F. (1995). *Women's health care: A comprehensive handbook*. Thousand Oaks, CA: Sage.

Fordham, S. (1996). *Blacked out: Dilemmas of race, identity, and success at Capital High*. Chicago: University of Chicago Press.

Foreit, K. G., Agor, T., Byers, J., Larue, J., Lokey, H., Palazzini, M., Patterson, M., & Smith, L. (1980). Sex bias in the newspaper treatment of male-centered and female-centered news stories. *Sex Roles, 6*, 475–480.

For water cooler paramours, the ties that (legally) bind. (1998, February 22). *New York Times*, p. WK7.

Fox, S. 1991 *Toxic work*. Philadelphia: Temple University Press.

Fox, T. G. (1998, July 12). Policing the net. *The Hartford Courant*.

Frable, D. E. S., & Bem, S. L. (1985). If you're gender-schematic, all members of the opposite sex look alike. *Journal of Personality and Social Psychology, 49*, 459–468.

Frank, E., Brogran, D., & Schiffman, M. (1998). Prevalence and correlates of harassment among U.S. women physicians. *Archives of Internal Medicine, 158*, 352–362.

Frank, F. W. (1989). Language planning, language reform, and language change: A review of guidelines for non-sexist usage. In F. W. Frank & P. A. Treichler (Eds.), *Language, gender, and professional writing: Theoretical approaches and guidelines for nonsexist usage* (pp. 105–133). New York: The Modern Language Association of America.

Franklin, D. W., & Sweeney, J. L. (1988). Women and corporate power. In E. Boneparth & E. Stroper (Eds.), *Women, power, and policy: Toward the year 2000* (pp. 48–65). New York: Pergamon.

Franks, P., & Clancy, C. M. (1993). Physician gender bias in clinical decisionmaking: Screening for cancer in primary care. *Medical Care, 31*, 213–218.

Freedman, R. (1986). *Beauty bound*. Lexington, MA: Lexington Books.

Freeman, J. (1973). The origins of the women's liberation movement. *American Journal of Sociology, 78*, 792–811.

Freeza, H., Padova, C. D., Pozzato, G., Terpin, M., Baraona, E., & Lieber, C. S. (1990). High blood alcohol levels in women: The role of decreased gastric alcohol dehydrogenase activity and first-pass metabolism. *The New England Journal of Medicine, 322*, 95–99.

French, H. W. (1997, February 2). Africa's culture war: Old customs, new values. *New York Times*, pp. E1, 4

Freud, S. (1983/1933). Femininity. In M. W. Zak & P. A. Motts (Eds.) *Women and the politics of culture* (pp. 80–92). New York: Longman.

Freudenheim, M. (1997, November 2). Nurses treading on doctors' turf. *New York Times*, p. WK7.

Friedan, B. (1963). *The feminine mystique*. New York: W. W. Norton.

Friedman, J. (1993, May 2). The founding mother. *The New York Times Magazine*, pp. 50, 60, 64, 66.

Friedman, R. C., Hurt, S. W., Aronoff, M. S., & Clarkin, J. (1980). Behavior and the menstrual cycle. *Signs, 5*, 719–738.

Frieze, I. H., Parsons, J. E., Johnson, P. B., Ruble, D. N., & Zellman, G. L. (1978). *Women and sex roles*. New York: W. W. Norton.

Fulani, L. (Ed.) (1988). *The psychopathology of everyday racism and sexism*. New York: Haworth.

Fullilove, M., Lown, A., & Fullilove, R. (1992). Crack hos and skeezers: Traumatic experiences of women crack users. *Journal of Sex Research, 29*, 275–287.

Funk, N., & Mueller, M. (Eds.) (1993). *Gender politics and post-communism*. New York: Routledge.

Funk, T. (1996, August 11). Black women are heeding the call to the ministry. *Philadelphia Inquirer*, p. G6.

Furstenberg, F. F., & Cherlin, A. (1991). *Divided families*. Cambridge: Harvard University Press.

Gabin, N. F. (1990). *Feminism in the labor market: Women and the United Auto Workers, 1935–1975*. Ithaca, NY: Cornell University Press.

Gabriel, M. (1998). *Notorious Victoria*. Chapel Hill, NC: Algonquin Books of Chapel Hill.

Gadon, E. M. (1989). *The once and future goddess*. New York: Harper and Row.

Gailey, C. W. (1987). Evolutionary perspectives on gender hierarchy. In B. B. Hess & M. M. Ferree (Eds.), *Analyzing gender* (pp. 32–67). Newbury Park, CA: Sage.

Gallagher, M. (1995, March). *Women and the media*. New York: United Nations.

Gallup, G., & Castelli, J. (1989). *The people's religion*. New York: Macmillan.

Gammon, C. (1992). Lesbian and gay studies emerging in Canada. In H. L. Minton (Ed.), *Gay and lesbian studies* (pp. 137–160). New York: Haworth Press.

Gargan, E. A. (1991, December 13). Ultrasound skews India's birth ratio. *New York Times*, p. A13.

Garrison, C. G., McClelland, A., Dambrot, F., &. Casey, K. A. (1992). Gender balancing and the criminal justice curriculum and classroom. *Journal of Criminal Justice Education, 3*, 203–222.

Gastil, J. (1990). Generic pronouns and sexist language: The oxymoronic character of masculine generics. *Sex Roles, 23*, 629–643.

Gazzaniga, M. (1992). *Nature's mind*. New York: Basic Books.

Geis, F. L., Brown, V., Jennings (Walstedt), J., & Porter, N. (1984). TV commercials as achievement scripts for women. *Sex Roles, 10*, 513–525.

Gelles, R. J. (1993). Alcohol and drugs are associated with violence—They are not its cause. In R. J. Gelles & D. R. Loseke (Eds.), *Current controversies on domestic violence* (pp. 182–196). Newbury Park, CA: Sage.

Gendler, M. (1979). The restoration of Vashti. In E. Koltun (Ed.), *The Jewish woman* (pp. 241–247). New York: Shocken Books.

Gerami, S. (1996). *Women and fundamentalism: Islam and Christianity*. New York: Garland.

Gerber, J., & Weeks, S. L. (1992). Women as victims of corporate crime: A call for research on a neglected topic. *Deviant Behavior, 13*, 325–347.

Gerbner, G. (1993). *Women and minorities on television: A study in casting and fate*. A Report to the Screen Actors Guild and the American Federation of Radio and Television Artists. Available from the author, Annenberg School of Communications, University of Pennsylvania.

Gerson, M., Alpert, J. L., & Richardson, M. S. (1984). Mothering: The view from psychological research. *Signs, 9*, 434–453.

Gertzog, I. N. (1984). *Congressional women.* New York: Praeger.

Gettelman, T. E., & Thompson, J. K. (1993). Actual differences and stereotypical perceptions in body image and eating disturbance: A comparison of male and female heterosexual and homosexual samples. *Sex Roles, 29,* 545–562.

Gibb, F. (1998, January 29). Judge gives "drink rape" girl advice on Pimm's. *London Times,* p. 4.

Giddings, P. (1984). *When and where I enter.* New York: William Morrow.

Gidengil, E. (1995). Economic man—social woman? The case of the gender gap in support for the Canada–United States Free Trade Agreement. *Comparative Political Studies, 28,* 384–408.

Gilbert, M. J., & Collins, R. L. (1997). Ethnic variation in women's and men's drinking. In R. W. Wilsnack & S. C. Wilsnack (Eds.), *Gender and alcohol* (pp. 357–378). New Brunswick, NJ: Rutgers Center of Alcohol Studies.

Gilbert, L. A., & Scher, M. (1999). *Gender and sex in counseling and psychotherapy.* Boston: Allyn and Bacon.

Gilfus, M. (1992). From victims to survivors to offenders: Women's routes of entry into street crime. *Women and Criminal Justice, 4,* 63–89.

Gilkes, C. T. (1985). Together and in harness: Women's traditions in the sanctified church. *Signs, 10,* 678–699.

Gilligan, C. (1982). *In a different voice: Psychological theory and women's development.* Cambridge, MA: Harvard University Press.

Gilligan, C., Lyons, N. P., & Hanmer, T. J. (Eds.) (1990). *Making connections: The relational worlds of adolescent girls at Emma Willard School.* Cambridge, MA: Harvard University Press.

Gilligan, C., Taylor, J. M., & Sullivan, A. (1995). *Between voice and silence: Women and girls, race and relationship.* Cambridge, MA: Harvard University Press.

Gillum, R. F., Mussolino, M. E., & Madans, J. H. (1997). Coronary heart disease incidence and survival in African-American women and men. *Annals of Internal Medicine, 127,* 111–118.

Gilmore, D. O. (1990). *Manhood in the making.* New Haven, CT: Yale University Press.

Gimbutas, M. (1989). *The language of the goddess.* New York: Harper and Row.

Ginzburg, C. (1991). *Ecstacies: Deciphering the witches' sabbath.* New York: Penguin.

Giovannini, M. J. (1992). The relevance of gender in postpartum emotional disorders. In T. L. Whitehead & B. V. Reid (Eds.), *Gender constructs and social issues* (pp. 209–231). Urbana: University of Illinois Press.

Girl, 14, wins case charging sex harassment. (1996, October 4). *New York Times,* p. A16.

Gitlin, M. J., & Passnau, R. O. (1990). Psychiatric symptoms linked to reproductive function in women: A review of current knowledge. *American Journal of Psychiatry, 146,* 1413–1422.

Gjerdingen, D. K., Froberg, D. G., & Fontaine, P. (1990). A causal model describing the relationship of women's postpartum health to social support, length of leave, and complications of childbirth. *Women and Health, 16,* 71–87.

Glaberson, W. (1993, September 10). Gay journalists leading a revolution. *New York Times,* p. A20.

Glass, J. (1990). The impact of occupational segregation on working conditions. *Social Forces, 68,* 779–796.

Glass, R. (1982, January 24). Some fear abuses in premenstrual tension decisions. *Philadelphia Inquirer,* p. 8C.

Glenn, E. N. (1987). Gender and the family. In B. B. Hess & M. M. Ferree (Eds.), *Analyzing gender* (pp. 348–380). Newbury Park, CA: Sage.

Glenn, E. N. (1992). From servitude to service work: Historical continuities in the racial division of paid reproductive labor. *Signs, 18,* 1–43.

Glenn, S. A. (1990). *Daughter of the Shtel: Life and labor in the immigrant generation.* Ithaca, NY: Cornell University Press.

Gluck, S. B. (1987). *Rosie the riveter revisited.* New York: Twayne.

Goering, L. (1996, May 21). Fighting lucrative sex trade a losing battle. *Chicago Tribune,* p. 4.

Gold, M. (1983). Sexism in gynecologic practices. In M. Fooden, S. Gordon, & B. Hughley (Eds.), *Genes and gender IV: The second X and women's health* (pp. 133–142). New York: Gordian.

Goldberg, C. (1996a, March 26). Virtual marriages for same-sex couples. *New York Times,* p. A12.

Goldberg, C. (1996b, October 5). Political battle of the sexes is sharper than ever: Suburbs' soccer moms, fleeing the G.O.P., are much sought. *New York Times,* pp. 1, 24.

Goldberg, C. (1997, October 7). Women at the helm of New Hampshire politics. *New York Times,* p. A14.

Golden, S. (1992). *The women outside: Meanings and myths of homelessness.* Berkeley: University of California Press.

Goldhaber, M. K., Poland, M. R., &. Hialt, R. A. (1988). The risk of miscarriage and birth defects among women who use visual display terminals during pregnancy. *American Journal of Industrial Medicine, 13,* 695–706.

Golding, J. M. (1988). Gender differences in depressive symptoms: Statistical considerations. *Psychology of Women Quarterly, 12,* 61–74.

Goldman, A. L. (1990a, June 26). Reform Judaism votes to accept active homosexuals in rabbinate. *New York Times,* pp. A1, A21.

Goldman, A. L. (1990b, September 19). A bar to women as cantors is lifted. *New York Times,* p. B2.

Goldman, A. L. (1990c, November 18). Ecumenist in charge: Joan B. Campbell. *New York Times,* p. 32.

Goldman, A. L. (1992, November 29). Even for ordained women, church can be a cold place. *New York Times,* p. E6.

Goldman, R. J., & Goldman, J. D. G. (1982). *Children's sexual thinking.* London: Routledge and Kegan Paul.

Goldner, M. (1994). *Accounting for race and class variation in the disjuncture between feminist identity and feminist beliefs: The place of negative labels and social movements.* Paper presented at the Annual Meeting of the American Sociological Association, Los Angeles, CA.

Goldsmith, B. (1998). *Other powers.* New York: Alfred A. Knopf.

Goldstein, L. F. (1979). *The constitutional rights of women.* New York: Longman.

Gole, N. (1996). *The forbidden modern: Civilization and veiling.* Ann Arbor: University of Michigan Press.

Goleman, D. (1990, May 29). As bias crime seems to rise, scientists study roots of racism. *New York Times,* pp. C1, C15.

Goleman, D. (1996). *Emotional intelligence.* New York: Bantam Books.

Golombok, S., & Fivush, R. (1994). *Gender development.* Cambridge: Cambridge University Press.

Golombok, S., & Tasker, F. (1996). Do parents influence the sexual orientation of their children? *Developmental Psychology, 32,* 3–11.

Golub, S. (1992). *Periods: From menarche to menopause.* Newbury Park, CA: Sage.

Gonzalez, A. (1982). Sex roles of the traditional Mexican family. *Journal of Cross-Cultural Psychology, 13,* 330–339.

Good, T. L., & Brophy, J. E. (1987). *Looking in classrooms.* New York: Harper & Row.

Goodenough, R. G. (1990). Situational stress and sexist behavior among young children. In P. R. Sanday & R. G. Goodenough (Eds.), *Beyond the second sex* (pp. 225–252). Philadelphia: University of Pennsylvania Press.

Goodstein, L. (1992). Feminist perspectives and the criminal justice curriculum. *Journal of Criminal Justice Education, 3,* 165–182.

Goodstein, L. (1998, February 6). Unusual, but not unorthodox: Causing a stir, 2 synagogues hire women to assist rabbis. *New York Times,* pp. B1, 4.

Goodstein, L., & Connelly, M. (1998, April 30). Teenage poll finds a turn to the traditional. *New York Times,* p. A20.

Goodwin, J. (1994). *Price of honor.* Boston: Little, Brown.

Gordon, L. (1976). *Woman's body, Woman's right.* New York: Grossman Publishers.

Gordon, M. R. (1990, January 4). Woman leads G.I.'s in Panama combat. *New York Times,* p. A12.

Gordon, M. R. (1993, April 24). Pentagon report tells of aviators' debauchery. *New York Times,* pp. 1, 9.

Gordon, M., & Creighton, S. J. (1988). Fathers as sexual abusers in the United Kingdom. *Journal of Marriage and the Family, 50,* 99–106.

Gordon, M. T. & Riger, S. (1991). *The female fear: The social cost of rape.* Urbana, IL: University of Illinois Press.

Gorman, C. (1992, January 20). Sizing up the sexes. *Time,* p. 4251.

Gornick, M. E., Eggers, P. W., Reilly, T. W., Mentneck, R. M., Fitterman, L. K., Kucken, L. E., & Vladeck, B. C. (1996). Effects of race and income on mortality and use of services among Medicare beneficiaries. *New England Journal of Medicine, 335,* 791–799.

Gortmaker, S. L., Must, A. Perrin, J. M., Sobol, A. M., & Dietz, W. H. (1993). Social and economic consequences of overweight in adolescence and young adulthood. *New England Journal of Medicine, 329,* 1008–1012.

Gould, S. J. (1980). *The panda's thumb.* New York: W. W. Norton.

Gould, S. J. (1981). *The mismeasure of man.* New York: W. W. Norton.

Graham, E. (1986, June). African women fight clitoris cutting. *off our backs,* p. 18–19.

Graham, P. A. (1978). Expansion and exclusion: A history of women in American higher education. *Signs, 3,* 759–773.

Grant, J. (1986). Black women and the church. In J. B. Cole (Ed.), *All American women* (pp. 359–369). New York: Free Press.

Gray, M. (1979). *Margaret Sanger.* New York: Richard Marek Publishers.

Greeley, A. M. (1990). *The Catholic myth.* New York: Charles Scribner's Sons.

Green, J. (1993, June 13). Out and organized. *New York Times,* pp. V1, V7.

Green, V. (1993). *Doped up, knocked up, and . . . locked up? The criminal prosecution of women who use drugs during pregnancy.* New York: Garland.

Greene, K. W. (1989). *Affirmative action and principles of justice.* New York: Greenwood.

Greenfeld, L. A. (1996). *Child victimizers: Violent offenders and their victims.* Washington, DC: U. S. Department of Justice, Bureau of Justice Statistics.

Greenfeld, L. A. (1997). *Sex offenders and offenses.* Washington, DC: U.S. Department of Justice, Bureau of Justice Statistics.

Greenfeld, L. A. (1998). *Violence by intimates.* Washington, DC: U.S. Department of Justice, Bureau of Justice Statistics.

Greenhouse, L. (1998, March 5). High court widens workplace claims in sex harassment. *New York Times,* pp. A1, 18.

Greenhouse, S. (1993, November 14). If the French can do it, why can't we? *New York Times Magazine,* pp. 59–62.

Greenhouse, S. (1997, November 8). Nike shoe plant in Vietnam is called unsafe for workers. *New York Times,* pp. A1, D2.

Greer, G. (1992). *The change.* New York: Alfred A. Knopf.

Greif, G. L. (1985). *Single fathers.* Lexington, MA: Lexington Books.

Griffin, L. W., Williams, O. J., & Reed, J. G. (1998). Abuse of African American elders. In R. K. Bergen (Ed.), *Issues in intimate violence* (pp. 267–284). Thousand Oaks, CA: Sage.

Griffin, S. (1995). *The eros of everyday life.* New York: Doubleday.

Grigsby, J. S. (1992, November). Women change places. *American Demographics,* pp. 46–50.

Gross, J. (1990, October 12). Prostitutes and addicts: Special victims of rape. *New York Times,* p. A14.

Gross, J. (1992, December 7). Divorced, middle-aged and happy: Women, especially, adjust to the 90s. *New York Times,* p. A14.

Gross, J. (1994, January 4). Gay candidate making history in a state race. *New York Times,* p. A6.

Gross, L. (1991). Out of the mainstream: Sexual minorities and the mass media. *Journal of Homosexuality, 21,* 19–46.

Gruber, J. E. (1998). The impact of male work environments and organizational policies on women's experiences of sexual harassment. *Gender & Society, 12,* 301–320.

Gruber, J. E., & Bjorn, L. (1982). Blue-collar blues: The sexual harassment of women autoworkers. *Work and Occupations, 9,* 271–298.

Guinier, L., Fine, M., & Stachel, D. L. (1994). Becoming gentlemen: Women's experiences at one Ivy League law school. *University of Pennsylvania Law Review, 143,* 1–113.

Gutis, P. S. (1989, August 31). What is a family? Traditional limits are being redrawn. *New York Times,* pp. C1, C6.

Haas, L. (1992). *Equal parenthood and social policy: A study of parental leave in Sweden.* Albany: State University of New York Press.

Haddad, Y. Y. (1985). Islam, women and revolution in twentieth-century Arab thought. In Y. Y. Haddad & E. B. Findly (Eds.), *Women, religion and social change.* (pp. 275–306). Albany: State University of New York Press.

Hafner, R. J., & Minge, P. J. (1989). Sex role stereotyping in women with agoraphobia and their husbands. *Sex Roles, 20,* 705–711.

Hagan, K. L. (1992). *Women respond to the men's movement.* San Francisco: Pandora.

Hale-Benson, J. E. (1986). *Black children: Their roots, culture and learning styles* (rev. ed.). Provo, UT: Brigham Young University Press.

Hall, L. (1992). Beauty quests—A double disservice: Beguiled, beseeched, bombarded—Challenging the concept of beauty. In D. Dreidger & S. Gray (Eds.), *Imprinting our image: An international anthology by women with disabilities* (pp. 134–139). Toronto: gynergy books.

Hall, R. M., &. Sandler, B. R. (1985). A chilly climate in the classroom. In A. G. Sargent (Ed.), *Beyond sex roles* (pp. 503–510). New York: West.

Hamer, D. H., Hu, S., Magnuson, V. L., & Pattatucii, A. M. L. (1993). A linkage between DNA markers on the X chromosome and male sexual orientation. *Science, 261,* 321–327.

Hamilton, M. C. (1988). Using masculine generics: Does generic "he" increase male bias in the user's imagery? *Sex Roles, 19,* 785–799.

Haney, D. Q. (1996a, March 28). Heart disease worse for Blacks. *Chattanooga Times,* p. F4.

Haney, D. Q. (1996b, October 15). *Overweight now the norm.* Breckenridge, CO: Associated Press. (Internet).

Hansen, F. J., & Reekie, L. (1990). Sex differences in clinical judgments of male and female therapists. *Sex Roles, 23,* 51–64.

Hanson, S. M. H. (1988). Divorced fathers with custody. In P. Bronstein & C. P. Cowan (Eds.), *Fatherhood today: Men's changing role in the family* (pp. 166–194). New York: John Wiley.

Harbeck, K. M. (1992). Introduction. In K. M. Harbeck (Ed.), *Coming out of the classroom closet: Gay and lesbian students, teachers, and curricula* (pp. 1–7). New York: Haworth Press.

Hardenbergh, M. (1996). *Women and front-page news.* Paper presented at the Annual Meeting of the Association for Education in Journalism and Mass Communication, Anaheim, CA.

Hardie, E. A. (1997). Prevalence and predictors of cyclic and noncyclic affective change. *Psychology of Women Quarterly, 21,* 299–314.

Harding, S. G. (1979). Is the equality of opportunity principle democratic? *Philosophical Forum, 10,* 206–223.

Harrington, A. (1987). *Medicine, mind, and the double brain.* Princeton, NJ: Princeton University Press.

Harrington, M. (1962). *The other America.* New York: Macmillan.

Harris, B. (1983). The myth of assembly-line hysteria. In M. Fooden, S. Gordon, & B. Hughley (Eds.), *Genes and gender IV: The second X and women's health* (pp. 65–86). New York: Gordian.

Harris, J. (1993, March 28). The babies of Bedford. *The New York Times Magazine,* p. 26.

Harris, M. B., & Knight-Bohnhoff, K. (1996). Gender and aggression II: Personal aggressiveness. *Sex Roles, 35,* 27–41.

Harrison, J. B. (1984). Warning: The male sex role may be dangerous to your health. In J. M. Swanson & K. A. Forrest (Eds.), *Men's reproductive health.* (pp. 11–27). New York: Springer.

Hart, M. M. (1980). Sport: Women sit in the back of the bus. In D. F. Sabo & R. Runfola (Eds.), *Jock: Sports and male identity* (pp. 205–211). Englewood Cliffs, NJ: Prentice-Hall.

Hartjen, C. A. (1978). *Crime and criminalization.* New York: Holt, Rinehart and Winston.

Hartmann, H. I. (1987). Internal labor markets and gender: A case study of promotion. In C. Brown & J. A. Pechman (Eds.), *Gender in the workplace* (pp. 59–106). Washington, DC: The Brookings Institute.

Hartmann, H. I.,. Roos, P. A., & Treiman, D. J. (1985). An agenda for basic research on comparable worth. In H. I. Hartmann (Ed.), *Comparable worth: New directions for research* (pp. 3–33). Washington, DC: National Academy Press.

Hass, N. (1998, February 22). A TV generation is seeing beyond color. *New York Times,* pp. AR1, 38.

Hatch, M. (1984). Mother, father, worker: Men and women and the reproduction risks of work. In W. Chavkin (Ed.), *Double exposure* (pp. 161–179). New York: Monthly Review Press.

Hawkesworth, M. (1997). Challenging the received wisdom and the status quo: Creating and implementing sexual harassment policy. *NWSA Journal, 9,* 94–117.

Hayden, S. (1994). Interruptions and the construction of reality. In L. H. Turner & H. M. Sterk (Eds.), *Differences that make a difference* (pp. 99–106). Westport, CT: Bergin and Garvey.

Heidensohn, F. (1992). *Women in control? The role of women in law enforcement.* New York: Oxford University Press.

Height, D. (1989, July 24–31). Family and community: Self-help—A Black tradition. *The Nation, 249,* 136–138.

Hekma, G., & van der Meer, T. (1992). Gay and lesbian studies in the Netherlands. In H. L. Minton (Ed.), *Gay and lesbian studies* (pp. 125–136). New York: Haworth Press.

Hekmat, A. (1997). *Women and the Koran.* Amherst, NY: Prometheus Books.

Helgeson, V. S. (1990). The role of masculinity in a prognostic predictor of heart attack severity. *Sex Roles, 22,* 755–774.

Helgeson, V. S. (1994). Long-distance romantic relationships: Sex differences in adjustment and breakup. *Personality and Social Psychology Bulletin, 20,* 254–265.

Helgeson, V. S. (1995). Masculinity, men's roles, and coronary heart disease. In D. Sabo & D. F. Gordon (Eds.), *Men's health and illness* (pp. 68–104). Thousand Oaks, CA: Sage.

Hellinger, D., & Judd, D. R. (1991). *The democratic facade.* Pacific Grove, CA: Brooks/Cole.

Henig, R. M. (1993, October 3). Are women's hearts different? *The New York Times Magazine,* pp. 58–61, 68–69, 82, 86.

Henley, N., Hamilton, M., & Thorne, B. (1985). Womanspeak and manspeak: Sex differences and sexism in communication. In A. G. Sargent (Ed.), *Beyond sex roles* (pp. 168–185). New York: West.

Henshaw, S. K. (1995). Factors hindering access to abortion services. *Family Planning Perspectives, 27,* 54–59, 87.

Herbert, B. (1996, July 12). Trampled dreams. *New York Times,* p. A8.

Herdt, G. H., & Davidson, J. (1988). The Sambia 'Turnim-man': Sociocultural and clinical aspects of gender formation in male pseudohermaphrodites with 5 alpha-reductase deficiency in Papua New Guinea. *Archives of Sexual Behavior, 17,* 33–56.

Herek, G. M. (1991). Myths about sexual orientation: A lawyer's guide to social science research. *Law and Sexuality, 1,* 133–172.

Herek, G. M., & Berrill, K. T. (1992). *Hate crimes.* Newbury Park, CA: Sage.

Herek, G. M., & Glunt, E. K. (1997). An epidemic of stigma: Public reaction to AIDS. In P. Conrad (Ed.), *The sociology of health and illness* (pp. 125–132). New York: St. Martin's Press.

Herman, J. L. (1988). Considering sex offenders: A model of addiction. *Signs, 13*, 695–724.

Hess, B. B., & Ferree, M. M. (1987). Introduction. In B. B. Hess & M. M. Ferree (Eds.), *Analyzing gender* (pp. 9–30). Newbury Park, CA: Sage.

Hess, R. D., & Miura, I. T. (1985). Gender differences in enrollment in computer camps and classes. *Sex Roles, 13*, 193–203.

Hesse-Biber, S. (1989). Eating patterns and disorders in a college population: Are college women's eating problems a new phenomenon? *Sex Roles, 20*, 71–89.

Heywood, C. (1987). Heterosexist theology: Being above it all. *Journal of Feminist Studies in Religion, 3*, 29–38.

Hicks, J. P. (1998, February 9). Road gets tougher for political pioneer. *New York Times*, p. B3.

Higginbotham, E. B. (1993). *Righteous discontent.* Cambridge, MA: Harvard University Press.

Higgins, P. J. (1985). Women in the Islamic Republic of Iran: Legal, social, and ideological changes. *Signs, 10*, 477–494.

Hilkert, M. C. (1986). Women preaching the gospel. *Theology Digest, 33*, 423–440.

Hill, M. A. (1980). *Charlotte Perkins Gilman: The making of a radical feminist, 1860–1896.* Philadelphia: Temple University Press.

Hinds, M. D. (1990, March 17). Use of crack is said to stifle the instincts of parenthood. *New York Times*, p. 8.

Hine, D. C. (1989). *Black women in white: Racial conflict and cooperation in the nursing profession, 1890–1950.* Bloomington: Indiana University Press.

Hine, D. C., & Thompson, K. (Eds.) (1997). *A shining thread of hope: The history of Black women in America.* New York: Broadway Books.

Hines, M., & Kaufman, F. R. (1994). Androgen and the development of human sex-typical behavior: Rough-and-tumble play and sex of preferred playmates in children with congenital adrenal hyperplasia (CAH). *Child Development, 65*, 1042–1053.

Hirsch, E. D. (1987). *Cultural literacy.* Boston: Houghton Mifflin.

Hirsch, M., & Keller, E. F. (1990). Conclusion: Practicing conflict in feminist theory. In M. Hirsch & E. F. Keller (Eds.), *Conflicts in feminism* (pp. 370–385) New York: Routledge.

Hite, S. (1987). *Women and love: A cultural revolution in progress.* New York: Knopf.

Hochschild, A. R. (1989). *The second shift.* New York: Viking.

Hochschild, A. R. (1997). *The time bind: When work becomes home and home becomes work.* New York: Henry Holt and Company.

Hodson, D., & Skeen, P. (1987). Child sexual abuse: A review of research and theory with implications for family life educators. *Family Relations, 36*, 215–221.

Hoffman, J. (1996, January 8). Egg donations meet a need and raise ethical questions. *New York Times*, pp. 1, 10.

Hoff-Wilson, J. (1987). The unfinished revolution: Changing legal status of U.S. women. *Signs, 13*, 7–36.

Holden, C. (1987). Why do women live longer than men? *Science, 238*, 158–160.

Holden, K. C., & Smock, P. J. (1991). The economic costs of marital dissolution: Why do women bear a disproportionate cost? *Annual Review of Sociology, 17*, 51–78.

Hole, J., & Levine, E. (1984). The first feminists. In J. Freeman (Ed.), *Women: A feminist perspective* (pp. 533–542). Palo Alto, CA: Mayfield.

Holland, D. C., & Eisenhart, M. A. (1991). *Educated in romance: Women, achievement and college culture.* Chicago: University of Chicago Press.

Holloman, J. L. S. (1983). Access to health care. In President's commission for the study of ethical problems in medicine and biomedical research. *Securing access to health care* (pp. 79–106). Washington, DC: U.S. Government Printing Office.

Holmes, S. A. (1996, December 27). With more women in prison, sexual abuse by guards becomes a troubling trend. *New York Times*, p. A18.

Holmes, S. A. (1998, April 15). FCC requirement on minority hiring is voided by court. *New York Times*, pp. A1, 22.

Hood, E. F. (1984). Black women, White women: Separate paths to liberation. In A. M. Jaggar & P. S. Rothenberg (Eds.), *Feminist frameworks* (pp. 189–201). New York: McGraw-Hill.

hooks, b. (1990). A conversation about race and class. In M. Hirsch & E. F. Keller (Eds.), *Conflicts in feminism* (pp. 60–81). New York: Routledge.

Horner, M. S. (1972). Toward an understanding of achievement-related conflicts in women. *Journal of Social Issues, 28*, 157–175.

Horney, K. (1967). *Feminine psychology.* New York: Norton.

Horwitz, A. V. (1982). Sex-role expectations, power, and psychological distress. *Sex Roles, 8*, 607–623.

House, J. S. (1986). Occupational stress and coronary heart disease: A review and theoretical integration. In P. Conrad & R. Kern (Eds.), *The sociology of health and illness* (pp. 64–72). New York: St. Martin's Press.

Hout, M., &. Greeley, A. M. (1987). The center doesn't hold: Church attendance in the United States, 1940–1984. *American Sociological Review, 52*, 325–345.

Howe, F. (1984). *Myths of coeducation.* Bloomington, IN: University of Indiana Press.

Howe, K. (1985). The psychological impact of a women's studies course. *Women's Studies Quarterly, 13*, 23–24.

Hoyenga, K. B., & Hoyenga, K. T. (1993). *Gender-related differences.* Boston: Allyn and Bacon.

Hsiung, P. (1996). *Living rooms as factories: Class, gender, and the satellite factory system in Taiwan.* Philadelphia: Temple University Press.

Hu, S., Pattatucci, A. M. L., Patterson, C., Li, L., Fulker, D. W., Cherny, S. S., Kruglyak, L., & Hamer, D. H. (1995). Linkage between sexual orientation and chromosome *Xq28* in males but not in females. *Nature Genetics, 11*, 248–256.

Hu, Y., & Goldman, N. (1990). Mortality differentials by marital status: An international comparison. *Demography, 27*, 233–250.

Hubbard, R. (1990). The political nature of human nature. In D. L. Rhode (Ed.), *Theoretical perspectives on sexual difference* (pp. 63–73). New Haven, CT: Yale University Press.

Hubbard, R., & Wald, E. (1993). *Exploding the gene myth.* Boston: Beacon Press.

Huie, V. A. (1994). Mom's in prison: Where are the kids? In D. J. Curran & C. M. Renzetti (Eds.), *Contemporary societies: Problems and prospects* (pp. 481–484). Englewood Cliffs, NJ: Prentice Hall.

Hunt, M. E. (1991). The challenge of 'both/and' theology. In M. A. May (Ed.), *Women and church* (pp. 28–33). New York: Friendship Press.

Hunter, A. G., & Sellers, S. L. (1998). Feminist attitudes among African American women and men. *Gender & Society, 12,* 81–99.

Hunter, S. M. (1992, August). Women in corrections: A look at the road ahead. *Corrections Today,* pp. 8–9.

Hurtado, A. (1996). *The color of privilege.* Ann Arbor: University of Michigan Press.

Hurtig, A. L., & Rosenthal, I. M. (1987). Psychological findings in early treated cases of female pseudohermaphroditism caused by virilizing congenital adrenal hyperplasia. *Archives of Sexual Behavior, 16,* 209–223.

Husni, S. (1997). *1997 Guide to new consumer magazines.* New York: Oxbridge Communications.

Hyde, J. S. (1984). How large are gender differences in aggression? A developmental meta-analysis. *Developmental Psychology, 20,* 722–736.

Hyman, P. (1979). The other half: Women in the Jewish tradition. In E. Koltun (Ed.), *The Jewish woman* (pp. 105–113). New York: Schocken Press.

Immarigeon, R., & Chesney-Lind, M. (1990). *Women's prisons: Overcrowded and overused.* Paper presented at the Annual Meeting of the American Society of Criminology, Baltimore, MD.

Imperato-McGinley, J., Peterson, R. E., Gautier, T., Looper, G., Danner, R., Arthur, A., Morris, P. L., Sweeney, W. J., & Shackleton, C. (1982). Hormonal evolution of a large kindred with complete androgen insensitivity: Evidence for secondary 5 alpha-reductase deficiency. *Journal of Clinical Endrocrinology Metabolism, 54,* 15–22.

Inciardi, J. A. (1993). *Criminal justice.* Orlando: Harcourt, Brace, Jovanovich.

Inciardi, J. A., Lockwood, D., & Pottieger, A. E. (1993). *Women and crack-cocaine.* New York: Macmillan.

Innes, C. A. (1988). *Drug use and crime.* Bureau of Justice Statistics Special Report. Washington, DC: National Institute of Justice.

Inter-Parliamentary Union. (1997). *Men and women in politics: Democracy in the making.* Geneva: Author.

Isaaks, L. (1980). *Sex role stereotyping as it relates to ethnicity, age and sex in young children.* Unpublished doctoral dissertation, East Texas State University.

Isasi-Diaz, A. M. (1991). Hispanic women in the Roman Catholic Church. In M. A. May (Ed.), *Women and church* (pp. 13–17). Grand Rapids, MI: Wm. B. Eerdmans Publishing Co.

Island, D., & Letellier, P. (1991). *Men who beat the men who love them.* New York: Harrington Park.

Israel orthodox attack skirts. (1996, July 31). Jerusalem, Israel: Associated Press. (Internet).

Jacklin, C. N. (1989). Female and male: Issues of gender. *American Psychologist, 44,* 127–133.

Jacob, H. (1989). Another look at no-fault divorce and the post-divorce finances of women. *Law and Society Review, 23,* 95–115.

Jacobs, J. A. (1983). *The sex segregation of occupations and women's career patterns.* Unpublished doctoral dissertation, Harvard University.

Jacobs, J. A. (1992). Women's entry into management: Trends in earnings, authority, and values among salaried managers. *Administration Science Quarterly, 37,* 282–301.

Jacobs, J. A., & Lim, S. T. (1995). Trends in occupational and industrial sex segregation in 56 countries, 1960–1980.

In J. A. Jabobs (Ed.), *Gender inequality at work* (pp. 259–293). Thousand Oaks, CA: Sage.

Jacobs, J. A., & Steinberg, R. J. (1990). Compensating differentials and the male-female wage gap: Evidence from the New York State comparable worth study. *Social Forces, 69,* 439–468.

Jacobsen, J. P., & Levin, L. M. (1995, September). Effects of intermittent labor force attachment on women's earnings. *Monthly Labor Review,* pp. 14–19.

Jacquet, C. H. (Ed.) (1988). *Women ministers in 1986 and 1987: A ten year view.* New York: Office of Research and Evaluation, National Council of Churches.

Janofsky, M. (1997, April 1). Women in the Marines join the firing line. *New York Times,* p. A10.

Japp, P. M. (1991). Gender and work in the 1980s: Television's working women as displaced persons. *Women's Studies in Communication, 14,* 49–74.

Jarratt, E. H. (1990). Feminist issues in sport. *Women's Studies International Forum, 13,* 491–499.

Jayakody, R., & Chatters, L. M. (1997). Differences among African American single mothers: Marital status, living arrangements, and family support. In R. J. Taylor, J. S. Jackson, & L. M. Chatters (Eds.), *Family life in Black America* (pp. 167–184). Thousand Oaks, CA: Sage.

Jayawardena, K. (1986). *Feminism and nationalism in the third world.* London: Zed Press.

Jeffery, P., Jeffery, R., & Lyon, A. (1988). *Labor pains and labor power: Women and childbearing in India.* London: Zed Books.

Jehl, D. (1993, February 25). High level grumbling over pace of appointments. *New York Times,* p. A16.

Jensen, R. (1995). Pornographic lives. *Violence Against Women, 1,* 32–54.

Jewell, K. S. (1988). *Survival of the Black family: The institutional impact of U.S. social policy.* New York: Praeger.

Johnson, D. (1996, February 12). No-fault divorce is under attack. *New York Times,* p. A10.

Johnson, D. (1997, March 17). New messages sent at Navy boot camp. *New York Times,* p. A10.

Johnson, K. (1997, February 2). Black workers bear big burden as jobs in government dwindle. *New York Times,* pp. 1, 36–37.

Johnson, S., Guenther, S., Laube, D., & Keettle, W. (1981). Factors influencing lesbian gynecologic care: A preliminary study. *American Journal of Obstetrics and Gynecology, 140,* 20–28.

Johnson-Odim, C. (1991). Common themes, different contexts: Third world women and feminism. In C. T. Mohanty, A. Russo, & L. Torres (Eds.), *Third world women and the politics of feminism* (pp. 314–327). Bloomington: Indiana University Press.

Johnston, D. (1992, April 24). Survey shows number of rapes far higher than official figures. *New York Times,* p. A14.

Johnston, D. (1993, October 11). In protest, agent to leave the F.B.I. *New York Times,* p. A11.

Johnston, D. (1995, September 20). F.B.I. hitting snag in talks about bias. *New York Times,* p. A18.

Johnstone, R. L. (1988). *Religion in society.* Englewood Cliffs, NJ: Prentice-Hall.

Joiner, T. E., & Blalock, J. A. (1995). Gender differences in depression: The role of anxiety and generalized negative affect. *Sex Roles, 33,* 91–108.

Jones, J. H. (1993). *Bad blood: The Tuskegee experiment.* New York: Free Press.

Jones, M. G., & Wheatley, J. (1990). Gender differences in teacher-student interactions in science classrooms. *Journal of Research in Science Teaching, 27,* 861–874.

Jordon, E., & Cowan, A. (1995). Warrior narratives in the kindergarten classroom: Renegotiating the social contract? *Gender & Society, 9,* 727–743.

Joseph, G. (1981). Black mothers and daughters. In G. Joseph & J. Lewis (Eds.), *Common differences: Conflicts in Black and White feminist perspectives* (pp. 75–126). New York: Anchor.

Jurgens, J. J., & Powers, B. A. (1991). An exploratory study of the menstrual euphemisms, beliefs, and taboos of Head Start mothers. In D. L. Taylor & N. F. Woods (Eds.), *Menstruation, health, and illness* (pp. 35–40). New York: Hemisphere.

Jurik, N. C. (1985). An officer and a lady: Organizational barriers to women working as correctional officers in men's prisons. *Social Problems, 32,* 375–388.

Jurik, N. C., & Halemba, G. J. (1984). Gender, working conditions and the job satisfaction of women in a non-traditional occupation: Female correctional officers in men's prisons. *Sociological Quarterly, 25,* 551–566.

Kaiser Family Foundation. (1998, March 27). *New KFF/YM Magazine survey of teens on dating, intimacy, and sexual experiences.* Menlo Park, CA: Author.

Kahn, K. F., &. Goldenberg, E. N. (1991). The media: Obstacle or ally of feminists? *The Annals of the American Academy of Political and Social Science, 515,* 104–113.

Kahn, S. S., Nessim, S., Gray, R., Czer, L. S., Chaux, A., & Matloff, J. (1990). Increased mortality of women in coronary bypass surgery: Evidence for referral bias. *Annals of Internal Medicine, 112,* 561–567.

Kalinowski, J., & Buerk, D. (1995). Enhancing women's mathematical competence: A student-centered analysis. *NWSA Journal, 7,* 1–17.

Kamerman, S. B., & Kahn, A. J. (1988). *Mothers alone.* Dover, MA: Auburn House Publishing Co.

Kammeyer, K. C. W. (1987). *Marriage and family.* Boston: Allyn and Bacon.

Kane, E. W., & Sanchez, L. (1992). *Pushing feminism out?: Family status and criticism of gender inequality at home and work.* Paper presented at the Annual Meeting of the American Sociological Association, Pittsburgh, PA.

Kannapell, A. (1998, February 17). Heading slowly into the ice age. *New York Times,* pp. B1, 6.

Kanter, R. M. (1977). *Men and women of the corporation.* New York: Basic.

Katz, R. C., Hannon, R., & Whitten, L. (1996). Effects of gender and situation on the perception of sexual harassment. *Sex Roles, 34,* 35–42.

Kaufman, D. R. (1991). *Rachel's daughters: Newly orthodox Jewish women.* New Brunswick: Rutgers University Press.

Kay, F. M., & Hagan, J. (1995). The persistent glass ceiling: Gendered inequalities in the earnings of lawyers. *British Journal of Sociology, 46,* 279–310.

Kay, H. H. (1988). *Sex-based discrimination.* St. Paul, MN: West.

Kaye, E. (1993, June 6). So weak, so powerful. *New York Times,* pp. V1, V10.

Kelly, E. S. (1998, June 2). Teaching doctors sensitivity on the most sensitive of exams. *New York Times,* p. F7.

Kelly, G. F. (1995). *Sexuality today.* Dubuque, IA: Brown and Benchmark.

Kelly, R. M., Saint-Germain, M. A., & Horn, J. D. (1991). Female public officials: A different voice? *The Annals of the American Academy of Political and Social Science, 515,* 77–87.

Kemper, T. D. (1990). *Social structure and testosterone.* New Brunswick: Rutgers University Press.

Kerber, L. K., Greeno, C. G., Maccoby, E. E., Luria, Z., Stack, C. B., & Gilligan, C. (1986). On *In a Different Voice:* An interdisciplinary forum. *Signs, 11,* 304–333.

Kessleman, A. (1990). *Fleeting opportunities: Women shipyard workers in Portland and Vancouver during World War II and Reconversion.* Albany: State University of New York Press.

Kessler, S. J. (1996). The medical construction of gender: Case management of intersexed infants. In B. Laslett, S. G. Kohlstedt, H. Longino, & E. Hammonds (Eds.), *Gender and scientific authority* (pp. 340–363). Chicago: University of Chicago Press.

Kessler-Harris, A. (1982). *Out to work: A history of wage-earning women in the United States.* New York: Oxford University Press.

Kessler-Harris, A. (1990). *A woman's wage: Historical meanings and social consequences.* Lexington, KY: University Press of Kentucky.

Kilborn, P. T. (1995, March 17). White males and the manager class. *New York Times,* p. A14.

Kilborn, P. T. (1996, November 12). Welfare mothers losing bonus to track fathers. *New York Times,* p. A12.

Kilborn, P. T. (1997, March 12). 5 women say sex charges in army case were coerced. *New York Times,* p. A14.

Kim, E. (1996, August 16). Sheriff says he'll have chain gangs for women. *Tuscaloosa News,* p. 1A.

Kimball, R. (1990). *Tenured radicals: How politics has corrupted higher education.* New York: Harper and Row.

Kimmel, M. (1995). *Manhood in America.* New York: Free Press.

Kimmel, M. S., & Messner, M. A. (Eds.) (1998). *Men's lives.* Boston: Allyn and Bacon.

King, D. R. (1988). Multiple jeopardy, multiple consciousness: The context of a Black feminist ideology. *Signs, 14,* 42–72.

Kinzer, S. (1997, May 27). Beating the system, with bribes and the big lie. *New York Times,* p. A4.

Kinzer, S. (1998, March 17). A woman, her scarf and a storm over secularism. *New York Times,* p. A4.

Kirschstein, R. L. (1996). Women physicians—Good news and bad news. *New England Journal of Medicine, 334,* 982–983.

Klag, M. J., Whelton, P. K., Corech, J., Grim, C. E., & Kuller, L. H. (1991). The association of skin color with blood pressure in U.S. Blacks with low socioeconomic status. *Journal of the American Medical Association, 264,* 599–602.

Klass, P. (1988, April 10). Are women better doctors? *The New York Times Magazine,* pp. 32–35, 46–48, 96–97.

Klatch, R. (1988). Coalition and conflict among women of the new right. *Signs, 13,* 671–694.

Klein, A. M. (1995). Life's too short to die small. In D. Sabo & D. F. Gordon (Eds.), *Men's health and illness* (pp. 105–120). Thousand Oaks, CA: Sage.

Klein, E. (1984). *Gender politics.* Cambridge, MA: Harvard University Press.

Klein, M. (1975). *Envy and gratitude and other works, 1946–1963.* New York: Delta.

Kocieniewski, D. (1995, October 14). Judge ordered victim, 15, to re-enact sexual abuse in court. *New York Times*, pp. 21–22.

Koehler, M. S. (1990). Classrooms, teachers, and gender differences in mathematics. In E. Fennema & G. C. Leder (Eds.), *Mathematics and gender* (pp. 128–148). New York: Teachers College Press.

Koeske, R. (1980). Theoretical perspectives on menstrual cycle research. In A. Dan, E. Graham, & C. P. Beecher (Eds.), *The menstrual cycle* (pp. 8–24). New York: Springer.

Kolata, G. (1993, October 26). Cloning human embryos: Debate erupts over ethics. *New York Times*, pp. A1, C3.

Kolata, G. (1998, March 10). Harrowing choices accompany advancements in fertility. *New York Times*, p. F3.

Kolker, A., & Burke, B. M. (1992). *Sex preference and sex selection: Attitudes of prenatal diagnosis clients.* Paper presented at the Annual Meeting of the American Sociological Association, Pittsburgh, PA.

Kolker, C. (1998, May 6). More women, children seek shelters, study says. *Houston Chronicle*, p. 1.

Kolodny, A. (1993). Raising standards while lowering anxieties: Rethinking the promotion and tenure process. *Concerns: Women's Caucus for the Modern Languages, 23*, 16–40.

Kong, D. (1998, April 7). Mergers with Catholic hospitals cut access to abortion, study finds. *Boston Globe*, p. A10.

Kosberg, J. I. (1988). Preventing elder abuse: Identification of high-risk factors prior to placement decisions. *The Gerontologist, 28*, 43–50.

Koser, N. W. (1992). Feminist pedagogy in criminology. *Journal of Criminal Justice Education, 2*, 81–94.

Koss, M. (1991). Changed lives: The psychological impact of sexual harassment. In M. A. Pauldi (Ed.), *Ivory power: Sexual harassment on campus* (pp. 73–92). Albany: State University of New York Press.

Koss, M., Gidycz, C., & Wisniewski, N. (1987). The scope of rape: Incidence and prevalence of sexual aggression in a sample of higher education students. *Journal of Consulting and Clinical Psychology, 55*, 162–170.

Kozol, J. (1988). *Rachel and her children: Homeless families in America.* New York: Fawcett Columbine.

Kraft, D. (1997, June 11). Women praying with men stoned. Jerusalem, Israel: Associated Press. (Internet).

Kramer, R. (1986). The third wave. *Wilson Quarterly, 10*, 110–129.

Kramarae, C., & Spender, D. (1992). Exploding knowledge. In C. Kramarae & D. Spender (Eds.), *The knowledge explosion: Generations of feminist scholarship* (pp. 1–24). New York: Teachers College Press.

Kranichfeld, M. L. (1987). Rethinking family power. *Journal of Family Issues, 8*, 42–56.

Kreiger, N., & Sidney, S. (1996). Racial discrimination and blood pressure: The CARDIA study of young Black and White adults. *American Journal of Public Health, 86*, 1370–1378.

Krieger, S. (1982). Lesbian identity and community: Recent social science literature. *Signs, 8*, 91–108.

Kristof, N. D. (1991, November 5). Stark data on women: 100 million are missing. *New York Times*, pp. C1, C12.

Kristof, N. D. (1996, April 14). Asian childhoods sacrificed to prosperity's lust. *New York Times*, pp. 1, 8.

Kuebli, J., Butler, S. A., & Fivush, R. (1995). Mother-child talk about past emotions: Relations of maternal language and child gender over time. *Cognition and Emotion, 9*, 265–283,

Kuhn, T. S. (1970). *The structure of scientific revolutions.* Chicago: University of Chicago Press.

Kurz, D. (1995). *For richer, for poorer: Mothers confront divorce.* New York: Routledge.

Kushner, H. I. (1985). Women and suicide in historical perspective. *Signs, 10*, 537–552.

Lacan, J. (1977). *Ecrits: A selection.* London: Tavistock.

Lackey, P. N. (1989). Adults' attitudes about assignments of household chores to male and female children. *Sex Roles, 20*, 271–281.

LaCroix, A. Z., & Haynes, S. G. (1987). Gender differences in the health effects of workplace roles. In R. C. Barnett, L. Biener, & G. K. Baruch (Eds.), *Gender and stress* (pp. 96–121). New York: Free Press.

Ladner, J. (1971). *Tomorrow's tomorrow.* Garden City, NY: Doubleday.

Lake, C. C., & Breglio, V. J. (1992). Different voices, different views: The politics of gender. In P. Ries & A. J. Stone (Eds.), *The American woman, 1992–93* (pp. 178–201). New York: W. W. Norton.

Lakeoff, R. (1990). *Talking power: The politics of language in our lives.* New York: Basic Books.

Lakoff, R. (1991). You are what you say. In E. Ashton-Jones & G. A. Olson (Eds.), *The gender reader* (pp. 292–298). Boston: Allyn and Bacon.

Lamar, J. V. (1988, February 15). Redefining a woman's place. *Time*, p. 27.

Lambeck, L. C. (1998, February 10). Black kids "irrationally" singled out for special ed: Report." *Connecticut Post*.

Lambert, B. (1998, April 24). Gay school? What gay school? On Long Island, an abrupt reversal. *New York Times*, p. B1, B8.

Landrine, H., & Klonoff, E. A. (1997). *Discrimination against women: Prevalence, consequences, remedies.* Thousand Oaks, CA: Sage.

Landry, D. J., & Forrest, J. D. (1995). How old are U.S. fathers? *Family Planning Perspectives, 27*, 159–161, 165.

Langolis, J. H., & Downs, A. C. (1980). Mothers, fathers, and peers as socialization agents of sex-typed play behaviors in young children. *Child Development, 51*, 1217–1247.

Lanis, K., & Covell, K. (1995). Images of women in advertisements: Effects on attitudes related to sexual aggression. *Sex Roles*, 639–649.

Lantz, P. M., House, J. S., Lepkowski, J. M., Williams, D. R., Mero, R. P., & Chen, J. (1998). Results from a nationally representative prospective study of U.S. adults. *Journal of the American Medical Association, 279*, 1703–1708.

Lapointe, J. (1998, February 18). U.S. women first at gold in ice thriller. *New York Times*, pp. A1, C2.

Larson, J. H. (1988). The marriage quiz: College students' beliefs in selected myths about marriage. *Family Relations, 37*, 3–11.

Laumann, E. O., Gagnon, J. H., Michael, R. T., & Michaels, S. (1994). *The social organization of sexuality.* Chicago: University of Chicago Press.

Lawlor, J. (1998, April 26). For many blue-collar fathers, child care is shift work, too. *New York Times*, p. BU11.

Lawmaker's rape view stirs ire. (1995, April 20). Raleigh, NC: Associated Press. (Internet).

Lawrence, R., & Johnson, D. (1991). *Women in corrections: The prospects for equality.* Paper presented at the Annual

Meeting of the American Society of Criminology, San Francisco, CA.

Lawrence, W. (1987). Women and sports, In S. E. Rix (Ed.), *The American woman, 1987–88* (pp. 222–226). New York: W. W. Norton.

Lawson, C. (1989, June 15). Toys: Girls still apply makeup, boys fight wars. *New York Times*, pp. C1, C10.

Lawson, C. (1996, February 15). Fun at the toy fair: Babies that fly! *New York Times*, p. C2.

Lawson, C. (1997, February 13). What the next sled of toys are up to. *New York Times*, p. C2.

Lazier-Smith, L. (1989). A new "genderation" of images of women. In P. J. Creedon (Ed.), *Women in mass communication* (pp. 247–260). Newbury Park, CA: Sage.

Leach, W. (1980). *True love and perfect union: The feminist reform of sex and society*. New York: Basic Books.

Leaper, C., Carson, M., Baker, C., Holliday, H., & Meyers, S. (1995). Self-disclosure and listener verbal support in same-gender and cross-gender friends. *Sex Roles, 33*, 387–404.

LeBlanc, A. N. (1996, June 2). A woman behind bars is not a dangerous man. *New York Times Magazine*, pp. 34–40.

LeClere, F. B., Rogers, R. G., & Peters, K. (1998). Neighborhood social context and racial differences in women's heart disease mortality. *Journal of Health and Social Behavior, 39*, 91–107.

Leder, G. C., & Fennema, E. (1990). Gender differences in mathematics: A synthesis. In E. Fennema & G. C. Leder (Eds.), *Mathematics and gender.* (pp. 188–200). New York: Teachers College Press.

Lee, F. R. (1989, July 17). Doctors see gap in Blacks' health having a link to low self-esteem. *New York Times*, p. A11.

Lees, S. (1989). Learning to love: Sexual reputation, morality and the social control of girls. In M. Cain (Ed.), *Growing up good* (pp. 19–37). Newbury Park, CA: Sage.

Lehrman, K. (1993, September/October). Off course. *Mother Jones*, pp. 45–51.

Leinen, S. (1993). *Gay cops*. New Brunswick, NJ: Rutgers University Press.

Lemle, R. (1984). *Alcohol and masculinity: A review and reformulation of sex role, dependency, and power theories of alcoholism*. Paper presented at the Annual Meeting of the American Psychological Association, Toronto, Canada.

Lenskyj, H. (1986). *Out of bounds*. Toronto: The Women's Press.

Lentz, B. F., & Laband, D. N. (1995). *Sex discrimination in the legal profession*. Westport, CT: Quorum Books.

Lepowsky, M. (1990). Gender in an egalitarian society: A case study from the Coral Sea. In P. R. Sanday & R. G. Goodenough (Eds.), *Beyond the second sex* (pp. 169–224). Philadelphia: University of Pennsylvania Press.

Lepowsky, M. (1994). Women, men and aggression in an egalitarian society. *Sex Roles, 30*, 199–211.

Lerner, G. (Ed.) (1972). *Black women in White America*. New York: Vintage.

Lerner, G. (1993). *The creation of feminist consciousness*. New York: Oxford University Press.

Lesperance, F., & Frasure-Smith, N. (1996). Negative emotions and coronary heart disease: Getting to the heart of the matter. *The Lancet, 347*, 414–415.

Letellier, P. (1996). Twin epidemics: Domestic violence and HIV infection among gay and bisexual men. In C. M. Renzetti & C. H. Miley (Eds.), *Violence in gay and lesbian domestic partnerships* (pp. 69–82). New York: Haworth.

Leung, J. J. (1990). Aspiring parents' and teachers' academic beliefs about young children. *Sex Roles, 23*, 83–90.

LeVay, S. (1991). A difference in hypothalamic structure between heterosexual and homosexual men. *Science, 253*, 1034–1037.

Levine, A., & Cureton, J. (Eds.) (1998). *When hope and fear collide: A portrait of today's college student*. San Francisco: Jossey-Bass.

Levine, J. (1997). *Working fathers*. Reading, MA: Addison-Wesley.

Lewin, T. (1992a, April 20). Battered men sounding equal-rights battle cry. *New York Times*, p. A12.

Lewin, T. (1992b, October, 21). Lutherans asked to decide on blessing of gay unions. *New York Times*, p. A16.

Lewin, T. (1995, April 26). Age found to widen income gap for sexes. *New York Times*, p. A19.

Lewin, T. (1997a, March 15). New guidelines on sexual harassment tell schools when a kiss is just a peck. *New York Times*, p. 8.

Lewin, T. (1997b, October 9). In California, wider test of same-sex schools. *New York Times*, pp. A1, A22.

Lewin, T. (1997c, September 15). Women losing ground to men in widening income difference. *New York Times*, pp. A1, 12.

Lewin, T. (1997d, September 5). Equal pay for equal work is No. 1 goal of women. *New York Times*, p. A20.

Lewin, T. (1998a, May 1). Birth rate for teen-agers declined sharply in the 90s. *New York Times*, p. A21.

Lewin, T. (1998b, March 7). Fewer children per care provider is good for all, study finds. *New York Times*, p. A6.

Lewin, T. (1998c, June 8). Report tying abortion to welfare is rejected. *New York Times*, p. A10.

Lewis, C., Scully, D., & Condor, S. (1992). Sex stereotyping of infants: A re-examination. *Journal of Reproductive and Infant Psychology, 10*, 53–63.

Lewis, G. B., & Nice, D. (1994). Race, sex, and occupational segregation in state and local governments. *American Review of Public Administration, 24*, 393–410.

Lewis, L. A. (1990). *Gender politics and MTV*. Philadelphia: Temple University Press.

Lewis, M., & Simon, R. I. (1986). A discourse not intended for her: Learning and teaching within patriarchy. *Harvard Educational Review, 56*, 457–472.

Lewis, N. A. (1993, November 24). U.S. restrictions on adult-TV fare are struck down. *New York Times*, pp. A1, A20.

Lewis, R. (1998, April 19). Is that love in the air? More people are saying "I do." *Philadelphia Inquirer*, pp. A1, 12.

Liebert, R., Neale, J. & Davidson, E. (1992). *The early window: The effects of television on children and youth*. New York: Pergamon Press.

Liebman, M. (1995, December 6). Christian bigotry can breed violence, gay bashing. *Los Angeles Times*.

Lightfoot-Klein, H. (1989). *Prisoners of ritual: An odyssey into female genital circumcision in Africa*. New York: Harrington Park Press.

Lincoln, C. E., & Mamiya, L. H. (1990). *The Black church in the African American experience*. Durham, NC: University of North Carolina Press.

Lindeqvist, K. (1996). Fighting repressive tolerance: Lesbian studies in Sweden. In B. Zimmerman & T. A. H. McNaron (Eds.), *The new lesbian studies* (pp. 229–233). New York: Feminist Press.

Lindgren, J. R., & Taub, N. (1993). *The law of sex discrimination*. Minneapolis: West.

Little, C. B. (1983). *Understanding deviance and control: Theory, research and public policy*. Itasca, IL: F. E. Peacock.

Littlewood, R., & Lipsedge, M. (1989). *Aliens and alienists: Ethnic minorities and psychiatry*. London: Unwin Hyman.

Limbert, C. A. (1995). Chrysalis, a peer mentoring group for faculty and staff women. *NWSA Journal, 7*, 86–99.

Lipsyte, R. (1998, March 5). Severing ties to a second home. *New York Times*, pp. C1, 5.

Liston, B. (1998, May 31). Abortion foes threaten to turn tactics on gay event. *Boston Globe*, p. A2.

Lloyd, K. M., & South, S. J. (1996). Contextual influences on young men's transition to first marriage. *Social Forces, 74*, 1097–1119.

Lobao, L. (1990). Women in revolutionary movements: Changing patterns in Latin American guerrilla struggle. In G. West & R. L. Blumberg (Eds.), *Women and social protest* (pp. 180–204). New York: Oxford University Press.

Lobel, T. E., Bempechat, J., Gewirtz, J. C., Shoken-Topaz, T., & Bashe, E. (1993). The role of gender-related information and self-endorsements of traits in preadolescents' inferences and judgments. *Child Development, 64*, 1285–1294.

Lock, J., & Kleis, B. N. (1998). A primer on homophobia for the child and adolescent psychiatrist. *Journal of the American Academy of Child and Adolescent Psychiatry, 37*, 671–672.

Lockhart, L. L. (1991). Spousal violence: A cross-racial perspective. In R. L. Hampton (Ed.), *Black family violence* (pp. 85–101). Lexington, MA: Lexington Books.

Lofland, L. H. (1975). The "thereness" of women: A selective review of urban sociology. In M. Millman & R. M. Kanter (Eds.), *Another voice* (pp. 144–170). New York: Anchor/Doubleday.

London, K. A. (1991). *Cohabitation, marriage, marital dissolution and remarriage: United States, 1988*. Washington, DC: U.S. Government Printing Office.

Longer menstrual cycles in active, lean women. (1996, October 14). New York: Reuters. (Internet).

Longino, H., & Doell, R. (1983). Body, bias, and behavior: A comparative analysis of reasoning in two areas of biological science. *Signs, 9*, 206–227.

Lorber, J. (1986). Dismantling Noah's ark. *Sex Roles, 14*, 567–580.

Lorber, J. (1993). Believing is seeing: Biology as ideology. *Gender & Society, 7*, 568–581.

Lorber, J. (1998). *Gender inequality: Feminist theories and politics*. Los Angeles: Roxbury.

Lorber, J., Coser, R. L., Rossi, A. S., & Chodorow, N. (1981). On the *Reproduction of Mothering*: A methodological debate. *Signs, 6*, 482–514.

Loredo, C., Reid, A., & Deaux, K. (1995). Judgments and definitions of sexual harassment by high school students. *Sex Roles, 32*, 29–45.

Loring, M., & Powell, B. (1988). Gender, race and DSM-III: A study of psychiatric behavior. *Journal of Health and Social Behavior, 29*, 1–22.

Lott, B. (1987). *Women's lives: Themes and variations in gender learning*. Monterey, CA: Brooks/Cole Publishing Company.

Love, A. A. (1998, June 9). Wage gap between the sexes narrowing. *Atlanta Constitution*, p. 1.

Lovejoy, O. (1981). The origins of man. *Science, 211*, 341–350.

Lovenduski, J. (1986). *Women and European politics*. Amherst: University of Massachusetts Press.

Luckenbill, D. F. (1986). Deviant career mobility: The case of male prostitutes. *Social Problems, 33*, 283–296.

Luebke, B. F., & Reilly, M. E. (1994). *Women's studies graduates: The first generation*. New York: Teachers College Press.

Luker, K. (1984). *Abortion and the politics of motherhood*. Berkeley: University of California Press.

Luker, K. (1996). *Dubious conceptions: The politics of teen pregnancy*. Cambridge: Harvard University Press.

Lunneborg, P. W. (1990). *Women changing work*. New York: Bergen and Garvey.

Lurie, N., Slater, J., McGovern, P., Ekstrum, J., Quam, L., & Margolis, K. (1993). Preventive care for women: Does the sex of the physician make a difference? *New England Journal of Medicine, 329*, 478–482.

Lutz, J. S. (1991, Spring). Feminism: Cornerstone of political correctness. *Campus*, p. 1.

Lynn, N. B. (1984). Women and politics: The real majority. In J. Freeman (Ed.), *Women: A feminist perspective* (pp. 402–422). Palo Alto, CA: Mayfield.

Lynn, R. (1994). Sex differences in intelligence and brain size: A paradox resolved. *Personal and Individual Differences, 17*, 257–271.

Maccoby, E. (1988). Gender as a social category. *Developmental Psychology, 24*, 755–765.

MacCorquodale, P., & Jensen, G. (1993). Women in law: Partners or tokens? *Gender & Society, 7*, 582–593.

MacDonald, C. L., & Sirianni, C. (1996). The service society and the changing experience of work. In C. L. MacDonald & C. Sirianni (Eds.), *Working in the service society* (pp. 1–26). Philadelphia: Temple University Press.

MacDonald, E. (1992). *Shoot the women first*. New York: Random House.

MacDonald, K., & Parke, R. D. (1986). Parent-child physical play: The effects of sex and age on children and parents. *Sex Roles, 15*, 367–378.

MacFarquhar, N. (1996). Mutilation of Egyptian girls: Despite ban, it goes on. *New York Times*, p. A3.

MacKinnon, C. (1986). Pornography: Not a moral issue. *Women's Studies International Forum, 9*, 63–78.

Madriz, E. I. (1997). Images of criminals and victims: A study of women's fear and social control. *Gender & Society, 11*, 342–356.

Maghan, J., & McLeish-Blackwell, L. (1991). Black women in correctional employment. In J. B. Morton (Ed.), *Change, challenge, and choices: Women's role in modern corrections* (pp. 82–99). Laurel, MD: American Correctional Association.

Maher, F. A., & Tetrault, M. K. T. (1994). *The feminist classroom*. New York: Basic Books.

Mandel, R. B., & Dodson, D. L. (1992). Do women officeholders make a difference? In P. Ries & A. J. Stone (Eds.), *The American woman, 1992–93* (pp. 149–177). New York: W. W. Norton.

Manegold, C. S. (1993, May 9). Among Blacks, new voices emerge. *New York Times*, pp. 25, 32.

Mann, C. R. (1989). Minority and female: A criminal justice double bind. *Social Justice, 16(4)*, 95–114.

Mann, C. R. (1993). *Unequal justice: A question of color*. Bloomington: Indiana University Press.

Mann, C. R. (1995). Women of color and the criminal justice system. In B. R. Price & N. J. Sokoloff (Eds.), *The criminal justice system and women* (pp. 118–135). New York: McGraw-Hill.

Manning, A. (1998, February 23). Operating with sexism. *USA Today,* p. 1D.

Mannix, M., Bernstein, A., & Flynn, M. K. (1996, June 23). These nifty sites show why more women are frequenting the Internet. *U.S. News and World Report,* pp. 58–60.

Mansnerus, L. (1997, November 16). Sometimes the punishment fits the gender. *New York Times,* p. WK1.

Maquieira, V. (1989). Boys, girls and the discourse of identity: Growing up in Madrid. In M. Cain (Ed.), *Growing up good* (pp. 38–54) Newbury Park, CA: Sage.

Mares, M. (1996). *Positive effects of television on social behavior: A meta-analysis.* Paper presented at the Annenberg Washington Conference on Children and Television, Washington, DC.

Margolis, D. R. (1993). Women's movements around the world: Cross-cultural comparisons. *Gender & Society,* 7, 379–399.

Marieskind, H. I., & Ehrenreich, B. (1975). Toward socialist medicine: The women's health movement. *Social Policy,* 6, 34–42.

Marini, M. M., & Brinton, M. (1984). Sex typing in occupational socialization. In B. F. Reskin (Ed.), *Sex segregation in the workplace: Trends, explanations, remedies* (pp. 192–232). Washington, DC: National Academy Press.

Markens, S. (1996). The problematic of "experience": A political and cultural critique of PMS. *Gender & Society,* 10, 42–58.

Marshall, E. (1992). Sex of the brain. *Science,* 257, 620–621.

Martin, B. (1978). Conservative Judaism and reconstructionism. In B. Martin (Ed.), *Movements and issues in American Judaism* (pp. 103–157). Westport, CT: Greenwood Press.

Martin, C. L. (1989). Children's use of gender-related information in making social judgments. *Developmental Psychology,* 25, 80–88.

Martin, D. (1993, February 15). After Wood and Baird, illegal-nanny anxiety creeps across many homes. *New York Times,* p. A13.

Martin, J. R. (1994). *Changing the educational landscape.* New York: Routledge.

Martin, M. C. & Kennedy, P. F. (1996). The measurement of social comparison to advertising models: A gender gap revealed. In J. Curran, D. Morley & V. Walkerdine (Eds.), *Cultural studies and communications* (pp. 104–124). London: Arnold.

Martin, M. K., & Voorhies, B. (1975). *Female of the species.* New York: Columbia University Press.

Martin, S. E. (1989). *Dealing with the "double whammy": The impact of race and gender on women in policing.* Paper presented at the Annual Meeting of the American Sociological Association, San Francisco, CA.

Martin, S. E. (1990). *On the move: The status of women in policing.* Washington, DC: The Police Foundation.

Martin, S. E. (1992). The changing status of women officers: Gender and power in police work. In I. L. Moyer (Ed.), *The changing roles of women in the criminal justice system* (pp. 281–305). Prospect Heights, IL: Waveland Press.

Martin, S. E., & Jurik, N. C. (1996). *Doing justice, doing gender.* Thousand Oaks, CA: Sage.

Marty, M. E. (1992). Fundamentals of fundamentalism. In L. Kaplan (Ed.), *Fundamentalism in comparative perspective* (pp. 15–23). Amherst, MA: University of Massachusetts Press.

Marty, M. E., & Appleby, R. S. (1992). *The glory and the power.* Boston: Beacon Press.

Martyna, W. (1980). Beyond the "he/man" approach: The case for nonsexist language. *Signs,* 5, 482–493.

Marzolf, M. T. (1993). *Women making a difference in the newsroom.* Paper submitted to the Commission on the Status of Women in Journalism and Mass Communication, AEJMC, Kansas City, KS.

Massachusetts to look at sex bias in courts. (1986, August 10). *New York Times,* p. 37.

Masse, M. A., & Rosenblum, K. (1988). Male and female created they them: The depiction of gender in the advertising of traditional women's and men's magazines. *Women's Studies International Forum,* 11, 127–144.

Mates, R. (1997, April 4). Financial abuse of elderly hits close to home. *Toronto Globe and Mail,* p. 1.

Math theory gains ground: Girls classes help them learn. (1994, November 6). *New York Times,* p. 48.

Matthews, W., Booth, M., Turner, J., & Kessler, L. (1986). Physicians' attitudes toward homosexuality—Survey of a California County medical society. *Western Journal of Medicine,* 144, 106–110.

Mauer, M., & Hurling, T. (1995). *Young Black American and the criminal justice system: Five years later.* Washington, DC: The Sentencing Project.

Mauldin, T. (1991). Economic consequences of divorce or separation among women in poverty. In S. S. Volgy (Ed.), *Women and divorce, men and divorce* (pp. 163–177). New York: Haworth.

Mauro, T. (1998, March 12). Corps of clerks lacking in diversity. *USA Today,* pp. 12A–13A.

Mayall, A., & Russell, D. E. H. (1993). Racism in pornography. In D. E. H. Russell (Ed.), *Making violence sexy* (pp. 167–177). New York: Teachers College Press.

Mazur, A., Booth, A., & Dabbs, J. M. Jr. (1992). Testosterone and chess competition. *Social Psychology Quarterly,* 55, 70–77.

Mazur, A., & Lamb, T. A. (1980). Testosterone, status, and mood in human males. *Hormones and Behavior,* 14, 236–246.

McAdoo, H. P. (1986). Societal stress: The Black family. In J. B. Cole (Ed.), *All American women* (pp. 187–197). New York: Free Press.

McAdoo, J. L. (1988). Changing perspectives on the role of the Black father. In P. Bronstein & C. P. Cowan (Eds.), *Fatherhood today: Men's changing role in the family* (pp. 79–92). New York: John Wiley.

McCaulay, M., Mintz, L. & Glenn, A. A. (1988). Body image, self-esteem, and depression-proneness: Closing the gender gap. *Sex Roles,* 18, 381–391.

McClary, S. (1991). *Feminine endings: Music, gender and sexuality.* Minneapolis: University of Minnesota Press.

McClellan, D. S. (1994). Disparity in the discipline of male and female inmates in Texas prisons. *Women and Criminal Justice,* 5, 71–97.

The McClintock Collective. (1990, May). Gender inclusive science and technology education. *Refractory Girl,* pp. 34–36.

McConnell-Ginet, S. (1989). The sexual (re)production of meaning: A discourse-based theory. In F. W. Frank & P. A. Treichler (Eds.), *Language, gender, and professional writing: Theoretical approaches and guidelines for nonsexist usage* (pp. 35–50). New York: Modern Language Association of America.

McCormack, A. (1985). The sexual harassment of students by teachers: The case of students in science. *Sex Roles, 13,* 21–31.

McCormick, T. M. (1994). *Creating the nonsexist classroom.* New York: Teachers College Press.

McCracken, E. (1993). *Decoding women's magazines.* New York: St. Martin's Press.

McCrate, E., & Smith, J. (1998). When work doesn't work: The failure of current welfare reform. *Gender & Society, 12,* 61–80.

McDonald, M. (1996, April 8). Is God a woman? *MacLean's Magazine.*

McFadden, R. D. (1995, November 28). Subway fire attack prompts uproar over action movie. *New York Times,* pp. A1, B4.

McGrath, E., Keita, G. P., Strickland, B. R., &. Russo, N. F. (1990). *Women and depression.* Washington, DC: American Psychological Association.

McGregor, R., & Lawnham, P. (1993, August 5). Japan apologizes to sex slaves. *The Australian,* p. 8.

McIntosh, P. (1984). *Interactive phases of curricular revision: A feminist perspective.* Wellesley Working Papers Series, No. 124. Wellesley, MA: Wellesley College Center for Research on Women.

McKee, K. B. (1996). The child as image: Photographic stereotypes of children. In P. M. Lester (Ed.), *Images that injure* (pp. 107–112). Westport, CT: Praeger.

McKinley, J. C. (1996, May 4). In peace, warrior women rank low. *New York Times,* p. 4.

McLaren, A. (1990). What makes a man a man? *Nature, 346,* 216–217.

McLarin, K. (1996, January 7). Radcliffe alumnae get tough with Harvard. *New York Times Education Life,* pp. 19, 39–41.

McMinn, M. R., Troyer, P. K., Hannum, L. E., & Foster, J. D. (1991). Teaching nonsexist language to college students. *Journal of Experimental Education, 59,* 153–161.

McMinn, M. R., Williams, P. E., & McMinn, L. C. (1994). Assessing recognition of sexist language: Development and use of the Gender-Specific Language Scale. *Sex Roles, 31,* 741–755.

McNamara, J. A. K. (1996). *Sisters in arms.* Cambridge, MA: Harvard University Press.

McNamara, R. P. (1994). *The Times Square hustler: Male prostitution in New York City.* Westport, CT: Praeger.

McNeil, D. G. (1995, September 10). For gay Zimbabweans, a difficult political climate. *New York Times,* p. 3.

McPhillips, K. (1993). Women-Church and the reclamation of sacredness. *Journal of Feminist Studies in Religion, 9,* 113–118.

McQuiston, J. T. (1997, March 16). Caller objects to integration of lead role in Passion play, but threat report is denied. *New York Times,* p. B6.

McRobbie, A. (1996). *More!:* New sexualities in girls' and women's magazines. In J. Curran, D. Morley & V. Walkerdine (Eds.), *Cultural studies and communications* (pp. 172–194). London: Arnold.

Media Education Foundation. (1995). *Dreamworld II: Desire, sex and power in music video.* Videotape available from the author: 26 Center St., Northampton, MA 01060.

Media Report to Women (MRTW). (1993a, Spring). *Newspaper gender gap widening says Newspaper Association of America.* p. 5.

Media Report to Women (MRTW). (1993b, Winter). *Brief: Also from WCI and Unabridged Communications.* p. 6.

Media Report to Women (MRTW). (1993c, Winter). *Briefs: The Associated Press in December.* p. 6.

Media Report to Women (MRTW). (1993d, Fall). *EEOC rules in favor of TV anchorwoman in discrimination complaint.* p. 1.

Media Report to Women (MRTW). (1993e, Winter). *One-third of women journalists report sexual harassment on the job.* p. 2.

Media Report to Women (MRTW). (1993f, Fall). *Canada cracks down on TV violence; U.S. programmers, advertisers resist restrictions.* pp. 1–3.

Media Report to Women (MRTW). (1995, Fall). *And one more poll: The kids speak up about TV and its shortcomings.* pp. 8–9.

Media Report to Women (MRTW). (1996a, Summer). *Women utilize fewer media for '96 campaign news.* pp. 1–2.

Media Report to Women (MRTW). (1996b, Spring). *Front page news coverage of women declines yet again in 1996.* pp. 8–10.

Media Report to Women (MRTW). (1996c, Winter). *Women candidates still receiving less than serious coverage, panel says.* p. 4.

Media Report to Women (MRTW). (1996d, Spring). *Women politicians said to attract different coverage than men.* pp. 5–8.

Media Report to Women (MRTW). (1996e, Summer). *Women, Men and Media roundtable assesses backlash in news coverage.* pp. 5–6.

Media Report to Women (MRTW). (1996f, Spring). *AARP study confirms prime-time TV shows limited roles for older women.* p. 4.

Media Report to Women (MRTW). (1996g, Winter). *Women, minority reporters slide into background on TV networks in 1995.* p. 12.

Media Report to Women (MRTW). (1996h, Winter). *Briefs: More stats to raise your blood pressure.* p. 10.

Media Report to Women (MRTW). (1996i, Winter). *NAA "departure study" pinpoints newspaper women's dissatisfaction.* pp. 1–2.

Media Report to Women (MRTW). (1997a, Spring). *Briefs: Only 51% of adults read daily newspapers at least four times a week.* p. 9.

Media Report to Women (MRTW). (1997b, Summer). *Twin Cities newspaper study: Women only 21% of names in the news.* pp. 4–6.

Media Report to Women (MRTW). (1997c, Spring). *Media reinforce some stereotypes, break others.* pp. 1–3.

Media Report to Women (MRTW). (1997d, Fall). *Briefs: The Screen Actors' Guild reports that women's voices make up only 25% of those heard in commercials.* p. 13.

Media Report to Women (MRTW). (1997e, Fall). *Briefs: Seen in The Wall Street Journal, Oct. 20, 1997: A full-page ad of a naked woman.* p. 13.

Media Report to Women (MRTW). (1997f, Spring). *Briefs: More marketing, less value.* p. 9.

Media Report to Women (MRTW). (1997g, Spring). *Briefs: ABC charged premium rates for the coming-out episode of "Ellen," which aired April 30.* p. 10.

Media Report to Women (MRTW). (1997h, Winter). *U.S. TV ratings have parents underwhelmed, concerned, confused.* pp. 1, 3.

Media Report to Women (MRTW). (1998a, Spring). *Prime-time stereotyping of women persists on all networks.* pp. 1–3.

Media Report to Women (MRTW). (1998b, Spring). *Men's magazines now following women's magazines' formula.* p. 6.

Media Report to Women (MRTW). (1998c, Spring). *Briefs: "Ellen" is out of the closet and off the air.* p. 9.

Media Report to Women (MRTW). (1998d, Spring). *Miller: Why women are giving up on newspapers.* pp. 7–8.

Media Report to Women (MRTW). (1998e, Winter). *Women's sports magazines seeking identity, advertisers.* pp. 1–3.

Meier, B. (1993, February 14). Effective? Maybe. Profitable? Clearly. *New York Times,* pp. F1, F6.

Meier, B. (1996, November 21). Bias complaints against Wall St. firms. *New York Times,* p. D4.

Meigs, A. (1990). Multiple gender ideologies and statuses. In P. R. Sanday & R. G. Goodenough (Eds.), *Beyond the second sex* (pp. 99–112). Philadelphia: University of Pennsylvania Press.

Meredith, N. (1986). The gay dilemma. In L. Simkins (Ed.), *Alternative sexual lifestyles* (pp. 113–117). Acton, MA: Copley Publishing Group.

Meredith, R. (1997, September 20). Strip clubs under siege as saleman's haven. *New York Times,* pp. A1, D3.

Mernissi, F. (1977). Women, saints, and sanctuaries. *Signs, 3,* 101–112.

Messias, D. K. H., Im, E., Page, A, Regev, H., Spiers, J., Yoder, J. D., & Meleis, A. I. (1997). Defining and redefining work: Implications for women's health. *Gender & Society, 11,* 296–323.

Messner, M. (1987). The meaning of success: The athletic experience and the development of male identity. In H. Brod (Ed.), *The making of masculinities* (pp. 193–210). Boston: Allen and Unwin.

Messner, M. (1989). Sports and the politics of inequality. In M. S. Kimmel & M. A. Messner (Eds.), *Men's lives* (pp. 187–190). New York: Macmillan.

Messner, M. (1992). Boyhood, organized sports, and the construction of masculinity. In M. Kimmel & M. Messner (Eds.), *Men's lives* (pp. 161–176). New York: Macmillan.

Messner, M. A. (1998). The limits of "the male sex role": An analysis of the men's liberation and men's rights movements' discourse. *Gender & Society, 12,* 255–276.

Messner, M. A., Duncan, M. C., & Jensen, K. (1993). Separating the men from the girls: The gendered language of televised sports. *Gender & Society, 7,* 121–137.

Metzger, G. (1992, November). T.V. is a blonde, blonde world. *American Demographics,* p. 51.

Meyer, M. (1996, March 18). No sex and violence: Wholesome computer games aimed at young girls hit the market. *U.S. News and World Report,* p. 69.

Michael, R. T., Gagnon, J. H., Laumann, E. O., & Kolata, G. (1994). *Sex in America: A definitive study.* Boston: Little, Brown.

Mies, M., & Shiva, V. (1993). *Ecofeminism.* London: Fernwood Publications/Zed Books.

Miethe, T. D., & Moore, C. A. (1986). Racial differences in criminal processing: The consequences of model selection on conclusions about differential treatment. *Sociological Quarterly, 27,* 217–237.

Mifflin, L. (1998, April 17). Increase seen in number of violent TV programs. *New York Times,* p. A16.

Miles, T. (1995, April 25). Girls complain of "poor" school careers advice. PA News (Internet).

Milkman, R. (1987). *Gender at work: The dynamics of job segregation by sex during World War II.* Berkeley, CA: University of California Press.

Millbrath, L. W. (1965). *Political participation.* Chicago: Rand McNally.

Miller, A. S., & Hoffman, J. P. (1995). Risk and religion: An explanation of gender differences in religiosity. *Journal for the the Scientific Study of Religion, 34,* 63–75.

Miller, C., & Swift, K. (1991a). One small step for genkind. In E. Ashton-Jones & G. A. Olson (Eds.), *The gender reader* (pp. 247–258). Boston: Allyn and Bacon.

Miller, C., & Swift, K. (1991b). Women and names. In E. Ashton-Jones & G. A. Olson (Eds.), *The gender reader* (pp. 272–286). Boston: Allyn and Bacon.

Miller, C. L. (1987). Qualitative differences among gender-stereotyped toys: Implications for cognitive and social development in girls and boys, *Sex Roles, 16,* 473–488.

Miller, J. (1992, December 27). Women regain a kind of security in Islam's embrace. *New York Times,* p. E6.

Miller, J. G. (1996). *Search and destroy: African-American males in the criminal justice system.* New York: Cambridge University Press.

Miller, M. (1998, July 27). Going to war over gays. *Newsweek,* p. 27.

Miller, N. (1992). *Single parents by choice.* New York: Plenum.

Miller, S. L. (1994). Gender-motivated hate crimes: A question of misogyny. In D. J. Curran & C. M. Renzetti (Eds.), *Contemporary societies: Problems and prospects* (pp. 229–235). Englewood Cliffs, NJ: Prentice Hall.

Miller, S. L. (1998). The tangled web of feminism and community policing. In S. L. Miller (Ed.), *Crime control and women* (pp. 95–112). Thousand Oaks, CA: Sage.

Miller, S. M., & Kirsch, N. (1987). Sex differences in cognitive coping with stress. In R. C. Barnett & G. K. Baruch (Eds.), *Gender and stress* (pp. 278–302). New York: Free Press.

Miller-Bernal, L. (1992). *To be or not to be a feminist: Students' views of feminism.* Paper presented at the Annual Meeting of the American Sociological Association, Pittsburgh, PA.

Millman, M., & Kanter, R. M. (Eds.) (1975). *Another voice.* New York: Anchor.

Minority enrollment drops. (1997, November 2). *Atlanta Constitution.*

Minority women lag white men and women in management circles. (1997, October 22). New York: Associated Press. (Internet).

Minton, H. L. (1992). The emergence of gay and lesbian studies. In H. L. Minton (Ed.), *Gay and lesbian studies* (pp. 1–6). New York: Haworth Press.

Mintz, L. B., & Betz, N. E. (1986). Sex differences in the nature, realism, and correlates of body image. *Sex Roles, 15,* 185–195.

Mitchell, A. (1998, February 17). Congresswoman angry over silence on scandal. *New York Times,* p. A12.

Mitchell, F. (1997). Keeping it all in the family: Sexual harassment policies and informal resolution in small colleges. *NWSA Journal, 9,* 118–125.

Mitchell, J. (1974). *Psychoanalysis and feminism.* New York: Random House.

Mohanty, C. T. (1991). Cartographies of struggle: Third World women and the politics of feminism. In C. T. Mohanty, A. Russo, & L. Torres (Eds.), *Third World women and the politics of feminism* (pp. 1–47). Bloomington: Indiana University Press.

Mohr, J. (1978). *Abortion in America.* New York: Oxford University Press.

Moir, A., & Jessel, D. (1989). *Brain sex.* London: Carol Publishing Group.

Mollenkott, V. R. (1991). Heterosexism: A challenge to ecumenical solidarity. In M. A. May (Ed.), *Women and church* (pp. 38–42). Grand Rapids, MI: Wm. B. Eerdmans Publishing Co.

Money, J., & Ehrhardt, A. A. (1972). *Man and woman, boy and girl.* Baltimore: Johns Hopkins University Press.

Money, J., & Matthews, D. (1982). Prenatal exposure to virilizing progestins: An adult follow-up study on twelve young women. *Archives of Sexual Behavior, 11,* 73–83.

Montgomery, R. J. V., & Datwyler, M. M. (1990, Summer). Women and men in the caregiving role. *Generations 14,* pp. 34–38.

Moore, A. M. (1997). Intimate violence: Does socioeconomic status matter? In A. P. Cardarelli (Ed.), *Violence between intimate partners* (pp. 90–100). Boston: Allyn and Bacon.

Moore, M. (1997). Student resistance to course content: Reactions to the gender of the messenger. *Teaching Sociology, 25,* 128–133.

Morash, M., & Haarr, R. (1995). Gender, workplace problems, and stress in policing. *Justice Quarterly, 12,* 113–140.

Morello, C., & Katel, P. (1998, March 20). Warning signals were simply seen as boyhood bravado. *USA Today,* pp. 1A–2A.

Morello, K. B. (1986). *The invisible bar: The woman lawyer in America.* New York: Random House.

Morgan, M. (1982). Television and adolescents' sex-role stereotypes: A longitudinal study. *Journal of Personality and Social Psychology, 43,* 947–955.

Morgan, M., Rapkin, A. J., & Goldman, L. (1996). Cognitive functioning in premenstrual syndrome. *Obstetrics and Gynecology, 88,* 961–966.

Morrissey, E.. (1986). Power and control through discourse: The case of drinking and drinking problems among women. *Contemporary Crises, 10,* 157–179.

Mosher, D. L., & Sirkin, M. (1984). Measuring a macho personality constellation. *Journal of Research in Personality, 18,* 150–163.

Moyer, I. L. (1991). *Women's prisons: Issues and controversies.* Paper presented at the Annual Meeting of the American Society of Criminology, San Francisco, CA.

Moyo, M. (1996, November 21). Gender equality polarizing women. Bulawayo, Zimbabwe: PanAfrican News Agency. (Internet).

Mueller, C. (1991). The gender gap and women's political influence. *The Annals of the American Academy of Political and Social Science, 515,* 23–37.

Munt, S. R. (1996). Beyond backlash: Lesbian studies in the United Kingdom. In B. Zimmerman & T. A. H. McNaron (Eds.), *The new lesbian studies* (pp. 234–239). New York: Feminist Press.

Murray, S. O. (1996). *American gay.* Chicago: University of Chicago Press.

Murphy, B. O. (1994). Women's magazines: Confusing differences. In L. H. Turner & H. M. Sterk (Eds.), *Differ-*

ences that make a difference (pp. 119–128). Westport, CT: Bergin and Garvey.

Mydans, S. (1992, November 21). Quietly, Christian conservatives win hundreds of local elections. *New York Times,* pp. 1, 9.

Mydans, S. (1994, March 13). Female agents sue F.B.I., alleging discrimination. *New York Times,* p. 28.

Mydans, S. (1996, October 10). Blame men, not Allah, Islamic feminists say. *New York Times,* p. A4.

Myers, D. J., & Dugan, K. B. (1996). Sexism in graduate school classrooms: Consequences for students and faculty. *Gender & Society, 10,* 330–350

Myers, M. A., & Talarico, S. M. (1986). The social contexts of racial discrimination in sentencing. *Social Problems, 33,* 236–251.

Myers, S. L. (1997, December 16). Pentagon is urged to separate sexes. *New York Times,* pp. A1–26.

Nagel, S., & Weitzman, L. J. (1972). The double standard of American justice. *Society, 9,* 171–198.

Nanda, S. (1990). *Neither man nor woman: The Hijras of India.* Belmont, CA: Wadsworth.

National Collegiate Athletic Association (NCAA). (1992). *NCAA gender-equity study: Summary of results.* Overland Park, KS: NCAA.

National Demographics and Lifestyles. (1994). *The lifestyle market analyst.* Wilmette, IL: SRDS.

National Institute Against Prejudice and Violence. (1990, January–February). Group violence in the U.S.A. *NIAPV Forum,* pp. 1, 56.

National Opinion Research Center. (1989). *General social survey.* Chicago: Author.

Natividad, I. (1992). Women of color and the campaign trail. In P. Ries & A. J. Stone (Eds.), *The American woman, 1992–93* (pp. 127–148). New York: W. W. Norton.

Nature of clothing isn't evidence in rape cases, Florida law says. (1990, June 3). *New York Times,* p. 30.

Navarro, M. (1996, April 4). Abortion clinics report drop in harassing incidents. *New York Times,* p. B14.

Nechas, E., & Foley, D. (1994). *Unequal treatment.* New York: Simon and Schuster.

Neighbors, H. W. (1997). Husbands, wives, family, and friends: Sources of stress, sources of support. In R. J. Taylor, J. S. Jackson, & L. M. Chatters (Eds.), *Family life in Black America* (pp. 277–292). Thousand Oaks, CA: Sage.

Nelson, M. (1979). Why witches were women. In J. Freeman (Ed.), *Women: A feminist perspective* (2nd ed.) (pp. 451–468). Palo Alto, CA: Mayfield.

Nelson, M. B. (1992). *Are we winning yet?* New York: Random House.

Nemy, E. (1992, June 18). "What? Me Marry?" Widows Say No. *New York Times,* p. C1, C8.

Neuberger, J. (1983). Women in Judaism: The fact and the fiction. In P. Holden (Ed.), *Women's religious experience: Cross-cultural perspectives* (pp. 132–142). London: Croom Helm.

Nevels, L. (1990). *Mentoring relationships and women.* Paper presented at the Annual Meeting of the Mid-Atlantic Association of Student Officers of Housing, Women's Issues Group, Glasboro, NJ.

New Zealand judge: Rape as exciting. (1996, July 7). Wellington, New Zealand: Reuters. (Internet)

Nicholi, A. M. (1991). The impact of family dissolution on the emotional health of children and adolescents. In B. J. Christensen (Ed.), *When families fail . . . The social costs* (pp. 27–41). New York: University Press of America.

Nichols, P. C. (1986). Women in their speech communities. In S. McConnell-Ginet, R. Borker, & N. Furman (Eds.), *Women and language in literature and society* (pp. 140–149). New York: Greenwood.

Nicoloff, L. K., & Stiglitz, E. A. (1987). Lesbian alcoholism: Etiology, treatment, and recovery. In Boston Lesbian Psychologies Collective (Eds.), *Lesbian psychologies* (pp. 283–293). Urbana: University of Illinois Press.

Niebuhr, G. (1996a, May 8). Open attitude on homosexuality makes pariahs of some churches. *New York Times*, pp. A1, B13.

Niebuhr, G. (1996b, April 25). Methodists keep rule against homosexuality. *New York Times*, p. A16.

Niebuhr, G. (1996c, May 28). Episcopal bishop hails victory on gay priests. *New York Times*, p. B4.

Niebuhr, G. (1997, October 12). Rabbis still resist interfaith marriage, study shows. *New York Times*, p. 28.

Niebuhr, G. (1998, April 17). Laws aside, some in clergy quietly bless gay "marriage." *New York Times*, pp. A1, 20.

Nieves-Squires, S. (1991). *Hispanic women: Making their presence on campus less tenuous*. Washington, DC: Association of American Colleges and Universities.

Nilsen, A. P. (1991). Sexism in English: A 1990s update. In E. Ashton-Jones & G. A. Olson (Eds.), *The gender reader* (pp. 259–270). Boston: Allyn and Bacon.

Niven, D. (1998). *The missing majority: The recruitment of women as state legislative candidates*. Westport, CT: Praeger.

Norris, J., & Kerr, K. L. (1991). *Hypermasculinity and violent pornography: Does alcohol consumption affect macho men's judgments?* Paper presented at the Annual Meeting of the American Society of Criminology, San Francisco, CA.

Nossiter, A. (1996, September 27). 6-year-old's sex crime: Innocent peck on cheek. *New York Times*, p. A14.

Norton, M. B. (1997). *Founding mothers and fathers*. New York: Alfred A. Knopf.

Oakley, A. (1980). *Becoming a mother*. New York: Schocken.

Odeon, K. (1997). *Great books for girls*. New York: Ballantine Books.

Offen, K. (1988). Defining feminism: A comparative historical approach. *Signs, 14*, 119–157.

Ogden, A. S. (1986). *The great American housewife*. Westport, CT: Greenwood.

Older Women's League. (1989). *Failing America's caregivers: A status report on women who care. Mother's day report 1989*. Washington, DC: Older Women's League.

O'Leary, K. D. (1993). Through a psychological lens: Personality traits, personality disorders, and sources of violence. (pp. 7–30). In R. J. Gelles & D. R. Loseke (Eds.), *Current controversies on domestic violence*. Newbury Park, CA: Sage.

O'Neill, W. L. (1969). *Everyone was brave*. New York: Quadrangle.

Onishi, N. (1996, October 3). Harassment in 2d grade? Queens kisser is pardoned. *New York Times*, pp. A1, B8.

Onishi, N. (1997, February 16). Reading Torah, women's group tests tradition. *New York Times*, pp. 43, 49.

Orenstein, P. (1994). *Schoolgirls: Young women, self-esteem and the confidence gap*. New York: Anchor/Doubleday.

Osmond, M. W., Wambach, K. G., Harrison, D. F., Byers, J., Levine P., Imershein, A., &. Quadagno, D. M. (1993).

The multiple jeopardy of race, class, and gender for AIDS risk among women. *Gender & Society, 7*, 99–120.

Ovens, H. J., & Permaul-Woods, J. A. (1997). Emergency room physicians and sexual involvement with patients: An Ontario study. *Canadian Medical Association Journal, 157*, 663–684.

Padevic, I. & Orcutt, J. D. (1997). Perceptions of sexual harassment in the Florida legal system: A comparison of dominance and spillover explanations. *Gender & Society, 11*, 682–698.

Padevic, I. A. (1992). White-collar work values and women's interest in blue-collar jobs. *Gender & Society, 6*, 215–230.

Padevic, I. A., & Reskin, B. F. (1990). Men's behavior and women's interest in blue-collar jobs. *Social Problems, 37*, 613–628.

Page, D. C., Fisher, E. M. C., McGillivray, B., & Brown, L. G. (1990). Additional deletion in sex-determining region of human Y chromosome resolves paradox of X,t(Y;22) female. *Nature, 346*, 279–281.

Pagelow, M. D. (1981). Secondary battering and alternatives of female victims to spouse abuse. In L. H. Bowker (Ed.), *Women and crime in America* (pp. 277–298). New York: Macmillan.

Pagels, E. (1979). What became of God the mother? In C. P. Christ & J. Plakow (Eds.), *Womanspirit rising* (pp. 107–119). San Francisco: Harper and Row.

Paglia, C. (1992). *Sex, art, and American culture*. New York: Vintage.

Palmer, L. (1993, November 7). The nurses of Vietnam, still wounded. *The New York Times Magazine*, pp. 36–43, 68, 72–73.

Papper, B., & Gerhard, M. (1997, October). Moving forward, falling back. *RTNDA Communicator*, pp. 25–30.

Paradise, L. V, & Wall, S. M. (1986). Children's perceptions of male and female principals and teachers. *Sex Roles, 14*, 1–7.

Parlee, M. B. (1982, September). New findings: Menstrual cycles and behavior. *Ms.*, pp. 126–128.

Parlee, M. B. (1983). Changes in moods and activation levels during the menstrual cycle in experimentally naive subjects. *Psychology of Women Quarterly, 7*, 119–131.

Parsons, T. (1955). The American family: Its relations to personality and to the social structure. In T. Parsons & R. F. Bales (Eds.), *Family, socialization and interaction process* (pp. 3–33). Glencoe, IL: The Free Press.

Patterson, C. J. (1992). Children of lesbian and gay parents. *Child Development, 63*, 1025–1042.

Patterson, P. (1996). Rambos and himbos: Stereotypical images of men in advertising. In P. M. Lester (Ed.), *Images that injure* (pp. 93–96). Westport, CT: Praeger.

Paul, M., Daniels, C., & Rosofsky, R. (1989). Corporate response to reproductive hazards in the workplace: Results of the family, work, and health survey. *American Journal of Industrial Medicine, 16*, 267–280.

Pear, R. (1987, March 22). Number of Blacks in top jobs in administration off sharply. *New York Times*, p. 30.

Pearlman, S. F. (1987). The saga of continuing clash in the lesbian community, or will an army of exlovers fail? In Boston Lesbian Psychologies Collective (Eds.), *Lesbian psychologies* (pp. 313–326). Urbana, IL: University of Illinois Press.

Peck, S. (1985). *Halls of jade, walls of stone: Women in China today*. New York: Franklin Watts.

Peplau, L. A. (1986). What homosexuals want. In L. Simkins (Ed.), *Alternative sexual lifestyles* (pp. 118–123). Acton, MA: Copley Publishing Group.

Perception: Crime rate rising. (1993, October 28). *USA Today*, p. 6A.

Peretti, P. O., & Sydney, T. M. (1985). Parental toy choice stereotyping and its effects on child toy preference and sex-role typing. *Social Behavior and Personality, 12,* 213–216.

Perlez, J. (1991, July 29). Kenyans do some soul-searching after the rape of 71 schoolgirls. *New York Times,* pp. A1, 7.

Perry, D. G., & Bussey, K. (1979). The social learning theory of sex differences: Imitation is alive and well. *Journal of Personality and Social Psychology, 37,* 1699–1712.

Petro, C. S., & Putnam, B. A. (1979). Sex-role stereotypes: Issues of attitudinal changes. *Signs, 5,* 41–50.

Pfost, K. S., & Fiore, M. (1990). Pursuit of nontraditional occupations: Fear of success or fear of not being chosen? *Sex Roles, 23,* 15–24.

Philips, R. D., & Gilroy, F. D. (1985). Sex-role stereotypes and clinical judgments of mental health: The Brovermans' findings reexamined. *Sex Roles, 12,* 179–193.

Phillips, P. (1998). *Censored, 1998.* New York: Seven Stories Press.

Phillips, S. P., & Schneider, M. S. (1993). Sexual harassment of female doctors by patients. *New England Journal of Medicine, 329,* 1936–1939.

Picard, A. (1997, October 9). Gang rape nets 2-year sentences. *Globe and Mail.*

Pike, D. L. (1992). Women in police academy training: Some aspects of organizational response. In I. L. Moyer (Ed.), *The changing roles of women in the criminal justice system* (pp. 261–280). Prospect Heights, IL: Waveland.

Pillemer, K., & Finkelhor, D. (1988). The prevalence of elder abuse: A random sample survey. *The Gerontologist, 28,* 51–57.

Pinccinelli, M., & Homen, F. G. (1997). *Nations for mental health: Gender differences in the epidemiology of affective disorders and schizophrenia.* Geneva: World Health Organization.

Pinel, J. P. J. (1997). *Biopsychology.* Boston: Allyn and Bacon.

Pliner, P., Chaiken, S., & Flett, G. L. (1990). Gender differences in concern with body weight and physical appearance over the life span. *Personality and Social Psychology Bulletin, 16,* 263–273.

Poe-Yamagata, E., & Butts, J. A. (1996). *Female offenders in the juvenile justice system.* Washington, DC: U.S. Department of Justice.

Pogrebin, L. C. (1982, February). Big changes in parenting. *Ms.,* pp. 41–46.

Pogrebin, L. C. (1992). *Deborah, Golda, and me: Being female and Jewish in America.* New York: Crown Publishers.

Pogrebin, R. (1997a, September 21). Adding sweat and muscle to a familiar formula. *New York Times,* pp. BU1, 14–15.

Pogrebin, R. (1997b, October 25). Success and the Black magazine. *New York Times,* pp. D1, 3.

Pohli, C. V. (1983). Church closets and back doors: A feminist view of Moral Majority women. *Feminist Studies, 9,* 529–558.

Polivy, Janet, & Herman, C. Peter (1985). Dieting and binging: A causal analysis. *American Psychologist, 40,* 193–201.

Poll: More women in politics. (1996, March 27). New York: Associated Press (Internet).

Pollard, D. S. (1990). Black women, interpersonal support, and institutional change. In J. Antler & S. K. Bilken (Eds.), *Changing education: Women as radicals and conservators* (pp. 257–276). New York: State University of New York Press.

Pollock-Byrne, J. M. (1990). *Women, prison and crime.* Pacific Grove, CA: Brooks/Cole.

Poole, K. T., & Zeigler, L. H. (1985). *Women, public opinion, and politics.* New York: Longman.

Pope, K. S., Sonne, J. L., & Holroyd, J. (1993). *Sexual feelings in psychotherapy.* Washington, DC: American Psychological Association.

Popkin, B. M., Siega-Riz, A. M., & Haines, P. S. (1996). A comparison of dietary trends among racial and socioeconomic groups in the United States. *New England Journal of Medicine, 335,* 716–720.

Porter, K. (1997). *Improvements in poverty and income in 1995 tempered by troubling long-term trends.* Washington, DC: Center on Budget and Policy Priorities.

Portrait of the electorate, 1992. (1992, November 5). *New York Times,* p. B9.

Portrait of the electorate, 1996. (1996, November 10). *New York Times,* p. 28.

Poussaint, A. F., & Comer, J. P. (1993). *Raising Black children.* New York: Plume.

Powers, A. (1993, February 14). No longer rock's playthings. *New York Times,* pp. H1, H34.

Pratt, N. F. (1980). Transitions in Judaism: The Jewish American woman through the 1930s. In J. W. James (Ed.), *Women in American religion* (pp. 207–228). Philadelphia: University of Pennsylvania Press.

Prentky, R. A., Knight, R. A., & Lee, A. F. S. (1997). *Child sexual molestation: Research issues.* Washington, DC: U.S. Department of Justice, National Institute of Justice.

President's Council on Physical Fitness and Sport. (1997). *Physical activity and sport in the lives of girls.* Washington, DC: U.S. Department of Health and Human Services.

Press, A. L. (1991). *Women watching television: Gender, class, and generation in the American television experience.* Philadelphia: University of Pennsylvania Press.

Prestage, J. L. (1991). In quest of African American political woman. *The Annals of the American Academy of Political and Social Science, 515,* 88–103.

Preston, J. A. (1995). Gender and the formation of a women's profession: The case of public school teaching. In J. A. Jacobs (Ed.), *Gender inequality at work* (pp. 379–407). Thousand Oaks, CA: Sage.

Price, B. R., Sokoloff, N. J., & Kuleshnyk, I. (1989, November). *Is police work changing as a result of women's contributions?* Paper presented at the Annual Meeting of the American Society of Criminology, Reno, NV.

Price-Bonham, S., & Skeen, P. (1982). Black and White fathers' attitudes toward children's sex roles. *Psychological Reports, 50,* 1187–1190.

Project on the Status and Education of Women. (1986). Studying men . . . formally. *On Campus With Women, 16*(#2), 11.

Punishment is 18 months for killing cheating wife. (1994, October 19). *New York Times,* p. A20.

Purcell, P., & Stewart, L. (1990). Dick and Jane in 1989. *Sex Roles, 22,* 177–185.

Pyke, K. D. (1994). Women's employment as gift or burden? *Gender & Society, 8,* 73–91.

Quality of day care affects child development. (1997, April 4). Washington, DC: Reuters. (Internet).

Quebec to appeal rape case. (1997, October 9). *Toronto Star*, p. A33.

Quester, G. H. (1982). The problem. In N. L. Goldman (Ed.), *Female soldiers—combatants or noncombatants?* (pp. 217–236). Westport, CT: Greenwood Press.

Quinn, F. X. (1998, February 11). Maine voters repeal gay rights law. *Atlanta Constitution*, p. 1.

Quinn, P., & Allen, K. R. (1989). Facing challenges and making compromises: How single mothers endure. *Family Relations, 38*, 390–395.

Rabbi group OKs gay unions. (1996, March 28). Philadelphia: Associated Press. (Internet).

Ragins, B. R., & Scandura, T. A. (1995). Antecedents and work-related correlates of reported sexual harassment: An empirical investigation of competing hypotheses. *Sex Roles, 32*, 429–455.

Raiborn, M. H. (1990). *Revenues and expenses of intercollegiate athletics programs*. Overland Park, KS: The National Collegiate Athletic Association.

Raines, H. (1983, November 27). Poll shows support for political gains by women in U.S. *New York Times*, pp. 1, 40.

Ramos, I., & Lambating, J. (1996). Risk taking: gender differences and educational opportunity. *School Science and Mathematics, 96*, 94–98.

Rankin, D. (1987, May 31). Living together as a way of life. *New York Times*, p. F11.

Raskin, P. A., & Israel, A. C. (1981). Sex-role imitation in children: Effects of sex of child, sex of model, and sex-role appropriateness of modeled behavior. *Sex Roles, 7*, 1067–1077.

Rayman, P. (1993). *Pathways for women in the sciences*. Wellesley, MA: Center for Research on Women.

Raymond, J. G. (1990). Fetalists and feminists: They are not the same. In S. Ruth (Ed.), *Issues in feminism* (pp. 257–261). Mountain View, CA: Mayfield.

Rayner, B. (1997, August 10). Stamping out scourge of genital mutilation aid worker educates men, women about dangers of female circumcision. *Ottawa Sun*.

Real, T. (1997). *I don't want to talk about it*. New York: Scribner.

Recer, P. (1997, April 4). Studies find children of lesbian couples well-adjusted. *Rocky Mountain News*, p. 36A.

Reid, G. M. (1994). Maternal sex-stereotyping of newborns. *Psychological Reports, 75*, 1443–1450.

Reid, P. T. (1982). Socialization of Black female children. In P. Berman (Ed.), *Women: A developmental perspective* (pp. 137–155). Bethesda, MD: National Institutes of Health.

Reid, R. L., & Yen, S. S. C. (1981). Premenstrual syndrome. *American Journal of Obstetrics and Gynecology, 139*, 85–104.

Reid, S. T. (1987). *Criminal justice*. St. Paul, MN: West.

Reilly, M. E., Lott, B., & Gallogly, S. M. (1986). Sexual harassment of university students. *Sex Roles, 15*, 333–358.

Reinharz, S. (1992). *Feminist methods in social research*. New York: Oxford University Press.

Reiss, I. L. (1986). *Journey into sexuality: An exploratory voyage*. Englewood Cliffs, NJ: Prentice-Hall.

Renzetti, C. M. (1987). New wave or second stage? Attitudes of college women toward feminism. *Sex Roles, 16*, 265–277.

Renzetti, C. M. (1992). *Violent betrayal: Partner abuse in lesbian relationships*. Newbury Park, CA: Sage.

Renzetti, C. M. (1996). The poverty of services for battered lesbians. *Journal of Gay and Lesbian Social Services, 4*, 61–68.

Renzetti, C. M., & Curran, D. J. (1986). Structural constraints on legislative reform. *Contemporary Crises, 10*, 137–155.

Renzetti, C. M. & Curran, D. J. (1998). *Living sociology*. Boston: Allyn and Bacon.

Reskin, B. (1993). Sex segregation in the workplace. *Annual Review of Sociology, 19*, 241–270.

Reskin, B. A., &. Hartmann, H. I. (Eds.) (1986). *Women's work, men's work: Sex segregation on the job*. Washington, DC: National Academy Press.

Reskin, B. F., & Roos, P. A. (1990). *Job queues, gender queues: Explaining women's inroads into male occupations*. Philadelphia: Temple University Press.

Rheingold, H. L., & Cook, K. V. (1975). The content of boys' and girls' rooms as an index of parents' behavior. *Child Development, 46*, 459–463.

Rhoads, S. E. (1994). *Incomparable worth*. New York: Cambridge University Press.

Rhode, D. L. (1997). *Speaking of sex*. Cambridge, MA: Harvard University Press.

Rhodes, J. (1991). Television's realist portrayal of African-American women and the case of "L.A. Law." *Women and Language, 14*, 29–34.

Riding, A. (1992, November 17). New catechism for Catholics defines sins of the modern world. *New York Times*, pp. A1, A17.

Riding, A. (1993, January 9). European inquiry says Serbs' forces have raped 20,000. *New York Times*, pp. 1, 4.

Ries, P., & Stone, A. J. (Eds.) (1992). *The American woman, 1992–93*. New York: W. W. Norton.

Riger, S. (1988). Comment on "Women's History Goes to Trial: EEOC v. Sears, Roebuck and Company." *Signs, 13*, 897–903.

Riger, S., Foster-Fishman, P., Nelson-Kuna, J., & Curran, B. (1995). Gender bias in courtroom dynamics. *Law and Human Behavior, 19*, 465–480.

Rimer, S. (1993, December 8). Gay rights law for schools advances in Massachusetts. *New York Times*, p. A18.

Rimer, S. (1996, October 23). Blacks urged to act to increase awareness of the AIDS epidemic. *New York Times*, pp. A1, 16.

Rimer, S. (1997, November 25). Children of working poor are day care's forgotten. *New York Times*, pp. A1, 22.

Riordan, T. (1994, May 29). Even in a "big tent," little insults, little compromises. *New York Times*, p. F5.

Ripper, M. (1991). A comparison of the effect of the menstrual cycle and the social week on mood, sexual interest, and self-assessed performance. In D. L. Taylor & N. F. Woods (Eds.), *Menstruation, health, and illness* (pp. 19–33). New York: Hemisphere.

Risch, N., Wheeler, E. S., and Keats, B. J. B. (1993). Male sexual orientation and genetic evidence. *Science, 262*, 2063–2065.

Risen, J., & Thomas, J. L. (1998). *Wrath of angels*. New York: Basic Books.

Ritzer, G. (1980). *Sociology: A multi-paradigm science*. Boston: Allyn and Bacon.

Robert Wood Johnson Foundation. (1993). *Substance abuse: The nation's number one health problem*. Princeton, NJ: Author.

Roberts, S. (1995, April 27). Women's work: What's new, what isn't. *New York Times*, p. B6.

Robertson, C., Dyer, C. E., & Campbell, D. (1988). Campus harassment: Sexual harassment policies and procedures at institutions of higher learning. *Signs, 13,* 792–812.

Robertson, J., & Fitzgerald, L. F. (1990). The (mis)treatment of men: Effects of client gender role and lifestyle on diagnosis and attribution of pathology. *Journal of Counseling Psychology, 37,* 3–9.

Robinson, J. G., & McIlwee, J. S. (1989). Women in engineering: A promise unfulfilled? *Social Problems, 36,* 455–472.

Robinson, L. S. (1992). A good man is hard to find: Reflections on men's studies. In C. Kramarae & D. Spender (Eds.), *The knowledge explosion* (pp. 438–447). New York: Teachers College Press.

Robinson, R. A. (1996). Bearing witness to teen motherhood: The politics of violations of girlhood. In D. Dujon & A. Withorn (Eds.), *For crying out loud: Women's poverty in the United States* (pp. 107–119). Boston: South End Press.

Robinson, W. V., & Gosselin, P. G. (1998, Janaury 29). Many workplaces ban certain relationships. *Boston Globe,* p. A1.

Robson, R. (1992). *Lesbian (out)law.* Ithaca, NY: Firebrand Books.

Rogers, J. K., & Henson, K. D. (1997). "Hey, why don't you wear a shorter skirt?": Structural vulnerability and the organization of sexual harassment in temporary clerical employment. *Gender & Society, 11,* 215–237.

Rogers, L., & Walsh, J. (1982). Shortcomings of the psychomedical research of John Money and co-workers into sex differences in behavior: Social and political implications. *Sex Roles, 8,* 269–281.

Roiphe, K. (1993). *The morning after.* Boston: Little, Brown.

Roland, H. A. (1993*). Relationships of gender and rape with acceptance of sexual perceptions of music videos.* Paper presented at the Annual Meeting of the Association for Education in Journalism and Mass Communication.

Romero, M. (1992). *Maid in America.* New York: Routledge.

Roof, W. C., & Roof, J. L. (1984). Review of the polls: Images of God among Americans. *Journal for the Scientific Study of Religion, 23,* 201–205.

Roopnarine, J. L. (1984). Sex-typed socialization in mixed-age preschool classrooms. *Child Development, 55,* 1078–1084.

Roos, P. (1985). *Gender and work: A comparative analysis of industrial societies.* Albany: State University of New York Press.

Root, M. P. P. (1990). Disordered eating in women of color. *Sex Roles, 22,* 525–536.

Roscoe, W. (1991). *The Zuni man-woman.* Albuquerque: University of New Mexico Press.

Rosen, L. W., Shafer, C. L., Dummer, G. M., Cross, L. K., Deuman, G. W., & Malmberg, S. R. (1988). Prevalence of athogenic weight-control behaviors among Native American women and girls. *International Journal of Eating Disorders, 7,* 807–811.

Rosenberg, H. G. (1984). The home is the workplace: Hazards, stress, and pollutants in the household. In W. Chavkin (Ed.), *Double exposure* (pp. 219–245). New York: Monthly Review Press.

Rosenberg, J., Perlstadt, H., & Phillips, W. R. F. (1993). Now that we are here: Discrimination, disparagement, and harassment at work and the experience of women lawyers. *Gender & Society, 7,* 415–433.

Rosenfeld R. A., & Kalleberg, A. L. (1991). Gender inequality in the labor market: A cross-national perspective. *Acta Sociologica, 34,* 207–225.

Rosenfeld, R. A., & Spenner, K. I. (1992). Occupational sex segregation and women's early-career job shifts. *Work and Occupations, 19,* 424–449.

Rosenhan, D. L. (1973). On being sane in insane places. *Science, 179,* 250–258.

Rosenwasser, S. M., Rogers, R. Fling, S., Silvers-Pickens, K., & Butemeyer, J. (1987). Attitudes toward women and men in politics: Perceived male and female candidate competencies and participant personality characteristics. *Political Psychology, 8,* 191–200.

Rospenda, K. M., Richman, J. A., & Nawyn, S. J. (1998). Doing power: The confluence of gender, race, and class in contrapower sexual harassment. *Gender & Society, 12,* 40–60.

Ross, C. E., & Bird, C. E. (1994). Sex stratification and health lifestyle: Consequences for men's and women's perceived health. *Journal of Health and Social Behavior, 35,* 161–178.

Rosser, P. (1989). *The SAT gender gap: Identifying the causes.* Washington, DC: Center for Women Policy Studies.

Rossi, A. S. (1973). *The feminist papers.* New York: Bantam.

Rossi, A. S., & Rossi, P. E. (1977). Body time and social time: Mood patterns by menstrual cycle phase and day of the week. *Social Science Research, 6,* 273–308.

Rossi, P. (1989). *Down and out in America: The origins of homelessness.* Chicago: University of Chicago Press.

Rothblum, E. D. (1982). Women's socialization and the prevalence of depression: The feminine mistake. *Women and Therapy, 1,* 5–13.

Rothman, B. K. (1984). Women, health and medicine. In J. Freeman (Ed.), *Women: A feminist perspective* (pp. 70–80). Palo Alto, CA: Mayfield.

Rothman, B. K. (1989). *Recreating motherhood.* New York: W. W. Norton.

Rothman, B. K. (1992). *Now available in the freezer section: Packaging the frozen embryo.* Paper presented at the Annual Meeting of the American Sociological Association, Pittsburgh, PA.

Rowbotham, S. (1989). *The past before us: Feminism in action since the 1960s.* London: Unwin Hyman.

Rowbotham, S. (1997). *A century of women in Britain and the United States.* New York: Viking.

Rubin, G. (1975). The traffic in women. In R. R. Reiter (Ed.), *Toward an anthropology of women* (pp. 157–211). New York: Monthly Review Press.

Rubin, J. Z., Provenzano, F. J., & Luria, Z. (1974). The eye of the beholder: Parents' views on sex of newborns. *American Journal of Orthopsychiatry, 44,* 512–519.

Rubin, L. (1991). *Erotic wars.* New York: Harper Row.

Rubin, R. T., Reinisch, J. M., & Haskett, R. F. (1981). Postnatal gonadal steroid effects on human behavior. *Science, 211,* 1318–1324.

Ruble, D. N. (1977). Menstrual symptoms: A reinterpretation. *Science, 197,* 291–292.

Ruether, R. R. (1988). *Women-church.* San Francisco: Harper and Row.

Ruhlman, M. (1997). *Boys themselves: A return to single-sex education.* New York: Henry Holt and Company.

Runfola, R. (1980). The Black athlete as super-machismo symbol, In D. S. Sabo & R. Runfola (Eds.), *Jock: Sports and male identity* (pp. 79–88). Englewood Cliffs, NJ: Prentice-Hall.

Rush, S. E. (1998, Winter). Why can't you see her? A mother assails color blindness in schools. *Outlook,* pp. 5–7.

Rushton, J. P., & Ankney, C. D. (1996). Brain size and cognitive ability: Correlations with age, sex, social class and race. *Psychonomic Bulletin and Review, 3*, 21–36.

Russell, D. E. H. (1986). *The secret trauma.* New York: Basic Books.

Russell, D. E. H. (1990). *Rape in marriage.* (rev. ed.) Bloomington, IN: Indiana University Press.

Russell, D. E. H. (1993). Introduction. In D. E. H. Russell (Ed.), *Making violence sexy,* (pp. 1–20). New York: Teachers College Press.

Rustad, M. (1982). *Women in khaki.* New York: Praeger.

Ruzek, S. (1987. Feminist visions of health: An international perspective. In J. Mitchell & A. Oakley (Eds.), *What is feminism? A re-examination* (pp. 184–207). New York: Pantheon.

Ryan, L. T. (1994, February 20). Swimsuit model or victim stories, who will cover for me? *New York Times,* p. S11.

Rynbrandt, L. J., & Kramer, R. C. (1995). Hybrid non-women and corporate violence: The silicone breast implant case. *Violence Against Women, 1,* 206–227.

Sachs, A., & Wilson, J. H. (1978). *Sexism and the law.* New York: The Free Press.

Sacks, K. (1979). *Sisters and wives.* Westport, CT: Greenwood Press.

Sadker, M., & Sadker, D. (1994). *Failing at fairness.* New York: Charles Scribner's Sons.

Saletan, W. (1998). Electoral politics and abortion: Narrowing the message. In R. Solinger (Ed.), *Abortion wars: A half century of struggle, 1950–2000* (pp. 111–123). Berkeley, CA: University of California Press.

Saltzman, A. (1996a, July 8). A look at the research: Lots on girls, little on boys. *U.S. News and World Report,* pp. 52–53.

Saltzman, A. (1996b, August 19). Life after the lawsuit. *U.S. News and World Report,* pp. 57–61.

Samuels, S. U. (1995). *Fetal rights, women's rights: Gender equality in the workplace.* Madison, WI: University of Wisconsin Press.

Sanday, P. R. (1981). *Female power and male dominance: On the origins of sexual inequality.* New York: Cambridge University Press.

Sanday, P. R. (1990). *Fraternity gang rape: Sex, brotherhood, and privilege on campus.* New York: New York University Press.

Sanday, P. R. (1996a). Rape-prone versus rape-free campus cultures. *Violence Against Women, 2,* 191–208.

Sanday, P. R. (1996b). *A woman scorned.* New York: Doubleday.

Sandmair, M. (1980). *The invisible alcoholics.* New York: McGraw Hill.

Sanders, M., & Rock, M. (1988). *Waiting for prime time: The women of television news.* New York: Harper Collins.

Sandler, B. R., & Hall, R. M. (1986). *The campus climate revisited: Chilly for women faculty administrators, and graduate students.* Washington, DC: Project on the Status and Education of Women.

Sanger, D. E. (1994, May 27). Job-seeking women in Japan finding more discrimination. *New York Times,* p. A9.

Sapiro, V. (1986). *Women in American society.* Palo Alto, CA: Mayfield.

Sarbin, T. R., & Miller, J. E. (1970). Demonism revisited: The XYY chromosomal anomaly. *Issues in Criminology, 5,* 170–195.

Sargent, J. D., & Blanchflower, D. G. (1994). Obesity and stature in adolescence and earnings in young adulthood: Analysis of a British birth cohort. *Archives of Pediatric and Adolescent Medicine, 148,* 681–687.

Sarri, R. C. (1986). Gender and race differences in criminal justice processing. *Women's Studies International Forum, 9,* 89–99.

Saussy, C. (1991). *God images and self esteem.* Louisville, KY: Westminster/John Knox.

Sayer, S. (1996). "Out of the blue": Lesbian studies in Aotearoa/New Zealand. In B. Zimmerman & T. A. H. McNaron (Eds.), *The new lesbian studies* (pp. 240–243). New York: Feminist Press.

Sayers, J. (1987). Science, sexual difference, and feminism. (pp. 68–91) In B. B. Hess & M. M. Ferree (Eds.), *Analyzing gender.* Newbury Park, CA: Sage.

Schmalz, J. (1992, October 11). Gay politics goes mainstream. *The New York Times Magazine,* pp. 18–21, 29, 41–42, 50, 53.

Schmalz, J. (1993, March 5). Poll finds an even split on homosexuality's cause. *New York Times,* p. A14.

Schmitt, E. (1988, December 26). Suburbs wrestle with steep rise in the homeless. *New York Times,* pp. 1, 36.

Schmitt, E. (1994a, January 14). Aspin moves to open many military jobs to women. *New York Times,* p. A22.

Schmitt, E. (1994b, May 9). Gay troops say the revised policy is often misused. *New York Times,* pp. A1, 14.

Schmitt, E. (1995, March 13). The new rules on gay soldiers: A year later, no clear results. *New York Times,* pp. A1, 16.

Schneider, F., Gur, R. C., Gur, R. E., & Muenz, L. R. (1994). Standardized mood induction with happy and sad facial expressions. *Psychiatry Research, 51,* 19–31.

School program in San Francisco seeks to reassure gay youths. (1996, May 19). *New York Times,* p. 17.

Schools' books on gay families stir Seattle. (1997, November 2). *New York Times,* p. 24.

Schoolyard teasing now has a new name. (1994, June 3). *CQ Researcher,* pp. 494–496.

Schrof, J. M. (1993, September 27). Feminism's daughters. *U.S. News and World Report,* p. 68.

Schrott, H. G., Bittner, V., Vittinghoff, E., Herrington, D. M., & Hulley, S. (1997). Adherence to National Cholesterol Education Program treatment goals in postmenopausal women with heart disease: The Heart and Estrogen/Progestin Replacement Study (HERS). *Journal of the American Medical Association, 277,* 1281–1286.

Schuppel, R., Buchele, G., & Koenig, W. (1998). Sex differences in selection of pacemakers: A retrospective observational study. *British Medical Journal, 316,* 1492–1495.

Schur, E. M. (1984). *Labeling women deviant.* New York: Random House.

Schussler Fiorenza, E. (1979). Women in the early Christian movement. In C. P. Christ & J. Plaskow (Eds.), *Womanspirit rising* (pp. 84–92). San Francisco: Harper and Row.

Schussler Fiorenza, E. (1983). *In memory of her: A feminist theological reconstruction of Christian origins.* New York: Crossroad.

Schuster, M. A., Bell, R. M., & Kanouse, D. E. (1996). The sexual practices of adolescent virgins: Genital sexual activities of high school students who have never had vaginal intercourse. *American Journal of Public Health, 86,* 1570–1576.

Schwager, S. (1987). Educating women in America. *Signs, 12,* 333–372.

Schwartz, L. A., & Markham, W. T. (1985). Sex stereotyping in children's toy advertisements. *Sex Roles, 12,* 157–170.

Schwartz, L. M., Fisher, E. S., & Wright, B. (1997). Treatment and health outcomes of women and men in a cohort with coronary artery disease. *Archives of Internal Medicine, 157,* 1545–1552.

Schwartz, M. D. (1988). Ain't got no class: Universal risk theories of battering. *Contemporary Crises, 12,* 373–392.

Schwartz, M. D., & DeKeseredy, W. S. (1997). *Sexual assault on the college campus.* Thousand Oaks, CA: Sage.

Schweder, R. A. (1997, March 9). It's called poor health for a reason. *New York Times,* p. E5.

Sciolino, E. (1990, January 25). Battle lines are shifting on women in war. *New York Times,* pp. A1, D23.

Sciolino, E. (1996, October 5). Political battle of the sexes is sharper than ever: For many White men Clinton's the reason to vote for Dole. *New York Times,* pp. 1, 24.

Sciolino, E. (1997, May 4). The Chanel under the chador. *New York Times Magazine,* pp. 46–51.

Scott, D. (1994). *The power of connections in corporate-government affairs: A gendered perspective.* Paper presented at the Annual Meeting of the American Sociological Association, Los Angeles, CA.

Scott, D. B. (1996). Shattering the instrumental-expressive myth: The power of women's networks in corporate-government affairs. *Gender & Society, 10,* 232–247.

Scott, K., & Schau, C. (1985). Sex equity and sex bias in instructional materials. In S. Klein (Ed.), *Handbook for achieving sex equity through education* (pp. 218–260). Baltimore, MD: Johns Hopkins University Press.

Scully, D., & Marolla, J. (1985). "Riding the bull at Gilley's": Convicted rapists describe the rewards of rape. *Social Problems, 32,* 251–263.

Sears, J. T. (1992). Educators, homosexuality, and homosexual students: Are personal feelings related to professional beliefs? In K. M. Harbeck (Ed.), *Coming out of the classroom closet: Gay and lesbian students, teachers, and curricula* (pp. 29–79). New York: Haworth Press.

Seavy, A. A., Katz, P. A., & Zalk, S. R. (1975). Baby X: The effect of gender labels on adult responses to infants. *Sex Roles, 1,* 103–109.

Seeking Corp. PAC money. (1986, Spring). *Women's Political Times,* p. 6.

Seelye, K. Q. (1998, July 18). Republicans introduce two bills in fight against homosexuality. *New York Times,* p. A12.

Segal, L. (1990). *Slow motion.* New Brunswick, NJ: Rutgers University Press.

Segregation anew. (1997, June 1). *New York Times,* p. 16E.

Segura, D. A., & Pierce, J. L. (1993). Chicanao family structure and gender personality: Chodorow, familism, and psychoanalytic sociology revisited. *Signs, 19,* 62–91.

Seidler, V. J. (1991). *Recreating sexual politics.* London: Routledge.

Senn, C. Y. (1993). The research on women and pornography: The many faces of harm. In D. E. H. Russell (Ed.), *Making violence sexy* (pp. 179–193). New York: Teachers College Press.

Serbin, L. A., Moller, L., Powlishta, K., & Gulko, J. (1991). *The emergence of gender segregation and behavioral compatibility in toddlers' peer preferences.* Paper presented at the Annual Meeting of the Society for Research in Child Development, Seattle, WA.

Sergeant gets 25-year term for 6 rapes at Aberdeen. (1997, May 7). *New York Times,* p. A18.

Sex offender MDs still practicing. (1997, June 4). Washington, DC: Associated Press. (Internet).

Sexual harassment: Little boys, big corps. (1996, October 4). Washington, DC: Reuters. (Internet).

Shakin, M., Shakin, D. & Sternglanz, S. H. (1985). Infant clothing: Sex labeling for strangers. *Sex Roles, 12,* 955–964.

Shanley, M. L. (1993). "Surrogate mothering" and women's freedom: A critique of contracts for human reproduction. *Signs, 18,* 618–639.

Shapiro, H. (1997, December 12). Western Wall posters warn women against "inviting" harassment. *Jerusalem Post.*

Shapiro, L. (1990, May 28). Guns and dolls. *Newsweek,* pp. 56–65.

Shaywitz, B. A., Shaywitz, S. E., Pugh, K. R., Constable, R. T., Skudlarski, P., Fulbright, R. K., Bronen, R. A., Fletcher, J. M., Shakweiler, D. P., Katz, L., & Gore, J. C. (1995). Sex differences in the functional organization of the brain for language. *Nature, 373,* 607–608.

Sheldon, A. (1990). Pickle fights: Gendered talk in preschool disputes. *Discourse Processes, 13,* 5–31.

Shelton, B. A. (1992). *Women, men and time: Gender differences in paid work, housework and leisure.* Westport, CT: Greenwood.

Shelton, B. A., & John, D. (1993). Does marital status make a difference? *Journal of Family Issues, 14,* 401–420.

Shenon, P. (1994, August 16). China's mania for baby boys creates surplus of bachelors. *New York Times,* pp. A1, A8.

Shenon, P. (1997, February 26). New study faults Pentagon's gay policy. *New York Times,* p. A10.

Shenon, P. (1998, January 21). New finding on mixing sexes in military. *New York Times,* p. A12.

Sherman, B. L., & Dominick, J. R. (1986). Violence and sex in music videos: TV and rock 'n' roll. *Journal of Communication, 36,* 94–106.

Sherman, J. A. (1971). *On the psychology of women: A survey of empirical studies.* Springfield, IL: C. C. Thomas.

Sherman, J. A. (1982). Mathematics the critical filter: A look at some residues. *Psychology of Women Quarterly, 6,* 428–444.

Sherry, A., Lee., M., & Varikiotis, M. (1995, December 14). For lust or money. *Far Eastern Economic Review,* pp. 22–28.

Shilts, R. (1993). *Conduct unbecoming: Gays and lesbians in the military.* New York: St. Martin's Press.

Shulman, A. K. (1980). Sex and power: Sexual biases of radical feminism. *Signs, 5,* 590–604.

Sidel, R. (1986). *Women and children last.* New York: Penguin Books.

Sigel, R. S. (1996). *Ambition and accommodation: How women view gender relations.* Chicago: University of Chicago Press.

Signorelli, N. (1997). *A content analysis: Reflections of girls in the media*. Menlo Park, CA: Children Now and the Kaiser Family Foundation.

Silveira, J. (1980). Generic masculine words and thinking. *Women's Studies International Quarterly, 3*, 165–178.

Silverstein, B., Perdue, L., Peterson, B., & Kelly, E. (1986). The role of the mass media in promoting a thin standard of bodily attractiveness for women. *Sex Roles, 14*, 519–532.

Simon, R. (1975). *Women and crime*. Washington, DC: U.S. Government Printing Office.

Simon, R. J., & Danziger, G. (1991). *Women's movements in America*. New York: Praeger.

Simon, R. J., & Landis, J. (1991). *The crimes women commit, the punishments they receive*. Lexington, MA: Lexington Books.

Simons, M. (1997, December 31). Child care sacred as France cuts back the welfare state. *New York Times*, pp. A1, 8.

Since coming out is in, a guide for the TV audience. (1997, February 23). *New York Times*, p. E7.

Sinclair, A. H., Berta, P., Palmer, M. S., Hawkins, J. R., Griffiths, B. L., Smith, M. J., Foster, J. W., Frischauf, A., Lovell-Badge, R., & Goodfellow, P. N. (1990). A gene from the human sex-determining region encodes a protein with homology to a conserved DNA-binding motif. *Nature, 346*, 240–244.

Skitka, L. J., & Maslach, C. (1990). Gender roles and the categorization of gender-relevant behavior. *Sex Roles, 22*, 133–150.

Slocum, S. (1975). Woman the gatherer: Male bias in anthropology. In R. R. Reiter (Ed.), *Toward an anthropology of women* (pp. 36–50). New York: Monthly Review Press.

Small, M. A., & Tetreault, P. A. (1990). Social psychology, "marital rape exemptions," and privacy. *Behavioral Sciences and the Law, 8*, 141–149.

Smallwood, J. (1997, March 28). Women might leap early in future. *Philadelphia Daily News*, p. 126.

Smart, C. (1982). The new female offender: Reality or myth? In B. R. Price & N. J. Sokoloff (Eds.), *The criminal justice system and women* (pp. 105–116). New York: Clark Boardman.

Smith, D. E. (1993). The standard North American family. *Journal of Family Issues, 14*, 50–65.

Smith, E. (1982). The Black female adolescent. *Psychology of Women Quarterly, 6*, 261–288.

Smith, P. M. (1985). *Language, society, and the sexes*. New York: Basil Blackwell.

Smythe, M., & Meyer, J. (1994). On the origins of gender-linked language differences: Individual and contextual explanations. In L. H. Turner & H. M. Sterk (Eds.), *Differences that make a difference* (pp. 51–60). Westport, CT: Bergin and Garvey.

Smythe, T. C. (1996). Growing old in commericals: A joke not shared. In P. M. Lester (Ed.), *Images that injure* (pp. 113–118). Westport, CT: Praeger.

Snarey, J. (1993). *How fathers care for the next generation*. Cambridge: Harvard University Press.

Snell, T. L., & Morton, D. C. (1994). *Women in prison*. Washington, DC: U.S. Department of Justice.

Snell, W. E., Jr., Belk, S. S., & Hawkins, R. C. II (1987). Alcohol and drug use in stressful times: The influence of the masculine role and sex-related personality traits. *Sex Roles, 16*, 359–374.

Snow, J. T., & Harris, M. B. (1989). Disordered eating in southwestern Pueblo Indians and Hispanics. *Journal of Adolescence, 12*, 329–336.

Snow, M. (1992, October 6). Mindworks: Question on gender brings out stereotypes. *Minneapolis Star Tribune*, pp. 1E, 3E.

Snow, M. E., Jacklin, C. N., & Maccoby, E. E. (1983). Sex-of-child differences in father-child interaction at one year of age. *Child Development, 54*, 227–232.

Snyder, G. (1997). *Children's television commercials and gender-stereotyped messages*. Paper presented at the Annual Meeting of the Association for Education in Journalism and Mass Communication, Chicago, IL.

Snyder-Joy, Z. K., & Carlo, T. A. (1998). Parenting through prison walls: Incarcerated mothers and children's visitation programs. In S. L. Miller (Ed.), *Crime control and women* (pp. 130–150). Thousand Oaks, CA: Sage.

Sokoloff, N. J. (1992). *Black women and White women in the professions: Occupational segregation by race and gender, 1960–1980*. New York: Routledge, Chapman and Hall.

Sommer, B. (1983). How does menstruation affect cognitive competence and psychophysiological response. In S. Golub (Ed.), *Lifting the curse of menstruation* (pp. 53–90). New York: Haworth Press.

Sommers, C. H. (1994). *Who stole feminism?* New York: Simon and Schuster.

Song, Y. I. (1991). Single Asian American women as a result of divorce: Depression affect and changes in social support. In S. S. Volgy (Ed.), *Women and divorce, men and divorce* (pp. 219–230). New York: Haworth.

Sonne, J. L., & Pope, K. S. (1991). Treating victims of therapist-patient sexual involvement. *Psychotherapy, 28*, 174–187.

Sontag, D. (1993, September 27). Women asking U.S. asylum expand definition of abuse. *New York Times*, pp. A1, 13.

Sorenson, E. (1994). *Comparable worth: Is it a worthy policy?* Princeton, NJ: Princeton University Press.

Southern Baptists say women should "submit graciously" to their husbands. (1998, June 10). Salt Lake City, UT: Associated Press. (Internet).

Spanier, B. (1995). Biological determinism and homosexuality. *NWSA Journal, 7*, 54–71.

Spender, D. (1981). The GateKeepers: A feminist critique of academic publishing. In H. Roberts (Ed.), *Doing feminist research* (pp. 186–202). London: Routledge and Kegan Paul.

Sperry, R. (1982). Some effects of disconnecting the cerebral hemispheres. *Science, 217*, 1223–1226.

Spielberger, C., & London, P. (1985). Rage boomerangs. In C. Borg (Ed.), *Annual editions: Health 85/86* (pp. 77–79). Guilford, CT: The Dushkin Publishing Group.

Spohn, C. (1990). *An analysis of the "jury trial penalty" and its effects on Black and White defendants*. Paper presented at the Annual Meeting of the American Society of Criminology, Baltimore, MD.

Stacey, J. (1986). Are feminists afraid to leave home? The challenge of conservative pro-family feminism. In J. Mitchell & A. Oakley (Eds.), *What is feminism? A re-examination* (pp. 208–237). New York: Pantheon.

Stacey, J. (1990). *Brave new families*. New York: Basic Books.

Stacey, J., & Thorne, B. (1985). The missing feminist revolution in sociology. *Social Problems, 32*, 301–316.

Stanko, E. A. (1985). *Intimate intrusions*. London: Routledge and Kegan Paul.

Stanko, E. A. (1992). Intimidating education: Sexual harassment in criminology. *Journal of Criminal Justice Education, 3,* 331–340.

Stanko, E. A. (1996). Warnings to women: Police advice and women's safety in Britain. *Violence against Women, 2,* 5–24.

Stanko, E. A. (in press). Women, danger, and criminology. In C. M. Renzetti & L. Goodstein (Eds.), *Women, crime and justice: Contemporary perspectives.* Los Angeles, CA: Roxbury.

Stanley, L. (1992). The impact of feminism on sociology in the last 20 years. In C. Kramarae & D. Spender (Eds.), *The knowledge explosion: Generations of feminist scholarship* (pp. 254–269). New York: Teachers College Press.

Stansell, C. (1986). *City of women.* New York: Alfred A. Knopf.

Staples, R. (1995). Health among African American males. In D. Sabo & D. F. Gordon (Eds.), *Men's health and illness* (pp. 121–138). Thousand Oaks, CA: Sage.

Staples, R., & Jones, T. (1985). Culture, ideology and Black television images. *The Black Scholar, 16,* 10–20.

Starr, P. (1982). *The social transformation of American medicine.* New York: Basic Books.

Starhawk (1979). Witchcraft and women's culture. In C. P. Christ & J. Plaskow (Eds.), *Womanspirit rising* (pp. 259–268). San Francisco: Harper and Row.

Stark, E. (1990). Rethinking homicide: Violence, race, and the politics of gender. *International Journal of Health Services, 20,* 3–26.

Statham, A., Richardson, L., & Cook, J. A. (1991). *Gender and university teaching: A negotiated difference.* Albany: State University of New York Press.

Steenland, S. (1987). Women in broadcasting. In S. E. Rix (Ed.), *The American woman 1987–88* (pp. 215–221). New York: Norton.

Steffensmeier, D., Kramer, J., & Streifel, C. (1993). Gender and imprisonment decisions. *Criminology, 31,* 411–446.

Steffensmeier, D. J. (1982). Trends in female crime: It's still a man's world. In B. R. Price & N. J. Sokoloff (Eds.), *The criminal justice system and women* (pp. 117–130). New York: Clark Boardman.

Steil, J. M., & Turetsky, B. A. (1987). Marital influence levels and symptomatology among wives. In F. J. Crosby (Ed.), *Spouse, parent, worker: On gender and multiple roles* (pp. 74–90). New Haven: Yale University Press.

Stein, D. K. (1978). Women to burn: Suttee as a normative institution. *Signs, 4,* 253–268.

Steinbacher, R., & Gilroy, F. D. (1985). Preference for sex of child among primiparous women. *The Journal of Psychology, 119,* 541–547.

Steinberg, J. (1997, September 18). All-girls school may violate rights of boys, officials say. *New York Times,* pp. B1, B9.

Steinberg, R. J. (1990). The social construction of skill. *Work and Occupations, 17,* 449–482.

Steinberg, R., & Haignere, L. (1985). *Equitable compensation: Methodological criteria for comparable worth.* Paper presented at the conference on "Ingredients for Women's Employment Policy," Albany, NY.

Steinberg, R.J., & Cook, A. (1988). Policies affecting women's employment in industrial countries. In A. H. Stromberg & S. Harkess (Eds.), *Women working* (pp. 307–328). Mountain View, CA: Mayfield.

Steinem, G. (1978, November). Erotica and pornography: A clear and present difference. *Ms.,* pp. 53–54, 75–78.

Steinfels, P. (1992, July 19). Vatican condones some discrimination against homosexuals. *New York Times,* p. 7.

Steinfels, P. (1994, May 14). Female concept of God is shaking Protestants. *New York Times,* p. 8.

Steinfels, P. (1995a, November 19). Vatican says the ban on women as priests is "infallible" doctrine. *New York Times,* pp. 1, 13.

Steinfels, P. (1995b, November 14). Women wary about aiming to be priests. *New York Times,* p. A17.

Steinfels, P. (1996, May 12). New York to hear Mass in Latin, language of Catholic discontent. *New York Times,* pp. 1, 16.

Steinmetz, S. K. (1978). The battered husband syndrome. *Victimology, 2,* 499–509.

Steinmetz, S. K. (1993). The abused elderly are dependent: Abuse is caused by the perception of stress associated with providing care. In R. J. Gelles & D. R. Loseke (Eds.), *Current controversies on family violence* (pp. 222–236). Newbury Park, CA: Sage.

Stevens, P. E. (1998). The experiences of lesbians of color in health care encounters: Narrative insights for improving access and quality. *Journal of Lesbian Studies, 2.*

Stiehm, J. H. (1985). The generations of U.S. enlisted women. *Signs, 11,* 155–175.

Stillion, J. M. (1995). Premature death among males. In D. Sabo & D. F. Gordon (Eds.), *Men's health and illness* (pp. 46–67). Thousand Oaks, CA: Sage.

Stoddart, T., & Turiel, E. (1985). Children's concepts of cross-gender activities. *Child Development, 56,* 1241–1252.

Stolberg, S. G. (1997a, May 16). Senate tries to define fetal viability. *New York Times,* p. A18.

Stolberg, S. G. (1997b, December 14). For the infertile, a high-tech treadmill. *New York Times,* pp. 1, 36.

Stolberg, S. G. (1998, January 11). Shifting uncertainties in the abortion war. *New York Times,* p. WK3.

Stombler, M., & Martin, P. Y. (1994). Bringing women in, keeping women down: Fraternity "little sister" organizations. *Journal of Contemporary Ethnography, 23,* 150–185.

Stombler, M., & Padevic, I. (1994). *Getting a man or getting ahead: A comparative analysis of African American and Euro-American fraternity little sister programs on college campuses.* Paper presented at the Annual Meeting of the American Sociological Association, Los Angeles, CA.

Stone, L., & James, C. (1995). Dowry, bride-burning, and female power in India. *Women's Studies International Forum, 18,* 125–134.

Stone, M. (1976). *When God was a woman.* New York: Harcourt Brace Jovanovich.

Stoneman, Z., Brody, G. H., & MacKinnon, C. E. (1986). Same-sex and cross-sex siblings: Activity choices, roles, behavior, and gender stereotypes. *Sex Roles, 15,* 495–511.

Strate, L. (1992). Beer commercials. In S. Craig (Ed.), *Men, masculinity and media* (pp. 78–92). Newbury Park, CA: Sage.

Straus, M. A. (1993). Physical assaults by wives: A major social problem. In R. J. Gelles & D. R. Loseke (Eds.), *Current controversies on family violence* (pp. 67–87). Newbury Park, CA: Sage.

Straus, M. A., & Gelles, R. J. (1990). How violent are American families? Estimates from the National Family Violence Resurvey and other studies. In M. A. Straus & R. J. Gelles (Eds.), *Physical violence in American families* (pp. 95–132). New Brunswick, NJ: Transaction Publishers.

Straus, M. A., & Smith, C. (1990). Family patterns and child abuse. In M. A. Straus & R. J. Gelles (Eds.), *Physical violence in American families* (pp. 245–262). New Brunswick, NJ: Transaction Publishers.

Strauss-Noll, M. (1984). An illustration of sex bias in English. *Women's Studies Quarterly, 12*, 36–37.

Striegel-Moore, R. H., Silberstein, L. R., & Rodin, J. (1986). Toward an understanding of the risk factors in bulimia. *American Psychologist, 41*, 246–263.

Strober, M. H., & Arnold, C. L. (1987). The dynamics of occupational segregation among bank tellers. In C. Brown & J. A. Pechman (Eds.), *Gender in the workplace* (pp. 107–158). Washington, DC: The Brookings Institution.

Strober, M. H., & Lanford, A. G. (1986). The feminization of public school teaching: Cross-sectional analysis, 1850–1880. *Signs, 11*, 212–235.

Strober, M. H., & Tyack, D. (1980). Why do women teach and men manage? A report on research on schools. *Signs, 5*, 494–503.

Stunkard, A. J., Harris, J. R., Pedersen, N. L., & McClearn, G. E. (1990). The body-mass index of twins who have been reared apart. *The New England Journal of Medicine, 322*, 1483–1487.

Sudetic, C. (1995, November 28). Token clerk is threatened in 3d attack. *New York Time*, p. 1

Suffragette's racial remark haunts college. (1996, May 5). *New York Times*, p. 30.

Surprises in a study of life expectancies. (1997, December 4). *New York Times*, p. A24.

Sutker, P. B., Patsiokas, A. T., & Allain, A. N. (1981). Chronic illicit drug abusers: Gender comparisons. *Psychological Reports, 49*, 383–390.

Sutlive, V. H. (1991). *Female and male in Borneo*. Williamsburg, VA: The Borneo Research Council.

Swarns, R. L. (1998, April 14). Mothers poised for workfare acute lack of day care. *New York Times*, pp. A1, B8.

Syme, S. L., & Berkman, L. F. (1997). Social class, susceptibility, and sickness. In P. Conrad (Ed.), *The sociology of health and illness* (pp. 29–35). New York: St. Martin's Press.

Taeuber, C. M. (1992). *Sixty-five plus in America*. Washington, DC: U.S. Department of Commerce, Bureau of the Census.

Taeuber, C. M., & Valdisera, V. (1986). *Women in the American economy*. Current Population Reports, Series P-23, #146. Washington, DC: U.S. Government Printing Office.

Tallichet, S. E. (1995). Gendered relations in the mines and the division of labor underground. *Gender & Society, 9*, 697–711.

Tannen, D. (1990). *You just don't understand*. New York: William Morrow.

Tannen, D. (1994a). *Gender and discourse*. New York: Oxford University Press.

Tannen, D. (1994b). *Talking from 9 to 5*. New York: William Morrow and Company.

Tanner, N., & Zihlman, A. (1976). Women in evolution. Part I: Innovation and selection in human origins. *Signs, 1*, 585–608.

Tavris, C. (1992). *The mismeasure of woman*. New York: Simon and Schuster.

Taylor, V. (1990). The continuity of the American women's movement: An elite-sustained stage. In G. West & R. L. Blumberg (Eds.), *Women and social protest* (pp. 277–301). New York: Oxford University Press.

Taylor, V. (1996). *Rock-a-by-baby: Feminism, self-help and postpartum depression*. New York: Routledge.

Teilmann, K. S., & Landry, P. H., Jr. (1981). Gender bias in juvenile justice. *Journal of Research in Crime and Delinquency, 18*, 47–80.

Teltsch, K. (1992, July 22). As more people need care, more men help. *New York Times*, pp. B1, B4.

Terry, R. M. (1978). *Trends in female crime: A comparison of Adler, Simon, and Steffensmeier*. Paper presented at the Annual Meeting of the Society for the Study of Social Problems, San Francisco, CA.

Theberge, N. (1993). The construction of gender in sport: Women, coaching, and the naturalization of difference. *Social Problems, 40*, 301–313.

Theberge, N. (1997). "It's part of the game": Physicality and the production gender in women's hockey. *Gender & Society, 11*, 69–87.

The *Forbes* four hundred. (1996, October 14). *Forbes Magazine*, pp. 100–320.

The year of the Michaels. (1996, December 16). *Forbes Magazine*, pp. 244–249.

Thoits, P. A. (1987). Negotiating roles. In F. J. Crosby (Ed.), *Spouse, parent, worker: On gender and multiple roles* (pp. 11–22). New Haven: Yale University Press.

Thomas, D. (1993). *Not guilty: The case in defense of men*. New York: Morrow.

Thompson, B. W. (1994). *A hunger so wide and so deep: American women speak out on eating problems*. Minneapolis: University of Minnesota Press.

Thompson, C. (1964). *Interpersonal psychoanalysis: The selected papers of Clara M. Thompson*. New York: Basic.

Thompson, E. H. (1991). Beneath the status characteristic: Gender variations in religiousness. *Journal for the Scientific Study of Religion, 30*, 381–394.

Thompson, L., & Walker, A. J. (1989). Women and men in marriage, work, and parenthood. *Journal of Marriage and the Family, 51*, 845–872.

Thompson, S. (1984). Search for tomorrow: On feminism and the construction of teen romance. In C. Vance (Ed.), *Exploring female sexuality* (pp. 350–357). London: Routledge and Kegan Paul.

Thorne, B. (1982). Feminist rethinking of the family: An overview. In B. Thorne (Ed.), *Rethinking the family* (pp. 1–24). New York: Longman.

Thorne, B. (1992). Feminism and the family: Two decades of thought. In B. Thorne (Ed.), *Rethinking the family: Some feminist questions* (pp. 3–30). Boston: Northeastern University Press.

Thorne, B. (1993). *Gender play: Girls and boys in school*. New Brunswick, NJ: Rutgers University Press.

Thorson, E., & Mendelson, A. (1996). *Perceptions of news stories and news photos of Hillary Rodham Clinton*. Paper presented at the Annual Meeting of the Association for Education in Journalism and Mass Communication, Anaheim, CA.

Thun, M. J., Day-Lally, C. A., Calle, E. E., Flanders, W. D., & Heath, C. W., Jr. (1995). Excess mortality among cigarette smokers: Changes in a 20-year interval. *American Journal of Public Health, 85*, 1223–1230.

Thys-Jacobs, S., Alvir, J. M. J., & Fratarcangelo, P. (1995). Comparative analysis of three PMS assessment instruments—The identification of premenstrual syndrome with core symptoms. *Psychopharmacology Bulletin, 31,* 389–396.

Tidball, M.E. (1980). Women's colleges and women achievers revisited. *Signs, 5,* 504–517.

Tiemann, K. A., Kennedy, S. A., & Haga, M. P. (1998). Rural lesbians' strategies for coming out to health care professionals. *Journal of Lesbian Studies, 2.*

Tiger, L., & Fox, R. (1971). *The imperial animal.* New York: Oxford University Press.

Tobias, S., & Weissbrod, C. (1980). Anxiety and mathematics: An update. *Harvard Educational Review, 50,* 63–70.

Toner, R. (1996, February 9). Candidates weigh cost of office to families. *New York Times,* p. A24.

Treichler, P. A., & Frank, F. W. (1989a). Introduction: Scholarship, feminism, and language change. In F. W. Frank & P. A. Treichler (Eds.), *Language, gender, and professional writing: Theoretical approaches and guidelines for nonsexist usage* (pp. 1–32). New York: The Modern Language Association of America.

Treichler, P. A., & Frank, F. W. (1989b). Guidelines for nonsexist usage. In F. W. Frank & P. A. Treichler (Eds.), *Language, gender, and professional writing: Theoretical approaches and guidelines for nonsexist usage* (pp. 137–278). New York: The Modern Language Association of America.

"True love waits" for some teenagers. (1993, September 27). *New York Times,* p. A12.

Tuchman, G. (1979). Women's depiction by the mass media. *Signs, 4,* 528–542.

Tuchman, G., Daniels, A. K., & Benet, J. (Eds.) (1978). *Hearth and home: Images of women in the mass media.* New York: Oxford University Press.

Tucker, M. B., & Mitchell-Kernan, C. (Eds.) (1995). *The decline in marriage among African Americans: Causes, consequences and policy implications.* New York: Russell Sage.

Tucker, N. S. (Ed.) (1995). *Bisexual politics: Theories, queries, and visions.* New York: Haworth.

Turner, C. S. V., & Thompson, J. R. (1993). Socializing women doctoral students: Minority and majority experiences. *The Review of Higher Education, 16,* 355–370.

Turner, H. A., Pearlin, L. I., & Mullan, J. T. (1998). Sources and determinants of social support of caregivers of persons with AIDS. *Journal of Health and Social Behavior, 39,* 137–151.

Turner, L. H., & Sterk, H. M. (1994). Introduction: Examining "difference." In L. H. Turner & H. M. Sterk (Eds.), *Differences that make a difference* (pp. xi–xvi). Westport, CT: Bergin and Garvey.

25 million women lack pensions (1996, July 30). Washington, DC: Associated Press. (Internet).

Tyack, D., & Hansot, E. (1990). *Learning together: A history of coeducation in American public schools.* New Haven, CT: Yale University Press.

Umansky, E. M. (1985). Feminism and the reevaluation of women's roles within American Jewish life. In Y. Y. Haddad & E. B. Findly (Eds.), *Women, religion and social change* (pp. 477–494). Albany: State University of New York Press.

United Nations. (1997). *Report on the world social situation, 1997.* New York: Author.

United Nations. (1998). *Maternity protection at work.* New York: Author.

Uribe, V., & Harbeck, K. M. (1992). Addressing the needs of lesbian, gay and bisexual youth: The origins of PRO-JECT 10 and school-based intervention. In K. M. Harbeck (Ed.), *Coming out of the classroom closet: Gay and lesbian students, teachers, and curricula* (pp. 9–28). New York: Haworth Press.

U.S. Bureau of Prisons agrees to reforms in settlement of sex suit. (1998, March 4). San Francisco, CA: Associated Press (Internet).

U.S. Department of Commerce, Bureau of the Census. (1976). *Historical statistics of the United States, Colonial Times to 1970, Part I.* Washington, DC: U.S. Government Printing Office.

U.S. Department of Commerce, Bureau of the Census. (1985). *Statistical abstract of the United States, 1985.* Washington, DC: U.S. Government Printing Office.

U.S. Department of Commerce, Bureau of the Census. (1991). *Statistical abstract of the United States, 1991.* Washington, DC: U.S. Government Printing Office.

U.S. Department of Commerce, Bureau of the Census. (1993). *Statistical abstract of the United States, 1993.* Washington, DC: U.S. Government Printing Office.

U. S. Department of Commerce, Bureau of the Census. (1994). *Statistical abstract of the United States, 1994.* Washington, DC: U.S. Government Printing Office.

U.S. Department of Commerce, Bureau of the Census. (1996). *Statistical abstract of the United States, 1996.* Washington, DC: U.S. Government Printing Office.

U.S. Department of Commerce, Bureau of the Census. (1997). *Statistical abstract of the United States, 1997.* Washington, DC: U.S. Government Printing Office.

U.S. Department of Defense. (1997). *Military manpower statistics.* Washington, DC: Author.

U.S. Department of Education. (1997). *1994 Elementary and secondary school civil rights compliance report.* Washington, DC: Author.

U.S. Department of Health and Human Services, National Center for Health Statistics. (1991). *Health, United States, 1991.* Washington, DC: U.S. Government Printing Office.

U.S. Department of Health and Human Services, National Center for Health Statistics. (1995). *Health, United States, 1994.* Washington, DC: U.S. Government Printing Office.

U.S. Department of Health and Human Services, National Center for Health Statistics. (1996). *Health, United States, 1995.* U.S. Government Printing Office.

U.S. Department of Health and Human Services, National Center for Health Statistics. (1997). *Health, United States, 1996–97.* Washington, DC: U.S. Government Printing Office.

U.S. Department of Health and Human Services. (1998). *Child maltreatment 1996. Reports from the states to the National Child Abuse and Neglect Data System.* Washington, DC: Author.

U.S. Department of Justice, (1991). *Women in prison.* Washington, DC: U.S. Government Printing Office.

U.S. Department of Justice. (1994). *Violence against women.* Washington, DC: U.S. Department of Justice.

U.S. Department of Justice, Bureau of Justice Statistics. (1994). *HIV in prisons and jails.* Washington, DC: U.S. Government Printing Office.

U.S. Department of Justice, Bureau of Justice Statistics. (1996). *Sourcebook of criminal justice statistics, 1996.* Washington, DC: Author.

U.S. Department of Justice, Bureau of Justice Statistics. (1997). *Criminal victimization in the United States, 1994.* Washington, DC: Author.

U.S. Department of Labor. (1994). *Working women count! A report to the nation.* Washington, DC: Women's Bureau, U.S. Department of Labor.

U.S. Department of Labor. (1997a). *The glass ceiling initiative: Are there cracks in the ceiling?* Washington, DC: Author.

U. S. Department of Labor. (1997b). *National census of fatal occupational injuries, 1996.* Washington, DC: Author.

U.S. Department of Labor. (1998a). *The employment situation: May 1998.* Washington, DC: Author.

U.S. Department of Labor. (1998b, January). *Employment and earnings.* Washington, DC: Author.

U.S. Department of State. (1994). *Country reports on human rights practices for 1993.* Washington, DC: U.S. Government Printing Office.

U.S. House of Representatives, Select Committee on Children, Youth and Families. (1990, June 28). *"Victims of Rape," fact sheet.*

U.S. National Center for Education Statistics. (1996). *Digest of education statistics, 1996.* Washington, DC: U.S. Department of Education.

U.S. Senate Special Committee on Aging. (1991). *Aging America.* Washington, DC: U.S. Government Printing Office.

Ussher, J. (1989). *The psychology of the female body.* London: Routledge.

Vanderstaay, S. (1992). *Street lives.* Philadelphia: New Society Publishers.

Van Goozen, S., Frijda, N., & Van De Poll, N. (1994). Anger and aggression in women: Influence of sports choice and testosterone administration. *Aggressive Behavior, 20,* 213–222.

Van Voorhis, P., Cullen, F. T., Link, B. G., & Wolfe, N. T. (1991). The impact of race and gender on correctional officers' orientation to the integrated environment. *Journal of Research in Crime and Delinquency, 31,* 555–572.

Verhovek, S. H. (1998, January 1). As woman's execution nears, Texas squirms. *New York Times,* pp. A1, 12.

Vivian, J. (1993). *The media of mass communication.* Boston: Allyn and Bacon.

Voakes, P. S. (1997). *The newspaper journalists of the '90s.* Reston, VA: American Society of Newspaper Editors.

Vobejda, B. (1997a, June 18). For many girls, first sex was "not wanted." *Washington Post,* p. A14.

Vobejda, B. (1997b, December 5). Abortion rate in U.S. off sharply. *Washington Post,* p. A1.

Voelker, R. (1998). Teen health risks. *Journal of the American Medical Association, 279,* 1599.

Voss, L. S. (1997). Teasing, disputing, and playing: Cross-gender interactions and space utilization among first and third graders. *Gender & Society, 11,* 238–256.

Wadden, T. A., et al. (1997). Exercise in the treatment of obesity: Effects of four interventions on body composition, resting energy expenditure, appetite, and mood. *Journal of Clinical and Consulting Psychology, 65,* 269–275.

Waite, T. L. (1992, December 8). Sexual behavior levels compared in studies in Britain and France. *New York Times,* p. C3.

Waldron, I. (1995). Contributions of changing gender differences in behavior and social roles to changing gender differences in mortality. In D. Sabo & D. F. Gordon (Eds.), *Men's health and illness* (pp. 22–45). Thousand Oaks, CA: Sage.

Walker, A., & Parmar, P. (1993). *Warrior marks: Female genital mutilation and the sexual blinding of women.* New York: Harcourt Brace.

Wallace, R. A. (1992). *They call her pastor.* Albany: State University of New York Press.

Wallis, C. (1989, December 4). Onward, women! *Time Magazine,* p. 8089.

Walsh-Childers, K. (1996). Women as sex partners. In P. M. Lester (Ed.), *Images that injure* (pp. 81–86). Westport, CT: Praeger.

Walzer, S. (1996). Thinking about the baby: Gender and divisions of infant care. *Social Problems, 43,* 219–234.

Warr, M. (1985). Fear of rape among urban women. *Social Problems, 32,* 238–250.

Warren, M. A. (1985). *Gendercide: The implications of sex selection.* London: Rowman and Allanheld Publishers.

Watt, S., & Cook, J. (1991). Racism: Whose liberation? Implications for women's studies. In J. Aaron & S. Walby (Eds.), *Out of the margins: Women's studies in the nineties* (pp. 131–142). London: The Falmer Press.

Wayne, L. (1996, September 6). Loopholes allow presidential race to set a record. *New York Times,* pp. 1, 26.

Weaver, J. (1992). The social science and psychological research evidence: Perceptual and behavioural consequences of exposure to pornography. In C. Itzen (Ed.), *Pornography: Women, violence and civil liberties* (pp. 284–309). Oxford: Oxford University Press.

Weaver, M. J. (1995). *New Catholic women: A contemporary challenge to traditional religious authority.* Bloomington, IN: Indiana University Press.

Webber, J. (1983). Between law and custom: Women's experience of Judaism. In P. Holden (Ed.), *Women's religious experience: Cross-cultural perspectives* (pp. 143–162). London: Croom Helm.

Webster, J. (1996). *Shaping women's work: Gender, employment and information technology.* New York: Longman.

Wechsler, H., Dowdall, G. W., Davenport, A., & Castillo, S. (1995). Correlates of college student binge drinking. *American Journal of Public Health, 85,* 921–926.

Weidman, J. L. (Ed.) (1984). *Christian feminism.* San Francisco: Harper and Row.

Weiser, B. (1997, June 11). Sex and race discrimination occurs in federal courts, a study finds. *New York Times,* p. B6.

Weisner, T. S., Garnier, H., & Loucky, J. (1994). Domestic tasks, gender egalitarian values and children's gender typing in conventional and nonconventional families. *Sex Roles, 30,* 23–54.

Weisner, T. S., & Wilson-Mitchell, J. E. (1990. Nonconventional family lifestyles and sex typing in six year olds. *Child Development, 61,* 1915–1933.

Weissman, M. M. (1980). Depression. In A. M. Brodsky & R. Hare-Mustin (Eds.), *Women and psychotherapy* (pp. 97–112). New York: The Guilford Press.

Weitz, R. (1991). *Life with AIDS.* New Brunswick, NJ: Rutgers University Press.

Weitzman, L., & Rizzo, D. (1976). *Images of males and females in elementary school textbooks.* Washington, DC: Resource Center on Sex Roles in Education.

Weitzman, L. J. (1985). *The divorce revolution.* New York: Free Press.

Weitzman, L. J., Eifler, D., Hokada, E., & Ross, C. (1972). Sex-role socialization in picture books for pre-school children. *American Journal of Sociology, 77,* 1125–1150.

Weitzman, N., Birns, B., & Friend, R. (1985). Traditional and nontraditional mothers' communication with their daughters and sons. *Child Development, 56,* 894–896.

Welch, S. D. (1985). *Communities of resistance and solidarity: A feminist theology of liberation.* Maryknoll, NY: Orbis Books.

Wellington, A. J. (1994). Accounting for the male/female wage gap among Whites, 1976 and 1985. *American Sociological Review, 59,* 839–848.

Wenger, N. K. (1997). Coronary heart disease: An older woman's major health risk. *British Medical Journal, 315,* 1085–1095.

Wennards, C., & Wold, A. (1997). Nepotism and sexism in peer review. *Nature, 307,* 341.

Werthheimer, B. M. (1979). "Union is power": Sketches from women's labor history. In J. Freeman (Ed.), *Woman: A feminist perspective* (pp. 339–358). Palo Alto, CA: Mayfield.

Wertz, R. W., & Wertz, D. C. (1986). Notes on the decline of midwives and the rise of medical obstetrics. In P. Conrad & R. Kern (Eds.), *The sociology of health and illness* (pp. 134–146). New York: St. Martin's Press.

Westley, L. A. (1982). *A territorial issue: A study of women in the construction trades.* Washington, DC: Wider Opportunities for Women.

Weston, K. (1991). *Families we choose: Lesbians, gays, kinship.* New York: Columbia University Press.

Where French course is cause celebre. (1990, March 4). *New York Times,* p. 35.

Whipp, B. J., & Ward, S. A. (1992). Will women soon outrun men? *Nature, 355,* 25.

Whitaker, A., Johnson, J., Shaffer, D., Rapoport, J. L., Kalikow, K., Walsh, B. T., Davies, M., Braiman, S., & Dolinsky, A. (1990). Common troubles in young people: Prevalence disorders in a nonreferred adolescent population. *Archives of General Psychiatry, 47,* 487–496.

White, D. (1995). *Above the political glass ceiling: A comparison of men and women members of Congress.* Paper presented at the Annual Meeting of the Eastern Sociological Society, Philadelphia, PA.

White, J. C., & Dull, V. T. (1998). Room for improvement: Communication between lesbians and primary care providers. *Journal of Lesbian Studies, 2.*

White, P. G., Young, K., & McTeer, W. G. (1995). Sport, masculinity, and the injured body. In D. Sabo & D. F. Gordon (Eds.), *Men's health and illness* (pp. 158–182). Thousand Oaks, CA: Sage.

Whitehead, H. (1981). The bow and the burden strap: A new look at institutionalized homosexuality in Native North America. In S. B. Ortner & H. Whitehead (Eds.), *Sexual meanings* (pp. 31–79). New York: Cambridge University Press.

Widom, C. S., & Ames, A. (1988). Biology and female crime. In T. E. Moffitt & S. A. Mednick (Eds.), *Biological contributions to crime causation* (pp. 308–331). Dordrecht: Martinus Nijhoff Publishers.

Wikan, U. (1984). Shame and honour: A contestable pair. *Man, 19,* 635–652.

Wilbanks, W. (1987). *The myth of a racist criminal justice system.* Belmont, CA: Wadsworth.

Wilkerson, I. (1991a, August 14). To save its men, Detroit plans boys-only schools. *New York Times,* pp. A1, A17.

Wilkerson, I. (1991b, January 25). Blacks wary of their big role in military. *New York Times,* pp. A1, A2.

Wilkie, J. R. (1993). Changes in U.S. men's attitudes toward the family provider role, 1972–1989. *Gender & Society 7,* 261–279.

Willentz, J. A. (1991). Invisible segment of a veterans population: Women veterans, past omissions and current corrections. In M. L. Kendrigan (Ed.), *Gender differences: Their impact on public policy* (pp. 173–188). New York: Greenwood Press.

Williams, B. (1987). Homosexuality: The new Vatican statement. *Theological Studies, 48,* 259–277.

Williams, C. L. (1992). The glass escalator: Hidden advantages for men in the "female" professions. *Social Problems, 39,* 253–267.

Williams, C. L. (1995). *Still a man's world: Men who do women's work.* Berkeley: University of California Press.

Williams, C. W. (1991). *Black teenage mothers.* Lexington, MA: Lexington Books.

Williams, J. A., Jr., Vernon, J. A., Williams, M. C., & Malecha, K. (1987). Sex role socialization in picture books: An update. *Social Science Quarterly, 68,* 148–156.

Williams, J. E. (1985). Mexican American and Anglo attitudes about sex roles and rape. *Free Inquiry in Creative Sociology, 13,* 15–20.

Williams, L. A. (1988). Toxic exposure in the workplace: Balancing job opportunity with reproductive health. In E. Boneparth & E. Stroper (Eds.), *Women, power and policy: Toward the year 2000* (pp. 113–130). New York: Pergamon.

Williams, W. L. (1986). *The spirit and the flesh.* Boston: Beacon.

Williamson, N. E. (1976). *Sons or daughters.* Beverly Hills, CA: Sage.

Wilson, E., & Ng, S. H. (1988). Sex bias in visual images evoked by generics: A New Zealand study. *Sex Roles, 18,* 159–168.

Wilson, W. J. (1987). *The truly disadvantaged.* Chicago: University of Chicago Press.

Wise, E., & Rafferty, J. (1982). Sex bias and language. *Sex Roles, 8,* 1189–1196.

Wise, M. (1997, October 29). It's official: Two women are referees. *New York Times,* pp. C1, 2.

Withorn, A. (1986). Helping ourselves. In P. Conrad & R. Kern (Eds.), *The sociology of health and illness* (pp. 416–424). New York: St. Martin's Press.

Witkin, H. A., Mednick, S. A., Schulsinger, F., Bakkestrm, E., Christiansen, K. O., Goodenough, D. R., Hirschhorn, K., Lundsteen, C., Owen, D. R., Philip, J., Rubin, D. B., and Stocking, M. (1976). Criminality in XYY and XXY men. *Science, 193,* 547–555.

Witt, L., Paget, K. M., & Matthews, G. (1994). *Running as a woman: Gender and power in American politics.* New York: Free Press.

Wolf, N. (1991). *The beauty myth.* New York: William Morrow.

Wolfe, A. (1998). *One nation, after all.* New York: Viking.

Wolowitz, H. M. (1972). Hysterical character and feminine identity. In J. Bardwick (Ed.), *Readings on the psychology of women* (pp. 307–313). New York: Harper and Row.

Women candidates. (1992, July 22). *Time*/CNN opinion poll conducted by Yankelovich Partners, Inc., Washington, DC.

Woods, N. F., Dery, G. K., & Most, A. (1982). Recollections of menarche, current menstrual attitudes, and perimenstrual symptoms. In S. Golub (Ed.), *The transition from girl to woman* (pp. 87–97). Lexington, MA: D.C. Heath.

Woog, D. (1995). *School's out*. Los Angeles: Alyson Publications.

Wooley, S. C., & Wooley, O. W. (1980). Eating disorders: Obesity and anorexia. In A. M. Brodsky & R. Hare-Mustin (Eds.), *Women and psychotherapy* (pp. 135–158). New York: The Guilford Press.

Woollett, A., White, D., & Lyon, L. (1982). Fathers' involvement with their infants: The role of holding. In N. Beail & J. McGuire (Eds.), *Fathers: Psychological perspectives* (pp. 72–91). London: Junction.

Worden, A. P. (1993). The attitudes of women and men in policing: Testing conventional and contemporary wisdom. *Criminology, 31*, 203–237.

World Bank. (1991). *World development report*. New York: Oxford University Press.

World Bank. (1996). *World development report*. New York: Oxford University Press.

World Health Organization. (1960). *Constitution*. Geneva: Palais des Nations.

Wright, J. C., Huston, A. C., Truglio, R., Fitch, M., Smith, E. & Piemyat, S. (1995). Occupational portrayals on television: Children's role schemata, career aspirations, and perceptions of reality. *Child Development, 66*, 1706–1718.

Wright, R. (1996). The occupational masculinity of computing. In C. Cheng (Ed.), *Masculinities in organizations* (pp. 77–96). Thousand Oaks, CA: Sage.

Wright, R., & Jacobs, J. A. (1995). Male flight from computer work: A new look at occupational resegregation and ghettoization. In J. A. Jacobs (Ed.), *Gender inequality at work* (pp. 334–376). Thousand Oaks, CA: Sage.

Wroblewski, R., & Huston, A. C. (1987). Televised occupational stereotypes and their effects on early adolescents: Are they changing? *Journal of Early Adolescence, 7*, 283–297.

Yamanaka, K. & McClelland, K. (1994). Earning the model-minority image: Diverse strategies of economic adaptation by Asian-American women. *Ethnic and Racial Studies, 17*, 79–114.

Yee, S. J. (1992). *Black women abolitionists*. Knoxville: The University of Tennessee Press.

Yoon, J. (1996, March 2). In sexist Korea, a rare victory for women. Seoul, South Korea: Reuters. (Internet).

Zappone, K. (1991). *The hope for wholeness*. Mystic, CT: Twenty Third Publications.

Zate, M. (1996, January-February). Breaking through the glass ceiling. *Hispanic Business*, pp. 30–24.

Zavella, P. (1987). *Women's work and Chicano families*. Ithaca, NY: Cornell University Press.

Zerbe, K. J. (1993). *The body betrayed: Women, eating disorders, and treatment*. Washington, DC: American Psychiatric Press.

Zicklin, G. (1992, August). *Re-biologizing sexual orientation: A critique*. Paper presented at the Annual Meeting of the Society for the Study of Social Problems, Pittsburgh, PA.

Zimmer, L. E. (1986). *Women guarding men*. Chicago: University of Chicago Press.

Zimmer, L. E. (1987). How women reshape the prison guard role. *Gender & Society, 1*, 415–431.

Zimmer, L. E. (1988). Tokenism and women in the workplace: The limits of gender-neutral theory. *Social Problems, 35*, 64–77.

Zimmerman, B., & McNaron, T. A. H. (Eds.) (1996). *The new lesbian studies: Into the twenty-first century*. New York: Feminist Press.

Zoba, W. M., & Lee, H. (1996, April 8). Ministering women. *Christianity Today*, pp. 14–21.

Zoch, L. M. (1997). *Women as sources: Gender patterns in framing the news*. Paper presented at the Annual Meeting of the Association for Education in Journalism and Mass Communication, Chicago, IL.

Zupan, L. L. (1992). The progress of women correctional officers. In I. L. Moyer (Ed.), *The changing roles of women in the criminal justice system* (pp. 323–343). Prospect Heights, IL: Waveland Press.

Zuravin, S. J. (1987). Unplanned pregnancies, family planning problems, and child maltreatment. *Family Relations, 36*, 135–139.

NAME INDEX

SUBJECT INDEX

Photo Credits: 1, © Photo by Jean-Claude LeJeune/Stock Boston; 31, © Barbara Campbell/Liaison International; 57, © D. Young/Wolff/PhotoEdit; 81, © Spencer Grant/Photo Researchers; 119, © T. Nourok/PhotoEdit; 149, © Elderfield/Liaison; 191, © Nancy Pierce/Black Star/Photo Researchers; 234, © Rhoda Signey/The Image Works; 276, © N. R. Rowan/Stock Boston; 307, © Polak/SYGMA; 339, © Jon Riley/Tony Stone Images.